# THE GOSPEL
# IN HYMN

not

Back together with th
under which partic
Does it seem p
Soldier
autho

# THE GOSPEL IN HYMNS

## OTHER BOOKS BY THE AUTHOR

DAILY LIFE IN BIBLE TIMES
THE ARTS AND RELIGION (EDITOR AND CONTRIBUTOR)
PICTURES IN THE UPPER ROOM
ART AND CHARACTER
CHRIST AND HIS GOSPEL IN RECENT ART
THE USE OF ART IN RELIGIOUS EDUCATION
JESUS AND HIS TEACHINGS: THE APPROACH THROUGH ART
HISTORY OF THE HEBREW COMMONWEALTH
ART STUDIES IN THE LIFE OF CHRIST
THE GOSPEL IN ART
ON NAZARETH HILL

# The
# Gospel in Hymns

## BACKGROUNDS
## AND
## INTERPRETATIONS

By

Albert Edward Bailey

CHARLES SCRIBNER'S SONS, NEW YORK
1950

22789

To my daughter

MARION BAILEY SPARLING

# PREFACE

I have attended church, Bible school, young people's meeting and week-day prayer meeting (off and on) for upwards of sixty years. On these occasions I have sung an average of at least ten hymns a week, or 520 a year; total, at least, 31,000 hymns. Yet I can count on the fingers of one hand the persons who in all that time ever said a word about either the hymn or its author. Nobody in charge of those services ever called my attention to the glorious heritage that was mine—the saints and heroes, the experiences of sorrow and of joy, of sin, defeat, triumph, aspiration, vision, that are embodied in those hymns.

To this last statement there was one grand exception. When as a boy I came from the country to the Academy at Worcester, Massachusetts, I fell under the spell of a preacher who was also a scholar. Though from a sense of loyalty I attended regularly the drab services of another denomination, occasionally on a Sunday evening I used to visit his church to hear a sermon devoted to the interpretation of hymns. There for the first time I learned about St. Francis, St. Bernard, Zinzendorf, the Greek hymns, and the glorious company of English poets who have lived through the centuries within the covers of our hymnal; and to the end of my days I shall bless Dr. William V. W. Davis for mountain-panoramas that have inspired my whole religious life.

What a pity that so few teachers and preachers are now opening this Delectable Country to our boys and girls.

## BASIS OF SELECTION IN THIS STUDY

The choice of the hymns to be studied is of course a crucial matter. The choice was not mine: it was that of ten different hymnal committees of different denominations. The result is what might be called an ecumenical hymnary. First, the official hymnbooks of eight leading denominations in the United States and Canada were selected, to which were added an independent book of outstanding excellence and a popular Anglican compilation. This shows what is being offered to tens of millions of English-speaking Christians. From these ten books were chosen for study those hymns which are found in at least six of them. However, in order to fill certain time-gaps when hymnody had not yet awakened, or the merits of certain poets had not yet been widely recognized, a few hymns have been considered even though they are found in fewer than six books. Here is the list of the hymnals used:

| Symbol | Denomination | Title and Date |
|--------|--------------|----------------|
| A | Anglican (Canadian) | *The Hymn Book,* 1938 |
| B | Baptist-Disciples | *Christian Worship,* 1941 |
| C | Congregational Christian | *Pilgrim Hymnal,* 1935 |
| E | Episcopal (United States) | *The Hymnal,* 1940 |
| L | United Lutheran | *Common Service Book,* 1918 |
| M | Methodist | *The Methodist Hymnal,* 1939 |
| N | Undenominational | *New Church Hymnal,* 1937 |
| P | Presbyterian | *The Hymnal,* 1937 |
| S | Anglican (English) | *Songs of Praise,* 1931 |
| U | United Church of Canada | *The Hymnary,* 1930 |

There is no telling how many people actually use these hymnals; but since the denominations listed are the largest in the United States and Canada it is reasonable to suppose that no other hymnals can compete in wide use with those chosen. When a hymn occurs in at least six of these books, it is what might be called fairly representative of contemporary Christian thought or sentiment.

From another angle also the chosen hymns are important: they ignore superficial denominational differences. The hymnals fall into two distinct categories: ritualistic and non-ritualistic. *Songs of Praise,* for example, is a thoroughly liturgical book. Its editor, Percy Dearmer, was an ecclesiologist and a Canon of St. Paul's, London. In 1906 he was one of the editors of the *English Hymnal,* highest of High Church; but in the intervening twenty years he realized that religion had to do with other aspects of life than ritual, and he broadened his interests to include the Social Gospel. Similarly the *Hymn Book* of the Canadian Anglicans is based upon and reproduces 426 hymns from *Hymns Ancient and Modern,* the Church of England hymnal, of which probably 75,000,000 copies (all editions) have been sold. The Episcopal *Hymnal* of 1940 is the latest and best of the Churchly books. The *Common Service Book* of the United Lutherans is also liturgical, deriving much of its inspiration from sixteenth century German ideals. These four books emphasize the Christian year, the ancient creeds, the Sacraments and the saints' days.

From these books of the liturgical type it is a far cry to the Baptist-Disciples *Christian Worship* in which Worship, the Christian Life, the Kingdom of God and Christian Society hold a prominent place. This differing point of view is shared largely by the Presbyterian, Congregational and Dr. Smith's *New Church* hymnals. As a consequence, if a hymn is included in both the first and second categories, and especially if it is found in all ten books, we may be sure that it belongs to the whole Protestant Church without distinction of creed or liturgy. Out of a total of 313 hymns analyzed in this book, 59 hymns are found in all but one hymnal and 59 in all. These hymns might be said to constitute *the* true ecumenical hymnary.

Even so this collection of widely accepted hymns does not constitute the ideal hymnal. Many valuable lyrics have been and still are being written, and are not yet included by hymnal editors. The average hymnal becomes out of date in one generation and, therefore, is apt to lag behind the ideal by twenty years or so. In other words, there will never be a perfect compilation, merely one that keeps alive the best until there is something better.

### ORGANIZATION OF MATERIAL

The theory underlying the organization of this book is that hymns are partly an individual and partly a social product. Few hymns were written in a vacuum. While the experience that inspired them may have been personal, the form and subject-matter were conditioned in part at least by the author's setting in time and place, by his historical, religious and social environment. We cannot properly understand a hymn apart from this fact. This is why the material of this book is chronological in arrangement. But the chronology does not begin with our earliest Christian hymn, about 200 A.D., for that hymn was not English but Greek. The time-scheme is that of the English hymn, which began at zero in the sixteenth century; and it introduces us to hymns in the order in which they appear in English from that date to the present. By this means we are able to understand why Milton paraphrased Psalms—and what particular Psalms; out of what intolerance and persecution sprang Bunyan's "He who would valiant be"; why the Wesleys needed to stress personal salvation from sin and to cultivate the religious life so strenuously through hymns. We discover why and when the old Latin Breviaries and the Greek Service Books were ransacked and translated; who devised prayer-meeting hymns in Germany and England, and why; when, why and where Gospel Songs sprang into being; and finally why hymns of the Social Gospel did not arise in Watts' day in England but in our own lifetime. All this orientation is a necessary preliminary to real appreciation.

Then at the risk of explaining the obvious I have tried to tell what the words of the hymns actually say and imply. This is to enlighten our young people who have been singing hymns without thinking about them. The words often mean very little to them until, years afterward it may be, or by accident or circumstance they are led to consider their true significance. Even then they will sometimes miss the author's thought because of the theological implications buried in certain phrases, or because they do not accurately visualize the poet's imagery, derived so often from infrequently read books of the Old Testament. I have tried, therefore, to throw light on such matters.

# ACKNOWLEDGMENTS

Over the years while this book was taking shape many people have given me information from their knowledge and experience. To all of these I say thank you. The following persons and institutions, however, deserve special notice:

The custodians of the Bodleian Library and the Ashmolean Museum in Oxford, England; the British Museum, London; the Bibliothéque Nationale, Paris; the Archives Division of the Harvard University Library; Dr. Kenneth S. Gapp of the Princeton Theological Seminary Library, where is preserved Dr. Benson's invaluable collection of books on Hymnody; my son Stephen who, while a student at Oxford, drove his mother and me to the haunts and homes of hymn-writers throughout England and Wales; Rev. Theodore Theodorides of Cambridge, Massachusetts, who translated orally for me portions of a book in modern Greek about Mar Saba; Dr. Leroy A. Campbell, Head Master of Worcester Academy, who translated a paragraph from the Latin poem of Alan of Lille, twelfth century; Dr. William W. Rockwell of Union Theological Seminary for minute and valuable criticisms; Miss S. Elizabeth DeVoy and Mr. William Savage and their assistants at Charles Scribner's Sons, whose infinite patience and cooperation have made publication possible; my daughter Lois Bailey Wills for her valuable judgments of matter and form; and especially my wife for her constant evaluations and clerical help.

A book of this size and scope naturally has many direct quotations from other sources. I am grateful to those authors or publishers who have graciously given me permission to quote from their works and an attempt has been made to give acknowledgment in the footnotes. If proper credit has not been given in any case it is an inadvertent omission and apologies are here offered.

ALBERT E. BAILEY

WORCESTER,
MASSACHUSETTS.

# TABLE OF CONTENTS

# ILLUSTRATIONS

# THE GOSPEL IN HYMNS

# HISTORICAL SUMMARY

## CHAPTER ONE: THE GREAT REJECTION

| | |
|---|---|
| 1509–47 | HENRY VIII. Married Catherine of Aragon. |
| 1517 | Luther challenges the Roman Church. |
| | In England: growing liberalism in religion; scorn of Roman abuses; rising sense of national importance; intolerance of foreign control. |
| 1533 | Henry secretly marries Anne Boleyn. |
| | English clerical court nullifies his marriage with Catherine. |
| | Pope excommunicates Henry. |
| | Cranmer made Archbishop of Canterbury: ruled against masses for the dead, indulgences, Purgatory. Luther's ideas seep in. |
| 1534 | Parliament declares Henry head of Catholic Church in England. |
| | Payment of tribute to the Pope stopped. |
| 1536–7 | Dissolution of monasteries. |
| 1539 | Vicar General Cromwell publishes the *Great Bible* in English. Every church in England ordered to have a copy. |
| 1544 | Cranmer's first Liturgy in English. |
| | All through Henry's reign, Catholic dogma and discipline were retained. It was treason to deny Henry's supremacy over the Church, but it was heresy to depart from Catholic dogma: punishment: burning or hanging. |
| 1547–54 | EDWARD VI. Advisors largely Protestant. The unwisdom of radicals produced a reaction after his death. |
| 1547 | By royal command, Epistle and Gospel to be read in English in church; Communion in "both kinds" (both bread and wine) for all people. |
| 1549 | *The Booke of Common Prayer.* Use made compulsory by Parliament. |
| | Sternhold: Certayne Psalmes . . . drawè into Englishe mètre (37 only). |
| 1552 | *The Second Prayer Book* of Edward VI. |

# CHAPTER ONE

# THE GREAT REJECTION

IF VIVACIOUS TWENTY-YEAR-OLD ANNE BOLEYN had not snared with her dark eyes the heart of forty-one-year-old Henry VIII there might not have been any English hymnody.

Of course in the providence of God, the lyric soul of England's religion and the spirit of democracy and reform deeply imbedded in centuries of English history would doubtless have found some way to express themselves. But historically it is a fact that this love affair was the first of a chain of events that led to a break with the Church of Rome, the establishment of a liturgy in English and the provision that hymns in English might be publicly sung only if the words were taken from the Bible. Without those purgations our hymns would have remained Latin.

Though Parliament voted to break with Rome, it was one thing to vote a new order into existence but quite another to uproot a national way of life. Henry, therefore, had some difficulty in establishing his supremacy as head of the Roman Catholic Church in England. To be sure, the English people for years had been strongly dissatisfied with some aspects of the Church: many of the clergy were ignorant, often immoral, and could not be tried by the king's courts; great monastic houses were rich and greedy; clerics of all orders were eternally begging for more property; and from the compulsory annual payment of dues to Rome there seemed to be no adequate return in benefits. Therefore, provided only that the Church remained Roman Catholic in doctrine, the majority of the people, even most of the clergy and monks, did not object to a change in head. English Henry VIII, who was leading his nation toward greater strength both at home and abroad, might even be a good exchange for Italian Clement VII who seemed to be on the losing side of nearly every quarrel.

First came the "purification" of the Church and especially of the monastic houses. In order to break up the influential body of clerical landlords and to give the lay peers a majority in the House of Lords, Henry began a ruthless dissolution and plundering of the monasteries. One quarter of the realm

3

of England was thus transferred to Henry, together with gold, jewels, plate and other valuables totaling $150,000,000. The noble medieval buildings of 800 establishments were emptied and left to the mercy of the elements or used by the neighbors as a quarry. You may be sure that the motive of all this was not purification but avarice.

Fortunately other influences assisted Henry in his work, though he did not fully recognize the fact. The intellectual revival called the New Learning, and the ideas of Luther and his reformation were seeping in from Italy and Germany. This made it easier for Henry's Vicar General, Thomas Cromwell, to make many changes that loosened the hold of Catholicism on the people. He abolished from Oxford University the medieval scholastic philosophy; he discouraged the veneration of saints, images and relics, the making of processions and pilgrimages, observing feasts and saints' days, burning candles. This was a necessary part of the Great Rejection and it helped clear the ground for the Hymnody that was to come.

But there were some die-hards, especially among the Franciscan friars and Carthusian monks. Henry took pains that those should die hard. He ordered a rigorous extermination of them by the brutal methods in vogue— they were "broken on the wheel," hanged, "drawn and quartered." The stories of these Catholic martyrs who died for conscience sake shine among the annals of heroism.

Though Henry and his loyal Archbishop, Cranmer, were able to effect the break with Rome, they found themselves with a new problem on their hands. They had a national Church that had been Roman Catholic and still was, with its entire service of prayers, hymns, sacraments and Mass in Latin; now they had to make it over into an English Church in order that the people might have no excuse to go back to Roman ways. We shall understand this problem better if we look for a moment at the Latin ritual with which these innovators had to deal.

For 1200 years or more the Roman Church had been building up a stately service that by 1520 was in its general plan universal throughout central and western Europe. This ritual was largely the work of the monastic orders and was used in its complete form only by them. A monk's life during the day was divided into eight "Hours," for each of which there was a special ritual called the "Office." It is easy to see that if a man had any serious work to do, like supporting a family, he could not spend his time performing "Offices." Some allowance had to be made for non-monks. Therefore, in the parish churches a man was thought to be doing his full duty if he attended "Lauds" in the morning and "Vespers" in the evening; and very few did even that.

These Church Offices were not as simple as at first appears. Not only were there eight canonical Hours but the Office was changed to fit the great festivals of the Church year and the saints' days. Thus practically there was a different set of Offices for every day of the year. The immense literature that grew up to provide material for these Offices was gathered into books, which had become so voluminous that before the days of Henry VIII the Church had standardized them and cut them down to two: (1) the *Breviary*, detailing the various Offices for the use of the clergy; (2) the *Missal*, which gives the ritual of the Mass, most important of the Sacraments. These books enable a person to follow intelligently the services of the Church year if he knows Latin.

In the Breviary, selections from the immense treasure of the Hymns were

*Left*, Archbishop Cranmer, martyred March 21, 1556, under Bloody Mary. *Right*, King Edward VI, crowned at the age of 9, died at 16.

preserved. Since the days of St. Benedict, sixth century, a hymn had been sung by the choir at each of the Hour Offices. The hymns were based upon the details of the Church year or on the doctrines of the Church or on themes appropriate to the adoration of God, Christ, the Blessed Virgin and other saints.

In the new ritual that had to be made for the national Church, Cranmer *omitted all hymns*. There were practical reasons behind this act. Ordinary citizens could not read Latin—or English, for that matter; and without choirs of monks who knew the intricacies of plainsong tunes, singing by the congregation was impossible. Therefore, by a stroke of the Archbishop's pen, into the discard went the hymns. Not until the middle of the nineteenth century were any of these Latin hymns recovered for the English-speaking Church. The story of that recovery is told in Chapter IX.

Henry VIII died in 1547. His successor was his son Edward, a boy of nine years. After much political maneuvering, young Edward VI was placed under the care of men who favored the New Learning from Italy and the religious doctrines of Martin Luther that were seeping in from Germany. The King therefore was easily induced to give assent to many changes that swung

Psalter of Westminster Abbey, late 12th century.

the new English Church still further from the Church of Rome. Archbishop Cranmer continued to be the guiding spirit in all this.

Now let us watch Cranmer as he tried to preserve religion while breaking with Rome.

First, he threw away all the eight Hours but two, which means that henceforth there shall be only two services a day called Morning and Evening Prayer, reminiscent of the old Matins and Vespers.

Second, by order of Parliament Cranmer and his associates revamped the Roman Breviary: modified the Latin material, translated it, condensed it, and produced in 1549 the first *Book of Common Prayer* in English. This is the first great landmark in the history of the English Church. Parliament made the use of this book compulsory. In 1552 when Protestant views were rapidly being adopted by all classes, this Prayer Book was revised in the direction of the Reformation theology, and with slight modifications is in use today by all Anglican Churches (the Established Church of England) and with other slight modifications, by the Protestant Episcopal Church of the United States.

Third, he substituted English for Latin as the language of the liturgy, so that all people might understand completely what the service contained. As a matter of fact, it was the Prayer Book and the newly translated Bible that standardized the English language throughout the realm.

Finally, Cranmer and those who followed through with his ideals changed the altar into a communion table; put out the candles, removed the sacred images and the pictures; smashed the stained glass windows with their figures of saints. Gradually the increasingly Protestant temper of the people swept away all traces of Roman custom. It was indeed a great rejection.

One vitally important fact emerges from this brief review: *the Hymn has disappeared.* Its place is usurped by selections of scripture and by the *Te Deum* of the fourth century, which is more of a creed than a hymn. Cranmer has made a clean sweep of the hymnic treasure of the centuries. The English Church must start from the beginning, if at all, in its expression of religion in non-Biblical lyric terms.

But there was left one consolation of which the Church at once availed itself: Psalms, many of which are really Jewish hymns, were permitted freely *in private devotions.* Says the "Act of Uniformity for the Use of the Common Prayer in English" (1549):

> Provided also that it shal be lawful for al men, as well in churches, chapels, oratories, or other places, to use openly any Psalm or Prayer taken out of the Bible, at any due time; not letting or omitting thereby the service, or any part thereof mentioned in the said book.

The case of Thomas Sternhold illustrates how this permission was used.

## Private Psalm Singing

(An imaginative reconstruction based on contemporary data)

The scene: Whitehall Palace, London, in the year 1548.

Thomas Sternhold, a Groom of the Robes under Henry VIII and Edward VI, has been singing softly to himself and playing his organ in his private apartments in the royal palace. Having finished, he leaves the room to go about his duties, and find in the corridor immediately behind the portière the boy-king Edward, aged eleven.

"Your Majesty! How you startled me! I am at your service, Sire."

"I was only listening, Master Sternhold. The music was so pretty! I wish you would sing some more."

"Your Majesty is very gracious to be pleased with my simple music. I was singing only for my own Godly solace. But if it pleases your Majesty to enter my humble apartment I shall do my best to sing again."

"That I desire, Master Sternhold."

They enter. Thomas places a chair for the King and seats himself at a small organ. It has only one keyboard. A few pipes rise above the console, very much as in the instrument one sees in medieval pictures of St. Cecilia playing. Thomas pulls a cord and summons a boy to pump for him. After a few preliminary notes Thomas sings:

My shepherd is the living Lord,
   Nothing therefore I need,
In pastures faire with waters calm
   He set me for to feed.

He did convert and glad my soule
   And brought my mind in frame,
To walk in paths of righteousness
   For his most holy name.

(Three more stanzas)

The King clapped his hands in delight.

"Where did you find the words, Master Sternhold? Or did you write them?"

"They are the words of the Twenty-third Psalm in the Bible, Your Majesty. Only in order to sing them to a regular tune I had to change them somewhat."

"And did you make up the music?"

"No, Your Majesty. One of my friends who recently returned from Geneva sang this tune to me. He says that a certain Monsieur Louis Bourgeois composed it."

"It is very pretty, and the words make me feel good."

"Your Majesty, I have hopes that if I can compose several of these Psalms in the popular ballad meter and print them in a book, it will induce many of the gentlemen and ladies of Your Majesty's court to sing them, and to drop the amorous and obscene songs with which they now delight themselves; for they would be very mete to be used of all sorts of people privately, for their Godly solace and comfort; laying apart all ungodly songs and ballads which tend only to the nourishing of vice and corrupting of youth. Such a work, I am sure, would have met with the approval of Your Majesty's father, King Henry of blessed memory, who ever labored for the spiritual welfare of his subjects."

"Master Sternhold, will you sing me another?"

Thomas then strikes up a ballad tune and sings Psalm 78:

"Give ear, my children, to my Law, etc."

"Master Sternhold, I desire and I command that you write out all the Psalms you have turned into ballads, and give them to the printer at once."

"You do me great honor, Your Majesty. It is my pleasure as well as my bounden duty to comply."

"Now I will go, Master Sternhold. When will the book be ready?"

"At the earliest possible moment, Your Majesty. And it shall be dedicated to Your Majesty!"

"Our thanks, Master Sternhold."

So it came to pass that there shortly appeared (1549) a little book of nineteen paraphrases by Thomas Sternhold, entitled *Certayne Psalmes, chosē out of the Psalter of Dauid and drawē into Englishe metre by Thomas Sternhold, grome of ye kynge's Maiesties robes.* In the Dedication to the twelve-year-old king appeared these words: "Albeit I cannot give Your Majesty great loaves or bring into the Lord's barn full handfulls . . . I am bold to present a few crumbs which I have picked from under my Lord's board."

This is the beginning of an endless procession of Metrical Psalters that served the very purpose hinted in the "Act of Uniformity," namely, for use in private devotions; and within a few years, when to Sternhold's paraphrases were added those of Hopkins and others, this Psalter was admitted for use into the Office of Morning and Evening Prayer. It was this version of Sternhold and Hopkins with some revisions that dominated the Established Church and the non-conforming Churches as well for ten generations until the genius of Isaac Watts broke its stranglehold and led the way to the use of true hymns of "human composure." The story of this long domination by the Psalters and the final liberation will be told in the two following chapters.

## HISTORICAL SUMMARY

CHAPTER TWO: THE REFORMATION: ENTER THE PSALTERS

1554–8    MARY, Queen. Advisors Catholic. Persecution of Protestants and their exodus to Europe.

1555–6    Martyrdoms of Ridley, Latimer and Cranmer.

1556      John Calvin: *Form of Prayer and Ministration of the Sacraments*. Translated by English exiles in Geneva.

1558–1603 ELIZABETH, Queen. Protestantism made by law the religion of the realm. Climaxed by defeat of the Spanish Armada, 1588.

1559      *Act of Supremacy* made Elizabeth the head of the Church of England.

          *Act of Uniformity* made mandatory the use of Second Prayer Book of Edward VI.

1561      The *Genevan Psalter* published.

1562      Sternhold and Hopkins: *One and Fiftie Psalmes of David in Englishe Metre*, the so-called "Old Version."

1564      *Scottish Psalter.*

1570      Elizabeth excommunicated by the Pope. Reformation fully established. Beginning of the Anglican Church.

# THE REFORMATION: ENTER THE PSALTERS

THE NEWLY ESTABLISHED CHURCH had to go through fire. Edward died of tuberculosis at the age of sixteen, and his older half-sister Mary succeeded to the throne in 1553. She had been reared in the Roman faith. At once she restored the Mass, reinstated Roman Catholic bishops who had been ousted under Edward. Leading Protestants were arrested, others fled to the continent. As Mary redoubled her efforts to suppress the new English Church and restore the authority of Rome, resistance increased. This in turn stiffened Mary's severity, until in 1555 her persecution took extremest form. The fires of martyrs burned all over England. Famous men were sent to the stake. Bishop Ridley, who had helped compile the Prayer Book, and ex-Bishop Latimer, who was an eloquent preacher of the new faith, were burned in the town ditch at Oxford near the present Martyrs' Memorial.

"Be of good comfort, Master Ridley, and play the man," cried Latimer, when the faggots were lighted. "We shall this day light such a candle, by God's grace, in England, as I trust shall never be put out."

Archbishop Cranmer, who had been responsible for so much of the new movement under both Henry and Edward, followed them in the flames. For three years the persecution raged until "Bloody Mary" died in 1558. Her half-sister Elizabeth, daughter of Anne Boleyn, was proclaimed Queen by the Protestants, whose beliefs and policies she shared. Then there were great rejoicing and a second housecleaning. Before long Elizabeth set about to remove all traces of her sister's work. Her Parliament passed the "Act of Supremacy," which gave the Crown jurisdiction over all ecclesiastical persons, and consolidated the new Church by passing the "Act of Uniformity" which forbade the use of any form of public worship other than the Second Prayer Book of Edward VI. These historic events gave the needed impetus to the development of Psalmody as the almost universal medium of church praise in England. And thereby hang several tales.

The thousands of Protestants who had fled Bloody Mary's reign took refuge—some in Germany, home of the Reformation, but most in Switzerland. There on the shores of blue Lake Geneva, they came under the powerful influence of John Calvin, minister to a Protestant congregation. Calvin was rapidly becoming the chief exponent of Protestantism in Europe. He was a tyrant in discipline as well as in theology: in his Church Universal there were to be no bishops but only ministers elected by the congregation, and elders, likewise elected, to enforce morality. Prohibited were card-playing, singing of profane songs, and all amusements on Sunday. When it came to Divine Service there was to be a uniform order in which the singing

Martyrdom of Ridley and Latimer, in the "Oxford ditch" October 16, 1555. (Find the martyrs, the guardsmen, and the preacher of the sermon.)

of Metrical Psalms formed an important part. Flocking back to England and Scotland after Elizabeth's coronation, these exiles brought chiefly three things: first, a strong belief in the right of the congregation to select their own clergy—an idea which, though rejected by the Anglican Church, was destined to have a tremendous political as well as religious influence; second, an unshakable Protestant Calvinistic theology; and lastly, an enthusiasm for congregational singing. English Protestants were bound to sing.

The new singing began in one small church in London, spread to other city churches, country churches, and into the open. Bishop Jewell writes:

> The practice of joining in church music has very much conduced to this [greater interest in religion] . . . You may now sometimes see at Paul's Cross after the sermon, six thousand persons, young and old, of both sexes, all singing together and praising God. This sadly annoys the mass-priests and the devil. For they perceive that by these means the sacred discourses sink more deeply into the minds of men, and that their own kingdom is weakened and shaken at almost every note.

Although Elizabeth herself detested these public songs which she called "Geneva jiggs," singing in her reign became almost a passion, an orgy, and the Psalms were "roared aloud" not only in church but in every street! Shakspere takes a fling at the Puritans of his day, "singing Psalms to horn-pipes." This "Geneva-wise" singing was alway in unison; the Puritans had a special abhorrence of antiphonal singing and of part-singing because it savored of popery. As one of them put it:

> Concerning the singing of Psalms, we allow of the people's joining with one another in a plain tune, but not of tossing the Psalm from one side to the other, with the intermingling of organs.

Singing thus became a powerful instrument of propaganda for the reformed faith, whether Established, Puritan or Dissenting. In Cromwell's day (1649–1658), when the Puritans were in power, the Psalms were set to popular tunes and jiggs which were "too good for the devil," and were sung everywhere—at Lord Mayors' dinners, by soldiers on the march and at parade, and by families "who had windows fronting on the streets; for the hypocritical brotherhood did not always care to sing unless they were heard!" As late as 1692 Richard Baxter wrote in the Preface to his *Paraphrase of the Psalms of David in Meter:*

> And Godly Families have still been differenced from the ungodly by open singing the Praises of God, when the other sing wanton and idle songs. Good Christians will not be ashamed, that such Psalms of Praise be heard by their Neighbors into the Streets, when Players, or Ballad-singers are not ashamed, more openly to sing amorous, foolish, ungodly, or abusive Songs.

Having thus proved to their own satisfaction that the Psalms in meter were the best possible material for use and therefore that nothing else ought to be used, the returning exiles proceeded to enforce such use. This was done by act of Parliament for the Established Church, and by order of the Presbyterian and other General Assemblies for all whose consciences would not allow them to endorse the Established Church. The astounding result was that the Church, both Anglican and non-conforming, became a psalm-singing Church and remained so, well into the nineteenth century. Within that time it produced at least 326 metrical versions of the Psalms. Everybody with a pretense of scholarship seemed to try his hand at translation. Among the more prominent paraphrasers were Queen Elizabeth, Lord Bacon, Lord Fairfax, Coverdale, Sir Philip Sidney, Spenser, King James I, Milton, Addison, and hosts of lesser poets.

The earliest of these metrical versions of Psalms, technically called Psalters, is that of *Sternhold and Hopkins,* later called

### THE OLD VERSION

After the death of Thomas Sternhold, a friend of his named Hopkins collected the paraphrases he had made (See Chap. I, end), added thirty-nine of his own, gathered still others from friends, and in 1562 published the entire Book of Psalms with the following title page:

ONE AND FIFTIE PSALMES
OF DAVID IN ENGLISHE METRE,
whereof 37 were made by Thomas
Sterneholde: and the rest by others,
Conferred with the Hebrewe, and in
certeyne places corrected as the
texte, and sens of the Prophete
required

Jam. 5

Yf any be afflicted let him pray,
and if any be merye, let him singe
Psalmes.

Of this version the British Museum preserves 200 different editions—eloquent testimony to a long and valuable service to the cause of religion. In the Established Church it had almost universal use and approval.

Although this Psalter was the best of its time, it was used reluctantly by the stricter Puritans. The words took too much liberty with the sacred text. Cotton Mather of Boston in his *Magnalia* (1702) speaks of the common Puritan feeling about it: "it was an offence unto them."

### THE SCOTTISH PSALTER

The second notable Psalter to appear in this sixteenth century Reformation period was published in Scotland. When the Scottish exiles who had fled from the persecutions of Mary Queen of Scots returned from Geneva, they resolved to make a Psalter completely suited to their taste. Using their Geneva experience they compiled a new version for their Presbyterian kirks. Some of the Psalms they took bodily from the Geneva book, seventy-six more they took bodily from Sternhold and Hopkins, while the remaining numbers were new renderings made by themselves. This work was published in 1564, was reprinted and revised several times, until a hundred years later in 1650 it was given its final form.

Many of the Psalms in this Psalter have found use beyond the borders of the Scottish kirk. They appear, for example, in the present *Hymnary* of the United Church of Canada, and a few of them still appear in the denomi-

John Calvin in his study, Geneva. On the shelf and table are his expositions of the various Biblical books; leaning against the stove (lower right) is his attack on his Protestant rivals, the Anabaptists, in his hand, the *Institutes* which became the standard treatise on theology for the western Protestant world. It is Calvin's theology that pervades practically all English hymns, except Wesley's, up to the later 19th century.

*Left,* Sermon at St. Paul's Cross, 1616. The Bishop of London is preaching from the octagonal pulpit (left). In the gallery box are King James I, his Queen and Charles, Prince of Wales; adjoining are the Archbishop of Canterbury and courtiers. *Right,* Present St. Paul's Cross. The old Cross was demolished under the Commonwealth, 1643, because it was a cross and therefore "popish." At the Restoration the Paul's Cross sermons were removed into the cathedral itself and still belong to the Sunday morning preachers.

national hymnals of the United States. Perhaps the most widely used is the anonymous rendering of Psalm 23, sometimes assigned to Francis Rous:

*The Lord's my shepherd, I'll not want*

One of the writers whose metrical Psalm in this Psalter has survived to the present was

### WILLIAM KETHE (*active 1555–93*) Scottish ?

KETHE'S early life is unknown to us. He was a clergyman and probably was or became a Puritan, for he went into exile in Frankfort during the Marian persecution of 1555; then moved to Geneva. There he seems to have been engaged in translating the Scriptures into what is known as the

*Geneva Bible,* most widely used by the Puritans and brought to America in the *Mayflower.* He also assisted with the Anglo-Genevan metrical Psalter. In this version appeared his renderings of twenty-five Psalms. His work had enough popular appeal to warrant their inclusion in the Sternhold and Hopkins (1562), the Scottish Psalter (1564) and others; and one appears in our modern hymnals, Psalm 100:

### *All people that on earth do dwell* [1560]

In part, what gave this Psalm popularity was Louis Bourgeois' tune to which it was set, now called "Old Hundredth." Originally this tune had a sprightly rhythm. It was tunes like these that won from Queen Elizabeth the scornful phrase "Geneva jiggs."

To conclude, therefore, we find that by the end of the sixteenth century not only the English or Anglican Church but the Scottish National Church and, in general, the miscellaneous bodies of Protestants that were organizing outside the established Churches, were all committed to the use of Psalms of David as hymns. It was the theological beliefs derived from John Calvin that united all Protestants in this practice: only God's own Word was worthy to be used in praising Him.

The influence of these Psalters is incalculable. Their exalted language became part and parcel of Christian thought and speech; the Messianic ideas contained in some of them strengthened the belief that Jesus was the Christ ordained from the foundation of the world to be the Saviour of mankind; the wide range of their emotions touched all the chords of the heart—faith, trust in divine protection, courage in danger, a sense of being the chosen people for whom heaven is in store. This was truly a magnificent contribution to the religious life of the world.

CHAPTER THREE: THE FIGHT FOR FREEDOM

| | | |
|---|---|---|
| 1603–25 | JAMES I. Puritan clergy ask freedom in ritualistic details: James orders them to conform or leave the ministry. | *Writers* |
| 1611 | *King James Version* of the Bible. | |
| 1620 | English settlement of New England begins. | Milton, 1623–48 |
| 1625–49 | CHARLES I. Religious differences: Archbishop Laud represses Puritans and Presbyterians. | |
| 1637–8 | Troubles with Scottish Covenanters; Presbyterianism established. | Herbert, 1633 |
| 1642–7 | Civil War: Col. Cromwell develops cavalry regiment of Puritans: Struggle for power between Presbyterians and Separatists (Independents). Cromwell favored the latter. | |
| 1645 | Archbishop Laud executed: victory of Presbyterians and Independents over Anglicans. | |
| 1648 | Presbyterian majority in Parliament voted to suppress all heresy. | |
| 1649 | Charles I executed. England declared to be a COMMONWEALTH, without king or House of Lords. Cromwell master. | |
| 1653 | Cromwell and army ejected Presbyterians from Parliament and made Independents supreme. Cromwell made Lord Protector. | |
| 1654 | Puritan religion established, supported by tithes. Ministers, any brand of Puritanism (neither Anglican nor Catholic). | |
| 1658 | Cromwell died: an Interregnum | |
| 1660–85 | CHARLES II. | |
| 1661 | *Corporation Act:* Office-holders must take Sacrament administered by Anglican Church (Non-conformists thus excluded from Parliament). | |
| 1662 | *Act of Uniformity:* Clergymen and schoolmasters refusing to consent to everything in Prayer Book, excluded from holding a benefice. 2000 clergy resigned. (Henceforth, all who refused to assent were called Dissenters.) | |
| 1664 | *Conventicle Act:* Any person attending a Dissenting meeting punished up to 7 years' transportation. | |
| 1665 | *Five Mile Act:* Dissenting ministers never to come within five miles of former preaching-places. | |
| 1673 | *Test Act:* Office-holders must swear disbelief in Catholic doctrine of Transubstantiation, and receive Sacrament by Anglican clergymen (Catholics thus driven from office: Dissenters usually conformed.) | Baxter, 1672, 1681<br>Ken, 1674 |
| 1685–9 | JAMES II (a Roman Catholic). | Bunyan, 1684 |
| 1686 | Judge Jeffries persecutes Dissenters but favors Roman Catholics. | |
| 1687 | James issues *Declaration of Indulgence*, suspending all laws against Catholics and Dissenters. Anglican clergy resist. Seven bishops jailed but acquitted. | |
| 1689–1702 | WILLIAM AND MARY. Parliament declared for Protestant succession hereafter. *Toleration Act* (1689) gave Dissenters (except Unitarians and Catholics) right to worship publicly. | Tate & Brady,<br>1696, 1700 |

# THE FIGHT FOR FREEDOM

THE HYMNS OF THE SEVENTEENTH CENTURY are closely associated with the history of the times. That century was filled with struggles in which nearly every hymn writer was actively engaged and a victim of persecution. Before entering upon an account of the historic contest that ended at last in the legal toleration of the religious sects, we must define some of the principal terms used, for these terms will be constantly employed in this chapter.

*Catholic:* Literally the words means Universal and is applied to various sects that claim a world-wide authority. *Cf.* the phrase in the Apostles' Creed in the Anglican Prayer Book: "I believe in the Holy Catholic Church." Ordinarily the term is limited to the Roman Church, the government of which is exercised by authority from the top—from Pope, through cardinals, archbishops, bishops, et al.—rather than by authority from the bottom, as in democratic Congregational or Baptist Churches. Its theology is that of Thomas Aquinas, thirteenth century.

*Protestant:* One who protests against the authority or the belief of the Roman Catholic Church. The term covers all of the Churches which are mentioned below.

*Anglican:* The word is the same as "English" when applied to religious matters. The Anglican Church is the "Established" English Church which began its independent existence when Parliament proclaimed Henry VIII to be the head of the Church in England and declared the Church's independence of Rome. The term covers all Churches that hold the same faith (beliefs), order (government by bishops, priests and deacons), and worship (the use of the Prayer Book),—mostly in the British Empire. The Episcopal Church in America is essentially, though not technically, Anglican.

*Established Church:* One supported by the civil authority and paid for out of taxation. The Constitution of the United States forbids Congress ever to

19

"establish" a religion. With us, therefore, religious bodies have to support themselves by voluntary offerings.

*Puritan:* One who opposed the traditional forms of faith, order, and worship of the Anglican Church and strove for "purer" or simpler forms. Puritans objected to prescribed clerical vestments, to kneeling at the reception of the Lord's Supper, to the use of the ring in marriage and the sign of the cross in baptism. They felt that authority should come from the people rather than from the bishops and clergy. At first the Puritans did not advocate withdrawal from the Established Church.

Puritans became strong in the reigns of Elizabeth and James I, and were the dominant political party in the days of the Commonwealth. The term came to cover several varieties, namely:

*Independents* (Separatists, Congregationalists): Puritans who separated themselves from the Established Church and set up their own organizations on a democratic, self-governing basis. In theology they were Calvinistic. (See "The Theology of Watts' Hymns" in Chap. IV.) They were severely persecuted under Elizabeth and James I. Many fled to Holland and later to America—20,000 of them by 1640.

*Presbyterians:* A form of independent Church in which the government is by presbyters, or elders, elected by the members of individual church bodies; and the whole collection of churches is regulated by a system of courts made up of ministers and elders. These courts are called Synods, Sessions, General Assemblies: In theology, the Presbyterians are Calvinists. The Scottish Church was Established Presbyterian until 1929, when it ceased to be established but remained Presbyterian.

*Baptists:* Churches that are congregational in government, mostly Calvinistic in theology, and insist that church membership is open only to adult believers who have been baptized by immersion, as opposed to baptism of infants and baptism by sprinkling or pouring. They were an offshoot of an old continental sect—the Anabaptists. The first English Baptist Church dates 1611; the first Baptist Church in America was established by Roger Williams in Providence in 1639. There are various brands.

*Non-conformists:* This new term arose in 1662 to cover anyone who refused to conform to the ritual and discipline of the Established Church. Primarily it applied to the 2000 clergymen who would not submit to the Act of Uniformity of 1662 and so were put out of their Churches. The Act required every schoolmaster and every clergyman to express his unfeigned consent to everything contained in the *Book of Common Prayer.*

*Dissenter:* One who dissented from the doctrines of the Established Church: loosely a synonym for Non-conformist; though strictly speaking, non-conformity has to do with acts, while dissent has to do with belief.

## THE STORY OF THE STRUGGLE

It seems incredible that the professed followers of the Prince of Peace should have fought one another in England with ferocious savagery for 150 years. Their fury is accounted for by the fact that religion was mixed up with politics, with greed and the lust for power.

First of all, Protestantism was a protest against the immorality of the Catholic clergy from parish priest to pope, and against a foreign Church that was bleeding the English people of their money. The fast-rising national spirit of England was irked that an Italian should claim the power of heaven and hell over Englishmen and should constantly strive to subordinate their civil rulers to his authority. These factors largely account for the readiness with which England changed from Catholicism to Protestantism, and for the persecutions perpetrated by both sides.

But second, the Protestant sects soon began to war against one another, and for an added reason. They had made the mistake of substituting for an infallible Church, as the source of religious authority, an infallible Bible. When it came to understanding that Bible, every man felt that his interpretation of it was the right one, and the only right one. Now since the Bible was the inspired Word of God, every man's interpretation of it carried the weight of infallibility. If a Christian differed from another Christian on any matter of religion, his first duty was to find a passage of scripture that seemed to back up his belief, and his second duty was to convert his opponent or crush him as a heretic. The struggle among the sects resolved itself, one might say, into a battle between proof-texts.

Furthermore, within the Anglican Church there were offices and "livings" to be dispensed, and the holders received both money and social position. Since the Church was established by act of Parliament, whoever controlled Parliament controlled the Church with its rich pickings. The seventeenth century which we are now considering represents the attempts by Protestant blocs to reform the Established Church by political means, and, on the part of those who rejected that Church, the attempt to escape control. The tragedy is that all parties felt that God Almighty was on their side. It was the Puritan's belief that he was fighting God's battles which gave him his political audacity.

We shall follow for a few moments this tremendous struggle called the Puritan Revolution.

Elizabeth saw the Protestant Church firmly established. But that Church had two enemies: the Roman Catholics who wanted to get back into power, and some Puritans who wanted to change the Church over into what they believed to be a more scriptural form. The enthusiasm caused by the defeat of the (Roman Catholic) Spanish Armada, and the eternal vigilance toward the political plots of the Jesuits against Elizabeth, kept Catholic power at a low ebb for nearly a century. But the Puritans were argumentative and aggressive. They showed in season and out that ritual, choirs, organs, pictures and statues, stained glass, clerical vestments, signs of the cross, genuflexions, candles, altars, and such like, were superstitious relics of popery and had no warrant in the Word of God.

In the reign of James I more and more Puritans were elected to Parliament; the religious quarrels became more and more a matter of politics. As Parliament became more independent the King became more autocratic. James asserted that God was on the side of the monarch and the bishops ("No bishop, no king"), just as the House of Commons asserted that God was on the side of the people. In 1603 a thousand clergymen petitioned James that those who thought it wrong to wear surplices and to use certain other ceremonies be excused from doing so. James flew into a passion, and his answer showed how closely religion and politics were mixed: "A Scottish Presbyterian agreeth as well with a monarchy as God with the devil."

Under Charles I the tension between King and Parliament, between established religion and Puritanism, became heightened. Charles's Archbishop Laud was the instrument of cruel repression of all dissenting tendencies. Clergymen were deprived of their livings if they refused to conform to the Prayer Book or even to remove the communion table to the east end of the chancel. Scotland, which had become largely Presbyterian, was stirred to revolt. When their General Assembly was dissolved by the King's commission, the members continued to sit on the ground that they possessed the divine right to settle all the affairs of the Church independently of the King. Needing Scottish support in its war against Charles, Parliament sent a delegation to Edinburgh. The result was a "Solemn League and Covenant" (1643) in which both parties agreed to be loyal to their several Churches, which must henceforth be governed "according to the Word of God." The Scots then sent armies to fight Charles.

The civil war lasted from 1642 to 1646. Charles was defeated and executed. Early in this war Archbishop Laud had been beheaded, Parliament abolished the Prayer Book, overthrew Episcopacy, and from 1646 Presbyterianism was the legal form of Church government in England. Cromwell and his army tried to prevent a tyranny by the Presbyterians, so that during the Commonwealth (1649–60) he ruled that no inquiry was to be made whether a minister were a Presbyterian, Independent, or what not, so long as he were a Puritan. But on Cromwell's death, Parliament, tired of the tyranny of the army on which Cromwell had depended, made terms with Charles II and restored the ancient government by "Kings, Lords, and Commoners."

At first Charles II favored toleration of all sects, but Parliament would have none of it through fear of the return of Catholics to power. So the bishops were reinstated and the authority of the Established Church was restored with a vengeance. In 1662 Parliament passed the *Act of Uniformity* by which all dissenting clergy were expelled from their pulpits. Presbyterians as well as Independents fell under the ban, also Baptists, Quakers and others.

**LIKE COACHMAN, LIKE CAUSE**
*or.*
**AN EMBLEM**
*Of what we must expect, if Low-Church gets uppermost*

This cartoon was drawn in 1717 or later as a veiled attack on the religious policy of George I, who favored Whigs and Low-Church; the allusions are to the stirring times of Cromwell.

*The Coach,* labelled "Commonwealth," symbolizes the Puritan Revolution. Inside, Oliver Cromwell shouts, "No monarchy." At the rear axle are the headsman's axe and a gibbet with noose. The word "Covenant," attached to the rear post, signifies help received from the Scottish Covenanters in putting down monarchy and episcopacy. The coachman is the Devil.

*The Horses* represent the means by which the Commonwealth secured its victory: Republican Tyranny, Presbytery, Moderation; on the tugs of the harness are Slavery, Rebellion, Occasional Conformity (a device by which a nonconformist could keep his job). The postillion blowing his trumpet is "B. H (oad) ly," then Bishop of Bangor. His blast reads, "Tantara L.C. (Low-Church)."

The *Victims* being trodden down are: the Monarchy represented by King Charles I, crushed under the rear wheel. Under the hoofs of the wheel-horses lie "Liberty of the Subject" and "Magna Carta." Under the center team lie "Loyalty" and the "Earl of Strafford," who had fought against arbitrary imprisonment. Under the leading team, "Episcopacy," "Archbishop Laud" and the *Book of Common Prayer.*

Parliament followed it up two years later with the *Conventicle Act* by which any person was forbidden to attend a religious meeting not in accordance with the Established Church; and the *Five Mile Act* (1665) which forbade a clergyman to come within five miles of his former preaching-places. Punishments for Non-conformists were meted out on an ascending scale ending with a seven-year "transportation," which meant being sent to the Barbadoes or other tropical places, there to work as slaves. Pepys, the writer of the famous *Diary*, says of these victims: "They go like lambs without any resistance. I would to God they would conform, or be more wise and not be catched." These repressive measures were devised to prevent Dissenters from acquiring and wielding political power.

Though Charles II professed to be a Protestant, at heart he was a Catholic. His successor, James II, was an avowed Catholic. The struggle now shifted from a war between the sects to a war of all the sects against Rome. Finally came the "Glorious Revolution" of 1688 and the Protestants called in William of Orange with his Protestant troops. James had to flee. Parliament elected William and Mary as joint sovereigns, decreed that henceforth no Catholic could be king of England, and by the *Toleration Act* gave the Dissenters (except Unitarians and Catholics) a legal right to worship publicly. Thus the century of struggle for religious freedom ended with at least a partial victory.

Fortunately through all this wrangling the Churches had in common one feature: in their services they used the Psalter, and they derived mutual satisfaction in singing those Psalms in which David cursed his enemies. But there were those who held that the current Psalters had departed too much from the sense of the sacred Hebrew text. This was particularly true of the Independents, to whom fault-finding with the Established Church was second nature.

### THE AINSWORTH PSALTER

Among the bands of those Independents who had fled to Holland was one Henry Ainsworth, a learned man acquainted with Hebrew. For the use of his flock in Amsterdam he made a fairly literal paraphrase which was so highly thought of that it came to be bound up with the Geneva Bible, used largely by the Independents. When certain of these exiles went to Plymouth, Massachusetts, in 1620, they carried with them this Bible and the Ainsworth, as later the Massachusetts Bay Colony was to bring Sternhold and Hopkins. Thus the rivalry was transplanted to America.

Nothing of Ainsworth has survived in our hymnals.

### HYMNS OF "HUMAN COMPOSURE"

David's Psalms may have satisfied the belligerents of this age, but many of them were too remote from the inner life of a truly religious Christian. Neither could Parliament suppress the lyric soul of England; it might forbid the use of hymns of "human composure" in the two stated services of the Church, but it could not prevent a poet from writing or from singing in his own home, or in social gatherings. A few of these privately used hymns have survived in our hymnals and will now be considered.

A contemporary broadside, 1688. Two men in the habit of scholars are turning a grindstone while King William III, attended by his Queen, forces the Pope's nose against the stone. Mourners on the left are two monks, two priests and a cardinal who holds the Papal cross while he weeps. Witnesses on the right are Schomberg, who as a Protestant was forced out of his office as Marshal of France when the Edict of Nantes was revoked, and who fled to England to become a general under King William. His companions are (?) a noble and a commoner.

### Rev. GEORGE HERBERT (1593–1632) Anglican

GEORGE HERBERT was the gentle rector of Bemerton, near Salisbury. Izaak Walton in 1661 wrote the lives of several of his friends, including Herbert; and thus we have an intimate picture of one of the loveliest characters that grace the history of English literature. Walton says of Herbert when he was a boy of twelve at the Westminster School under the shadow of the great Abbey in London: "The beauties of his pretty behavior and wit shined and became so evident and lovely in this his innocent age, that he seemed to be marked out for piety, and to become the care of heaven and of a particular angel to guard and guide him."

The angel must have tutored him well, for when Herbert went to

*Left,* George Herbert, from a rare print prefixed to Herbert's poems. *Center,* George Herbert's church at Bremerton. *Bottom,* Herbert's rectory, restored by him.

Cambridge University at the age of fifteen, he was "perfect in the learned languages, and especially in the Greek tongue." He became a great master of music—was honored by being made "University Orator," whose function was to greet distinguished visitors with an oration in Latin. He became Master of Arts at twenty-two, made many friends among notables like Lord Bacon and King James I. He was easily on the road to court preferment, but his influential friends died. He, therefore, followed his true bent, took Holy Orders and became rector of the poor country church at Bemerton, far from the world's tumult. The tumble-down parsonage he rebuilt at his own expense, and engraved on the mantel, where you may still read the words:

### To My Successor

If you chance for to find
A new house to thy mind,
And built without thy Cost:
Be good to the Poor,
As God gives thee store.
And then, my Labour's not lost.

The care of the poor seems to have been one of his chief concerns. He was constantly giving, largely through his wife, who shared in all his ministrations. Of the response of his people Walton writes: "Some of the meaner sort of his Parish did so love and reverence Mr. Herbert that they would let their plow rest when Mr. Herbert's bell rung to prayers, that they might also offer their devotions to God with him, and would then return back to their plow."

Herbert's devotion to music continued. When he had composed the words for a hymn or anthem, he would set them to music and sing them to the accompaniment of his lute or viol. Twice a week he walked to Salisbury to hear music in the cathedral, and then met with a company of friends to sing and play his part at a "private musick meeting."

Herbert lived only four years after coming to Bemerton, but in the meantime he made the world richer by his life and his poetry. He seems to have been completely dedicated to holy living. As he once put it, "We live in an age that hath more need of good examples than precepts." Considering the schisms, the wranglings and the persecutions that characterized that age, it is remarkable to find this holy atmosphere at Bemerton—this oasis of which the life-giving spring was the saintliness of the rector. It was a mystic sainthood, revealed to us in his poems.

The hymns that still survive in our hymnals are all taken from a little book which before his death he gave to a friend to be published, as he said, "if he can think it may turn to the advantage of any dejected soul." It was *The Temple: or Sacred Poems and Private Ejaculations*, published 1633.

## Let all the world in every corner sing     [1633]

This hymn was called by its author an "Antiphon"; by which he meant that it was to be sung alternately by two bodies of singers. The chorus was to sing, wherever it occurred,

> Let all the world in every corner sing,
> My God and King

and a soloist or the people in the church were to sing the rest. When so sung it would certainly be effective.

> *Stanza 1.*   We must visualize the universe ringing with praise—the highest heaven and the fruitful earth beneath. The poet here gives us in his own words a reminiscence of many passages in the Psalms.
> *Stanza 2.*   The two kinds of praises that must resound: the official worship of the Church expressed in Psalms, and the heart's private devotions. We can easily discern which type most strongly appealed to Herbert; for while the Psalms were compulsory in church and could be heard only at Morning and Evening Prayer, the praises of the heart could arise every hour, an eternal improvisation.

## Teach me, my God and King     [1633]

This second hymn has some quaint ideas that need to be made clear. Herbert entitled the poem *The Elixir*. This word "elixir" takes us at once into the realm of medieval chemistry or alchemy. In those pre-scientific days the "philosophers," as they were called, were always looking for two elusive substances: the touch-stone which would turn everything to gold, and the elixir which would endow one with perpetual youth. The word "elixir" and its near-synonym "tincture" sometimes stand for both substances; it was thought capable of causing the most astonishing changes both material and spiritual. In this poem Herbert says he has found an elixir that will change the basest metal into gold. It is the little phrase "For Thy sake." Anyone can use it if he will always remember that God is present; it is easy then to make all of one's actions an offering to Him (stanza 1).

This imagery of alchemy is obscured by the changes that John Wesley made in the original. Stanza 3 (in the Methodist Hymnal) is Wesley's endeavor to get round the medieval imagery which the common people for whom he labored could not understand. Herbert wrote it thus:

> *All may of Thee partake*
>      That is, any base metal has the power of assimilating this magic elixir
> *Nothing can be so mean,*
> *Which with this tincture ("For Thy sake")*
> *Will not grow bright and clean.*

So the metal lead, with the "tincture" or "elixir" added, the alchemist believed, would become shining gold.

In stanza 5, Herbert gives an illustration of his general statement:

*A servant with this clause*
> That is, if he uses this magic phrase "For Thy sake"

*Makes drudgery divine;*
> Makes ordinary work become an offering to God

*Who sweeps a room, as for thy laws,*
> In a way to embody God's law of perfection

*Makes that and the action fine.*
> Makes the room clean and the action noble.
> "Fine" is here used as in "24 carats fine," that is, pure gold.

*This is the famous stone*
*That turneth all to gold;*
*For that which God doth touch and own*
> That is, doth apply the touch-stone to and doth acknowledge as His

*Cannot for less be told.*
> Cannot be counted as of lesser value.

All this was too specific for Wesley: he had to dignify (and blur) it with generalities.

John Wesley rated Herbert very high as a religious poet. When he compiled his first hymnbook in 1737 for the use of his parish in Savannah, Georgia, out of seventy hymns in all, six of them were adapted from Herbert; only two authors had more than he. Perhaps the best tribute to the religious quality of Herbert comes from Richard Baxter who lived and wrote in the same century (see below). He writes:

> I must confess that next to the Scripture poems there are none so savory to me as Mr. George Herbert's. Herbert speaks to God like one that really believeth in a God, and whose business in the world is most with God.

## JOHN MILTON (1608–1674) Independent

MILTON, the mighty bard of *Paradise Lost* which so enthralled our ancestors, was the finest representative of the more liberal aspects of seventeenth century Puritanism. From his early days a lyric poet, in his middle life he became deeply involved in politics, and by his fighting pamphlets he did more than any other man to justify at home and abroad the political acts of the Puritans; then in his blind old age he wrote the great English epic poems that have no rival in any language with the exception of Dante's *Divine Comedy*. In our hymnbooks he is represented by as many as four poems, of which we give only one.

*Let us with a gladsome mind*    Ps 136      [1623]

Wonderful that so many hymnals should enshrine the work of a fifteen-year-old boy! When Milton wrote this hymn in 1623 he lived at his father's house in Bread Street, London, and was a student at St. Paul's School. That school was a logical place for a boy of his ancestry. His grandfather had changed from Catholicism to Protestantism while attending Christ Church College, Oxford. His father had been disinherited in Elizabeth's reign for

John Milton, age 21. The busts are Homer, left, and Virgil, right.

reading the Bible, and now the boy with seeds of liberalism in his blood was drinking at that famous fount of liberalism, the school founded in 1512 by John Colet, Dean of St. Paul's Cathedral. This school was established for the express purpose of setting aside the quibbling, logic-chopping education of the medieval schoolmen, and of giving a chance for the New Learning from Italy to enter, with its emphasis upon Greek studies and upon liberalizing philosophy. Colet set no limits whatever to the kind of student admitted, whether high or low, rich or poor; nor did he bind his school to any form of religion, for he saw that the forms were bound to change; and he aimed at fitting his pupils to meet the needs of the day in which they lived. In all England there was not another such nourisher of freedom.

When Milton finished there it was said of him, "He was as scholarly, as accomplished and as handsome a youth as St. Paul's had ever sent forth."

While there Milton wrote this paraphrase of Psalm 136, evidently for his own delight or for that of his father and his teachers. That he turned to the Bible for his inspiration was natural considering his heritage, and that he paraphrased a Psalm shows clearly what was in his day the chief outlet for a religiously inclined poet. Young Milton is here just imitating his elders, only he did a better job than they.

At sixteen years, Milton entered Christ College, Cambridge. This was the liberal university of his day, more so than Oxford, and from it were destined to come many of the Puritan leaders, among them John Harvard, founder of Harvard University in Cambridge, Massachusetts.* Here Milton distinguished himself in English and Latin poetry and left the impression on his contemporaries that he was a genius to be heard from. As a college exercise he wrote his magnificent *Ode on the Morning of Christ's Nativity,* begun Christmas morning, 1629. At this time he was twenty-one years old. While the poem is far too elaborate for use as a hymn, editors have been tempted to make use of parts of it. Stanzas 13–15 have been so used in *Songs of Praise,* under the first line, *Ring out, ye crystal spheres.*

In 1648, moved by the stress of the civil war between Charles I and Parliament, with all its accompanying religious tensions, Milton wrote a metrical translation of Pss 80–88, using the original Hebrew. Because the Puritans were such sticklers for respecting the very words of the Bible, without additions or subtractions, Milton printed the Hebrew text at the side of his version and then indicated by italic type the words which he himself had added to those of the Holy Ghost, a method you can still see employed in the King James version of the Bible (2 Peter 1:21, A. V.). Editors of hymn books have made selections from these 128 verses in order to construct hymns of singable length. Here is an example:

*The Lord will come and not be slow    Pss 82, 85–6    [1648]*

If you turn to the particular Psalms in the Bible from which these stanzas are taken you will find Ps 85 is a plea for God's pardon for sins committed; Ps 86 a plea for God's help in time of trouble; and Ps 82 is a plea for God to put an end to the injustices under which the nations suffer. To Milton's mind, these inspired passages fitted exactly the unhappy lot of England. In the year just passed, the army had defied civil law by revolting against Parliament; the Presbyterians were scheming with France and Scotland to bring about a Scottish invasion of England on behalf of King Charles I; the Independent (Congregational) members of Parliament were expelled by a mob; a Presbyterian Parliament had rejected a scheme for

* Also Oliver Cromwell, Henry Dunster, first President of Harvard University, Cromwell's General Lord Fairfax, and some of the Pilgrim fathers.

toleration of all sects but Roman Catholics. In the current year, 1648, there were uprisings in Wales and Kent, the fleet deserted Parliament for the Prince of Wales in France; Parliament voted to suppress all heresy; King Charles was playing fast and loose with all parties and was imprisoned by the army; and in January of the following year his head was cut off.

With these tremendous events in mind, read the verses selected for this hymn:

*Stanza 1.* The great and terrible day of the Lord is at hand; he will judge the earth with righteousness.
*Stanza 2.* Then truth and justice will once more flourish among men.
*Stanza 3.* For God has the power and the right to rule over all nations.
*Stanza 4.* And all nations must and shall submit.
*Stanza 5.* He alone can accomplish these wonders, for He is God alone.

Milton's use of these Psalms is just another instance of how men through all ages have looked to the Bible for hope and inspiration, and to God for the establishment of freedom and justice throughout all the world. (See Watts: "Our God, our help in ages past.") Our present generation in the midst of universal change does the same.

### Rev. *RICHARD BAXTER* (*1615–1691*) Anglican-Non-conformist

RICHARD BAXTER was one of the most remarkable men of his generation. For the most part self-educated, he published 168 books on a great variety of topics. Though licensed to preach by the Anglican Church, his conscience would not allow him to accept fully the views of any sect— "He grew too puritan for the Bishops and too Episcopalian for the Presbyterians"—and that meant trouble in those days of fierce sectarianism. He could not keep out of politics, and that meant more trouble; for he favored Cromwell (to a certain extent), and as chaplain in his army took part in seven battles. Yet he rebuked Cromwell for usurping the chief place in the State. He helped bring about the restoration of Charles II, yet he helped dethrone James II. At first not much of a preacher, he became the prince of preachers in London. When most Puritan clergymen disapproved of music in church, he was an ardent champion. Persecuted for twenty years, he died a most honored citizen, and two hundred years after his death members of all creeds raised a monument to his character and his deeds in the town of Kidderminster.

In this same Kidderminster he performed a miracle and that at the very beginning of his career. When the Long Parliament began its work in 1640, it undertook to reform the clergy of the Established Church. The attitude of some of these ministers toward their flock had become scandalous. They took their pay from their people's tithes yet gave nothing in return; they were lazy, without sense of obligation, and in many cases dissolute. As Milton wrote in his poem *Lycidas*, "The hungry sheep look up, and are not fed." The result after a century of Protestantism added to previous centuries of Romanism was that parts of England were simply not civilized. The town of Kidderminster was especially noted for its ignorance and depravity, so that some of its citizens complained to the committee which Parliament had named to hear grievances. This committee finally forced

"The Reverend and Learned
Mr. Richard Baxter, 1673."

the rector of Kidderminster, whose salary was £200—equivalent today to about $5000—to give up £60 a year to provide a preacher who would do something. Young Baxter, age twenty-six, was chosen. With some intermissions he stayed nineteen years. He changed that town and the surrounding country beyond anyone's belief. Brutality gave place to something like manners; ignorance yielded to skilled teaching until it was said that irreligious people became not the rule but the exception.

That was the work of a practical man; but Baxter was also a poet. Most hymnals carry two of his hymns—and be it noted that they are not paraphrases of the Psalms but original lyrics. He showed his courage when he wrote, "I durst make hymns of my own"—for most writers did not dare.

### Lord, it belongs not to my care     [1681]

As you read this sweet song of resignation and trust, you might think it was composed by some dear old lady in the quiet of her home, perhaps after reading the 23rd Psalm. It breathes a gentle faith in the leadership of God and implicit trust that whatever He sends is good. It holds fast to the example of Christ and looks forward to that union with Him in heaven which will be the crowning joy of serving Him here below. Actually the hymn is an expansion of Phil. 1:21, "For me to live is Christ and to die is gain." But behind that hymn is this record of Baxter's from 1661 to 1681:

> Not allowed to resume his old pastorate at Kidderminster.
> Forbidden to preach in the diocese of Worcester.
> Deprived of all rights as a clergyman by the Act of Uniformity.
> Sent to prison for "keeping a conventicle"—holding meetings in a private house.
> Arrested for preaching in London; the meetinghouse he built for himself closed by the authorities after his first sermon.
> Arrested in his house, though very sick, and carried away at the risk of his life. Though later released that he might die at home, his goods and books were seized.
> His wife, to whom he had been happily married for twenty years, died after a long and painful illness. He says about this hymn in a later edition (1689), "This covenant, my dear wife, in her former sickness, subscribed with a cheerful will."

And after the poem was written these things befell him:

> Three times brought before the court, though scarcely able to stand, and finally made to sign a bond for £400 in security for his good behavior.
> Hounded by the infamous chief-justice Jeffreys for "libelling the Church in his paraphrase of the New Testament." After calling Baxter "an old rogue, an old schismatical knave, a hypocritical villain, a conceited, stubborn, fanatical dog, a snivelling Presbyterian," Judge Jeffreys proposed that he should be whipped at the cart's tail through London. But Baxter was let off with a fine of 500 marks and eighteen months in jail (he was now seventy years old and for twenty-five years had been very much of an invalid).

When next we sing this hymn let us remember that it came out of great tribulation.

### Bishop THOMAS KEN (1637–1711) Anglican

KEN is associated first of all with the angler Izaak Walton who married Ken's half-sister. Early left an orphan, Thomas went to live in their cottage near the river Dove in west-central England—and doubtless went fishing! When Walton moved to London, Thomas, a lad of fourteen, was sent to Winchester College.

Winchester, earliest of the English public (by which is meant private) schools had been founded in 1382 by William Wykham, who was both

*Top*, Winchester College. Ken attended as a boy and later became Chaplain. *Center*, Thomas Ken as Bishop of Bath and Wells. *Right*, Wells Cathedral, worn entrance to the Chapter House.

Bishop of Winchester and Lord Chancellor of the realm. Previously he had magnificently founded New College, Oxford, and now invested some of his ample means in this school for ninety-six boys who were presumably to be sent later to New College. And ample means he had! The bishopric alone yielded him the equivalent of $300,000 a year.

Ken lived at Winchester College during its worst period—the Commonwealth. Soldiers of Parliament profaned with rough horse-play the great cathedral, almost under whose eaves the school nestled; they paraded the streets in surplices stolen from the sacristy. The schoolboys like the citizenry at large were split into two camps, Roundheads and Cavaliers; and you may be sure that the Roundheads would not be too gentle with an undersized Anglican like Ken. Schoolmasters too were tough. In the schoolroom above the Master's throne was engraved a verse in Latin hexameters which freely translated runs, "Learn, leave, or be licked." Ken left behind one hint that he was a boy: carved in the stone of the cloister walk one may still read "T. KEN."

At New College, Oxford, things were even worse than at Winchester. The managers were illiterate Presbyterians and Independents of the severest type. Owen, the vice chancellor of the university, hated the Anglican forms of worship so much that when the Lord's Prayer was used he sat down and put on his hat. When the Restoration came in 1660, all the Puritan riff-raff was swept away, the old scholars were restored, the Puritan rules were abolished, and the university went "stark, staring mad" in its new freedom. Ken was a student there through both these phases. The experience confirmed in him his love for decency, morality, and the dignity of the Church.

A clergyman now, he returned to Winchester as chaplain to the bishop in whose palace his old step-brother-in-law, Izaak Walton, was now living. He was also a Fellow in his old school, and a Prebendary, or member of the cathedral staff. Remembering the dearth of religion in his school days, and to counteract the restoration drift toward immorality, he now wrote the *Manual of Prayers* for the Winchester boys; and to this *Manual* he later added his Morning and Evening Hymns listed below. All the while he was growing in power as a preacher, so much so that he was appointed chaplain to Charles II. The King was greatly impressed by his sermons in which "little Ken tells me of my faults." But "little Ken" had his nerve with him! When the King came to Winchester on one of his periodical visits to the sumptuous palace he was building there, bringing among others his mistress Nell Gwyn, the king's "harbinger" picked Ken's house as the best place to lodge Nell. Ken refused to take her. He said, "A woman of ill repute ought not to be endured in the house of a clergyman, least of all in that of the King's chaplain . . . Not for his kingdom will I comply with the King's commands." It is said that Ken put his house in charge of a builder for repairs and had the roof taken off. King Charles greatly admired his courage. Shortly after, when the King was being urged to appoint this one or that one as Bishop of Bath and Wells, he broke off all arguments with: "Odd's fish! Who shall have Bath and Wells but little Ken who would not give poor Nelly a lodging!" So "little black Ken" went forthwith to the Episcopal palace at Wells.

Ken had more than one later occasion to show the stuff that was in him, especially under James II. He lost his bishopric in 1691 because, having sworn fealty to James II, he could not in good conscience swear fealty to William and Mary while James was alive and had been deposed (as he thought) unjustly. All of which proves that to the end Ken gave supreme authority only to his conscience.

This true and loyal character of Ken's shines through the hymns that have come down to us:

### Awake, my soul, and with the sun     [1674]

Written for the boys of Winchester College with the recommendation that they "be sure to sing the Morning and Evening hymn in their chamber devoutly." For 300 years before this time the boys had sung the Latin hymn, "*Jam lucis orto sidere*"—"Now that the daylight fills the sky." We must picture their early rising—literally "with the sun" or even earlier in winter (at 5 o'clock); the reluctance of the boys to get out of their truckle-beds in the cold dormitory ("Shake off dull sloth, and joyful rise"), and the singing of this hymn before breakfast, just as one might whistle to keep up one's courage. Some phrases suggest the author's recollections of glad morning adventures with his angling step-brother, but most of them are strong appeals to conscience, to diligence, self-improvement, living as under the eye of God. This is good tonic for a boy if he thinks about it while he sings.

### Glory to thee, my God, this night     [1674]

### (All praise to thee, my God, this night)

This also is from the Winchester hymns sung by the boys first from manuscript, then from printed sheets, until at last it and "*Awake, my soul*" were incorporated into the school hymnal. The thoughts are so simple that they need no explanation: thanks for the day just passed, prayers for forgiveness, for rest, and for freedom from fear of death. One might say that the thoughts are rather morbid for youngsters to entertain every night;—but then, we live in a different age.

Bishop Ken was a thorough musician. He used to sing both these hymns as part of his own devotions, accompanying himself upon an organ in his room or upon a lute or a viol.

### Rev. JOHN BUNYAN (1628–1688) Independent-Baptist

THE once-despised sect of the Baptists furnished English literature with one of its greatest writers and English hymnody with a sturdy song. Bunyan's *Pilgrim's Progress* in which that song occurs has been read by more English-speaking people and translated into more languages than any book except the Bible. But the present generation is, for the most part, ignorant of the book.

The story tells how the hero named Christian, a native of the *City of Destruction*, oppressed with a sense of impending doom, undertakes a pilgrimage to the *Celestial City*. On the way he gets stuck in the *Slough of Despond*, reaches the *Strait Gate* where a wise Interpreter instructs him about the way. At a wayside Cross his heavy pack of sins falls off; he climbs the hill *Difficulty* to a castle where the guardian's two daughters give him armor for the fights he is bound to have. Soon the road is barred by the fiend *Apollyon* with whom he wages a long but victorious fight. He passes through the town of *Vanity Fair* where all kinds of shows and frivolities are in full swing; there he is beaten, put in an iron cage, pilloried, and sees his companion *Faithful* burned at the stake. Next he falls into the clutches of *Giant Despair*, lord of *Doubting Castle*, who thrusts him into a dungeon and beats him within an inch of his life. Finally from the *Delectable Mountains* he catches a glimpse of the holy city, from which only a deep river called *Death* divides him. Crossing this, he is welcomed into the *Celestial City* by troops of angels with songs of victory.

No abstract like this can do justice to the vivid portrayal of the scores of persons involved, their lively conversations, their hopes and fears, temptations, battles, successes, or of the courage, faith and loyalty with which they meet all crises.

Bunyan wrote this allegory while he was in jail. He was one of those Non-conformists whose conscience would not allow them to accept the Prayer Book and liturgy of the Established Church. What would the State Church care for him, a poor traveling tinker whose wife said that at their marriage they had neither a spoon nor a dish between them! But the Baptists were seeking the outcast and the lost. They took him in at their Bedford meeting and in due time inspired him with the resolve to become a preacher of the gospel that he might mend the souls of people as well as their pots and pans. Then the Church and the State rose in their dignity and sent the tinker to jail (1660) for preaching in a "conventicle," or illegal meeting. On promise of pardon if he would stop preaching he replied: "If I were out of prison today, I would preach the gospel again tomorrow, by the help of God!" What can you do with a prisoner like that but keep him in jail? They kept him in jail for the better part of twelve years. During that confinement he wrote nine books!

Released by the "Declaration of Indulgence" of Charles II in 1672, Bunyan was called to be the pastor of the Congregational (Baptist) church of Bedford that met in a barn. From this center he preached throughout the shire so successfully that his enemies dubbed him "Bishop Bunyan." Then Parliament revoked the Declaration of Indulgence, Bunyan lost his license to preach, persisted in preaching—once, tradition says, "disguised as a wag-

*Top*, The "Den" at Bedford, where Bunyan wrote *Pilgrim's Progress*. *Left*, Bunyan's prison door, now preserved at the Bunyan Baptist meeting-house, Bedford. *Right*, Statue of Bunyan in Bedford Park.

goner and preaching in a smock-frock with a cart-whip in his hand." But he was spied upon and soon jailed again. The original warrant for his arrest is still in existence, addressed to the constables of Bedford. It stated, among other things, that notwithstanding the King's past clemency and indulgent grace:

> yett once John Bunnyon of your said Towne, Tynker, hath divers times within one month last past in contempt of his Majestie's good laws preached or teached at a Conventicle meeteing or assembly under colour or pretense of exercise of Religion in other manner than according to the Liturgie or Practice of the Church of England.

During this second imprisonment he wrote *Pilgrim's Progress* (published 1678), which begins with the words:

> As I walk'd through the wilderness of this world, I lighteed on a certain place where there was a Denn, and I laid me down in that place to sleep; and as I slept, I dreamed a Dream.

That "Denn" was a tiny gate-house prison half way across a narrow bridge that spanned the river Ouse in Bedford town. If you want to know what sort of judges and jurors and spies sent him there, read in *Pilgrim's Progress* the description of the trial of Faithful at Vanity Fair,—the judge, Lord Hate-good; the jury, Mr. Blindman, Mr. No-good, Mr. Malice, Mr. Love-lust, Mr. Live-loose, Mr. Heady, Mr. High-mind, Mr. Enmity, Mr. Lyar, Mr. Cruelty, Mr. Hate-light, and Mr. Implacable. That is a good sample of the administration of justice in the heresy-hunting seventeenth century.

All this preliminary material is necessary to the full appreciation of the poem which has survived in our hymnals:

### He who would valiant be    [1684]

These verses come from the second part of *Pilgrim's Progress*, written six years after the first part, which describes how Christian's wife and children made the same pilgrimage. The lines occur at the close of the conversation between Mr. Great-heart and Mr. Valiant-for-Truth, in which the latter tells of a battle he fought with three men who tried to prevent his continuing his pilgrimage, and of the trials that had beset other determined wayfarers. Of course Mr. Bunyan never intended that his verses should be sung in church; indeed, in our "cultured" times, editors have seen fit to tone down their picturesque particulars into colorless generalities. To get the full flavor we must see the original:

> Who would true Valour see,  
> Let him come hither;  
> One here will Constant be,  
> Come Wind, come Weather.

> There's no Discouragement,  
> Shall make him once Relent,  
> His first avow'd Intent,  
>     To be a Pilgrim.

Whoso beset him round,
With dismal Storys,
Do but themselves confound;
His strength the more is,
No Lyon can him fright,
He'll with a Gyant Fight,
But he will have a right,
    To be a Pilgrim.

Hobogoblin, nor foul Fiend,
Can daunt his Spirit:
He knows, he at the end,
Shall Life Inherit.
Then Fancies fly away,
He'll fear not what men say,
He'll labor Night and Day,
    To be a Pilgrim.

In the England of Bunyan's day, wind and weather, lions and giants, hob-goblins and foul fiends, were physical and spiritual realities to tinkers and carters, farmers and blacksmiths, as they are not to the well-dressed occupants of the pews of our day who have ridden to church in their motor-cars. Baptists and Presbyterians are no longer jailed or transported, or Quakers whipped at the cart's tail through the town for not attending an Episcopal church. But for Bunyan this poem that summed up the qualities demanded of a Pilgrim who followed his conscience come what might, was true to the life. It was as a matter of fact a miniature autobiography and spiritual description of Bunyan himself.

In contrast to this fighting hymn of Bunyan, here is a non-controversial, spontaneous folk-song, far removed from the war of creeds that otherwise dominates this page of English history:

ANONYMOUS: English Carol. c. seventeenth cent.

## The first Noël the angels did say

The popularity of this carol is shown by its presence in nine of our ten hymnals. It deserves to be popular, for it gives a purely narrative song on a level children can comprehend. We need not be troubled by the shepherds seeing the star in the East, contrary to the Bible account, nor wonder how the star could go north-west to find Bethlehem. We only enjoy the frank naïveté and the reverent spirit of the lyric, and can see the waits standing in the snow before the shining windows of the manor house until the squire or the lord comes out with the wassail-bowl and a coin, or whatever custom prescribes.

"Nowell" is the English form of the French "Noël" which in turn derives from the Latin for "Birthday." A carol is a popular religious song meant to be sung outside a church rather than within.

The original consisted of nine stanzas of which five are usually chosen.

### THE TATE AND BRADY PSALTER

This belligerent century closes with a new metrical version of the Psalms. For the past hundred years and more the Established Church had given the Sternhold and Hopkins Psalter tyrannous sway over itself and over many dissenting sects. Its chief virtue was its faithfulness to the original

Hebrew, its chief defect was its hopelessly unpoetical character. Now England was beginning to emerge from its fighting stage. The *Toleration Act* of 1689 gave Dissenters a legal standing and so removed the persecution incentive. The English people were beginning to feel the influence of the literary models of France, for this was the era of Louis XIV in which French literature reached its height of classical style. In the light of the elegancies of Molière, Racine, Corneille, how uncouth the language of England seemed! Dryden was introducing the Heroic Couplet as the proper verse of polite society; and other authors were trying to attain the conciseness and polish which marked his literary work and which were destined to flower in the elegant prose of the eighteenth century. No wonder Sternhold and Hopkins seemed out of date.

Two men at the court of William and Mary undertook a new metrical version of the Psalms more in keeping with the literary pretensions of the age. One was Nahum Tate (1652–1715), an Irishman who as perhaps the least unpoetical of the Protestant poets had been appointed Poet Laureate; and Nicholas Brady (1659–1726), another Irishman, chaplain to William III. This "New Version," as it was called, was published in 1696 and because from the start it had royal sanction it was used largely in the Established Church. But the Non-conforming Churches would have little to do with it because it took too much liberty with the inspired Word. Today we can see little difference between the old Psalters, certainly not enough to quarrel over.

Nevertheless some verses in this "rhetorical paraphrase," called "Tate and Brady," stand out so conspicuously from the earlier versions that modern editors have very generally adopted them. Here they are:

*As pants the hart for cooling streams*   Ps 42: 1–2, 5, 9, 11

*Through all the changing scenes of life*   Ps 34: 1, 3–4, 7–9, 22

At a later date (1700) the authors added a supplement to their versions. It contained a few original hymns, all of which have sunk into oblivion except one. That one is, perhaps, the happiest description we have of the appearance of the angels to the shepherds. It is thought that Nahum Tate was the sole author. If so, this is his monument:

*While shepherds watched their flocks by night*   [1700]

At this point it will be well to pause long enough to take account of stock. Up to the year 1700, English hymnody as we know it was practically non-existent. The Protestant Church began its liturgical life by rejecting the accumulated treasure of Latin Hymns, and then on a false theory of the nature of Praise in worship, tried to make the Jewish Psalms express Christian adoration. The tyranny of David became complete in both the Established and the Non-conforming Churches. The hymns considered here were not written as hymns but as private devotions. We now await the arrival of a revolutionary spirit to open the floodgates of religious song.

# HISTORICAL SUMMARY

| | | *Writers* |
|---|---|---|
| 1702–14 | QUEEN ANNE: Strong for Anglican Church and Tories. Rise of Deism: reason the sole test of religion; God revealed in a world of law. | Watts, 1707–19 |
| 1711 | Jonathan Swift uses satire against Whigs, Catholics and Dissenters. *Occasional Conformity Act:* penalized Dissenters who received Anglican Sacrament to get office but continued to attend Dissenting Churches. | Addison, 1712 |
| 1714 | *Schism Act:* no one could keep a school without license from Anglican bishop. | |
| 1714–27 | GEORGE I: Favorable to Whigs, Dissenters and traders. Much political corruption: Tories stood for religious intolerance and contempt for trade; Whigs for toleration and weakening power of king. Both used bribery. | |
| 1726–29 | Voltaire visits England: pours unsparing ridicule on organized religion. | Doddridge, |
| 1727–60 | GEORGE II. | 1735–55 |
| 1736 | Butler: *Analogy of Religion*—the divine regnancy of conscience over behavior. | Wesleys, 1738–47 |
| 1738 | Revivals begin under Whitefield and the Wesleys. Leaders and converts persecuted. | Cennick, 1742 Williams, 1745 |
| 1744 | Methodism established. Evangelical wing develops in Anglican Church. | Byrom, 1749 |
| 1751–83 | England wins territory in India. Bishop Berkeley (d. 1753) attacks Deism: nothing really exists but mind and ideas. | |
| 1757 | Hume: *Natural History of Religion.* Experience the source of all knowledge; miracles, so-called proofs of Christianity, never existed. | Steele, 1757 |
| 1760–1820 | GEORGE III. | |
| 1767–85 | Revolutionary inventions in textile industry; steam engine; northern cities pose problems in politics and religion. | Grigg, 1765 Cowper, 1768–79 Olivers, 1770 |
| 1778 | "Gordon riots" against Catholics. | Fawcett, 1773–82 |
| 1778–82 | Violence in Ireland between Catholics and Protestants. | Newton, 1774–79 |
| 1779 | Agitation for economic and political reform. | Toplady, 1776 |
| 1789– | French Revolution. | Heath, 1781 |
| 1792 | Wm. Carey first missionary to India. Baptist Missionary Society founded. | Perronet, 1789 |
| 1794 | Paley: *Evidences of Christianity:* Design in nature proves existence of a Designer. | |
| 1795 | Tom Paine: *Age of Reason:* A criticism of common ideas of God and morality. | |

## CHAPTER FOUR

# THE REVOLUTIONARY DR. WATTS
# AND HIS CONTEMPORARIES

IMAGINE A LITTLE MAN FIVE FEET HIGH; a large head made bigger with a huge wig; a hooked nose; small piercing eyes; a frail and sickly body; the whole combination looking more like an embryo than a fully developed organism: that was the illustrious Rev. Isaac Watts (1674–1748), Dissenter, Congregationalist.

A beautiful and accomplished young lady once upon a time fell in love with him through his poetry, having never seen him. When the two met, her disillusionment was instantaneous while he fell deeply in love with her. He shortly asked her to marry him; whereupon she declined him in her most gracious manner and added with no doubt the best of intentions, "Mr. Watts, I only wish I could say that I admire the casket as much as I admire the jewel." Pretty plain talk; but young Watts took it sweetly and the two remained good friends for more than thirty years. Watts never married.

Perhaps the poor health that clung to him all his days was pre-natal in its origin. While his mother was carrying him, his father was jailed for "playing the deacon in the Independents' meeting house"; shortly after Isaac was born the father was again arrested and put into St. Michael's prison at Southampton. Tradition says that his mother used to sit on a stone mounting-block opposite the jail and nurse her baby while conversing with her husband beyond the bars. The father was jailed a third time in 1683 and finally compelled to leave town, in accordance with the *Conventicle* and *Five-Mile Acts* mentioned on page 24. So Isaac, Sr., hid himself for two years in London, where he plied the business of clothier, and ultimately became well-to-do. Young Isaac thus knew something about persecution, though as a man he found that Dissenters were tolerated and had even become respectable.

Isaac was precocious. His father, who for a time ran a successful boarding school, was his early tutor and made hay with his young genius while the sun shone. He began to teach Isaac Latin when the boy was four years old. He, or someone else, taught Isaac Greek when he was eight or nine, French

*Left,* the Reverend Dr. Isaac Watts. *Below,* In Watts' own hand, a list of "memorable affairs" in his early life.

Coincidents

Memorable Affairs in my Life

1683: my father persecuted & imprisoned for Nonconformity 6 months. after that forced to leave his family & live privately in London for 2 years

1685/7 1688: K: Ch: 2: Dyed & K: Ja: 2d procl

| | |
|---|---|
| I was Born. | July 17. 1674 |
| Began to Learn Latin of my father | ..... 1678 |
| & Latin school & wrote & writeing | - - - 1680 |
| was Propositor of ye Latin school | - - - 1683 |
| Began to Learn Greek | - - - 1683 or before |
| Had ye small Pox | - - 1683 |
| Learnt - French | 1684, 1685 - 7 |
| Learnt Hebrew | - - 1687, or 8 |

1688: Nov. 5: Prince of Orange landed in Engl

1692: Sept. 8: at noon an Earthquake & an England & in other nations

| | |
|---|---|
| Fell under Considerable Convictions of Sin | - 1688 |
| & was taught to trust in Christ I hope, | - 1689 |
| Had a great & dangerous Sickness | 1689 |
| Left ye grammar school & came to London to Mr Rows, to study Phil: | - 1690. |
| Paid a 6 weeks visit to Southton | 1692 |

when he was eleven, Hebrew when he was thirteen. This learning was interrupted by smallpox when he was nine, and culminated when he was fourteen in what might have been expected in a non-conforming Calvinistic family:—as Isaac put it, "Fell under considerable conviction of sin." Poor boy! He ought to have been playing more ball. He made the proper entry next year: "And was taught to trust in Christ, I hope"—so modest was this young saint about presuming to know that he had been "elected" to stand among the saved! We must not omit the next item in his list, for perhaps it is a result of all the others: "1689. Had a great and dangerous illness."

His precocity showed itself in insatiable reading, and in versifying in season and out. His conversation was so annoyingly metrical that after various prohibitions against rhyming, his father started to whip him, whereupon the rhymester cried out through his tears:

> O father, do some pity take,
> And I will no more verses make.

As a sample of his early poetizing as well as of his Calvinistic theology, listen to this acrostic—the first letters of each line spelling out his name, ISAAC WATTS. He wrote it when he was seven years old!

> I am a vile polluted lump of earth;
> So I've continued ever since my birth;
> Although Jehovah grace does daily give me,
> As sure this monster Satan will deceive me.
> Come therefore, Lord, from Satan's claws relieve me.
>
> Wash me in thy blood, O Christ,
> And grace divine impart;
> Then search and try the corners of my heart,
> That I in all things may be fit to do
> Service to Thee, and sing thy praises too.*

As he matured, some friends offered to send Isaac to Oxford University; but since in that case he would be obliged to become an Anglican, he declined the opportunity. Thereafter for eight years he studied with a Mr. Rowe, "philosophy, etc.," in a Non-conformist academy at Stoke Newington, then a northern suburb of London. Having thus prepared himself for the ministry, in 1701 when he was twenty-six years old he was called to be pastor at Mark Lane Independent Chapel in London. His parishioners soon loved and admired him. When he shortly became ill they provided an assistant to do most of the work. He preached there when he was able for twenty-two years and through life held no other pastorate.

This Mark Lane congregation was a remarkable one. The members were largely drawn from the class of merchant princes and were among the

* From Arthur P. Davis: *Isaac Watts*, p. 7.

prominent men of the city. Their argosies sailed the seven seas. Their town houses were palaces in the immediate vicinity of the chapel, in what is now the financial section of London east of the Bank of England; their country houses were apt to be up Stoke Newington way, which was the favorite seat of the aristocrats of Puritanism, many of them descendants of Cromwell and his friends. One of Watts' parishioners, Sir Thomas Abney, was chosen Lord Mayor of London in 1700. Sir Thomas, fond of his brilliant but sickly pastor, invited Watts to spend a week at his country seat—with unexpected results. He stayed thirty-six years till he died!

When Sir Thomas invited him up he was living at an estate called "Theobald's" about ten miles beyond Stoke Newington. The house was in a magnificent park. The gardens were the finest in England, with their "lakes, canals, bridges, haw-haws, quincunxes [whatever those are!], labyrinths, terraces and summer-houses." Watts had his special apartments, his favorite walks among the trees, his out-of-door sanctuary for writing. Practically all of the works that made Watts famous, except his early hymns, were written here. Here he wrote his *Logic,* used as a textbook by the universities. Here he finished *The Knowledge of the Heavens and the Earth Made Easy; or the First Principles of Astronomy and Geography. Explained with the Use of Globes, Maps, etc.* He took a lively interest in the three Abney daughters, especially in their moral and religious education. In fact, Watts was a pioneer in this field, as in so many others. For these girls he wrote *Divine and Moral Songs,* not published till 1720, which became a classic for a hundred years. The annual average sale in England alone was 80,000. Six generations of children were brought up on:

> Let dogs delight to bark and bite,
>   For God hath made them so.
>
> But, children, you should never let
>   Such angry passions rise;
> Your little hands were never made
>   To tear each other's eyes.
>
> How doth the busy little bee
>   Improve each shining hour.
>
> In works of labor or of skill
>   I would be busy too;
> For Satan finds some mischief still
>   For idle hands to do.

When Sir Thomas died in 1722, Lady Abney moved into the village of Stoke Newington, taking her old friend with her, and occupied another mansion set in the midst of twenty-five acres of lawn and grove. Here Watts continued his writing, which by the time of his death included, besides the works mentioned, books on Grammar, Pedagogy, Ethics, Psychology, 3 volumes of sermons, 29 treatises on theology—a total of 52 works in all; this in addition to his poetry. Both Aberdeen and Edinburgh Universities conferred on him the Doctorate in Divinity. A monument to him stands in Abney Park, one in Southampton Park, and one in Westminster Abbey; in Southampton are a Memorial Hall, and a Watts Museum on the site of his birthplace.

### THE HYMNS OF ISAAC WATTS

When Isaac was fifteen years old he turned loose his rhyming tendencies in the religious field. He was driven to it by the lamentable singing in the churches of his day, Anglican and Non-conformist. As he later put it, "The singing of God's praise is the part of worship nighest heaven, and its performance among us is the worst on earth." One Sunday after returning from some particularly atrocious service, he was railing at it, when his father exclaimed, "Give us something better, young man." Before the evening service, Isaac had written his first hymn:

> Behold the glories of the Lamb
> Amidst his Father's throne;
> Prepare new honors for his name,
> And songs before unknown.

The hymn was lined out and sung that night at the Independents' meeting, Southampton—that is, read line by line by the clerk and sung after him, line by line, by the congregation.

Thus began the Revolution.

That revolution consisted in breaking the strangle-hold of David on the liturgy of the Church, Anglican and Dissenting, and the substitution of hymns of "human composure."

We should remember that Watts was not the first writer of hymns in English, as his title "the Father of English Hymnody" would imply. But he was the first to think out the theory of congregational praise and to furnish a well-rounded body of material for the Church to use. His theory was (1) that our songs were a human offering of praise to God, and that therefore the words ought to be our own. This contrasted with the Calvinistic theory to which the Church had held, that the inspired words of the Bible, particularly of the Psalms, were the only fit offering of praise man could make. Watts' arguments were sound, and they finally won out even against long and determined opposition. (2) Watts maintained that if the Psalms were to be used, they should be Christianized and modernized.

Out of these two convictions arose the two kinds of hymns that made Watts the most famous religious poet of his day. The first were the hymns of "human composure"—Watts' own; the second were the hymns based on the Psalms but shot through with Watts' own imagination. In these "Imitations of the Psalms," as he called them, he made David speak like King William III; England and Scotland take the place of Israel and Judah. Thus the Psalmist became "an orthodox and patriotic English Christian of the early eighteenth century."

## 1. THE HYMNS OF HUMAN COMPOSURE

For the next eighteen years after his first boyish attempt Watts wrote hymns, and when he began to preach his congregation sang them. They were composed in simple meters that all Christians knew and sung to whatever familiar tune the Clerk chose at the time. You will notice that Watts constructed his hymns to assist the practice of "lining out": as he himself put it, "I have seldom permitted a stop in the middle of a line, and seldom left the end of a line without one, to comport a little with the unhappy Mixture of Reading and Singing, which cannot presently be reformed."

This accumulating material was finally published in 1707 (enlarged edition, 1709) under the title, *Hymns and Spiritual Songs.* Watts intended, he says, "to write down to the Level of Vulgar Capacities, and to furnish Hymns for the meanest of Christians." In this attempt he succeeded. The common people sang him gladly and literally "thumbed the first edition out of existence." Here was poetry they could understand.

We shall now consider the more famous of these hymns.

## *When I survey the wondrous cross*     [1707]

This hymn, written for use in the Communion Service, was inspired by Paul's impassioned declaration in Gal 6:14. As a climax to his argument that one does not have to become a Jew before he can become a Christian, and that the Law in which the Jew glories cannot possibly save anyone, Paul exclaims, "But far be it from me to glory save in the cross of our Lord Jesus Christ, through which the world hath been crucified to me, and I unto the world."

*Stanza 1.* "Survey" suggests not only sight but contemplation; the deliberate attempt on the part of the communicant to realize what Christ's death meant to the world. The cross is "wondrous" because in this one instance a Roman instrument of torture and death has become God's instrument for saving mankind. "Prince of Glory" suggests the highest exaltation. Watts believed that Christ had been a "Prince" in heaven before the world was created (Col 1:15–17). The tragedy is that he should have come to earth only to be rejected and killed. That also is part of the wonder and the mystery. "Pour contempt": when I consider this exaltation and sacrifice, all I have ever achieved is as nothing and all I have taken pride in is by comparison contemptible (Phil 3:7–8).

*Stanza 2.* "Boast." Paul frequently referred to his Jewish ancestry, his perfect keeping of the Law, his education as a Pharisee, as possible grounds for boasting; but see 1 Cor 2:2. "Vain things": each person can make his own inventory of the worthless things to which he clings. They can all be summarized in "the lust of the flesh, the lust of the eyes, and the pride of life" (1 Jn 2:16). "Sacrifice them": one has to choose between keeping the "vain things" that go with the worldly life, and accepting the "blood of Christ," which is the symbol of Christ's sacrifice and of our salvation (Mt 26:28).

*Stanza 3.* One of the most beautiful stanzas in any hymn. In Jn 19:34 a soldier, to prove that Jesus was dead, pierced his side with a spear, "and straightway there came out blood and water." Watts takes from that the idea of "mingled," and then by the alchemy of his imagination changes the revolting physical details into their spiritual equivalents, "sorrow and love." Then in the final couplet he loses himself in adoration, until even the crown of thorns becomes more priceless than a monarch's diadem.

*Stanza 4.* This survey, this endeavor to assess the value of Christ's sacrifice, reaches a climax of personal resolve. Though man's sins through the ages are infinite in quantity, as large as the bulk of the material universe, Christ's atonement is adequate—and more. God therefore needs nothing from me in the way of further payment. Yet personal gratitude to Christ makes its own irresistible demand. Insignificant though I am, I can at least give myself, "my soul"—the essence of me that makes me an individual, "my life"— all the activities of my days, "my all"—whatever I possess of wealth and inward power.

In this combination of imagery, insight and passion, Watts reaches the heights of devotional poetry.

### *There is a land of pure delight*    [1709]

This is a work of pure imagination in which the glories of heaven are suggested rather than described. There are perhaps three sources for Watts' imagery:

1. The experiences of the Israelites in prospect of the Promised Land.

"And Moses went up from the plains of Moab unto mount Nebo . . . and Jehovah showed him all the land" (Deut 34:1-4).

Watts could not have improved upon the ardor of his vision if he had actually climbed Nebo. The  view thence is entrancing: At one's feet the robin's-egg blue of the Dead Sea, and the twisting narrow jungle in which the Jordan hides; straight ahead, the opalescent mountains of Judea; to the right, the violet haze over the rolling hills of Ephraim and Gilead. The imagery breaks down when we recall that Israel had to fight to possess this land. Nevertheless, for many centuries the river Jordan has been used as a symbol of death that must be crossed if one would enter, and the land itself a symbol of heaven.

2. Watts' knowledge of Scripture.

His mind was saturated with the words of the Bible: every experience of his recalled these words, so that most of his hymns are disguised translations of Biblical phrases. The New Testament pictures of heaven which he is here recalling are found mostly in the Book of Revelation, chaps. 21–22.

3. The scenery near Watts' early home, Southampton.

While the poet was deeply engaged with his hymn-writing as well as his preaching in London, he fell into one of his frequent sick spells, and to recoup he paid a six-weeks visit to his parents at Southampton (May, 1706). It is very probable that this hymn was written during that visit. In those days Southampton was a small village lying within the fork of two rivers. The estuary known as Southampton Water lapped the town walls and the old prison in which Watts' father had three times languished, while just across it to the south-west lay the long lush meadows of Marchwood. It is more than likely that the sight of this peaceful and fruitful land glowing in the afternoon sun beyond the placid river, inspired the lines:

> Sweet fields beyond the swelling flood
> Stand dressed in living green.

The frail health that so often interrupted Watts' work no doubt made him think of death. At the time of writing this hymn he was only thirty-two years old, an age when most young men are full of lusty life. This natural dread of death is expressed in stanza 4, sometimes omitted by editors:

> But timorous mortals start and shrink
> To cross the narrow sea;
> And linger trembling on the brink
> And fear to launch away.

and also in the phrases: "Those gloomy doubts that rise," "Death's cold flood," "Fright us from the shore." But to Watts' mind, the glories of heaven are enough to overcome man's natural aversion to death. These glories may be seen even here and now "With faith's illumined eyes."

Death and heaven play a far less important part in our present-day thought than they did in olden times. Medieval hymns were wont to dwell upon the glories and pleasures of heaven which were regarded as a reward for the toils and sufferings of the earthly life. But the number of these in our current hymnals is small and most of those that are printed are never sung. This hymn by Watts is probably the best of its kind.

In addition to the above hymns, Watts is today represented in our ten hymnals by thirty-three others!

## 2. THE PSALMS IMITATED

The arguments by which Watts was led to substitute "hymns of human composure" for the metrical Psalms, were quite valid. Many a Dissenting congregation was convinced by them and proceeded to use the hymns. Yet the prejudice in favor of Psalms was deep and persistent. Watts himself knew perfectly well that the Psalms were a veritable treasure of praise. What he objected to was the undiscriminating way in which this treasure was used: the failure of the Church to discard the obsolete, the heathen, the un-Christian elements found therein, and to suffuse what was left with the spirit of the gospel. Very early, in fact before he published his hymns, he had tried his hand at "improving" the Psalms. He kept at this work for more than ten years, until in 1719 he published *The Psalms of David Imitated in the Language of the New Testament, and Apply'd to the Christian State and Worship.* These lyrics were not metrical translations, nor even paraphrases; they were inspired by Psalms and they followed in general the thoughts of the original, but they contained a great deal of Watts. Watts put it tersely in a letter to Cotton Mather of Boston in 1717: " 'Tis not a translation of David that I pretend, but an imitation of him, so nearly in Christian hymns that the Jewish Psalmist may plainly appear, and yet leave Judaism behind."

Watts tried to forestall criticism of this revolutionary treatment of Scripture by giving in his Preface some of his reasons. These are stated with such keenness and delightful humor that it makes pleasant reading even after two hundred years:

> I could never persuade myself that the best Way to raise a devout Frame in plain Christians was to bring a King or a Captain into their Churches and let him lead and dictate the Worship in his own Style of Royalty, or in the Language of a Field of Battel. Does every menial Servant in the Assembly know how to use these words devoutly—"A Bow of Steel is broken in mine Arms," Ps 18:34? Would I encourage a Parish-Clerk to stand up in the midst of a County Church, and bid all the People joyn with his Words and say, "I will praise thee upon a Psaltery; or, I will open my dark Saying upon the Harp . . ." Why must all that will sing a Psalm at Church use such words as if they were to play upon Harp or Psaltery, when Thousands never saw such an Instrument? . . . Have not your Spirits taken Wing and mounted up near to God and Glory with the Song of David on your Tongue? But on a sudden the Clerk has proposed the next Line to your Lips with . . . Burnt-Offering or Hyssop, with New-Moons and Trumpets and Tumbrils in it, with Confessions of Sins which you never committed, cursing such Enemies as you never had, giving Thanks for such Victories as you never obtained . . . How have all your Souls been discomposed at once, and the Strings of Harmony all untuned!

It must be confessed that with a few notable exceptions the "improved Psalms" were only mediocre. Yet because they were the work of the renowned Isaac Watts and were certainly an advance over most earlier work, they speedily made their way into general use. In Dissenting congregations they largely superseded both the Old Version (Sternhold and Hopkins) and the New Version (Tate and Brady). Within a hundred years Watts absolutely dominated the field, both in Psalmody and Hymnody. For example, in the most famous American compilation, that by Rev. James Winchell of Boston, 1832, there were 337 selections from the *Psalms Imitated* and 350 of Watts' hymns. In an Appendix, additional hymns of Watts appeared to the number of 74. Thus out of a total of 1220 hymns that included such prolific writers as Doddridge, John Newton, Cowper, Anne Steele, Stennett (for the most part now all forgotten), and Charles Wesley, Watts claimed 761!

We shall now consider a few of Watts' *Psalms Imitated* to see what he did to the originals.

### *Jesus shall reign where'er the sun*     [1719]

This is the most widely used and probably the finest missionary hymn ever written. In it Watts took the 72nd Psalm, which according to the Authorized Version of the Bible was a prayer of David for his son Solomon and a prophecy of the glories of his reign, and transformed it into a celebration of the conquests of Christ among the heathen. The reader will understand this technique if he looks up the Biblical references.

*Stanza 1.*   Jesus shall reign where'er the sun, Ps 72:8, 5, 17.
*Stanza 2.*   Behold! the islands, with their kings, vv. 10, 11.
*Stanza 3.*   There Persia, glorious to behold, v. 17.
*Stanza 4.*   For him shall endless prayer be made, vv. 15, 11.
*Stanza 5.*   Peoples and realms of every tongue, vv. 15, 17.
*Stanza 6.*   Blessings abound where'er he reigns, v. 4.
*Stanza 7.*   Where he displays his healing power, vv. 12–14.
*Stanza 8.*   Let every creature rise and sing, vv. 18–19.

This is a remarkable performance. Fused in the crucible of Watts' mind, the various Scripture verses have regrouped themselves, and the material with the Hebrew parallelisms removed has issued in a totally new creation. The Psalm has been "imitated in the spirit of Christianity," though scarcely a word of the original has survived. At one point (stanzas 2–3, now omitted) his imagination has run away with his good sense: the kings of Sheba and Seba have issued as Europe, Persia and India. At another place Watts has lugged in by the heels Father Adam and his curse. But time has removed this tinsel; what is left is pure gold.

In vivid imagery Watts sees the Great Commission of Christ realized (Mt 28:19–20), the gospel preached to all nations, the Golden Age of the

Greeks, the Messianic Kingdom of the Jews, the Kingdom of God of the Christians ushered in and the work of redemption completed. This was for Watts a gospel ideal realized by the imagination alone in a kind of rapture. For when this hymn was written (1719) the great missionary movement had scarcely begun. It was not until 1779 that William Carey began to preach the obligation of the Protestant Church to the heathen. Even at that late date, an Anglican bishop expressed the attitude of his Church toward missions in his contemptuous remark to Carey: "Young man, if God wants to save the heathen, He will do it without any help from you." But God used Carey and He has used this hymn by Watts to keep alive in His Church the obligation and the hope expressed in the Great Commission.

### *Joy to the world, the Lord is come*        [1719]

This is an imitation of Ps 98:4, 6b–8, 9; with reminiscences of Gen 3:17–18 and Rom 5:20.

Ps 98 is a song of rejoicing at the marvellous ways in which God has protected and restored His people; a kind of "Praise God from whom all blessings flow" that might have sprung from the heart of an Israelite after reading the stories of the Old Testament or upon experiencing some present deliverance like the return from the Babylonian captivity or like the rescue from the persecutions of the days of the Maccabees. The song looks forward also to the time when Jehovah will be the God of the whole earth and Israel's Law will be accepted by all nations.

Watts gives the Psalm a fresh interpretation. He turns it into praise for the salvation of God's saints, a salvation that began when God became incarnate in the Babe of Bethlehem who was destined to remove the "curse" entailed by Adam's fall. The old Jewish Psalm thus became a Christian song of rejoicing, a Christmas carol. It is one of the most joyous Christmas hymns in existence; not in the sense of merry-making but in the deep and solemn realization of what Christ's birth has meant to mankind. Two of our hymnals have omitted the stanza in which the "curse" rears its head; and the Unitarians change the offending line to "As far as sin is found." With these omissions and changes the hymn has universal acceptance.

### *Our God, our help in ages past*

By universal consent this hymn is one of the grandest in the whole realm of English Hymnody. It is found in practically every hymnal. No other embraces in such moving language the whole scope of history, faith in a God who realizes His purposes through history, and the solidarity of a nation which in times of crisis places its hope in the Eternal. Such a hymn is the product of three elements. The first is the original Jewish Ps 90 on which the hymn is based:

*Stanza 1.* Our God, our help, Ps 90:1.
*Stanza 2.* Under the shadow, v. 17b.
*Stanza 3.* Before the hills, v. 2.
*Stanza 4.* A thousand ages, v. 4.
*Stanza 5.* Time like an, v. 5.
*Stanza 6.* Our God, our help, v. 14.

The unknown Jewish author of this Psalm, so many scholars think, was moved to write it because of a national calamity. King Josiah in a great reformation had wiped out the idolatrous religions indigenous to Canaan and imported from Assyria, and according to the theology of the reformers who had backed the King, God should have rewarded the nation with His blessing. But in 609 B.C. while the King was still young he was killed in battle and the Egyptian conqueror became dictator of the helpless nation. But this Psalmist tells his people that calamities have happened before, will happen again; and after the nation has atoned for its sins, God the changeless and the eternal will still be man's refuge and defense.

The second element in the hymn is contemporary English history, of August, 1714. Queen Anne, daughter of Roman Catholic James II, though herself a Protestant, had in her latter days surrounded herself with ministers who in case of her death favored the succession to the throne of her Catholic brother. These men had forced through Parliament the "Schism Act," which was aimed at the suppression of Dissenters, and was the opening wedge, so the Dissenters firmly believed, for the return of persecution, exiles, executions, and the re-establishment of Catholicism in England. A terrible storm seemed to be gathering which would wreck all that had been accomplished by the Reformation and the brief era of Toleration. That act was to have become operative on Sunday, August 1, 1714. But the Queen was suddenly taken ill and died on that very day.

> The news of the miraculous upsetting of the Catholic plans flew east, west, north and south. Men ran through town and village shouting, "The Queen is dead! The Queen is dead!"—That most militant and masterful London preacher, Thomas Bradbury, on the following Sunday took for his text: "Go, see now this cursed woman and bury her; for she is a king's daughter." *

By a previous *Act of Settlement and the Succession* (1701) Anne's successor was to be a Hanoverian Protestant prince. He became king of England as George I. Under him persecution was prevented and popery became no longer a menace. It was in the midst of these alarms and crises that Watts wrote this hymn. (For details, see Thackeray's *Henry Esmond*, chaps. X–XIII.)

The third element in the hymn was the genius of Watts. He saw the

* Thomas Wright: *Life of Isaac Watts*, pp. 118–19.

possibility of making the Jewish past celebrate the Protestant English present. His dramatic fusion of old imagery with new phrases preserved the majesty of the Psalm and added a fervor of faith by which all English-men felt that indeed they were God's chosen people:

> Sufficient is Thine arm alone,
> And our defence is sure.

No wonder that this transformed Psalm is sung on all occasions of national sorrow or rejoicing. It has become the second national anthem of England.

### Before Jehovah's awful throne     [1719]

This paraphrase of Ps 100 was published in 1719, long after most of Watts' hymns had been written (1707). By that time the simplicity and directness of expression which made his hymns easily comprehensible to the common people were giving place to a more flowery style that had been made fashionable by Addison, Pope and others (See below). Take for example the use of adjectives: in the original Psalm there are only four, three of them in the last verse, while in the hymn there are fourteen, each of them preceding its noun with military precision. Stanzas 3 and 4 of the hymn illustrate also the trick of parallelism so much in vogue in eighteenth century literary circles: "crowd thy gates" . . . "fill thy courts"; "with thankful songs" . . . "with sounding praise"; "wide as the world" . . . "vast as eternity" . . . "firm as a rock." These devices are not defects; in fact, for the most part they add to our pleasure, and in Stanza 4 they reach a sublimity that really moves us. However, they are indication of the literary fashion of the times.

Watts' Calvinism appears in a few unsuspicious lines and phrases. In the second couplet of stanza 1 and in stanza 2 the absolute supremacy of God is announced, not only in creation but in destruction. These are moral terms, not physical. Hell was God's provision for those whom he should create for perdition, just as the "fold" was made for those who were elected for salvation. Stanzas 3 to 5 are filled with the rejoicing of those who like Watts were assured of a predestined heaven: "We are his people, we his care." Unrepentant sinners can have no share in the "vast eternity" of God's love. That is why in all Watts' hymns there is no pleading with sinners to repent and be saved: they are powerless to change the status determined for them before the foundation of the world (See below, "The Theology of Watts' Hymns"). It took the Wesleys to popularize a change in these ideas (See Chapter V).

It is surprising that so many hymnals are preserving this typically Wattsian bit of antiquity.

### From all that dwell below the skies     [1719]

"The classic of English doxologies," a paraphrase of Ps 117.

In the Jewish original there is naturally no suggestion of any redemptive work by Christ, but only in God's "merciful kindness." Watts, however, equates Redeemer with Creator because of the theological concepts found in Paul and the Fourth Gospel (Jn 1:1, 3, 12; Col 1:14, 16). These passages couple creation and redemption in the same person.

The first stanza is a good illustration of a literary device known as "chiastic arrangement": outer line *a* is synonymous with outer line *d*; inner lines *b* and *c* are synonymous. Watts was a thorough classical scholar and knew all the tricks of the rhetoricians.

Seventeen other Psalm paraphrases by Watts have survived in our hymnals. A useful method of studying them is to compare them with their originals, see what old imagery Watts has retained, what new imagery or ideas he has added, to what extent the Psalm has been "Christianized," and to identify the emotions called forth by the finished whole.

## THE THEOLOGY OF WATTS' HYMNS

For the most part, Watts' hymns are rhymed theology, and the theology is derived from John Calvin, who in turn got his basic ideas from Augustine and Paul. In the course of the years some Churches have greatly modified their beliefs and in the process have gradually dropped from their hymnals the hymns that no longer express their point of view. As a consequence the modern user of hymnals is not aware of the true views of Dr. Watts. To find their original Calvinism one must search the discarded hymns and the lyrics that appeared in his earlier *Horae Lyricae,* some of which never got into the hymnbooks. We shall then be astonished at the kind of ideas which dominated the Church in the eighteenth century.

God is an absolute and arbitrary ruler:

> Life, death, and Hell, and worlds unknown
> Hang on his firm decree.

> Chained to his throne a volume lies,
> With all the fates of men,
> With every angel's form and size
> Drawn by th' eternal pen.

> His providence unfolds the book,
> And makes his counsels shine;
> Each op'ning leaf and ev'ry stroke
> Fulfils some deep design.

> Here he exalts neglected worms
> To scepters and a crown;
> Anon the following page he turns
> And treds the monarchs down.

> Not Gabriel asks the reasons why,
> Nor God the reason gives,
> Nor dare the favorite angels pry
> Between the folded leaves.

MAN is "totally depraved":

> Adam, our father and our head,
> Transgress'd and justice doom'd us dead.
> The fiery law speaks all despair,
> There's no reprieve, no pardon there.

> Lord, I am vile, conceived in sin,
> And born unholy and unclean;
> Sprung from the man whose guilty fall
> Corrupts his race and taints us all.

We can now understand why young Isaac aged fifteen should fall "under considerable conviction of sin." All children were supposed to do that.

> My crimes awake; and hideous fear
> Distracts my restless mind;
> Guilt meets my eyes with horrid glare,
> And Hell pursues behind.

The only relief from despair lies in the thought that Jesus has paid the penalty of sin, and that if I am among the fortunate "elect" I shall be rescued by Him:

> Is there no shelter from the eye
> Of a revenging God?
> Jesus, to thy dear wounds I fly;
> Bedew me with thy blood.

> Those guardian drops my soul secure,
> And wash away my sin;
> Eternal justice frowns no more,
> And conscience smiles within.

This is in accordance with the doctrine of "foreordination and election":

> May not the sovereign Lord on high
> Dispense his favors as he will;
> Choose some to life while others die,
> And yet be just and gracious still?

How may one be sure that he is among the elect? The only way to settle it is to put your trust in Christ and see what happens. If you are not among the elect you will find that you can't be moved to put your trust in Him; and if you do feel that you trust Him, that sense of security may have been raised by the Devil just to deceive you. So you can never tell. The author knew a dear old saint who as she approached her ninetieth year was assailed by fearful doubts whether she was going to be saved after all. It was the resurgence in her second childhood of the fears that had tormented her first childhood, before she had received the assurance of being accepted. Assurance, if attained, is an anchor to the soul:

> When I can read my title clear
>   To mansions in the skies,
> I'll bid farewell to every fear
>   And wipe my weeping eyes.
>
> Should earth against my soul engage,
>   And fiery darts be hurled,
> Then I can smile at Satan's rage,
>   And face a frowning world.

How is Christ able to save all mankind and pay the penalty of every-one's sin? Only because *He is* GOD and so was able to endure an infinite punishment and pay an infinite debt accumulated by the sin of the infinite number of human beings who have been born and will be born before the end of the world comes. This belief involves the doctrine of the Trinity: God existing in three Persons—

> Their glory shines with equal beams;
> Their essence is forever one;
> Though they are known by different names,
> The FATHER GOD and GOD THE SON.

Because Jesus was God, the *Incarnation* became possible:

> Jesus, the God whom angels fear,
>   Comes down to dwell with you.

The Incarnation was the necessary preliminary to accomplishing the Atonement—the At-one-ment that reconciles:

> Alas, and did my Saviour bleed,
>   And did my Sovereign die?
>
> When God, the mighty Maker, died
>   For man, the creature's sin.
>
> Justice was pleased to bruise the God,
> And pay its wrongs with heavenly blood;
> What unknown racks and pains he bore!
> Then rose; The Law could ask no more.

Without that sacrificial act, you and I cannot possibly escape damnation.

Having then risen to His seat on the right hand of God, Jesus becomes the special *Intercessor* for sinners; points out to God who are the elect so that vengeance may not light on them, and pleads for them if they fall into sin:

> Before his Father's eye
>     Our humble suit he moves;
> The Father lays his thunders by,
>     And looks, and smiles, and loves.
>
> Lift up your eyes to the heavenly seat
>     Where your Redeemer stays;
> Kind Intercessor, there he sits,
>     And loves, and pleads, and prays.

When the fullness of time has come, the days of man's probation end. The trumpets announce the *Final Judgement* in which the eternal status of every man shall be revealed. Then the long bliss and the long torments of eternity will begin. If you are not among the elect, the prospect is terrific:

> Eternal plagues and heavy chains,
> Tormenting racks and fiery coals,
> And darts t'inflict immortal pains,
> Dyed in the blood of damnèd souls.
>
> There guilty souls of Adam's race
> Shriek out and howl beneath Thy rod;
> Once they could scorn a Saviour's grace,
> But they incensed a dreadful God.

How do we know that this is all true? It is written in the *Bible*, which is an inerrant revelation of God to man, supernaturally given:

> 'Twas by an order from the Lord
> The ancient prophets spoke his word;
> The Spirit did their tongues inspire,
> And warmed their hearts with heavenly fire.

There is no other revelation. The heathen have been given only light enough to secure their condemnation.

I am sure you will agree with me that this religion is nothing short of dreadful. For those of us who are not theologians or philosophers but just ordinary individuals, it outrages our sense of justice, contradicts our reason, makes God a monster, Christ a play-actor in the tragedy of human history, and robs man of his freedom without which a moral life is impossible. Yet the sincerity of Watts, his skill in dramatizing and emotionalizing this theology, his success in getting his hymns sung throughout the English-speaking world, have all conspired to perpetuate his brand of Calvinism even into the twentieth century. It is today the theology of the Fundamentalists. Gradually, however, the hymnbooks have sloughed off the worst expressions of this belief, leaving as a permanent deposit a small body of hymns that are unsurpassed as an expression of universal Christianity.

## THE POETRY OF WATTS' HYMNS

Watts' hymns admirably illustrate Milton's statement that poetry should be "simple, sensuous, and passionate."

1. He is "simple." Anyone with average intelligence can understand what he means. Watts knew how to be intricate and learned if he chose. In his first published poems, *Horae Lyricae,* he wrote lyrics with involved metrical structures, some in Latin; imitated odes of the Greek Pindar, and in a long preface justified himself before "Judges of Wit" by classical quotations and references to foreign critics. But he was wise enough to see that if hymns were to serve the common man they must be simple. His meters are therefore the standard three—Common, Long, Short; and the language and thought are brought down to the level of "Vulgar Capacities." This simplicity is one of the underlying reasons for the almost complete domination of Watts' hymns in the Dissenting Churches for 150 years.

2. His hymns are also "sensuous"—that is, appealing to the senses. This quality shows in the pictures conjured up by his nouns, adjectives and even verbs: heaven is a land where "everlasting spring abides"; on "wings of faith" we rise to see the saints in heaven who once had "wet their couch with tears"; "His name like sweet perfume shall rise"; "the prisoner leaps to loose his chain"; "Time, like an ever-rolling stream"; "nor thorns infest the ground"; "O, may my heart in tune be found like David's harp of solemn sound." These images are familiar to ordinary people either because they come from the constantly read Bible or because they come from everyday experience with nature.

3. The hymns are "passionate"—that is, charged with emotion. They shed a glow of joy or resound with praise. Even the cold logic of Calvinism catches fire: God is apprehended emotionally, in awe, or dread, or fear; as love, or power, or infinity; Christ is full of human sympathy that evokes from the individual a personal response; man is filled with hope or fear, with joy or penitence; he is torn by doubts or enraptured by the certainties of heaven. In Watts at his best, there is nothing drab or passive; all is vivid and active.

But in Watts at his ordinary level or at his worst, there is plenty of commonplaceness; machine-made lines furnish the modern preacher with metrical prose that sums up briefly for the congregation what has already been said at length in the sermon.

Time has relieved us of most of this uninspired material. Down to the middle of the nineteenth century Watts was almost intact. Winchell's edition of Watts (1832) contained 761 of his Psalms and hymns—everything he had written; *The Psalmist* (1843), still used in the writer's home church when he was a boy contained 303 hymns by Watts; the *Methodist Hymnal* of 1905 gave 53; and in the ten hymnals which are the basis of the present study, published 1918–1941, Watts appears from a maximum of 28 times (in *The Hymnary*, United Church of Canada) to 10 (in *Pilgrim Hymnal*, Congregational); in all, 56 different hymns. Ten of these are found in all ten hymnals! Other authors with wider aims and with a more diversified experience have more fully expressed the religion of the present age.

### *JOSEPH ADDISON (1672–1719)* Anglican

ADDISON is the bright star of early eighteenth-century literature in England. The work by which he is best known and loved is found in the paper which he and Dick Steele managed together for several years, *The Spectator*. Of his purpose in writing these essays Addison said: "The great and only end of these speculations is to banish vice and ignorance out of the territories of Great Britain." It is an extraordinary tribute to an author who wrote primarily for fashionable women and the habitués of coffee-houses that he should have attempted to preach and that he should have gotten away with it. He actually broke the tradition left by the Restoration writers that to be brilliant one had to be obscene. Macaulay said of him that "since his time the open violation of decency has always been considered amongst us a sure mark of a fool."

Addison was not only a writer and a moralist but a man of affairs. What made him famous and opened the doors to a high political career was his poem "The Campaign," written in praise of Marlborough at the battle of Blenheim. Because this poem made the headlines, the Whigs saw his propaganda value; he was elected to Parliament and then appointed successively Under Secretary, Secretary for Ireland, and finally Secretary of State. Yet, in an age of extreme political corruption, Addison's honesty was never questioned; when the Whigs were overwhelmingly defeated, Addison, the Whig, was re-elected to Parliament. "The most cruel pamphleteers respected him; his uprightness, his talent, seemed exalted by common consent above discussion. He lived in abundance, activity, and honors, wisely and usefully, amid the admiration and constant affection of learned and distinguished friends, . . . amid the applause of all good men and all the cultivated minds of England." *

In *The Spectator* appeared not only Addison's essays and that lovable creation of his, Sir Roger de Coverley, whose eccentricities gave Addison a chance to poke fun at a lot of contemporary foibles and vices, but also his

---

* Taine, H. A.: *History of English Literature*, II:110.

four hymns, all published in 1712 within a space of two months. There can be little doubt that the appearance of Watts' hymns was the spark that kindled Addison's brief but noble fire.

### The spacious firmament on high    [1712]

This hymn appeared in *The Spectator* for August 23, 1712, following an essay on "The Strengthening of Faith." In that essay Addison offers four suggestions, the last of which is frequent retirement from the world for the purpose of religious meditation:

> In our retirements everything disposes us to be serious. In courts and cities we are entertained with the works of men; in the country with those of God. . . . Faith and devotion naturally grow in the mind of every reasonable man, who sees the impressions of divine power and wisdom in every object on which he casts his eye. The Supreme Being has made the best arguments for his own existence, in the formation of the heavens and the earth: and these are arguments which a man of sense cannot forbear attending to, who is out of the hurry and noise of human affairs. . . . The Psalmist has very beautiful strokes of poetry to this purpose, in that exalted strain: "The heavens declare the glory of God. . . ."
>
> As such a bold and sublime manner of thinking furnished very noble matter for an ode, the reader may see it wrought into the following one.

Then after the current fashion of the preachers who capped their sermons with an original hymn, Addison appends his own paraphrase of the nineteenth Psalm, which has from that day to this been the classic hymn to the glories of the Heavens and their Creator. Read Ps 19:1–6 and see how wonderfully Addison expands and enriches the original.

This is typical eighteenth century "literary" work, far removed from the Dissenter's simple hymn which was deliberately written down to "vulgar capacities." In the first place, it is composed in heroic couplets, a form that was imported from France, brought to its perfection and all but universally used in the eighteenth century. In this scheme the unit is two rhyming lines. In the second place, the ideas are dressed up in a very conscious way by attaching an adjective wherever possible to each noun and by disposing the phrases in a kind of pattern:

> All the stars . . .
> All the planets . . .
> Confirm the tidings . . .
> Spread the truth . . .

Then again, the ode shows the typical attitude of the upper classes toward God. In that age the dawning scientific spirit had in a way put

God out of His universe and removed Him from that close personal relationship with man which He held in the hymns of Watts, Doddridge and Anne Steele. It became the fashion to refer to God as the "Great Original" or the "First Cause," leaving the operation of the universe and even the acts of men to natural law. This way of looking at God and the universe is called "Deism." Addison uses "Great Original" in his hymn, and he also calls God "Hand," with a capital letter. You will also notice that the heavenly voices are heard by "Reason"—with a capital letter—rather than by Faith. That is another indication of the increasing trust in Reason as the revealer of all truth. In fact, in the history of thought, the eighteenth century is known as the "Age of Reason."

These literary details and points of view were as much a part of the eighteenth century as were the costumes and manners of the time: the powdered periwig, the lace cuffs and collars, the low bow with a sweep of the arm, the stately minuet. The original Psalm that Addison paraphrases is primitive, like David's shepherd's cloak, and strong with the naked strength of noun and verb; in all of it there is but one descriptive adjective. We feel in it also the solemn awe of David who knew nothing of science and could only wonder and worship. But the civilized and literary Addison adds to the Psalm the details that make a more vivid picture; he personalizes and dramatizes the heavenly bodies. For these reasons and because of the exhilarating tune of Haydn to which it is set, the hymn is always enthusiastically sung. Its sweep, its stateliness and its sincerity make it the favorite hymn of nature in all our hymnody.

## When all thy mercies, O my God    [1712]

This is a morning hymn of thanks (like that of Bishop Ken, p. 37), as shown by the words "rising soul." It appeared in *The Spectator* for August 9, 1712 following an essay on Gratitude. Whereas in his paraphrase of Ps 19 Addison conformed quite closely to the literary fashion of his day, in this lyric he returned to the earlier plebeian pattern of Watts. The rhythm is the Common Meter of the ballads; the stanzas have four lines. He still shows his fondness for adjectives, and some of his verbs will have to be looked up in the dictionary for special eighteenth century shades of meaning. Apparently Addison never expected his verses to be sung in church, for the original has thirteen stanzas!

In cutting down the number of stanzas to four or five, our present editors have spoiled the fine sequence of the original in which God's constant guidance and blessings are shown: first to Addison's "infant heart," then along the "paths of youth" that led "up to man"; through "sickness" and "health." These stages are then summed up in "every period of my life." By thus lengthening out the time element, Addison strengthens the feeling of the long-continued goodness of God. He also reveals the genuinely religious quality of his own soul: he believes that God is good and just, because in his own character he finds those same qualities. He loved deep and serious things, he lived willingly in God's presence, and he trusted the future in which he believed goodness would triumph. To help along that goodness was his constant concern, not by ranting, or crusading, but by being himself good. "When he was about to die," says Hippolyte Taine, "he

*Left,* Dr. Philip Doddridge. *Right,* Joseph Addison.

sent for his step-son, Lord Warwick, whose careless life had caused him some uneasiness. He was so weak that at first he could not speak. The young man, after waiting a while, said to him: 'Dear sir, you sent for me, I believe; I hope that you have some commands; I shall hold them most sacred.' The dying man with an effort pressed his hand and replied gently: 'See in what peace a Christian can die.'"

The poem shows a more intimate side of Addison's religion than does "The spacious firmament." God is not the distant First Cause of the deists, but that near and loving Person which the human heart demands; one who marks the sparrow's fall and gives good gifts unto His children. Conversely, Addison is the grateful child of God who, daily aware of God's mercies, expresses with sincerity the thankfulness of his heart. At the same time, we observe that the theology of the Church, whether Anglican or Dissenting, is completely ignored: there is no reference to Christ and His Atonement, there is no infant damnation, and no morbid "conviction of sin." In fact, this hymn springs from that general attitude toward God that we call "natural religion" rather than "revealed religion." This fact makes it available for all sects, even for most non-Christian religions. Doubtless that is why practically every hymnal contains it.

It was natural that the success of Watts' hymns should stir up many preachers who felt either the poetic impulse or the desire to end every sermon with a hymn which would clinch the message of the day. The Dissenting Churches produced many such versifiers and their output was voluminous. "Time like an ever-rolling stream" has borne most of these songs away; but surviving in our current hymnals are the following:

### Rev. PHILIP DODDRIDGE (1702–1751) Congregationalist

WHEN Doddridge was twenty-six years old he met Dr. Watts, aged fifty-four, to consult him about the founding of a Non-conformist Academy in the Midlands. The friendship thus begun continued until Watts' death. Doddridge was a rising young preacher. He recognized the tremendous usefulness of hymns as an aid in preaching. His parishioners were of the humblest people—"poor men in smock frocks and hobnail boots, and poor women in cloaks and pattens." He said of his parish at Kibworth, "I have not so much as a tea-table in my whole diocese, and but one hoop petticoat." But being human, these people could be stirred by such hymns as:

> Give me the wings of faith to rise
> Within the veil, and see
> The saints above, how great their joys,
> How bright their glories be.

Therefore without pretending in any degree to be a rival of his friend, Doddridge began to supplement Watts by writing his own closing hymns. This practice he kept up all his life until at his death he left behind manuscript copies of more than four hundred.

His pastorate at the Chapel Hill Congregational Church in Northampton lasted twenty-two years; at the same time he managed his Academy in which he prepared 200 young men for the ministry. An indefatigable worker, he never wasted a minute; even while he was shaving and dressing he had a student read to him, and when he rode out to preach in a distant village he took along a manuscript in his saddlebag.

Doddridge was the first Non-conformist leader to show any sympathy for the work of the two great evangelists who were responsible for the religious awakening of the eighteenth century, Whitefield and Wesley (See next chapters). Most church people were either indifferent or hostile. When Doddridge offered prayer at Whitefield's Tabernacle, even his good friend Watts remonstrated at such a "sinking of character," but in spite of a storm of protest, he later opened his pulpit at Northampton to Whitefield. These acts arouse our admiration for Doddridge's character and courage.

Doddridge fought tuberculosis for years and finally succumbed at the age of 49. When Lady Huntingdon (one of Whitefield's financial backers) made it possible for him to take a voyage to Lisbon for his health, he said to her in parting, "I can as well go to heaven from Lisbon as from my own study at Northampton." From that journey he never returned. He was buried in the English cemetery at Lisbon near the novelist Henry Fielding.

In 1938 the writer visited Doddridge's church at Northampton. It stands in a poverty-stricken, tumble-down neighborhood. About it are abandoned slum houses, some of which were being torn down while the inhabitants were being moved to new housing projects in other parts of the town. In the little study used by Doddridge are the table on which he wrote his hymns, his rush-bottomed ladder-back armchair, and the little cupboard of pigeonholes in which he kept his sermons. On the walls are framed pictures and pertinent documents mostly in Doddridge's hand, and a sketch of himself at his mother's knee before the Dutch fireplace.

Louis Benson * draws this picture of his home: "His earliest recollection was of his mother explaining the scenes of Bible history pictured on the blue-and-white Dutch tiles lining the fireplace: Eve's apple tree with the serpent, Noah at the window of the ark, a very large Jonah coming forth from a very small whale, Peter crossing the sea of Galilee in a Dutch three-decker, the prodigal son in a periwig, and the rest. She would tell him of her father, driven from his Bohemian home by religious persecution, and show him the Luther's Bible in black stamped leather he brought away beneath the peasant clothes he wore; of his father's father also, one of the Church of England clergy ejected in 1662 for conscience sake."

In this study a few years later (1783), a poor journeyman shoemaker named William Carey disrobed and walked down the hill a few hundred yards to be baptized in the river; that shoemaker became the first Protestant missionary to India, and probably the greatest.

Doddridge's hymns proved to be a useful supplement to Watts' and as such were widely used. But they have largely followed Watts into oblivion. Only nineteen are found in any of our standard hymnals, and of these only five are generally used.

### Awake, my soul, stretch every nerve    [1755]

This hymn capped a sermon preached from Phil 3:12–14.

The imagery that underlies all the stanzas is taken from the Greek games, with which Paul, the writer of Philippians, was quite familiar: in fact, while he was preaching at Corinth, the Isthmean games were being held only four miles away. In the hymn we catch the tenseness of the

* *Studies of Familiar Hymns*, Second Series, p. 169, by Louis F. Benson, copyright, 1923. Used by permission of The Westminster Press.

contest: the straining nerve, the utter expenditure; we see the cloud of witnesses in the great stadium, their eyes fixed on the runners; we hear the shouts of the partisans who called to their favorite athlete to beat his rivals; we rise in our seats when the victor staggers across the line into the arms of his trainer, and then is led proudly to the judges' stand where the Proconsul of Achaea himself places the wreath of pine twigs on the hero's brow, more to be desired than any monarch's crown on earth.

In the hymn the race is spiritualized into a symbol of the strenuous religious life in which heaven is the prize. The poet is using, almost paraphrasing, another passage from Paul, as he thought (Heb 12:1–2). And as for the prize, 1 Cor 9:25. This is undoubtedly Doddridge's best hymn, one of the immortals.

### O God of Bethel (Jacob) by whose hand        [1736]

This hymn is a good illustration of "hymn tinkering." In varying versions from the original of 1736 to the *Hymns Ancient and Modern* of 1889, the addressee is given as "O God of Bethel," "God of Jacob," "of Abraham," "God of Ages," "of Israel," "O God," "God of our fathers." One wonders why Jacob, Abraham and Israel are any better than Bethel, since all three blur the sharpness of the story on which the hymn is based—Gen 28:20–22. It is the story of Jacob's vow made at Bethel after he had had his dream of the ladder reaching to heaven. See how closely Doddridge followed the original scripture (his original text).

> If Thou, through each perplexing path
>     Wilt be our constant guide
> ("If God will be with me, and will keep me in the way that I go")

> If thou wilt daily Bread supply
>     And Raiment wilt provide
> ("and will give me bread to eat, and raiment to put on")

> If thou wilt spread thy Shield around
>     Till these our wanderings cease
> And at our Father's loved Abode
>     Our Souls arrive in Peace
> ("So that I come again to my father's house in peace")

> To thee as to our Covenant God
>     We'll our whole selves resign
> And count that not our tenth alone
>     But all we have is thine.
> ("Then shall the Lord be my God—and of all that thou shalt give me I will surely give the tenth unto thee.")

This stanza is now never sung.

In the old days when every Christian knew his Bible, each phrase in the hymn would at once suggest the original words, and part of the joy in singing the hymn was that constant recognition of Jacob's parallel situation. But today when only the exceptional person would recognize the story it makes little difference that the "tinkerers" have spoiled the picture.

Chapel Hill Church, Northampton, in Doddridge's day.

The hymn is often used at times of national crisis or rejoicing, and thus is a good second to Watts' "Our God, our help in ages past."

### Great God, we sing that mighty hand     [1755]

Original caption: "Help obtained from God. Acts 26:22. For New Year's Day." The text describes Paul's defense before Agrippa.

Looking for a text for a New Year's sermon, Doddridge happened to light upon this passage, which, though it has nothing to do with New Year's, suggested to his imagination the passing of time ("I stand unto this day testifying"), and so gave him a springboard from which to start. If we had the sermon before us we could doubtless see how each stanza of the hymn was a kind of summary of his "firstly," "secondly," etc. in the discourse. Reversing the process we may say that Doddridge's "firstly" was praise to God for the way He had supported us by His mercies through life from each year's beginning to its end. His "secondly" would be that these mercies would include protection from accident and sickness, provision for our physical wants and wisdom for our tasks. "Thirdly," this experience is solid basis for our trust in the future, and "fourthly," God's presence in our lives is the source of our joy, our peace and our hope.

This would be a fine sermon for those who to date had escaped danger and want, but the pastor is here forgetting for the moment those who have failed, been trampled upon, lost their jobs, suffered through sickness, been maimed or killed in war. He will have to preach another sermon and write another hymn for these.

### Miss ANNE STEELE (1716–1778) Baptist

THIS lady is sometimes referred to as "Mrs." When fairly young she was engaged to a Mr. Elscourt. On the wedding day a short time before the ceremony, the groom went down to the river for a bath, got beyond his depth and was drowned. Miss Steele never recovered from the shock.

When she was fourteen years old she united with her father's Baptist Church. At an early age also she began writing poetry, but not until she was forty-one did she publish anything, and then under the name of "Theodosia." Her father wrote in his diary: "This day, Nanny sent part of her composition to London, to be printed. I entreat a gracious God, who enabled and stirred her up to such a work, to direct in it and bless it for the good of many. . . . I pray God to make it useful and keep her humble." This prayer was answered. For nearly a hundred years Miss Steele's hymns were a good third to Watts' and Doddridge's in the hymnals of the Dissenting Churches. *The Psalmist*, 1843, gave Watts 303, Doddridge 59, Steele 54.

In her childhood the poet had an accident that made her an invalid through life, and for the last nine years she was confined to her chamber. This life of suffering breathes through her hymn, "Father, whate'er of earthly bliss," and a general atmosphere of tenderness, of trust and of communion with Christ characterize all her work. It is no doubt because of her sentimentality that all but one of her 144 hymns are now forgotten, namely:

### Father of mercies, in thy word    [1760]

The Reformation erased for its followers the belief in an infallible Church, but preserved its belief in an infallible Bible. While the Anglicans kept enough of the Roman emphasis still to place their Church and its sacraments toward the fore-front of their loyalties, the Dissenters had suffered so much at the hands of the Establishment that they were quite willing to form new Churches of their own and continue to derive their comfort and inspiration solely from the Word. This was particularly true of the Baptists to whom Miss Steele belonged.

"Endless glory" from "celestial lines" is supreme praise for the Bible (st. 1), but that evaluation comes from the experience of believing what the Book says. In sorrow, such as the poet continually knew, the Bible was like a spring of cool water (st. 2). Since the Old Testament was regarded as almost wholly prophecy or allegory which found its fulfillment in Christ, and the New Testament contained Christ's own words and the interpretation of these by His early followers, all of them inspired and inerrant, any portion of the Bible was the "Redeemer's voice," which raises a sensitive soul like

Miss Steele's to a state of ecstasy (st. 3). Under these circumstances, it is no wonder that her nine-year confinement to a sick room became a foretaste of Paradise (st. 4-5).

The study of the historic origins of the Bible has revealed in these days a multiplicity of environments and points of view, heathen and Christian, which we must learn to evaluate. In this process, we discover a gradation of insights and inspirations in the poets and sages of Israel, in the social gospel of the prophets, and in the words and works of the great Teacher who is Light and Life and Love. This changes our experience of reading from an unvarying stratosphere flight of emotional enjoyment where Miss Steele remained, to the exhilaration of mountain-climbing, where peaks and valleys give us a truer perspective and a more practical grasp of the verities of life, its tragedies and failures both personal and social, its imperatives of duty and love. We have outgrown Miss Steele intellectually as well as emotionally. But it is also true that in our less frequent reading of the Bible we have failed to reach Miss Steele's reverence for the greatest book ever written, or to receive from it that courage and inspiration to high action which we sorely need.

## Rev. JOSEPH GRIGG (c. 1720–1768) Presbyterian

GRIGG was born in poverty. In his youth he worked as a mechanic until he was twenty-five, but since that hampered his idealism he gave it up and became a clergyman. After four years of preaching he married a well-to-do widow, resigned his assistant-pastorate and spent the rest of his life in literary work. Only two of his hymns have survived, only one in general use:

## Jesus, and shall it ever be        Published 1765

The remarkable thing about this hymn is that it was written when the author was ten years old! To be sure, it was somewhat crude and had to be revised, but it stands witness to the precocity and morbid sentiment of a boy who thought he had "crimes" (altered to "sins" or "guilt") to be washed away at his early age. But that was a hang-over from the Calvinistic idea of Total Depravity.

The hymn has a constant value for all of us in its last line, a reminder of our high duty to honor our Master by our lives. It has had a special meaning in these latter days for adults like those in Norway and other subjugated countries who were compelled to choose between their loyalty to Jesus, or their God, or their conscience, and loyalty to a godless State. What ordinarily looks like sentiment becomes in times of persecution the sternest of realities.

# HISTORICAL SUMMARY

## CHAPTER FIVE: THE AGE OF THE WESLEYS

| | | *Writers* |
|---|---|---|
| 1702–14 | QUEEN ANNE: Strong for Anglican Church and Tories. Rise of Deism: reason the sole test of religion; God revealed in a world of law. | Watts, 1707–19 |
| 1711 | Jonathan Swift uses satire against Whigs, Catholics and Dissenters. | |
| | *Occasional Conformity Act:* penalized Dissenters who received Anglican Sacrament to get office but continued to attend Dissenting Churches. | Addison, 1712 |
| 1714 | *Schism Act:* no one could keep a school without license from Anglican bishop. | |
| 1714–27 | GEORGE I: Favorable to Whigs, Dissenters and traders. Much political corruption: Tories stood for religious intolerance and contempt for trade; Whigs for toleration and weakening power of king. Both used bribery. | |
| 1726–29 | Voltaire visits England: pours unsparing ridicule on organized religion. | Doddridge, |
| 1727–60 | GEORGE II. | 1735–55 |
| 1736 | Butler: *Analogy of Religion*—the divine regnancy of conscience over behavior. | Wesleys, 1738–47 |
| 1738 | Revivals begin under Whitefield and the Wesleys. Leaders and converts persecuted. | Cennick, 1742 Williams, 1745 |
| 1744 | Methodism established. Evangelical wing develops in Anglican Church. | Byrom, 1749 |
| 1751–83 | England wins territory in India. Bishop Berkeley (d. 1753) attacks Deism: nothing really exists but mind and ideas. | |
| 1757 | Hume: *Natural History of Religion.* Experience the source of all knowledge; miracles, so-called proofs of Christianity, never existed. | Steele, 1757 |
| 1760–1820 | GEORGE III. | |
| 1767–85 | Revolutionary inventions in textile industry; steam engine; northern cities pose problems in politics and religion. | Grigg, 1765 Cowper, 1768–79 Olivers, 1770 |
| 1778 | "Gordon riots" against Catholics. | Fawcett, 1773–82 |
| 1778–82 | Violence in Ireland between Catholics and Protestants. | Newton, 1774–79 |
| 1779 | Agitation for economic and political reform. | Toplady, 1776 |
| 1789– | French Revolution. | Heath, 1781 |
| 1792 | Wm. Carey first missionary to India. Baptist Missionary Society founded. | Perronet, 1789 |
| 1794 | Paley: *Evidences of Christianity:* Design in nature proves existence of a Designer. | |
| 1795 | Tom Paine: *Age of Reason:* A criticism of common ideas of God and morality. | |

# THE AGE OF THE WESLEYS

ON THE BASE of Dr. Watts and his contemporaries with their hymns of praise came the Wesleys with their hymns of personal religious experience. Following the apathy of the Established Church and middle-class Dissenters toward the social and economic degradation of the poor, came the Great Awakening with its deep concern for the individual that within two generations flowered in the humanitarian work of John Howard, prison reformer, William Wilberforce, apostle of the abolition of slavery, and the elder Earl of Shaftesbury, pioneer in social legislation. The dynamic behind these social changes came from the two brothers John and Charles Wesley, and only to a lesser degree from George Whitefield and his devoted followers. Before we can understand the hymns that embody the gospel of the Methodists and Evangelicals we must glance at the social and religious backgrounds of this tremendous upheaval.

The restoration of 1660 reinstated in power the Anglican Church. That Church was naturally a stout defender of the monarchy from which it derived its privileges, class distinctions, wealth and power. Reciprocally the landed aristocracy and gentry lined up loyally behind the Church; the hierarchy and the "squirearchy" dominated the nation. The wealth of the Church, derived from universal taxation, attracted to its high offices ambitious men whatever their qualifications of character or ability. In the eighteenth century the Archbishop of Canterbury was little more than a wire-puller and a social climber. The Primate and the Bishop of Durham each drew revenues of $100,000 a year, equivalent in purchasing power today to $250,000 or more. The higher offices of the Church were all for sale. The more important "livings" (that is, pastorates) were secured by wire-pulling. Many a rector held simultaneously two, three, or four "benefices" all of which provided him with ample means but exacted from him no comparable duties. He hired a "curate" to look after each parish paying him about a shilling a day and pocketing the rest of the income. In a certain parish in Wiltshire the parson received £300 a year, but there was neither church nor parsonage. Out of 11,000 livings in the kingdom there were over 6000 where the incumbent was non-resident. The ordinary working rector had to be content with £50 a year; indeed, Wesley's father, a capable, thrifty and hard-working clergyman, was for months kept in prison because he could not pay debts incurred for the bare necessities of life. And as for sermons, the eminent jurist Sir William Blackstone, after taking the trouble to hear every preacher of note in London, reported that he "did not hear a single discourse which had more Christianity in it than the writings of Cicero"; from what he heard he could not discover "whether the preacher was a follower of Confucius, of Mohammed or of Christ." By expelling the Dissenting clergymen in 1662, the Established Church rid itself of the only really zealous workers for morality and religion, and largely caused a stoppage of effort for reform.

But the Dissenting sects were also delinquent. They had fallen from their high state of vitality that had been engendered by persecution, for they were now tolerated. They came mostly from the middle class—skilled workers, shopkeepers, merchants who were getting rich from expanding overseas trade. They had no special quarrel with things as they were, and no enthusiasm to spread the gospel among the suppressed classes. While Watts was enjoying a comfortable living in the home of a rich merchant and fighting for a renovated Psalmody and a Gospel hymnody for Church people, the "elect" of the Calvinist creed, he had no idea that the business of the Church was to seek and save the lost and remake the social structure of the world.

From all accounts, that social structure was in sad need of a revolution. Beneath the wealthy upper classes who were completely worldly, largely callous and immoral, and the self-satisfied middle class who had little to complain of, was the vast sodden throng of the under-privileged, neglected by Church and State alike. These people existed in a condition little above savagery. They were brutalized by a penal code and a prison system which staggers present-day imagination. Adults and even children of both sexes could be legally hanged for 160 different offences—from picking a pocket for more than a shilling to snaring a rabbit on a gentleman's estate. Charles Wesley writes in his *Journal* that he preached in jail to 52 felons waiting to be hanged, among them a child of ten. One of the most popular shows was the mass hangings held every six weeks at Tyburn Hill, London. For lesser crimes there were the pillory, the stocks, the scold's bridle, the whipping-post, the branding-iron, transportation to slavery, and the atrocious jail. John Wesley wrote in a letter to the *London Chronicle*, January 2, 1761: "Of all the seats of woe on this side hell, few, I suppose, exceed or even equal Newgate" (the famous London prison).

One of the tragedies of the eighteenth century was the high death rate among children. Official records show that in London, three out of four children of all classes died before their fifth birthday. But the mortality

"GIN LANE" BY HOGARTH.

*Start left middle and go clockwise.* Man and dog gnaw same bone. Carpenter pawns saw and coat at prosperous pawnshop owned by S. Gripe. Tattered woman pawns kitchen utensils to get drink. Parish beadle directs putting woman's body in coffin; her child crying on the ground. Drunken man impales child on a spit. A house falls to ruins. Good house belongs to undertaker—sign of a coffin. In nearer house, barber hangs himself in garret. Remaining good house owned by "Kilman," the distiller. In street two young girls from St. Giles Charity School are toasting one another. Two drunken beggars are fighting, crutch vs. stool. Drunken woman is carried off in wheelbarrow while boy pours last glass down her throat. Mother gives baby a drink to keep it from crying. A peddler cries, "Buy my ballads and I'll give you a glass of gin for nothing." He has pawned waistcoat, shirt and stockings; his body is a skeleton. Center, a diseased intoxicated woman takes snuff while baby falls to death over rail. Gin shop under street named "Gin Royal"; over door, "Drunk for a penny, Dead drunk for twopence, Clean straw for nothing."

among the poor was higher, made so by the callousness of those who cared
for orphans and foundlings in the work-houses, namely, the churchwardens.
The parish register in Greater London for 1750–1755 shows that in many
places all the children died within twelve months of entry. Some wardens
took bastard children off their mothers' hands at so much per head, spent
the money in hilarous living and let the babies die. In one parish in Westminster, out of five hundred bastards so received over a series of months,
only one survived.

Harlotry was scandalously flourishing among all classes. Gin drinking
became a national curse and was responsible for much of the crime and a
good deal of the poverty. In 1750 the consumption of this "cheap, fiery,
poisonous drink" was 11,000,000 gallons. In the parish of St. Giles, London,
out of 2000 houses more than one in every four was a gin-shop. The sign
on many of these read, "Drunk for one penny. Dead-drunk, tuppence. Free
straw" (on which to sleep off the effects). This was such a profitable
business that the manufacturers of liquor became wealthy, and the trade
became a vested interest in which many who were high in Church and
State had a stake.

It is not difficult to trace the ramifications of this hellish gin business
into every area of life. Drink led to debts and thence to prison, deportation
and slavery, to crime of every kind, with its inhuman punishments, to a
passion for the cruel sports of bull- and bear-baiting, and cock-fighting, and
prize-fighting among even women champions, to ruinous gambling which
became a national obsession among high and low alike; to the immoralities
that accompanied obscene theatrical performances—every theater surrounded by taverns and brothels. That is why John Wesley prohibited his
Methodists from attending the theater, which he called "the sink of all
profaneness and debauchery."

Add to these overwhelming factors the evils of ignorance and illiteracy,
and you have a degenerate picture. In the fifty years preceding the rise of
the Wesleys and Whitefield, England reached its lowest pitch of moral
degradation. Hogarth has pictured it for all time in his paintings and
engravings: "Rake's Progress," "Marriage à la Mode," "Election Day," "Beer
Street and Gin Lane," and the like. Hogarth also lampooned Wesley and
Whitefield in "A Medley."

This black situation became a challenge to the three great evangelists.
They tackled the problem of reform, not from the economic or social point
of view, but from the religious. They believed that the spirit of God could
change the hearts of men, could make them desire a better life here, and,
trusting in the saving power of God through Christ, could break the chains
of sin and cause them to rise to a sobriety and dignity which was theirs by
right. Historians can trace the revolutionary effects of their preaching in all
fields: personal morality, health, politics, the penal code, class barriers,
economic and personal slavery, education, literature, music, and the religious
life of all sects.

Nevertheless, the Established Church of their day would have none of them. All these men were forbidden to preach in any church: their "enthusiasm" was condemned as an excitation of the devil. A certain rector named John Kirby called John Wesley a "mystery of iniquity," an "emissary of Satan," whose religion is "as opposite to Christianity as heaven is to hell,"

Burning of the Epworth Rectory, February 9, 1709. "Mrs. Wesley, who was ill, barely escaped with her life. 'Jacky' appeared at the window and cried for help. Men climbed on each other's shoulders and he leaped into their arms."

and whose "damnation will be just." * William Cobbett, perhaps the most powerful political pamphleteer in English history, called the sect "nasty, canting, dirty, lousey Methodists." **

In spite of all this calumny both John and Charles Wesley lived and died in full communion with the Church of England. Methodism was not established as a separate Dissenting sect until 1808.

## Rev. JOHN WESLEY (1703–1791) Anglican

JOHN WESLEY was a phenomenal man. Until the days of the airplane he travelled more miles—a quarter of a million, mostly on horseback; he preached more sermons—upwards of forty thousand; he converted probably more people—at least 100,000—than any person who ever lived.

Saved in childhood by a hair's breadth from being burned to death

* Taken from J. W. Bready: *England Before and After Wesley* (1938), to whom and also to E. Halévy: *History of the English People* (1924), I am indebted for many of the facts in this chapter.

** G. D. H. Cole and Raymond Postgate: *The Common People, 1746–1938*, p. 265, when his father's enemies set the rectory on fire, nearly taken off in his fifties by a "galloping consumption," he nevertheless lived to be nearly ninety. An undersized man of delicate appearance, he yet had nerves of iron, could ride horseback twenty to sixty miles a day—once he rode a hundred in twenty-four hours. An indefatigable man, he rose at four in the morning, retired at ten P. M. and never wasted a minute. He read hundreds of volumes while travelling—would drop the reins on the horse's neck and

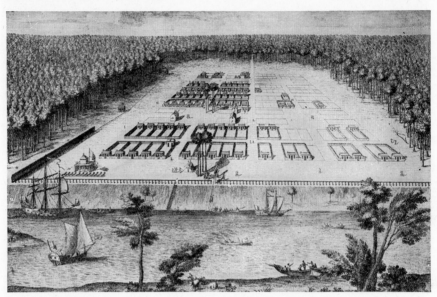

Savannah, Georgia, in 1747, where John Wesley translated German hymns into English and printed them in the first Anglican hymnal ever published. The German authors translated were Gerhardt, Tersteegen and Zinzendorf.

with both hands hold the big books to his near-sighted eyes. In later years when friends had given him a chaise he boarded up one side of it, put in some book-shelves and a writing-board and so kept up his incessant work.

He wrote voluminously, published 233 original works besides editing or translating other men's. For sixty-six years he kept a diary in cipher or shorthand which accounted for every hour in every day, and kept besides a full-length Journal. "At the age of 83 he was piqued to discover that he could not write more than fifteen hours a day without hurting his eyes; and at 86 he was ashamed to admit that he could not easily preach more than twice a day. In his 86th year he preached in almost every shire in England and Wales and often rode thirty to fifty miles a day."

A learned man, he could read Hebrew, Greek and Latin, and could not only read but preach in German, French, Italian; he also mastered enough Spanish to pray in it!

Gentle of speech, yet he could make his resonant voice heard out of doors by an audience of 30,000. Never a rabble-rouser and never stooping to the language of the street, he could sway a crowd of uneducated men as the wind stirs a grain field. Never belligerent or aggressive, he faced and neutralized mob after mob bent on bodily injury or death.

A master of organization, he so laid the foundations of his Societies that instead of disintegrating after his death they grew to be the largest present-day body of Protestants in the world.

So much for a general summary of his lifework. What interests us here is his impact upon hymnody—and it was epochal.

On his voyage to America with his younger brother Charles, where he was to serve as Chaplain to the English colony at Savannah, he found twenty-six Moravians on board. He immediately began the study of German so that he could converse with them and learn about their religion. These people were enthusiastic singers; in their daily meetings for prayer they sang lustily out of their *Gesangbuch* compiled by Count Zinzendorf, about whom more anon. Especially in a storm they out-vied the elements. This from Wesley's *Journal*, January 25, 1736, describing their behavior in a gale:

> In the midst of the Psalm wherewith their service began, the sea broke over, split the mainsail in pieces, covered the ship and poured in between the decks . . . A terrible screaming began among the English. The Germans looked up, and without intermission calmly sang on. I asked one of them afterwards, "Was you not afraid?" He answered, "Thank God, No."

This experience convinced Wesley of the vitality of the Moravian religion and of the immense value of singing. In the Church of England, it must be remembered, there was no hymn-singing, and now that the enthusiasm generated by the Reformation and the fight for tolerance had waned, Psalm-singing had fallen into its worst estate. At once Wesley began to translate some of the German hymns, particularly those of Paul Gerhardt, Tersteegen and Zinzendorf. These hymns will be considered in detail in Chap. XI.

On arrival at Savannah Wesley continued to translate, sing and use hymns. He was very methodical and practical about it. First he translated, then he sang by himself, then he tried out the hymn in his early morning devotions when a handful of people met for mutual comfort and help; then in sick-rooms where people far from home and friendliness caught eagerly at this new source of courage and hope; then in larger gatherings on weekday evenings and Sunday he taught the people to sing not only his translations, but other poems culled from various sources. The value of each selection was tested by actual use.

In 1737 at Savannah, Georgia, he printed these hymns and Psalms in a book, *Collection of Psalms and Hymns*—the first Hymnal ever used in an Anglican Church. About half the seventy selections were from Isaac Watts. The Wesleys were represented by five hymns from his father and

John Wesley preaching at the Market Cross, painted by William Hatherell.

five from his brother Samuel; brother Charles had not yet begun to write. The most important source was George Herbert, now introduced into English hymnody for the first time. But the book got Wesley into trouble: his parishioners objected to the use of anything but Psalms.

John did not stay long in Georgia. He was too straight-laced, too much of a disciplinarian, too lacking in tact, and he was victimized by unscrupulous females who found him attractive and whom he tried unsuccessfully to reform. He was finally indicted by a grand jury on a number of ridiculous charges, but "skipped the country" before the trial came off and took ship for England, hoping to lay his case before the Colony's Trustees. This complete failure in his first encounter with the world gave him such a jolt that it led him to search for a better religion than the one he had. It drove him into the arms of the Moravian colony which met in Aldergate, London. In one of their meetings on May 24, 1738, he was "converted," that is, had a deep emotional experience which convinced him that what he thought were his sins were forgiven and that Christ and he now lived in close personal relationship. His brother Charles had gone through this experience only three days earlier, and thus the point of view of both was changed. John had gone to Georgia, he confessed, "in the hope of saving my own soul: I cannot hope to attain the same degree of holiness here [England] which I may there." But now he himself no longer counted; he became the messenger of Christ's saving love to a sinful world. From this fateful period, when together the brothers crossed the line which separates smug religious self-interest from total abandonment of self to a divine vocation, John and Charles worked as a team in which the gifts of each found ample and long-continued use.

John's main contribution to hymnody was his editing, organizing and publishing of the hymns of Charles. Under his directing genius Methodist hymnody became the most powerful evangelizing influence England ever knew. His smallest contribution was the hymns he personally wrote. They were few in number. Those that have survived in our hymnals are:

> "We lift our hearts to thee"
> "Author of life divine" (half by Charles)

His most extensive contribution is translation from the German. Our hymnals contain the following which are interpreted in Chap. XI:

> "Jesus, thy boundless love to me" (Gerhardt)
> "Give to the winds thy fears" (Gerhardt)
> "Commit thou all thy griefs" (Gerhardt)
> "O thou to whose all-searching sight" (Zinzendorf)
> "Thou hidden Love of God" (Tersteegen)
> "Lo, God is here! Let us adore" (Tersteegen)

We must now take a preliminary glance at Charles.

## Rev. CHARLES WESLEY (1707–1788) Anglican

CHARLES was the eighteenth child of Susanna and Samuel Wesley. By good fortune he was able to attend Westminster School, London, where his older brother Samuel was a master. It was a tough experience for an undersized boy of eight. He and his schoolmates rose at 5:15 A.M., which in winter was long before daylight, washed in the cold cloisters superintended by monitors, attended Latin prayers, then studied Latin till breakfast at eight. Classes till dinner at noon, followed by "construes" (translation) for two hours; then after an interval, studies were resumed till supper time. Bed at eight. The boys had to talk Latin at all times. Then there were the other boys to get along with, many of them rough customers who were glad to perpetuate the brutal traditions of the school. Charles gave proof of his grit by defending a small Scottish boy named Murray against the school bully. This was good preparation for the encounters with mobs in his later life.

Charles went to Christ Church, Oxford, in 1726, age nineteen. The University was a dull place. "The professors never lectured, the exams were a farce, and the statutes were a dead letter. Only those who wished to study did so." Charles liked fun and had a capacity for friendship, but brother John, just elected a Fellow of Lincoln College, kept him steady. It was really Charles' set of friends that formed the nucleus of "Holy Club" which John took over and made famous.

On graduation Charles took holy Orders and shipped to Georgia as private secretary to Governor Oglethorpe. He and John sailed together. Charles fell into trouble through the venom of adventuring females, lost the confidence of the Governor who treated him outrageously, and sailed for home before John did. "I could not be more trampled on were I a fallen minister of state. The people have found out that I am in disgrace . . . The servants that used to wash my linen sent it back unwashed . . . Today Mr. Oglethorpe gave away my bedstead from under me and refused to spare one of the carpenters to mend me up another."

The brothers met again at the Moravian rooms at Aldergate, went through the conversion experience and found their true selves by complete surrender to the love of Christ and the will of God. Henceforth John and Charles were partners in one of the most dramatic and fruitful episodes in religious history, the mission to the poor and outcast in the United Kingdom. Says D. M. Jones in *Charles Wesley, A Study*: "John was the calm general that directed operations, Charles was the brilliant cavalry leader who plunged into the thickest of the fray." *

Charles began his mission by working with the felons in Newgate Prison, London, and following them to the gallows at Tyburn, as will later be recounted in detail. Then when John took over the direction of White-

* Published by Skeffington & Son, Ltd., London, 1919.

field's out-of-door preaching at Bristol and in Wales, Charles moved to Bristol, August, 1739, and with that as a center began a fifteen-year period of itinerant evangelism in which he showed extraordinary energy, courage, self-sacrifice, and a power in preaching that surpassed even John's.

To document what he and John endured in the way of persecution, here is what happened at Devizes in February, 1747. The mob opposition was worked up by the local Anglican clergyman who went from house to house to make the absurd charge that he had heard Charles preach blasphemy at the University. When the crowd got underway, the leaders proved to be led by "the chief gentlemen of the town," accompanied by "the jealous curate, dancing for joy." They surrounded the house where Wesley and his aides were staying, they broke the windows, ripped off the shutters and drove the preachers' horses into the pond. Next day they got out the fire engine and deluged the house in which Wesley had taken refuge, flooding all the rooms and ruining the stock-in-trade of the shopkeeper on the street floor. Local leaders of the Methodist society were ducked in the pond. When Wesley and his companions left town, singing as they went a hymn Charles had composed, "Thine arm hath safely brought us," they rode out between two lines of scowling faces.**

Somehow Wesley always seemed to be the victor: "At Tasfield," reads the *Journal*, "I found a great mob about our house, and bestowed an hour upon taming them. An hundred or more I admitted into the room, and when I had got them together, for two hours exhorted them to repent in the power of love. The rocks were melted on every side, and the ringleaders of the rebels declared they would make disturbances no more."

If it was hard on the preachers, it was worse on the converts. They were outrageously treated—stoned, mauled, ducked, hounded with bulldogs, threatened; homes looted, businesses ruined. Anyone who walked through a town could pick out by their ruinous condition the houses where Methodists lived. This opposition of the ignorant and brutalized populace is understandable in that half-savage eighteenth century, but why the ringleadership of the clergy and the "Gentlemen of the town"? The clergy regarded these preachers as poachers on their private domain. The clergy had been set over their parishes by their bishops; their duty was to maintain morning and evening prayer, to christen and marry and bury, and theoretically at least they were the spiritual overseers of their flock. They resented the intruders who preached a different doctrine and had such astonishing success. They represented the spiritual *status quo* and wanted to be let alone. The fact that their parishioners were poor and degraded was beside the point. Did not the Bible say, "The poor ye have always with you"? God made men in classes; it was not the business of the Church to unmake them. The "Gentlemen" (squires et al.) also were upholders of the economic, social and political *status quo*, the condition of special privilege for them-

** Summarized from Jones: *op. cit.*, who took his facts from Wesley's *Journal*.

selves. They demanded that the lower classes be kept in their places. They acquired merit in their own eyes by doling out limited charity to the poor, but they feared to have the poor rise to a condition where they did not need charity. Methodism raised the fallen, set them on their feet, made them honest, industrious, and inspired them with ambition. That was a threat to society; it bordered on treason. In self-defence the old order banded together to send the Methodist cohorts to Hell whence they came.

WESLEY'S HYMNS

The "conversion" of Charles released within him his gift of song. On the very next day he wrote his first hymn, "Where shall my wandering soul begin." Thereafter hardly a day or an experience passed without its crystallization into verse. Charles composed in his study, his garden, on horseback—anywhere. The result, 6500 hymns on hundreds of Scripture texts and on every conceivable phase of Christian experience and Methodist theology. Sensing their tremendous use in arousing sinners, encouraging saints, and educating all in the mysteries of Christian faith, John began to select and publish hymn-tracts in small collections; others were larger, the hymns grouped according to subject. Over a period of fifty-three years the total publications numbered fifty-six! The smaller inexpensive collections were for use in revival services and in the Class meetings. The culmination of the series was the comprehensive Hymnal of 1780: *A Collection of Hymns for the use of the People called Methodists* (three shillings, sewed).

John wrote a Preface to it in which he summed up its purposes and its excellences:

> Large enough to contain all the important truths of our most holy religion . . . In what other publication of this time have you so full and distinct an account of Scriptural Christianity? Such a declaration of the heights and depths of religion, speculative and practical? So strong cautions against the most plausible errors? And so clear directions for making our calling and election sure: for perfecting holiness in the fear of God?

As we might put it today, this hymnbook is intended as a complete manual of religious education. Nothing shows more clearly John's organizing mind and the various aspects of Christian experience through which a soul should pass, if it followed the Methodist line, than the arrangement of hymns in this book. It is worth giving in detail:

Part I.  Introductory Hymns
     Section   I.  Exhorting and beseeching to return to God
     Section  II.  Describing the pleasantness of religion; the goodness of God; death; judgment; heaven; hell
     Section III.  Praying for a blessing

Part II.  Convincing
Section    I.  Describing formal religion
Section   II.  Describing inward religion
Part III. Praying
For Repentance; for Mourners convinced of Sin; for Mourners
brought to the Birth; for those convinced of Backsliding;
for the Recovered
Part IV.  For Believers
Rejoicing; Fighting; Praying; Watching; Working; Suffering;
Groaning for full Redemption; brought to the Birth; Saved;
Interceding for the World
Part V.   For the [Methodist] Society
Meeting; Giving thanks; Praying; Parting

How strange a religion this seems; so intense, purposeful, introspective, and yet so socially concerned; humble yet militant—as if religion, salvation, character, the will to save others, were the most important things in the world. We who go on Sunday to our fine churches see the congregation in its Sunday best, hear the choirs present their anthems and the organ roll, listen to a well-organized sermon on something-or-other, greet our friends and ride home well-satisfied with our Four Freedoms, would hardly know what to do with a hymnbook like this.

By way of contrast to our own church services, let us look at a Class meeting in Kingswood, outside of Bristol, in the coal country: twelve members with John Cennick for a leader—later a notable evangelist in the Welsh Revival, and author of "Children of the Heavenly King." (See Chap. VI.)

### An Imaginative Reconstruction

The room is a small school building contributed by the other societies for the poor colliers of this region. The evening is Wednesday, after dark and after supper. Cennick is there first; he lights the candles, builds a fire in the grate. Soon the people arrive: an old lady with a cane, a couple of miners in their heavy boots and rough smocks, the grime not wholly removed from hands and face; the town simpleton who longs for company; the village drunk recently snatched from the burning; a carter, a shepherd, a farmer and wife. None of them has an education, most of them cannot read or write, every last one of them is poor—some of them desperately poor; they have worked all their lives and have never been farther away from home than Bristol (four miles). Of such is the Kingdom of God in Kingswood.

Cennick greets them as they come in: "The Lord bless you, brother." "Thank the Lord you could come, sister." "How's the sick girl, Mrs. Stow?" "How's the lamb that broke her leg, Danny?" They nod to one another as they take their seats on the benches, glad to feel the warmth of friend-ship and a common aspiration. Cennick strikes up an old familiar hymn by Charles Wesley, "O for a thousand tongues to sing my dear Redeemer's praise." The tune is lively, Cennick is a good singer, everybody joins whether he can sing or not. It makes one feel good to sing after twelve hours in the coal pit. The leader prays *ex tempore* and calls for another hymn. The ex-drunkard asks for "Soldiers of Christ, arise!" Most of the people know that also.

The leader then says that Mr. Charles Wesley has written a new hymn which he desires all the Kingswood class to learn. He wrote it when he heard of the stoning of some of the members of the class last week, and the setting on fire of Mr. Barrow's hay-rick by the same ruffians. From his Bible Cennick takes a piece of paper on which are written in Mr. Wesley's own hand the words of "O Thou, to whose all-searching sight."

"It is to be sung in times of trouble and persecution, says Mr. Wesley, and he wrote it especially for us."

Cennick then reads the whole hymn, then re-reads the first stanza, sings the first stanza alone to a tune some of them have heard, he re-reads the first two lines and asks them to try to sing them with him. This they attempt to do. And so on till the first two stanzas have been rehearsed. That is enough for tonight. We shall tackle the other stanzas on Sunday evening.

Here are stanzas 3 and 6: *

> If in this darksome wild I stray,
> Be thou my light, be thou my way;
> No foes, no violence I fear,
> No fraud, while thou, my God, art near.

> If rough and thorny be the way,
> My strength proportion to my day;
> Till toil, and grief, and pain shall cease,
> Where all is calm, and joy, and peace.

The leader then turns to the subject of the evening. "What should a Christian do if he falls into sin?"—that is, "backslides." The subject has been announced at the previous meeting and everybody has been thinking about it. Cennick introduced the subject by reading Charles Wesley's hymn, "Depth of mercy, can there be," which he had taught them to say by heart on previous occasions. He then explained it line by line, and from the Bible read the verses that said the same thing. The talk was a kind of run-ning commentary on the hymn and the Bible and the infinite mercy of God. Here is the framework on which it was built:

* As found in the Hymnbook of 1780, Part IV, Section IV, "For Believers Suffer-ing." Hymn 338. Sung to *Pudsey*, L. M.

"CREDULITY, SUPERSTITION AND FANATICISM" BY HOGARTH, 1762.

*The Preacher:* His voice, a bull-roar; under his gown, a clown's jacket. From his right hand dangles a witch sucked by a cat; on the broom she rides is a Biblical quotation, "I speak as a fool." From left hand dangles devil with gridiron, a warning that his hearers better get converted. In cloud, cherub messenger-boy brings letter for "St. Money-Trap," a slur on the revival movement as a racket. Thermometer (upper right) labelled "Whitefield's Scale of Vociferation," running from natural voice to bull-roar.

*The Clerk* with wings, attended by cherubs. On sheet, quotation from a Whitefield hymn, "Only Love to us be given; Lord, we ask no other heaven": interpreted sensually by (1) vulgar lovers below the pulpit; (2) by thermometer, lower right, where the mercury rises from Methodist brain resting on Wesley's *Sermons* and Glanvil's *On Witches,* pauses at "Luke-warm," and may descend through Low Spirits, Sorrow, Agony . . . to Suicide, or may rise through Love Heat, Lust, Ecstacy, Convulsion Fits, Madness, to Raving. That is what Methodist religion will do to one.

*The Congregation:* Motley crowd of debased persons: Lower left, Mary Toft giving birth to rabbits—which she claimed to do. Under desk, bewitched boy vomits hobnails, pins, etc. Left, a Jew lays down bloody sacrificial knife and cracks louse between thumbnails. Outside the window a Turk smokes and says by implication, "If this be Christianity, Great Prophet, I thank Thee I am a Mohammedan."

"Depth of mercy, can there be": Ex 34:6–7; 2 Chron 16:34; Ps 33:18–19; 86:5
"Can my God his wrath forbear": Micah 7:18–19; 1 Tim 1:13–15

And so through the rest of the hymn.

The last part of the Class meeting is taken up with "testimony." Each person present tells "what the Lord has done for him" since they last met together: encouragement in time of distress, strength in time of weakness, old habits losing their grip, prayer a greater help, singing the hymns as they went about their work a source of joy, greater kindness in their treatment of others, forgiveness of enemies, deep sorrow over failures.

So these humble folks, once ignorant and some of them depraved, were learning what the spiritual life is, how God is merciful and Christ a friend.

And so the social life of England was being measurably raised from the Slough of Despond into which centuries of neglect had plunged it— less ignorance, less gin drinking and gambling, less cruelty, a greater sense of responsibility, a deeper loyalty to conscience.

The Methodist Revival did not concern itself with the reformation of social institutions. It did not tackle evils from the legislative end. It did work a moral transformation in the lives of thousands of people and thus prepared the public conscience and raised up the leaders to enact the legislative reforms of the nineteenth century. John Wesley has expressed the rationale of it: "The sure hope of a better age is a better man."

Yet the Wesleys were perfectly conscious that institutions needed reformation. They spoke fiercely against human slavery, war, inhuman prisons, barbarous laws, the abuse of privilege, power and wealth, the liquor traffic. In France it took a bloody revolution to break old bonds and liberate the lower classes. The Wesleys are credited with forestalling a bloody revolution in England, largely through the educative influence of such meetings as we have just attended.

### METHODIST BELIEFS

Charles Wesley's hymns are a textbook of Methodist theology. The quality of that theology aroused plenty of contemporary opposition. Most of the religious people of the eighteenth century in and out of the Established Church were Calvinists; they held views about God and man like those of Dr. Watts. But the Wesleys were heretics; they rejected Calvin and embraced Arminius, the Dutch theologian (1560–1609). The main point of difference between the two was the matter of "election." Watts, following Calvin, believed that God had chosen some men to be saved and some to be damned: man could do nothing to change his fore-ordained state. Wesley, following Arminius, believed that man is free; he himself can decide whether he will be saved. Christ's death on the cross atoned for the sins of all men, not a chosen few; God's pardon through the cross is offered to all ("Free Grace"). Salvation is a matter of accepting what Christ has accomplished and God has offered. Men are therefore subject to persuasion, and it is the function of the Christian to endeavor to bring men to a decision.

While therefore Watts can praise God and Christ for the salvation which he (fortunately) was elected to receive, he has no word of invitation to sinners, just as in his preaching he had no passion for the saving of souls. But the Wesleys were on fire for saving souls, and their hymns pleaded with sinners to come to the Water of Life. You can pick out from them scores of lines like the following that reflect these fundamental beliefs:

*The Universality of Salvation*

Come, almighty to deliver,
Let us all thy grace receive.

&ast;   &ast;   &ast;

He now stands knocking at the door
  Of every sinner's heart;
The worst need keep him out no
    more,
  Nor force him to depart.

*Reformation of the Life*

He breaks the power of cancelled
    sin,
  He sets the prisoner free;
His blood can make the foulest
    clean,
  His blood avails for me.

*The Invitation to sinners*

Come, sinners, to the Gospel feast;
Let every soul be Jesus' guest;
Ye need not one be left behind,
For God hath bidden all mankind.

&ast;   &ast;   &ast;

Sinners, turn! Why will ye die?

*Conscience quickened*

I want a Godly fear,
  A quick-discerning eye,
That looks to Thee when sin is
    near
  And sees the tempter fly.

*Social Obligation*

A charge to keep I have

&ast;   &ast;   &ast;

To serve the present age,
  My calling to fulfil;
O may it all my powers engage
  To do my Master's will.

On the negative side read Charles Wesley's attack on Calvinism—a selection from a fifteen-stanza hymn taken from Hymns on *God's Everlasting Love*, 1741.

*"The Horrible Decree"*

Ah, gentle, gracious Dove,
And art thou grieved in me?
That sinners should restrain thy
    love
And say, "It is not free;
It is not free for all;
The *most* thou *passest* by,
And mockest with a fruitless call
Whom thou hast doomed to die."

O HORRIBLE DECREE,
Worthy of whence it came!
Forgive their hellish blasphemy
Who charge it on the Lamb,
Whose pity him inclined
To leave his throne above,
The Friend and Saviour of man-
    kind,
The God of grace and love.

FAMOUS WESLEY HYMNS INTERPRETED

*Jesus, Lover of my soul*     [1739]

This is the most famous of all Charles Wesley's 6500 hymns. It is found in all our hymnals and has been translated into all the languages of the missionary world.

No one knows the circumstances under which the hymn was written. All the stories about doves or hawks flying through his window or into his cabin and taking refuge in his bosom from a storm are sentimental legends. The stories of his composing it while lying under a hedge or in a spring-house after having been beaten up by a mob are equally legendary. When it was written in 1739, he had not become an itinerant evangelist, or been mobbed. The best explanation is that it came spontaneously from the depths of his soul, and bears the marks of three tremendous experiences that occurred during his early life.

The first of these was the near foundering of his ship during a great storm on the Atlantic when returning from Georgia to England in the fall of 1736. He had gone out as secretary to Governor Oglethorpe but had made a failure in personal adjustment. He sailed home disheartened in mind and sick in body. Doubtless the storm within his own soul made the hurricane on the ocean doubly frightening and memorable.

Now turn to his *Journal* for 1736 in which this experience is recorded:

Thurs. Oct. 28. The captain warned me of a storm approaching. In the evening at eight it came, and rose higher and higher. . . . There was so prodigious a sea that it quickly washed away our sheep and half our hogs, and drowned most of our fowl. Our ship had been new-calked at Boston; how carefully it now appeared: for being deeply laden the sea streamed in at the sides so plentifully that it was as much as four men could do by continual pumping to keep her above water. I rose and lay down by turns, but could remain in no posture long; strove vehemently to pray, but in vain. I prayed for . . . faith in Jesus Christ, continually repeating his name, till I felt the virtue of it at last, and knew that I abode under the shadow of the Almighty.

It was now about three in the afternoon and the storm at its height. I endeavored to encourage poor Mr. Brig and Cutler, who were in the utmost agony of fear. I prayed with them and for them till four; at which time the ship made so much water that the captain, finding it otherwise impossible to save her from sinking, cut down the mizzen mast. In this dreadful moment, I bless God, I found the comfort of hope; and such joy in finding I could hope, as the world could neither give nor take away . . .

I went to my poor friend Appee, declared the difference between one that feareth God and one that feareth Him not. . . . He said that all his refuge, in time of danger, was to persuade himself there was none. Mr. Cutler frequently calling upon God to have mercy upon his soul, Appee confessed that he greatly envied him, as he had no manner of concern for his own. I advised him to pray. He answered, it was mocking God to begin praying in danger when he had never done it in safety. . . .

I returned to Mr. Brig and Mr. Cutler and endeavored from their fear to show them the want of religion, which was intended for our support on such occasions; urged them to resolve, if God saved them from this distress, that they would instantly and entirely give themselves up to Him. . . .

Toward morning the sea heard and obeyed the divine voice, 'Peace, be still.'

Friday, Dec. 3. At six the pilot came on board. In half an hour we reached the shore. I knelt down and blessed the Hand that has conducted me through such inextricable mazes.

In the light of this narrative read the first two stanzas of the hymn: "Jesus, lover of my soul" and "Other refuge have I none."

The second great experience that entered into the composition of this hymn was Charles Wesley's spiritual awakening and sudden cure which occurred on May 21, 1738. It was the turning point in his career. From a self-distrustful and over-anxious clergyman with uncertain aim, he became a flaming evangelist, a veritable voice of God, swaying with his eloquence vast out-of-door audiences all over England and Wales and in Ireland. He pleaded wth the lowest of men, the outcasts of society, to accept the free salvation of Christ and to lead lives of holiness.

For some time Wesley had been in the grip of an intermittent fever that accompanied pleurisy and dysentery. On the day of his "conversion" he was desperately ill. In his lodgings in London, alone in his room upstairs, he had an hallucination that a Mrs. Musgrove entered his room and said: "In the name of Jesus of Nazareth, arise, and believe, and thou shalt be

healed of all thy infirmities." She then faded away. Wesley called down after
her but was told that she had not been in the house. Then he went to the
Bible for comfort. His *Journal* tells the rest:

*Left,* John Wesley. A portrait by Frank O. Salisbury from all available data.
It now hangs in John Wesley's study in the house adjoining the Wesley Chapel
on City Road, London. *Right,* Charles Wesley, after the original painting
owned by the Wesley family.

> I arose and looked into the Scripture. The words that first pre-
> sented were, 'And now, Lord, what is my hope? Truly, my hope is
> even in Thee.'
>
> Afterwards I opened upon Isaiah 40:1, 'Comfort ye, comfort
> ye my people . . . and cry unto her that her warfare is accom-
> plished, that her iniquity is pardoned.' . . . I now found myself at
> peace with God. . . .
>
> At midnight I gave myself up to Christ: assured I was safe,
> sleeping or waking. Had continued experience of his power to over-
> rule all temptations; and confessed, with joy and surprise, that he
> was able to do exceedingly abundantly for me, above what I can
> ask or think.

His brother John testifies, "His bodily strength returned also from that
hour."

Compare this entry with stanza 3 of the hymn, usually omitted, "Wilt
thou not regard my call?" and stanza 4, "Thou, O Christ, art all I want."

The final experience that sunk deep into the soul of Charles Wesley
and lent its subconscious pressure and imagery to the creation of this hymn,

was his ministration to the felons in Newgate prison. One of these occurred during the week of July 12–19, 1738, and climaxed in the execution of ten of them at Tyburn Hill. We will let the *Journal* tell the story:

> July 12. Preached at Newgate to the condemned felons, and visited one of them in his cell, sick of a fever—a poor black that had robbed his master. I told him of One who came down from heaven to save lost sinners, and him in particular; described the sufferings of the Son of God, His sorrows, agony and death. He listened with all the signs of eager astonishment; the tears trickled down his cheeks while he cried, 'What! Was it for me? Did God suffer all this for so poor a creature as me?' I left him waiting for the salvation of God . . .
>
> July 17. At Newgate I preached on death (which they must suffer the day after tomorrow). At one (o'clock) I was with the black in his cell. Two more of the malefactors came. I had great help and power in prayer. One rose and said he felt his heart all on fire so as he never found himself before; he was all in a sweat; believed Christ died for him . . . The black was quite happy. The other criminal was in an excellent temper; believing or on the point of it.
>
> July 18. I administered the sacrament to the black, and eight more; having first instructed them in the nature of it . . . At night I was locked in with Bray in one of the cells. We wrestled in mighty prayer. All the criminals were present, and all delightfully cheerful. The soldier in particular found his comfort and joy increase every moment. Another, from the time he communicated, has been in perfect peace. Joy was visible on all their faces. We sang
>
> > Behold the saviour of mankind,
> >     Nailed to a shameful tree!
> > How vast the love that Him inclined
> >     To bleed and die for thee.
>
> > [—Sam. Wesley, Sr. See *Methodist Hymnal* 136]

July 19. I rose very heavy, to visit them for the last time. At six I prayed and sang with them all together. All the ten received [the sacrament].

> At half-hour past nine their irons were knocked off and their hands tied. I went in a coach. By half-hour past ten we came to Tyburn, waited till eleven: then were brought the children appointed to die. I got upon the cart and Sparks and Broughton [two friends of his]: the Ordinary [prison chaplain] endeavored to follow, when the prisoners begged he might not come; and the mob kept him down.

I prayed first, then Sparks and Broughton. We had prayed before that our Lord would show there was a power superior to the fear of death. They were all cheerful; full of comfort, peace and triumph; assuredly persuaded Christ had died for them, and waited to receive them into paradise.

The black had spied me coming out of the coach, and saluted me with his looks. As often as his eyes met mine, he smiled with the most composed, delightful countenance I ever saw. Read caught hold of my hand in a transport of joy. Newington seemed perfectly pleased. Hudson declared he was never better, or more at ease, in mind and body. None showed any natural terror of death: no fear, or crying or tears. I never saw such calm triumph, such incredible indifference to dying. We sang several hymns; particularly,

Behold the Saviour of mankind, etc.

and the hymn [by Watts] entitled, 'Faith in Christ,' which concludes,

A guilty, weak and helpless worm,
Into Thy hands I fall:
Be Thou my life, my righteousness,
My Jesus, and my all.

We prayed Him in earnest faith to receive their spirits. I could do nothing but rejoice: took leave of each in particular. Mr. Broughton bade them not be surprised when the cart should draw away. They cheerfully replied, they should not . . . We left them going to meet their Lord, ready for the Bridegroom. When the cart drew off, not one stirred or struggled for life, but meekly gave up their spirits. Exactly at twelve they were turned off. I spoke a few suitable words to the crowd; and returned, full of peace and confidence in our friends' happiness. That hour under the gallows was the most blessed hour of my life.

Now read the second half of stanza 4, and the final stanza, "Plenteous grace with thee is found."

The tremendous sincerity of this hymn is born from the depth of great experiences like these; and the language, as always, comes from the Bible.

It is evident, however, that the influence of this great hymn is on the wane. I have not heard it sung in church for many years. The reason is that its language and imagery are foreign to most of our twentieth-century conditions. We who have been born into respectable families, brought up in the atmosphere of religion and accustomed to community life on a plane of decency, can hardly sing with sincerity

I am all unrighteousness;
False and full of sin I am.

We have our faults and our sins, but we are not drunkards and criminals as were many of those to whom this hymn was originally addressed. Nor do we relish the amatory suggestions of the first two stanzas, which are clearly

An execution at Tyburn Hill, London, where Charles Wesley labored to convert prisoners from Newgate. *Left,* Victim in cart, his coffin behind him, being harangued by a Methodist lay-preacher out of a book of Wesley's Sermons. *Center,* Cab containing the Newgate Prison chaplain who is obliged to attend but has no interest in the felon. *Right,* Jibbet with executioner on top smoking his pipe. And what a crowd of rascally men, women and children! Engraving by Hogarth.

a hang-over from Wesley's association with the Moravians. The hymn is the reflection of lower-class eighteenth-century conditions and of the passionate evangelistic temper of the Great Revival.

### Love divine, all loves excelling    [1747]

In contrast to "Jesus, Lover of my soul," this hymn is more than holding its own in the affections of the contemporary Church. It voices the universal recognition that God is the kind of person Jesus would call Father, that man needs a moral reconstruction, and that the efficient means to our spiritual growth is the indwelling spirit of Christ. We do not have to call ourselves bad names but we do have to aspire and struggle and transform "under the eyes and by the strength of God." As in all other hymns of Wesley the tapestry is woven with threads from the Bible.

Stanza 1. This is a prayer to Christ as the incarnation of the love of God, a love greater in quantity and quality than any earthly love we have known. Christ is called the "Joy of heaven" because he is the center of the affection of all the saints of the Church above, the object of adoration of men and angels. "Come" is not a past-participle, suggesting the Incarnation of long ago, but an imperative, a prayer that He now descend again; in fact it is a five-fold prayer that Christ shall come, fix, crown, visit, enter. Christ is asked to "crown" (complete and glorify) all His other acts of grace by becoming a permanent guest in our soul. Our prayer is based not upon any deserts of our own but solely upon the compassionate character of Jesus. The visitor will enter with a gift so precious that the heart trembles with anticipated joy.

The scripture recalled in this stanza is found in 1 Jn 4:8; Col 2:9; Rev 5:11–14; Jn 14:16–17; 2 Tim 1:14; Rev 21:3; Mt 9:36; Ps 86:15; 106:4.

*Stanza 2.* The prayer continues that certain longed-for results shall follow the indwelling Spirit of love: trouble relieved, rest secured, the desire to sin removed, release from the bondage of sin. The "rest" is the state of moral perfection which the Wesleys believed could be obtained in this life. The "bent to sinning" has been altered in most hymnals to "love of." The phrase refers to the theological idea that man was conceived in sin and is forever prone to sin. "End of faith" is a vocative: it is synomous with Christ who is being addressed. "Alpha and Omega" are the first and last letters of the Greek alphabet. The prayer is that Christ shall be both the originator of our faith and the end or object of that faith.

Scripture: Jn 20:22; 14:1; Mt 19:29; Heb 4:3; 4:8, 9, 11; Is 59:7; Prov 21:10; Rev 1:8, 11; Col 3:11; 2 Cor 3:19; Gal 5:1.

*Stanza 3.* The chief idea is the desire never to be separated from the presence of God, either in time or eternity. The "temples" are our bodies.

Scripture: Ps 109:21; 2 Pet 2:9; Jas 4:6; Mal 3:1; 1 Cor 6:19; Heb 13:5; Rom 1:9; Rev 7:15; Ps 138:2; 145:2; 146:2.

*Stanza 4.* This stanza embodies one of the most cherished ideals of the Wesleys. John especially elevated the ideal into a tenet of faith which he pugnaciously maintained against all comers: namely, that it was possible to live without sinning; in fact, that he had himself so lived. His motive for going to Georgia, you will remember, had been to attain to greater holiness than he could achieve at home; after his return, his rules for Holy Living formed the underlying discipline of his daily life; and the announcement of his perfectionist doctrine was one of the hardest things his friends had to bear. It brought him to verbal blows with Augustus Toplady, under whose name the controversy will be considered.

The "new creation" is one of the persistent metaphors of the New Testament: Jn 3:3; 2 Cor 5:17; Gal 6:15; 2 Pet 3:14; Jude 24. The progressive growth and final perfection of character is intimated in the last quatrain: 2 Cor 3:18; Rev 4:10.

Readers will be astonished at the number of scriptural references attached to these hymns to show how permeated they are with Bible language. Since every word of Scripture if correctly interpreted was thought to be true, nothing could give either sermon or hymn more cogency than to fill it with scriptural language. The fact that one could cite a text on either side of most religious quarrels did not bother the theologians at all. They quoted the Devil's dictum in Job 2:4 with as great assurance as Jehovah's in the previous verse! Throughout the prolific period of hymn-writing in the eighteenth century, therefore, scriptural language and allusion abound.

### O for a thousand tongues to sing      [1749]

This hymn was written on May 21, 1749, the anniversary of Charles' conversion. The opening line is thought to have been inspired by a chance remark of Peter Böhler, the Moravian leader who was the chief instrument in the awakening of the Wesleys: "Had I a thousand tongues, I would praise Him with all of them."

Charles had not yet learned by experience what are the requirements of a good hymn. Six stanzas have proved to be about the limit of length, with a preference for four; but this poem has nineteen! Moreover, the subject-matter of a hymn should be of general rather than of private import; but this poem had reference primarily to Charles' personal experience in conversion. For these reasons the editors of hymnbooks have rejected thirteen stanzas and cut out the personal and part of the theological matter. Here are stanzas 2, 4 and 5 which justify the title placed on the hymn in its first edition: "For the Anniversary Day of One's Conversion."

On this glad day the glorious Sun
  Of Righteousness arose,
On my benighted soul he shone,
  And filled it with repose.

Then with my heart I first believed,
  Believed with faith divine;
Power with the Holy Ghost received
  To call the Saviour mine.

I felt my Lord's atoning blood
  Close to my soul applied;
*Me, me* He loved—the Son of God
  For *me*, for *me* He died.

These stanzas illuminate the psychology of Charles' conversion. The general fact of Christ's atonement had always been known to him: all the Churches taught that Christ's death on the cross had paid the debt incurred by Adam's fall, and Charles had accepted that teaching as an intellectual proposition. But on May 21st the spotlight from the cross fell upon his own soul; he was singled out by redeeming Love as one particular individual for whom the Saviour had died. That personal application of the general principle brought with it a flood of emotion which energized his will and made him ever afterward a flaming ambassador of Christ to other individuals.

Such an experience is the essence of the Methodist spiritual life. The Sacraments were useful and Methodists were urged to be faithful to them. The essential foundation of the religious life and its course of sustaining power is that vital contact.

*Stanzas 1–2.* These modern opening stanzas are the seventh and eighth in the original poem. Here begin the less personal portions, the general praises that are suited to the common use. They conform to Watt's theory that the primary function of a hymn is praise. *Stanza 3.* The praise now concentrates on definite themes. The effect of the name of Jesus is said to be almost magical—it works like a "charm" to change the whole emotional groundwork of life. *Stanza 4.* Here are presented the effects of Christ's atoning work upon the individual life. Two figures of speech are used. The first is borrowed from the eighteenth-century treatment of prisoners: men were bound with shackles that were riveted on. As the jailor "knocks off" the irons when a prisoner is released, so Christ knocks off the shackles of sin from the individual life; the prisoner is a free man, unhampered by his past. The second figure is taken from the Jewish ritual of sacrifice when on the Day of Atonement rivers of blood from thousands of animals were shed for the sole purpose of washing away national and individual sin. The transfer of Jewish ideas to Christian use is found in the New Testament Epistles, especially in the letter to the Hebrews (See Heb 9:12–14; also 1 Jn 1:7). *Stanzas 5–6.* This is a metrical version of Christ's reply to the query of the imprisoned John the Baptist, "Art thou he that should come or do we look for another?" In answer Christ cited the effects of his ministry, which all could see (Mt 11:5).

The last six stanzas of the original enumerate the classes of sinners who are cleansed by the sacrifice of Christ: harlots, publicans, thieves, murderers, sons of lust or pride. Christ can "wash the Ethiop white." This catalogue is a reflection of Charles' evangelistic work among the rascals of Newgate prison.

### Soldiers of Christ, arise    [1749]

Three stanzas are all that have survived from an original sixteen published in 1749 while Charles was in the midst of his vigorous, not to say violent, campaigns of evangelism all over England and Ireland. Encounters with mobs, like that at Devizes in 1747, only two years before the publication of the hymn, are clearly reflected in the warlike imagery and in the splendid courage and faith that animates the whole. What to us are figures of speech, encouraging, stimulating, relating to the inner conflicts of our personal religious life, were to Wesley and his contemporaries real fighting words in which spiritual energies had to be summoned to meet physical danger, man-handling and imminent death. In singing this hymn we must bear this fact in mind.

Charles had a specific use for his hymn. In its published form it had the title, "The Whole Armour of God, or Confirmation." This indicates that the hymn was to be used in the endeavor to "con-firm" or make strong a new convert, or in a "Confirmation" service, when the convert publicly takes the vows of faithfulness to Christ and His Church.

The imagery is taken from Eph 6:10–18.

John Bunyan had already made literary use of this famous bit of Scripture. In his *Pilgrim's Progress*, before Christian left the Palace Beautiful where he had been entertained and instructed, he was shown the Armory, in which was

> all manner of Furniture, which their Lord had provided for Pilgrims, as Sword, Shield, Helmet, Breastplate, *All-prayer*, and Shoes that would not wear out. . . . And when they came there, they harnessed him from head to foot with what was of proof, lest perhaps he should meet with assaults in the way. He being therefore thus accoutred, walketh out to the Gate.

Very fortunate it was, for on going thence into the Valley of Humiliation, Christian encountered a foul fiend, Apollyon, with whom he fought "above half a day." But for this armor, poor Christian would there have died in his tracks.

The fact that the armor used by Christian was of the Roman type removes it from the realm of present-day reality. Shall we urge one another to fight our spiritual war with tommy-guns, Garand rifles, bazookas, flame-throwers, tanks, half-tracks, air umbrellas, amphibians, gas masks, vitamin rations, atomic bombs and radio-activity? War has become so mechanized, and the conflict in most cases so impersonal that the military figure no longer can energize us to our spiritual struggles. Perhaps that is the reason why this hymn, found in so many of our hymnals, is so seldom sung in church.

## *Ye servants of God, your Master proclaim*    [1744]

This hymn was first published in one of the "hymn tracts"—that is, small collections of hymns on a single subject, which the Wesleys issued for use in their Class meetings. This tract was entitled, *Hymns for Times of Trouble and Persecution*. It appeared in 1744 when the Wesleys were in the midst of their evangelistic campaigns and when their converts were suffering more and worse attacks from mobs led by the clergy and the "gentlemen of the town." The direction given with this hymn was, "To be sung in a tumult."

The four stanzas in our hymnals do not reveal this purpose: as they stand they are a glorious paean of praise to God and to His Son, our Lord.

They are a reflection in verse of the praises which John heard in heaven from his prison on Patmos (Rev 7:9–12).

As such, it is one of the grand hymns of adoration which any Christian can sing with a minimum of mental reservation.

But as is so often the case the stanzas that our modern editors omit as being not applicable to our present circumstances reveal exactly the author's purpose. Here they are:

> The waves of the sea have lift up their voice,
> Sore troubled that we in Jesus rejoice;
> The floods they are roaring, but Jesus is here;
> While we are adoring, He always is near.
>
> Men, devils engage, the billows arise,
> And horribly rage, and threaten the skies;
> Their fury shall never our steadfastness shock;
> The weakest believer is built on a Rock.

These stanzas are full of the fighting and conquering spirit that enabled the despised fanatics called Methodists to survive and make their tremendous contribution to the religious, the moral, the social life of their age. Combine these two dissimilar parts of the hymn—the fighting stanzas and the stanzas of confidence in the over-ruling power of God—and we get the hidden source of Methodist courage. We can almost see some little band, at Kingswood or Falmouth, stand together in the midst of flying brickbats, bucketfuls of muddy water, and curses, and with shining faces raise this battle-cry of victory and thanksgiving.

### Hark, the herald angels sing    [1738]

This is one of the favorite Christmas hymns, sung thousands of times every year all round the world. Like most of Charles' hymns which time has spared, it was written in his early productive period before 1739, within a year of his conversion while the inspiration of his newly-made contact with God was still fresh. The original poem had ten stanzas.

The story of the angel visit to the shepherds (Lk 2:8–14) rings joyfully in the first stanza; in the second and fifth all men are summoned to join in the triumphal celebration. Then in stanzas 3, 4, 6–10, exultant poetry turns into prosaic theological teaching. In these omitted or modified stanzas we are introduced to ancient explanations of the Garden of Eden story, the preexistence of Jesus as Deity, His descent from heaven to be incarnated as man, the curse pronounced upon the serpent, the cancellation of Adam's sin by Christ, the "second birth" which man may now experience, and the new life lived in union with Christ. These ideas made the hymn particularly serviceable in the Class meetings soon to be established (1740) by John, in which the particular beliefs of Methodists were taught.

All this does not readily appear in the hymn as we know it because practically all editors have cut out the last four stanzas in which most of the theology is found. They have also changed other lines in the endeavor to improve the poetry. Our hymn is therefore a composite. What suits the ideas and temper of one age often has to be modified to survive in another.

### Christ the Lord is risen today       [1739]

This Easter hymn, written in that first year after Charles' conversion, rivals in popularity the Christmas hymn just considered. Part of our enthusiasm in singing it is no doubt due to the tune to which it is set, with the joyful refrain "Hallelujah!" at the end of every line. Charles did not write "Hallelujah." Some editor, perhaps Martin Madan, wedded the words to an older tune (1708) and to fill in the extra measures inserted the Hebrew ejaculation found so frequently in Pss 106–150, meaning "Praise Jah!" (Jehovah).

In the exultant phrases of this hymn are reflected the various incidents of the crucifixion and the resurrection: the battle fought upon the cross with death—apparently lost but finally won; the eclipse of the sun, symbol of temporary defeat; the measures taken by Pilate to prevent the stealing of the body; the (traditional) descent into hell, as in the Apostles' Creed, to receive the punishment due to the sins of mankind and to liberate the Old Testament saints who had been kept in Limbo; the ultimate conquest over death by which, in the language of the *Te Deum*,

> When thou hadst overcome the sharpness of death,
> Thou didst open the Kingdom of Heaven to all believers.

In stanza 4 there is an echo of Paul's exultant climax to his teaching about the resurrection in 1 Cor 15:55. In stanza 5 we have the assurance, voiced originally by Paul, that all followers of Christ will conquer death as did their Master. The last six stanzas of the original hymn are omitted in contemporary hymnals.

### Rejoice, the Lord is King       [1746]

Based upon Phil 4:4. Of the original six stanzas five are in common use.

There is an exultancy about this hymn that fits it particularly for processionals on Easter Day. By his resurrection Jesus has demonstrated that He is King, worthy of His subjects' adoration, thanks and triumphing (stanza 1); that He is Saviour, His mission of redemption now accomplished (stanza 2); that His kingdom never will be destroyed since its enemies Death and Hell are now in His power (stanza 3); that now He is awaiting the submission of all His enemies (stanza 4); and that as Lord and Judge He will some day take His servants to His heavenly abode (stanza 5).

Not yet has the Church learned to translate this apocalyptic imagery into the vision of a redeemed society upon earth. It will still take more than a century for science, evolutionary philosophy and atomic energy to compel a re-interpretation of Jewish Messianism. Individuals separately must be saved, but only as a means of saving the United Nations on earth, in time as well as for eternity.

### Christ whose glory fills the skies     [1740]

A true lyric, superior as poetry to most; a morning hymn which is also a prayer for spiritual illumination. There is no dogma here which one is obliged to accept in order to be saved, only an appreciation of what Christ accomplishes in one's inner life. The figure is that which pervades the Gospel of John: Christ as Light. As the sun conquers the gloom of night, so Christ brings joy by scattering whatever darkness beclouds the soul.

### Come, thou long-expected Jesus     [1744]

The point of view is that of Israel's Messianic expectation: Christ born a King who is destined to reign forever over the hearts of all men.

### Forth in thy name, O Lord, I go     [1749]

A prayer for faithfulness to the daily task and the consciousness of the inspiring presence of Christ.

### Hail the day that sees him rise     [1739]

For Ascension Day. The poet visualizes not only Christ's ascension, but His triumphal entry into heaven and the blessing sent down thence to the disciples on earth.

### Lo, he comes with clouds descending     [1760]
(Revised by John Cennick and M. Madan)

A celebration of the Second Advent, when Christ comes to receive into glory all His saints and to rule the universe forever.

### O for a heart to praise my God     [1742]

Longing for holiness, humility, resignation and love.

Summary of Wesley's hymns found in our ten hymnals:

Listed above, 14 hymns, three of which are found in all ten hymnals
Others,        64 hymns, found in from one to four of the hymnals
Total,         79 hymns, the largest number by any hymn-writer

CHAPTER SIX: EVANGELICALS AND DISSENTERS

| | | Writers |
|---|---|---|
| 1702–14 | QUEEN ANNE: Strong for Anglican Church and Tories. Rise of Deism: reason the sole test of religion; God revealed in a world of law. | Watts, 1707–19 |
| 1711 | Jonathan Swift uses satire against Whigs, Catholics and Dissenters. | |
| | *Occasional Conformity Act:* penalized Dissenters who received Anglican Sacrament to get office but continued to attend Dissenting Churches. | Addison, 1712 |
| 1714 | *Schism Act:* no one could keep a school without license from Anglican bishop. | |
| 1714–27 | GEORGE I: Favorable to Whigs, Dissenters and traders. Much political corruption: Tories stood for religious intolerance and contempt for trade; Whigs for toleration and weakening power of king. Both used bribery. | |
| 1726–29 | Voltaire visits England; pours unsparing ridicule on organized religion. | Doddridge, |
| 1727–60 | GEORGE II. | 1735–55 |
| 1736 | Butler: *Analogy of Religion*—the divine regnancy of conscience over behavior. | Wesleys, 1738–47 |
| 1738 | Revivals begin under Whitefield and the Wesleys. Leaders and converts persecuted. | Cennick, 1742 Williams, 1745 |
| 1744 | Methodism established. Evangelical wing develops in Anglican Church. | Byrom, 1749 |
| 1751–83 | England wins territory in India. Bishop Berkeley (d. 1753) attacks Deism: nothing really exists but mind and ideas. | |
| 1757 | Hume: *Natural History of Religion.* Experience the source of all knowledge; miracles, so-called proofs of Christianity, never existed. | Steele, 1757 |
| 1760–1820 | GEORGE III. | |
| 1767–85 | Revolutionary inventions in textile industry; steam engine; northern cities pose problems in politics and religion. | Grigg, 1765 Cowper, 1768–79 Olivers, 1770 |
| 1778 | "Gordon riots" against Catholics. | Fawcett, 1773–82 |
| 1778–82 | Violence in Ireland between Catholics and Protestants. | Newton, 1774–79 |
| 1779 | Agitation for economic and political reform. | Toplady, 1776 |
| 1789– | French Revolution. | Heath, 1781 |
| 1792 | Wm. Carey first missionary to India. Baptist Missionary Society founded. | Perronet, 1789 |
| 1794 | Paley: *Evidences of Christianity:* Design in nature proves existence of a Designer. | |
| 1795 | Tom Paine: *Age of Reason:* A criticism of common ideas of God and morality. | |

# EVANGELICALS AND DISSENTERS

THE WESLEYAN MOVEMENT was part of a greater revival of religion that both antedated and paralleled it. This larger awakening had its earliest focal point in Wales, it had another among the Dissenting Churches in England, and a third in the Established Church. George Whitefield was the dynamic behind the first group and to a large extent the second; Selina, Countess of Huntingdon, was patron saint of both first and second groups, chiefly the latter; while the third group, lacking organization, received inspiration from Whitefield, Huntingdon and from Methodism. Altogether the Revival is the most notable event in religious history since the Protestant Reformation. It began in the eighteenth century and continued into the nineteenth.

This movement is named "Evangelical" because it emphasized the kind of religion found in the Gospels (the Latin word for "the Gospel" is *Evangelium*). We read in these four New Testament books that this person or that one "came to Jesus"; or "they brought him to Jesus"; or "He said unto him, 'thy sins are forgiven'"; or "thy faith hath made thee whole"; or "go and sin no more." The Gospel is the story of Christ's personal contact with people and of the good news that sins may be forgiven, souls saved, sicknesses cured. It is a story of right relations among men, and between God and man, established by love. Somehow in the previous 1700 years the Church had lost sight of that simple message, had built up a gospel of Sacraments by which one could be saved by being baptized in infancy, kept righteous by confession and partaking of the Mass or the Communion, encouraged to holy living by attendance upon Morning and Evening Prayer or listening to sermons. All this was formal and impersonal; it represented what the Church could do for you almost automatically. The Revival restored to men the personal touch of Jesus; it emphasized conversion; it aroused a hatred of sin and a passion to get rid of it, an enthusiasm for spreading the Good News among those who needed it most—the unchurched, the socially outcast, the poverty-stricken, the ignorant, the criminal. Methodism was the most potent element in this revival because it was

104

led by an organizing genius; but the other groups were strong leavening forces which left a permanent mark upon the religious life of England and the world.

Within the Established Church, the Evangelicals, who placed lesser emphasis upon the Sacraments as a means of Grace and more upon faith, prayer, active work for the physical welfare and moral redemption of others, came to be known as the Low Church party, as against the Sacramentarians who became the High Church party. These groups still exist, although the latter have called themselves "Anglo-Catholics." (See Chap. VIII, The Oxford Movement; and Chap. XII, High Church Hymns.)

We must now consider the leading personalities in these groups, together with the hymns inspired by the revival. For hymns now became a vehicle of the Gospel second only to preaching in inspirational power. Before the revival there had been little singing; there had been no enthusiasm for religion that demanded release in song. After it, singing became a recognized part in religion, whether private or public. Today, thanks to the Evangelicals and Methodists, there is hardly ever a religious service without hymn-singing.

Chief among the inspirers, though they themselves wrote no hymns that have survived, but only edited and published the hymns of others, was:

### Rev. GEORGE WHITEFIELD (1714–1770)
#### Anglican: Calvinistic Methodist

THE life of Whitefield reads like a novel—the story of a poor boy who through genius and indomitable will became famous. Taken from school at fifteen he became bartender in his mother's inn at Gloucester. Somehow he managed to prepare for Oxford, where he worked his way by doing menial tasks for the Fellows. He met the Wesleys as a member of the Holy Club, and he entered so enthusiastically into their discipline that he took sick and left college. This brought on a crisis in his religious life comparable to a Wesleyan "conversion." Having been ordained in the Anglican Church at the age of 22, he began an evangelizing tour in Bristol and other west-England towns, which owing to his power as a speaker was immensely successful. After 1738, when the Anglican clergy became distrustful of his methods and closed their churches to him, he took to preaching in the open. He preached everywhere—in the streets, on the steps of a windmill, on a table in the market-place, from a wall, in a brickyard, on a bowling green. Sermons were sometimes two hours long! Here are two entries from his journal:

May 28. Preached in a field belonging to one Mr. Rudge to about 10,000 people.
May 30. Preached at Newington Common to about 15,000 people.

Preached in the evening at a place called Mayfair, near Hyde Park Common (London). The congregation, I believe, consisted of near 80,000 people . . . Yet they kept a deep silence during the whole of my discourse . . . God strengthened me to speak so loud that most could hear, and so powerfully that most, I believe, could feel.

He came to America seven times. His preaching in New England in 1740 was the cause of the greatest spiritual upheaval this country ever saw— the "Great Awakening." He died and was buried in Newburyport, Massachusetts.

Whitefield's stimulation of hymnody came by powerfully aiding the Welsh revival which thrived on the creation of hymns, and by editing a widely-used hymnbook.

### HYMNS OF THE WELSH REVIVAL

Before the Wesleys had begun their outdoor preaching in 1739, or Whitefield his revival work in 1736 in Bristol, a young Welshman named Howell Harris began to talk religion to his fellow-countrymen by calling at people's homes. Then he gathered groups to hear him preach and became so successful that he enlisted many preachers lay and ordained to help him spread the gospel throughout Wales. Whitefield and John Wesley encouraged the movement and did some preaching, but since they did not speak Welsh they were handicapped. By 1741 the revival in full swing was arousing both great enthusiasm and violent opposition. Then came the unfortunate split over theology between Whitefield and John Wesley. While in New England in 1740, Whitefield had become acquainted with the Rev. Jonathan Edwards of Northampton, Massachusetts, and by him was persuaded to become an uncompromising Calvinist (see under Watts); whereas by that time Wesley had become just as uncompromising an Arminian (see under Wesley). When Whitefield returned to England in 1741, the two men tried to reconcile their differences, but without success. The Welsh preachers stuck by Whitefield and formed a separate denomination called the Calvinistic Methodists. The split still exists.

The Welsh people were great singers. From earliest times their bards had sung the deeds of warriors, kings and patriots; and after they became Christianized they mingled religion with their worship of national heroes. Taliéssin, bard of the sixth century, is said to have written,

No musician is skilful unless he extols the Lord, and no singer is correct unless he praises the Father.

Sacred poems have survived in Welsh from the fourteenth and fifteenth centuries. In the Protestant Reformation of the sixteenth century, one Prichard, vicar of Llandvery, turned his sermons into quaint verses, printed them under the title of *The Welshman's Candle*, and set his ignorant parishioners to singing them. This opened a new era in Welsh hymnody.

When Harris began his revival, he turned most naturally to song as an instrument of the gospel; but he was handicapped for want of hymns in the Welsh language. He therefore reverted to the old Welsh custom of bard contests—the "Eisteddfod" which is still a national institution—to see which of his preachers could produce the best hymns. The result was most happy, for

*Copyright by Western Mail Photograph Department, Cardiff, Wales*

A recent *Eisteddfod* or Welsh singing festival.

besides creating many useable hymns the contest brought to light a poet of great excellence one of whose hymns we shall now consider, the Poet Laureate of the Welsh Revival.

### Rev. WILLIAM WILLIAMS (1717–1781) Calvinistic Methodist

WILLIAMS was born in a solitary farmhouse in the parish of Pantycelyn. The house is still standing, a low-lying building of stone in an open field some distance from the highway. The barn with its characteristic odors is close at hand within the same enclosure. The most interesting room in the house is the kitchen, stone walled, stone floored, a broad raised hearth above which rises a huge stone fireplace and oven. From the beams of the ceiling and from pegs on the walls hang the family stores for the winter: circular loaves of bread, hams, flitches of bacon, and whatever else would keep by drying. A general aroma of sour milk and dry meat pervades this "home, sweet home." To enter the house is like stepping back two hundred years. The Williams family still lives there.

When Williams was twenty years old, preparing to take a medical course, he heard how Howell Harris was upsetting everyone with his fanatical preaching. His curiosity was aroused and he went one Sunday morning to see for himself. He found Harris preaching in Talgarth churchyard to people coming out of the regular service, standing on a flat tombstone and warning all and sundry of hellfire to come. The preacher was only twenty-four years old, but he knew how to play on human emotions. Williams succumbed and there formed the purpose to become a preacher like Harris. Shortly he became a deacon in the Established Church, but his sympathy was not with the formal and lifeless religion of the Establishment; it was rather with the pulsing, passionate preaching of such Dissenters as Harris. He therefore never became an ordained clergyman; instead he took all Wales for his parish and for the next 43 years travelled 95,900 miles.

It was a hard life that he entered. He was always in the open, soaked with rain, chilled by snow, bronzed by wind and sun, attacked by mobs usually led by "a gentleman of the neighborhood"—as once in Cardiganshire a crowd of ruffians carrying guns and cudgels fell upon him and beat him within an inch of his life. Though he was a great preacher, the chief source of his influence was his hymns. He wrote 800 of them all in Welsh. Like all Welshmen he loved the beauty of his native land, its rolling hills and cloud-swept mountains, its tumbling brooks, its narrow valleys and caverns of darkness, the sea breaking upon its rocky shore. This love of nature which was for a Welshman so intimately twined with religion breathed through all of Williams' poetry and endeared it to every heart. People who could not read caught the hymns by ear; others who were illiterate learned to read that they might enjoy them. They thus became a mighty educational and cultural force, and more than all else, they assured the triumph of the Revival.

Unfortunately most of Williams' hymns are still untranslated. Some of them, indeed, did appear in English dress, but they have gradually faded out of our American hymnals until only one is left. Here it is:

### Guide me, O thou great Jehovah    [1745]

First take a look at stanza 1 as it is written in Welsh:

> Arglwydd, arwain trwy'r anialwch
> Fi, bererin gwael ei wedd,
> Nad oes ynof nerth na bywyd,
> Fel yn gorwedd yn y bedd:
> Hollalluog
> Ydyw'r un a'm cwyd i'r lan.

The first stanza was translated into English by the Rev. Peter Williams in 1771, the other two by the author himself in 1772, and the combination was printed in a leaflet for use in Trevecca College, South Wales, supported by the Countess of Huntingdon as a training school for preachers. Thereafter it appeared in various collections in England and so was transmitted to us. It has been translated into many languages.

The imagery of the hymn is drawn wholly from the Bible. Its general setting is the march of the Israelites from Egypt to Canaan. It may be helpful to see in the parallel arrangement below, just how the poet's mind worked in transforming an ancient story into something that could sustain the religious life of his own and any time.

Birthplace of William Williams, Pantycelyn, Wales.

> Guide me, O thou great Jehovah,
> Pilgrim through this barren land.

In the Bible there are many references to Israel's journey through the Wilderness: Ps 78:52; Deut 8:15; Heb 11:13. Life is a pilgrimage, as Bunyan saw and pictured in *Pilgrim's Progress*—from birth to death, through vicissitudes and hardships, with the goal constantly in view of achieving the good life, here and hereafter.

> I am weak, but thou art mighty;
> Hold me with thy powerful hand.

Ps 6:2; Deut 9:29; Ps 139:10. The sustaining and guiding hand of God in the experience of individuals and in history. *Cf.* "O God, beneath thy guiding hand, Our exiled fathers crossed the sea."

> Bread of heaven,
> Feed me till I want no more.

Ex 16:4–18; Jn 6:48–51. The spiritual life is nourished by partaking of Christ. Here the symbolism merges into the partaking of the Lord's Supper, in which the bread represents Him who can satisfy the soul's need.

> Open now the crystal fountain
> Whence the healing streams do flow.

Num 20:2–13; Ps 78:15–16; 1 Cor 10:4; Rev 22:1–2. Water is the symbol of salvation, either by (1) Baptism, the waters of which are said to cleanse from sin and cause one to be born again; or (2) the teachings of Christ or His direct contact with the soul (Jn 4:14). The poet may also have had in mind the death of Christ as an atonement for sin. In that case the healing streams are the blood of the cross. *Cf.* Toplady's "Rock of Ages."

> Let the fiery, cloudy pillar
> Lead me all my journey through.

Ex 13:21. This is another symbol of divine Providence in human life.

> Strong deliverer
> Be thou still my strength and shield.

Ex 14:27–31; Ps 18:2; 28:7.

> When I tread the verge of Jordan
> Bid my anxious fears subside.

Josh 3:1–17. In Christian symbolism Jordan stands for the river of death; the waters that threaten to overwhelm are the cause of the "anxious fears." From the Calvinistic viewpoint the fears are real, for one can never tell surely whether he be among the elect until he has actually crossed.

> Death of death's and Hell's Destruction,
> Land me safe on Canaan's side.

Josh 3:17; Rev 1:18; 2 Tim 1:10; Heb 2:14. The first obscure line reduced to lowest terms means Christ: He conquered death by rising on Easter morning, and hell by saving men from it, and so He is called the "Destruction" of both. "Canaan's side" is heaven.

> Songs of praises
> Will I ever give to thee.

Ps 27:6; 34:1; Rev 7:9–17.

Another strong preacher in the Welsh revival and in the English was

### Rev. *JOHN CENNICK* (1718–1755) Various

CENNICK had a checkered religious career. He was born of Quaker stock, was brought up in the Established Church, was converted at nineteen, assisted John Wesley as his first lay preacher, transferred his allegiance to Whitefield at the time of the split, and ended his days as a Moravian. Perhaps that instability hints at an over-emotionalized nature, a suggestion borne out by the hard time he had in getting converted. To be sure, he had been carefully trained in religion by his mother, but the teaching left him with an overwhelming sense of his own sinfulness. While learning a trade in London he fell into deep despondency until his only wish was for death, yet the thought of death with its possible consequences was full of terror. After some weeks of spiritual chaos, one day in church in 1737 he had a sudden realization of God's forgiving love, and the cloud lifted. That was his "conversion," the beginning of a new life.

Desiring to do something about it, he consulted both John Wesley and Whitefield. They gave him a job as teacher in a school they had recently founded for the children of coal miners at Kingswood, just outside of Bristol. There he not only taught but helped in the Class meetings and in preaching. He also came in contact with Howell Harris, the Welsh revivalist, and joined him in out-of-door evangelistic tours. He also discovered his own talent for poetry. By the time he transferred his allegiance to Whitefield in 1741 he had written enough hymns to fill a small book, by the next year another, and by the following a third. Whitefield liked the hymns, partly because Cennick used to have them sung antiphonally, that is, to have part of the congregation sing half a stanza and another part the second half —a practice still kept up by us in community sings or week-night prayer meetings. Cennick's total output was 500 hymns, all written during the four years he helped Harris and Whitefield. Of these, time has weeded out all but one. That one is

### Children of the heavenly King     [1742]

The hymn originally had twelve stanzas, of which not more than six appear in our hymnals; five are usual.

We do not know under what special circumstances the hymn was written. Its tone is so gentle, its spirit so unruffled, that we cannot associate it with the rough turmoil of an evangelist's life. There is a feeling that life is transitory but the future is full of hope, of the joy of reunion in heaven with the faithful souls who have gone before. In some of the omitted stanzas this picture of heaven is enlarged; the pilgrimage ended, the Saviour's welcome, the rewards bestowed, the thrones assigned. In only one or two words is there a hint that the earthly pilgrimage was having for him and his companions any dangers: "Fear not, brethren"; "undismayed go on"; "gladly leaving all below." This background of trouble is almost submerged by the happiness and the singing. Yet we must visualize, if we can, the hardships through which Cennick travelled during the four years of his evangelizing.

Both Cennick and Howell Harris have left written accounts of what happened to them at Swindon. Piecing the details together we get the following:

Before they began to preach, a mob gathered, evidently bent on doing them bodily harm. They brought horns, guns and a fire engine besides the usual clubs, stones, eggs, dung, rotten fruit and dead animals. They fired the guns over the preachers' heads so close that the faces of both were "as black as tinkers" with the powder. They covered them with dust from the highway and then with the fire engine sprayed them with filthy water from the ditches. While they were deluging Harris, Cennick preached; when they changed to Cennick, Harris took up the talking. Thus antiphonally exhorting, they walked through the town, until the engine broke down and the mob was forced to use buckets! Cennick continues: "Mr. Goddard, a leading gentleman of the town, lent the mob his guns, halberd, and engine, and bade them use us as badly as they could, only not to kill us; and he himself sat on horseback the whole time, laughing to see us thus treated."

> Children of the Heavenly King,
> As ye journey, sweetly sing!

Surely it took courage, sustained by a sense of the Saviour's presence and by faith in God's approval, to combine such a life with such a song.

Chronologically at this point emerges a hymn-writer who had no connection with revivals, whether Wesley's, Whitefield's or the Welsh. He is

## JOHN BYROM (1692–1763) English, Anglican

BYROM was one of the unique personalities of the eighteenth century: he was one of the tallest men in the kingdom (he met only two who were taller), and he invented shorthand. We might add that he was one of the queerest-looking—a sort of caricature, with a long Dutch nose, inquisitive eyes, round shoulders, protruding neck; he wore a broad-brimmed slouch hat and carried a long cane. Everybody must have turned to look at him as he passed by.

He was not a clergyman, as most hymn writers were, but a physician and surgeon. He took his training in medicine at the University of Montpellier in France while in exile on account of his loyalty to the House of Stuart dethroned by Parliament in 1688. The Stuarts in the person of the "Pretender" were still trying to regain the throne; in fact, in 1745 the Pretender's forces took possession of Manchester where Byrom lived. Byrom satirized the situation in Jacobite lines that became very popular:

God bless the King—I mean the faith's defender;
God bless—no harm in blessing—the Pretender;
But who Pretender is, and who is King,
God bless us all that's quite another thing.

These facts would indicate that Byrom was a courageous individualist, quite capable of going counter to prevailing sentiment. This was true not only in politics but in religion. Presumably an Anglican, yet he was deeply read in the writings of the Mystics—Fénélon, William Law, Jacob Boehme and others—and therefore was prepared to be tolerant of Methodism; in fact, he often sought the society of Methodists and their leaders. On the other hand, he was equally friendly with Evangelicals, knew Doddridge and with him called on Lady Huntingdon. Yet he never joined any of these societies. He was independent to the last. A bit of doggerel from his volumes shows where he stood—or didn't stand—theologically:

Flatter me not with your *Predestination,*
Nor sink my spirits with your *Reprobation.*
From all your high disputes I stand aloof,
Your *Pre's* and *Re's,* your *Destin* and your *Proof,*
And formal, *Calvinistical* Pretense,
That contradicts all Gospel and good Sense.

Byrom's system of shorthand made him famous. Nothing in that line up to 1864 caused so great a sensation. It was taught officially at both Oxford and Cambridge Universities; it was used by the clerk of the House of Lords. "On June 16, 1742, His Majesty George II secured to John Byrom, M.A., the sole right of publishing for a certain term of years [21] the art and method of shorthand invented by him."

This shorthand impinges upon hymnody in an interesting way. Both John and Charles Wesley studied the system under Byrom; Charles in particular became so proficient in it that he beat his master at it and produced pages that looked like copper-plate. While he was secretary to Governor Oglethorpe in Georgia he used it to take down conferences between the Governor and the Indians. Throughout his ministry he kept his journals in shorthand, and composed most of his hymns that way, often while riding horseback.

Byrom was elected a Fellow of the Royal Society when Sir Isaac Newton was President of it.

As a poet, Byrom does not rank high. At his death he left a manuscript of poems which was afterward published in two volumes. The verses touch on all kinds of subjects—hymns for different Church days, translations from German, French and Latin, rhymed letters to people, anecdotes, Biblical subjects; on the Origin of Evil, Free Grace, Predestination, etc. He was evidently more sympathetic with Wesley's theology (Arminianism) than with Whitefield's (Calvinism). His one surviving hymn appeared in the second volume of his poems, published posthumously.

### *Christians, awake, salute the happy morn*     [1749]

This hymn was a Christmas present from Byrom to his daughter Dolly. Sometime earlier he had asked Dolly what she wanted for Christmas and she replied, "Please write me a poem." When she came down to breakfast Christmas morning, 1749, she found this hymn on her plate, with the inscription "Christmas day for Dolly." A year later the Byroms were awakened by hearing this carol sung under their windows. The singers were the parish choir of Manchester, and the tune was "Yorkshire," composed by the organist John Wainwright especially for it, and still used.

The poem originally had 48 lines but the modern tendency toward brevity has cut it to 36 or 24. It is organized about the gospel story.

---

The second inspirer of hymn-writers besides Whitefield was

### SELINA, COUNTESS OF HUNTINGDON (1707–1791)
#### Anglican, Independent

THIS gifted woman was for fifty years a true fairy godmother to the preachers and hymn-writers of Evangelical mind whether Dissenting or Anglican.

Selina came from a noble family and married an earl. She was "converted" through the influence of her sister who had attended Methodist meetings. Lord and Lady Huntingdon knew both Whitefield and the Wesleys, attended the "love feasts" at Fetter Lane, and followed John Wesley when he pulled out of the Moravian fellowship. In fact the first Methodist Conference was held in their house. Widowed at 49, she assumed entire care of her property and the upbringing of her seven children. She was a brilliant modern-type woman, an executive of high order and what we Americans would call a "go-getter."

Since she belonged to the Anglican Church her sympathy was more with Whitefield's theology than with Wesley's. While she never broke with Wesley, she made her London drawingroom a center of Whitefield influence. This great evangelist preached there frequently to the brilliant social set, the duchesses, lords and ladies, ministers of state, who could not very well refuse the countess' invitation. One, however, did refuse in no uncertain terms—the Duchess of Buckingham. She replied to the invitation:

I thank your Ladyship for the information concerning the Methodist preachers; their doctrines are most repulsive, and strongly tinctured with impertinence and disrespect towards their superiors, in per-

*Left*, Selina, Countess of Huntingdon. *Right*, John Byrom, drawn in 1822.

petually endeavoring to level all ranks, and do away with all distinctions. It is monstrous to be told, that you have a heart as sinful as the common wretches that crawl on the earth. This is highly offensive and insulting; and I cannot but wonder that your Ladyship should relish any sentiments so much at variance with high rank and good breeding.*

But the countess won out; she finally got the Duchess to come and hear Whitefield!

The countess became interested also in itinerant preaching which found its clientele at the opposite end of the social scale. She subsidized the preachers and finally began to build chapels for them where the need was great, to finance which she sold some of her jewels. Before her death she had erected more than seventy. Her benefactions are estimated to have cost her £100,000, or half a million dollars. For use in her chapels, she edited hymnbooks. These, as in the case of the Wesley hymnal, became powerful aids in evangelizing. On the musical side she was a friend and special patron of Handel, Giardini, (most famous violinist of his day and leader of the Italian Opera in London) who wrote tunes for her hymnbooks (e.g., "Italian Hymn"), as did another famous Italian musician, Giordano (e.g., "Cambridge").

The countess had intended to remain Anglican. But as her chapels grew in number the opposition within the Church stiffened, until at last she was

* *Life and Times of Selina, Countess of Huntingdon,* 1844.

compelled to register them all as Dissenting congregations. She then withdrew from the Church and organized her missions as virtually a separate sect called "Lady Huntingdon's Connexion." This organization continued for a hundred years.

Among the hymn-writers she was friend to Watts, Doddridge, Cennick, W. Williams, Charles Wesley, Olivers, Toplady and Perronet. Among those whom she especially patronized only three are represented in our hymnals.

### Rev. THOMAS OLIVERS (1725–1799) Methodist

OLIVERS, early left an orphan, was converted by Calvinist Whitefield, but shortly changed his allegiance to Arminian Wesley. He became one of Wesley's hard-riding circuit preachers—rode 100,000 miles in twenty-five years. Later Wesley made him editor of his *Arminian Magazine*. Wesley stood his lack of education, his faults and his independence for twelve years, then dismissed him.

The hymn we are about to consider in a paraphrase and Christianization of a Jewish "Doxology," called a *Yigdal*, which in turn was based upon a metrical version of the Thirteen Articles of Faith composed in 1404 by Rabbi Daniel ben Judah Dayyam. The Articles in turn had been drawn up in prose by the greatest of Jewish scholars, Maimonides (1130–1205). The old Hebrew *Yigdal* is still used in the daily services of our American synagogues.

Olivers' paraphrase was written after hearing the original sung in the Great Synagogue, London. In his own version he gave a Biblical reference for nearly every line. Of Olivers' twelve stanzas, ten have been used by our various hymnal editors. What different choices have been made from these ten are indicated below.

### *The God of Abraham praise*     Tr. Olivers, 1770

### *Praise to the living God*     Tr. Max Landsberg and Newton Mann, 1914

*Stanza*  1. "The God of Abrah'm praise"   A C E L S U
*Stanza*  2. "The God of Abrah'm praise, At whose supreme command"   A C U
*Stanza*  3. "He by himself hath sworn"   E C U
*Stanza*  4. "Tho' nature's strength decay"   L S
*Stanza*  5. "The goodly land I see"   A L S
*Stanza*  6. "There dwells the Lord our King"   A E L S U
*Stanza*  7. "Before the great THREE-ONE"   L S
*Stanza*  8. "The God who reigns on high"   E L S
*Stanza*  9. "Before the Saviour's face"   A L
*Stanza* 10. "The whole triumphant host"   A E L S U

This paraphrase does not compare in dignity and depth with the original: "I" was never mentioned; God was all. And, of course, all of Olivers' Christian theology and his allusions to the journey of the Israelites from Egypt to Canaan are pure additions. To help appreciate what Olivers did not give us and to show the superiority of the recent translation of Landsberg and Mann, a prose translation of the *Yigdal* is now given:

Extolled and praised be the living God, who exists unbounded by time.

He is one of unparalleled unity, invisible and eternal.

Without form or figure—incorporeal—holy beyond conception.

Prior to all created things—the first, without date or beginning.

Lo! He is Lord of the world and all creation, which evince His greatness and dominion.

The flow of His prophetic spirit has He imparted to men selected for His glory.

No one has appeared in Israel like unto Moses; a prophet, beholding His glorious semblance.

God has given the true law to His people, by the hands of His trusted prophets.

This law, God will never alter nor change for any other.

He perceives and is acquainted with our secrets,—sees the end of all things at their very beginning.

He rewards man with kindness according to his work; dispenses punishment to the wicked, according to his misdeeds.

At the end of days by Him appointed, will He send our Messiah, to redeem those who hope for final salvation.

God, in His great mercy, will recall the dead to life. Praised be His glorious name for evermore.*

The new translation found in E M N and P is much closer to the original. All Christian doctrine so much stressed in Olivers' day is eliminated, leaving what may be called a universal religion acceptable largely to Jew and modern Christian alike.

### Rev. *AUGUSTUS TOPLADY* (1740–1778) Anglican

DR. LOUIS F. BENSON ** has given us the most readable and vivid account of this man of contradictions. I shall borrow freely from him.

Toplady, like most of the eighteenth century hymn writers, came from the middle class. His father, a major in the British army, was killed at the siege of Cartagena when the boy was a few months old. His mother sent him to Westminster School which was a poor place for a sickly, neurotic

* From J. Julian: *A Dictionary of Hymnology*, pp. 1149–50.
** *Studies of Familiar Hymns*, Second Series, Westminster Press, 1923.

lad. But he had a fighting spirit; he composed a daily prayer to be kept from quarreling with his schoolmates. He was precociously religious. In his diary he writes, "I am now arrived at the age of eleven years. I praise God I can remember no dreadful crime; and not to me but to the Lord be the glory, Amen."

His mother spoiled him and his uncles and aunts detested him. The child repaid them in kind. In his diary he writes: "Aunt Betty is so vastly quarrelsome; in short, she is so fractious, and captious, and insolent, that she is unfit for human society." At twelve years he preached sermons to those who would listen, at fourteen he became a writer of hymns, at nineteen he published a volume of them. Having moved to Ireland to attend Dublin University, he was "converted" at the age of sixteen while listening to a Methodist revivalist as he preached in a barn, and was "brought nigh to God." Thereupon he prepared for the ministry.

Though converted to Methodism, he was later convinced by his studies that the correct theory of salvation was not Arminian but Calvinist. He therefore entered the Established ministry as one of the early members of the Evangelical or Low Church party. Ever after, he was the most militant not to say vituperative supporter of Calvinism. The emphasis placed by him upon sin and redemption is shown by the headings under which he arranged the hymns collected for use at his Huguenot chapel in London: Original Sin, Election Unchangeable, Electing Grace, Efficacious Grace, Imputed Righteousness, Preserving Grace, Assurance of Faith. These titles impress us with the intensely theological nature of eighteenth century Christianity. Belief was of fundamental importance, truth was established by proof-texts from the Bible, and anyone who did not believe as you did was anathema!

Toplady naturally came into violent collision with John Wesley the champion of Arminianism (the doctrine of Free Grace for all, not for the elect alone), and the two men waged their battles in public by means of pamphlets, sermons, letters, tracts and hymns. Toplady charged Wesley with lying and forgery; and he wrote, "I believe him to be the most rancorous hater of the gospel-system, that ever appeared in this island"; at another time, "Wesley is guilty of Satanic shamelessness," of "acting the ignoble part of a lurking, sly, assassin," of "uniting the sophistry of a Jesuit with the authority of a pope"—this about a man who was fifty years older than he and by this time one of the most honored men in England. Wesley on the other hand kept the controversy on a more impersonal plane, though he did say in the preface to his sermon on Free Grace, "I dare not speak of the deep things of God in the spirit of a prize-fighter or a stage player," and on another occasion, "I do not fight with chimney-sweeps."

The only excuse for resurrecting this ancient controversy is to point the moral that when theology assumes the place of supremacy in the religious life, Christian love degenerates. "Little children, love one another" is a

better working instrument of salvation than Calvinism, Arminianism, Bar-
thianism, Fundamentalism, Unitarianism, Existentialism or any other ism.
The head divides but the heart unites. Toplady's one immortal hymn is

### Rock of Ages, cleft for me    [1776]

This world-famous hymn was a shot in Toplady's battle of the creeds.
Its author printed it in *The Gospel Magazine*, 1776, as the climax to an
article intended to show that as England could never pay her national debt,
so man could never liquidate his sin account, and he gave it the title,

Westminster Abbey and Westminster School from the air. The cross-shaped
building in the center is the Abbey. At lower right is the Dean's Yard (with
trees). Westminster School, founded by Queen Elizabeth, is the group of
buildings above the yard.

### A living and dying PRAYER for the HOLIEST BELIEVER in the World

This was a slap at Wesley's claim that a believer could live without sinning.
The remarkable thing is that the hymn outlived its ancient pugnacity and
the neglect it suffered for thirty years, then gradually became the Number
One hymn in the affection of all Christians. Such a triumph shows that it
contains a genuine inspiration for the human heart.

It is astounding that this fighting poet should have stolen his weapons
from his antagonist! Dr. Benson calls attention to the fact that in Wesley's
*Hymns on the Lord's Supper*, published thirty years before Toplady wrote
this hymn and still being used in its eleventh edition, a paragraph of the
Preface reads as follows:

O Rock of Israel, Rock of Salvation, Rock struck and cleft for me, let those two Streams of Blood and Water which once gushed out of thy side, bring down Pardon and Holiness into my soul. And let me thirst after them now, as if I stood upon the Mountain whence sprang this Water; and near the Cleft of that Rock, the Wounds of my Lord, whence gushed this sacred Blood.

And in Hymn XXVII in that same collection, the opening line runs

Rock of Israel, cleft for me.

Toplady's hymn is Christian plagiarism of the first order!

If we assume that Toplady borrowed his imagery from John Wesley we must also confess that Wesley took his from the Bible. In the Book of Exodus there are stories of two cleft rocks: (1) the rock struck by Moses when the Israelites were perishing of thirst in the wilderness; from it water miraculously gushed forth (Ex 17:1–6); (2) the rock in the cleft of which Moses hid when Jehovah passed by that his prophet might see his glory and yet not die (Ex 33:17–23). These Israelitish stories were Christianized by St. Paul, who, using the then-current allegory to explain Scriptures said:

Moreover, brethren, I would not that ye should be ignorant, how that all our fathers . . . did drink the same spiritual drink; for they drank of that spiritual Rock that followed them: and that Rock was Christ. (1 Cor 10:1, 4.)

Toplady, who like Wesley knew the Scripture by heart, borrowed the phrase "Rock of Ages" from the marginal reading of Isa 26:4 in the King James Version.

What then did Toplady himself contribute to this hymn?

A moving quality that came from the depths of a passionate nature. We feel it as we read—the utter abandon of a soul which knows itself to be helpless except for Divine Grace.

A sincerity that no one can doubt. Toplady believed that what he wrote was true. Remember, this is the expression of Calvinist theology, according to which men are born damned; if any are saved, it is because Christ by his death on the cross paid the penalty due to sin, and because God has specifically chosen them for salvation. Good works avail nothing. That helplessness expressed in stanza 2 the poet had fully realized in his own experience.

A vividness conveyed by the pictures borrowed from Wesley and the Bible and from Calvinism but fully exploited by him—the Rock, the cleft, the water and blood, the unavailing labor, zeal, tears; the naked, helpless, foul sinner clinging desperately to the cross and imploring aid; the death-bed, the soaring among the stars, the vision of the final Judgement when souls are sent to their everlasting weal or woe.

A unity of structure: the hymn begins with a prayer for immediate aid, looks forward toward continuing aid till eternity begins, and at the final Judgement it closes with the prayer with which it began,

> Rock of Ages, cleft for me,
> Let me hide myself in thee.

In our day, theology has ceased to interest the mass of mankind; few Christians know whether they are Arminian, Calvinist, or what, or can tell the meaning of those once fighting words. But every one of us has felt the sting of sin, helplessness in the grip of failure, a sense of moral worthlessness, perhaps even a desperation such as led Margaret Fuller once to pray, "O God, if there be a God, save my soul, if I have a soul!" Happy indeed are we if we can find beneath the imagery of this hymn the reality for ourselves of God's saving help.

Because it contains this basic appeal beneath such moving imagery, this hymn has met the need of all sorts and conditions of men from the derelict snatched from the gutter by the Salvation Army to Prime Minister Gladstone, at whose funeral it echoed through the dim spaces of Westminster Abbey.

And as an omen of ultimate Christian unity, be it remembered that when Toplady published his collection of hymns in 1776, his own "Rock of Ages" and Charles Wesley's "Jesus, lover of my soul," stood, in spite of theology, side by side.

## Rev. EDWARD PERRONET (1721–1792) Anglican, Independent

THE Perronet family were French Huguenots who because of the persecution in France fled to Switzerland and later to England. Edward's father had been associated with the Evangelical Movement in the Established Church, as well as with the Wesleys and Whitefield. Edward himself was brought up in the Establishment. But since he had a critical mind he was keenly aware of the Church's defects. He once wrote, "I was born and I am like to die in the tottering communion of the Church of England; but I despise her nonsense." This is doubtless the reason he threw himself strenuously into evangelistic work with the Wesleys in the 1740's and 50's. Yet he never became the unquestioning servant that John Wesley exacted. The break came when Wesley demanded that none of his preachers should administer the Sacraments, but that for these rites they should attend parish churches with their flocks. Perronet claimed the right to administer. Accordingly he left the Methodists to become one of the chaplains of the Countess of Huntingdon. But the Countess objected so strongly to his violent criticism of the Church that he finally went "on his own" as pastor of a small Congregational chapel in Canterbury.

His emotional nature found ready outlet in writing hymns and other forms of poetry which he published anonymously in 1785. While many of his hymns are as worthy of survival as others that have persisted, only one of his is still found in common use. That one is the universally sung

### *All hail the power of Jesus' name*    [1789]

The editors had a hard time tracing down the authorship of this hymn. As late as 1892 it was still in doubt, although the great Julian's *Dictionary of Hymnology* thought that Perronet wrote it. Final proof came 126 years after it was first printed, when Dr. Louis F. Benson, minutely examining a copy of *Occasional Verses,* said to have been written by Perronet (the volume mentioned above), discovered the poet's name in an acrostic: the first letters of the lines of a poem "On Sleep" spell EDWARD PERRONET. In this same little book the hymn is found.

The hymn is a salutation to Jesus in memory of His Resurrection. It uses Biblical imagery and phraseology throughout, as did many eighteenth century hymns. See the references below.

The author calls upon various classes of beings to acclaim the risen Lord as He rises to heaven for His everlasting coronation:

*Stanza 1*. Angels are summoned, and in the omitted next stanza the Seraphs, highest of the nine ranks of angels. Mt. 28:9; Phil 2:9–11; Rev 7:1; Heb 2:9; 1 Tim 6:15; Rev 19:12, 16.

*Stanza 2*. The stars. The one who "fix't this floating ball" is Christ. Ps 148:3; Job 38:7; Col 1:16; Heb 2:1; 1 Sam 15:29.

*Stanza 3*. Martyrs. Rev 6:9–10; Is 11:1.

*Stanza 4*. The Jews. In Rom 9 Paul argues to show that the true seed of Israel is the Church (Is 45:25; Gal 3:29). The "fall" is the sin of Adam in the Garden. Gen 3; 1 Tim 2:6; Acts 15:11.

*Stanza 5*. Sinners. Lam 3:19; Mt 27:34; Rev 4:4, 10.

*Stanza 6*. All Mankind. Rev 7:9–12; 5:11–13.

*Stanza 7*. Us personally. This stanza was added by Rev. John Rippon, an editor.

When read critically the hymn is choppy and monotonous. Ingenuity has exhausted itself to find a rhyme-word for "all"; the result is "fall," "ball," "call," "fall," "gall," "ball," "fall." Nevertheless the images conjured up by the words and by the remembered Scripture parallels are vivid and splendid, and the imperatives of the verbs are highly exciting, especially when sung by a great congregation. There is no doubt that the success of the hymn is due largely to the two grand tunes to which it has been set. "Miles Lane," which has always been the English favorite, was written by a nineteen-year-old chapel organist in London, William Shrubsole. A phrase from this tune is carved on Shrubsole's tombstone at Bunhill Fields, London. "Coronation," the almost universal American setting, was written in 1793 by a self-taught musician, Oliver Holden, of Charlestown, Massachusetts. A verse from the hymn is engraved on Holden's tomb. Thus both America and the mother country are bound together by these contributions to the immortality of this paean of praise.

### ANONYMOUS c. 1757

### Come, thou almighty King

THE unknown author was contemporary with the Wesleys and the hymn first appeared with one other in a little leaflet such as the Wesleys used to publish. That is all we know about its origin. It was evidently written in imitation of the British national anthem beginning "God save our gracious King" which had appeared about fifteen years earlier and was sung originally to the same tune. Its value is attested not only by its almost universal use in English but by its translation into many languages.

The hymn is a prayer for the presence of Christ to inspire a congregation in the hour of worship. God is addressed under three forms: as Father, the timeless "Ancient of Days" whose function is to rule (stanza 1); as Incarnate Word, the spirit of holiness whose function is to bless and conquer (stanza 2); as Comforter, the indwelling source of joy and power (stanza 3); and finally as the mystic combination, the Holy Trinity, in whose presence we shall spend an eternity of love and adoration (stanza 4).

---

Besides the two strong inspirers of Dissenting hymnody already described in this chapter—Whitefield with his Welsh Calvinists and Lady Huntingdon with her independent congregations—there is a third person who gave impetus to Evangelical hymnody. He was

### Rev. JOHN NEWTON (1725–1807) Anglican

HERE is a man who probably did more than any other to forward the Evangelical spirit in the Established Church. That was a spirit of fervent personal devotion to Christ and of earnest desire to save men to a better life. How badly that spirit was needed is shown in Wakeman's *History of the Church of England*:

> The bishops were still amiable scholars, who lived in dignified ease apart from their clergy, attended the king's levee regularly, voted steadily for the party of the Minister who had appointed them, entertained the country gentry when Parliament was not sitting, wrote learned books on points of classical scholarship, and were occasionally seen driving in state through the muddy country roads on their way to the chief towns of their diocese to hold confirmations. Of spiritual leadership they had little idea. Church patronage,

which was mainly in the hands of the land-owning class, was largely used to make provision for life for the younger sons of the patrons . . . The intense and simple piety of the Evangelical Revival never succeeded in leavening the solid mass of English churchmanship.*

With such a spirit at the top of the hierarchy, precious little elixir of true religion could trickle down from above. It had to spring up from below— a "grass roots" religion like that stimulated by Whitefield, the Wesleys and the Countess. That a gradual spiritualization of the Church did result is certain; it was due to the Evangelicals.

No prophet would ever have picked John Newton to be a leader in spirituality. He started life as a pretty bad boy—if we may trust his possibly exaggerated account of himself.**

John's pious mother died when he was seven. His father, a Mediterranean sea captain, soon married again and sent the boy to a boarding-school "where the imprudent severity of the master almost broke my spirit, and relish for books." He left school forever at ten years, went to sea with his father at eleven. Adolescence found John rather tempestuous, but with spells of being religious. He fell in love at first sight with an English girl under fourteen, and the thought of her was his good angel for seven years. In 1743 at the age of eighteen he was "impressed" on a man-of-war, that is, compelled by force to enlist. His father could not get him released, but procured his becoming a midshipman—a cadet in training for promotion as officer. However, he hated the life, deserted, was caught, put in irons, whipped publicly and degraded to a common sailor. This disgrace embittered him. Since the warship was glad to get rid of him, he exchanged for a slave ship bound for Africa. "There I could be as abandoned as I pleased without any control." Once there, he quit ship and took service with a white slave dealer on an island off Sierra Leone. Now he was virtually a slave himself, half starved, and abused unmercifully by the slaver's black wife. Finally he was taken off by a sea captain at the request of John's father, to whom John had written of his condition.

The ship was on a trading voyage collecting gold, ivory, dyer's-wood and beeswax. After a long cruise he came back to England via Brazil and the Newfoundland Banks. To pass the time he read much in a book he found on board—Thomas a Kempis' *Imitation of Christ*, which sowed the seeds of his conversion. The crisis came during a great storm that nearly caused the ship to founder—he had to man the pumps from 3 A.M. till noon. Provisions spoiled or were washed overboard; the crew had nothing to eat for four weeks except fish which they lay-to to catch on the Banks. The result of the fright—he couldn't swim!—was his conversion.

* H. D. Wakeman, *op. cit.*, published by Rivington's, London, 1890, 1914.
** *An Authentic Narrative of some Remarkable and Interesting Particulars in the Life of * * * * * * (John Newton), Communicated in a series of Letters to the Rev. M. Haweis,* 3rd ed., London, 1765.

*Top, left,* John Newton. *Top, right,* Newton's church at Olney. *Bottom,* Plan of slave ship, drawn c. 1790. Every available foot was used, giving a capacity of up to 600 Negroes. This is only half the ship's lower deck.

Next Newton became captain of a slave ship. Those were days when the moral iniquity of the slave business had not impressed itself upon the public conscience. The business had many dangers—storms, fever, treachery of crews, insubordination of slaves. He had several hairbreadth escapes. All of the time he was trying to establish himself in his religious life and to educate himself by reading. As captain he held public worship for his crew of thirty twice every Sunday. "At one time there was a conspiracy amongst my own people to turn pirates and take the ship from me; but two men were taken ill, one died, and the plot was discovered in good time." At last the inhuman aspects of the business began to pall on him, and taking advantage of a serious illness when at home, he got out of it. Meantime he had married his girl four years before.

While earning a living as tide surveyor at the port of Liverpool, he was diligently studying for the ministry, came under the influence of White-field, wavered between the Dissenting Churches and the Established, but finally cast his lot with the latter. Many times in the ten years he was rejected for orders by his bishop; but at last, under pressure from Lord Dartmouth (for whom Dartmouth College is named) who was an avowed Evangelical and special helper of Lady Huntingdon, the Bishop of Lincoln ordained him and sent him to Lord Dartmouth's little village of Olney as curate to the vicar of Olney, who was one of the absentee kind. He stayed there fifteeen years (1764–1779).

Now his real life began. His interest in common folks, his earnestness in preaching the gospel, his genuine goodness—and perhaps his reputation for having had a shady past—attracted young and old. Especially effective was the story of his early life and conversion, which he often told. His congregations grew until he had to build a gallery in the church to hold the crowds. But he did not depend upon the stated Morning and Evening Prayer to make men religious. He begged from Lord Dartmouth the use of a large old manorhouse, former residence of the Earl's family, and in it held devotional meetings: on Thursday afternoons to teach children the Bible and religion, in the evenings to teach the older people. No orthodox rector ever did a thing like that! And worse still, he used *hymns* instead of singing Psalms from Sternhold and Hopkins! Not finding just the hymns he wanted, even in Watts, to express the simple, heartfelt religion he was teaching, he began to write some, and best of all, he enlisted his neighbor William Cowper in the same task. The result was the famous *Olney Hymns*, published 1779—a book of revival hymns designed, like the Wesley hymnal that came out the next year, to be a book of instruction in the Evangelical faith, for singing, reading and memorizing. The use of this book spread in time over all the English-speaking world.

After Olney, a London church claimed Newton for twenty-eight years until his death in 1807—the very year that the good Evangelical whose conversion Newton had aided, William Wilberforce, succeeded in putting

through Parliament a bill that abolished slavery forever in all British domains.
Newton's tombstone reads:

JOHN NEWTON

CLERK

ONCE AN INFIDEL AND LIBERTINE

A SERVANT OF SLAVES IN AFRICA

WAS

BY THE RICH MERCY OF OUR LORD AND SAVIOUR

JESUS CHRIST

PRESERVED, RESTORED, PARDONED,

AND APPOINTED TO PREACH THE FAITH

HE HAD LONG LABORED TO DESTROY.

Newton was more remarkable for his goodness than for his greatness.
Considering the enduring influence of his life, one may claim his as a
shining example of the truth Will Durant recently uttered (1943): "A good
man who is not great is a hundred times more precious than a great man
who is not good." At 82 Newton said:

My memory is nearly gone, but I remember two things, that I am
a great sinner, and that Christ is a great Saviour.

No one ever more neatly summed up the spirit of the great eighteenth-
century revival.

## The Olney Hymns

This collection, of which Cowper wrote 67 and Newton 281, had for
its purpose according to Newton's Preface "a desire of promoting the faith
and comfort of sincere Christians." In other words, religious education took
first place over the conversion of sinners. Begun in the happy days when
Cowper was comparatively well, it was finished by Newton alone because
of his friend's relapse into insanity.

The three divisions in the book show why the hymns were written.
In Part I were collected verses on Scripture texts, used to climax a sermon
or to illustrate prayer-meeting talks about Bible characters. The method was
first the story in verse, then the moral or allegory based upon it. Here is a
sample to show the intellectual level of the Olney flock:

Poor Esau repented too late
That once he his birthright despised
And sold for a morsel of meat
What could not too highly be prized.

> He stands as a warning to all
> Wherever the Gospel should come;
> O hasten and yield to the call,
> While yet for repentance there is room.

Part II is devoted to "Occasional Subjects," poems relating to particular seasons or events. Under the sub-topic "Time how swift" we find paradoxically the beautiful hymn "As with ceaseless course the sun," once found in most hymnals. Part III, "On the Progress and Changes of the Spiritual Life," contains some autobiographical verses by Cowper (see p. 133). These hymns afforded Cowper an outlet for feelings which if unexpressed might have become pathological, and Newton a lively source of instruction for his people. Newton's own robustness and moral health turned them all into an instrument of good for thousands of people. *Olney Hymns* became the hymnbook of the Low Church party in the Established Church and was reprinted in England and America for a hundred years. Individual hymns from it are still found in every hymnbook.

NEWTON'S CONTRIBUTION TO OLNEY HYMNS

### *Glorious things of thee are spoken*    [1779]

A hymn in praise of the Church, found in Bk. I of the *Olney Hymns* and based upon Is 33:20–21. Quite as appropriately it could be related to Ps 87 in which occur the words of the first line of the hymn.

The dignity and nobility of this hymn are very uplifting. Especially when sung by a great congregation to Haydn's matchless tune "Austria," it attains the very heights of worshipful praise. But when we ask just what the author meant by it and when we try to visualize the city we are baffled. It seems to be a conglomerate of many vague figurative elements.

> *Stanza 1.* Zion is the poetic name for Jerusalem, the capital city of Palestine since the time of David, and the seat of the Temple which was the focal point of Jewish worship. But in early Christian times the physical city, destroyed by Titus, became sublimated into an ideal city of the future. This new habitation is inspiringly described in Rev 21:2–3. Then follow two verses which are usually interpreted as describing heaven (vv. 4–5). This is a prophet's vision of something in the future: it can be the state of the Church on earth, the Church in heaven or a regenerated social order of living people, or what? Whatever it is, it will endure, founded like the house in the parable (Mt 7:24–25) upon a rock—the "Rock of Ages" which is Christ. For protection it is surrounded by walls which the poet calls Salvation.
>
> *Stanza 2.* Now the figure changes. We see its inhabitants crowding about a spring of the water of life. Newton had in mind the story

of the smiting of the rock in the wilderness (Ex 17:1–6) when Moses saved the Israelites from death by thirst. But this story also underwent a transformation in New Testament times. Christ declared that he was the Water of Life; and in the Book of Revelation the spring becomes a river (22:1). And the river nourishes the Tree of Life, and the people dwell beneath its shade in peace and plenty, as the nomads of the desert rest in the oasis under the palms and call it Paradise, a Persian word meaning a grove of trees.

*Stanza 3.* Again the poet reverts to the Old Testament. Now appears the "pillar of cloud by day and of fire by night" that guided Israel through the wilderness and rested like a living presence upon the Tabernacle (Num 9:15).

That too is sublimated into the New Testament imagery of a miraculous illumination, which may be spiritual as well as physical; for in the New Jerusalem men "shall need no candle, neither light of the sun; for the Lord God giveth them light" (Rev 22:5). Their food also, which in the wilderness had been "manna" (Ex 16:4–18), now is supplied by the "tree of life, which has twelve manner of fruits, and yielded her fruit every month" (Rev 22:2).

All these picturesque details convey the general idea of that ultimate state of the redeemed when God shall supply all their needs, physical and spiritual, in some place that is secure, beautiful and everlasting. This is a perpetual human ideal that has never yet been realized on earth, and may never be, but men have always cherished it and worked toward it. Jesus called it the "Kingdom of God."

It will be interesting to compare with this hymn Alexander Pope's poem beginning, "Rise, crowned with light, imperial Salem, rise," which is an attempt to realize in pageantry the coming of the Messiah as world ruler and then to turn to modern hymns by people who have caught the vision of man's social destiny upon earth, as distinct from a static condition of blessedness in heaven:

"Hail the glorious golden city, Pictured by the seers of old"—Felix Adler, 1878

"The fathers built this city, In ages long ago"—Wm. G. Tarrant, 1895

"Where cross the crowded ways of life"—Frank Mason North, 1903

"O Holy City seen of John, Where Christ the Lamb doth reign" —W. Russell Bowie, 1909

"The city, Lord, where thy dear life Didst pave the nobler way" —Wm. E. Dudley, 1929

Still others are appraised in Chapter XIX. This comparison will show the difference between the eighteenth-century way of looking at religion, salvation, life, and the twentieth-century way.

### *How sweet the name of Jesus sounds*    [1779]

This hymn is found in Book I of *Olney Hymns*: "On select texts of Scripture." The particular text illustrated is Song of Solomon 1:3—"Because of the Savor of thy good ointments thy name is as ointment poured forth." The hymn title, "The name of Jesus," shows that Newton interpreted the ancient collection of lovesongs in the allegorical fashion: Solomon becomes Jesus and his sweetheart becomes the Church, called in Rev 21:9 "the bride of Christ."

In Newton's thought, the chief virtue of ointment is to heal, therefore in the first two stanzas the healing, soothing, calming effects of the name of Jesus are stressed. Then the word "name" suggests to the writer some other names which the Jews applied to their God and which the Christian Church promptly took over, and other names applied to Jesus in the New Testament. These are all grouped in stanzas 3 and 4—an imposing but not an exhaustive list. We recognize at once the Biblical origin of all these metaphors. A concordance will give specific references to the appropriate passages.

Editors have changed one word in stanza 3. Instead of "Brother," Newton wrote "Husband" in view of his text (S of S 1:3) and in allusion to Rev 21:9. But the editors felt that the men of a congregation could hardly sing that term with any sincerity, and they changed it.

In stanzas 5 and 6 the poet realizes that he cannot adequately exalt the Name until he reaches heaven, but declares that he will never cease trying.

### *May the grace of Christ, our Saviour*    [1779]

This is a benediction to be sung at the end of any service, Sunday in church or weekdays in cottage prayer-meetings such as Newton instituted at Olney. It is based upon the Trinitarian formula—Father, Son and Spirit—that has been standard from the days of the Apostles' Creed. Christ is the medium through which God's grace is transmitted, Love is the essence of God's nature, whereby He sought the redemption of man, the Holy Spirit is that added token of divine interest whose function is to "guide us into all truth" (Jn 16:13). This prayer, if fulfilled, results in the spiritual union of all men, and of men with God, an experience that cannot by any other means be duplicated.

The Episcopal *Hymnal* (E 216) has made an interesting change in the nature of this little hymn. The editors have changed "us" to "them" (stanza 1); "we" to "they" (stanza 2), and placed it under the heading "Matrimony." By such simple means they have produced a most appropriate benediction upon a newly-married couple and have emphasized the spiritual element in marriage, which alone can make heaven upon earth.

We now consider the other partner in *Olney Hymns*, and his contribution.

## WILLIAM COWPER (1731–1800) Anglican

HIS was a tragic life, beginning in a frail childhood, dogged periodically by fits of melancholia and outright insanity, but glorified by devoted friendship and extraordinary success as a poet. In his published volumes he signed himself "William Cowper of the Inner Temple, Esq." which means that he was a lawyer by profession. Indeed, his first mental breakdown was caused by his being nominated to a clerkship in the House of Lords and his anxiety over the preliminary examination before the House.

*Left,* Cowper House, Olney, now the Cowper Museum. From a print of 1812. *Right,* Cowper's summer house in the back garden, where much of his poetry was written. The fence separates it from Newton's rectory lawn.

On this occasion he bought poison, and placed a penknife at his heart, but hadn't the courage to kill himself by either means. Then he tried hanging himself with a garter, but the garter broke. After that, an asylum for eighteen months. During this detention he was "converted" in the Evangelical manner; that is, he realized a personal contact with Christ and a sense of sin forgiven. This was in 1764 when he was 33 years old.

After his release he went to live at Huntingdon, near Cambridge. There he met the Rev. Mr. Unwin and family, who took him to board. His happy life was interrupted by the accidental death of Mr. Unwin, but providentially the Rev. John Newton of Olney called to offer his sympathy. Thus began a new life indeed. Newton prevailed upon him and Mrs. Unwin to move to Olney, where he secured for them a house near the vicarage; in fact, the lots adjoined in the rear so that he and Cowper could meet daily without having to use the streets. Here Cowper began to realize the healing power of friendship. Newton was his good angel. He interested the invalid in gardening, carpentering, a printing press, pets of all kinds—rabbits, dogs, guinea-pigs, canaries, goldfinches, a magpie, a jay, a starling, and finally he proposed that they write together a book of hymns—the *Olney Hymns* described above. Thus happily they lived and worked together. They conducted together the village prayer meetings, visited the poor and sick, distributed the alms supplied by a wealthy friend of Newton's. On Sunday, from his special pew in the new-built gallery of the parish church, Cowper listened to his friend's heart-warming gospel. In this way, by the double stimulus of healthy interests and the friendship of a godly man, Cowper spent some of the happiest years of his life. And when in 1773 Cowper again passed into the valley of the shadow, he clung to his friend as to an angel of God. This was a frightful period. The voices and visions returned,

From left: Lady Austen, Cowper, Mrs. Unwin. These are the friends who gladdened and inspired Cowper's later life and are responsible for the poetry that placed Cowper in the front rank of the eighteenth-century writers.

the awful sense of sin, a conviction that he was doomed to a place in hell lower than Judas, and that God demanded that he kill himself and hasten to his final doom. Again he attempted suicide. But the cloud lifted and Cowper enjoyed twenty years of comparative health.

At the suggestion of two other good angels, Mrs. Unwin and Lady Austen, Cowper used his new period of sanity in writing secular poetry. His second volume, *The Task*, brought him fame and a secure place in English literature. For a century, his *Royal George*, and *John Gilpin's Ride* were in all the reading-books of the schools, while the literary historians credit him with having brought about a return from the artificialities of eighteenth-century poetry to a natural style and a love of nature. He was the precursor of Wordsworth, Scott, and the early nineteenth-century singers. But this fame was the fruit of his later years; his hymns lay in an earlier period and a different area of life.

All hymn-lovers would rejoice in a pilgrimage to Olney. The house where Cowper lived is now a museum—a red brick house on the south-east corner of the market-place. It is filled with all kinds of relics of the poet: books by him and about him, portraits of the poet and his friends, the original iron grates in the fireplaces, gate-legged tables, rush-bottom chairs, and the kitchen fireplace of stone so huge that it holds seats within on each side. There are two attractive paintings: one represents the poet at tea with Mrs. Unwin and Lady Austen, the other shows him getting breakfast, absent-mindedly boiling his watch over the grate and holding an egg in his hand! In a bedroom on the second floor was written the hymn, "God moves in a mysterious way."

But best of all are the gardens behind the house: the first one a wild mass of flowers, containing at its farther end a glassed-in shelter for Cowper's pew taken from the village church when the gallery was pulled down. Then through a gate one enters a second garden, arranged formally and attractively, while on the far side one discovers Cowper's summer house where he composed in good weather.

Another gate leads to the lawn and garden of the vicarage which backs up to this property. Through this gate came the friendly Newton each day.

## COWPER'S CONTRIBUTION TO OLNEY HYMNS

*God moves in a mysterious way*        [1774, published 1779]

Found in *Olney Hymns*, Bk. III, under the title, "Conflict: Light shining out of Darkness."

The word majestic best describes this hymn. It reveals at work in the world a God who preserves the grandeur of the ancient Jehovah and the personal concern of the Christian's Father.

Out of the Old Testament come the pictures of stanzas 1 and 2: the Lord striding over the oceans and riding the storm-clouds (2 Sam 22:7–20); from Job the mines hidden in the earth and the treasuries out of which he draws his gifts for men (Job 28: 1–3; 38:22–23). Then in stanzas 3 to 6 the poet addresses comforting words to the fearful, bids them remember their limitations of understanding, and boldly asserts his faith in the goodness of God in spite of all appearances.

This is the Calvinism we have met earlier in Dr. Watts (Chap. IV). But whereas the good doctor boldly asserted the dogma that God is sovereign, all-powerful, arbitrary and not to be questioned, Cowper takes a more trustful attitude and assures us that in due time the event will interpret God's purposes for man's good. Poetry and an attitude of faith can make even Calvinism comforting!

We do not know under what circumstances Cowper wrote this hymn. It is somehow connected with his mental breakdown in 1773 when he made an attempt upon his life; probably written about six months afterward in 1774 when the cloud had lifted somewhat. An unverified story has it that, resolved to drown himself in the river Ouse at a spot about three miles out of town, he called a cab and told the driver to take him to the place. For some reason—perhaps purposely—the driver could not find the spot, and after coursing about for an hour deposited the poet again at his own door. Even though the story may be fiction, the title of the hymn holds true, "Light shining out of darkness." This is the last hymn Cowper ever wrote.

The main thesis of the hymn had already been documented more than once in the poet's own life. His first fit of insanity had landed him in St. Alban's Asylum; yet that misfortune was what led to his brother's visits and his own "conversion." That was "light shining out of darkness." Again, happily established in the Unwin home, he was crushed by another disaster —the death of Mr. Unwin and the threatened break-up of that providential haven. But this calamity brought Mr. Newton upon the scene, and the new home, happiness and creativity at Olney.

> Judge not the Lord by feeble sense,
>     But trust him for his grace;
> Behind a frowning Providence
>     He hides a smiling face.

Still other incidents in his life justify his conclusion that faith and confidence are better than despair.

In a broader sense, the thesis of the hymn expresses the Christian attitude toward disasters of the world like the recent war. Since Jesus believed in a God who cares and who works unceasingly to accomplish His purposes, we too are justified in believing that a thousand times in human history God has directed the course of events toward His own ends— the evolutionary redemption of the human race. This is the "telefinalism" so wonderfully explained in Lecomte du Noüy's *Human Destiny*, 1947.

### O for a closer walk with God     [1769]

Written on December 9, 1769, before he had begun work with Newton on the *Olney Hymns*. In that collection it was placed in Bk. I, "On select texts of Scripture." The particular verse illustrated is Gen 5:24, "And Enoch walked with God: and he was not; for God took him." The title was "Walking with God."

This is one of the sweetest and saddest lyrics of our hymnody, and most poignant when it is viewed as a revelation of the inner life of its author. While it expresses phases of the spiritual life common to all of us, our varying intensities of emotion and devotion, it indicates in Cowper a special period of depression that came a few months after moving to Olney before he had become fully adjusted to his new life there. Its special occasion was the serious illness of Mrs. Unwin, his faithful friend and housekeeper. Cowper wrote: "She is the chief of blessings I have met with in my journey since the Lord was pleased to call me . . . I began to compose the verses yesterday morning before daybreak but fell asleep at the end of the first two lines; when I awaked again, the third and fourth were whispered to my heart in a way which I have often experienced."

This anxiety and dread reminds him, by contrast, of a former happy experience alluded to in stanzas 2 and 3: the poet thinks back to those days in St. Alban's asylum when his brother visited him, brought the healing message of the gospel that finally swept over him like a flood and washed away all his past. That was his "conversion" and the beginning of his mental restoration. The next twelve months of convalescence before his release from St. Alban's were bright with joy and hope. In stanzas 4 and 5 recurs the sense of guilt—as if the poet knew that his own hated sins had brought about his present spiritual decline, and then the resolve that he would rid himself at whatever cost of the obstacles to perfect fellowship with God. The last stanza is faith's beautiful return to former blessedness. Appropriately, the words are largely a repetition of stanza 1. The former longing for peace has become a definite assurance that the light on the road will grow stronger and the goal surer.

## Sometimes a light surprises [1779]

This hymn is also from *Olney Hymns*, Bk. III, under the heading, "Joy and Peace in Believing."

This hymn breathes the very soul of trust, a perfect echo of the words of Christ on the Mount about the Father's care. The majesty—one might almost say awe—of "God moves in a mysterious way" gives place to a child-like peace, calm in the assurance that clear shining will follow rain. Recalling what has been said above about the poet's periods of depression, one can clearly read between the lines of the hymn the sad autobiography. But the accent is on the hopeful side: a "light surprises"; there is "healing in his wings"; "sweetly," "cheerfully," "confiding," "rejoice." In this poem, the head has stopped reasoning, the heart is trusting. Such a poem transcends individual bounds and becomes universal in its appeal and its inspiration. These Biblical passages were evidently in the author's mind:

Stanza 1. Mal 4:2; 2 Sam 23:4.
Stanza 2. Ps 35:9; 116:13; Is 12:2.
Stanza 3. Mt 6:25–30.
Stanza 4. Hab 3:17.

## Rev. *JOHN FAWCETT* (*1739–1817*) Baptist

THE life of this useful man might be taken as a kind of norm for dissenting clergymen in the eighteenth century: poverty, self-education, a gruelling ministry, growing influence, ultimate recognition. Many clergymen did not attain to the final goal, but Fawcett did.

Born in bleak Yorkshire, left an orphan when he was twelve, he was promptly "bound out" as apprentice to a tailor in Bradford. The indentures of that time constituted a contract of slavery. The hours of work for this thirteen-year-old were from 6 A.M. to 8 P.M.! Somehow he learned to read. He mastered *Pilgrim's Progress* by candle-light when his master thought he was asleep, hiding the gleam under an earthen "bushel" and lying on the floor of his attic chamber. From that book he got his first religious ideas, especially the necessity of conversion.

When fifteen he heard Whitefield preach in an open field to 20,000 people who had flocked thither from miles around. John could not resist the appeal; he even told the evangelist he wanted to become a preacher. Whitefield gave him his blessing.

John now joined a tiny Baptist church which held meetings in private houses in Bradford, gradually accustomed himself to public speaking, and was advised by visiting clergymen to preach in the villages round about as he had opportunity. At eighteen years of age he married a girl five years older than himself, with whom he lived happily for many years. Soon the Baptist flock in nearby Wainsgate became interested in him and asked him to become their pastor. Wainsgate was not even a village; it was a straggling group of houses on the top of a barren hill. From it was an extensive view— hill after hill, all as bald as an eagle's head—great bleak moors between which were narrow valleys with streams at the bottom. The people were all farmers and shepherds, poor as Job's turkey; an uncouth lot whose speech one could hardly understand, unable to read or write; most of them pagans cursed with vice and ignorance and wild tempers. The Established Church had never touched them; only the humble Baptists had sent an itinerant preacher there and he had made a good beginning. Now they wanted John to come and live there. A farmer had recently given a piece of land and the men had built a little house which held one hundred people—horribly damp, with no furniture but stools on which to sit.

So enticed by a great opportunity rather than by the promised salary of not over twenty pounds a year, John was ordained minister in 1765, and he and Mary went up there to live. There was no parsonage, so they "boarded round." His house-to-house contacts, his simple goodness, his devotion to everyone's welfare but his own, speedily won the love of all. His congregation grew so that a gallery had to be erected in the meeting house.

But children began to arrive in the pastor's family—four of them within five years; and although the "meeting" voted to raise John's salary to twenty-five pounds if he would take out the "raise" in wool and potatoes, the family found it hard to survive the winter storms on porridge for breakfast, potatoes for dinner and potatoes for supper. At length light broke. A message from London told that Dr. Gill, pastor of Carter's Lane Baptist Church, was old and incapacitated; would Mr. Fawcett come down and let the congregation hear him preach? Mr. Fawcett went and saw and conquered. He returned with the call in his pocket—much larger salary, much wider field of usefulness, chance for self-improvement for which he had been starved. He and Mary decided to accept. The announcement was made to the church, the farewell sermon was preached, the bulky items of

Interior of the present Wainsgate Church, erected 1815 and enriched with rare and beautiful marble, the gift of wealthy woolen manufacturers who moved their factories and looms up into this wool country following the Industrial Revolution in the 1830's. Present membership, 90.

his furniture and some of his older books were sold and the day of departure arrived. The two-wheeled cart came for the rest of his belongings, and likewise came the parishioners to say good-by.

Shall we draw on our imagination and dramatize what followed?

(Noise of a small crowd; sniffling and soft crying among the women.)

*John:* "Back the cart up here, Tom. Put the big things in first."

*First parishioner:* "We're sorry to see you go, Mr. Fawcett."

*John:* "It is hard to break away, Mr. Gubbins. You people have been very good to us."

*Second parishioner:* "What are we poor folks goin' to do, Mr. Fawcett!"

*John:* "Put the box of books under the table, John. ——Yes, but I've been here seven years now. You ought to have a change."

*Third parishioner*: "We don't want no change, Mr. Fawcett. We love our pastor!"

*Woman parishioner* (sobbing): "O Mrs. Fawcett, don't go and leave us! What shall we do when you ain't here any more!"

*Mary* (starting to cry): "It doesn't seem as if I could stand it, either!"

*John*: "Here, Tom, put that heavy box in front of the wheels. Any more weight behind will lift old Dobbin off his feet."

(Sounds of sobbing.)

*John*: "Now, Mary, you get up on the seat and I'll hand the children up —littlest first . . . Number two—up he goes! —Number three—up he goes! . . . Number four. Is there room for Tom on the seat? I'll sit on the load. Good-by, everybody! God bless you and send you a better man than I am." (Sobbing increases.) Calls of "Good-by"—"Don't go!"—"Please don't go, Mrs. Fawcett" —"I'll always remember that you married me, Mr. Fawcett" —"You'll come back to see us sometime?"

*Mary*: "I can't stand it, John! I know not how to go." (Crowd still calling.)

*John*: "Lord help me, Mary, nor can I stand it! We will unload the wagon. Tom, get down again; we won't go. I'll hand down the children." (To the crowd) "We have changed our minds! We are going to stay! (Noise of crowd stops)—"you don't seem to understand: we have decided not to go to London. (To Tom) Take the stuff off the cart, Tom, and carry it back into the house. (Pandemonium breaks loose.) Shouts of "Hurrah!"— "Praise the Lord!"— "Halleluia!"— "They're goin' to stay!"

❋     ❋     ❋     ❋     ❋

So the heart had its way over the head. The Fawcetts stayed for a ministry of fifty-four years in Wainsgate and nearby Hebden Bridge. Next Sunday Mr. Fawcett preached from the text in Luke 12:15, "A man's life consisteth not in the abundance of the things he possesseth," and after the sermon he lined-out, and the congregation sang, the hymn he had written the previous midnight:

### *Blest be the tie that binds*     [1782]

This self-sacrificing decision on the part of John and Mary Fawcett brought a new impulse to the preacher's mind, and a new power. He opened a training school for young preachers, published a volume of hymns, built a new meetinghouse, wrote several books, among these an "Essay On Anger" which became a particular favorite of King George III. This monarch offered Mr. Fawcett any benefit he could confer, but the offer was declined with the statement that "he lived among his own people, enjoyed their love; God had blessed his labors among them, and he needed nothing which even a king could supply." In 1811, Brown University in Providence, Rhode Island, conferred upon him the degree of Doctor of Divinity. The hymn and one other, listed below, are his monument. For nearly two hundred years they have been the parting benediction upon all kinds of religious gatherings the world around.

### Lord, dismiss us with thy blessing    [1773]

This is more distinctly a dismission hymn than is "Blest be the tie"; nevertheless it is sung much less frequently. It is a prayer that we may make practical use of the gospel of which we have been partakers and be conscious henceforth of God's presence with us. This is an appropriate but uninspired prayer. The last stanza, which introduces angel transportation to heaven and endless reigning with Christ over some unidentified domain, is so foreign to modern thought that editors have rewritten practically all of it.

### Rev. GEORGE HEATH (1745–1822) Dissenting

HEATH'S biography is short. He was educated in a Dissenting Academy at Exeter, England; became pastor of a Presbyterian Church but was dismissed for "bad conduct"; later became a Unitarian minister. This hymn is his sole monument.

### My soul, be on thy guard    [1781]

The subject is steadfastness. The underlying image is a soldier on duty. Various aspects of spiritual warfare are hinted and the whole is characterized by earnestness and devotion. The hymn has been a standby for a hundred and sixty-five years.

### ANONYMOUS: "K" or "KN" Baptist?

### How firm a foundation, ye saints of the Lord    [1787]

This hymn first appeared in Rippon's Selections. Dr. John Rippon, pastor of a Baptist church in London from 1773 to 1836, made himself famous and rich by publishing a hymnbook consisting of Watts and "A Selection of Hymns from the Best Authors." In that collection appeared this hymn with the author indicated as "K–." Later reprints also gave "Kn," and one, "Keen." Since the precentor in Dr. Rippon's church was one named R. Keene, composer of the tune to which the hymn was originally set, we may conclude that R. Keene wrote the words. But there our knowledge stops. The hymn is certainly characteristic of the late eighteenth century.

Rippon's Selections won immediate popularity. Within three years, Baptists in Philadelphia reprinted this hymn, and in five years Rippon's whole book was published in New York. While the Established Church in England has never included the hymn in its collections, in America it is sung generally and enthusiastically, partly no doubt because of the splendid tune "*Adeste Fideles*" to which it is set in five of our hymnals.

The hymn is really a sermon in verse. In the first stanza the foundation of the Christian faith is said to be the Bible in which God has given us all we need. Those gifts are specified in the following stanzas and are here documented with the appropriate references.

*Stanza 2.* Josh 10:25; Is 41:10.
*Stanza 3.* Is 43:2a; Josh 2:10; 2 Sam 22:17; Ps 18:16; Is 43:5a; 1 Kings 1:29.
*Stanza 4.* I Peter 4:12; 2 Cor 12:9; Is 1:25; Zech 13:9.
*Stanza 5.* Job 5:26; Is 46:4; 40:11.
*Stanza 6.* Jn 13:23; Ps 16:10; Acts 2:27; Deut 31:6, 8; Heb 13:5.

*ANONYMOUS*, Anglican, Evangelical

## *Praise the Lord! Ye heavens adore him*      [1801]

THIS hymn is one of five printed in a four-page tract and pasted into a book called *Psalms, Hymns, and Anthems of the Foundling Hospital*, London. The hospital was a remarkable establishment founded in 1739 for deserted children, but after 1760 was reserved for illegitimate children whose mothers were known. (See Chap. V for a description of such "hospitals" in the eighteenth century.) The founder was a merchant sea-captain named Thomas Coram who for a time was a ship builder in Taunton, Massachusetts, but returned to England in 1703 to become a promoter of colonies in Georgia (See under the Wesleys, Chap. V) and Nova Scotia; and he devoted his latter years to charitable enterprises like the Foundling Hospital. Among the pictures in the Board Room was a very appropriate one by Hogarth called "The Finding of Moses," and Raphael's cartoon of "The Massacre of the Innocents." The organ in the chapel was a gift from the composer Händel who took a great interest in this institution and for several years conducted special performances of *The Messiah* to promote this foundation. It was quite the thing for fashionable Londoners to visit here, especially on Sundays. At the morning service the children all sang, led by trained voices, and at dinner they could be seen dressed in their quaint and distinctive costumes. The institution was moved early in the twentieth century and the building demolished.

While nothing is known about the author, we can perhaps in imagination hear the children singing this Psalm of praise in their famous chapel on "High Holborn" in down-town London—the street through which criminals went from Newgate prison to their hanging at Tyburn (Chap. V).

The hymn is a paraphrase of Psalm 148. It expresses praise to God for His wonderful works of creation, governed by law, and for His promises to man of victory over sin and death.

CHAPTER SEVEN: THE AGE OF ROMANTICISM

| | | *Hymnists* |
|---|---|---|
| 1760–1820 | GEORGE III (cont.). | Largely |
| 1790–1833 | "Clapham Sect" seeking to apply Evangelical religion to social reform. | Evangelical |
| | French Revolution continues. | |
| 1795 | London Missionary Society founded. | |
| 1798 | Wordsworth: *Lyrical Ballads.* | |
| 1799 | Church Missionary Society founded (Evangelical). | |
| 1800 | Napoleon First Consul. | |
| | Coleridge: *Ancient Mariner.* | |
| 1804 | Napoleon Emperor; war with England. | |
| | British and Foreign Bible Society founded. | |
| 1805 | Scott: *Lay of the Last Minstrel.* | |
| 1809 | Byron: travels resulting in *Childe Harold.* | Kelly, 1809–20 |
| | | Heber, 1811–27 |
| 1813 | Southey Poet Laureate. | |
| | Wesleyan (Meth.) Missionary Society founded. | Marriott, 1813 |
| | Parliament opens E. India territory to missions. | |
| 1815 | Battle of Waterloo. | |
| | Passage of *Corn Law*; depression and riots in England. | |
| 1816 | Shelley: *Alastor.* | Moore, 1816 |
| 1817 | Keats: *Poems.* | Montgomery, 1816–43 |
| | | Keble, 1819–22 |
| 1820–30 | GEORGE IV. | |
| | Industrial revolution in full swing; much violent agitation for reform. | Edmeston, 1820–21 |
| 1823 | Limitation of death penalty for petty crimes. | Milman, 1823 |
| | | Lyte, 1824–37 |
| | | Bowring, 1825 |
| 1825 | Trades Unions legalized. | |
| 1828 | Repeal of Corporation and Test Acts. | Stowell, 1828 |
| 1829 | Catholic Emancipation Act. | Reed, 1829 |
| 1830–37 | WILLIAM IV. | |
| 1830 | Riots against tithes, poor laws, etc. | Bathurst, 1831 |
| | Revolution in France frightens England. | Eb. Elliott, 1832 |
| 1832 | Reform Bill eliminating "rotten boroughs" and giving industrial cities seats in Parliament. | Grant, 1833 |
| | | Ch. Elliott, 1834 |
| | | Anon. 1836 |

# THE AGE OF ROMANTICISM

HYMNS ARE A FORM OF LITERATURE. The English hymn, however, began inauspiciously as an attempt to rhyme the Book of Psalms without disturbing too much its inspired prose. It developed without benefit of art because Dr. Watts, though a man of learning and quite competent to please the Classic Muse, chose deliberately to "write down to the Level of Vulgar Capacities and to furnish Hymns for the meanest of Christians." Throughout the eighteenth century the hymn served mainly the religious needs of non-conforming middle-to-lower-class Christians who valued it for other qualities than its poetry. Most of Charles Wesley's 6000 hymns were rhymed theology and exhortation; most of the hymns of Beddome, Anne Steele, Doddridge, Stennett, were Biblical phrases and pious prose chopped up into stove lengths. They stood quite aloof from the justly famous literature of Pope and others of the Augustan Age: the latter was created for the delight of the educated leisure class; the former were the refuge, the solace and the hope of the underprivileged.

But this condition could not last. As the eighteenth century drew to a close the great middle class of non-conforming England was gaining in culture, and many Anglicans of the gentry, even of high social and political status, were joining the Evangelical wing of their Church. In this way there grew up a well-educated, democratic, idealistic, socially-minded body of religious people who became increasingly conscious of the inadequacy of the hymns and Psalms the Church was singing. They were ready for something better.

Then as if in answer to prayer broke the Romantic Movement as it is called, a resurgence of the emotions from beneath the hard crust of Reason and classic form that had bound secular literature and art.

No doubt political events had assisted at the birth. In England the democratic movement had been growing in intensity, the demand for reform of abuses, the extension of the franchise, the restraint of privilege. The rebellion of the American colonies added fuel and the French Revolution released all the baser, as well as the loftier passions of men, drenched the land in blood, and caused all the monarchs of Europe to totter on their thrones. With emotion dominant in the realm of action, how could it be restrained in the arts?

The English genius responded generously. In 1798 appeared Wordsworth's *Lyrical Ballads* which included "Tintern Abbey," the poet's poetical creed, his feeling for nature and man. Then came Coleridge's "Ancient Mariner," his masterpiece of romance and moral insight. Southey's "Lodore" was revolutionary when one remembers the classic swains and nymphs who peopled the eighteenth-century literary landscape; in 1813 Southey became Poet Laureate. In 1809 Byron broke upon a startled world with "Childe Harold." Shelley in 1816 captured the very spirit of poetry in "Alastor," and later in the "Hymn to Mont Blanc," "Ode to the West Wind," and "Skylark." In 1817 Keats published his first volume. With such inspirations let loose upon the literary world at that time, what hymn-writer could remain unaffected!

From the first decade of the nineteenth century therefore we discern in the religious poetry of the Church, whether Anglican or non-conformist, a new note that is best symbolized by the word "literary," a true lyric expression of emotion and a regard for elegance of form. Not all hymn writers were equally successful craftsmen, but all aimed at the new ideal. One of the earliest and best was

## Bishop REGINALD HEBER (1783–1826)

HEBER was a child of fortune; he had a goodly heritage. Born in a home of wealth and culture, he had every opportunity to develop the precocity which appeared in him in childhood. When he was five he had already read the Bible so diligently that he could give chapter and verse for chance quotations. Hearing the conundrum, "Where was Moses when the light went out?" he instantly replied, "On Mt. Nebo, for there his lamp of life went out." At seven he translated a Latin classic into English verse. So kind-hearted and generous was he that his parents found it "necessary to sew into the lining of his pockets the banknotes given him for his half-year's spending money when he went away to boarding school so that he might not give them away in charity on the road."

He entered Oxford at seventeen. Within two years he had won two prizes for poetry. Taking holy orders after graduation in 1807, he became rector of his father's church in the little village of Hodnet in western England twelve miles northwest of Shrewsbury. The Gothic building of red sandstone with an octagonal tower on one corner stands on a hill overlooking the village at close range. Rose trees bloom in the church yard and hang over the embankment wall. Having independent means, Heber abandoned the little thatched vicarage near the church, built the present imposing house, laid out the grounds and on a hill some distance away a large garden. The brick house is set in magnificent trees: elms 120 feet high, tulip, lime and yew; a formal garden with little box hedges and well-kept lawns. A grass walk goes straight up the hill a hundred yards to a place where Heber once had a summer house. Here he used to read and write his sermons and hymns in face of a magnificent prospect of woods and fields, of hedgerows, farms, cow pastures and villages. The little structure has gone but the tile flooring was recently uncovered. We can see how all this loveliness crept unawares into the hymns that have become the world's delight.

Heber lived sixteen years at Hodnet as squire and vicar. They were happy years. One of his first tasks was to improve the singing in his church, where like most Anglican congregations they were still singing Sternhold and Hopkins. He writes to a friend: "My Psalm-singing continues bad. Can you tell me where I can purchase Cowper's *Olney Hymns* to put in the seats? Some of them I admire much, and any novelty is likely to become a favorite and draw more people to join in the singing." But being a Church-man, his services governed by the Prayer Book and the ecclesiastical year, he did not find anywhere the hymns he wanted. He resolved to get up a hymnal of his own, to compose hymns connected with the Epistles and the Gospels appointed to be read on specific days in church, to be sung in the services after the Nicene Creed and before the sermon. Some of these hymns were published in the *Christian Observer* from 1811–16; the rest were published after his death.

His hymnal was to contain other hymns besides his own. He invited contemporary friends like Walter Scott, Southey, Milman and others to contribute. Milman alone responded. He tried to get the Bishop of London to authorize its publication, but that conservative prelate thought "the time was not ripe." It was not published till after Heber's death. He was the first in England to apply the touchstone of literary excellence to hymns, to liberate the meters from the tyranny of Common, Long and Short, and to make use of contemporary rhythms and stanza structure.*

Appointed Bishop of Calcutta in 1823 he went to India where he spent three years at ceaseless labor. He brought to his task a splendid enthusiasm and efficient administrative ability. Since his diocese extended over most of India, distances and climate wore heavily upon him. On a visit to the Madras Presidency, scene of the successful labors of the German missionary Schwartz, he came to Trichinopóly, the town under the towering rock which rises like Gibraltar out of the plain. Scheduled to preach at Schwartz's chapel at 10 A.M., the crowd was so great that he went into the yard and spoke from the steps of the mission house. His subject was the evils of the caste system. He must have suffered a touch of sun without realizing it. Returning about midday to the house of a judge with whom he was staying,

---

* Charles Wesley had made some experiments along this line: *e.g.*, "Nancy Dawson."

*Top, left,* Bishop Reginald Heber. *Top, right,* Wrexham Church, c. 1470. Here Heber's "From Greenland's icy mountains" was first sung. Eli Yale is buried in the churchyard near the tower. *Bottom, left,* The Rock of Trichinopoly, South India; beneath its height Heber preached his last sermon. *Bottom, right,* The pool in Trichinopoly in which Heber died.

he went for a bath in the swimming pool under the trees of the garden. When he did not return the family sent a servant, who found him drowned, probably as the result of an apoplectic stroke. The pool is now enclosed with a rail, and on it a memorial stone put up by Edward VII when he was there as prince in 1875. He is buried in the English church at Trichinopoly; a good window to his memory has been placed over the high altar and a slab in the north wall.

### *Brightest and best of the sons of the morning*     [1811]

This earliest of Heber's hymns was written for use on Epiphany Sunday, that is, on or about January 6th. On this date the liturgical Churches which organize their year around events in the life of our Lord, celebrate the Adoration of the Wise Men. The significance of this event is hinted in the "Collect" for Epiphany: "O God, who by the leading of a star didst manifest thine only-begotten Son to the Gentiles." The Gospel to be read on that day is the story of the Wise Men, Mt 2:1–12. One can imagine how impressive to those who had been accustomed to sing only metrical Psalms would be the singing of this lyric which adorns and interprets the straightforward Gospel story with beautiful imagery from nature.

The first stanza centers our interest upon the star, here called a "son of the morning." Behind this phrase there are scriptural reminiscences. In Job 38:7, for example, we read, "When the morning stars sang together, and all the sons of God shouted for joy," which in accordance with the rules of Hebrew poetry would indicate that the stars are personified as sons. Then the poet expands "brightest and best" by describing the star's function of scattering darkness and giving guidance, of adding beauty and revealing the Redeemer. No other star ever did that.

Then the poet's imagination fills in with details not mentioned in scripture: the dew drops on his cradle, the beasts of the stall which the artists seldom fail to picture, the angels adoring—as well they may, since he is both Maker and Monarch of them as well as Saviour of mankind.

In stanza three the worshiping kings become ourselves; the original frankincense is sublimated by the poet's fancy into "odors of Edom"; the forest and the mine provide a picture background for the myrrh and the gold, while gems and pearls are added for good measure. Having thus conjured up in our imagination the costliness of such an offering, we discover that in God's sight these gifts are far less dear to him than is the love of our hearts.

It was very kind of Mr. Heber, the darling of fortune, as he sat creating this gorgeous tapestry in his summer house on the hill and looking at the broad domain over which it had pleased God to set him as squire and vicar, to commend in his final line of one stanza the prayers of the poor. Does God love to have poor people beg him for the things they desperately need, as Heber was glad to hand out a dole to them from his palatial vicarage? But we must not be hard on the good poet. He and his Church had not yet begun to realize that God hates poverty as much as he hates pride.

## By cool Siloam's shady rill     [1812]

Written to be sung on the first Sunday after Epiphany. On that day the lesson from the Epistle is Rom 12:1–5; and the Gospel lesson is Lk 2:41–52, the story of Jesus' visit to the Temple at twelve years.

With this scriptural setting in mind it is easy and delightful to follow the poet's fancy. First the Palestinian landscape with its lilies of the valley and its roses of Sharon, two flowers that have been poetically assigned as symbols of Jesus himself by the theologians of a past generation (Song of Songs 2:1). Siloam and its rill are mentioned because of their proximity to the Temple on Mt. Zion where the meeting of Jesus with the doctors occurred—as Milton put it (*Paradise Lost* I. 10–11).

> . . . Sion hill
> . . . and Siloa's brook that flowed
> Fast by the oracle of God.

This lovely picture in no way corresponds with the Jerusalem topography, for Siloam is not shady nor is there any rill in the Kidron valley except after a downpour, but the poet's purpose is to give an imaginative simile for the young adolescent now opening his heart and life to God, as the flowers open their petals to the sun.

The last two stanzas are a prayer that through the grace—the undeserved favor—of this divine youth and man, we may be kept close in spirit and character to Him throughout our earthly course.

## The Son of God goes forth to war     [1812]

Written for use on St. Stephen's day, December 26th. The collect for this day is a paraphrase of the vision of Stephen as recorded in Acts 7:54–60: "Grant, O Lord, that, in all our sufferings here upon earth for the testimony of thy truth, we may stedfastly look up to heaven, and by faith behold the glory that shall be revealed; and, being filled with the Holy Ghost, may learn to love and bless our persecutors by the example of thy first Martyr, Saint Stephen, who prayed for his murderers to thee, O blessed Jesus, who standest at the right hand of God to succour all those who suffer for thee, our only Mediator and Advocate. Amen." The Epistle for the day is the passage in Acts mentioned above; and the Gospel is Mt 23:34, which opens up to the imagination the long lines of prophets and wise men that will follow Jesus and Stephen to a martyr's death.

With these passages in mind, Heber proceeds to visualize that line, beginning with Jesus Himself. In the first stanza Jesus appears as the Messiah of prophecy and apocalypse, He who was to be sent by God as the warrior to conquer the unrighteous nations of the world, to be crowned king and reign forever from Jerusalem over a kingdom of Jews. Though Jesus Himself repudiated that role, "My kingdom is not of this world," Jn 18:36; "The kingdom of God is within you," Lk 17:21, nevertheless the early Church took it up with enthusiasm, put themselves in the place of the rejected Jews and looked forward confidently to a Second Coming of Jesus as conqueror and king. His army, says the poet, will consist of all those through the ages who are willing to "drink his cup of woe." This is a reminiscence of the request of the mother of James and John that her two sons might have the chief offices in His kingdom, and of Jesus' reply, "Are ye able to drink the cup that I drink?"—meaning to undergo the suffering of death on the cross (Mk 10:38).

So the grand review begins. First the king, with his blood-red banner (red to symbolize the blood He shed on the cross, and because of His love, whose symbolic color is red); then Stephen the first martyr; then the Twelve valiant saints, the Apostles, every one of whom met a martyr's death; and last a foreshortened view of the long army of martyrs of all ages, "men and boys, the matron and the maid."

Now the background scenery changes from earth to heaven. We stand with John of the Revelation before the throne (Rev 7:9–17).

In the final couplet this vast array includes us—if need be.

### From Greenland's icy mountains      [1819]

This hymn was written in the old vicarage of St. Giles, Wrexham, ten miles southwest of Chester. The house has since been replaced by a business block. On the abutment of the near-by railroad bridge may be seen a memorial tablet erected in 1926 on the centenary of Heber's death, which reads:

> To the glory of God and in memory of Reginald Heber,
> Bishop and poet . . . who in the old vicarage near this site
>     in 1819 wrote the missionary hymn,
>         From Greenland's icy mountains.
> "Go ye into all the world and preach the gospel to every
>     creature."

The fifteenth-century parish church of Wrexham has one other title to fame besides its connection with this hymn: it is the burial place of Elihu Yale for whom Yale University is named. Its porch was restored in 1901 by graduates of that University on the two hundredth anniversary of the founding of the college, in recognition of Yale's bounty. This gentleman, appropriately enough, made his great wealth in India, where he was the governor of the East India Company's settlement at Madras only a couple of hundred miles from where Heber died.

The occasion of the writing was a Royal letter that authorized collections to be taken in every church and chapel in England to aid the Society for the Propagation of the Gospel. Heber's father-in-law, Dean Shiply, who was vicar and dean of the church in Wrexham, had asked Heber to deliver the first of a series of evening lectures on the subject of missions. On the previous Saturday, when a group was seated round the table in the vicarage, the dean asked Heber to write something that might be sung at the missionary service next day. Heber at once went over to a corner of the room and while the conversation continued began to write. In a few minutes his father-in-law asked, "What have you written?" Heber then read the first three stanzas. "That will do very well," said the dean. "No, the sense is not yet complete," replied Heber, and he proceded to add the final stanza. Next morning it was sung at the service in the Wrexham church and has since been sung all round the world. As the date will show, it was written before Heber had any idea of going to India as a missionary.

What gives this hymn its power is partly the vividness of its imagery. Instead of saying that the heathen are calling for our help from various parts of the world, the poet flashes upon our screen a series of snapshots: icy mountains, coral strand, sunny fountains, golden sands, ancient rivers, palmy plain—each distinct, pictorial, stimulating to our memory and our imagination. Heber had never seen these places but he had read about them. Greenland he vaguely knew through the reports of seventeenth-century explorers, India through the growing empire of the British East India Company and the very recent missionary work of William Carey (India has no coral strands except in this poem); he could visualize some of Africa's rivers by a name on the map—Gold Coast, and the antiquity of the rivers from what he had read of the civilizations that long ago flourished on the banks of the Nile, the Euphrates, the Ganges and the Yangtse. Stanza 1 therefore is what an imaginative Oxford graduate with a flair for poetry could have organized in five minutes.

But lovely scenery does not of itself produce noble men. Where God's gifts of nature are most prodigal, men seem to be most blind to the giver (stanza 2). For that reason, we who are blessed with the true faith are obligated to carry the light to those that sit in darkness (stanza 3). Again, in the final stanza, the brilliant pictures are resumed in an impassioned call to wind and wave to bear the tidings to the ends of the earth as a preparation for the Second Coming of Christ to rule a ransomed world forever.

While this hymn has had an almost universal appeal, the contemporary Church is beginning to hedge. The British *Songs of Praise* omits it altogether, for what reason I cannot guess; the Unitarians cannot sing it because of the theology implied in stanza 4; the Episcopal hymnal cuts out stanza 2, perhaps because the editors had heard that the educated heathen vociferously object to being called vile. Perhaps, too, the present debacle in our western civilization makes us hesitate to claim "wisdom from on high" when we continue to exploit the vile heathen for our own advantage, and deny them the very opportunities the gospel promises them. But for a good many decades the hymn will doubtless continue to epitomize at least the ideals of Christian missions and inspire the Church to sacrificial effort.

Heber's hymn is a good illustration of the fact that hymns are in part the product of the times. The Protestant Church was just awakening to its responsibilities to the pagan world. While Catholicism was earliest in the field, following the vast geographical discoveries of the thirteenth through the fifteenth centuries, and had planted the banner of the Cross in many places in the Far East (Franciscans in Asia, thirteenth century; Jesuits in South America, India, Japan, sixteenth century); the Protestants became aroused to the needs of Asia only as the eighteenth century was drawing to a close (Baptist Missionary Society, 1792 to support Carey; London Missionary Society [Interdenominational] 1795; Scottish Missionary Society [Presbyterian], 1796; Anglican Church Missionary Society [Evangelical wing], 1799; Wesleyan Missionary Society, 1813). The East India Company with the backing of Parliament had all along forbidden missionary work within its sphere of operations; but when these obstructions were removed by Act of Parliament in 1813, Heber himself became an enthusiastic propagandist. "From Greenland's icy mountains" could hardly have been created previous to this awakening and would never have attained its popularity except for this general enthusiasm.

### *Bread of the world, in mercy broken*        Published 1827

Written for the celebration of Holy Communion.

This is an emotional expression of what the Eucharist or Lord's Supper means to us who partake. That masterful phrase, "bread of the world," removes us from the simple historic act that occurred in the Upper Room; it suggests to us the Feeding of the Five Thousand as interpreted by the Fourth Gospel. This multitude upon the Galilean hillside becomes in his thought the countless millions of disciples through all the ages, with the great Teacher dividing unto them the loaves and saying, "And the bread that I will give is my flesh, which I will give for the life of the world" (Jn 6:51). Similarly, "wine of the soul" somehow suggests the stimulating draught of life that through the years has renewed and kept dominant the spiritual qualities of Man's nature. Yet behind the imagery and the emotion is the Calvinistic theology revealed by the last line of stanza 1, "And in whose death our sins are dead"—that is, by His death on the Cross Christ cancelled the sins of the world.

Stanza 2 is a trifle obscure. Apparently the poet asks Christ to look upon each individual as he comes to the Lord's table, upon the sorrowing, upon the repentant sinner, and then prays that the sacrament may be a reminder of the spiritual food which comes to us by God's grace. If this interpretation is correct, Heber was not a believer in the miraculous transformation of the bread and wine into the body and blood of Christ, which is the Roman

Catholic interpretation, or even in the "Real Presence," which is the Anglican doctrine that Christ is actually present in the elements along with the real bread and wine. He believes rather in the symbolic or suggestive function of the Sacrament: what feeds our soul is the spiritual touch of Christ as we endeavor through this rite to make contact with Him. Whatever our interpretation, this hymn will supply an emotional preparation.

## *Holy, holy, holy, Lord God Almighty*     Published 1827

Written for Trinity Sunday which occurs eight weeks after Easter. The festival is dedicated to the theological interpretation of God as existing in three Persons, Father, Son and Holy Spirit, as proclaimed by the Council of Nicaea in 325 A.D. The tune by Dykes to which the words are usually sung is for this reason named "Nicaea." On Trinity Sunday the Gospel lesson to be read is Jn 3:1–15 in which Christ teaches Nicodemus the function of the Spirit and of the Son.

No hymn has greater dignity and uplifting power; none is more thoroughly liturgical, fit to be sung by vast multitudes in grand cathedrals, while the organ rolls its thrilling thunders through "long-drawn aisle and fretted vault." The hymn consists almost entirely of epithets—words that seek to define the nature of the God we worship. He is Lord, God, the Almighty, the Holy, merciful, mighty, the one who was and is and is to come; His glory hidden in darkness; unique, perfect in power, love, purity; the Triune—both one and three, incomprehensible though that may be to mortal mind. These are powerful words, filled with the emotion with which centuries of Christian teaching and worship have charged them. They are conjuring words, evoking the visions of John's Revelation where all the angelic hosts join with cherubim, seraphim and the Church Triumphant in adoration, while the stars and the sea, the whirlwinds and the thunders furnish the orchestration. That this hymn of Heber's satisfies the needs of the Church Universal is proved by its presence in all the hymnals used in this study.

The doctrine of the Trinity is uniquely Christian. Triads of gods are very ancient,—a father, a mother, a son. Thus in Egypt there was Lord Osiris, his wife Isis, his son Horus; but they were three distinct personalities, a projection into the heavens of the family on earth which is the fundamental unit of society. The Hindu religion had its triads, and long after Christianity was born the Brahmins attempted to reconcile their various hostile sects by the doctrine of the three-fold manifestation of the single supreme power of Brahma, Vishnu and Siva. But two historic religions have stoutly maintained that there is only one God: the Jewish—"Hear, O Israel, the Lord our God is One" (Deut 6:4); and Islam—"O ye people of the Book! [Christians] Believe in God and his Apostles, and say not 'Three' [there is a Trinity]—Forbear. God is only one God! Far be it from his glory that he should have a son!" (Koran, Sura iv. 169).

In fact, it has been the great stumbling-block in the Christian pathway, divisive and deadly. Words cannot recount the quarrels, schisms, anathemas, exiles, excommunications, murders, wars, that have sprung from this attempt to raise a figure of speech that expresses the functions of God as creator, redeemer and inspirer, into a metaphysical dogma the acceptance of which is essential to salvation. The old Greek theologians would better have spent their time persuading men to live like Jesus than to have forged these chains for the intellect of man and to have deluged the world with blood through the centuries.

In singing this hymn we may either accept the trinitarian formula as true, mentally retranslate the formula into a statement of function—how God works; or do as the Unitarians have done—substitute for the last line of stanzas 1 and 4 the last line of stanza 2, and so cut the Gordian knot; or, as the Baptists have done less poetically—substitute for the same lines "God over all, and blest eternally." In any case we can feel the inspiration of a grand hymn of praise, worthy to have come from the Bible itself.

### *God that madest earth and heaven*      Published 1827

Heber wrote only one stanza. This is a choice evening prayer based on the thought that since God made night as well as day for man's good, it is fitting to ask for His blessing as darkness comes. It is vastly superior to Watts's "Now I lay me," which has frightened many a child with "If I should die before I wake!" It prays for all that mortal man can reasonably ask: protection, sleep, holy dreams, and hopes for the morrow.

To this little gem Archbishop Whately of Dublin added in 1855 a second stanza. It is based upon the Roman Catholic antiphon (a piece of devotional verse or prose sung antiphonally by the choir) used at Compline (the service held at curfew just before bedtime), as follows:

*Salve nos, Domine, vigilantes, custodi nos dormientes, et vigilemus in Christo et requiescamus in pace.*

Times change and editors will edit. What the good bishop wrote is not what most of you read in your hymnals. His last stanza has been tinkered with to avoid mentioning the trump of Doomsday. But the thought of lying peacefully in the ground until the trumpet calls us to the resurrection of the body and an eternal life in the form of an angel is too antiquated for some moderns. Therefore they discard Bishop Whately entirely and substitute a stanza written by the American Unitarian hymnist, Frederick C. Hosmer, in 1912. Thus B C M N. This ending lands us upon earth, with another chance.

It is a great tribute to Heber's genius that in spite of a style which is somewhat too florid for modern taste, all of his hymns are still in use and eight of them are found in five or more of our standard hymnals.

*Rev. THOMAS KELLY (1769–1854)* Irish, Anglican; later Independent

KELLY, though Irish, was an Anglican clergyman whose Evangelical preaching was so earnest and effective especially on the subject of "justification by faith"—a doctrine taboo by High Church—that the Archbishop of Dublin closed to him all the pulpits of his diocese. The status of the Establishment in Ireland was so precarious (see Chap. VIII) that any tendency toward liberalism was regarded as dangerous. Rather than stop preaching the gospel as he saw it, Kelly first preached in unconsecrated buildings and finally, being a man of means, built several places of worship for his own use. He was a learned man, a musician, a magnetic preacher, a generous and friendly soul who gave liberally to those in need, especially during the famine of 1847. "During the latter a poor man of Dublin is said to have comforted his wife by saying, 'Hold up, Bridget! Bedad, there's always Mr. Kelly to pull us out of the bog, after we've sunk for the last time.'"

Kelly's hymns, written over a period of sixty years, numbered 765, of which three are still in common use. They are on the whole commonplace, not having been seriously influenced by the literary revival that was contemporary with them. The two listed below, however, are above the average and are in every way worthy.

## *Look, ye saints, the sight is glorious*      [1809]

The hymn was entitled "The Second Advent" and is based on Rev 11:15. It is a shout of exultation as the poet sees in imagination the ineffable glories that accompany Christ's return, the contrast between Christ's earthly degradation and His heavenly splendor—angels and saints adoring, the enthronement, the coronation, the music, the shouting.

Those editors who look upon the Second Coming as a poetic drama created by the imagination of John rather than a coming historic event, yet who want to preserve the hymn for its emotional uplift, classify it in their hymnals under "Ascension," "The Everlasting Christ," "His Abiding Presence," "His Exaltation." In these catagories the hymn is still useful as emphasizing the supreme place held by Christ in the thought and love of Christendom.

## *The head that once was crowned with thorns*      [1820]

Primarily an Ascension Day hymn based on Heb 2:9, the hymn presents the contrast between the shame and suffering of Christ's earthly life and His eternal glorification; also the joy of the Christian to know that if he bears his own cross below he shall reign with Christ above. These ideas are recollected from such passages of Scripture as 2 Tim 2:12; Eph 3:18–19; Rev 3:12. Such an intertwining of Biblical ideas is characteristic of an eighteenth rather than of a nineteenth century preacher's mind.

## Rev. JOHN MARRIOTT (1780–1825)

MARRIOTT wore the "old school tie" of Rugby and got his degree with honors from the aristocratic Christ Church (college) of Oxford. In recognition of his services as tutor in the family of the Duke of Buccleuch, the Duke presented him with the Rectory of a little church in Warwickshire. This means that Marriott had a job for life as rector, salary paid out of tithes collected by the government—a method of church support quite alien to America. In this system parishioners have nothing to say in choosing their rector: the choice rests with the owner or controller of the estates of the district. Moreover the rector does not have to stay put: he can hire a "curate" to run the parish and himself go where he pleases. In Marriott's case his wife's health made it desirable for them to live in Devonshire near the sea. So in that region he became curate successively to several parishes. Thus he drew two salaries—one from Warwickshire (the difference between his stipend and what he paid his curate), and one as curate in the Devonshire parish. This undemocratic and often irresponsible arrangement, subject to so much abuse, a little later became the source of social and political agitation.

Marriott himself was a thoroughly fine man. Sir Walter Scott thought enough of him to dedicate to him the second canto of *Marmion*. But Marriott was too modest to publish his own hymns. After his death they appeared in print; only one has survived to our day:

### *Thou whose almighty word*    [c. 1813]

This is a missionary hymn of high order, antedating by six years Heber's famous "From Greenland's icy mountains."

Written twelve years before his death, it was shortly thereafter read at a meeting of the London Missionary Society and then published, 1825.

The theme line is the last one in each stanza, "Let there be light!" There follow successively four time elements. Each of them is an inspiration to missionary effort:

*Stanza 1.* The original creative work (Gen 1:2–3). So the Church prays that the darkness of heathenism the world around may be dissipated by the gospel.

*Stanza 2.* The ministry of Christ and His contemporaries (Mal 4:2; Is 9:2). We now pray that these promises may apply, not to apostate Israel, but to the suffering nations of mankind.

*Stanza 3.* The gift of the Spirit at Pentecost. The imagery still clings to Gen 1:2–3 but adds the lovely picture from Noah (Gen 8:8, 11) and three others (Gen 8:8, 11; Mk 1:10; Jn 1:32; 1:14; Acts 2:16–17, 21).

*Stanza 4.* The reminiscences of stanzas 1–3 are now fused into the Trinitarian formula: "Wisdom" is God the Father of Gen 1; "Love" is God the Son at His baptism; "Might" is God the Holy Spirit at Pentecost. And the triple attributes of the Three now become the ocean of the Gospel whose radiant tide shall encircle the globe.

This architectural structure with vivid imagery and high feeling make this hymn a work of art.

## THOMAS MOORE (1779–1852) Irish, Nominally Roman Catholic

THE short and simple annals of this poet are: born in Dublin, educated at Trinity College, Dublin, studied for the Bar, held for a short time a government post in Bermuda, did a great deal of literary work. For a while he was the social lion of London because he appeared in fashionable homes to sing his own poetry to his own accompaniment. His *Irish Melodies* contain some of his best work. Political satire was also one of his specialties. Financial difficulties and family disappointments made of him a total wreck some seven years before he died. He lives only in his poetry, which all agree is of high merit. Only one of his thirty-two hymns has survived:

### Come, ye disconsolate      1816, revised 1831

The hymn is an invitation to pray. Whatever one's sins and sorrows, they can be assuaged for the truly penitent by pouring them out before God. The "Mercy seat" is the Christian poetic adaptation of the gold top on the "Ark of the Covenant" in the Old Testament, on which Jehovah sat between the two cherubims (Ex 25:17–22) and made His will known to Moses. Compare Cowper's "Jesus, where 'er thy people meet" and Stowell's "From every stormy wind that blows." The invitation is made emotionally attractive by such words as "Comforter" (Jn 14:16–18), "Bread of Life" (Jn 6:32–33), "waters flowing" (Rev 22:1–2), "feast of love"—a reminiscence of the "agape" or love feast celebrated by the early Church, a common meal preceding the Lord's Supper.

The last line must not be misunderstood: "heaven" is here not the eternal abode of the blessed but is a poetic word for God. The Chinese have their Temple of Heaven, meaning the highest deity. What is to be realized in prayer is not the assurance of heaven but the actual presence of God. That experience nullifies sorrow.

The galloping dactyls of this hymn are unusual and hardly suited to the pace of prayer. Fortunately, though, the tune *Consolation* to which they are invariably sung disguises and softens the movement.

## JAMES MONTGOMERY (1771–1854) Scottish, Moravian

THIS author wrote more hymns in common use today (twelve) than any writer except Charles Wesley (twenty) and Watts (eighteen). One cannot call him a great poet, but he knew how to express with sincerity, fervor, simplicity and beauty the emotions and aspirations of the common Christian. Out of his work we might almost construct a definition of a hymn: religious verse that expresses the spiritual life in forms of beauty suitable for public worship.

In the primary background for this hymn-writing lies his piety. Montgomery was brought up in the atmosphere of religion, first by his clergyman father and then, after his parents sailed as missionaries to the West Indies when he was six years old, by the Brethren of Fulneck (Yorkshire) who kept a boys' boarding-school—one might almost call it a monastery. "There," says Montgomery, "whatever we did was done in the name and for the sake of Jesus Christ, whom we were taught to regard in the amiable and endearing light of a friend and brother." This attitude of informal familiarity is illustrated by the prayer of one of the boys after a change in the menu:

> O Lord, bless us little children and make us very good. We thank thee for what we have received. Oh, bless this good chocolate and give us more of it.

James began to write poetry at ten years, stimulated thereto by the splendid heritage of Moravian hymns used by the Brethren. At fourteen he "flunked out" of school and was set to work in a bakeshop. When he was sixteen he ran away, a pack of clothing on his back, a few specimens of his verse and three shillings sixpence in his pocket. At his first night's stand he applied high salesmanship to an unusually benevolent gentleman and sold him a poem for a guinea, which staked him till he found a job. Later London lured him; there he could sell no poetry but clerked in a bookshop. Next, in answer to a want ad he went to Sheffield (1792) and got a job on a radical weekly, the *Sheffield Register*. Here he began his life's work.

Shortly after, when the editor had to leave England for fear of prosecution for his political articles, Montgomery took over the paper, changed its name to the *Iris* and maintained it for thirty-one years. He became a fearless social leader. The French Revolution was in full blast. The British Government was trying to raise an army for an expected war with France, but Sheffield, though an upstart manufacturing town that had no political power, was growing by leaps and bounds and was all for fighting for the rights of man and ousting the aristocrats. Montgomery had the temerity to reprint a song celebrating the fall of the Bastille and was jailed for it in York Castle. Shortly after his release he printed a tirade against the way the military commander had put down a riot in town, and was jailed again for seditious libel. In prison he spent his time writing poetry!

In 1825 he gave up his paper to devote himself to literary and philanthropic pursuits—composing poetry and lecturing about it, advocating foreign missions, and the like. He also tackled local problems, as when he tried to humanize the lot of boy chimney-sweeps; world problems, as when he worked for the abolition of the slave trade and forswore the use of sugar till it should be accomplished. He became Sheffield's first citizen. A reformed government in 1833 gave him a royal pension of £200 a year. He bought a magnificent estate called The Mount at the west end of the town and lived there in comfort till his death.

In his religious life he learned to be tolerant. He left for a time the Moravian fold and did some "free thinking"; around the time of his York imprisonments he joined freely in public worship with Anglicans, Independents, Baptists and Methodists, while in local charities he cooperated cordially with the outlawed Catholics, Unitarians and Quakers. But he returned to the Moravians when he was about forty-three.

His total output of hymns was 400. He edited and published three hymnbooks: *Songs of Zion,* paraphrases of the Psalms, 1822; The *Christian Psalmist,* 1825, containing 103 of his own hymns; *Original Hymns for Public, Social and Private Devotion,* 1853. All of his other voluminous poetical work has died a natural death, but his hymns seem destined for immortality— unless the forms and substance of the religious life radically change.

## *Hail to the Lord's anointed*      [1821]

The hymn is based upon Ps 72, long regarded as a prophecy of the Messiah: first by the Jews, who thought that Solomon wrote it with his Messianic successor in mind, then by Christians who applied it to Jesus. The translators of the King James version thought that David wrote it, and so they added the words now found in that version to interpret its meaning. None of these words, given just under the Psalm number, belong to the original. Montgomery took them all as gospel truth.

It will be instructive to compare Montgomery's paraphrase with that of Watts' "Jesus shall reign where'er the sun," inspired by the same Psalm. (See page 53.)

### Biblical References

*Stanza 1.* Psalm heading and v. 1b.
*Stanza 2.* Ps 72:4b, 2a.
*Stanza 3.* Ps 72:12, 4a.
*Stanza 4.* Ps 72:14, 6.

It is evident at once that Montgomery has stuck less closely to his text than did Watts. In the early days before Watts broke the spell, such freedom would have been considered sacrilege, but in this period when literary form was more valued than faithfulness to the inspired Word it was reckoned a virtue. Montgomery absorbed from the Psalm the essential intent of the Psalmist as he saw it, then proceeded to create his own imagery. "Songs for sighing," "darkness turn to light," "condemned and dying," and all the last six lines have no parallel in the original.

This is less of a missionary hymn than one might expect. Watts stressed the universal extent of Christ's kingdom, the gifts brought to the Lord from the ends of the earth, and gave the scene all the pageantry of an Indian durbar. Montgomery glorifies rather the redemptive function of Christ and the new social order that His justice will bring. His poem is more prayer than prophecy, or shall we say it is prophecy in large part unfulfilled but still capable of inspiring the Church to work for its fulfillment! While our hymnal editors have felt it desirable to cut out three whole stanzas of Watts' pedantic nonsense and his Calvinism, they have given us Montgomery intact.

### Angels from the realms of glory     [Dec. 24, 1816]

Of the many Christmas hymns based upon the stories in Matthew and Luke this is one of the best. It is pictorial, emotional, well organized. A few comments suffice to make everything clear:

*Stanza 1.* Angels are told not to stay in Bethlehem but tell the good news to all the world. Angels, called Sons of God, were poetically said to have sung when God created the world (Job 38:7b). They are now asked to celebrate the fulfillment of creation's unfinished task.

*Stanza 2.* "God with man is now residing"—a reference to Is 7:14 in which a promised child was to be called Emmanuel, "God with us." Mt 1:23 interprets this as applying to Jesus.

"Yonder shines the infant Light." Possibly alluding to the legend that when Jesus was born, light from His body illumined the whole cave. The capital letter however would remind us of what Jesus once said about Himself (Jn 8:12).

*Stanza 3.* Reference to the Magi, i.e. the astrologers whose profession it was to study the heavens and by the stars to interpret future events. They had already divined that a king of the Jews had been born (Mt 2:2). See also Hag 2:7, interpreted by the Church as referring to Jesus (Mt 2:2).

*Stanza 4.* The poet now passes beyond the Bible story and sees the pious of all ages gathering in their churches at Christmas time. They hope that Christ will come again to rule the earth; fear that they may possibly not be among the "elect." See also 1 Thess 4:16 referring to His Second Coming; and Mal 3:1 when He claims His spiritual heritage as world ruler.

The original had a fifth stanza beginning

> Sinners, wrung with true repentance,
> Doomed with guilt to endless pains, etc.

With its vanishing emphasis upon eternal hell the modern Church has omitted these lines and so saved the rest of the hymn to a longer life.

### O Spirit of the living God    [1823]

Another evidence of the writer's fervor in the cause of missions. Not only were his parents missionaries to the West Indies and died there, but the Moravian sect to which he belonged was from early times devoted to

*Left,* James Montgomery, age 35. *Right,* "The Mount," his residence, built on the highest point of Sheffield "at a safe distance from the smoke, the smells, the bustle, and all the goings-on of human life in this strange place"—Montgomery.

the cause—long before the English Protestant sects saw their duty or caught the inspiration. (See Chap. XI, German Hymns.)

This is a prayer, filled with reminiscences of scriptural and theological phrases, that the messengers of the Cross may be able to win the whole world for Christ.

> *Stanza 1.* "Grace" is defined as undeserved favor, the initiative taken by divine love toward reconciliation and forgiveness.
> "Plenitude" means fullness, adequacy, enough to cover all needs (Rom 5:20).
> Our race is "apostate" because, according to the theology of Montgomery's Church, it was involved in sin by Adam's fall; all men have therefore been born damned. Only "grace" can save them.

*Stanza 2.* "Tongues of fire" is an allusion to the descent of the Holy Spirit on Pentecost (Acts 2:3–4).

"Reconciling word" (2 Cor 5:20).

"Unction": that quality in language or manner which excites fervent religious emotion. Theoretically this stems from the speaker's having been "anointed" for his task.

*Stanza 3.* The last line may suggest God's mercy triumphing over His wrath against sinners (a theological concept), or that man's mercy toward his fellows may prevail over his anger at them (an ethical concept).

This is one of Montgomery's less successful hymns. Along with others, this hymn has been preserved largely because the editors needed a hymn on this subject to fill a gap.

### In the hour of trial  [1834]

Like so many hymns of the seventeenth to eighteenth centuries this one has a Biblical background. The writer presupposes that we shall instinctively recognize it from the allusions in the words. Here the writer had in mind the incident of Peter's denial of his Lord in the courtyard of the High Priest (Mk 14:54, 66–72).

*Stanza 1.* "In the hour of trial": a reminder of what Jesus said to Peter after the latter had so vehemently protested his loyalty (Lk 22:31–32).

"Base denial": Mk 14:70–71.

"With a look recall": Lk 22:61–62.*

*Stanza 2.* "With its witching pleasures." John once described the pleasures of the world as "the lust of the flesh and the lust of the eyes and the pride of life" (1 Jn 2:16); and added, "This is not of the Father"—by which phrase he excluded them from the life of a Christian. By "sordid treasures" the poet means wealth pursued as an end in itself without social responsibility, that is, Greed, which eats out the spiritual life.

"Bring to my remembrance." One function of the life of Jesus is to remind us of true values. Gethsemane teaches us the terrible consequences of betrayal; it should have taught Peter just that. Calvary teaches us that greed and the lust for power stop at nothing in their mad career, not even murder. Intent upon getting what we want when we want it we do not realize the fearful consequences of untransformed desire, and we need to be reminded.

*Stanza 3.* The imagery of Montgomery's original third stanza is a

* For a picture of this incident with an interpretation of it, see A. E. Bailey: *The Gospel in Art*, pp. 329–331.

little too strong for modern taste. We do not think of sickness, accident and other disasters as punishment sent by God, or ourselves as sacrificial victims to some irrational demand of deity, as Isaac must have thought of himself (Gen 22:6–10). The last line recalls the words of Jesus in Gethsemane (Mt 26:39).

There are three chief attitudes we may take towards suffering: rebellion, submission, the endeavor to find something helpful in the experience. The last is Faith's drinking the cup. This attitude may enable us to

> rise on stepping-stones
> Of our dead selves to higher things.

Montgomery's original stanzas 3 and 4 have been rightfully omitted from all our hymnals except the Canadian *Hymn Book* and the Presbyterian *Hymnal*. Mrs. Frances A. Hutton has written two substitutes in which poetic imagery has given place to rhymed prayer.

*Stanza 4.* Again Mrs. Hutton objects to the vivid pictures of the grave and the flashing glory: her generalities are less spectacular. Both are an affirmation of the Christian's faith in immortality as taught by Jesus.

The hymn has been greatly loved; it seems especially to appeal to young people. It was the favorite hymn of my aviator-son who was killed in the service of his country.

## Prayer is the soul's sincere desire    [1818]

A collection of beautiful metaphors that describe prayer: hidden fire, a sigh, a falling tear, an upward glance, vital breath. The plain prose of the first line is as good a definition of prayer as one can find in short compass.

## Go to dark Gethsemane    [1825]

The lessons one may learn from three of the final incidents in the life of Jesus: Gethsemane—learn the spirit of prayer; the Pretorium—learn how to bear the Cross; Calvary—learn how to die.

### Rev. JOHN KEBLE (1792–1866) English, Anglican

PREPARED for the university by his father in the home vicarage, Keble entered Oxford at 14, proved to be a high-ranking scholar, was elected a Fellow of Oriel College when not yet 19 years old, and won university prizes for English and Latin essays—an unusual record. He was ordained a priest at 24 and tutored at Oriel for five years. On the death of his mother he went home to assist his father as curate of his country parish and there remained till his father's death twelve years later. That did not prevent him from accepting at the same time the Professorship of Poetry at Oxford in 1831.

In 1833 he preached the memorable Assize sermon which started the Oxford Movement (see Chap. VIII). He also helped along that movement by writing four of the ninety tracts by which the movement was publicized; but in 1835 he retired from public view to become vicar of Hursley, a small village near Winchester. There he passed the rest of his 31 years as a devoted and hard-working parish priest.

Though Keble did much other writing, his fame rests on his *Christian Year*, from which all his hymns are culled. The sub-title of this work reads, "Thoughts in verse for the Sundays and Holy Days throughout the Year." In the Preface Keble gives as his purpose, "bringing thoughts and feelings into more entire unison with those recommended and exemplified in the Prayer Book"—a truly "High Church" aim. Accordingly there are poems for each of the fifty-two Sundays, for Christmas, for each of the Saints Days, Holy Communion, Baptism, Confirmation, Matrimony, Burial, and even Gunpowder Treason, King Charles the Martyr, and the Restoration of the Royal Family! The poems were written between 1819 and 1827; that was while he was assisting his father as curate.

This book was so sincerely pious and so stimulating to the religious consciousness of his day that it ran through ninety-five editions in his own lifetime. Though it was then acclaimed an unexcelled masterpiece of poetry, modern taste relegates it to a very humble position. Nevertheless it is important for our study because it represents so fully the romantic spirit of the early nineteenth century.

The trouble is, it is too "romantic," too much patterned after Wordsworth and the other Lake Poets, who saw a spirit abroad in every cloud and flower, responsive to every passing human emotion. The *Christian Year* might be called a book of nature poems quite as reasonably as a book of piety. But Keble's nature pictures are vague, evolved in his own study. "There is no observation behind his images, no thought behind his emotion, no emotion behind his thought—nothing but simple assertion." Moreover, his language is that of conventional literary sentiment. He speaks of sweet spring, soft as Memnon's harp, transporting chords; mountain hoary; deepening glen; the willow, her free arms flinging, wearing her willing smile.

> Thus I learn Contentment's power,
> From the slighted willow bower,
> Ready to give thanks and live
> On the least that heaven may give.

—all this dedicated to the First Sunday After Epiphany!

This poetry is far removed from the fervent Calvinism of Watts, the prose-meters of dear old Doddridge, the evangelistic fervor of Wesley and even the literary piety of Cowper. It is piety soaked in romanticism. That kind of romanticism is now dead; with the advent of Tennyson and Browning it gave place to something less artificial.

Keble was more than a romanticist: he was the spark plug of the reactionary development dealt with in the next chapter—the Oxford Movement. That function of his stemmed from a mental and spiritual set against all

*Copyright National Portrait Gallery, London*

*Left,* John Keble. *Right,* Keble College, Oxford, opened in 1870. In its library is the manuscript of Keble's *Christian Year;* in the chapel, Hunt's painting *Light of the World.*

change, transmitted to him by his father. It was passed on to his pupil, Hurrell Froude, and through Froude to Newman who developed it to its logical conlucison. Geoffrey Faber, in his *Oxford Apostles* (1934), says of Keble and his ideas:

> He adorned them with his own sweetness of character, preserved them with his invincible obstinacy, shared them feverently with his pupils and friends, and popularized them by his facile lyre. But they remained simply the ideas which his father had taught him—devotion to the memory of king Charles the Martyr, belief in the principles of the non-jurors [the prelates like Bishop Ken (Chap. III) who would not swear allegiance to William and Mary]; hatred of Dissent, or Erastianism [the doctrine of the supremacy of the State in ecclesiastical matters], of liberal thinking; and loyalty to the idea of a priestly Apostolic Church.
>
> Nothing ever had the least effect upon Keble's opinions. They were

unalterable, inaccessible. If he could avoid controversy he avoided
it; if he could not avoid it he lost his temper . . . If you did not
agree with him, there was something morally wrong with you.
His ascendency rested apparently on personality. A man so charming, so boyish and unaffected, so pure and sweet and good, so
humble and so devout, so learned and so eloquent, so capable of
indignation for the truth, must have seemed to those who shared
his vision of the truth a living proof of their own rightness.*

On the basis of such an appraisal it is easy to trace Keble's influence on the
immensely significant movement described in Chapter VIII. He is still
further commemorated by the founding of Keble College, Oxford, now a
place of pilgrimage for art lovers because the chapel contains Holman
Hunt's famous picture "The Light of the World."

### New every morning is the love       [1822]

In the *Christian Year* the first poem is named "Morning." It begins
with five stanzas of description given in characteristically romantic fashion.
Man's spirit is touched into worship by the beauty of nature:

> Hues of the rich unfolding morn,
> That, e'er the glorious sun be born,
> By some soft touch invisible
> Around his path are taught to swell;—
>
> Thou rustling breeze so fresh and gay,
> That dancest forth at opening day,
> And brushing by with joyous wing,
> Wakenest each little leaf to sing;—(Sts. 1–2)

This is very pretty but it is not a hymn; you cannot imagine singing it in
church. But when you come to Keble's stanza 6 an authentic strain of
religious meditation begins. The editors have therefore chosen original
stanzas 6–9 and 14 as having the true hymnic elements: they can be sung
by a congregation and they are worthy of the universal use they have
attained.

*Stanza 1.* Our return to consciousness from the mystery of sleep
and from the dangers of night prove God's love.
*Stanza 2.* The new day will be full of new experiences—mercies,
perils, sins forgiven, holy thoughts, hopes.
*Stanza 3.* If we hallow all these, God makes them precious.
*Stanza 4.* Religion will transfigure both the old and the new.
*Stanza 5.* Daily self-denial in common tasks is a road to God.
*Stanza 6.* May we merit heaven, and make life and prayer agree.

* Published by Scribner's, New York; Faber and Faber, London.

The village of Hursley.

Keble's church at Hursley.

## Sun of my soul, thou Saviour dear    [1820]

In the *Christian Year* this poem is named "Evening" and is based upon Lk 24:29. Of the original fourteen stanzas most hymnals give from four to six, though never Keble's first stanza:

'Tis gone, that bright and orbed blaze,
Fast fading from our wistful gaze;
Yon mantling cloud has hid from sight
The last faint pulse of quivering light.

The thought alternates between day and night—nature and its changes reveal God and His providence: prayer for the constant and unobscured vision of Christ; for His presence in life or death; for the sinful, the sick, the poor, and those who mourn; prayer for tomorrow's journey and the final immersion in God's love.

## Blest are the pure in heart    [1819]

Written for "The Purification for Saint Mary the Virgin," otherwise called "The Presentation of Christ in the Temple," observed on February 2nd. The Gospel for the day is Lk 2:22–40 which describes the event.

The poem is a paean of praise over the first visit of Jesus, who is Priest, King, God, to His Temple at Jerusalem, accompanied by the invisible armies of heaven. In allusive language Mary, Joseph, Simeon and Anna are presented. Since that day, uncounted throngs have met Him in His temple—which is the humble and contrite heart.

Little of all this appears in our hymn. The editor of a hymnal in 1836 chose stanzas 1 and 17 of the original poem, and to round them out to the standard length of a hymn added two stanzas of his own. In a sense we may regard all four stanzas as Keble's, for Keble saw and authorized the use of the hymn in that form which is the one used today. The hymn exalts purity of heart: it is an extended commentary on Mt 5:8, the text affixed to the original poem by Keble himself.

Keble also translated hymns from the Greek. See "Hail! gladdening Light."

## JAMES EDMESTON (1791–1867) Anglican

ONE of the few hymn writers who was not a clergyman. He was a celebrated London architect and surveyor. Though grandson of an Independent minister, early in life he joined the Anglican Communion and in later years became a churchwarden. His Evangelical bent characteristically led him to be a constant visitor to the London Orphan Asylum, where he found inspiration for many of his children's hymns. Altogether he wrote 2000 of them—one every Sunday! which he read at family prayers, an

Evangelical "means of grace." Some of his hymns were written for cottage prayer-meetings, another Evangelical institution, and doubtless in his case an aftermath of the family's Independent tradition. Of his 2000 hymns only two survive in general use, the most popular of which, described by Julian as one of the finest evening hymns in the English language, is

### Saviour, breathe an evening blessing     [1820]

The introduction to this hymn in Edmeston's *Sacred Lyrics* where it first appeared was: "At night their short evening hymn, 'Jesus Mahaxaros' (Jesus, forgive us) stole through the camp—Salte's *Travels in Abyssynia.*"

The words are so simple that they need no explanation. It is well, however, to note the Scriptural basis for some of them:

Stanza 1 is a typical confession and petition suitable for an evening bedside prayer. Stanza 2 is based upon Ps 91:5–6, 10–11; Stanza 3, upon Ps 139:11–12. Stanza 4 is Edmeston's paraphrase of Dr. Watts' child-prayer which beyond doubt his mother taught him to use:

> If I should die before I wake,
> I pray thee, Lord, my soul to take.

Various editors have modified the original hymn by new phrases, omissions, or the addition of whole stanzas. Bishop Bickersteth in 1870 added two stanzas beginning "Father, to thy holy keeping" and "Blessed Spirit, brooding o'er us." Godfrey Thring added in 1882, "Be thou nigh should death o'ertake us." They would better have left Edmeston alone.

### Lead us, heavenly Father, lead us     [1821]

Written for the children of the London Orphan Asylum, it is a three-fold prayer for the Triune God's supervision, forgiveness, and the ensuing blessings of joy, peace and love. The words need no explanation; but most people are not aware of how they are impregnated with Scripture, which of course the writer knew by heart through his daily reading at family prayers. Some of these inspiring passages are here given:

*Stanza 1.* God, being not simply a god to be placated, but a *Father*, will protect us from evil: Ps 17:8; Mt 6:13; Jn 17:35; 1 Cor 10:13; direct our affairs: Ps 32:8; 73:24; Is 58:11; give us unfailing security: Ps 32:7; 121:7–8; 2 Tim 4:18; give us nourishment both physical and spiritual: Ps 23; 40:11; Rev 7:17. Thus all blessings we may desire are ours: Deut 11:26–27; Ps 24:4–5; Mal 3:10.

*Stanza 2.* God also is *Saviour:* He forgives because having partaken of our human nature He knows our weakness: Heb 2:18; He can enter into our suffering: Jn 11:32–36; He was tempted: Heb 4:15; He was weary: Jn 4:6; He was often solitary: Mk 1:12–13; Lk 9:10 (A.V.).

*Stanza 3.* God is also *Spirit* (completing the Trinity) and therefore can give us gifts that are distinctly spiritual: Acts 2:1–4;
13:52; joy, love, peace: Jn 14:27; Rom 5:1; 14:17; 15:13; Gal 5:22;
Phil 4:7; Heb 13:20–21.

*Rev. HENRY HART MILMAN* (1791–1868) English, Anglican

MILMAN was one of the choice spirits of the early nineteenth
century. An Oxford man (Brasenose College), he showed his brilliant parts
while still an undergraduate by winning the Newdigate prize for poetry,
and three other literary prizes. Then successively he became Fellow of
Brasenose, Professor of Poetry at Oxford, Canon of Westminster, and Dean
of St. Paul's Cathedral, London. All through his life he did literary work of
a high order: he wrote dramas, translated Greek plays, wrote a History of
the Jews, a History of Latin Christianity, besides other volumes of conspicuous merit. For each of his three religious dramas he received £500.
He was one of the most popular of the romantic poets. His hymns represent
the romantic or literary spirit at its best; all thirteen of his were written for
Heber's proposed hymnal, which the Bishop of London turned down as
premature (see above under Heber), and therefore date before Heber
went to India in 1823. Both he and Heber were High Church, but the
latter died before the Oxford Movement made the name a fighting word,
and the former never became a partisan.

*Ride on! ride on in majesty!*　　[Before 1823]

Written for Palm Sunday; probably the best on that subject. The
point of view is that of Mt 21:1–11, which sees in the act of Jesus the
fulfillment of ancient prophecy (Zech 9:9). And in general it follows the
theological interpretation of Jesus as God, who to carry out a pre-ordained
plan came to earth and went through the appearance of enacting a tragedy
in order that man might be saved from hell. The "appearance" is hinted
in such phrases as "humble beast," "lowly," "to die," "sad and wondering
eyes," "approaching sacrifice," "last and fiercest strife," "bow thy meek
head to mortal pain." But these are only seeming realities. The truth,
hidden from the eyes of Jesus' contemporaries, is revealed to us in such
words as "majesty," "thy triumphs now begin," "angel armies of the sky,"
"sapphire throne," "anointed Son," "Take, O God, thy power and reign."
Through the humble and tragic events of a mortal drama the poet allows
us to see the cosmic significance of a vast plan of redemption, conceived
"before the foundation of the world." The skillful way in which the poet
has blended sight and insight, together with the dignity and exaltation of
his language, makes this a superb piece of poetry.

*Rev. HENRY FRANCIS LYTE (1793–1847)* Scottish, Anglican Evangelical

LYTE lives only in his hymns. Born in Scotland in humble circumstances, left an orphan when still a child, educated first as a charity student at a boys' school in Ireland, then at Trinity College, Dublin, where he had a hard struggle with poverty, he entered the ministry of the Anglican Church at the age of 21 and was assigned to a small parish in Ireland. He might have remained a typical professional priest who reads morning and evening prayer regularly, baptizes, marries and buries his parishioners, and otherwise enjoys private studies or sports. A hint that this was originally true of Lyte lies in a stanza omitted from "Abide with me":

> Thou on my head in early youth didst smile;
> And, though rebellious and perverse meanwhile,
> Thou hast not left me, oft as I left Thee.

But a change came over him. A neighboring clergyman, possibly of that worldly type, sent for him in his last sickness in great agony of soul because he was unpardoned and unprepared to die. They both turned to the Bible to find out if they could how men could be saved, and in the process both of them had a religious experience that the Methodists would call conversion. That experience made a great change in the life and the preaching of Lyte, but the strain of it all caused a long illness and left him with asthma and a tendency to consumption.

After being moved from one parish to another, in the course of which he fell in love with an heiress and married her, Lyte was transferred in 1823 to Lower Brixham in Devonshire. That town was one of the scores of picturesque places that stud the coast of England. From the pier on which William of Orange landed in 1688 to help Parliament get rid of Catholic James II, the fishermen's houses climb steeply, look down upon the fleet of trawlers for which the town is famous, as they snuggle into the tiny harbor or sweep out into the Channel towards Cherbourg. Here Lyte labored for twenty-four years. His people were busy, shrewd, somewhat rough and disorderly, but warm-hearted; to them he gave himself in sacrificial service. He gathered a Sunday school of nearly eight hundred children in the days when schools were few, and trained some seventy teachers for the children. For this parish he wrote all of the hymns that made him famous the world around—"hymns for his little ones, hymns for his hardy fishermen and hymns for sufferers like himself." His heavy duties wore upon a constitution that was never robust. Finally in 1844 he broke down. Thereafter he had to spend his winters on the French Riviera where he could rest in the presence of the sea he loved, coming home summers to be with his church. Returning to Nice in September 1847, he died almost immediately. He lies buried there in the English cemetery overlooking the Mediterranean.

He left to the world three hymns that seem to be immortal:

### Jesus, I my cross have taken     [1824]

Based upon Mk 10:28. Originally in six stanzas.

Out of disappointment and ill-health came this passionate cry of surrender. Lyte wrote it the year after he was assigned to Brixham. As noted above, he had passed through an experience which meant the entire reconstruction of his inner life and which had worn upon his already frail health. Then had come his quick shifts to three parishes to find a climate he could endure, and finally this tiny fishing village. His sensitive nature must have

The fishing village of Brixham where Lyte ministered for 24 years.

shrunk from contact with these burly and often immoral people, but he learned to love them, to devote himself to them sacrificially, and won their hearts completely so that his church was crowded every Sunday. He visited the fishermen on their boats and took care that a Bible was placed on every ship before it left port. Larger social questions also engaged his support, especially Wilberforce's agitation for the abolition of slavery. At first it was a hard struggle, but he took courage from the example of his Master. He too could put aside his ambitions, scholarly or social, accept his limitations, and with bleeding feet walk his *Via Dolorosa* behind his Lord. Read through this hymn and see how many phrases express the reaction of his sensitive spirit to the inevitable. Like a true mystic he takes refuge in Christ; he learned how to accept suffering and use it. The record of his twenty-four years at Brixham tells the story of his self-conquest and the hymns that survive still further document it.

### Praise, my soul, the King of heaven     [1834]

Lyte's stanza 4 is omitted in all our hymnals; also instead of "Alleluia, Alleluia" in line five he wrote "Praise him, praise him."

The hymn is based upon Ps 103 but the rendering is too free to suggest the original phraseology. In fact, the little collection of Psalm paraphrases which he printed in 1834 for his own congregation was titled *Spirit of the Psalms*. Certainly this hymn is the spirit and not the letter.

It is wonderful to see what ten years of work in little Brixham did to Lyte. Contrast the near-despair of "Jesus, I my cross have taken" with the exultation of this hymn. No longer do "human hearts and looks deceive" him; whether the world may "despise and leave" him no longer counts. Introspection and self-pity have changed to thankfulness that God in His mercy has enabled him to rise to the challenge of a great task. "Ransomed, healed, restored, forgiven"—these words have in them the ring of a man who has climbed out of despair into sunshine and self-forgetfulness. Ill-health still dogs his steps, but "well our feeble frame he knows," and every down curve somehow flattens out and then rises. No wonder his own praise seems so inadequate that he calls upon angels and the heavenly bodies to join in his "Alleluia." This is Christian life at its best and fullest.

## Abide with me   [1847]

The original had eight stanzas. The omission of three has improved the hymn.

The last few years of Lyte's life at Brixham were unhappy. During his long absences on account of his health, dissensions arose in his church. Some members withdrew and joined the Plymouth Brethren; his choir also that had contributed so much, refused to function further. But he still clung to the hope that he might yet make some lasting contribution to the spiritual life of his people. That hope was fulfilled in his final hymn—and more than fulfilled. It was written on his last Sunday at Brixham, after the sermon and the Communion Service at which he officiated.

Several conflicting accounts of the origin of this hymn have arisen. The most probable was printed in *The British Weekly*, April 3, 1947, condensed as follows:

> Charles Potter, the gardener of the parsonage "Berry Head" from his youth to a ripe old age, asserts that after tea on that last Sunday, Lyte walked in the valley garden in front of the home, then down to the rocks, where he sat and composed. It was a lovely sunny day and the sun was setting over distant Dartmoor in a blaze of glory. On the left lay Brixham harbor like a pool of molten gold, with its picturesque trawling vessels lying peacefully at anchor. After the sun had set Lyte returned to his study. His family thought he was resting, but he was putting the finishing touches to his immortal hymn.

Immediately thereafter the hymn was printed with its original tune in leaflet form. Its great service to the world, however, began when the Anglican

Church abandoned its three-century-long devotion to metrical *Psalms* and published the hymn in its first hymnal, *Hymns Ancient and Modern,* in 1861. The hymn is now found in practically every hymnbook printed in the English language.

The hymn is wholly about death. The imagery, to be sure, is taken from the phenomenon of the passing day in its several sequences—falling eventide, deepening darkness, growing dimness, fading glories, but these are only metaphors which suggest the ebbing tide of life. When this description is finished the poet turns in stanza three to his spiritual need in this critical hour, then to his courage vouchsafed by his Lord's presence, and finally to his triumphant hope. Everything now vanishes but the Cross, which in turn is the herald of heaven's morning.

The fact that this hymn about death is so frequently sung, especially at young people's meetings, is undoubtedly due to the music which Dr. Monk wrote for it and which so perfectly interprets it. Singularly, the composition which took Dr. Monk only ten minutes was inspired both by a glorious sunset and a great personal sorrow. Today no one ever sings it to any other tune.

## SIR JOHN BOWRING (1792–1872) Unitarian

SIR JOHN ranks high among the geniuses of the English-speaking world. First of all he was one of the greatest linguists who ever lived. Over a period of forty years he published translations of poetry from the Russian, Batavian, Spanish, Polish, Serbian, Bohemian, Magyar, Czech and Hungarian languages. He mastered Chinese in record time. He early became interested in social progress: advocated free trade, abolition of the Corn Laws, favored parliamentary reform, Catholic emancipation, popular education, prison reform, abolition of flogging in the navy, the release of the Manx people from feudal tyranny. These were topics filled with dynamite in the 1820's and '30's.

Next the government commandeered him to investigate commercial relations, a task that took him to France, Switzerland, Italy, Syria, Germany, Siam. Successively he was a member of Parliament (twice), consul at Canton and superintendent of trade with China; governor of Hong Kong (1854), invested with supreme naval and military power. Apparently from the dusty records Sir John was, with one exception, the most unpopular governor Hong Kong ever had. Sir Henry Parkes, the governor of Amoy, wrote of him: "He is full of conceit and without any very clear idea of political principles on a large scale." His high-handed policy, his insolence in dealing with the Chinese, brought on the second Opium War (1856–58). During the hostilities the mandarins put a price on his head. He had a narrow escape when the attempt was made to wipe out the entire British colony by putting arsenic in the bread. He did not die but his health was impaired and Lady Bowring later died from the effects. In this war China was beaten ingloriously, Peking was looted and burned, and the Celestial Empire was forced to cede Kowloon (opposite Hong Kong) to England, open up Tientsin and ten river ports to trade, and grant permission for missionaries to preach and hold property anywhere. It is humiliating to know that Christian privileges in China are based upon opium and war!

Though Sir John was technically retired in 1860, his public services continued long after—commissioner to Italy, "minister plenipotentiary and envoy extraordinary" at posts from Hawaii to the various courts of Europe. All his life his pen was busy with translations, original poetry, economic and religious essays. Many honors and decorations were conferred upon him, including membership in most of the learned societies of Europe. In his eightieth year he addressed 3000 people in Plymouth with all the energy of youth. He was buried in Exeter within a stone's throw of the house where he was born.

How can we reconcile the tough diplomat which was Sir John with the Christian gentleman, the most hated governor of Hong Kong with the sweet singer whose hymns still inspire the Christian Church the world around? A study of the dates of his life gives the answer. The hymns that have lived were all written when he was about 30 years old, when his poetic interests were uppermost, when the idealism of youth made him the champion of the downtrodden and the underprivileged. But with his rise to power other traits emerged, and while no one ever breathed a syllable against his personal character, his public acts are a commentary on Lord Acton's dictum, "Power corrupts." In the endeavor to uphold and expand the unholy imperialistic aims of Great Britain, he lost sight of the principles that alone make for public virtue, forced opium upon China and robbed her of treasure and her sovereignty. "God is love, his mercy brightens" and "In the cross of Christ I glory" were relegated to a water-tight compartment that had no relation to power politics. That failure to carry through, to harmonize personal with civic and political virtue, has been one of the perpetual tragedies of religion, and both humanity and the Church have paid the price.

### *In the Cross of Christ I glory*     [Published 1825]

There is a tradition in Macao, thirty-five miles up-river from Hong Kong, that when Bowring wrote this hymn he had in mind the cross that still surmounted the ruined church of St. Paul's in that town. Surely the ruin might be taken as a symbol, for Macao was a forlorn relic of the far-flung Portuguese Empire that reached its eastern limits here in 1557. But the dates show that this hymn was written thirty years before Bowring ever saw Macao. The imagery came out of the poet's imagination buttressed by his survey of world history, as the theme was inspired by Paul: "Far be it from me to glory save in the cross of our Lord Jesus Christ" (Gal 6:14).

A traveler like Sir John would often have been reminded of wrecked empires, civilizations and religions. The Pyramids are ruined relics of an

Egyptian Empire built by devotees of the mighty gods Re and Ptah. Babylon lies buried around the ziggurat of the god Marduk; the noble religion of Ahuramazda died when Alexander set the torch to Persepolis; Zeus lost his grip when Rome wiped Corinth off the map, and Jupiter, his Roman counterpart, fell when the barbarians sacked the Eternal City. The Cross had already begun to conquer both Rome and the religion of Mithra when Constantine saw it blazing in the sky before his battle of Mulvian Bridge, and although Thor and Allah both waged mighty wars against it, it never came down for long from the spires of Europe. When Sir John was a child, the leaders of the French Revolution had pulled down the

Sir John Bowring.

*Copyright National Portrait Gallery, London*

Cross from the churches of Paris, abolished Sunday and the Christian calendar, crowned Reason as their goddess and as a symbol enthroned a courtesan upon the high altar of the Church of the Madeleine. But before long all this passed and the Cross once more shone against the sky. Something like that must have passed before the poet's imagination.

In our own day the mightiest attack of all time had been thrown against the Cross—for in the last analysis, the Great War of 1941–45 was the struggle of a civilization based upon the ideals of Christianity to survive against the attack of a paganism based wholly upon materialism and atheism. But the armies of the pagans have been destroyed and the radiance of the Cross, we fervently hope and pray, will again stream over another wreck of time. So this is the documentation of stanza 1.

In the remaining stanzas the hymn becomes personal rather than historic. In times of defeat, fear, disappointment, the Cross stands by with its deliverance. The poet does not tell us how it is able to do this, but human experience has shown that contemplation of the sufferings of Christ and the lesson of victory through self-sacrifice implicit in the Cross are a powerful inspiration.

On the other hand, when things are going well, consciousness that our lives are linked with Christ and God puts the glory of eternity under our fleeting happiness.

In stanza 4 the same ideas are given in another way: the opposites in life are reconciled when we view them "under the aspect of eternity," and the resultant peace and joy are enhanced.

### God is love; his mercy brightens    [Published 1825]

Each stanza of this hymn ends with the refrain, "God is wisdom, God is love." This is the general theme which the other lines embroider with specific illustrations. Light upon our path, happiness aroused, the burden of sorrow lightened—these are evidences of God's wisdom and love (st. 1). Nothing is stable in a changing world except God's mercy—another proof (st. 2). His power to bring light out of darkness, good out of evil, is another proof (st. 3). His practice of weaving bright threads with dark ones in the tapestry of our lives is the final testimony of his wisdom and love (st. 4).

The theme is similar to that of Cowper's hymn, "God moves in a mysterious way." But whereas Cowper makes us feel the darkness and the storm so that the author's own pathological state is the dominant element, Bowring lets the light shine strongly over the landscape. For that reason we seldom sing Cowper's hymn but Bowring's is often used in church. That fact is commentary on a passage Bowring wrote in the preface to his *Hymns* in which these verses first appeared. The writer says (here condensed):

> I have often witnessed with delight the consoling influence produced by the recollection of some passage of devotional poetry, under circumstances the most disheartening, and suffering the most oppressive. Should any fragment of this little book, remembered in moments of gloom and anxiety, tend to restore peace, awaken fortitude, create or strengthen confidence in heaven, I shall have obtained the boon for which I pray.

This hymn is one such fragment which has fulfilled the author's prayer.

### Watchman, tell us of the night    [Published 1825]

The hymn was inspired by an obscure passage in the Bible (Is 21:11–12) written probably during the Exile when all small nations were under the heel of Babylon. It is a dialogue. An American translation clears up somewhat the obscurity:

Someone is calling me from Seir [Edom, south of the Dead Sea]:

> "Watchman, what hour of the night is it?
> Watchman, what hour of the night is it?"
The watchman says:
> "Morning comes, but also night;
> If you wish to know more, come again." *

Seir is evidently in trouble (night) and is looking for relief (morning). He is calling Judah to see if relief is in sight. Judah answers equivocally: "Yes, and No." That is, the future contains for both of us things good and bad. Keep in touch with me.

Bowring's hymn is a moving dramatization of the hopeful side of this oracle. It also interprets the "morning" in a Messianic sense: the new day is the coming of Christ the "Sun of Righteousness" who shall arise to bless the earth with peace and truth. To indicate this he adds to the Old Testament prophecy the New Testament imagery of the star the Wise Men saw in the East.

The three stanzas show us the steady progress toward the day:

*Stanza 1.* The morning star appears over the mountain rim.
*Stanza 2.* The star rises as the earth turns eastward; it shines on more and more areas of darkness.
*Stanza 3.* The dawn flushes the sky; then full day, the realization of the promise of the star.

While this is wholly a work of the imagination and has primary reference to the coming of Christ—prophesied long years ago, anxiously awaited, realized in the manger of Bethlehem—there are suggestions of meaning that are bound up with the times in which Bowring was living. They were trying times. The misery caused by the twenty years of the Napoleonic wars had been intense. Inflated prices, triple the former ones, placed wheat, meat and other foodstuffs quite beyond the reach of prevailing wages; village grazing lands held in common were being "enclosed" for private use by "get-rich-quick" landlords to the impoverishment of the rural masses; the Industrial Revolution was in full swing in which machines were throwing thousands out of work, turning some into hopeless migrants and driving others into the poorhouse. Everything seemed to be rigged up to make the rich richer and the poor poorer. England was on the edge of social upheaval, for there seemed to be no relief through parliamentary reform. But hope began to stir when Robert Owen began his agitation for better treatment of the poor. Trade Unions were made legal the very year this hymn was written. William Cobbett and other reformers began to publish radical magazines—though hundreds of editors were sent to jail again and again. Then repressive acts by Parliament grew less frequent; more and more leaders like Canning, Peel, Grey, were raising their voices for reform. Young Bowring himself edited the *Westminster Review* in cooperation with the radical Jeremy Bentham and

* Translated by J. M. P. Smith, University of Chicago Press.

fought for the needed reforms mentioned. These movements might well be symbolized by the Star of this hymn, the promised day, whose blessings were not to be confined to England alone but should "burst o'er all the earth." (Slavery was abolished in all British domains in 1833.) These matters will be more fully discussed in the next chapter of this book.

But Bowring may have had in mind also the growing missionary movement (see above under Heber). Only a generation previous, an Anglican bishop had told the young enthusiast, William Carey, "Young man, if God wants to save the heathen he will do it without any help from you." But Carey nevertheless became the first English missionary, and was at that time transforming the life of Bengal by his scholarship, his practical help for farmers and his Christian character and teaching, while, to aid in this work, the British and Foreign Bible Society was founded in 1804. The beloved Heber wrote his great missionary hymn in 1819 and went to India as Bishop of Calcutta in 1823. The symbolism of Bowring's hymn—"higher yet that star ascends," "the morning seems to dawn," "See, it bursts o'er all the earth"—may well envisage this mounting concern of those who had the gospel for those who had it not. This is doubtless the reason why "Watchman, tell us of the night" ranks with "Jesus shall reign" and "From Greenland's icy mountains" as one of the Church's great missionary hymns.

### Rev. HUGH STOWEL (1799–1865) English (Manx), Anglican

A POPULAR and effective preacher who never rose higher than Honorary Canon of Chester Cathedral, he wrote one hundred hymns, many of them for Sunday school children. Only one has survived:

### From every stormy wind that blows      [1828] (altered)

Compare the imagery of this poem with that of Moore's "Come ye disconsolate" above. Both allude to the "mercy seat," though this poem makes that figure of speech central to the thought.

*Stanza 1* suggests our troubles under the figures "stormy wind" and "swelling tide."
*Stanza 2* recalls the oil of ointment used upon Aaron (Ps 133:2) and the Old Testament symbolism of oil for "gladness" (Is 61:3).
*Stanza 3.* The blending of spirits is suggested by God's communing with the worshipper at the mercy seat (Ex 25:22).
*Stanza 4* gives the final result of prayer: inspiration and a timeless sense of union and glory. Is 40:31 gives the poet the "eagle" imagery.

### Rev. ANDREW REED (1787–1862) Congregational

TRAINED to be a watch-maker, he yielded to an inner call, studied at Hackney College and became a Congregational minister. Beginning with a church in East London, his congregation outgrew the building, and at the larger Wycliffe Chapel he continued for thirty years (1831–61). Following with great interest the social awakening of his time, he immersed himself in philanthropic work, and, being a most skilful organizer, he was the leading spirit in founding six great benevolent institutions—two asylums for orphans, two for idiots, one for infants and one for incurables—these at a cost of over $600,000. He was a great promoter also of missions, home and foreign. "I sprang from the people, I have lived for the people" is his summary of his life-work.

While all his mature work fell within the Victorian era when people's movements were in full swing, his hymns preceded the reforming 1830's.

### *Spirit divine, attend our prayers*     [1829]

In February 1829 the Congregational ministers of London held a Good Friday service in the slum section of East London with the purpose of arousing a religious revival in all British churches. Since this hymn had recently appeared in the *Evangelical Magazine*, the London Board requested that it be sung. It was, of course, very appropriate, but it is pretty prosaic poetry.

> *Stanza 1.* A prayer for the presence of God's spirit in the meetings.
> *Stanza 2.* A prayer for illumination—with no allusion to the Nicene characterization of Christ as "Light of light" (see Ambrose, Chap. IX).
> *Stanza 3.* A prayer for purification—the figure of fire that burns out impurities and suggests the spirit of sacrifice.
> *Stanza 4.* A prayer for peace—the figure of the dove, without reference to the Trinitarian doctrine of the Holy Spirit. The prayer was needed to subdue the warring factions that divided the Church then, as now.
> *Stanza 5.* A repetition of the essence of stanza 1, with the area expanded from a single sanctuary to the whole world.

The Oxford Movement with its re-emphasis upon the Apostolic Church and the Nicene formula of the Trinity has not yet arisen. The Spirit here is simply that of God at work in the hearts of men, without reference to creedal distinctions.

### *HARRIET AUBER* (1773–1862) Anglican

MISS AUBER was of French Huguenot extraction, her great-great-grandfather having fled from Normandy after the Revocation of the Edict of Nantes in 1685 whereby Protestantism in France became a crime. Her long life of 89 years was passed in the seclusion of tiny villages. She lives only in her poetry.

In 1829 she published *The Spirit of the Psalms* consisting mainly of devotional verse on scriptural subjects taken from both the Old and New Testaments. She hoped that her improved version of the Psalms might displace the old Sternhold and Hopkins version which still maintained its strangle-hold on the Anglican Church. Perhaps her work helped along the inevitable. Excerpts from this poetry gradually found their way into many hymnals, chiefly in America, but the spirit of the age has now passed her by, so that now only the following remains in common use:

### Our blest Redeemer, e'er he breathed     [1829]

This poetry version of the function of the Holy Spirit and His descent on Pentecost was written for use on Whitsunday, fifty days after Easter.

*Stanza 1.* A reminiscence of two passages: Jn 20:21–22; Jn 14:16.
*Stanza 2.* A description of the coming and of the function of the Holy Spirit: Acts 2:1–4.
*Stanza 3.* Jn 14:17.
*Stanzas 4–6.* In these last stanzas there is no Biblical phraseology; but anyone can feel in them the spirit of love and devotion which characterized this gentle poet. For her the Holy Spirit is admonisher, encourager, inspirer to virtue, victory and holiness.

### Rev. WILLIAM HILEY BATHURST (1796–1877) Anglican

BORN of a good family—his father a Rt. Hon. Member of Parliament—educated at Winchester School and Christ Church, Oxford, and a rector at Leeds, he resigned his living in 1852 because he could not reconcile his doctrinal views with the *Book of Common Prayer.* In his latter years he would be classified as Broad Church. But since his surviving hymn was written before the Oxford Movement was started he is here placed. He was author of more than two hundred hymns besides more than one hundred metrical versions of Psalms.

### O for a faith that will not shrink     [1831]

First published in his *Psalms and Hymns for Private Use,* with the caption "The Power of Faith—Lk 17:5."
The straightforward and unemotional verses list the situations in life that call for faith in God and His providence: enemies, sickness, poverty, times of stress and danger, perplexity, and the difficulty of pursuing the narrow way to the end. The possession of such a faith gives one a foretaste of heaven.

### EBENEZER ELLIOTT (1781–1849) English Unitarian

ELLIOTT, an iron merchant of Sheffield, was "the product of a Unitarian Sunday School." Whether he had any further connection with that denomination does not appear; we only know that in general the Unitarians, being deprived of the franchise, were very ardently behind the reform movements of the early nineteenth century. Elliott also was one of the notable agitators. His life takes us into one of the most desperate fights the English people ever waged against their government. It centered first around the Reform Act that certain Whig statesmen, backed by popular groups, were trying to force through a hostile Tory Parliament. By the reform they hoped to extend the franchise to individual workers and others who could not meet the property qualifications for voting and office-holding. Just before the turn of the century, for example, there were only 214,000 men in all England who could vote; and voting was so weighted in favor of the aristocrats, the Universities, the property-holders, that out of 530 members of Parliament, 300 of them were chosen by 162 favored people, 88 of whom were appointed directly by peers. But this agitation was closely connected also with the repeal of the Corn Laws (high tariffs on foodstuffs) which made earning a living on the part of poor people a desperate thing.

The reformers set out deliberately to create public opinion against what they regarded as injustice: they organized petitions—some of them signed by more than a million people, they founded societies and held conferences. The fight reached its pitch of intensity in the 1840's with the Chartist Movement. (See Chap. XII, Introduction, and under "Ring out, wild bells.") Elliott was in the thick of the fight. His weapon was poetry which he contributed to his local newspaper. So apt and poignant were his early verses that he won the nickname of "The Corn Law Rhymer." Out of these verses first gathered into a volume in 1831, here is a sample to show how vividly he pictured the desperate plight of the poor for whom he was fighting:

Tune: "Robin Adair"

Child, is thy father dead?
    Father is gone!
Why did they tax his bread?
    God's will be done!
Mother has sold her bed;
Better to die than wed!
Where shall she lay her head?
    Home we have none!

Father clamm'd thrice a week—
    God's will be done!
Long for work did he seek,
    Work he found none.

His one hymn to survive is

Tears on his hollow cheek
Told what no tongue could speak:
Why did his master break?
    God's will be done!

Doctor said air was best—
    Food we had none;
Father, with panting breast,
    Groan'd to be gone:
Now he is with the blest—
Mother says death is best!
We have no place of rest—
    Yes, we have one!

## *When wilt thou save the people?*     [1832]

*Stanza 1.* This is not a disloyal cry. Thrones and crowns are an
ancient English heritage and no one wants to abolish them—even
though William IV was as disreputable a monarch as any since
Charles II. But the prayer is for the common people who live in the
dark—people who ought to be nourished like roses but are treated
as if they were thistles.

*Stanza 2.* How can crime bring crime? The crime perpetuated by
the government of treating men like beasts brings retaliation in more
criminal acts on the part of men. Wilberforce, the great Emanci-
pator, used to inveigh against "our bloody laws," which would imprison for the slightest offense and hang for not much more. He once
wrote in his diary: "Hanging has been tried too long, and with the
success which might have been expected from it. The most effective
way to prevent greater crimes is . . . by endeavoring to repress that
general spirit of licentiousness which is the parent of every species
of vice." (See stanza 3:7 below.)

How can strength aid the strong? When the industrialists and the
commercial interests of England became rich they sided with the
Tories to preserve the privileges for themselves, not to give them to
the poor who needed them most. In this way the worker in the
factory or the mine creates the wealth that keeps him more securely
in his helpless position—he "toils for wrong."

Nature itself cries out against such a situation: Is the sun created to
shine only on the rich or does the beauty of the mountain exist only
for the pleasure of the peer? No! Their very universality protests
against the exclusive prerogatives of the upper classes.

*Stanza 3.* All men are God's children, as valuable in His sight as the
angels. God save them from sin—which is their personal contribution
to their own suffering; from oppression—which is chargeable to unjust economic and political laws; from despair—to which they are
driven by both the others.

Truly this is a cry the likes of which has not yet been heard in English
hymnody but which is destined to be raised with greater insistence as the
nineteenth century moves toward the twentieth. (See Chap. XII, The Victorian Era; XIII, American Hymnody, final sections.)

### SIR ROBERT GRANT (1779–1838) Scottish, Anglican

SIR ROBERT belonged to a famous Aberdeen family, which
strangely enough was not Presbyterian but Anglican. His father, Charles
Grant, was one of the early members of the Evangelical wing of the Church
to become influential in civic affairs, along with Wilberforce the Emanci-
pator, Zachary Macaulay, Governor of the freed slave colony of Sierra Leone,

James Stephen, Under Secretary to the Colonies, Lord Dartmouth, Colonial Secretary, and Lord Teignmouth, Governor-General of India. The Methodist "enthusiasm," developing first in the lower ranks of society, by 1800 had spread upward and into the Anglican fold until a genuine Christian force was leavening the governing class. The father Charles went as a young man to India, where he rose to be a member of the Board of Trade, and on returning to Scotland was elected to Parliament and finally was chosen chairman of the East India Company. He was a generous supporter of the Church's missionary work and was largely responsible for the removal of barriers to missions formerly maintained by the East India Company.

This residence in India accounts for the fact that his second son, Sir Robert, was born in that country, became a director of the East India Company, member of Parliament and finally Governor of Bombay. He also continued and enhanced the Evangelical influence of the family, for to his other accomplishments he added the art of poetry. Though he wrote little, he wrote well. Only one of his twelve hymns has survived in common use.

### *O worship the King, all glorious above*      [1833]

This hymn was written the year before he became Governor of Bombay. It is based on portions of Psalm 104, which is one of the most impassioned Biblical descriptions of the Creator and His works. Something of the original sweep and exaltation has been preserved in this hymn; and, while the descriptions are general in contrast to the specific nature-pictures of the Psalm, the emotional content is strong. Each of the epithets applied to God—King, Shield, Defender, Ancient of Days, Maker, Redeemer, Friend—arouses Biblical reminiscences, while the last two become intimate and personal. It is no small accomplishment to combine, as this hymn does, the majestic, the tender, and a smooth-flowing poetical rendering. Sir Robert offers a development of thought parallel to the six days of creation in Gen 1.

### CHARLOTTE ELLIOTT (1789–1871) Anglican, Low

THE perfect representative of the Evangelical wing of the Anglican Church is this saintly woman. She was granddaughter to a famous Evangelical preacher, daughter of another, niece of two others, and all her Christian training centered on piety rather than on what she called "Puseyite errors," that is, on the emphases of the Oxford Movement. Her life at Clapham (now part of London) and Brighton was secluded largely because of her illnesses, for with brief intermissions she was an invalid during her last fifty years. And so one who in her earlier days was natural and gay—within the limits set for "females" by the pious tradition of her time and environment—and one who wrote humorous poems, she became introspective, "acquainted with grief," and therefore particularly fitted to minister spiritually to those who were similarly afflicted. This is shown in the titles of her collected poems: *The Invalid's Hymn Book*, 1834, originally a compilation to which in its various editions she contributed 112 hymns; her own *Hours of Sorrow Cheered and Comforted,* 1836. This last contained such titles as: "A Vision, composed during a thunderstorm"; "To one deprived of hearing at church through deafness"; "On a restless night in illness"; "To a mother, on the death of a child of great promise"; "To one whose mind was disordered by grief." Later with a broader outlook, *Morning and Evening Hymns for a Week,* 1839, and *Thoughts in Verse on Sacred Subjects,* 1869. All told her hymns number about 150. One great satisfaction to her was the immense sale of her books. They evidently met a spiritual need.

### *Just as I am without one plea*      [1834]

Several myths have grown up about the composition of this hymn. The facts, however, seem to be these: While she was living at Brighton her clergyman brother was trying to establish a school where at nominal cost the daughters of poor clergymen might be educated. To assist in raising money he organized a bazaar in preparation for which all his parish were hard at work. On the opening day Miss Elliott, ill and unable to help, obsessed with her feeling of uselessness, wrote this hymn. "She gathered up in her soul the great certainties, not of her emotions but of her salvation—her Lord, his power, his promise—and deliberately set down for her own comfort the formula of her faith; restated to herself the gospel of pardon, peace and heaven."

The sale of this hymn aided the cause more than any bazaar; the title-pages of the various editions of *Hymns for the Week* contain the note, "Sold for the benefit of St. Margaret's Hall, Brighton."

The hymn was always printed beneath the text, "Him that cometh to me I will in no wise cast out" (Jn 6:37). This was warrant for the opening phrase of each stanza, "Just as I am." Acceptance of Christ for no preparation, no endeavor to make one's self worthy; "to rid my soul of one dark blot" absolute surrender is all that is needed. The price paid by Christ covers all possible sins. The successive stanzas mention some of the limitations and failures of which the soul is conscious: conflicts, doubts, fears, poverty of accomplishment, wretchedness, spiritual blindness; then enumerate the opposites that are found in Christ and may be had by surrender: sight, riches, healing of the mind, welcome, pardon, cleansing, relief. The contemplation of these contrasts drives one's will into action—"O Lamb of God, I come."

It is easy to recognize beneath the hymn the Calvinistic doctrine of the saving power of the blood of Christ, which constituted the orthodox Evangelical belief; and to note that the Church, the Sacraments, the Liturgy, are not mentioned or suggested. That emphasis is yet to come.

### *My God, my Father, while I stray*      [1834]

This is a hymn of surrender. In every stanza we are minded of the invalidism of the author. While one feels that the self-surrender intrudes too much and limits the usefulness of the hymn, that very quality gives it a poignancy which doubtless has brought help and blessing to many an afflicted soul. All hymns are not for everybody.

### *ANONYMOUS*, Anglican, Low

## *Saviour, like a shepherd lead us*    [1836]

The hymn was first published in *Hymns for the Young* compiled by Miss Dorothy Ann Thrupp (1779–1847), but no authorship was assigned to any in the collection. It may possibly have been written by Rev. Henry F. Lyte, author of "Abide with me."

The hymn is largely on the child's level. The only theological suggestion lies in "Thou hast bought us" (1:6). All the rest is a poetic rendering of the ideas contained in Ps 23, in Jesus' Parable of the Good Shepherd, and in the various Bible passages indicated below. This shows how saturated the author was with the thoughts and language of the Bible—one of the distinguishing marks of an Evangelical.

*Stanza 1.* Ps 23:1; Is 40:11; Ps 23:2; Ezek 34:14–15; Jn 10:9, 11, 15; 1 Cor 6:20; 7:23

*Stanza 2.* Jn 17:6, 9; Ps 23:3; Job 23:10; Jer 31:10–12; Mt. 18:12; Ezek 34:16; Ps 4:1

*Stanza 3.* Jn 6:37; Ps 103:10–12; Num 14:18a; Ps 33:18–19; 130:7; Lk 1:50; Heb 4:16; 1 Jn 1:9; Jn 8:36; Rom 6:18

*Stanza 4.* Ps 90:14; Prov 8:17; Heb 10:7; 1 Jn 4:19; Jn 13:1; Eph 2:4

# HISTORICAL SUMMARY

*Hymnists*
*Romanists*
*Translators*

1830–37    WILLIAM IV.

1830    Riots against tithes, poor laws, etc. Revolution in France frightens England.

1832    *Reform Bill* eliminating "rotten boroughs" and giving industrial cities seats in Parliament.

1833    Abolition of slavery. *Factory Act* reduces women's and children's working hours to 12 and 8!          Newman, 1833

Agitation for repeal of *Corn Laws.* Ten Anglican bishoprics in Ireland abolished. Whigs in power.

1833    Keble's sermon on "National Apostacy" starts the Oxford Movement.

1833–45    Tractarian propaganda for High Church Movement.          Chandler (tr) 1837
Mant (tr) 1837

1837–    Victoria Queen (See Chaps. XII-XV).

Oakeley (tr) 1841
Leeson, 1842

Caswall
  (tr) 1848–49
Campbell
  (tr) 1849
Faber, 1849–54
M. Bridges, 1851
Neale
  (tr) 1851–65
Collins, 1854
Palmer (tr) 1858
Procter, 1858–62
Baker
  (tr) 1859–61
Potter, 1860
Pott (tr) 1861
Ellerton
  (tr) 1868
R. Bridges
  (tr) 1899
Dearmer
  (tr) 1906–33
Draper (tr) 1910
Mattes (tr) 1913
Coffin (tr) 1916
Robbins
  (tr) 1939

## CHAPTER EIGHT

# THE OXFORD MOVEMENT

THE OXFORD MOVEMENT was the endeavor on the part of certain High Churchmen to rescue the Anglican Church from dangers so serious that so notable an Anglican as Headmaster Thomas Arnold of Rugby declared that nothing could save the Established Church as then constituted. This must not be confused with a twentieth century Oxford Group Movement called also the Buckmanite.

It will be necessary for a few moments to set this movement in the economic and political world of the early nineteenth century.

Fundamental is the economic fact of the industrial revolution. The introduction of steam, the removal of industries from the home and the village to large factories were causing a tremendous dislocation. Power looms were putting small weavers out of business. The factories were making more cloth at less cost, especially as child labor was freely used. Thousands of once independent workers were forced into unemployment. Farmers were up in arms; landlords, who had formerly rented land to scores or hundreds of tenants, now were able by the use of machinery to cultivate more acres with fewer men and to undersell everybody. The result was human tragedy, despair, and finally the revolt of the workers against a system that was crushing them.

In 1830 all over southern England there were riots. Laborers destroyed threshing machines and other new implements, burned the hay ricks of especially harsh landowners and ducked in the horse-ponds unpopular overseers of the poor. They demanded from the Church a remission of the hated tithes (Church taxes), and from the landlords a general lowering of rents; from the administrators of the Poor Laws they demanded doles that would enable them at least to subsist. But the rioters were put down mercilessly. Though throughout the whole uprising they had neither killed nor wounded a single person, the government hanged nine of them, transported 457 and sent as many more to prison. England feared a duplication of the French Revolution.

Somehow the rebellious people connected their misery in part with the failure of the Established Church to cope with their real needs and in part they regarded the Church as symbol of vested interests. They voiced their conviction in no uncertain terms. Writes R. W. Church, one of the leaders of the Oxford Movement, "The official leaders of the Church were almost stunned and bewildered by the fierce outbreak of popular hostility."

The counts against the Church were mainly three:

1. The worldliness and spiritual stagnation of the clergy.

All the abuses outlined in the early pages of Chapter V still persisted unchecked into the nineteenth century. Everybody, whether belonging to the Established Church or not, was taxed for the support of a hierarchy that made no adequate return. The people were still sullenly demanding that the government "expell from the parsonage Parson Dolittle and Parson Merryman, and replace them with Parson Lovegood." No wonder Hurrell Froude wrote, "Things are in a bad way down here. The laboring population as well as the farmers seem thoroughly indifferent to the welfare of parsons and squires"(!)

2. The hostility of the Church to all social and political reform.

In the late 1820's a Reform Bill was being debated. The dislocations of population caused by the factory system and the uprooting of farmers had led to the growth of large industrial cities like Sheffield, Leeds, Manchester, Birmingham. These cities had no representation in Parliament while the so-called "rotten boroughs," though they had few inhabitants *or none,* were still given a seat. The fight over the bill that would remedy this evil waxed hot. The squirearchy and the aristocracy who owned most of the land and therefore controlled most of the Parliamentary seats opposed all change. They of course belonged to the Established Church. The clergy, appointed to their "livings" by these same landed proprietors, were naturally on their side of the quarrel; and the bishops, many of whom sat in the House of Lords, were committed to uphold the system that gave them their power. The bill was defeated by the Lords in 1831 but was re-introduced and passed by a narrow margin in 1832.

The people never forgave the Church for its opposition, nor for its hostility to all proposed social reforms—the repeal of the Corn Laws which were keeping up the cost of living, the repeal of savage criminal laws, reducing hours of labor, especially for women and children; abolishing the slave trade; repealing the Test Act which compelled the receiving of the Sacrament from an Angelican clergyman as qualification for public office; the Roman Catholic Relief Act which abolished the requirement for office of taking oaths against the doctrine of Transubstantiation. During this agitation, prelates were being insulted in the streets; the palace of the Bishop of Bristol was burned by a mob.

3. The opposition of the Church to any change in its privileged position.

Parliament was determined to limit the Church's power. Lord Grey, the

OXFORD: CITY AND

*Colleges:* Balliol (E II), Brasenose (E III), Christ Church (B III), Corpus Christi (D IV), Exeter (D II–III), Keble (H° I), Magdalen (I IV), New

Whig Prime Minister, had warned the bishops to "set their house in order," but they held to the theory that the Church was a divine institution and had an authority of its own which the State could not challenge. This came out clearly in the struggle over the situation in Ireland. In that unhappy land more than seven million Catholics were taxed to support a Protestant Church numbering only 850,000 adherents. Twenty-two Anglican bishops drew salaries totaling $750,000 a year, and the rest of the Establishment cost the Catholic peasants $3,000,000 more. This foreign Church was maintained in

° [Keble] not built when this "air-view" was drawn.

E          F          G          H          I

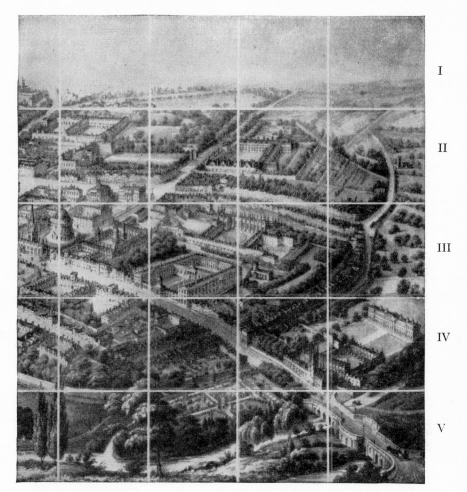

I

II

III

IV

V

UNIVERSITY, C. 1833.

(G III), Oriel (D–E III), Pembroke (A III), Queens (G III), Trinity
(F II), University (E–F III–IV), Wadham (G–H II).

Ireland by armed force. By the Act of 1833 Parliament suppressed two out
of four Anglican archbishoprics in Ireland, eight out of eighteen bishoprics.
Nevertheless, pressure from the Church in England caused the downfall of
the Whig Government that had passed the act. "It seemed intolerable to enthusiastic Churchmen that Parliament should interfere with God's heritage."
They forgot that the Parliament that had established the Church in the first
place (Act of Supremacy, 1559) had power to disestablish it.

This popular hostility to an antiquated and hide-bound Church was one
reason for the decline in Anglican membership and the growth of Dissenting

Churches. By 1800, one fourth of the population of England were acknowledged Dissenters. The new industrial cities were rewarding missionary fields for Methodists, Baptists, Congregationalists. This was the chief reason why the Establishment opposed the granting of the electorate to these cities: it knew that they would vote Whig and so increase the hostile radical element in Parliament.

The Oxford Movement in its first phase was the attempt of High Church to "vindicate its privileges under the threat of spoliation by a Whig government." Its second phase was an attempt, not primarily to reform abuses, but to defend the theory of a Catholic and Apostolic Church ordained by Christ Himself.

The movement began on July 14, 1833, with a sermon by John Keble, entitled "National Apostacy." It was preached at St. Mary's Church, Oxford, before His Majesty's judges of Assize, and written, says the preface to the printed edition, "In anticipation of legislation soon to be passed by which the Parliament (the members of which are not even bound to profess belief in the Atonement) assumes control over the Church; so that the Apostolic Church in this realm is henceforth only to stand, in the eyes of the state, as *one sect among many,* depending for any pre-eminence she may still appear to retain, merely upon the accident of her having a strong [political] party in the country."

Immediately some of the young Oxford dons set themselves to implement this teaching of the Church's divine origin and destiny. Brilliant though they were, they did not have the wisdom to see that the proper strategy was, first, disestablishment, then such devotion to the gospel of Jesus that Church reform and social amelioration would inevitably follow. So they attacked the problem from the theological end. Their campaign of tracts—ninety of them—sought to "rediscover that divine pattern, now preserved more truly than elsewhere in the Church of England." (See further under Newman, p. 194).

For ten years the movement held religious England with great tenacity, then it began to disintegrate, for following the theses of the tractarians themselves many of its members began to secede to the Roman Church. Those who did not go but whose leanings in doctrine and ritual went far in that direction became a rejuvenated High Church party. They called themselves Anglo-Catholics. In them the movement still lives.

## Rev. JOHN HENRY NEWMAN (1801–1890)

### Anglican, Roman Catholic after 1845

NEWMAN is such a key figure in the Oxford Movement, and his poem, "Lead, kindly light" is so universally beloved, that it seems necessary to allow him space disproportionate to his hymnic contribution. He has given a full account of himself, from his own defensive standpoint, in his *Apologia,* and he has been the subject of numerous studies by others. This account of him draws from three of these sources and especially from Geoffrey Faber's *Oxford Apostles* (1936), in which Newman is psychoanalysed.

John Henry was a difficult boy to bring up. He had occasional "scenes" with his father, usually the result of arguing. He had set-tos also with his strong-willed mother: "You see, John, you did not get your own way." "No," he retorted, "but I tried very hard."

Symptoms of these early impressions are the devices by which his inferiority was converted into a grand superiority—the ecstacy of untrammelled

St. Mary's Church, Oxford, official university church. Built 1472–88.

day-dreaming. He writes, "I used to fancy that life might be a dream, or I an angel, and all the world a deception, my fellow-angels by a playful device concealing themselves from me and deceiving me with the semblance of a material world." He rested in the thought, "There are only two supreme and luminously self-evident beings, myself and my Creator." Says Faber, "All the resources of his intellect were employed throughout his life to protect that dream from destruction."

In Trinity College, Oxford, where he matriculated at fifteen he had a hard time. In the midst of his final examination for his degree he collapsed and failed, in spite of twelve hours' study a day. At twenty he decided to take Holy Orders; at twenty-one he won a Fellowship at Oriel College and there met for the first time John Keble. He entered Oriel as an Evangelical, but, through contact with Keble especially, he gradually changed in the direction of High Church. He was excessively conscientious; felt uncharitable toward those who attended the theater, and suspected the morals of anyone who profaned Sunday by reading a newspaper. About now he began to believe in the doctrine of Apostolic Succession, a little later, in baptismal regeneration—both principles stressed by High Church. At twenty-three he became curate in a poor, populous and run-down Oxford parish, and through pastoral zeal built up a congregation larger than the church would hold. Contemporaneous hard work as tutor at Oriel caused another complete collapse—though Faber thinks it was hysteria due to his changing convictions and other deep-seated

John Henry Newman, age 43, eleven years after he had written "Lead, kindly Light." The next year (1845) he entered the Roman Catholic Church.

conflicts. When twenty-seven he was appointed vicar of St. Mary's, Oxford. It was only a parish church, but because of the magnificent building it was used for university functions—as it still is. Here his superb power as a preacher began to build a large congregation of university men. He served here fifteen years, almost up to the time he left the Anglican fold.

Political events now began to worry him (1830). In the early part of this chapter some of the disturbing events have been set forth: rising popular dissatisfaction with Tory squire and Tory parson, with the tyrannies of tradition, clericalism, hereditary power, social and economic misery and injustice, the fossilized institutions of Church and State, the rise of the industrialists for whom there was no place in either Church or State. Newman was scared by it; every institution he valued was in danger. "The French are an awful people!" wrote Newman apropos the Revolution of 1830; "This revolution seems to me the triumph of irreligion." His friend Keble became involved in an agarian riot; he rode out with a mob that was bent on destroying the farmers' machines, fearlessly and good-naturedly harangued them and begged them to desist, but they had no use for parsons and they put up a Methodist preacher to answer him. The latter advised Keble to go home for his own safety!

Then came the Whig victories, the Reform Bill, the Catholic Emancipation Bill and the move to disestablish the Anglican Church in Ireland. Newman and his friend Froude were panic-stricken and Newman again became ill. Froude developed tuberculosis and invited Newman to accompany him on a Mediterranean voyage. They left in December, 1832. Newman confesses that on this first adventure in travel he had a sense of being guided; he even felt that his guardian angel rode with him in the coach that took him to the port. Coasting along the Mediterranean they touched at Sicily. There Newman was shocked at the poverty and degradation of the peasantry and the degenerate morals of the priesthood.

Then Rome. The city terribly impressed and depressed him. He was now in contact with that Church which had excommunicated all members of the Anglican schism and was at this time rejoicing over the threatened disestablishment in Ireland. He and Froude, wondering if there were not some way of healing this breach in the Church of Christ, managed to get two interviews with Monsignor Wiseman who was Rector of the English College of the Roman Church in Rome. They discussed the conditions upon which the Anglicans might be received by Rome, at least partly, by some dispensation which would enable them to communicate (partake of the Mass) while still remaining clergymen of the Church of England. The Monsignor recognized the sincerity of the young men but had to tell them that no compromise was possible: the Anglican Church had spurned its Mother; it had only to repent and return to the true fold.

Froude now returned to England and Newman went alone to Sicily. There he had a wretched and all but fatal experience. The weather was bad, the inns were so flea-ridden that he could not sleep, the food was miserable, he strained his knee, he blistered his feet. Then came the dreadful Sicilian fever, but he pushed on, hardly able to hold himself on his mule. Finally he became too ill to move. They found a physician, who bled him with no good results. Faithful Gennaro, his Italian servant, stuck by him night and day; he was afraid Newman was going to die. "I shall not die, Gennaro," said Newman; "I have not sinned against light. God has a work for me to do in England. This fever is a punishment for my willfulness. I have always been willful: God is chastising me. But I shall get well."

After three weeks they ventured to move him to Palermo, though he nearly died on the way. Convalescing there, he used to watch eagerly for the coming of the daylight, murmuring rapturously to himself as the dawn gleamed through the shutter of the window, "O sweet light! God's best gift."

Over and over he repeated to Gennaro his intense and overpowering conviction that God had some work for him to do in England. When he grew stronger he began to visit the churches in Palermo with their lovely mosaics. They soothed his spirit, though he could not get over his qualms because they represented Rome. This conflict within him found expression in a remarkable poem written the very day he set sail for home:

> Oh, that thy creed were sound!
> For thou dost soothe the heart,
> Thou Church of Rome.
>
> There on a foreign shore
> The homesick solitary finds a friend.
> Thoughts, prisoned long for lack of speech, outpour
> Their tears; and doubts in resignation end.
> I almost fainted from the long delay
> That tangles me within this languid bay,
> When comes a foe, my wounds with oil and wine to tend!

Thus by the ministration of beauty his horror of Romanism was assuaged, which was the first step on the long path he was destined to tread.

At last an orange boat was found ready to sail for France; it was a lonely voyage and a slow one. On the way they were becalmed and be-fogged a week in the straits of Bonifazio between Corsica and Sardinia. There he wrote "Lead, kindly Light." (See below.) All the narrative given above is essential to the understanding of this autobiographical poem.

Newman landed in England in July, 1833, and the following Sunday heard Keble preach his Assize sermon on "National Apostasy" in St. Mary's pulpit—his own church. Ever afterward Newman kept that day sacred as the starting of the religious tasks to which he gave his all.

As the crusade of education took shape under Newman's dynamic leadership, the Oxford Movement came to be called the Tractarian Movement. That was because Newman's method of propaganda was the writing and distribution of *Tracts for the Times*—religious essays each upon some phase of the problem of arresting the spread of rationalism and liberalism, and of arousing deeper allegiance to the Anglican Church. He and his fellow Tractarians battled for Apostolic Succession [spiritual authority conveyed from Christ to Peter, first Bishop of Rome, and by him and his successor bishops in unbroken line to the present. This is claimed to be the only source of religious authority]; continuing revelation of truth through this Apostolic Church; freedom of this Church from any dictation by the State; the Sacraments administered by the Church as the sole means of Grace, as over against the Evangelical theory of salvation by prayer, preaching and conversion. The purpose became more and more to exalt the clergy into a sacerdotal caste and to bring the laity under the control of the priesthood with a view to a reunion of Christendom. The logic of the movement finally drove hundreds of Anglicans into the Roman Church. Newman himself went in 1845, to the discomfiture not to say horror of his dearest friends.

Newman now became an Oratorian: that is, a member of the Oratory of St. Philip Neri (founded in the sixteenth century). Authorized by the Pope, he founded the Order in England, and the community finally settled in Egbaston, then a suburb of Birmingham. In connection with it Newman

*Left,* The country retreat at Rednall about eight miles out of Birmingham, where the brothers went for change and rest. *Right,* The Oratory in Birmingham founded by Newman in 1847. Here he lived the rest of his life. His library, cardinal's robe and various mementos are still here.

established a school for boys. In 1910 a large memorial parish church was built beside it, served by the fathers of the Oratory. The whole establishment is a tribute to the influence of this great man and the love borne him by a vast circle from all creeds.

I had the privilege of visiting this Oratory in 1938. The monastery is a fascinating place. Newman's library has been preserved intact in a large two-story room. There are at least 10,000 volumes, most of them on history and the Church Fathers of the third to fourth centuries. It was the reading of these books that drew Newman to Romanism. In showcases are various relics: his birettas as Cardinal and his red skullcap and ring; manuscript of the *Dream of Gerontius,* and the original score of Elgar's Oratorio presented by the composer; also the printed *Bulla,* signed by the Vice Chancellor of Oxford University, which condemned his Tract No. 90 as contrary to the Thirty-Nine Articles and containing other dangerous errors. This "Bull" virtually read Newman out of the Anglican Church.

Up a circular winding stair and through a door one enters Newman's room. As each Father works and sleeps in the same room, here are all the articles that Newman used. In a series of cabinets are kept all the extant documents of Newman—even to his boyhood letters. One little volume written in his own hand gives the dates on which various of his friends had died, so that on the anniversaries he might pray for their souls.

When Newman was made a Cardinal, 1879, he was allowed a second room. Here where the bed used to be they screened off a portion as a chapel and erected an altar where he could say daily Mass. It is all as he left it— chair, *prie-dieu*, little clothespress where he kept his vestments appropriate to the seasons of the Church year, photographs of departed friends on the wall.

About eight miles out of town at Rednall Hill, Newman established a retreat where the brothers might go for rest and refreshment. It is a nine-acre farm on a strongly sloping hillside, the curving drive to the house lined with old trees. Just outside the house, screened by a hedge and backed by dense trees on rising ground, is the tiny cemetery where Newman lies buried in the same grave with Father St. John. Edward Caswall the hymnist lies next to them. It is as lovely a place to sleep as a man of God could wish.

## *Lead, kindly Light*    [1833]

The title originally given by Newman was "The Pillar of the Cloud," an allusion to Jehovah's guidance of the Israelites through the Wilderness (Ex 13:21–22). It is an immortal prayer for guidance, written in a period of home-sickness, of the emotionalism of convalescence, of bafflement in the religious problems with which he was wrestling; yet in the earnest desire to find the will of God and to do it. It is the supreme expression of spiritual surrender.

*Stanza 1.* True poetry seldom says directly what it means; it only hints it under some figure of speech. We have to reconstruct this incident. Not a breeze has ruffled the sea for a week; a gray fog-bank hangs motionless and blots out what usually is a brilliant landscape —rocky Sardinia to left, perpendicular cliffs of Corsica to right, and on all sides pinnacled islets that stab through the water like daggers. We can see Newman pacing the deck of his tiny orange-boat, by day following impatiently the captain as he tries to find his whereabouts on the chart, or by night guessing at the identity of the lighthouse flashes from rocky islet or headland that penetrate fitfully the rifts in the mist. What more perfect imagery could a poet invent to express utter spiritual bewilderment and helplessness? All this describes Newman's inner state: the fog and the night and the loss of all bearings picture exactly his perplexities about what he should believe and do. And the light he prayed for was God's guidance.

*Stanza 2.* This is a confession of sin: Newman tells the secrets of his soul in such general and figurative terms that we cannot guess the facts. But his whole life is a comment on this stanza. In his boyhood, for example, after a painful argument with his father he wrote: "I have been sadly deficient in meekness, long-suffering, patience and filial obedience. With God's assistance I will redeem my character." But those very words are more an implied condemnation of his father than a sign of repentance. Says his biographer,

Throughout his life he was a mixture of exaggerated humility and overweaning pride.

*Stanza 3.* If in stanzas I and 2 Newman wrote of his doubts and his wilfulness as if they were the night, so he must speak of his faith and his being guided as if they were the morning light. Just as in the darkness we lose sight of all the landmarks—the certainties, the clear duties and the ideals that have blessed us in the past, so with the light these verities look down upon us again with faces beautiful as angels. Newman here expresses the faith that, when he gets back to England, these faces will appear again to him. In using this hymn each of us must discover his own angels, whatever they are.

The frequent use of this hymn at funerals results from a total misapprehension of its meaning.

### HIGH CHURCH HYMNODY

The effect of this movement upon the liturgy of the Church was striking. It brought a new fervor and reverence into public worship, called upon art to enrich the altar and vestments, raised the quality of church music, inspired the writing of new hymns, and finally the compilation of a new and inclusive hymnal to supersede the old Metrical Psalter and the various individual attempts at hymn-collecting. This epoch-making book was called *Hymns Ancient and Modern;* its date, 1861.

It was inevitable that the devotees of the Oxford Movement, so immersed in the task of claiming for their Anglican Church lineal descent from the original Apostolic Church, should make an exhaustive study of ancient ecclesiastical history, doctrine and liturgy; and that in the study they should discover for the first time the wealth of hymns that had been preserved in the service books of both the Greek and Latin Churches. This was an exciting discovery. Newman was the first to call attention to the Roman Breviary (*Tracts for the Times,* No. 75, 1836); in the following year John Chandler published his *Hymns of the Primitive Church,* and Richard Mant his *Ancient Hymns from the Roman Breviary.* Again in 1838 Newman published two volumes of texts, titled *Hymni Ecclesiae;* in 1849 Caswall gathered his translated hymns into *Lyra Catholica.* And from this period to the present day, translations have been made from the ancient service books both in England and America, to the great enrichment of Protestant hymnody. All denominations are debtors to this movement.

During the first sixteen years the High Church people wrote almost no original hymns; they translated. The Latin and Greek hymns chosen for translation illustrate the various divisions of the Church Year as found in the Prayer Book: Advent, Christmas, Epiphany, Lent, Passiontide, Easter, Ascension, Whitsuntide, Saints' Days, Holy Communion. Closely related were the characteristic dogmas of Christianity and hymns appropriate to the two standard hours of prayer, Morning and Evening. In the succeeding decades, however, new poets arose who made their personal contribution to the growing body of churchly hymns. These will be considered in Chap. XII.

In this chapter we shall study the more important translators and the converts to Romanism.

A. THE TRANSLATORS

Many a scholar took a hand in the work of translating. Most of them have now sunk out of sight—like Bishop Richard Mant (1776–1848), Rev. Isaac Williams (1802–1865), Rev. William Irons (1812–1883), Rev. Robert Campbell (1814–1868), Rev. Benjamin Webb (1820–1885). Others are known for only one or two translations:

Rev. John Chandler (1806–1876), one of the first in the Oxford group to publish translations. He mistook the *Paris Breviary* for an ancient work. Most of its hymns were of the eighteenth century. Many by Charles Coffin. They have now practically disappeared from our hymnals.

Rev. Frederick Oakeley (1802–1880), who became a Romanist in 1845. (See Chap. IX Latin Hymns, Anonymous, eighteenth century: "O come, all ye faithful".)

Two translators, however, are outstanding and deserve our longer notice here.

### *Rev. EDWARD CASWALL (1814–1878)* Anglican, Roman Catholic

GRADUATE of Brasenose College, Oxford; became an Anglican clergyman; was deeply involved in the Oxford Movement; was admitted to the Roman Communion in 1847. After his wife died he became a priest and soon joined Dr. Newman at the Egbaston (Birmingham) Oratory. Thereafter his life was given in beautiful self-effacing service to his clerical duties and his ministrations to the unfortunate. His choice of hymns for translation shows the depth and tenderness of his nature, just as the quality of his literary work shows his poetic sensitiveness. While most of his original poetry has survived only in Romanist hymnals owing to its doctrinal slant, his translations are universally used and beloved—second only to Dr. Neale's. Our ten hymnals contain eighteen of these, and the following five have wide use:

See Chap. IX Latin Hymns, Anonymous, twelfth century: "Jesus, the very thought of thee."

See Chap. IX Latin Hymns, Anonymous, twelfth century: "O Jesus, king most wonderful."

See Chap. IX Latin Hymns, Anonymous, seventeenth century: "My God, I love thee; not because."

*Left,* Sackville College, warden's apartments. First floor, left, Dr. Neale's study where he wrote his hymns, translations and histories. *Right,* Dr. Neale's grave in East Grinstead and one of the old-man pensioners at the college.

See Chap. IX Latin Hymns, Anonymous, eighteenth century: "The sun is sinking fast."

See Chap. XI German Hymns, Anonymous, c. 1800: "When morning gilds the skies."

### *Rev. JOHN MASON NEALE (1818–1866)* Anglican

THE prince of translators, whose work has superseded that of most others in the Latin field and whose work stands practically alone in the Greek field.

Born almost under the eaves of St. Paul's Cathedral, London, in a family devoted to Evangelical religion, he went to Cambridge University but came under the influence of the Oxford Movement. This change was hastened and deepened by his intense interest in church architecture and liturgies. While in Cambridge he founded the Camden Society and became editor of that society's organ, *The Ecclesiologist,* the function of which was to arouse interest in all that pertained to the ancient churches of Britain. Excessive work impaired his health so that he did not stay long in the ministry; but when he was twenty-eight years old he was appointed Warden of Sackville College in East Grinstead. This was not an educational institution but a home for old men (later, women also), founded in 1608 and housed in fine Jacobean buildings. Its endowment yielded £14 a year for each of twelve pensioners and £28 for the warden! Did Neale not have independent means he could not have taken the position. But as it was, he found an asylum where his duties were few and where his beloved studies in church history and literature could be pursued continuously. He helped restore the dilapidated buildings, extended the benefits to several additional pensioners, and was wonderfully kind and friendly to all.

But he got into trouble. He reinstituted chapel services, dressed the altar with vestments in ancient style and used liturgies somewhat at variance with the Anglican. The Bishop of Chichester heard of his irregularities and forbade him to "continue to debase the minds of these poor people with his spiritual haberdasheries." Although Sackville College was a private foundation not subject to any bishop's jurisdiction, the matter was taken to an ecclesiastical court and Neale was defeated. For thirteen years he was "inhibited" from holding chapel services.

Neale took refuge in his study, surrounded himself with curious manuscripts of ancient liturgies, treatises on ecclesiology and architecture, books in every European language, Coptic and Syriac dictionaries, books on folklore, hymnology, history and theology. The room was crammed to every nook and corner—as it still is. There he spent his happiest hours and filled them with prodigious labor. The result was *History of Alexandria, History of the Eastern Church,* a book for children, *Translations of Mediaeval Hymns and Sequences, Hymni Ecclesiae, History of Antioch*—not to mention all. And he won the Setonian Prize for Poetry at the University ten years in succession.

Then came further trouble. He tried to simplify funeral customs at the College and make burial less expensive. One old lady objected on her deathbed to being buried "simply"; her relatives took up cudgels, revived the old accusation of the Bishop that Neale was a papist in disguise, enlisted the help of roughnecks of the village who mobbed the funeral, stoned windows and lighted fires. Neale tried to quiet the crowd but only two squads of police availed. The ringleaders were arrested but the attempts to poison the minds of the pensioners against their best friend continued. Some years later he and his Sisters of St. Margaret were mobbed at an out-of-town funeral: he was knocked down and the Sisters had to be rescued by the police, so easy was it for ecclesiastical bigotry to make a scapegoat out of an alleged "papist."

Neale's crowning accomplishment at East Grinstead was the establishment in 1854 of this Sisterhood of St. Margaret, a confraternity of women who devoted themselves to nursing and related ministrations to the poor and sick. The idea was inspired by the wretched living conditions of the peasantry in that district, fanned by Charles Kingsley's denunciations in his novels of the virtue-throttling slums in city and country, and organized after the pattern set by St. Francis of Assisi and others. The Order grew from humble beginnings till at present it has houses all over the world. It is the outstanding, if not the only social, result of the Oxford Movement. Organizing and conducting this work occupied most of Neale's time during the last decade of his life. The only scholastic honor ever awarded Neale was the degree of D.D. from Trinity College, Hartford, Connecticut, in 1860.

Sackville College is still a going concern. When I visited it in 1938 there were four men and twelve women inmates. One cultured old man of about eighty, immaculately groomed, was sunning himself on a seat by the door as we approached. He courteously showed us round, and later, the Warden himself—Lieut-Gen. Sir George MacMunn, Commander-in-chief in Mesopotamia during World War I—took us through Dr. Neale's study, the Great Hall and Chapel. The general was a keen man, still of soldierly bearing though well over eighty. We also visited the grave of Neale in the churchyard

John Mason Neale and family at Sackville College, 1855.

next door. It was a rich experience to come into such close contact with one of the choice spirits in the realm of hymnody, whose original poems as well as translations are used around the world after a hundred years.

Neale's contribution to hymnody is unsurpassed. Besides his translations he has given us two choice poems that savor of immortality. One is "Art thou weary," so intimately connected with the monastery of Mar Saba that it will be noted below under that head. The other is the Christmas carol, "Good king Wenceslaus," which is enough like an ancient folksong to deceive the elect. Altogether the hymnals used in this study contain 5 of his original hymns, 10 translations from the Greek and 31 from the Latin. The more important ones will be found under their appropriate heads: LATIN, GREEK.

### B. THE ROMANIST CONVERTS

Among the many sincere and talented people who made the transition from the Anglican High Church (Anglo-Catholic) party to the full Roman Catholic communion were several hymn writers. The most noted of all was

### Rev. FREDERICK WILLIAM FABER (1814–1863)
#### Anglican, Roman Catholic

BORN into the Anglican Church and brought up a strict Calvinist, Faber went to Oxford, took Holy Orders and began his work as rector. Following logically the teachings of his friend Newman, he began to lean more and more toward the beliefs and the ritualistic practices of Rome, and finally followed Newman into the Roman communion in 1845. With eight others he formed in Birmingham a community called "Brothers of the Will of God"; then when Newman established his Oratory these joined him. The Order of the Oratory, established in 1564 in Rome by St. Philip Neri, is an association of secular priests (not monks) who have assumed only the "internal bond of charity and the external bond of a common life and rule." Their life is founded upon prayer—hence the name of all their places of residence, "Oratory" (Latin, oratorium, a place of prayer). At first Faber lived at Newman's Oratory, but in 1849 Newman sent him to found an oratory in London. The work began in a former whiskey shop, then prospered and was moved to its present position at Brompton in the West End. Its splendid recent church (1884) is almost next door to the great South Kensington Museum. Father Faber was the moving and guiding spirit as long as he lived, a great preacher and a man of charming personality.

It was natural that the Oratory in London should be interested in music, for the great Palestrina had been choirmaster in the mother Oratory in Rome under St. Philip himself and had made it the chief center of sacred music. It is from this connection that the form of composition which unites Bible text with music takes its name, "Oratorio." Then too, Father Faber saw that the Catholics in England did not have a storehouse of English hymnody from which to draw their inspiration, such as he had drawn in his youth from the hymns of Newton, Cowper and the Wesleys. He therefore set himself to remove that handicap. By the time of his death he had written 150 hymns. All these were composed after he had become a Catholic. As we shall see below, they have to be edited for Protestant use. With this manipulation they have found a deep place in the heart of all communions.

### Faith of our fathers, living still      [1849]

The faith referred to in this hymn is the Roman Catholic faith. The little booklet describing Faber's Brompton Oratory Church shows in its opening paragraphs how the persecution alluded to in stanzas 1 and 2 fitted into the life of the founder of the Oratorians:

> St. Philip was in Rome preparing for his life's apostolate there when King Henry VIII was butchering the Carthusian martyrs in England as well as the holiest of his bishops: St. John Fisher, and the most illustrious of his subjects, St. Thomas More. Thus did he usher in the days which were to see England severed from the unity of Christendom. St. Philip died in 1595 when Queen Elizabeth and her government, by bitter and ruthless persecution, were completing that severance.*

*Oratory: Copyright by Photochrom Company, Ltd., Royal Tunbridge Wells*

*Left,* Reverend Frederick W. Faber. *Right,* London Oratory, Brompton Road.

Protestants, of course, overlook these facts of history and in singing these stanzas conjure up pictures of the Circus Maximus and the Catacombs in Rome, persecutions which antedate the rise of both Catholicism and Protestantism. Possibly some may prefer to recall what Catholic "Bloody Mary" did to the Protestants of England, and what Pope Pius V, Catherine de Medici and Louis XIV did to the Huguenots of France. On both sides, "the abuse of greatness is when it disjoins remorse from power."

The last couplet of stanza 2 seems to us unnatural and insincere. Nobody wants to be a martyr. Yet people in earlier days did long for precisely that end in order that they might win a higher place in heaven. It became an obsession. St. Philip the founder had it. Fired by that greatest of Jesuit missionaries, Francis Xavier, he wanted to go as a missionary to India, which would have meant almost certain death, but a Cistercian monk, with what authority is not stated, told him that "Rome was to be his Indies."

Original stanza 3 runs as follows:

* E. Kilburn, *A Walk Round the Church of the London Oratory,* 1938, Sands & Co., London.

> Faith of our fathers! Mary's prayers
> > Shall win our country back to thee;
> And through the truth that comes from God,
> > England shall then indeed be free.

It shows that the above interpretation of "dungeon, fire and sword" is true: the object of all true English Catholics was to win England back to Catholicism, which to the Catholic mind represents true freedom. It is easy to see why this stanza has had to be deleted from Protestant hymnals.

Stanza 4 is a noble expression of the Christian life. St. Philip's only weapon in his ministry in Rome was "the outflowing love of God." He used to say, "Only let a little love enter in and the rest will follow."

### My God, how wonderful thou art     [1849]

Most of our hymnals reduce the number of stanzas to four or five while the original had two others now not used at all.

The hymn is a beautiful expression of worship. Four stanzas describe the glories of God in exclamations of wonder, their imagery drawn largely from the Book of Revelation. Four others speak of His tenderness to His children, His desire that in spite of their fear, their waywardness, they will love Him and trust His friendship. This is the universal language of religion, used and understood by all races and creeds.

### O come and mourn with me awhile     [1849]

Written for Passiontide. It is seldom we find a hymn about the Crucifixion so free from theological bias as this one. No mention is made of Adam's sin and the removal of the curse by this act of atonement; nothing of cosmic significance is hinted, no grand transaction behind the scenes. The poet merely takes us by the hand and leads us to the foot of the cross. There love and pity do their work in our hearts. There in the presence of Him who suffered because sinful men would not let Him live in the same world with themselves we realize what our sin does to Him continually: we are Pilates who condemn Him because of our cowardice or our lust for power; we are Judas who betrayed Him for a bag of gold. But the sight of suffering and forgiving love breaks our stony hearts and lo! love is born.

This hymn is a white man's counterpart of the Negro's, "Were you there when they crucified my Lord?" and "He never said a mumblin' word."

### Hark, hark, my soul, angelic songs are swelling     [1854]

In this hymn we feel that sentiment has got the better of thought. We seem to be in that state of semi-consciousness which often precedes dying, and we experience a pleasing hallucination—or if you please, we are granted a vision of the heavenly land: angelic songs fitfully heard and drawing us after them; the voice of Jesus, sweet as evening bells; a sense of rest and home for the weary traveller, and of night dissolving into eternal day. It is a dream of light and color, of music and memory, of longing and hope and realization.

How much does it strengthen us for the stern realities of life? This hymn lies at the other pole from "Faith of our fathers" and shows Faber's versatility.

### There's a wideness in God's mercy    [1854; additions 1862]

This is one of the least poetical of Faber's hymns: that is, it consists of neither a visual nor an emotional realization of experience, but is a series of somewhat unrelated assertions, many of them commonplace and some of them with questionable theological implications. Most editors agree in omitting stanza 1 "Souls of men, why will ye scatter," and stanza 2 "Was there ever kindest shepherd," as destroying the unity of the hymn; others omit 5, 6, 7, 9, 10. Nearly all unite on 3, 4, 8, 11.

The solid core of 3, "There's a wideness," 8, "For the love of God is broader," 11, "If our love were but more simple," is simple, beautiful and true. Every Christian realizes that these propositions about the infinite Father coincide with Jesus' own teachings, just as the final stanza has been verified over and over in the experience of mankind.

Other lesser persons were stirred by the religious ferment of the times, among them a woman about whom little is known but whose hymns for children had large vogue in her day. She was

### JANE ELIZA LEESON  (1807–1882)  Apostolic, Romanist

MISS LEESON was a member of the Holy Catholic Apostolic Church. This was a freak sect organized in 1832 to take care of persons who "had been driven out of other congregations for the exercise of their spiritual gifts." Its local organizers, twelve in number, were called Apostles. Each congregation was presided over by its "angel" (Rev 2:1), and four and twenty priests (Rev 4:4), with subordinate deacons and acolytes. Their practices and preaching were based upon the interpretation of Old Testament prophecy and belief in the revival of the apostolic gifts of prophecy and healing. They laid great stress on ceremonials, symbolism, the "Real Presence" at the Eucharist. Their numbers gradually dwindled until the last "Apostle" died in 1901. Not finding permanent satisfaction in this fellowship, Miss Leeson finally joined the Roman Catholic Church. Her most enduring hymn is

### Saviour, teach me day by day    [1842]

A hymn for children. Each stanza ends with the line which is really the theme of the whole—"Loving him who first loved me." But love is empty of meaning unless it leads to action. This truth is emphasized in each stanza by a word or phrase: "to obey," (stanza 1), "prompt to serve" (stanza 2), "strong to follow" (stanza 3), "in obedience" (stanza 4), "to show," "singing" (stanza 5). A total absence of theological suggestion makes the hymn particularly usable with children.

## MATTHEW BRIDGES (1800-1894) Anglican, Romanist

THE dominant interests of this author were literature and history. His published works are largely religious poetry. Bridges was brought up in the Anglican Church but in 1848 he followed Newman into the Roman Church. His later years were spent in Canada. His two surviving hymns are

### Crown him with many crowns      [1851]

### Crown him the Son of God      Bridges and Thring

The "many crowns" were suggested by the Rev 19:12. The hymn is an imaginative search for what these many crowns might signify.

*Stanza 1.* The first crown represents Kingship in general, and is placed upon the head of "the Lamb upon his throne" following Rev 22:1. The music of the "heavenly anthem" comes from the worshipping angels and elders of Rev 5:11-14.

*Stanza 2* (omitted in most hymnals) "Crown him the Virgin's Son." The second crown belongs to Him as the Incarnate Son who fulfilled the ancient prophecies. He was the "Shiloh" or Messiah predicted in Jacob's dying song, Gen 49:10; the Branch of Jesse's Stem which Isaiah saw bearing fruit (Is. 11:1); the Shepherd King whose arm shall win the victory (Is 40:10-11). These obscure passages in the Old Testament were interpreted by the Jews of later years as prophecies of their Messiah, and by the Christians as Jesus, born at Bethlehem as God and Messiah and man.

*Stanza 3* "Crown him the Son of God": The third crown belongs to him as that unique person who had two natures; one pre-existent with God (Jn 1:1; 8:58; Col 1:15; Phil 2:6), the other able to become man (Phil 2:7-8) and as Babe of Bethlehem to appear as a creature of time and space, subject to the limitations of human frailty (Heb. 4:15; Is 53:4; Lk 9:22).

*Stanza 4* The fourth crown belongs to Him as Lord of Love (Jn 3:16; 15:13). Perhaps the finest comment to be found on this aspect of the King is Watts' hymn, "When I survey the wondrous Cross" (See above, Chap. IV).

*Stanza 5.* The fifth crown belongs to Him as Lord of Peace (Is 9:6-7; 52:7; 26:3; Ps 72:7-8; Rev 1:8; 22:13). Cf. Bickersteth's "Peace, perfect peace."

*Stanza 6.* The sixth crown is His as Lord of Years. This is an aspect of the third crown, yet with the addition of creative power (Col 1:16-17). Before time began He became Creator; after time merges with eternity He will merit our praises because at a historic point He became man's Redeemer.

Godfrey Thring (1823-1903) was not satisfied with only six crowns, possibly because seven was the Jewish sacred number and because Life is one of the aspects or gifts of Christ emphasized by John (1:4; 6:63; 11:25). He therefore added a seventh crown in a stanza of his own, frequently sung with those by Bridges:

> Crown him the Lord of Life,
> Who triumphed o'er the grave,
> And rose victorious in the strife
> For those he came to save;
> His glories now we sing
> Who died, and rose on high,
> Who died, eternal life to bring,
> And lives that death may die.

One of our hymnals (C) uses as first stanza, "Crown him the Son of God" by Bridges; then introduces a stanza from Thring for the second; then finishes with two from Bridges.

Dr. Percy Dearmer, editor of *Songs of Praise*, felt that this hymn of Bridges was not good enough for inclusion in his hymnal, "though the motive was a good one and had won favor." He therefore wrote a new one on the same theme beginning, "Crown him upon the throne." It emphasizes the social rather than the theological reasons why Christ should be crowned. If possible read No. 480 in *Songs of Praise* and decide whether his development of the theme is more fruitful for the twentieth century.

### Rev. HENRY COLLINS (1827–1919) Anglican, Romanist

AN OXFORD man who took Holy Orders in the Anglican Church upon graduation but almost immediately (1857) entered the Roman Church and three years later became a member of the Cistercian Order of Monks. His literary works are biographical and historical, pertaining to the interests of the Roman faith. His two hymns, written in the year of his graduation from Oxford while an Anglican, have both survived—one of them widely used.

### Jesus, my Lord, my God, my all    [1854]

This is in no sense a liturgical hymn. It is a prayer that a devout Christian of almost any sect may pray, though the phrase "my God" and the fact of its being a prayer to Jesus would cause Unitarians and the Humanists to avoid it. Here one "enters into his closet and shuts the door," exposes one's inmost soul for Jesus to see, and rejoices in communion with Him to whom heart and soul belong—a hymn almost too intimate to sing in a great congregation.

### ADELAIDE ANNE PROCTOR (1825–1864) Anglican, Romanist

THIS gifted writer, known all over the world as the author of *The Lost Chord*, has made a notable contribution to hymnody. Her talent no

doubt came from her father, Bryan Waller Proctor better known as "Barry
Cornwall," a popular poet and playwright in the mid-Victorian days. At an
early age she showed precocity in both languages and music, became a
favorite poet by the time she was twenty-eight. Through her father she became acquainted with such literary lights as Charles Lamb, Leigh Hunt and
Charles Dickens; in fact her first poems, written under the pseudonym of
"Mary Berwick," were published for a couple of years by Dickens in his
magazine without his knowing the real author. Once when dining with the
Proctors, Dickens showed the proof of a poem by this "Miss Berwick." Next
day Mrs. Proctor told him that her daughter was the real author. The young
lady had concealed her identity because she feared that Dickens might publish her poems through friendship rather than because of their real worth:
she took a chance and won! When her poems were collected and published
in 1858 Dickens wrote an enthusiastic introduction for the volume.

All Miss Proctor's hymns were written after her transfer to the Roman
Church in 1851 when she was twenty-six years old. Three of them have
survived in common use.

### *My God, I thank thee, who hast made*     [1858]

This beautiful prayer of thanksgiving concerns itself with six topics:

*Stanza 1.* Thanks for the beauty of the physical world and for the
beauty that operates in the moral realm, making "glorious" things
"noble and right."

*Stanza 2.* Thanks for the joy that springs from gentle thoughts and
deeds, which in turn spring from love.

*Stanza 3.* Thanks for pain which prevents us from relaxing into
ignoble ease and self-satisfaction; pain the revealer of true values,
the stimulus to action. This is a bit of intimate self-revelation. Miss
Proctor was frail, subject to increasing illnesses, and she died at
thirty-nine.

*Stanza 4.* Thanks for ideals: for the divine urge to leave behind
things of lesser value and soar to sublime heights. This is a poet's
way of saying what Paul said under different imagery in Phil
3:13–14.

*Stanza 5.* Thanks for the hope of greater spiritual satisfactions: the
urge in stanza 4 is not illusory but based upon faith in God's goodness.

*Stanza 6.* Thanks for the promise of heaven where comradeship with
the Saviour will be the realized goal of all desire.

This is one of the few hymns of the period in which there is not the
slightest trace of sectarian theology or liturgical usefulness. It is the private
outpouring of a thankful human soul.

## The shadows of the evening hours    [1862]

In all hymnals this poem is classified under "Evening," appropriate therefore for use in the church service of Evening Prayer or in one's private devotions at night.

*Stanza 1* is largely description.

*Stanza 2* shows intimations that the writer is conscious of approaching death. Her "sorrows" like incense rise in a dumb prayer for mercy. The obscure phrase "the brightness of the coming night" is a reference to the stars, symbols of hope, which will relieve the totality of darkness, whether of night or of death.

*Stanza 3* shows a growing realization that the time of her passing is not far away. But she still clings to the stars with their suggestions of infinity and of light beyond the dark.

*Stanza 4* is a prayer for peace. It is so phrased that we who are in the midst of life's activities can take the words literally—a night of rest after a day's toil, but those who are under sentence of death can take them figuratively—an eternity of rest after a life of pain.

Fortunately the average singer of these lines can rejoice in their poetic imagery, unaware of their sad autobiographical reference.

## Rev. THOMAS JOSEPH POTTER (1827–73) Anglican, Romanist

BROUGHT up an Anglican, he followed Newman into the Roman fold in 1847 and became a priest. Preaching was his gift. For that reason his chief work became to teach the art as Professor of Pulpit Eloquence and English Literature in the Foreign Missionary College of All Hallows, Dublin. A voluminous writer on his specialty, he also translated Latin hymns and wrote hymns of his own. Only one has survived.

## Brightly gleams our banner    [1860]

A processional written especially for use with children. It was published in *The Holy Family Hymns,* a collection of verses appropriate to the childhood of Jesus in His parental home. Its Roman approach is shown in original stanza 3 beginning "Mary, Mother, Ave!" and in stanza 5, "Jesus! Mary! Joseph! Sweet and holy Three." These stanzas never appear in Protestant hymnals, but the others form a very acceptable and widely used processional hymn.

The simplicity of the thoughts and imagery make interpretation almost unnecessary. We have to imagine ourselves marching like soldiers "through the desert" of this present world. The banners and the songs are a spirited accompaniment (stanza 1).

*Stanza 2.* A confession of sin: we are sometimes found, in army par-
lance, "AWOL" (absent without leave) from the ranks. This is not
a processional episode but something that checks the forward movement of the other lines.

*Stanza 3* resumes the processional imagery with a prayer for divine
protection in time of battle and sudden death.

*Stanza 4* is a pictured heaven of rest, worship and song after the
march is over, and discharge is won.

All that is left of the original are stanzas 1 and 2, and these have been
altered. W. W. How wrote the others. Found also in some hymnals is a
stanza beginning "Pattern of our childhood" written in 1869.

*Latin*
*Hymnists*

| | | |
|---|---|---|
| I cent. | Era of Apostolic Church. | |
| II–III | Era of Church Fathers. | |
| IV cent. | Era of Theologians. | |
| 323–37 | Constantine, first Christian Emperor. | |
| c.311–380 | Ulfilas spreads Arianism among barbarians. | |
| 325 | Council of Nicaea: c. 361 Trinitarian Creed of Athanasius. | |
| 378 on | Empire deluged with barbarians. | Ambrose, c. 374 |
| | | Niceta, c. 400 |
| V–X cent. | DARK AGES. | Prudentius, |
| 410 | Visigoths capture Rome. | c. 405 |
| 455 | Vandals sack Rome. | |
| 476 | Fall of Western Roman Empire. | |
| 496 | Franks under Clovis become Roman Christians. | |
| 529 | Benedict founds monastic rule at Cassino, Italy. | Fortunatus, |
| 590–604 | Pope Gregory I (Great) sends missionaries to England. "Plain-song" standardized; monasticism increasing; papal power rising. | c. 569 Gregory (?) |
| 622 | Rise of Mohammedanism; rapid spread toward Europe. | |
| 742–814 | Age of Charlemagne. Arianism in Europe eliminated. | |
| 800 | Charlemagne Holy Roman Emperor. | |
| | | Theodulph, c. 820 |
| | | Rab. Maurus, c. 830 |
| 850–1000 | Economic and political chaos; Italian universities founded. | |
| 910 | Monastery of Cluny founded. | |
| XI–XIII cent. | Era of the Crusades. | |
| XI–XIV cent. | MIDDLE AGES. Roman Church supreme. | Abelard, c. 1129 |
| | Center of learning shifts to France. Era of Schoolmen. | Bernard of |
| 1098 | Cistercian monastery of Citeaux founded. | Clairvaux, |
| 1112 | St. Bernard founds monastery of Clairvaux. | c. 1130 |
| | | Bernard of Cluny, c. 1145 |
| XIII cent. | Universities founded, cathedrals built, literature of Romance; age of strong heresies | |
| 1210 | Franciscan Order founded | |
| 1216 | Dominican Order founded | |
| | | Francis, 1226 |
| | | Jacopone da Todi, c. 1275 |
| | | Anon., XIII–XIV cent. |
| XV–XVI cent. | THE RENAISSANCE: Change of emphasis from religion to politics, commerce, discovery; wonderful advances in art; beginnings of science | Tisserand, c. 1490 |
| 1492 | Columbus discovers America | |
| 1517 | Luther begins Reformation | F. B. P., c. 1580 |
| | | Anon., XVII–XVIII cents. |

# LATIN HYMNS

WHEN THE TRACTARIANS decided to restore to the Church in English form the heritage of Latin hymnody they opened up a mine that was 1500 years old, very deep and rich. For they found in the Catholic Breviaries not only recently written or revised hymns of the seventeenth and eighteenth centuries, but genuine medieval hymns from the age of St. Thomas Aquinas and St. Francis (thirteenth cent.), hymns from the Romanesque age of the eleventh and twelfth centuries, from the age of Charlemagne (eighth and ninth cent.), from the rude days of the barbarian conquests (fifth and sixth cent.) and from the fourth century when the old Roman culture was still intact. One can readily imagine that these hymns reflect the various cultures that produce them, various social, artistic, theological and ritualistic traditions, and so they do. We shall now trace this story, tell something of the historic backgrounds and something of the great personalities that produced the hymns primarily, of course, for their own times.

But first it is necessary to understand that the ancient Church did not speak one language. The Tractarians were soon to find that fact and deal with it. For while their interest turned at first to the ancient Roman Church of which Protestantism was the offshoot, their researches led them into that vast world of Greek religious literature which antedated the Latin as well as paralleled it. That made them conscious afresh of the greatest split the Church ever experienced—a schism that rested primarily on a difference of language. A line running the length of the Adriatic and extending south to the Gulf of Libya in Africa was the boundary: all people living to the east were primarily Greek-speaking; peoples living to the west of that line became ultimately Latin-speaking. So it came about that the earliest Christians, who lived around the eastern shores of the Mediterranean, gave us our Bible in Greek and the earliest Church Liturgy in Greek. Even the earliest Church in Rome spoke Greek. We shall consider these facts at length when we study Greek hymns.

But Rome in the first century was the mistress of the world and her official language was Latin. Latin followed the Roman armies. Pompey greatly advanced the conquest of Spain and speeded up the Romanization process, so that today we find traces of 10,000 miles of Roman roads in Spain, aqueducts like that at Segovia, amphitheaters like that at Santiponce, and the Spanish language, which is only Latin bastardized by later conquerors. Julius Caesar conquered Gaul, and his successors so completely Romanized it that Roman civilization there outlived Rome itself and conquered the barbarian conquerors of Gaul. By the time Christianity had taken firm root in the West in the third century A.D., all Western countries had been Romanized and therefore latinized. Not only did all roads lead to Rome but all thought ran in Roman ruts. The provinces of Africa (old Carthage) and Mauretania (modern Algiers and Morocco) forgot their native tongues and Latin was everywhere spoken. It was to accommodate the Latin-speaking Church of north Africa that Jerome in the fourth century translated the Greek Bible into Latin, and his version has remained the Bible of the Roman Catholic world ever since.

We can follow the Romanization, then the Christianization and then the barbarization processes in such a Gallic town as Poitiers, for example, in west central France. Caesar's lieutenant conquered the town, then veterans were colonized there, then traders came, then settlers from Italy, until Poitiers became a Roman town with all the public buildings a little Rome would need—forum, theater, a large amphitheater, baths, temples with their statues, and villas, shops and houses. The Roman arena was dug up a few years ago. In 1902 a fourth-century statue of Minerva was found, indication that the Roman religion was established there.

## HILARY (c. 310–366)

INTO this Roman town and into this pagan religion was born the first man of Poitiers of whom we have distinct knowledge, Hilary. He saw the amphitheater and no doubt attended sports in it; he doubtless worshipped in the Minerva temple; he visited the baths on the ruins of which in the eleventh century the church of St. Germain was built.

Then into this provincial town, in the third century came a new force— the Christian religion. Who brought it we do not know, but by 330 A.D. at the latest a church was built there, which is still standing. It was a baptistry rather than a complete church, in which candidates were immersed in a tank of water—before the custom arose of baptizing by pouring. And so we may believe that in this oldest Christian building in France, Hilary was immersed (c. 353), he who afterwards became the first bishop and later was made a Doctor of the Church and a saint.

His most important characteristic was that he was a torrent of energy and eloquence. St. Jerome, who was a judge of talent, called him "the Rhone of Latin eloquence." Some other writer called him "the trumpet of the West."

Both of these tributes were given because he was the most famous defender of the Catholic faith against the first great heresy that split the Church—Arianism, which represents the root of what we call today Unitarianism. So stalwart a fighter was he that he got himself into trouble, first with Saturnius, the neighboring Bishop of Arles whom he attacked at a Church Council at Beziers (356 A.D.) because of his Arianism; and then with the Roman Emperor Constantius who was tainted with the same heresy. Constantius thought him so dangerous that he exiled him to Asia Minor—the other end of the world. But after a couple of years Hilary was allowed to return, though he couldn't get back his bishopric until there was a change of emperors.

His stay in Asia did him and the Church a good turn, for there for the first time he heard the Greek Church sing hymns. He was so captivated that on his return to Poitiers he tried his hand at hymn-writing—with no great success, we must confess, for the hymns were not well adapted to congregational use and did not find their way into the liturgy. But he used them in his fight to purge Gaul of heresy, and perhaps that was good enough.

Two of these hymns show the influence of his stay among the Greeks, for they are acrostics, an old Greek trick: that is, the first line begins with A, the next with B, and so on through the alphabet. That is not very good poetry, but it doubtless helped his Gallic Christians to remember and be able to recite lustily the articles of the Trinitarian faith enshrined in the poem. The other hymn that has survived celebrates the victory of Christ, the Second Adam, over the powers of evil (*Adae carnis gloriosa*). This hymn though prosaic and uninspired had the virtue of being written in the rhythm of the marching songs of the Roman soldiers. No doubt Hilary used this meter to make the singing popular—after the formula of the Salvation Army—and to facilitate its use as a processional. But according to Jerome, the Gauls in general didn't like hymns, and so Hilary's efforts went for naught.

After the good bishop died they made him patron saint of their city and built him a fine church over his tomb. What it looked like we do not quite know, for the present church of St. Hilaire dates from the tenth through eleventh centuries on the same site. But it enshrines the memory of a great man who made an unsuccessful attempt to introduce song into the liturgy of the Latin Church. None of his hymns appears in our English hymnals.

## NICETA OF REMESIANA

BEFORE this fateful fourth century comes to a close and the Great Depression of Barbarism settles down, three other men arise to make contributions to the Church's hymnody. The first is Niceta (c. 335–c. 414) missionary bishop of Remesiana, in Dacia (Serbia), on the great military road from Belgrade to Constantinople. His contribution was the "*Te Deum*," greatest of all the non-scriptural hymns in Latin. St. Jerome says of him that he spread Christianity among barbarians by his sweet songs of the cross.

## The "Te Deum"    [fourth century]

Scholars have employed their best skill for a century trying to attribute this hymn to the right person. They have rejected the legend that St. Ambrose and St. Augustine improvised it responsively when the former baptized the latter; they have thrown out the claims of Charlemagne and half a dozen others, and now have nearly all agreed that the late fourth century is the date, Dacia (Serbia) is the place, and Niceta is the author.

The Baptistry of St. John, Poitiers, c. 330 A.D., same date as the founding of Constantinople. The oldest Christian building in France. Without doubt St. Hilary was baptized in this structure.

This grand composition is partly a hymn of praise and partly a confession of faith. It was intended to take the place of hymns to Zeus and other pagan gods which the peasants of Dacia had sung from their childhood. Men must always worship—only the names change and sometimes the imagery.

Our English version is found in the First Book of Common Prayer, 1549.

*Stanza 1. We praise thee O God; we acknowledge thee to be the Lord.*

Here we are introduced to the Christian God, who has no name except the Lord and Father and the God of Hosts, and to the imagery of the Christian heaven, partly Hebrew in origin, where angels of various ranks (alluded to as "powers of heaven and the universe") chant eternally the old hymn of Isaiah—"Holy, holy, holy."

*Stanza 2. The glorious company of the Apostles praise thee.*

The background now expands as in a grand cinema spectacle. The glorious company of the Apostles approaches, and through invisible microphones their chorus swells into a grand anthem. Behind them marches the "goodly fellowship of the Prophets," who display their scrolls of prophecy and supplant with their melody the voices of the receding Apostles. Following them the Martyrs sweep in, clad in shining garments and bearing in their hands the emblems of their martyrdom and the martyr's palm. Now through a rift in the clouds we catch a glimpse of the earth swinging through space, and as the camera moves forward to give us a close-up, we see bands of saints worshipping in all the churches of the world; as the microphone is poised above them we hear the words of the new song which angels did not know, but only those redeemed spirits who had lived upon earth and been the subjects of redemption. That song is a confession of the orthodox Trinitarian faith in the Father of an infinite majesty, his true and only-begotten Son, and the Holy Ghost, the Comforter. That was the faith with which Niceta was destroying the worship of Zeus and the heresy of Arianism through the forests of Dacia; that was the vision of a glorious heaven of angels and a united brotherhood of the faithful on earth.

*Stanza 3. Thou art the King of Glory, O Christ.*

In the last stanza the Son is directly addressed; praise turns out to be a part of the Creed—that the Son took it upon Himself to deliver man, that He was miraculously born of a Virgin, that by His death on the cross He had overcome Death—which probably meant that He had cheated the Devil out of his expected prey—and therefore that the heaven so movingly shown in stanza I was hereafter available to all who would leave their heathenism and accept the Christian Creed. The stanza closes with a prayer that Christ will help His faithful ones now, and reward them hereafter.

*Added Stanza. O Lord save thy people and bless thine heritage.*

Some time later another section grew out of these three to express certain details which later generations thought should be included in any comprehensive statement of belief. It is made up largely of phrases culled from the Psalms. Nor can we help observing also that in composing his original three stanzas Niceta helped himself liberally to phrases from the Apostles' Creed, the *Sanctus*, and the *Gloria in Excelsis* already used in Church services. Altogether, therefore, the *Te Deum* as we now have it is a patchwork, but one that has served the Church nobly through 1500 years.

It would be impossible and useless to tell on what great occasions this anthem has been sung by the Church. The times are numberless. Not only did St. Benedict, founder of monasticism in the West, introduce it into his regular night service called Matins, but eventually it found place in every Catholic service book. When the English reformers threw away all the accumulated treasures of the ages they saved this precious hymn, and in translation introduced it into their Book of Common Prayer. There it has stayed ever since, to be chanted every day of the year by congregation or choir (Morning Prayer, after the first Scripture lesson). And on all occasions of public rejoicing when great congregations have gathered to express thanks and exultation, they use the words of this Dacian hymn—occasions as diverse as the massacre of St. Bartholomew when Pope Gregory XIII ordered it sung in all the churches of Rome to celebrate the killing of 70,000 Protestants throughout France, and the Victoria Diamond Jubilee in 1902, when the voices of the empire shook with it the very foundations of St. Paul's.

A far greater man, both as a churchman and as a molder of Christian hymnody was

## AMBROSE, BISHOP OF MILAN (340?–397)

AMBROSE was born at Treves (France) where his father was Prefect of *Gallia Narbonensis,* a huge province that embraced France, Britain, Spain and part of North Africa. The family was ancient Roman. On the death of the father, the family removed to Rome, and Ambrose began his extensive education for the law and administrative duties. He became an eloquent pleader in the courts and finally consular Governor of northern Italy with residence in Milan.

Those were stormy times. Barbarians were advancing like a flood beyond the Alpine wall; the empire was tottering. The Church was torn by fratricidal factions—Orthodox and Arian. For twenty years the Bishop of Milan had been an Arian. When the bishop died and a successor had to be elected, Ambrose, as consul, knowing that a riot was inevitable, went in person to the basilica to keep order and counsel moderation. His eloquent plea resulted immediately in his own election as bishop even though he was only a catechumen (one who was receiving instruction for membership in the Church). He was baptized, resigned his consular office and was consecrated bishop, gave away his property, devoted himself to studies suitable to his new office and became one of the ideal bishops of all time.

The world-shaking struggle for power, both ecclesiastical and secular, between the Western Catholic faith and the Eastern heresy of Arianism is so deeply imbedded in Latin hymnody that we must pause for a moment to review Arius, the founder, and the heresy itself.

Arius (c. 250–336 A.D.) was an influential presbyter in the church at Alexandria. He got into a contest with his bishop over the exact nature of Christ. He maintained that "if the Father was God, then the Son was a creature of the Father." He was willing to worship the Son as a kind of secondary God, a middle Being between God and the world, created before the world was, yet after God had been in existence. His bishop denied his assertions, called the Council of Alexandria (A.D. 321) which condemned them as heretical. The contest was then taken to the Council of Nicaea (A.D.

325). Though Arius' character was never impeached even by his enemies, the Council tore his confession of faith to pieces, three hundred of the bishops pronounced him and his writings anathema, burned his books and banished him to what is now Yugoslavia. There he spent his time in controversial writing and in composing songs so that his doctrines about the person of Christ might be popularized with all classes and conditions. He taught everybody to sing them—boys and girls, shop-keepers, longshoremen, sailors. They sang lustily whether they believed the teachings or not—march-

The Church of St. Ambrose, Milan, founded by that Saint in the 4th century. St. Ambrose here baptized St. Augustine in 387. The present structure on the same site was built in the 12th century.

ing songs, sailor chanties. The fashion and the songs spread like wildfire all over the northern barbarian world. Even the Emperor Constantine's sister was infected with the heresy. We have a contemporary record of what happened in Constantinople c. 398:

The Emperor Theodosius, an ardent defender of the Nicene Creed, had prohibited all Arians in his empire from using church buildings. Arians were still numerous in Constantinople but they had to worship in the open, outside the walls. However on Saturday and Sunday and the greater festival days they formed the habit of coming into the city at sunset and congregating in the porticoes and other places of public resort. There they sang all the night through!—antiphonal songs that preached the Arian doctrines, often accompanied by taunts and insults to the Orthodox. The Orthodox bishop Chrysostom feared that this singing might draw some of the simpler church people toward this heresy, and so under the patronage and at the cost of the Empress Eudoxia he organized in opposition a system of nightly processions of hymn-singers, accompanied by silver crosses, wax candles and other features of pageantry. Riots followed with bloodshed on both sides. One Orthodox victim was the empress's chief eunuch who had been appointed official conductor of the pageants. This led to the suppression by imperial edict of all public Arian singing, and the custom of Orthodox singing in churches especially at night and on special solemn occasions was thus firmly established, and has remained to this day.

Arius's compromise about the nature of Christ made it easy for pagans who believed in many gods to accept this kind of polytheism, and therefore the gospel of the Arian missionaries took fast hold on the barbarian tribes to the north—the Goths, Vandals, Lombards and others. As these tribes began to inundate the West they established Arian kingdoms in the Danube region, northern Italy, Gaul, Spain and even North Africa. The Romanized West that fought them as barbarians hated them with a mighty hatred as heretics. The controversy cost millions of lives and kept the Church divided. Though the Catholic faith of Athanasius finally prevailed, the heresy was never wholly extirpated but after various modifications survives today as Unitarianism. And the odium still continues. It barred Unitarians from full citizenship in England until 1828, and prevented the Federal Council of the Churches of Christ in America from admitting Unitarians and Universalists to membership. Surely this intolerance and hatred are an exorbitant price to pay for theological supremacy.

This struggle for power was naturally reflected in hymns. These became a kind of theological barrage, first effectively laid down in the West in Milan where Ambrose himself was being persecuted by Justina, mother of the boy emperor Valentinian. She was an Arian. The faithful flock of Ambrose used to gather at the basilica church to form a perpetual guard about their beloved bishop against possible violence from the Gothic (Arian) soldiers of the emperor. St. Augustine's mother Monica was one of these vigilantes. Augustine writes, "It was then that the custom arose of singing hymns and psalms, after the use of the Eastern provinces, to save the people from being utterly worn out by their long and sorrowful vigils." You may be sure that these hymns, composed by Ambrose, would be educational in character, militant propaganda not only to strengthen the morale of the faithful but to infect the heretical soldiery with the views of orthodoxy. How deeply they affected people, keyed up as they were by the tension of danger, is shown by Augustine in his *Confessions* (IX. 1):

What tears did I shed over the hymns and canticles, when the sweet sound of the music of Thy Church thrilled my soul! As the music flowed into my ears and Thy truth trickled into my heart, the tide of devotion swelled high within me, and the tears ran down, and there was gladness in these tears.

There seems to be little doubt that Ambrose was inspired to this hymnic propaganda by the example of Hilary (above). He improved upon his master by shortening and standardizing the form. He adopted for his meter the marching rhythm of soldiers, a 1-2, 1-2 step combined into a line of four feet; the number of lines in a strophe or stanza was fixed at four and the number of stanzas usually limited to eight. A line would diagram like this:

Splen-dór pa-tér- nae gló- ri-á

This was an old Latin classic meter, without rhyme and with syllables alternating short and long. This rhythm was easy for the unlearned to pick up; it became immensely popular and other writers tried their hand at it. As the liturgy of the Church developed, many such compositions were admitted into the official books under the title "Ambrosian Hymns"—which means, not written by Ambrose but in his meter—iambic tetrameter. When Benedict organized monasticism in the West (Monte Cassino, founded 529), he made the Ambrosian type of hymn standard for his liturgy, and therefore as the Benedictines spread over Europe these hymns became and remained well-nigh universal for 700 years, and the Ambrosian meter still persists in English hymnody as "Common Meter." Then in the thirteenth century other meters came to the fore.

Scholarship has tried for a long time to identify the genuine Ambrose, with the result that the probabilities are 18, though only four are guaranteed by the fact that Ambrose's contemporary Augustine has vouched for them. We shall study only three, none of which is absolutely authentic.

### Splendor paternae gloriae        [c. 374 A.D.]

O Splendor of God's glory bright        Tr Robert Bridges, 1899
O Jesus, Lord of heavenly grace        Tr Chandler and Louis Benson

The hymnals show three translators and various selections of stanzas. The most poetic rendering is that of Robert Bridges, 1899 (A E S); Benson, 1910, combined with Chandler, 1837, seems next in favor (M N P); and Chandler last (L). All eight stanzas are found only in S and A (Ancient Office Hymns).

Stanza 1. O Splendor of God's glory bright.
Christ is here addressed under the figure of the sun. This is a natural symbol: long ago Malachi used it (4:2) and Christians promptly interpreted it in Messianic terms (2 Cor 4:6). The Gospel of John is full of the same imagery (1:1–9 et passim). Even before Ambrose the Greek Church had adopted it in the famous hymn, "Hail, gladdening Light" (3rd cent.). The involved phrases here seem to echo

the attempt of the Athanasian Creed to show how Christ proceeded from the Father ("light from light"), was begotten, not created ("light's living spring"), and was coexistent with God in time and eternity ("all days illumining").

*Stanza 2. O thou true Son, on us thy glance.*
Christ is here identified with the Holy Ghost who is the rays that stream from the true Source to each individual believer.

*Stanza 3. The Father, too, our prayers implore.*
The Father here completes the trinity of light that shines with redemptive force on men (Lk 1:77–78).

*Stanzas 4–5. To guide whate'er we nobly do. Our mind be in His keeping placed.*
The attention now turns to the effect of the light upon us: it furnishes guidance, love, hope, patience, trust, loyalty, purity, faith. The tares are an allusion to the parable in Mt 13:24–30.

*Stanza 6. And Christ to us for food shall be.*
Here are many Scriptural echoes: Christ is bread (Jn 6:32–35), water (Jn 4:10–14; 7:37), wine (Lk 22:20; Jn 6:53–56)—but not the mocking kind (Prov 20:1).

*Stanza 7. Rejoicing may this day go hence.*
Three aspects of day are here introduced as symbols: the clarity of a cloudless dawn suggests the guilelessness we pray for; the heat of noon is the ardor of our faith; the gloom of twilight is that which our Light shall banish forever.

*Stanza 8. Morn in her rosy car is borne.*
Here are echoes of the Athanasian Creed in which the relationships of the Father to the Son are set forth in mystical and incomprehensible terms.

*Stanza 9. All laud to God the Father be*
A later Doxology added to keep the orthodox dogma ever in mind an an antidote to Arian poison.

Something of this elaborate imagery is due to the translators, as one may see by comparing Bridges with Chandler. But one may recognize in the hymn the educational purpose, the confidence and the aspiration that were all parts of St. Ambrose's fighting spirit.

## O Lux beata Trinitas

*O Trinity of blessed light*     Tr Neale, 1852
*O Light, O Trinity most blest!*     Tr Composite, 1890

There is no certainty that Ambrose wrote this hymn. The scholarly Episcopal *Hymnal*, 1940, ascribes it to an unknown sixth century author.

This is another propaganda—or shall we say fighting—hymn intended to confute the Arians and strengthen the Orthodox in their belief that God exists in three Persons. To use an incomplete analogy: as the sun's light is made up of three primary colors intermingled in ten thousand hues yet striking all objects as one united force, so the Light of the World is both Trinity and Unity, both illumination and power (stanza 1). The faithful are reminded of this analogy when they find this hymn in their Breviary to be sung at Vespers on Saturday.

Christians should reflect upon this glory at both the Morning Hour when praise is the dominant note, and at Evensong when prayer for protection during the night is more natural. Thus prayer and praise are perpetual expressions of worship (stanza 2).

Neale adds here a note to his translation: "Besides the natural sense of these words, they also mean that in the time of prosperity, which is like a morning when everything is bright and gay, we are to praise God, and in the time of trouble, which is like evening when the sky grows dark and the world gloomy, we are to cry for His help." *

In the Doxology (stanza 3) the term "Paraclete" is St. John's Greek word for Comforter, the Holy Spirit.

### AURELIUS CLEMENS PRUDENTIUS (348–413)
#### Spaniard. Roman Catholic

THE old Latin civilization produced yet another hymn writer in a different part of the far-flung empire, this time in Spain. The Iberian peninsula had been long known to the ancients because of its metals, particularly silver. Cretans, Greeks, Phoenicians had traded there before Carthage set up its colonies and Hannibal crossed it on his way to the Alps and Rome. Then Rome conquered it in a bloody war in which both Pompey and Julius Caesar had a part, and at last the barbarians submitted to the discipline and the blessings of Roman civilization. Roads, aqueducts, bridges, baths, temples, schools of philosophy—these followed, and an educational system at the bottom of which in primary schools boys learned to read and write Latin. This civilization was still flourishing when Prudentius was born in Saragossa in 348 A.D., a time when the empire had grown so far east that the capital had to be moved from Rome to Constantinople to be nearer the center of things.

Prudentius, the earliest Christian writer who was a real poet, went to the imperial schools in his native town, and, as he confesses in a biographical preface to his works, took his full share of the discipline that always went with learning—that is to say, "he wept under the rod of the schoolmaster." After learning his letters he studied the Latin poets, Horace and Virgil. When he was old enough he put on the "manly toga"—that is, came of legal age, and then to his literary studies were added the graces of rhetoric and the

* See J. M. Neale: *Collected Hymns, Sequences and Carols,* 1914, Hockler & Stoughton, London.

wanton ways of youth. He studied law and twice became a magistrate. So his life went on uneventfully in prosperous Spain while great things went on in the world outside. The Emperor Julian the Apostate had tried without success to stop the spread of Christianity, which was rapidly crushing paganism. Then came Theodosius, who called Prudentius to Rome and honored him with a court office. At Rome he was greatly impressed with the monuments and memories of the imperial city, its new Christian basilicas, and especially its sacred places of pilgrimage, tombs of Apostles and martyrs. There he gained also a sense of the superiority of Rome as over against the barbarian world.

He was now getting old—57! He therefore renounced the vanities of the world and spent the rest of his life in rigorous asceticism, and he found his activity and his delight in writing poetry. He wrote "to glorify God and atone for his sins," to sing the praises of God, fight heresy, trample on heathen rites and celebrate the Apostles and martyrs. He even appealed to the Emperor Honorius to stop the gladiatorial shows—and they were stopped in the Coliseum in 404 A.D. after the monk Telemachus was killed trying to part the gladiators. In his two-volume poem "Against Symmachus" he helped the fight of the Christian senators of Rome to oust from the senate chamber the altar and statue of Victory. This was part of the death struggles of paganism.

His poems were long-winded and had to be cut down for use in church. One volume called the *Cathemerinon* ("throughout the day") is a series of hymns that follow the various Hours with helpful thoughts, used in private devotions. They set forth the Christ of theology in all the particulars of the Apostles' Creed. From this book the Church finally culled for its Breviary

### *Corde natus ex parentis*      [c. 405 A.D.]

*Of the Father's love begotten*   Tr Neale, 1854, and H. W. Baker, 1859

*Of the Father's heart begotten*      Tr R. F. Davis, 1905

This is a fighting hymn.

*Stanza 1.* The very first line attacks the heresy of Arius that had recently blossomed so banefully to disrupt the Church. (See above under Ambrose.) Observe in how many words Prudentius takes up cudgels against Arius: "sole begotten"—not created; "ere the worlds began," "Alpha," "source of all things"—that is, the Son created the universe, "Omega"—He will exist to the end of time.
*Stanza 2. At his word the worlds were framéd.*
Christ is said to have been the subject of prophecy: "Promised since the world began" is an allusion to the alleged prophecy given in the Garden of Eden (Gen 3:15) and the continuance of such prophecies, even through heathen Sibyls (see S387) down to the time of the Roman Virgil *Eclogues* IV:5–7, "The age renews itself; Justice

returns and man's primeval time, and a new progeny descends from heaven."

*Stanza 3. O that birth forever blesséd.*

The poet here shows us the fulfillment of these prophecies in the Babe of Bethlehem and asserts the Orthodox position as found in the Apostles' Creed: "conceived by the Holy Ghost, born of the Virgin Mary."

*Stanza 4. This is he whom seers in old time.* Omitted in some hymnals.

*Stanzas 5–6. O ye heights; Thee let old men.*

Contemplation of these mysteries arouses such emotion that the poet breaks out in an apostrophe of praise, reminiscent of Ps 148:1–12; calls upon everything that hath breath to praise—not God, but the Son. "Power" and "Virtue" refer to two of the nine ranks of angels whom Dionysius the Areopagite saw when he visited heaven. Men, infants, matrons, virgins, children are all urged to join the chorus. Prudentius had a practical reason for urging this: the heretics were singing their heresies all over the East. Hilary had heard them in Asia Minor and tried to kindle a backfire of song in Gaul, but the light didn't catch. Augustine heard the Donatists singing their damnable heresies in Africa; the Gnostics and Neo-Platonists had been singing them in Syria and Egypt for two centuries, and the Arians themselves had been propagandizing with song for some seventy-five years. Let Christians beat them at their own game!

*Stanza 7. Christ, to thee.*

The final stanza tells these choirs what to sing. Sing the Orthodox dogma of the Trinity, officially established by the Council of Nicaea in A.D. 325. In this famous Council Athanasius was the champion against Arius. He insisted that the Son was of the *same substance* with the Father ("consubstantial" Neale calls it): that is, not created as Adam was created, but having "unfolded" out of the Father. Arius compromised by saying that the Son was of "similar substance" with the Father. Athanasius maintained that the son existed from all eternity, as did the Father ("co-eternal" Neale translates it), but Arius said No, the Father existed before the son.

You may be interested to read the full statement of the Orthodox position in the so-called Athanasian Creed, usually given in the Anglican Prayer Book, and found in the *Catholic Encyclopedia* under that head. No one can possibly understand what it means, yet every person in the world must believe every word of it without mental reservations or go to hell (*Cath. Enc.* II:33, first two sentences of the Creed)! One wonders how the Penitent Thief ever managed to get into heaven (Lk 23:39–43).

It is easy to see why the hymnal editors have softened down Neale and Prudentius, especially in the last stanza.

So comes to an end this first period of Latin hymnody. It covers the years when the Roman Empire was still intact and Christianity was spreading like leaven through all of the West. During this half-millennium the government and civilization of Europe were essentially Classical, that is, founded upon the idea of Law and Order inherited in germ from the Greek genius but enlarged and implemented by Rome. The final sixty-five years of that period saw the disruption and dissolution of that society by barbarian hordes which in 476 A.D. put an end to the Western Roman Empire. Christian Latin hymnody had its beginning during the final century of this period, as we have seen, by Hilary, Niceta, Ambrose and Prudentius. The verse structure of these poets was still classical: that is, it had no rhyme or accent, and the metrical feet showed an alternation of long and short syllables. The hymns were largely doctrinal, an antidote to the poison of Arian heresy.

### THE DARK AGE

The next half-millennium (500–1000 A.D.) is popularly called the Dark Age. In it the old order disappeared; the concept of government by law was superseded by the concept of loyalty to the will of a tribal chieftain. The age was "dark" because the "light" of Roman civilization was blotted out. But the light of Christianity was spreading across that darkness through the Church's missionary work carried on chiefly by Benedictine monks. Although some of the barbarian tribes had been Christianized while they were still in the East, their brand of Christianity was the heretical Arianism. Missionary activity was therefore directed against this heresy as well as against pure paganism. In the end, western Catholicism prevailed over eastern Arianism, but it was a long hard fight that literally cost the lives of millions.

In this struggle for survival hymnody played its part. The hymns were for the most part anonymous, though we have the names of half a dozen brilliant writers. In general we may say that the hymns express the fighting theology of the earlier classical period, they embody the fears and longings of men whose world was chaotic, they present Jesus as a King surrounded with the paraphernalia of the Old Testament and Apocalyptic imagery, and they are shaped to fit the requirements of the Christian year and of the daily Office as developed by the monks in their abbey churches. These hymns, therefore, appealed to the liturgically-minded High Churchmen of the Oxford Movement, to whom we are largely indebted for the translation of them, and they are preserved today in greatest number in the liturgical hymnals—the Anglican, Episcopalian and Lutheran.

We shall now trace the historical background of this Dark Age hymnody.

### THE BARBARIAN CONQUEST OF GAUL

As we have seen under Hilary, Gaul was completely Romanized after its conquest by Julius Caesar. But beginning with the fifth century A.D. the pressure of barbarian hordes was rising all along the empire's northeastern frontier until finally the barriers broke and the flood was on. In 406 the Vandals, Suevi and Alans crossed the Rhine frontier and inundated all of northern Gaul, while southern Gaul, bereft of the authority of the legions, disintegrated into civil war. Then in 410 Alaric's sack of Rome sent a thrill of horror through the world. Following him the Visigoths broke over the Alps into northern Italy but swept westward into southern Gaul and set up a kingdom at Toulouse. This tribe was Christian, but alas, of the Arian brand. By 450 the Burgundians had permanently occupied southern Gaul (hence the province of Burgundy) and the Visigoths held everything from the Loire River to the Pyrenees. In 451, Attila and his Huns swept like a tornado across Gaul, leaving devastation behind. Law and order collapsed. Among other fateful losses the public schools completely disappeared, and with them the Latin language for a while, so that for many generations no new literature of note was created.

The Germanic tribe that was destined to leave its mark and its name upon Gaul was the Frank. It broke across the lower Rhine in 431. By the end of that century their chieftain, Clovis (d. 511), had conquered all of Gaul except Burgundy and Provence. In 493 this pagan Clovis married a Burgundian princess Clotilda, who was an ardent Christian. He resisted all her prayers to forsake his heathen god until, confronted with a crucial battle against the Alamanni, he vowed that if Clotilda's God would grant him the victory he would become a Christian. He won the battle, went to Reims and there was baptized with 2000 of his warriors. This was an event of the first consequence, for it settled the destiny of France as a Catholic rather than an Arian Christian kingdom. Clovis then drove the Arian Visigoths out of southern France. Naturally he became the guardian of the Catholic Church and received in appreciation of his accomplishment the ardent support of the Popes.

The century that followed the invasions of the fifth was one of economic ruin and chaos. It seemed to civilized man that the end of the world was at hand, and, as always happens when the bottom drops out of economic and civil life, darkness fell also upon the human spirit. The world became irrational, the wildest superstitions took the place of reason. There was an immense growth in miracle stories, in the veneration of relics and belief in their miraculous powers. Worship of saints became organized as protection against the power of demons now augmented in men's minds to terrible proportions. No wonder that men fled from their insoluble problems to the shelter of the monasteries which in the sixth century began to multiply under the steadying hand of Benedict of Nursia, who in 529 established the monastery at Monte Cassino. The "Rule" of a Benedictine monastery seemed heaven beside the chaos of the world. So the monastic life became typical of these dark ages and set its stamp for a time upon the life and liturgy of the Church.

## GREGORY THE GREAT

Fortunately during this period of chaos a strong man came to power in Rome, Pope Gregory VII called the Great (590–604). He was the founder of the temporal power of the papacy. Born a patrician and bred for administrative duties, he gave up his wealth and power to become a monk. It was while he was abbot of St. Andrew's monastery in Rome that he saw the fair-haired Anglo-Saxon youths for sale in the slave market and remarked, "Not Angles but Angels—if they can be Christianized!"—the inspiration for his sending Augustine later as first monastic missionary to England. Gregory's missionary zeal was manifest from the start; he effected the conversion of the Lombard conquerers of northern Italy from Arianism to Catholicism, drove out the other tribes whom he could not convert and sent his missionaries to attack the paganism of Gaul and the Christian schisms elsewhere. In these campaigns his spearhead was the Benedictine order. Monasteries and nunneries sprang up all over Europe. They carried with them not only their Rule but the monastic liturgy and the exclusive use of plain-song melodies which Gregory himself is said to have collected and standardized. "Gregorian" music is still standard with the Catholic Church.

In our hymnals three hymns that have survived this turbulent sixth century are more or less doubtfully ascribed to Gregory the Great. These are:

*Audi benigne conditor*
*O kind Creator, bow thine ear*      Tr Canon Lacey, 1906
*Kind Maker of the world, O hear*      Tr Hymnal editors, 1941
*Ecce tempus idoneum*
*Now is the healing time decreed*      Tr Canon Lacey, 1906
*Rex Christi, factor omnium*
*O Christ, our King, Creator, Lord*      Tr Ray Palmer, 1858

These sixth century hymns have a haunting plaintiveness, as if they had been projected against a background of sin, suffering and fear. Christ is the Saviour whose streaming wounds are our ransom. He is the Conqueror who can defend our weakness. With fasting and prayer we plead for forgiveness. They are hymns for the Lenten season.

See also under the tenth century, anonymous, *Nocte surgentes vigilemus omnes*, formerly ascribed to Gregory.

## FORTUNATUS, VENANTIUS HONORIUS CLEMENTIANUS
### (c. 530–609)

FORTUNATUS was well-named, for Fortune smiled upon him during most of his life. Born in northern Italy in the days of the Ostrogothic domination, he was well educated in a school in Ravenna established by King Theodoric. While there he developed a severe eye trouble, but the disease was cured by the application of oil brought from a lamp hanging before the statue of St. Martin of Tours. In thankfulness he later made a pilgrimage to Tours (560) on horseback from the Po to the Danube, to the Rhine, to the Seine and Loire, improvising poems as he went along. He writes,

> I had for auditors, barbarians incapable of knowing the difference between a raucous voice and a sweet one, and of distinguishing the song of a swan from the cry of an owl . . . I sang my verses while my auditors kept time by clapping their hands and committing a thousand follies fit to revolt even the god Bacchus.

He and King Sigbert than travelled over the Frankish kingdoms together, the poet being variously useful as letter-writer and educated man, as public orator and as composer of flattering verse when bishops, nobles and their wives were guests of His Majesty. But in 567 Fortunatus left court and settled at Poitiers. He must have taken Holy Orders, for in 600 he became Bishop of Poitiers, and died prosperous and famous.

His arrival at Poitiers became the occasion of a Platonic romance that led shortly, among other things, to hymn-writing. The partner in the romance was ex-Queen Radegunde; and here is her story:

She had been born to a royal family in barbarian Thuringia. But this tribe was conquered in 529 by the Franks under Clotaire I and the princess was carried off as a prize of war. The conquerors quarrelled over her, then awarded her to the King. She was taken to Gaul and given tutors for her education. In due course the King commanded her to come to Vitry where he had made arrangements to marry her, but she fled by night. Clotaire re-captured her, brought her to Soissons and married her willy-nilly.

Radegunde had no taste for marriage with a barbarian nor for the pomp of courts. From her youth she had been strongly religious. So much was she devoted to prayer that the courtiers used to say, "The king has married a nun rather than a wife." She gave most of her income to the poor and to monastic houses. Finally she ran away from her husband and took refuge in a convent she had previously established, Sainte Croix, outside the walls of Poitiers. There are extant fifty-five letters between Fortunatus, Radegunde and her adopted daughter Agnes, abbess of the nunnery. Fortunatus sent them presents of wine—"good for Radegunde's weak stomach"—and eggs, with directions to eat up to two a day. Most of the letters were written to accompany or to acknowledge such gifts. Then Fortunatus acted as secretary to these two ladies. This devotion was the expression of the poet's almost superstitious reverence for the mystical religious life as exemplified by these two women.

The Queen was a typical mystic of that Dark Age period. Religious relics were her passion and she made her nunnery a regular museum of specimens from all over the world. Being a queen, she could bring pressure to bear on even the Emperor at Constantinople. "Once she begged the patriarch of

St. Martin dividing his cloak with a beggar, from the "Heures de Boucicaut," c. 1410, in the Musée Jacquemart-André, Paris.

Constantinople to get for her a relic of a saint named Mammes whose tomb was in Jerusalem. The patriarch held mass at the tomb and demanded before all the people in a loud voice, 'I conjure you, confessor and martyr of Christ, if the blessed Radegunde is a true servant of God, make known your power in the midst of the nations and grant that the relics of yours which the faithful soul desires she may obtain.' Then he opened the tomb and touched in turn each of the members of the saint in order to see which one Radegunde had desired. As he touched the fingers of the saint's right hand, one of them detached itself and he sent it by messenger to the queen. With what joy she received it! And all the week she and the sisters of the nunnery spent their nights singing psalms and thanking God that he had found her worthy of such a gift." *

All of this is quite characteristic of the barbarous age in which she lived, and leads directly to consideration of a characteristic hymn of Fortunatus:

## Vexilla regis prodeunt

*The royal banners forward go*    Tr Canon Percy Dearmer, 1933
*The royal banners forward go*    Tr Neale, 1851
*The royal banners forward go*    Tr Neale, altered, 1940
*The royal banners forward go*    Tr S.P.V., 1670
*The royal standard forward goes*    Tr J. C. Mattes, 1913

When the hymn was appropriated for use at Passiontide in the eighth century some of the original stanzas were omitted and two others were added —of course not by Fortunatus.

*Stanza 1. The royal banners forward go.* The interpretation of the Crucifixion here given is that of Catholic theology: Christ by His death on the cross suffered the penalty due to our sins and saved us from eternal punishment (if we are baptized).

*Stanza 2. Where deep for us the spear was dy'd.* The blood and water flowing from Christ's wounds serve as a bath to cleanse us from present sins.

*Stanza 3. Fulfill'd is all that David told.* This death was the fulfillment of prophecy spoken by David, Ps 96:10, "Tell it out among the heathen that the Lord reigneth"; and according to a reading of a second century text, "reigneth *from the tree.*"

*Stanza 4. O tree of beauty! tree of light!* The wood of the cross clothed by Christ's blood as with a garment, becomes a thing of beauty, of light, of royal dignity.

*Stanza 5. On whose dear arms, so widely flung.* The arms of the cross are like a balance on which coin is weighed—the price Christ paid to cancel humanity's debt to Satan. This idea, "to spoil the

* F. J. E. Raby: *History of Christian Latin Poetry*, Clarendon Press, Oxford, 1927.

Fortunatus and Queen Radegunde at the Abbey of Ste. Croix, a mural
in the Hôtel de Ville at Poitiers painted by Puvis de Chavannes, 1874.
The Queen, in white, and her adopted daughter, the Abbess Agnes,
listen to Fortunatus as he declaims one of his poems.

spoiler of his prey," reflects the early theology of Origen (c. 185–
c. 254) in which by Adam's sin the Devil took a mortgage on all of
Adam's posterity. By Christ's death Satan was deprived of what he
really wanted, the chance to torture all humanity.

Quite characteristic of the florid style of Fortunatus are the varying
figures of speech he employs. These are especially prominent in stanzas
4 and 6.

This hymn was written to celebrate the reception at Radegunde's nunnery of a relic of the True Cross.

It seems that Radegunde had greatly desired such a relic, for her
reverence for the cross had led to her founding of this convent named
Sainte Croix. She therefore sent word to the Frankish King Sigebert asking
that he petition the Emperor, Justin II at Constantinople, for a piece of the
cross. The King did so, the Emperor responded and anon sent messengers
with two "evangelaries," books containing the four Gospels or such parts of
them as are read at Mass. These were decorated with gold and precious
stones and filled with relics including the wood of the cross. When the box
reached Poitiers, the Bishop and all the people made great preparation to
receive it with the devotions due to such a prize. But the devil set his agents
to work to prevent its reception into the city, and he did so by forcing the
messengers to deposit it in a monastery at Tours. The Queen, baffled at the
moment of success, sent word to Sigebert while she and her nuns spent the
time in prayers and tears and self-torture, begging God to incline the heart
of the King to a righteous decision. The King then commanded the Bishop
of Tours to carry the relics with all honor and deposit them in the nunnery
of Radegunde. This was done. For that reception Fortunatus composed the
*Vexilla regis.*

We should try to visualize the scene: the ancient city of Poitiers, its
walls crowded with all its citizenry in holiday dress; the nuns of Sainte
Croix outside the walls, with the Abbess Agnes and Queen Radegunde, kneeling in prayer before the nunnery door; the Bishop of Poitiers and his clergy,
the poet Fortunatus at their head, all issuing from the gates in solemn procession with censers and candles to meet the procession of clergy and the
faithful approaching from Tours, holding lighted torches and chanting
liturgies, with the banners of King Sigebert gaily flying over them; the joyous
meeting; then the chant of Fortunatus rising for the first time from the lips
of the monk choir; the march back to the nunnery—the relics held high that
all might see; their reception by the Queen; the burst of joy, the shouts, the
plaudits, as the True Cross is carried within and deposited on the high altar
of the abbey chapel—all this on Nov. 19, 569.

We must hold this picture in mind as background for Fortunatus's contemplation of what the cross was and what it did for mankind. In this contemplation he reveals his own mystic approach to religion which was at the

same time a reflection of the age in which he lived. The theme is the mystery of what divine love accomplished by the cross.

### Salve, festa dies

### Welcome, happy morning; age to age shall say
### Tr John Ellerton, 1868

*Hail, Festival Day, to endless ages known*        Tr Canon Lacey, 1884
*Hail thee, Festival Day! blest day that art hallowed forever*
Tr Canon Percy Dearmer, 1925

If possible, read and enjoy the flowing lines of this paraphrase written in the original elegiac meter of Fortunatus. Dearmer's work is based upon former translations.

(Ellerton's translation):

*Stanza 1. "Welcome, happy morning!" age to age shall say;*
*Stanza 2. Earth with joy confesses, clothing her for spring,*
*Stanza 3. Months in due succession, days of lengthening light,*
*Stanza 4. Maker and Redeemer, Life and Health of all,*
*Stanza 5. Thou, of life, the Author, death didst undergo,*
*Stanza 6. Loose the souls long prisoned, bound with Satan's chain;*

This hymn is taken from a long poem of 110 lines addressed to Bishop Felix of Nantes on the subject of the Easter festival. The Church soon adapted portions of it to its liturgical needs and the poem has continued to the present day as one of the favorite Easter hymns. The various paraphrases only suggest the flavor of the elaborate metaphors of Fortunatus.

The original begins with a florid description of Spring when the sun calls all the earth back to light, the flowers are reborn, the birds return and the bees go forth again in search of nectar. In all this resurrected beauty the poet finds a symbol of the resurrection life. Noticeable throughout this hymn are the varied names or descriptions of Christ from the theological viewpoint: God, Creator, King, Vanquisher of Darkness, Maker, Redeemer, Life, Health, Son, Author of Life, True and Faithful Lord. The joy of Easter as reflected in the springtime breathes through stanzas 2–3; stanzas 4–5 sketch the story of the Incarnation and Atonement; theological concepts of redemption and deliverance appear in stanzas 1 and 6.

"Loose the souls long prisoned, bound with Satan's chain" is a reminiscence of the old belief that between the time of the Crucifixion and the Resurrection Christ "descended into Hell," as the Apostles' Creed puts it; that is, He preached His gospel to the righteous heroes of the Old Testament (such as Adam, Abel, Noah, David, et al.), who had been confined in "Limbo," the ante-chamber of Hell, won their acceptance and took them up to heaven. This act is technically known as the "Harrowing of Hell." Who says that Christianity has no mythology?

Ignoring some of the crudities we can still use and appreciate the hymn as an expression of the Christian joy that is linked with Easter and its promise of life after death.

It would seem then that Fortunatus has at least made a valuable contribution to the hymnody of the liturgical Churches. He was the last of the Romans: or better, the first Christian poet of the barbarians, acceptable to the rough age of conquest because he sang engagingly many themes that

*Left,* Queen Radegunde, wife of Clotaire. *Center,* Church of Ste. Radegunde, Poitiers, original built c. 560 by Queen Radegunde; the present structure dates from 1099. Inside is the chapel of the "Footstep of God"—an imprint left in the stone by Christ when He visited the Queen and foretold her death. In the crypt is Radegunde's tomb containing her original black marble sarcophagus, empty since 1562 when the Huguenots burned the Saint's remains. *Right,* King Sigebert (d. 575), a contemporary drawing of that king of the Franks who was son of King Clotaire, though not by Queen Radegunde. Fortunatus also wrote the marriage hymn when Sigebert wed. The king here carries the model of a church he has evidently given to a city.

touched their daily life, yet sympathetic with the inner meaning of Christianity as understood by mystic saints like Queen Radegunde. He is commemorated in nine out of the ten hymnals that are basic to our study.

*Angularis fundamentum*     Anonymous

*Christ is made the sure foundation*     Tr Neale, 1851 Alt.
*Christ is our Cornerstone*     Tr John Chandler, 1837

This hymn is part of *Urbs beata Hierusalem, Blessed city, heavenly Salem* in which is celebrated the New Jerusalem, coming down from heaven as a bride adorned for her husband (Rev 21:2). This metaphor, however, is speedily abandoned: the city becomes a genuine habitation built of gold and pearls, adorned with sculpture and prepared as the eternal home of the elect. Then in the original fifth stanza the Foundation is introduced.

This hymn is appropriate to the dedication of a church building. Some scholars think, however, that stanza 3 was not in the original. In that case the whole was a paean in praise of the heavenly Jerusalem to which the faithful of the dark days of the seventh century looked with longing. Contrasted with the poverty and squalor and sickness of that age, the brutality of barbarian invasions, the social chaos, heaven was a place that passed man's understanding in its safety, its beauty, its unchanging eternity. Observe the words that express these ideals: "sure foundation," "binding all the Church," "help forever," "confidence," "dedicated city," "exultant jubilation," "perpetual melody," "eternally," "gain-retain," "evermore." That city is the *summum bonum* granted by God to those that love Him.

The scriptural origins of the imagery are 1 Cor 3:11; 2 Tim 2:19; Eph 2:20–22; 1 Cor 2:9; 2 Tim 2:12; Rev 22:5.

The author has not neglected to fire a shot against the barbarian Arians: only those who acknowledge the "One in Three" can expect to praise Him in heaven (stanza 2), and for good measure a Doxology is added—omitted in our hymnals—in which the three Persons are declared to be "con-substantial, co-eternal," contrary to Arian assertion. (See above under Ambrose and Prudentius).

## THE AGE OF CHARLEMAGNE (742–814)

JUST beyond the middle of the Dark Age arose the one great secular genius who for a time seemed to shed the light of a new morning over the earth. He was Karl, king of the Frankish peoples, known to later times as Carolus Magnus or Charlemagne. Not only was he an insatiable fighter and conqueror—from Italy on the south and the Slavs on the east and the Danes on the north to Spain and the English Channel on the west. He was also a great organizer and civilizer, and especially after his coronation as Emperor by the Pope (800 A.D), a great propagandist for the Catholic faith. He became the shining light of the Dark Age who endeavored to bring something of the Roman civilization—its literature, education, art—together with the Christian religion, to the barbarous peoples over whom he ruled. His court became a brilliant assembly of men who founded schools and spread Christianity with the express purpose of bringing together, sometimes by ruthless methods, all the Germanic peoples into one great Christian empire. In this task he was greatly helped by an Englishman named Alcuin who became a sort of "Minister of Education," by another Englishman named Boniface (afterwards made a Saint) who became his "Minister of Propaganda" and worked with the conversion of the barbaric northern Saxons especially in mind, and by Theodulph of Orleans who was perhaps his outstanding poet.

## THEODULPH OF ORLEANS (c. 760–821)

THEODULPH was a great pastor, Bishop and poet. Perhaps his barbarian blood was responsible for enthusiasms which made him a leader in whatever he undertook, whether in learning, in poetry, in reforms both in social conduct and in church administration.

He was born in Spain of Ostrogothic parentage. His education was not confined to a study of the Church Fathers and such Christian poets as his fellow Spaniard Prudentius, but included heathen poets, as the Roman poets Virgil and Ovid were now called. He excused his Christian conscience by interpreting these poets allegorically. Dr. E. K. Rand * put it this way: "Keeping in mind the application of the allegorical method, the Christian reader may listen unharmed to the music of Virgil, and what is more surprising, he may wander without fear through the dangerous and alluring *Tales of Ovid*." Even Ovid's lascivious *Art of Love* was allegorized for nuns!

Charlemagne heard of Theodulph's genius and called him to his court at Aachen, c. 781. There he delighted the literary circle of scholars and courtiers with his poetry, until to reward him the King gave him the See of Orleans. Here his energy and enthusiasm found ample scope. Following his King's directions he established schools in connection with all the monasteries and cathedrals of his diocese. Going even beyond this he set up free schools in towns and villages so that the children of the poor might have instruction. Besides doing this work he became an outstanding organizer and reformer of the churches of Gaul, appointed thereto as a kind of inspector by the King himself. To help bolster Charlemagne's campaign to make the *filioque* theory of the Holy Ghost ** standard for his empire, he wrote an elaborate collection of the opinions of the Fathers on the subject. After Charlemagne had died (814) and was succeeded by his son Louis the Pious, a son of the former King Pepin named Bernard endeavored to seize the throne. Rightly or wrongly, Theodulph was accused of being in the plot, was deposed from his bishopric and imprisoned in a monastery in Angers. Here, having nothing else to do, he put his griefs into verse. It was during this imprisonment, also c. 820, that he composed the only hymn that has survived in common use. He died in prison in 821, probably from poison. It is not known where he was buried. Possibly it was in the little church he built at Germigny, most of which still exists—the oldest church in France.

### Gloria, laus et honor

### All glory, laud and honor    c. 820      Tr Neal, 1854

This hymn is used by the liturgical churches on Palm Sunday. It is a poetical rendering of the Gospel story of the Triumphal Entry (Mk 11:1–10; a different version in Jn 12:12–19). By this act Jesus is thought to have sym-

---

* *Ovid and His Influence*, copyright, 1925, Longmans.
** (That He proceeds from both the Father *and the* Son.)

Charlemagne founding his school at Aachen. Painting by Schnetz.

bolically presented Himself to the Jews as the Messiah, the son of David. In the poem we are asked to join in the procession of children and the choirs of angels above to sing praises to Christ as the Redeemer King.

Stanza 7 has obviously been omitted since the seventeenth century:

Be Thou, O Lord, the Rider,    That to God's Holy City
  And we the little ass;       Together we may pass.

We know from ancient books that Palm Sunday at Orleans was the occasion of a great celebration—a solemn blessing by the bishop, the distribution of palm branches, and then a pageant-like procession. Says Raby, quoting an earlier writer:

"At the head of the procession were bourne the Gospels, the dragon, the cross, and the banners; then followed a living representation of Jesus seated on an ass; last came the throng of people carrying branches and singing the Hosannahs. When the gates of the city were reached, they were closed, the procession halted while the Gospel was sung and a prayer was said for the city and its inhabitants. Then a choir of children sang, from the city walls, the *Gloria, laus et honor* and the refrain was taken up by the crowd. The gates were then opened and the ceremony ended at the cathedral." *

A pretty legend has grown up about this hymn. The scene is Angers where Theodulph was in prison by order of the Emperor Louis. On Palm Sunday the Emperor happened to be in town. As the grand procession, which the Emperor had joined, moved through the streets it halted by chance beneath the tower where Theodulph was kept. "Suddenly from above was heard the *Gloria, laus,* chanted loudly and melodiously. The emperor was charmed and asked the named of the unknown singer. He was told that it was Theodulph, his own prisoner. Then the gentle and merciful monarch was moved with compassion, and from that hour he delivered and pardoned him, and sent him back to his church, quit and absolved of the crime whereof he had been accused." There is no reason to suppose that the story is more than a pious legend invented by the people of Orleans for the glory and justification of their beloved bishop. It is at the same time testimony to the popularity of this magnificent hymn.

## RABANUS MAURUS (?) d. 856

ONE other hymn from this period cannot be ascribed with certainty, but nevertheless it has frequently been attributed to Rabanus Maurus.

This great man was a product of the school at the Benedictine monastery of Fulda in the forest of Buchonia, where now is the city of Fulda, Germany. This was an outpost of Christianity founded by Boniface in order that from it he might wage his campaign against the Saxons. Having become an enthusiastic student, Rabanus was sent next to Tours where he became the favorite pupil of the great Alcuin, then returned to Fulda to be its abbot (822–842) and finally achieved the highest place among the Germanic churchmen and theologians of his age. The hymn is ascribed to Rabanus by the *Catholic Encyclopedia,* but the great argument against his authorship is the fact that the hymn is better poetry than any other poetry we have from Rabanus. At any rate, out of this complex of partly Latinized barbarism, dawning and fading culture and crude missionary zeal in which power politics played a dominant role, out of the forests of Germany and the genius of some great scholar and cleric of this time came the

* F. J. E. Raby: *History of Christian Latin Poetry,* p. 175, Clarendon Press, Oxford, 1927.

## Veni, Creator Spiritus

The long-lived vitality of this hymn is attested by its constant presence in the Roman Catholic breviaries and by the numbers of translations made in our language since the Reformation. The following are found in our standard hymnals:

Creator Spirit, by whose aid      Tr John Dryden, 1693
Come, Holy Ghost, Creator blest
Tr Mant, 1837; Caswell, 1849; R. Campbell, 1850
Come, Holy Ghost, our souls inspire      Tr John Cosin, 1627
Come, O Creator Spirit, come      Tr R. Bridges, 1899

Of all the versions, Bridges, the English Poet Laureate, has made the closest and best translation; Cosin comes next, while Dryden's is really a paraphrase that partakes of the florid quality of late seventeenth-century literature. Unfortunately the hymnal editors have cut out from Dryden two important stanzas. To appreciate the hymn one really needs an exact prose translation of the whole original.

The point of view in the *Veni Creator* is intensely personal and emotional. The hymn is largely a prayer, expressed in its pleading imperatives: "Come," "visit," "pour" (stanza 1 Dryden's version); "inspire," "anoint" (stanza 2); "Descend with power," "teach," "reveal" (stanza 3—not much like the original). In the two omitted stanzas the prayers become even more vehement (Bridges' translation): *

> Our senses with thy light inflame,
> Our hearts to heavenly love reclaim;
> Our bodies' poor infirmity
> With strength perpetual fortify.

Then follows a prayer that must have been an instinctive cry in those dark ages of oppression and sudden death:

> Our mortal foe afar repel,
> Grant us henceforth in peace to dwell;
> And so to us, with thee for guide,
> No ill shall come, no harm betide.

The last stanza is the customary Doxology that affirms belief in the doctrine of the Trinity. But there is here also a fighting word which Dryden chooses to ignore but which Bridges preserves: *"utriusque,"* "who art of both." For centuries the Eastern Church had maintained that the Holy Spirit had proceeded from the Father alone (following Jn 14:26), whereas the Western Church held that the Spirit had proceeded from the Father and the Son equally (*filioque*, the Son also). This was a fighting proposition over which countless heads were cracked and countless anathemas were pro-

* Robert Bridges: *Yattendon Hymnal*, Clarendon Press, Oxford.

nounced, and it was one of the wedges that permanently split the Church into its two main branches of East and West, Greek and Roman. This western interpretation had been especially championed by the Church in Spain, and after Charlemagne came back from fighting the Moors in that country he resolved to line up his whole empire behind the *filioque* clause. So at the

*Left,* Portrait of Rabanus Maurus, drawn c. 1550. *Right,* Church of Germigny-des-Prés built in 806 by Theodulph of Orleans. The style is Byzantine; Romanesque developed later.

Council of Aachen (809) the doctrine of the "double procession of the Spirit" (from both Father and Son) was made mandatory for the German Church. Here it is in this hymn!

Dryden pads out the original form with some Biblical allusions: for example—

*Stanza 1,* line 2. The original calls the Spirit "Creator," implying throughout the hymn that He creates certain attitudes and gifts in us. But Dryden lugs in a cosmic idea from Heb 1:2, "by whom also he made the worlds"—not stopping to notice that the Biblical writer was referring to Christ as Creator, not the Holy Spirit.

*Stanza 1,* line 6. An allusion to 1 Cor 6:19.

*Stanza 2,* line 6 and *Stanza 3,* lines 3–6 are wholly Dryden.

*Stanza 2.* Dryden has fortunately preserved one important word of the orginal, "Paraclete." In reality it is a Greek word taken by the hymn-writer from the Fourth Gospel where it applies to the Holy Spirit (Jn 14:26). The word is translated in the Authorized Version as "Comforter," but we must remember that the original meaning of Comforter, both in Greek and Latin, is not one who comes to soothe but one who is called in to aid and strengthen. Percy Dearmer tells us (*Songs of Praise Discussed,* p. 111) of an entry in the Chronicles of the Monastery of St. Edmunds, that a certain school-master *comfortavit pueros baculo,* "fortified the boys with a stick"! Jesus promised this Strengthener in Jn 16:7; the promise is repeated in Acts 1:4–5, 8, and it was fulfilled by a mighty wind and tongues of flame on the day of Pentecost (Acts 2:1–4). Dryden alludes to this Pentecostal coming with power in his phrase "thrice holy fire."

The Emperor Charlemagne had been for a brief period a beacon light that seemed to herald a Chistendom united and something like a new universal civilization reborn. But with his death the light faded; darkness and disorder returned for a couple of centuries. Only one hymn had survival value until a new age was ushered in. That one is

*Nocte surgentes vigilemus omnes*     [*Tenth Century, Anonymous*]

> *Father, we praise thee, now the night is over*
> Tr Canon Percy Dearmer, 1906
> *Christ's loving children, for his hope abiding*
> Tr Robert Bridges, 1899

The unusual meter of the Bridges translation is the Greek "Sapphic": three lines with the rhythm $-\,\cup\cup-\cup\,\|-\cup-\cup-\cup$ and the fourth $-\cup\cup-\cup$.

While all but one of the hymnals credits Pope Gregory (sixth cent.) or says "ascribed to Gregory," the Episcopal *Hymnal* alone maintains that the author is unknown and the date tenth century.

The figure underlying the hymn is that of the faithful servant watching for the long-delayed coming of his Master (Lk 12:35–40). The joy of his coming lies in release from weakness and sin and suffering, the attainment of wholeness and joy in the mansions above. This was the only possible attitude for a Christian to take in that dark age when the light of civilization had well-nigh been extinguished by ignorance and the reign of anarchy. In that century heathen Norsemen had over-run all northern France and re-named it Normandy; heathen Danes were in complete control of England; the Mediterranean had become a Saracenic lake; Constantinople was suffering a series of naval raids by heathen Russians; the line of the most Christian King Charlemagne had become extinct; the first Saxon Holy Roman Emperor Otto I was crowned by Pope John XII, and the very next year deposed his benefactor. Truly, the world was very evil; the only hope an Apocalypse.

The modern attitude toward an evil world is not to flee from it but to remake it. This approach to evil is the biggest problem in the history of mankind.

## THE MIDDLE AGES (1000–1400)

WITH the hymns we are now about to consider we plunge into the middle of the Middle Age. The transition from the Dark Age had been slow and uncertain; in fact, during the tenth and eleventh centuries the spiritual and moral darkness of the Church reached a new blackness. The institution founded on Christ and St. Peter had become completely secularized. Church offices were bought and sold, and, contrary to their vows, the clergy married. So shocking had become the life of ecclesiastics that reform was bound to come. Fortunately into this crisis stepped Hildebrand who, as Pope Gregory VII (1073–1085), spearheaded a moral revolution among the clergy and then brought to a successful realization the ideal that the Papacy was supreme over all temporal rulers. This marked the complete triumph of the Catholic faith over all opponents.

Churchmen were now by far the most powerful class in Europe. They alone could read and write. Through the vast lands contributed to them, the revenues and fees that flowed to their coffers, they were also the wealthiest class, and through their powers of inquisition and excommunication by which they could consign any person, high or low, to the stake and to perdition, they held men in strictest control.

The spiritual functions of the Church were exercised not only by the Pope, the bishops and clergy; there were also the special organizations of monks who had long been the missionary arm of the Church, besides being the saviours of the arts and crafts of Roman civilization. Since its founding in 529 A.D. the order of Benedictines had supplanted most others and then had been "reformed," until at the beginning of the Middle Age there existed beside the old Benedictines the powerful orders of Cluny and of Citeaux whose monasteries came to dominate all western Europe. At the beginning of the thirteenth century the new itinerant orders of the Franciscans and Dominicans were also created. Henceforth most of the learning of the West was in the keeping of monks. These became the teachers in all schools, the founders of the universities that began to spring up in the thirteenth century. They also claim most of the hymn-writers whose works have survived to our day.

### TWELFTH CENTURY

In the earlier Christian centuries Italy had been the inheritor of Roman culture and in spite of barbarian inundations had managed to preserve some of its schools, teach the classical authors and produce some prose and verse. But with the twelfth century the creative center of Europe shifted to France. As far as learning was concerned, Paris was the center. That city became the battleground of rival philosophers who sharpened their wits by the study of logic and the practice of dialectic. But they found it rather difficult to decide how many angels could stand on the point of a needle—an oft-discussed

MAP OF PARIS IN THE 12TH CENTURY.

*Inside the Walls:*

A. Notre Dame, founded 1163 after Abelard's death, but on the site of the 6th century church he knew.

B. The Cathedral School, earliest and most famous of the three schools that were united c.1208 to form the University of Paris. Here Abelard studied dialectic and rhetoric under William of Champeaux c.1100–1108, and himself became professor 1113–8    C. The school of Theology connected with it.

D. Abbey of Ste. Genevieve (d. 512, patron saint of Paris). Founded by Clovis, 511. Here Abelard set up his own school, 1108, before becoming professor at the Cathedral School. The present Pantheon stands on the site.

E. The Bishop's palace.      F. The King's palace.

*Outside the Walls:*

1. Royal hunting lodge in country infested with wolves. King Philip Augustus (1180–1223) erected a castle here, where the Louvre now stands.

2. Abbey of St. Germain-des-Prés, founded in the 6th century. In Abelard's day the present church was being built.

3. Abbey St. Victor. Originally a hermitage, whither William of Champeaux fled when Abelard bested him in argument (1108). There William set up his rival school. It was made into an abbey in 1113.

4. Abbey of St. Martin-des-Champs. Named after the miracle-working Bishop of Tours (d.397). Its basilica of 1114 was the one Abelard knew.

5. Headquarters of the Knights Templar of France, the Order was founded in Jerusalem, 1118; became Cistercian in France, 1128, under the influence of St. Bernard; waxed immensely rich. Finally suppressed by the Church c.1312.

problem—when points differ in size and angels refuse to be measured. So in this century there begins to emerge the idea that the facts of experience are a more valid basis for philosophy than are major premises evolved by the mind. Churchmen found this to be a dangerous trend in that the rationalistic point of view challenged some of the theological dogmas on which salvation and the authority of the Church rested. This difference of opinion on an issue of the day is why Abelard and Bernard of Clairvaux became such mortal enemies.

Though the hymns of this century were written in part by churchmen of whom these two were types, they are not so different in their expression of religion; one can not wax lyrical over syllogisms. The one hymn of Abelard we still use is a lyric of escape from a life of intellectual combat to the calm of an eternal Sabbath in heaven, while the hymns ascribed dubiously to Bernard take refuge in a mystical union with Christ where no harsh facts disturb the peace of Faith. In reality, most hymns did not come from the great intellectual center of Paris but from the quiet country retreats of the monasteries where, in theory at least, contemplation and prayer alternated with labor and charity.

We must note also that in this century were perfected new forms of verse. The dignified long lines inherited from classical Latin, in which the distinctive feature was the alternation of long and short syllables, gave place to a variety of rhythms and structures in which rhyme and accent dominate. In this matter English poetry follows the medieval rather than the classical mode.

## PETER ABELARD (1079–1142)

ABELARD was probably the most brilliant of medieval scholars and teachers. At the same time he was handsome, passionate, egotistical, aggressive to brutality, a free thinker and utterly unworthy of the halo of romance which posterity has granted him.

Son of the lord of a Brittany village, he rebelled against his father's plan to make him a soldier; he became a wandering seeker after learning until, when he was twenty years old, he landed in Paris, center of scholastic instruction. Those were the days when the learned world shook with combat over the philosophies called Nominalism and Realism. The question at issue, briefly and imperfectly summarized, was—

Nominalism: "Are universal concepts merely names invented to express the qualities of particular things, and therefore later in origin than things themselves?"
Realism: "Are universals the only realities, independent of things and existing before things, eternal and indestructible like God Himself?"

Adolescent Abelard argued with his greybeard teacher, renowned William of Champeaux, beat him to a standstill and set up a rival school of his own just outside Paris. When a few years later William retired, Abelard aspired to succeed him at the cathedral school; but failing this, opened his own school in Paris, until in 1113 he was given the chair of rhetoric and dialectic he had coveted. To prepare further for this new post he took a course in theology at Laon under venerable Anselm. He out-smarted this

*Left,* Tomb of Abelard and Heloise at Père Lachaise, Paris. *Right,* Abelard and Heloise.

teacher also. Abelard was now the most renowned disputant in Europe. Pupils flocked to him from every country. He himself modestly admits that he had the world at his feet. He was not far wrong: nineteen cardinals and two popes came from the list of his pupils.

But his downfall was tragic. He got his eye on brilliant and beautiful Heloise, niece of Canon Fulbert of Notre Dame Cathedral; worked his charms on the canon to allow him to live at his house in the Latin quarter and become Heloise's tutor. "What shall I say more?" wrote Abelard; "We had only one house and soon we had only one heart!" When Heloise became pregnant Abelard absconded with her to the home of his sister in Brittany, where she gave birth to a son. The boy was baptized Peter-Astrolabe in a small romanesque chapel that still exists. Abelard wished to get legal control

over Heloise and married her in spite of her remonstrances that it would be
fatal to his progress.

   Uncle Fulbert, however, was not through with the case. Though pretending forgiveness he bribed a servant of Abelard, who one night entered
Abelard's chamber with a few accomplices, bound him to his bed and

What is left of the Oratory of Abelard, in the Abbey of the Paraclete.

castrated him. To hide his disgrace Abelard became a monk and forced
Heloise into a convent. This was in 1119; he was forty years old, she about
eighteen.

   Next year Abelard returned to his teaching. He opened a school in the
priory of Maisoncelles in the territory of the Count of Champagne. Three
thousand students flocked to him. But his teachings aroused the hostility of
the Church. The Council of Soissons declared them heretical. Bernard of
Clairvaux (see below) was his insistent opponent on the ground that Abelard's rationalism threw Faith out of the window. The Council burned his
heretical book and shut him up in a monastery. Released, he got into another
controversy that proved so hot he was forced to flee Paris and become a
hermit in a solitary place near Nogent-sur-Seine. But his old students flocked
to him and built a shelter for him which in gratitude he named the Paraclete
(the Comforter: Jn 14:16). The name angered his enemies.

   When Suger became the new abbot of St. Denis he virtually exiled
Abelard by appointing him abbot of St. Gildas in far-off Brittany. It was a
rascally place: the monks made his life miserable for ten years. They tried to

kill him many times, often by poison, but he had luck with them. Finally he fled.

But new dangers arose. Bernard, most powerful preacher and ecclesiastic in Europe, again charged him with heresy and got him condemned by the Council of Sens (1141). Abelard appealed to Rome. But Bernard held all the cards and the Pope upheld the Council. The disgraced scholar took refuge, a sick and mentally broken man, in the monastery of Cluny (see below under Bernard of Cluny); died in its near-by priory of St. Marcel and was buried in his old oratory, the Paraclete.

While Abelard was abbot of St. Giles, Heloise and her nuns got into trouble and were ousted out of their convent at Argenteuil. Since Abelard had the necessary authority he established them at his old abandoned retreat, the Paraclete. There Heloise remained abbess until her death in 1164, and there she was buried beside her lover. In 1817 the remains of both were transferred to the cemetery of Père Lachaise in Paris. Their tomb is still a trysting-place for lovers and for sentimentalists who look upon this pair as paragons of marital devotion. Heloise does, in fact, measure up; but not so her partner:

> "Tell me one thing only if thou canst," wrote Heloise to Abelard; "why, after our conversion, which thou alone didst decree, I am fallen into such neglect and oblivion with thee that I am neither refreshed by thy speech and presence nor comforted by a letter in thine absence. . . . Concupiscence joined thee to me rather than affection, the ardor of desire rather than love; and when therefore what thou desiredst ceased, all that thou hadst exhibited at the same time failed."

Ralph Adams Cram, in his Introduction to *Abelard's Historia Calamitatum* thus appraises the situation:

> Behind the sin of Abelard lay his intolerable spiritual pride, his selfishness and his egotism, qualities that society at large did not recognize because of their devotion to his engaging personality and their admiration for his dazzling intellectual gifts.

### *O quanta qualia sunt illa Sabbata* [c. 1129]

#### *O what their joy and their glory must be* Tr J. M. Neale, 1854

When Heloise and her nuns set up their new establishment at the abandoned oratory of the Paraclete they lacked almost everything. In particular they needed hymns for their services. Heloise wrote Abelard about their predicament. That genius set to work and shortly supplied them with a complete hymnal written by himself, ample enough to cover the important days of their liturgy. A twelfth century manuscript of this book still exists in Brussels and from it Neale translated *O quanta qualia,* scheduled to be sung on Saturday evenings in preparation for Sunday.

These hymns were bound to reflect the author's unhappy experiences, his stormy life at St. Gildas, his controversies over theology, his persecution by Bernard, which were soon to lead to his indictment and condemnation by the high ecclesiastics of the Church. He was getting worn out by his anarchic life. In this particular hymn the author envies the saints in heaven who have now forgotten their years of struggle in the peace of an eternal Sabbath. Even they could never tell all it means to them (stanzas 1 and 2). Nevertheless the several items of their perfect joy can be enumerated, and together they form a definition of heaven: It is called Jerusalem, which means the "city of peace"; in it, wish and fulfillment are forever joined, prayer and its answer (stanza 3). There by divine grace the discords of life are resolved into music (stanza 4). For this city we yearn as did the Babylonian exiles for their native Jerusalem (stanza 5). A Doxology with the Trinitarian formula concludes the hymn (stanza 6). Neale has preserved the original dactylic tetrameter.

Abelard in his earlier life wrote and sang many songs in praise of love in general and Heloise in particular, so that all the students of Paris knew them by heart. All his known hymns are preserved in the Brussels manuscript. *O quanta qualia* and a hymn on the Crucifixion are the sole survivors in contemporary hymnody.

### Period of BERNARD OF CLAIRVAUX (1090–1153)

THERE is doubt whether Bernard wrote the hymns that for many centuries have been attributed to him. Of the ten hymnals that are the basis of this study, four, including the Canadian Anglican *Hymn Book* of 1938, definitely credit the hymns to Bernard; one other says, "ascribed to Bernard"; two say, "anonymous eleventh century"; three, including the Episcopal *Hymnal* of 1940, say "anonymous twelfth century"; and one says "medieval Latin." The *Catholic Encyclopedia* pronounces against Bernard's authorship. Recently an eleventh century manuscript is said to contain most of the hymn.

Since it is generally agreed that, whoever wrote the hymn called the "Rosy Hymn" or the "Jubilee Rhythm," it reflects the type of religion that was St. Bernard's—the religion of mystic faith and emotional intensity. In describing the life and times of this saint we shall be painting an authentic background for the hymn itself. The monastic life was the typical religious life, and the hymn writers of his age were monks.

Bernard, greatest of the medieval saints, was born about two miles from Dijon, east-central France, to a noble family; his father was a knight and his mother a person of radiant goodness. He was third in a family of seven. He early showed a bent for piety and learning. As he grew to young manhood he became marked for his beauty—slender, with golden hair and "peaches-and-cream" complexion—and for his elegance of speech and gracious manner. At school he distinguished himself: the world was open to him—court, camp, university or Church. After his mother died when he was twenty-two years old, a vision of her, disappointed and reproving, took possession of his soul

Monastery of Clairvaux and environs (probably contemporary).

as he was riding toward the camp of the Duke of Burgundy to join his brothers who were besieging a castle. He retired to a roadside church to pray and there poured out his soul to God. From that hour his future course was fixed.

Immediately he tried to convert his brethren. They and his uncle all followed him. His youngest brother he found playing in the castle yard, too young to go.

"Well, brother Nivard, to you alone our land will have to look."

To which the boy replied: "Does that mean to you, heaven; to me, the earth? The division has not fairly been made." And he later followed his brothers into the monastery, as did his father. About thirty young noblemen in all went with Bernard to Citeaux.

This monastery had been founded only fourteen years before. It was a "reform" of the Cluny monastery in the sense that it endeavored to correct the laxity into which Cluny had fallen and to return to the original strictness of the Benedictine rule. It also revived manual labor; the monks becoming farmers and cattle-breeders. Thus they depended for their income wholly on the land. To help in the work they established a department of "lay brothers," attached to the monastery but not taking the vows of a monk. Expecting to expand, Citeaux made the rule that future houses would not be feudal subsidiaries of the present house, but when it came to spiritual discipline the authority of the Abbot of Citeaux should be absolute. Thus came into existence the Order of the Cistercians, destined to be a mighty spiritual and cultural power for two centuries to come.

Into this Order in 1112 came Bernard and his company, but so eminent was his leadership that in three years he was sent to found a branch house further north, not far from Troyes. The little group of twelve and their twenty-four-year-old Abbot found a promising site in the deep valley of the Aube river known as the Valley of Wormwood, a name they promptly changed to *Clara Vallis,* or in French, Clairvaux. It was a valley of forests, wholly wild and desolate, the haunt of robbers. To hew a home out of the wilderness was hard work. Their first winter was terrible. Having arrived too late in the season to sow, they were soon reduced to a diet of beechnuts and roots on which they nearly died. In addition Bernard's own self-discipline was so severe that he permanently wrecked his health. He never relaxed his succession of work, reading, prayer, preaching. His monks and lay brothers reclaimed waste lands, taught the ignorant peasants the arts of farming and vine culture, to which other arts were added as the monks themselves became proficient. Bernard had a genius for spiritual leadership. On the road one day he met a condemned robber being led to the gallows. He seized the halter, took the man to court and begged his life for the monastery, converted and made a useful man of him.

Under Bernard's inspiration new houses were founded. Within his lifetime Citeaux became the mother of 162 other monasteries; by the end of the twelfth century there were 500 Cistercian houses in Europe, all daughters of the parent house. In influence they surpassed old Cluny and her daughters, remained the chief religious power in western Europe for 300 years; then both orders declined before the rise of the mendicant orders of Franciscans and Dominicans. However, the buildings at Citeaux continued to be rebuilt until in the eighteenth century they were still of monumental proportions, but they were destroyed during the French Revolution. Parts of them were built into a large prison that occupies the site. In 1790 both orders of Cluniacs and Cistercians were dissolved.

We need not relate in detail the growing power of Bernard. He became a man of big affairs. He commanded kings, emperors and prelates and they obeyed him. He settled a war, all leaders being won by his impetuous eloquence. Single-handed he arbitrated the quarrels of rival popes and put Innocent II on his seat in Rome. His greatest feat was his last. In 1146 Christendom was confronted with a crisis. The Saracens had nearly exterminated the Latin Kingdom of Jerusalm set up by the Crusaders, and the Pope commissioned Bernard to preach a new crusade (the second). Broken in health though he was, his impassioned oratory subdued all opposition; the

St. Bernard of Clairvaux. Caption on the picture, in Latin, is thus translated:

"If Piety should wish to assume a fitting face,
Let it take, O Bernard, this portrait of thyself."

King and Queen of France and the Emperor of Germany took the cross at his hands, as did countless others of all degrees. Courts and towns were emptied of men. Women hid their husbands and sons to keep them out of reach of Bernard's powerful eloquence. Whenever he came to preach, crowds flocked out to meet him before he entered the city. When he demanded conversion as a condition to joining the crusade, multitudes of vicious men were changed as by a miracle. Single-handed he had aroused Europe to a great spiritual enterprise, and when the incompetence and sinfulness of its leaders made it a total loss, the blame fell upon him.

It was earlier, about 1140, that Bernard began his attack against the Schoolmen in general and Abelard in particular, as described above. Those famous logicians were elevating dialectic and reason above piety. But what mattered supremely to Bernard was not whether "universals" were first in creation or whether "things" existed before them! What counts in God's sight is a life of holiness: simplicity, devotion, prayer, preaching, ministering to the physical and spiritual wants of men. So he fought for his spiritual ideals in season and out till his victory over the great Free Thinker was complete. Abelard was condemned by the Church and died an outcast.

In spite of this extraordinary success as a man of affairs and a preacher, Bernard was a devoted mystic. Long hours were spent with the Bible, in contemplation and in prayer. His devotion to the Virgin Mary was intense and tender: as Dante makes him say, "The Queen of Heaven, for whom I am all on fire with love." It was said that the Virgin personally appeared to him while he was still in school, and that later when writing his sermons on the *Song of Songs*, in which he sets forth Mary as the Bride, type of the Church on earth, the Virgin appeared in his cell and by moistening his lips with milk from her breast bestowed on him his irresistible eloquence.

One can imagine the intensity of Bernard's thought, the poetic and allegorical imagery that arose in his mind to clothe the spiritual truths he found in Scripture, when one learns that he composed eighty-six sermons on the first two chapters of the *Song of Songs!* This power of fruitful contemplation combined with action is the root of the greatness that was his. It so impressed itself upon Dante that in the *Paradiso*, when Beatrice had led him through the crystal spheres of heaven to the highest one where the Great White Rose of redeemed humanity burst upon him, she surrendered her task as interpreter of mysteries to St. Bernard, who alone could present to him the ineffable vision of God Himself. This is Dante's way of saying that only a character developed by both action and contemplation can understand and interpret God.

Remembering, therefore, that this scant account of Bernard's life and personality must be considered not as an argument for Bernard's authorship of hymns but as background for appreciating the better aspects of medieval life out of which the poetry grew, we turn to the hymns themselves.

### *Jesu, dulcis memoria*      [twelfth century]
### *Jesus, the very thought of thee*      Tr Caswall, 1849

This "Jesus Hymn" or "Rosy Hymn" as it is called, or in Latin, *"Jubilus rhythmicus de nomine Jesu"* (Joyful rhythm on the name of Jesus), is a poem of 48 quatrains or 192 lines. Various poets have translated all or parts of it into English. The two *centos* or parts that have met with greatest favor are given below in the original Latin order, followed by a paraphrase which tries to gather up the spirit of the whole poem. The first two, "Jesus, the very thought of thee" and "O Jesus, King most wonderful," were translated by an English Roman Catholic; the last, "Jesus thou joy of loving hearts," by an American Congregationalist.

Though sundered far [in doctrine and practice] by faith they meet
Around one common mercy seat.

To enter into the spirit of this hymn we must visualize a monk kneeling in his tiny bare cell before his crucifix. It is the dark hour that precedes the dawn. Day will soon arise and with it will come the hard labor in the field and forest, dealing with rough Nature and with rougher men of the country, or with robbers or wicked monks who have found here the only place where they can be safe, but have not yet met with that change of heart for which the monastery stands. Oh, these human relationships that try one's soul! Oh, the monotonous succession of days and the grind of rigid discipline under the watchful eye of the abbot!

"But here is my chance for joy!"

The monk takes down the crucifix tenderly, holds it in one hand while with the other he caresses the twisted body of the Saviour and then raises it to his lips:

> Jesu, the very thought of Thee
>   With sweetness fills my breast;
> But sweeter far thy face to see
>   And in thy presence rest.

A pause.

Faintly from the distant kitchen comes the morning song of the scullion lad as he stirs the breakfast fire. The words are not discernible, only the melody. It is a distraction to the monk, but he closes his mind to the sound and repeats softly to himself, as his eyes wander over the little figure on the cross: "Jesu, Jesu, Jesu!"

> Nor voice can sing, nor heart can frame,
>   Nor can the memory find,
> A sweeter sound than thy blest name,
>   O Saviour of mankind.

Then his mind wanders back to the day when a monk found him in sin and meekly taught him the better way; the joy of both that one who had fallen need not stay down, and that the struggle to rise brought courage:

> O hope of every contrite heart,
>   O joy of all the meek,
> To those who fall, how kind thou art,
>   How good to those who seek!

And now he is here in this monastery where goodness is in the ascendant, where the love of Jesus for His humble brothers is so all-pervading and so deep that one cannot talk about it or even write it in poetry—though one often tries. It is peace that cannot be conveyed, only experienced:

> But what to those who find? Ah! this
>   Nor tongue nor pen can show;
> The love of Jesus, what it is,
>   None but his loved ones know.

The best part of this love is that it will never cease. Death may claim him, the world may depart as a scroll that is rolled together, but the joy will go with him across the gulf and will flame like a divine splendor time without end:

> Jesus, our only joy be thou,
>     As thou our prize wilt be;
> Jesus, be thou our glory now,
>     And through eternity.

### Jesu, Rex admirabilis

#### O Jesus, king most wonderful      Tr Caswall, 1849

But Jesus is not dead! The miracle foretold in Scripture took place: Death itself was vanquished and the Victim now reigns, not only in heaven but in my heart. This is a joy that encompasses all others:

> O Jesus, King most wonderful,
>     Thou conqueror renowned,
> Thou sweetness most ineffable,
>     In whom all joys are found.

Now that He is within me I begin to see values in their true relationship. If I possessed what the worldlings, even kings, enjoy, I would give them all for this love that burns within me.

> When once thou visitest the heart,
>     Then truth begins to shine;
> Then earthly vanities depart;
>     Then kindles love divine.

To what can I compare Him? He is the light of the world! He is a fountain from whom pours life eternal; a fountain from whom rise flames that consume every passion and warm my heart to ecstasy!

> O Jesus, light of all below,
>     Thou fount of life and fire,
> Surpassing all the joys we know,
>     And all we can desire.

Oh that every living soul could throw itself in worship at the feet of Jesus! That would transmute every desire into a burning and insatiable flame of love!

> May every heart confess thy name,
>     And ever thee adore;
> And seeking thee, itself in flame
>     To seek thee more and more.

Why then should I keep silent? Why love any other possession? I must
I must let my life speak for me until men see in me only Jesus:

> Thee may our tongues forever bless,
>   Thee may we love alone;
> And ever in our lives express
>   The image of thine own.

The monk now places the crucifix on its little shelf, crosses himself and
goes to the refectory and to his plowing.

Can you think of a better preparation for a day's work?

*Jesu, dulcedo cordium*     (Section of *Jesu, dulcis memoria*)

*Jesus, thou joy of loving hearts*    Tr (paraphrase) Ray Palmer, 1858

We shall have to abandon our imaginary monk kneeling in his cell before
a crucifix, and betake ourselves to a Congregational parsonage in Albany,
New York. It is a far cry in fact but not in spirit, for Dr. Palmer was a man
of deep religious faith not so far removed from that of St. Bernard and many
another medieval soul. No doubt that is why he found delight in reading
*Jesu, dulcis memoria.* (See further under Palmer, Chap. XIII.)

In translating the Latin Dr. Palmer did not take the stanzas consecutively
but picked out certain ones that especially met his own spirit, then he paraphrased rather than translated, free to give his own slant to the thought in
his own imagery. This can be seen by placing side by side his paraphrase and
certain stanzas from Neale and Caswall.

## BERNARD OF CLUNY (*twelfth century*)

"MORE than a thousand years ago [910 A.D.] on the site of William
Duke of Aquitaine's hunting lodge, the little monastery of Cluny was founded,
an event that seemed of such small importance that the founder hesitated
to turn out his hunting dogs in order to make room for the monks. Yet in less
than two hundred years the name of that small monastery had become
famous throughout Europe, and Cluny head of an international system;
where once the monks had built their wooden houses . . . arose a new and
famous school of architecture; where once the modest building had been
retarded through lack of funds, rose the church of St. Peter, the admiration
and wonder of the world; where once the dogs had barked, echoed the stately
ritual of the most famous musical center of Europe, and on the site of the
former hunting lodge rose a monastery so extensive in size that St. Louis of
France and his courtiers could stay there without one of the monks having to
leave his cell. Cluny . . . had by then become an international meeting-
place better known than Paris itself." *

* Lucy M. Smith: *The Early History of the Monastery of Cluny*, p. 1, P. Allen & Co.
Ltd., London, 1930.

The dominating idea governing the Cluniac Order was the centralization of authority. Whereas Benedictine monasteries had always been solitary, self-governing institutions, of course under papal charter, the Abbot of Cluny was the personal master of every subsidiary house and of every monk in it. The system was totalitarian. Fortunately, the abbots of Cluny were almost without exception men of superlative ability and character. Foremost among them was Peter the Venerable, abbot during the life of Bernard of Cluny whose hymns we are about to consider. Cluny finally became master of 314 monasteries—some say 2000!—in France, Italy, Germany, England, Scotland and Poland. These subsidiaries were founded especially along the famous

A sculptured capital from Cluny c. 1095. This figure stands for Tone I of the eight tones of the plainsong mode or scale, as is indicated by the inscription *Hic tonus orditur modulamina musica primus*. Prof. Conant writes: "The eight tones . . . express the love and high cultivation of music at Cluny and symbolize the richness of God's praise which was offered there."

pilgrimage roads that lead, for example, to Canterbury, Santiago di Compostela, and Rome. These became hostels for pilgrims and flourished on the sale of relics and souvenirs of the various shrines. Fortunately, also, the Cluniac monks became enthusiastic students of architecture, in fact, masters of the science of building. To them we are largely indebted for the development and spread of the Romanesque style which in the twelfth century reached the acme of its perfection. The abbey church at Cluny itself became the noblest specimen of Romanesque in the world as well as the largest before the construction of the new St. Peter's at Rome. It was 555 feet long. Begun in 1089, often enlarged, it was sacked by the Huguenots in 1562 but survived until 1790 when the monastery was suppressed and the buildings torn down by the people of the town.

Into this throbbing center of monastic life, about the year 1109 came one Bernard, possibly an Englishman, possibly born at Morlaix in Brittany, but more probably at Morlas in the Pyrenees. His sole title to fame rests on his authorship of a remarkable poem, *De Contemptu Mundi* ("Of Scorning the World"). The work, written c. 1145, consists of about 3000 lines in dactylic hexameter, lines divided into three sections by internal rhymes and linked in pairs by terminal rhymes (see below). The composition of such an intricate rhyme-scheme of such tremendous length called for all the poet's powers; in fact Bernard says that were it not for divine inspiration he could never have completed his task.

Bernard himself tells us about this inspiration:

> Often and of a long time I had heard the Bridegroom, but had not listened, saying, Thy voice is pleasant to Mine ears. And again the Beloved cried out: Open to Me, My sister. What then? I arose, that I might open to my Beloved. And I said: Lord, to what end that my heart may think, that my pen may write, and that my mouth may set forth Thy praise, pour both into my heart and pen and mouth Thy grace. And the Lord said, Open thy mouth. Which He straightway filled with the spirit of Wisdom and Understanding: that by one I might speak truly, by the other perspicuously. And I say it in nowise arrogantly but with all humility, and therefore boldly: that unless the Spirit of Wisdom and Understanding had been with me and flowed in upon so difficult a meter, I could not have compassed so long a work.

The result of this divine help is what Dr. Neale, who translated it in *The Rhythm of Bernard of Morlaix*, 1851, has called "one of the loveliest of medieval measures." Certainly Neale's hymns from it have enjoyed world-wide popularity.

Bernard is usually classified as a satirist because the larger part of his long poem is devoted to lambasting the iniquities of his time. Possibly he over-blackens his picture, but we know from other sources that life inside the monasteries as well as out had reached its lowest pitch of wickedness. In fact, Bernard's superior, Peter the venerable Abbot of Cluny, was forced to begin the reformation in his own monastery. Here is a summary of what Bernard fought, quoted from the *Catholic Encyclopedia*:

> The enormity of sin, the charm of virtue, the torture of an evil conscience, the sweetness of a God-fearing life alternate with heaven and hell as the theme of his majestic dithyramb. Nor does he dwell in generalities; he returns again and again to the wickedness of woman [*femina perfida, femina foetida, femina foetor*—"woman treacherous, woman bad smelling, woman a stink"], the evils of wine, money, learning, prejury, sooth-saying, etc.; . . . he cannot find words strong enough to convey his prophetic rage at the moral apostacy of his generation, in almost none of whom does he find spiritual soundness. Youthful and simoniacal bishops, oppressive

agents of ecclesiastical corporations, the officers of the Curia, papal legates, and the Pope himself are treated with no less severity than in Dante or the sculptures of medieval cathedrals . . . His highly-wrought pictures of heaven and hell were probably known to Dante; the roasting cold, the freezing fire, the devouring worm, the fiery floods, and again the glorious idyl of the Golden Age and the splendors of the Heavenly Kingdom are couched in a diction that rises at times to the height of Dante's genius.

Bernard begins his poem with a warning of impending doom. Neale's translation of this introductory section is found in two of our hymnals (E, L). Here are the first two stanzas:

| | |
|---|---|
| Hora novissima, | The world is very evil; |
| Tempora pessima | The times are waxing late; |
|    Sunt. Vigilemus! | Be sober and keep vigil; |
| Ecce minaciter | The Judge is at the gate: |
| Imminent Arbiter | |
|    Ille supremus. | |
| | |
| Imminet, imminet, | The Judge that comes in mercy, |
| Ut mala terminet, | The Judge that comes with might |
|    Aequa coronet, | To terminate the evil, |
| Recta remuneret, | To diadem the right. |
| Auxia liberet, | |
|    Aethera donet. | |

Interwoven with the pictures of human depravity glow the visions of heavenly splendor and the joys of the life everlasting. These are the portions which have survived in common use in our hymnals. One cento, "For thee, O dear, dear country" (Neale, 1851), is found in only two of our books (B, E); one other has had greater survival value: "Brief life is here our portion" (Neale, 1851), A, E, L, S, U; a third is in all ten:

## Urbs Syon aurea

### Jerusalem the golden   c. 1145     Tr Neale, 1851

*Stanza 1.* This is all Biblical imagery: Josh 5:6; Rev 1:17; 1 Cor 2:9; 2 Cor 3:18; Col 3:4.

*Stanzas 2–3.* Most of the phrases here are reminiscent of the Book of Revelation: 7:9–17; 19:9; 15:2. Chaps. 21–22 gather up into one glowing picture the hints that are scattered through the Old Testament, and other details of their own—music, the New Jerusalem, the River of the Water of Life. These are poetic images calculated to stir longing for a full realization of what we only fitfully enjoy in our earthly life. Dante amplifies this imagery, making the three chief

*Top*, Monastery of Cluny. A reconstruction by Dr. Kenneth J. Conant of Harvard University, after extensive excavations, 1928–38. The great church (left) was built c. 1120–25, and was therefore in existence when Bernard wrote *De Contemptu Mundi*. The earlier church (right) was built c. 960. The monastery itself was founded 910 and destroyed 1798–c.1823. *Bottom*, Typical house or "cell" of a medieval monk in an establishment like Cluny. Each brother lived alone.

elements of his Paradise: *motion*—the planets in their spheres and the circling hosts of angels and saints; *light*—colors of all kinds and the dazzling brightness of the Great White Rose of saints and of the vision of God; *music*—the hymns, the trumpets, the harps.

*Stanza 4.* The last stanza expresses longing for the satisfactions of heaven: beauty, praise, fellowship, rest, worship.

What shall we say about the adequacy of this Biblical-Dantesque imagery?

It is unsurpassed as a symbol of static bliss. But our modern conception of the religious life and of heaven makes necessary a re-translation of these symbols. It does not suit our temper to spend eternity cooped up in a cubical city, even if it is 1500 miles on a side (Rev 21:15–16), nor does the universe as we know it provide a place for such a town. We are not intrigued by the prospect of playing a harp and singing hosannahs throughout eternity. We must translate all this poetry into whatever will satisfy the vastly different intellectual and spiritual concepts of modern man. We demand opportunity for growth in knowledge, in character, in service. Our modern emphasis is on action rather than contemplation, righteousness rather than holiness, progress rather than attainment, civic and social ideals to be worked out here or anywhere.

### THE THIRTEENTH CENTURY

With St. Francis of Assisi we enter upon a new century that represents the culmination of medieval civilization. Books have been written to show that the thirteenth is the greatest of centuries, a thesis that has much to support it. In this century the Church became triumphant. It produced great churchmen like Popes Innocent III and Gregory IX who established their supremacy over the temporal powers; great monastics like Saints Francis, Dominic, and Edmund of Canterbury; great scholars like Albertus Magnus, St. Bonaventure, St. Thomas Aquinas; Roger Bacon the scientist, Robert of Sorbonne and twenty other founders of universities. It produced great temporal rulers, under the authority of the Church, like Philip Augustus, one of the ablest rulers of France, and St. Louis IX, one of the noblest; Edward I of England, the law-giver; Bruce of Scotland, the patriot. It produced great art and architecture: cathedrals—twenty of them—largely the work of the free communes and trade guilds; painting, released by Cimabue, Giotto and others from the fetters of Byzantine formalism; sculpture, reaching the heights of naturalism under the chisels of hundreds of nameless cathedral decorators. It produced great literature, the three most widely-known romances of the Middle Ages—*Renard the Fox*, the *Golden Legend*, the *Romance of the Rose;* great epics like the Celtic *Arthurian Legend*, the German *Niebelungenlied*, the Spanish *Cid;* it produced the Troubadours of Provence, the Meistersingers of Germany, Guido Cavalcanti, who with Dante created the modern Italian tongue; and Dante himself, greatest of all, the "morning star of the Renaissance." Strange indeed if this "Greatest of Centuries" should not produce also some of the greatest hymns.

On the other hand, the century developed great Protesters. There were revolts against the tyranny of the Church, against its teachings and its immorality. To deal with these heresies, the Church established the Inquisition and placed in its hands the right to murder thousands of progressive thinkers, culminating in the near-extermination of the sect of the Waldenses, and the extinction of the Albigerses. In this and the following century, too,

most of the fore-runners of the Reformation were hunted down and killed—
the Hussites of Bohemia, the Lollards in England. St. Francis himself barely
escaped, for the whole Franciscan movement was really a heresy, a revolt
from regimentation in doctrine and in life toward the freedom and love of
the original teaching of Christ.

The really distinctive movement of this century and the one that inspired
a grand hymnody was the rise of the Mendicant Orders, chiefly the Dominican and Franciscan. Both of these orders were protests against the apostacy
of the Church: the Dominican against its wealth and its neglect of a true
theology; the Franciscan against its wealth and its neglect of the welfare of
the common man. They were called Mendicant because they were under the
vow of poverty and so had to beg, and therefore the "Friars" worked outside
the monasteries rather than in them.

These reform movements were necessitated partly by the growth of
cities. The monasteries of the Benedictines, Cluniacs and Cistercians were
for the most part located on great feudal estates, leaving the town population
to the inadequate care of local church priests. Now that the center of gravity
was shifting to the towns, with consequent increase of poverty and misery
and crime, the need for spiritual ministrations became imperative. Hence the
Friars went from place to place, lived with the poor and preached the simple
life such as Christ and His disciples had lived. They were responsible for a
genuine religious revival that fixed its attention on the human aspects of
Christ and on the necessity of imitating Him. This new attitude is reflected
as clearly in the painting of Giotto and his successors as it is in the revolutionary life of the Franciscans.

In the realm of hymnody the Dominicans are represented by their
master-schoolman St. Thomas Aquinas. His hymns, as might be expected, are
theological or mystical expositions of the mysteries of the Eucharist. They
were written as a definite assignment by the Church, to supply the missal
with hymns and a sequence for the newly-created Office of *Corpus Christi*
(Sept. 8, 1264) in which the institution of the Eucharist and the doctrine of
Transubstantiation are celebrated. Since in our hymnals they are found in
only three (A, E and S), all liturgical in point of view, they will not be considered here. The three hymnists who find a place in our study are all Franciscans, for their human approach to religion would incline their hearts to
song, and modern response to them among Protestants has been wide-spread
in spite of their distinctive Catholic viewpoint.


## SAINT FRANCIS OF ASSISI (1182–1226) Italian

FRANCIS is the most popular saint in the calendar. Well he may
be, for his life has the simplicity, idealism and single-minded devotion of his
Master. Born in the Italian hill-town of Assisi, son of a wealthy cloth

merchant, he grew up carefree, developed a ready wit, sang merrily and became the leader of a gang of young blades with whom he got into all sorts of escapades. When he was about twenty Francis fought in a skirmish with neighboring Perugia, was captured and imprisoned for a year or more. A couple of illnesses during and after his confinement made him question the value of his way of life. One night after a sumptuous banquet he had prepared for his old cronies, the boys rushed into the streets for boisterous song and mischief, but soon discovered that Francis was missing. They finally found him staring at the ground in profound revery.

"What's the matter with you?" said one.

"He is thinking of taking a wife," said another.

"Yes," answered Francis with a smile; "I am thinking of taking a wife more beautiful, more rich, more pure than you could ever imagine." That was his way of announcing his decision to give up wealth, position and worldly ambitions and to wed "Lady Poverty."

Sometime later while praying in the ruined hermitage of St. Damian just outside Assisi he felt something marvellous take place: Jesus spoke to him from the crucifix, accepted him, his heart and his life. From that day Jesus became the very soul of his soul.

His father was angry at the change, publicly disinherited him. Thereupon Francis handed over to his father all the money he had on him, together with all his clothes, saying, "From henceforth I desire to say nothing else than 'Our Father who art in heaven.'"

Immediately Francis left town and wandered on the slopes of neighboring Mt. Subasio, singing his new-found joy to the vales and hills; then to the home of the lepers to serve them with his hands and his song. Taking up his abode in St. Damian he fashioned for himself a hermit's dress and began to visit Assisi to sing and preach in the public squares—enlisting the people to help him rebuild the forsaken and ruined shrines in the countryside. Gradually young men, inspired by his love and devotion, attached themselves to him. They all lived as did the poor people among whom they worked; they slept in haylofts, in leper hospitals or in the shelter of some church porch. They passed part of their day working with the peasants in the fields, telling them of their new-found joy in serving Christ. There was much hostility and persecution, but when the number of his followers became twelve, Francis took them to Rome to secure from Pope Innocent III permission "to live a life of absolute conformity to the precepts of the gospel." It took a dream to convince the pope, but he finally blessed and established the movement: the date, 1210.

Francis and his band now began their preaching tours. Their love for the humble, their message of repentance and hope took hold of the consciences of men and opened new vistas in their dull lives. In his home town of Assisi "the entire population was thrilled, conquered, desiring in future to live only in accordance with Francis' counsels." And everywhere his open-air sermons at street corners and public squares, in fields, had the same effect. His gospel was practical: men must prove their conversion by giving up their ill-gotten gains, renouncing their enmities and being reconciled with their adversaries.

It is needless to give in detail the activities of the next fourteen years: his missionary tours through Mediterranean lands, the rapid growth of his

St. Francis preaching to the birds (Sibra, Spanish, 1926). The most imaginative rendering of this oft-painted incident. Backgrounds realistic; but the orderly arrangement of the birds is most intriguing, suggestive of the unity of response to a great hypnotist.

movement, the Church's attempt to organize it and control it, which involved depriving Francis of all power, the mystic experience on Mount La Verna in which a vision of Christ on the cross smote into his body the "Stigmata"—the five wounds of Christ—his failing health and blindness, finally his death at the age of forty-five in the little hut at Portiuncula in the plain below the Assisi hills where he and his first twelve had begun their organized life. The important facts are not these, but the spirit that made him such a revolutionary force.

Francis took the life of Jesus as his ideal and the teachings of the gospel as his creed. Love was his driving force. It led him from the complexes of

ecclesiastical organization to one simple loyalty—to Jesus—from the world
of dogma where the intellect is regimented and the will chained, to the
world of the heart where love blossoms and where man finds in his fellow-
men his opportunity for companionship and service.

In such a personality there must arise also a love of nature, for the heart
that goes out in love to God's highest creatures cannot fail to embrace as well
His humbler ones, even the inanimate wind and sky. Many stories enshrine
this beautiful oneness with all things. They tell how he pleaded with the
people of Gubbio to feed the wolf who had ravaged their flocks, because
through hunger "Brother Wolf" had done this wrong. They tell how he
preached the duty of thankfulness and joy and praise to the birds who
crowded about him, of the nightingale who sang with him in the oak grove
of his retreat at Le Carceri, of the raven who woke him up for early matins,
but, when Francis was ill, aroused him an hour later! It was all one world for
Francis and for them—God's world.

And next to love came joy. He called himself and his disciples "God's
jugglers"—travelling men whose function it was to make mirth. "Is it not in
fact true," Francis would say, "that the servants of God are really like
jugglers, intended to revive the hearts of men and lead them into spiritual
joy?"

The moving end of his story will be told below in connection with his
hymn.

Francis was canonized a Saint only two years after his death—a most
extraordinary speed, and the great church that now stands over his tomb as
his memorial was begun the selfsame day.

### The Canticle of the Sun

*Altissimu, onnipotente, bon signore*      [1226]

*All creatures of our God and King*      Tr Rev. Wm. H. Draper, 1910
*Most High, omnipotent, good Lord*      Tr Howard C. Robbins, 1939

Strictly speaking, this hymn is not from the Latin, yet anyone who
knows Latin can read the original. In Francis' day all literary works were
written in Latin and so were not comprehensible to the common folk, the
vast majority of whom could not read or write. But the people had a language of their own—the "vulgar tongue." It was Latin debased by an admix-
ture of barbarian dialects planted in Italy during the invasions that overthrew
the Roman Empire, and simplified by dropping the elaborate inflectional
endings which make Latin so distasteful to American youngsters in our day.
Francis set this vulgar tongue aflame, infused into it his poetic joy and so
became the inspirer of a literary movement that reached a climax in Dante
and his friend Guido Cavalcanti. These were the first learned men to abandon Latin for the vulgar tongue in their poetry. It was they who by the

popularity of their works finally fused the countless dialects of the Italian peninsula into the standard language we know as Italian.

The language of this, neither Latin nor Italian, is a transitional speech.

This poem cannot be appreciated apart from the circumstances of its origin. Francis was now nearing his end. His periods of blindness and other symptoms of dissolution warned him that he must hasten home to die.

Convent of S. Damiano: the Little Cloister in which St. Francis actually composed his *Canticle of the Sun* in the presence of Clara.

Before going down to his hermitage in the valley he stopped at St. Damian to say farewell to Sister Clara, the first woman to be inspired by his gospel to forsake her wealth and station for Lady Poverty and to take the vows of the Order. Her conversion had attracted other women, and Francis had given them for a home the little monastery where he had taken his own first vows. There was a deep mystic love between these two which enabled Clara many times to understand his problems, to advise him with her sane judgement and inspire by her lofty faith.

So now Francis came to her for the last time. For fifteen days he had been so completely blind that he could not even distinguish light. Clara devoted herself to him, made him a reed hut in the little monastery garden and by her companionship brought comfort and courage to him. Gradually his customary joy returned. Sometimes the sisters would hear faint melodies issuing from the hut. "Then one day after a long conversation with Clara he took his place at the monastery table. The meal had hardly begun when suddenly he seemed to be rapt away in ecstasy, which lasted for some minutes. Then coming to himself he cried, 'Praise be to God!' He had just composed the Canticle to the Sun."

Following is a prose translation by Matthew Arnold (1883). With this compare the widely-used translation by the Anglican clergyman, William Draper, about 1910, written for a school children's Whitsuntide Festival at

Statue of St. Francis in front of Assisi Cathedral.

Leeds. It is found in all our hymnals except the Episcopal. One cannot fail to notice that Mr. Draper omits the distinctive mysticism of Francis—the "Brother" Sun and "Sister" Water—and preserves not much more than a catalogue of the different aspects of nature that might seem to praise their Maker. It is a far cry but adapted to a child's needs and made a thing of beauty by the superb music to which it is commonly set. By way of contrast, read if possible Dr. Robbins' more literal rendering which restores something of the mystic flavor (E).

Matthew Arnold's literal translation: †

Intro: O most high, almighty, good Lord God, to thee belong praise, glory, honor and all blessing!

† From P. Sabatier: *Life of St. Francis of Assisi*, p. 305, Scribner's, New York, 1894.

*Stanza 1.* Praised be my Lord God with all his creatures, and specially our brother the sun, who brings us the day and who brings us the light; fair is he and shines with a very great splendor: O Lord, he signifies to us thee!

*Stanza 2.* Praised be my Lord for our sister the moon, and for the stars, the which he has set clear and lovely in heaven.

*Stanza 3.* Praised be my Lord for our brother the wind, and for air and cloud, calms and all weather, by the which thou upholdest life in all creatures.

*Stanza 4.* Praised be my Lord for our sister water, who is very serviceable unto us, and humble and precious and clean.

*Stanza 5.* Praised be my Lord for our brother fire, through whom thou givest us light in the darkness; and he is bright and pleasant, and very mighty and strong.*

*Stanza 6.* Praised be my Lord for our mother the earth, the which doth sustain us and keep us, and bringeth forth divers fruits and flowers of many colors, and grass.

*Stanza 7.* Praised be my Lord for all those who pardon one another for his love's sake, and who endure weakness and tribulation; blessed are they who peaceably shall endure, for thou, O most Highest, shalt give them a crown.

Conclusion: Praise ye and bless the Lord, and give thanks unto him and serve him with great humility.

Good churchman that he was, Mr. Draper could not resist adding to the words of simple-minded Francis the theological formula, badge of all true believers, which he inherited from the fighting days when Orthodoxy was destroying Arianism:

> Praise, praise the Father, praise the Son,
> And praise the Spirit, three in one.

Neither could Francis resist adding another strophe, which only Dr. Robbins has seen fit to preserve. When at last they brought Francis to his little cell at Portiuncula to die, and before they took from him at his request all his clothing and laid him upon the bare earth so that he might die in the arms of his Lady Poverty, he composed one last stanza which is here reproduced:

---

* This stanza is perhaps a reminiscence of an experience earlier that year. The doctors who were trying to cure him finally decided to cauterize him by drawing a rod of white-hot iron across his forehead. When Francis saw them bringing the brazier and the rod he had a moment of terror; but immediately making the sign of the cross over the glowing iron said, "Brother Fire, you are beautiful above all creatures; be favorable to me in this hour; you know how much I have always loved you; be then courteous today."

(Francis)

Praised be my Lord for our sister,
the death of the body, from which
no man escapeth. Woe to him who
dieth in mortal sin! Blessed are they
who are found walking by thy most
holy will, for the second death shall
have no power to do them harm.

(Dr. Robbins, E)

For death our sister, praiséd be,
From whom no man alive can flee.
     Woe to the unprepared!
But blest be they who do thy will
And follow thy commandments still.*

### JACOPONE DA TODI (1230–1306) Italian

THIS remarkable man was a worldly-minded, some say avaricious,
lawyer till he reached the age of 40. Then the collapse of a staging at a
public spectacle killed his beautiful young wife, and in removing her remains
they found she wore next to her body a hair shirt—such as ascetics wore to
remind themselves by its constant irritation that they must mortify the flesh
in the interest of the spirit. This tragedy wrought a complete change in
Jacopone: he gave away all his property to the poor and became a Tertiary,
one who followed the rule of Francis without becoming a member of the
Order. His excesses of penance made people think he was crazy, but he
exulted in being "a fool for Christ's sake." After ten years he joined the
Franciscan Order. In his excessive zeal for the cause of "Lady Poverty" and
against the corruption of the Church, he so villified Pope Boniface VIII
that he was excommunicated and jailed for seven years. He died shortly
after release.

During his long years of devotion to the common people and to the
person of Christ, he composed and sang many dramatic songs called *laude,*
"praises," that glorified in rude and popular forms the life of poverty,
humility and service. Sometimes his themes changed to fierce denunciations
of the vanities of the world, the wickedness of the Church, or to contemplation of death and corruption. But his favorite themes seem to be the Passion
of Christ and the human sorrows of His Mother as she lived through with
her Son every detail of His six-hour agony on the cross. Something of the
dramatic quality of these *laude* is shown in this abbreviated selection from
one of them:

*A Voice from the Crowd:* "Lady of Paradise, thy Son is taken,
Jesus Christ the Blessed. Run, Lady, and see how they are smiting
Him; methinks they have slain Him; they have scourged Him so
much!" . . .
*The Mother:* "Oh, Pilate, do not allow my Son to be tortured, for
I can show thee that He is wrongly accused." . . .
*A Voice:* "Madonna, behold the cross which the people are carry-

* Used by permission of the author.

ing, whereon the true Light must be lifted up . . . Lady, he is
stretched on the cross!" *

In the fourteenth century these *laude* by Jacopone and others grew
into a great body of popular literature and were performed on all sorts of
occasions by a guild of lay brothers called *Laudesi*. These acting-jongleurs
popularized the Gospel story with emphasis on miracles, the Crucifixion,
events in the life of the Virgin, the punishments in Hell, and the joys of
Heaven. The poetic culmination of this dramatic-lyric popular poetry was
the *Stabat Mater*, only it is written in Latin instead of in the vulgar tongue,
and reaches the heights of literary perfection. Probably Jacopone wrote it,
though the evidence is not conclusive. At any rate it represents the sublima-
tion of the cruder vernacular poetry inspired originally by Francis.

It is difficult for Protestants to realize the intensity of devotion which
the Catholic Church has lavished for eighteen centuries upon the Virgin
Mary. Her cult began in Syria, attained some vogue in the third century,
increased in popularity in the West where Ambrose, Augustine, and Jerome
lent it the weight of their influence, and was implemented in theology when,
in the Council of Chalcedon, 451, Mary was officially declared to be Virgin
Mother of God. Thence her veneration grew into an integral part of popular
religion and of the Church's liturgy. Mary became the secret heart of every
monastery, the patron saint of nearly every cathedral, the persistent theme
of hymn-writers. In the later Middle Ages she outstripped Christ as the
dominant figure in heaven—the Queen crowned with twelve stars toward
whom the prayers of humanity were directed in absolute faith, "to whom the
Kings and Queens of France were coming constantly for help, and whose
absolute power was almost the only restraint recognized by Emperor, Pope
and clown." Everyone knew that it was Mary who dispensed Heaven and
Hell.**

Allan of Lille (twelfth century) has collected in an allegorical poem
some of the epithets applied to her by the mystics of his day:

> She is the star of the sea, the way of life, the gate of salvation, the
> norm of justice, the utmost bound of piety, the source of virtue,
> the mother of forgiveness, the inner chamber of modesty, a garden
> enclosed, a fountain sealed, an olive tree that makes fruitful, an
> odorous cedar, a luxurious park, a magic wand of beauty, a wine-
> cellar furnished with celestial liquors akin to heavenly nectar, a rose
> flourishing with never a thorn, gracious with never a fault, a
> spring of limpid clearness, a light that banishes clouds, hope of the
> wretched, medicine for the sick, protector of the saints, refuge of

---

* F. J. E. Raby: *History of Christian Latin Poetry*, p. 437, Clarendon Press, Oxford, 1927.

** Henry Adams: *Mont St. Michel and Chartres*, p. 162, Houghton, Mifflin, Boston,
1905, 1913.

the condemned, a path to the wanderer, to the blind a light, a
respite to the down-hearted, a rest to the weary.

## Stabat Mater dolorosa

At the Cross her station keeping        Tr Mant, 1837, and Caswall, 1849
  Near the Cross her vigil keeping        Tr compiled by Louis Benson

The hymn is a reminiscence of Jn 19:26–27.

We are here contemplating not so much the theological doctrine of the
Atonement as a sorrowful human spectacle. This is what the crucifixion of
her son meant to Mary.

Stanzas 1–2. A photographic picture of Mary's anguish.

Stanza 3. Our sympathy is deeply stirred by the sight of her
suffering.

Stanza 4. Augments her sense of outraged justice, and ours, for her
son was brought to His death not by His own sins but by those of
His people. The details of His torture: Mk 14:50; Acts 8:33.

Stanza 5. Here is the heart of the Franciscan devotion to Mary.
The contemplation of her suffering was the spring of their love for
her and so became the inspiration for greater love for her Son and
self-sacrificing ministry to all mankind.

Stanzas 6–10 of the original are omitted in our English translation.
These repeat over and over the prayer that the Virgin will "make
me" weep with her, enter into the sufferings of her Son, share the
punishment being inflicted upon Him for my sin, and finally that I
may be protected by her in the Great Judgement Day and share
in the resurrection of the body and the glory of Paradise.

The Stabat Mater though composed half a century after Francis' death
sums up with complete adequacy the motto of the Franciscan Order: "Far
be it from me to glory save in the Cross of Christ." And most intimately it
expresses the union of Francis' own heart with Christ's sufferings, that
"brooding on sorrow" that drove him to minister to the lepers, the outcasts,
the criminals, to embrace Lady Poverty and to brave persecution and death
in his missionary tours among the Saracens. His life was an incarnation of
those other grand passages from Paul: 2 Cor 5:14; Rom 8:35–37.

This Franciscan brooding on Christ's sufferings as a human experience
rather than a theological tenet exercised a tremendous influence on succeeding generations, both on literature and art, and it found a pathological
expression in the rise of certain heretical sects called "Flagellants." These
sporadic organizations harked back in spirit to the Hermits of earlier Christian centuries who used self-torture as a means of grace. We hear first of the
Flagellants in Perugia. Following the frightful plague of 1259 and the long-
continued economic and political anarchy of Italy, a despair had seized the

common folk and also a new hope in the appearance of Antichrist who would end the world and begin the millennium (2 Thes 2:1–12). Then appeared those weird processions, mounting at times to ten thousand people—men, women, clergy, laity, sometimes even children, marching through the towns with banners flying and scourging themselves for the sins of the world. Stripped to the waist they lashed themselves with leather thongs till the

"Stabat Mater Dolorosa," 1926. Painted by Dagnan-Bouveret.

blood ran down, chanting at the same time the hymns and the *laude* describing the passion of Christ and the sufferings of His mother. Like an epidemic they spread all over Italy, across the Alps and reached as far north as Poland. Then the Pope forbade such processions. But though suppressed for a time, the Flagellants broke out again after the Black Death in 1347 that destroyed half the population of Europe, and sporadically they have appeared down to our own times and country.*

* On March 26, 1948, the Penetente cult re-enacted the Crucifixion in the remote hamlets of the Sangre de Cristo mountains, New Mexico, and on the same date the Filipino Flagellants did the same on Balut Island.

The *Stabat Mater* reached the height of its vogue in these abnormal outbursts of penance and self-mortification and so by the end of the fourteenth century had established itself in the popular mind and heart all over Europe. It was not introduced into the Roman Breviary and Missal until 1727, where it is assigned to the Feast of the Seven Dolours of the Blessed Virgin Mary, the Friday after Passion Sunday. Its use has spread beyond the Catholic communion to the Protestants of all countries. There are over sixty translations of it in English alone.

## ANONYMOUS

*Veni, veni, Emmanuel*      Date of original unknown

*O come, O come, Emmanuel*      Tr Neale, 1851
      *Ditto*      Tr Hymnal Editors, 1940
      *Ditto*      Tr Neale, Henry Coffin, 1916
      *Ditto*      Tr Canon Lacey, 1906

This very popular hymn sung to a medieval plainsong melody has an interesting and checkered history. It began in the ninth century or earlier as a series of seven Antiphons—short verses sung at the beginning or close of the Psalm or of the *Magnificat* at Vespers during Advent, the four Sundays before Christmas. The word antiphon suggests that the lines were sung alternately by two choirs sitting opposite each other in the chancel. Here are the opening lines of the seven, with a translation of the key words:

1. *O Sapientia, quae ex ore altissimi*      "Wisdom"
2. *O Adonay et dux domus Israel*      "Lord"
3. *O Radix Jesse qui stas in sugnum*      "Root of Jesse"
4. *O Clavis David et sceptrum domus*      "Key of David"
5. *O Oriens, splendor lucis aeternae*      "Orient" (East)
6. *O Rex gentium et desideratus*      "King"
7. *O Emmanuel, rex et legifer*      "Emmanuel" (God with us)

Now a change comes. Sometime in the twelfth century, according to Neale, thirteenth century, according to Dr. Dearmer (English hymnodist), eighteenth century, according to the Julian Dictionary, someone took these seven separate sentences, threw away two, changed the order of the five remaining ones, wove them into a hymn and added a refrain. This made the text which Neale and the others translated. Lacey's translation is preferred because it preserves more of the medieval flavor and imagery. The key words of antiphons 7, 3, 5, 4, and 2, as given above, are here preserved in that order. They all derive ultimately from scripture passages:

Emmanuel, Is 7:14.
    The Church now separated from heaven is here compared to

Israel separated in its Babylonian exile from God's temple in Jerusalem.

Branch of Jesse, Is 11:1

By a mixture of metaphors the Branch becomes David, who rescued a lamb out of the mouth of a lion (1 Sam 17:34–35), then Christ who saves the Elect from an eternity in hell.

Dayspring, Lk 1:78

Key of David, Rev 3:7–8

Adonay. This is the Hebrew word for LORD. The Hebrew proper name for God was JAHVEH, the consonants of which are preserved in our word JeHoVaH; but since it is too sacred to pronounce, Adonay was substituted. This name JHVH was proclaimed to Israel at Mt. Sinai, where the Law was given to the accompaniment of lightning and thunder (Ex 19:16).

The whole spirit of the hymn is ancient in thought and imagery, remote from modern approaches to religion. It is preserved in our hymnals because of its usefulness in the Advent season and because the intriguing plainsong to which it is set appeals to our primitive instincts. Begin humming the tune and you will have difficulty in stopping.

## FOURTEENTH TO EIGHTEENTH CENTURIES

THE next five centuries were not productive of many hymns that have survived—an average of only two a century. This lack of creativeness paralleled a decline in the dominant position of the Church. There was, for example, the seventy year exile of the papacy to Avignon in France (1309–1377), when most popes were made by the French monarch, while Italy was in a state of political and social anarchy. Theological rifts were beginning to appear within the Church itself: the rise of John Wyclif and his heretical Lollards in England; of John Huss in Bohemia whose martyrdom proved to be the seed of a protesting sect, the United Brethren, and of the later general Reformation (See Chap. XI). Popular revolts, clerical abuses, stormy Church Councils, the abortive attempt to merge the Greek and Roman branches of the Church, and the growing strength of national governments kept Europe in a turmoil.

In the fifteenth century came the Italian Renaissance with the rise of humanism and the paganizing of the papacy. In the sixteenth century occurred the German Protestant Reformation; in the sixteenth and seventeenth centuries, the Anglican schism, and the gradual spread of Protestant views throughout northern Europe. All the Protestant movements were accompanied by the development of hymns in the vernacular, leaving to the Roman Church alone the use of its Latin hymnody. The Catholic service books were bulging by now with hymns, so that the task was one of pruning rather than expanding. The Catholic liturgy was officially reformed in the sixteenth century with the resulting exclusion of all but a handful of the thousands of hymns bequeathed by the centuries.

Following are briefly given the eight hymns of this period that have found general acceptance by Protestants:

### FOURTEENTH CENTURY

*Salve, caput cruentatum*      Anonymous

*O sacred head surrounded*      Tr H. W. Baker, 1861
*O sacred head sore (now) wounded*
Tr J. W. Alexander, 1830 (much altered)
*O sacred head, sore wounded*      Tr Robert Bridges, 1899

Most of the above translations were made not from the original Latin but from the German of that most famous pietist-poet, Paul Gerhardt, 1656 (See Chap. XI). Gerhardt translated from the Latin of St. Bernard of Clairvaux, as he thought, though modern scholars cannot trace the original before the fourteenth century.

It is difficult to select the proper English text, for Dr. Alexander's has been frequently "improved" and certain quatrains shuffled to new positions. Moreover, the original fifty lines of the Latin have been reduced in most hymnals to twenty-four English lines.

> *Stanza 1.* This tells what the eye sees—the wounds, the look of pain, the crown of thorns, the pallor and the marks of the beating, a contrast with the victim's former living beauty.
> *Stanza 2.* Here is given the reason for this transformation: it was for my sin He suffered (Is 53:5). Then the suppliant begs, as every mourner might who looks upon the dead face of his beloved, that He will open His eyes and speak as of yore.
> *Stanza 3* expresses the impossibility of adequate expression; begs for spiritual union that shall never end.

Whatever its date and author, the poem is thoroughly medieval and monkish in conception. It harks back to the age in which the crucifix became an important instrument of devotion. (See under *Jesu dulcis memoria*, above.) Every monk had a crucifix in his cell and made of it an object of intense concentration. In such an act the eye could not stay fixed on the total object, but must break it up into its component parts and follow them in fixed or irregular patterns while the mind keeps pace to interpret the special significance of each. In accordance with this psychological necessity, the author of this hymn addressed himself to the seven parts of the Saviour's body, giving to each part fifty lines—the feet, knees, hands, side, breast, heart, head. He entitled his meditation, "A rhythmic prayer to any one of the members of Christ suffering and hanging on the Cross."

In a German translation of the hymn dated 1454 is a note by the translator who supposed that Bernard of Clairvaux wrote the original—following a tradition which we suspect originated in Clairvaux:

> As now Saint Bernard had spoken these words with great earnestness of desire, the image on the cross bowed itself and embraced him with its wounded arms, as a sure token that to it this prayer was most pleasing.

This result might be expected to follow when a mystic soul concentrated with hypnotic fervor upon such an object. Though the modern mind does not usually profit by the contemplation of suffering, the medieval mind did. Not only are there many poems akin to this one (e.g. Theoctistus, Chap. X), but the European galleries are filled with pictures that spare us no single detail of the Saviour's wounds. Nevertheless there is valuable spiritual discipline to be derived from such contemplation. It helps us realize the price paid by most reformers who have bucked the intrenched privilege of the powerful in Church or state or society, and to appreciate how much the world has gained by their sacrifice. If, for example, World War II should prove to be the war that ends all wars, what honor would we not pay to the memory of those who wrought this great advance in civilization, and what soldier, tortured to a lingering death in German and Japanese concentration camps, would not rejoice in his own sacrifice? "He shall see of the travail of his soul and shall be satisfied."

LATE FOURTEENTH CENTURY

*In dulce jubilo*    Anonymous

*Good Christian men, rejoice*    Tr Neale, 1853

This Christmas carol is an excellent example of how the mind of a genius such as Neale works. The original carol was in so-called Latin, but really "dog-Latin"—a barbarous mixture, in this case, of Latin and German. Those who know either language will be interested in a stanza of the original, and in the literal translation.*

| | |
|---|---|
| In dulce jubilo | In sweet jubilation |
| Nu singet und seyt wonne | Now sing and be joyful! |
| Unsers herzen wonne | The joy of our hearts |
| Leyt in praesepio | Lies in a manger |
| Und leuchtet als die sonne | And shines like the sun |
| Matris in gremio | In the lap of his mother |
| Alpha es et O! | Alpha and Omega! |

From these two we can see how Neale caught the inspiration of the

---

* From R. G. McCutchan: *Our Hymnody*, 1937, p. 141, where the whole original will be found with literal translation.

original and transformed it into something suited to English sentiment. The
continued popularity of the carol is undoubtedly due in part to the swinging
fourteenth-century German melody to which it is set.

### Surrexit Christus hodie      Anonymous

### Jesus Christ is risen today      Tr Tate and Brady, 1698

There is no doubt that the almost universal use of this hymn is due
primarily to the vigorous and inspiring tune to which it is set (from *Lyra
Davidica,* 1708) and secondarily to the need of having a variety of hymns
about Easter upon which to draw. Otherwise the hymn is merely rhythmic
rhymed prose that gives the traditional theological interpretation of the fact
of Easter, and exhorts to praise. The Doxology, "Sing we to our God above,"
was added by Charles Wesley, 1740.

#### FIFTEENTH CENTURY

### O filii et filiae      Jean Tisserand (French)

### O sons and daughters, let us sing      Tr J. M. Neale, 1852

No data are available about the author except that he was French and
died in 1494. "The hymn is used in many French dioceses in the *Salut* or
solemn salutation of the Blessed Sacrament on the evening of Easter Day,"—
according to Julian's *Hymnology.*

One might call this hymn an Easter carol. It overflows with joy, not
only because of the triple *Alleluia* for introduction and the single *Alleluia*
refrain, but because of the triumphant factual note that sounds from each
stanza. To be sure, it is only a narrative, like the Christmas "Good King
Wenceslaus" and "The First Noel," for it puts into a triple rhyme the incidents of the post-resurrection story as given in the Gospels. But somehow
one catches the assurance that these incidents were real and that the very
repetition of them strengthens one's faith. Here in brief is the story by
stanzas:

    1. Introduction: invitation to praise
    2. The visit of the faithful women, Mt 28:1
    3. The angel and his message, Mt. 28:2–7
    4. The appearance to the Ten, Jn 20:19–20
    5. Doubting Thomas, Jn 20:24–25
6–7. The revelation to Thomas, Jn 20:26–28
    8. Christ's blessing to men of faith, Jn 20:29
    9. Conclusion: invitation to praise

Hymns of this kind are valuable educational material for younger
children. Their use fixes in mind the leading incidents of Resurrection Week
and adds the emotional contexts of joy and faith.

*Mater Hierusalem, civitas sancta Dei*      Anonymous

*O Mother dear, Jerusalem*      Tr F.B.P., 1580
*Jerusalem, my happy home*
Tr F.B.P., 1580 and J. Bromehead, 1795
*City of Peace, our Mother dear*      Tr W. Prid, 1585

This hymn has had a checkered career. It began as a 400-word prose description of heaven, drawn in part from phrases in the Book of Revelation (e.g., Chap. 21) and in part from the author's imagination and emotions. It was found in a book of *Meditations* ascribed to St. Augustine (354–430) but now proved to be a forgery of about 1480 A.D. Even before this prose guidebook to heaven was written, a famous Cardinal and Doctor of the Church, Peter Damian (c. 988–1072) had voiced his description of heaven in a hymn, *Ad perennis vitae fontem*. This hymn was sometimes bound up in the same manuscript with the prose *Meditations*. In the latter part of the sixteenth century two different Englishmen undertook to amalgamate and translate these two: they were a certain "F.B.P.," an unidentified Roman Catholic priest, and a certain "W. Prid." Both of these translators drew heavily on both Latin sources. Then appeared Rev. J. Bromehead, who in 1795 amalgamated many of the descriptive stanzas and added joys of his own. Modern hymnal editors have picked and chosen, with varying results.

There is no denying that the picture of heaven here given is attractive. It is a composite of all that the heart can desire in the way of physical comfort and beauty, the absence of all that a perverse fate and human depravity have created on earth. Very intriguing also are the saints whom F.B.P. picked out by way of historic review: David, maestro of orchestra and choir, with his harp for baton, the Blessed Virgin as Prima Donna, Saints Ambrose and Augustine rendering the Te Deum which tradition says they improvised antiphonally at the time of Augustine's baptism, Simeon and Zachariah, improvisatores of Lk 1:68–79 and 2:29–32, and finally Mary Magdalene who has forgotten her tears in the joy of being understudy to the Virgin.

While we cannot fail to enjoy this glorious picture we cannot help wondering why a modern compiler asks us to accept and sing such a concept in an act of worship. A medieval monk in his cell might believe that this vision is the *summum bonum* of all existence, but citizens of a contemporary Western democracy must regard it all as a fanciful escape from reality. In truth, we do not sing these hymns even though they are in our hymnal. Our religious interests are centered on other things.

*O Deus ego amo te*      Anonymous, 1669

*My God, I love thee; not because*      Tr Edward Caswall, 1849

*O God, I love thee; not that my*      Tr E. H. Bickersteth, 1889

Considerable controversy has raged over the authorship of this hymn, even over the original language. Some editors say, "Anonymous, Spanish"; others, "Spanish sonnet ascribed to Xavier," "Latin version of a Spanish sonnet ascribed to Xavier," "Anonymous Latin." The most recent scholarship rules out St. Francis Xavier (1506–1552), noted Jesuit preacher and missionary, though the hymn admittedly expresses his spirit, and it has established the fact that Caswall translated it from the Latin—rather bad Latin, they say.

In this hymn the author examines the motives he has for loving God (Christ). He rules out the obvious selfish motive of gaining heaven and escaping hell, and alleges that he is overwhelmed by the spectacle of God's offering himself—suffering manifold pains and disgrace, even dying—for his enemy, mankind. Such a spectacle of self-sacrifice and forgiveness eliminates all thought of self, stirs up love in return, praise, loyalty.

The detailed suggestion of suffering throws the poem into the category of most other medieval passion hymns, yet the subjective approach gives it an emotional intensity that is consonant with its Spanish origin.

*Finita iam sunt proelia*      Anonymous, 1695

*The strife is o'er, the battle done*      Tr Francis Pott, 1861

The joyous music of Palestrina has helped carry this hymn to its continuous popularity. Stripped of its Allelulias and the third line of each stanza, the words present the theological statement that the Crucifixion was a contest between Christ and the devil's legions, in which Christ won. This is proved by the fact that Christ did not stay dead. The victory enabled Him to close hell and open heaven—(as if heaven had not been open since the dawn of conscience in mankind, and hell were not still open today!). Translating the results from cosmic to personal terms: the punishment meted out to Christ because of our sins enables us to go scot-free. Our sole employment through eternity is to sing praises to Christ.

It is doubtful if contemporary Christians universally will accept this statement of the function of the Crucifixion or of the ideal of a future life.

The third line of each stanza gives the Christian's emotional reaction to the victory of Christ: a song of triumph, a shout of joy, ascriptions of praise.

### EIGHTEENTH CENTURY

*Adeste fideles*      John Francis Wade, 1744

*O come, all ye faithful*      Tr Frederick Oakley, 1841, altered
*Come hither, ye faithful*      Tr Edward Caswall, 1849

The facts about this "anonymous" Latin hymn were long obscure. However, in 1946, by chance an English vicar discovered a small manuscript of musical selections for chapel use among Roman Catholics, in which we are given certain data.

The author of the hymn was John Francis Wade, a man whose business apparently was to copy music for Catholic institutions and families in various places. He was an Englishman by birth but had early moved to Douai in France. There he wrote the hymn in 1744 and set it to the music which with few changes we still use. The first part of the air was probably written by him, because it was referred to as an "English" air, but it was helped out with phrases that sound like Handel, then in his prime.

An edition of Wade's MS was made in 1750 for the English Roman Catholic College in Lisbon, Portugal, which also was used in the chapel of the Portuguese embassy in London. Hence, when the words and music came into wide and ultimately universal use in England, the music was called "Portuguese Hymn."

But its popularity in all English-speaking countries is universal: hardly a congregation fails to sing it at every Christmas time. Such popularity is testimony to its genuine worth.

In the first place, the method of presentation is dramatic. The poet takes us by the hand and leads us with triumphant song to the cave of the Nativity in Bethlehem, shows us the Babe, and bids us adore.

Next, in a stanza that many hymnals omit or modify, we are given an explanation of what we see: it is not a human infant, but God. Here the language is taken literally from the ancient Greek creeds of the fourth century.

The choirs of angels now burst upon us, urged on to further song by our own exuberance. The shepherds enter the cave; they join us as we kneel in adoration. We speak to the child direct and make our offering of love and praise.

This is all so simple, so vivid in imagery, so sincere in emotion, that barring a few theological phrases a child can understand it and enter sympathetically into the experience of worship and joy.

# HISTORICAL SUMMARY
## CHAPTER TEN: GREEK HYMNS

|  |  | *Greek Hymnists* |
|---|---|---|
| 3rd cent. | Era of Church Fathers and tentative theologies. | Clement, c. 200 |
|  | Gnosticism the dominant heresy. | Anon. c. 250 |
| 323 | Constantine, first Christian emperor. |  |
| 325 | Council of Nicaea: |  |
| c. 361 | Athanasian Creed promulgated. |  |
|  | Rise of asceticism and monasticism in the East. |  |
| c. 340–420 | St. Jerome, famous ascetic (Palestine); translated Bible into Latin (the Vulgate). | Synesius, c. 420 |
|  | Neo-Platonism affecting Christianity. | Liturgy of St. |
| 5th cent. | Barbarians destroy Classic civilization in N. Africa. | James, c. 450 |
| 463 | Church of the Studium built (Constantinople). |  |
|  | Monophysite heresy strong in Near East. |  |
| 484 | Monastery of Mar Saba founded (Palestine). |  |
| 527–65 | Justinian Emperor: Byzantine Empire at its peak. |  |
| 622 | The "Hejira": Mohammed founds Islam. |  |
|  | Death struggle begins with Byzantine Empire. |  |
| 634–1917 | Mohammedanism controls Palestine (except Latin Kingdom, 1099–1187). |  |
| 726–842 | The Iconoclastic Controversy. |  |
|  | All hymn-writers defend the use of art in religion. | Andrew of Crete, c. 730 |
|  |  | John of Damascus, c. 750 |
| 787–826 | Theodore of the Studium, staunch supporter of the icons and of monastic discipline. | Anatolius, c. 810 |
|  | Eastern Orthodox Church (Greek) and Western Roman Church (Latin) increasingly hostile. | Joseph the Hymnographer, c. 850 |
|  |  | Theoctistus, c. 890 |
| 1054 | Final separation of Eastern and Western Churches. |  |

# CHAPTER TEN

# GREEK HYMNS

JUST AS THE LATIN HYMNS in English dress are a tribute to the learning, piety, and zeal of the leading spirits of the Oxford Movement, so are the Greek hymns. Every scholar knew and loved the Latin hymns; the Greek were practically unknown. But as it became evident to the developing High Church party that affiliation with the Roman Church was impossible except on the basis of absolute surrender, the minds of some of them turned sympathetically to the Eastern Orthodox Church, which, just as literally as the Roman, represents Apostolic Christianity.

Dr. Neale was one of these men. Having practically completed his translations from the Latin (*Medieval Hymns and Sequences*, 1852; *Rhythm of Bernard of Morlaix*, 1858; *Hymnal Noted*, 1854) he turned his rare talent upon the Greek liturgy and published in 1862 his *Hymns of the Eastern Church*. No one before him had ventured into this immense and complicated field. In the first place, the fully-developed liturgy is often in prose, and so no help is afforded through suggestion of structure and meter; then the "Canons" (see below) are tiresomely long and cannot be made serviceable to our English and American churches unless they are drastically trimmed down. Dr. Neale made his own selection of subject-matter and form, eliminating passages that would be offensive to Anglican sensibilities, like apostrophes to the Virgin Mary, and so produced some of the sweetest and most popular hymns to be found in all English hymnals.

Aside from the liturgies of the later centuries, the Greek Christians developed a large body of metrical hymns based on the ancient classical meters. Our earliest hint of their devotion to hymns comes from Pliny the Younger, who as governor of Bithynia (Asia Minor) in 112 A.D. had to perform the unpleasant duty of punishing Christians for their refusal to make sacrifiices to the emperor Trajan. Being a humane man he made a thorough investigation of the character of Christians in his province, found no evil in them, but only "that they met on a certain fixed day before it was light and sang an antiphonal chant to Christ as to a god."

That the practice of hymn-singing was widespread by the end of the first century is shown by the approval given in Eph 5:19—"speak to one another in psalms, hymns and sacred songs. Sing praise to God with all your hearts."

These hymns in the classical mode gradually ceased by the ninth century when the prose liturgies were fully developed. Since they were never incorporated into the service books, Neale did not translate any of them. After Neale's day other scholars continued his work, until now 27 different translated Greek hymns are found in our selected hymnals, nine of which are here to be studied.

## CLEMENT OF ALEXANDRIA ( TITUS FLAVIUS CLEMENS )

### ( c. 170–c. 215 A.D )

WITH the passing of the Apostolic Age the young Church entered a period not only of expansion but of controversy and persecution. The energetic center of propaganda had shifted from Jerusalem to Antioch to Ephesus, and by the end of the second century to Rome and Alexandria. Rome had the wealth and prestige as an organization, Alexandria had the early thinkers and apologists—the literary pugilists.

Well might this city be a center of intellectuality. Shortly after its founding by Alexander the Great in 332 B.C., its ruler, Ptolemy I ( 323–285 ), began the great Library which for a thousand years was the collection supreme of the literature of the world. For it the Greek translation of the Jewish Old Testament (the Septuagint Version) was made, and its librarians boasted that they had the works or a work of every Greek writer who ever lived. Being a cosmopolitan city, the learned men of all races flocked there. All the philosophical systems of the world had "schools" there—of the Platonists, Neo-Platonists, Stoics, Epicureans, Cynics, besides cults of all the Mystery Religions. Christianity entered early and, in the second century A.D., the city became a focal point of infection for the heresy called "Gnosticism" (from the Greek word meaning Knowledge), an amalgam of Platonism, Stoicism and Christianity.

Clement was a Gnostic. He became the head of a famous school which taught that Greek philosophy was not inconsistent with Christianity, but a handmaid to it. He taught that the *Logos* ( Jn 1:1) is the "source of all the intelligence and morality of the human race—the teacher of mankind everywhere." The Logos was, therefore, the source of all true philosophy: in fact, God gave philosophy to the Greeks until Christ should come with something better; as Paul said about the Jewish law, it was "a schoolmaster to bring us to Christ" (Gal 3:24). He taught also like Paul that knowledge should be added to faith, and then he advanced beyond Paul by saying that knowledge leads to a greater good than mere salvation—the knowledge of God. Clement had little interest in the earthly life of Jesus; the focus of his faith was the Logos, the revealer of Truth.

Under the severe persecution ordered by the Emperor Septimius Severus (202–3 A.D.) Clement was driven from Alexandria to be a wanderer the rest of his days. He was still alive in 211.

The sole hymn of Clement that has survived he attached to a prose volume variously called *The Pedagogue, The Instructor,* or *The Tutor.* The book aimed to instruct new converts from heathenism how to regulate their conduct in view of their new-found faith. That change was a difficult one. Their heathenism had been raw and uncontrolled; Christianity demanded self-conquest, direction, integration, obedience to Christ's new Law of Love.

In his *Instructor,* Clement spares no detail. Here are some of the subjects treated:

> Against embellishing the body; with whom we are to associate; behaviour in the public baths; exercises suited to a good life; clothes [simple, white]; ear-rings [no]; finger-rings [yes]; hair [not long, a beard]; painting the face [no]; walking [grave and leisurely]; amusements [don't loaf in barber shops, or throw dice]; public spectacles [no]; going to church; conduct out of church; the government of the eyes; love and the kiss of charity.

At the end he appends a poem of thanksgiving and praise to the Instructor (the Logos). Here it is, literally translated, and in the modern hymn form:

### Στόμιον πώλων ἀδαῶν

*Shepherd of tender youth*      Tr Rev. H. M. Dexter, 1846
*Master of eager youth, controlling, guiding*
Tr F. Bland Tucker, 1939

| *Literal* | *Dexter* |
|---|---|
| Bridle of colts untamed, | Shepherd of tender youth, |
| Wing of unwandering birds, | Guiding in love and truth, |
| Sure helm of ships, | Through devious ways; |
| Shepherd of royal lambs, | Christ our triumphant King, |
| Assemble thy simple children to praise | We come thy name to sing, |
| holily, to hymn guilelessly with innocent | Hither our children bring |
| mouths, Christ the guide of children. | To shout thy praise. |
| | |
| O King of Saints, all-subduing Word of | Thou art our holy Lord, |
| the most high Father, Ruler of Wisdom, | The all-subduing Word, |
| Support of sorrows, rejoicing in eternity, | Healer of strife; |
| Jesus, Saviour of the human race, Shepherd, Husbandman, Helm, Bridle, Heav- | Thou didst thyself abase, |
| | That from sin's deep disgrace |

enly Wing of the all-holy flock, Fisher of
men who are saved, catching the chaste
fishes with sweet life from the hateful
wave of the sea of vices—Guide us, Shepherd of rational sheep; guide, O holy
King, thy children safely along the footsteps of Christ; O heavenly Way, perennial Word, immeasurable Age, eternal
Light, Fount of mercy, Performer of
virtue.

Noble is the life of those who hymn God,
O Christ Jesus, heavenly milk of the
sweet breasts of the graces of the Bride,
pressed out of thy wisdom. Babes nourished with tender mouths, filled with the
dewy spirit of the rational pap, let us
sing together simple praises, true hymns
to Christ our King, holy fee for the teaching of life; let us sing in simplicity the
powerful Child.

O choir of peace, the Christ-begotten,
O chaste people, let us sing together the
God of peace.*

Thou mightest save our race,
  And give us life.

Thou art the great High Priest;
Thou hast prepared the feast
  Of heavenly love;
While in our mortal pain
None call on thee in vain;
Help thou dost not disdain,
  Help from above.

Ever be thou our Guide,
Our Shepherd and our Pride,
  Our Staff and Song;
Jesus, thou Christ of God,
By thy perennial word,
Lead us where thou hast trod,
  Make our faith strong.

So now, and till we die,
Sound we thy praises high,
  And joyful sing;
Infants and the glad throng
Who to thy Church belong,
Unite to swell the song
  To Christ our King!

Strangely enough, the translator of this hymn was not a member of the
Oxford Movement, nor an Anglican, but a young American Congregational
minister, a graduate of Yale College and Andover Theological Seminary. He
had been pastor in New Haven only two years when he made the above
paraphrase, which has had wider use than any subsequent one. Anyone can
see that it is not a translation but a lyric that expresses the sentiments stirred
in Mr. Dexter by reading the original, and those sentiments are totally at
variance with the original ideas and purposes of Clement. Clement did not
write for the "tender youth" (aged 6 to 12 years), delicately reared in a
modern Christian family. He was writing for the raw heathen who were
tackling the hardest task of their lives—to remake their whole pattern of
reactions in the lascivious and immoral environment of Alexandria. The first
line of the original gives us the point of view: "Bridle of colts untamed!"
According to Clement, the function of the Logos in human life is one of
control and direction. The Church has to break-in these rambunctious colts
and harness them to its wagon so that their energies may advance the

* From *The Ante-Nicene Fathers,* by Roberts and Donaldson. Vol II: Fathers of
the Second Century, pp. 295-6, Scribner's, New York.

Kingdom of God. Christ had the same idea when He said, "Take my yoke upon you" (Mt 11:29).

In the whole hymn Clement gives the Logos twenty-one different titles, each expressing some protecting or directing function necessary for the training of Christians. Of these Mr. Dexter uses only eight or so, and these he tones down or disguises. It goes to show how the metaphors and sentiments of one age are quite different from those of another. One function of a translator is to reconcile the two if possible. Mr. Dexter has practically abandoned the one for the other. Mr. Tucker has done a better job.


## ANONYMOUS, SECOND–THIRD CENTURY

### Φῶς ἱλαρὸν ἁγίας δόξης

*Hail! gladdening light, of His pure glory poured*
Tr John Keble, 1834
*O gladsome light, O grace of God the Father's face*
Tr Robert Bridges, 1899
*O brightness of th' Immortal Father's face*
Tr Edward W. Eddis, 1864


The scholars are not agreed as to the date of this lovely hymn. Prominent Englishmen say that it probably ante-dated Clement, end of second century; the Episcopal *Hymnal* and others say third century; in modern Greek Orthodox liturgical books it is attributed to Sophronius, Patriarch of Jerusalem, 629 A.D. Probably the third century is nearest the truth. Keble's translation is close to the original.

This hymn was probably sung in the family circle and no doubt also in church at candle-lighting time. It is sometimes captioned, "A Hymn for the Lighting of the Lamps."

Christians of earlier days, who lived closer to nature than we, sought to connect natural phenomena with their religion. Sunrise, sunset, night, calm and storm were occasions for thinking of God and Christ and for finding in the experience some metaphor that would embrace both the physical and the spiritual. So here, as clear daylight flushes into glorious sunset, which in turn is muted into the blue of night when stars shine out of infinity, so the poet is reminded of three aspects of deity: God the Father, Jesus Christ the Son, and the Holy Spirit—in essence all one. And yet, because through the Son we mortals have found eternal life, Him shall we praise especially in our evening hymn as the "Gladsome Light."

To sum it up in a literal translation of the Greek: "It behooveth to praise Thee at all times with holy songs, Son of God, who hast given life; therefore the whole cosmos glorifies Thee."

## SYNESIUS OF CYRENE (c. 375–c. 414)

CYRENE was the seat of a Greek colony in North Africa which during World War II was the scene of military operations around Tobruk, Derna and Benghazi. It was a flourishing center of wealth and learning, home of philosophers, poets, artists—one of whom made the famous Aphrodite of Cyrene statue found there 1913. Its apex of glory was around 100 B.C.; deserted and in ruins after the fourth century A.D. Synesius was its last great citizen.

And he was great: descended from Spartan kings, wealthy, a sportsman, a philosopher, a statesman, an orator, a man of noble character and a friend of St. Augustine of Hippo. In his youth he went to Alexandria to complete his education, became a disciple of the celebrated woman Neo-Platonist, Hypatia. Though not a very ardent Christian he was chosen Bishop of Ptolemais in Cyrene c. 410 A.D., and accepted on condition that he could retain his wife and his freedom to dissent from some of the tenets of the Church. His outstanding character alone made him acceptable to the Church in spite of these non-conformities.*

In his day the invasions of the Goths and of desert hordes began, which soon brought about the country's downfall. His death, usually set at 430, is more recently placed at 414.

## Μνώεο Χριστέ

*Lord Jesus, think on me*      Tr Allen W. Chatfield, 1876

This is a far cry from the belligerent Gnosticism of Clement (above). There is no pride of superior knowledge here, no *Instructor* telling young heathen how to hold their horses and learn the Christian discipline. A tired man is speaking: one who has run the entire gamut of life, tasted its power and its joy, its success and defeat, and now, having outlived his dearly beloved wife whom he would not give up to become a bishop, and all his sons who had been carried off by a plague, he looks forward to an uncertain future in which the whole fabric of society is disintegrating and the Western Empire tottering to its fall. His only recourse is to throw himself wholly upon the mercy and love of his Saviour. In this prayer-hymn he expresses what every Christian desires for himself when he deeply considers the values of human life, tries to examine life "under the aspect of eternity": forgiveness, the suppression of the passions, an inner purity, loyalty, quiet, some hand still to lead on, and a future life of light and joy. These universal desires, though expressed 1500 years ago, make this hymn contemporary to every age.

* See a fine characterization of him in Charles Kingsley's *Hypatia*, Chap. xxi, "The Squire-Bishop."

## ANONYMOUS: FROM THE LITURGY OF ST. JAMES

The Liturgy of St. James, one of the oldest in the world, was originally devised for use in the Church at Jerusalem; in fact it is often called the Liturgy of Jerusalem. Once it was supposed to have been the work of James the Less, brother of our Lord and first bishop of Jerusalem, but it seems to have taken its earliest form under Cyril of Jerusalem (fl. 347 A.D.), and was later modified and extended. Its primitive language was Greek, although in Syria the heretical churches of the Monophysite heresy (those who believed that Christ had only one nature, viz.; the divine) used it in the Syriac language.

In performance this liturgy leads up to the celebration of the Eucharist, our Communion. Since the Eucharist was an awesome rite in which, according to universal ancient belief, Christ was actually present under the guise of bread and wine, it should be approached only after due spiritual preparation. The Preface to the liturgy tells us how this conditioning was done.

First the celebrant says, "Let us give thanks unto the Lord," to which the people respond, "Meet and just." After this, the Preface goes on,

> We remember the sky, the earth and the sea, the sun and the moon, the stars and all creation both rational and irrational, the angels and archangels, powers, mights, dominations, principalities, thrones, the many-eyed Cherubim who also say those words of David: 'Praise the Lord with me.' We remember also the Seraphim, whom Isaias saw in spirit standing around the throne of God, who with two wings cover their faces, with two their feet and with two fly; who say: 'Holy, holy, holy, Lord of Sabaoth.' We also say these divine words of the Seraphim, so as to take part in the hymns of the heavenly host.

All this gives us the point of view from which to understand the hymn below:

Σιγησάτω πᾶσα σὰρξ βροτεία     Anon c. 5th cent.

*Let all mortal flesh keep silence*     Tr Rev. Gerard Moultrie, 1864

> *Stanza 1.* We are now standing before the altar where the Eucharist is to be celebrated. Silence and awe are befitting: "The Lord is in his holy temple."
>
> *Stanza 2.* We reflect upon the mystery: He was higher than all lords and kings, yet born on earth of an obscure village maiden. Now He will shortly be here before our eyes, His body in the bread, His blood in the wine, and we are to eat Him—take Him into our own bodies to nourish both them and our souls, to expel all sins we have committed since last we partook.

*Stanza 3.* Suddenly we are not alone: To witness this unique and incomprehensible mystery, all the hosts of heaven leave their thrones and descend in a body—all nine ranks of them, from angels (the lowest) through archangels, principalities, powers, virtues, dominations, thrones, to cherubs and seraphs. The vision blinds us, for the Source of all light is here, guarded by the effulgent hosts. Satan himself and all his minions of darkness flee in terror before them. *Stanza 4.* Now our attention centers upon the two highest orders: the cherubs who excel in knowledge, whose function it is to enlighten, the seraphs who excel in love and whose function it is to praise. The poet's imagery is suggested by Is 6:2–3, though the words of their song differ from Isaiah's; they convey not a description of God's character but they join with the seraphs in praise of the All-highest.

Now follows the consecration of the elements in which the miracle of Transubstantiation takes place, and the partaking of the Divine Food by all the Church.

## HYMNS FROM MAR SABA

The last place in the world to look for hymns would be the Wilderness of Judea in Palestine, yet out of it have come some of the most frequently-used and precious hymns in all our collections.

Leaving Jerusalem on horseback, you follow the Kidron valley southeastward across a wrinkled and treeless landscape, chalky at first, then browning as the harder rocks begin to crop. After a couple of hours two great ribs of limestone rise out of the ground like the springing of giant archways with a canyon in their hard embrace. Your horse mounts the western arch by a path which runs close to the edge, so steep in places that steps have been cut. The eastern wall rises opposite, twisting and turning parallel with yours, while between them the valley sinks ever deeper. And now as the valley turns sharply to the east, plastered against the cliff like a swallow's nest hangs the monastery of Mar Saba. The rocky canyon floor is 500 feet below.

You halt under a shattered tower and knock at a door in the wall. It is like the door of a fortress. A Greek monk in black robe and rimless, flat-roofed, stovepipe hat opens to you. Immediately you descend stone stairways between walls to the center of the monastery—the center perpendicularly and the center laterally—a little court with terraces of cells above and below, curious holes some of them, with narrow ledges in front protected by parapets, sometimes connected with one another by labyrinthine passages, and finally a heavily-buttressed chapel between you and the yawning depths.

To this desolate spot in 484 A.D. came an eighteen-year-old youth named

*Top, left,* Entrance to the Monastery of Mar Saba, wilderness of Judea. *Top, right,* A monk's cell. Rear window overlooks the deep gorge. On the door is the prayer, "Christ, stay with us." *Bottom, left,* Overlooking the gorge—proper background for "Art thou weary, art thou languid." *Bottom, right,* Mar Saba from within; cells in the face of the cliff.

Sabas. He wanted to be a hermit, and he lived like many others in the caves which honeycomb the canyon walls. After twenty years of this he was told in a vision exactly where he must build a monastery. It was in a cave which he reached only by climbing up a rope. Hearing of his sanctity, young men began to come to him. They were "toughies," the devil of discord was in them, and they and Sabas had a hard time. But in the end Sabas won out and he lived to be ninety-four. Meantime the fame of the monastery was spread abroad and it became the home of great men, some of whom left a permanent impression on the theology and the liturgy of the Greek Orthdox Church.

### STEPHEN THE SABAITE (c. 725–815)

THIS hymn-writer is introduced first of the Sabaite singers because he suggested to Dr. Neale a hymn that breathes the full monastic spirit and lays bare the motives which animated seekers after the holy life. Those were wretched days of pillage and bloodshed. In 611, Chosroes the Persian had ravaged Palestine and burned all the holy places. In 628 the Byzantine emperor re-conquered it. In 634 the Arabs swarmed in, beat back the Cross and planted the Crescent over Jerusalem—destined not to come down permanently till 1917. Internal rivalries and assassinations kept the country in turmoil and in poverty. The submerged peasant had no hope for any life that was endurable. His only escape was the desert and the so-called religious life. Stephen was one of these, only a boy of ten when he came to this region, and for five years he roamed around the Dead Sea, wearing a camel's hair costume in imitation of John the Baptist. Then he stayed put in the monastery, and in 790 became its Abbot. He lived to be 90 years old.

### Κόπον τε καὶ κάματον

*Art thou weary, art thou languid*      Tr J. M. Neale, 1862

On first publication Neale accredited the hymn to Stephen, but later acknowledged that there was so little of Stephen in it that his paraphrase would better be called an original poem. The inspiration came from an ancient volume in Constantinople out of which Neale took phrases here and there. Nevertheless the hymn can be put back into its old environment without a particle of violence. We might entitle it "the call of the religious life"— or more accurately "the monastic life."

We must dramatize it:

A young man makes his way along the rocky Kidron gorge. He was tired of the turmoil and blood of this wicked world, and was drawn by the reputation for holiness that St. Sabas enjoyed. He has walked the weary miles from Damascus and Jerusalem to this chasm, alone. It has been a tough journey; the sun bakes mercilessly down. (The guest-book of the monastery contains a Frenchman's comment as he registered his name: "Dieu! il fait chaud!") The abbot in his lofty cell sees the boy threading his way along, comes out on the narrow terrace and leaning over the parapet calls,

> "Art thou weary, art thou languid,
>     Art thou sore distressed?
> 'Come to me,' saith One, 'and coming,
>     Be at rest.' "

The boy looks up hopefully but uncertain. Who is this "One" who can give rest to the weary, peace to the struggling soul? "How shall I be able to recognize him if I come up to you?—

> "Hath he marks to lead me to him
>     If he be my guide?"

The not too reassuring answer comes down instantly from the terrace:

> "In his feet and hands are wound-prints,
>     And his side."

But such a One surely needs some sign of royalty. The boy had once seen the Omaiyad Caliph ride proudly through the streets of Damascus, with jewelled turban, flowing silk over gilded armor, flashing sword. All people touched forehead to earth in the presence of such wealth and power. Has this monk such a great One to offer?

> "Hath he diadem as monarch,
>     That his brow adorns?"

More hopeful comes the assurance:

> "Yea, a crown in very surety,
>     But of thorns."

After all, this is a hard life down here: starvation fare, gruelling labor, nights of vigil, penance that often prostrates. What do I get out of it?

> "If I find him, if I follow,
>     What his guerdon here?"

The abbot must tell the truth. He has not much to offer—

> "Many a sorrow, many a labor,
>     Many a tear."

Is that all he can offer?

> "If I still hold closely to him,
>     What hath he at last?"

The confident answer floats down:

> "Sorrow vanquished, labor ended,
> Jordan passed."

But I have led a wretched life—a life of outward violence and inner conflict. I am not worthy to hope for His guidance and His love.

> "If I ask him to receive me,
> Will he say me Nay?"

The voice of the black-gowned one on the terrace rings down like a trumpet:

> "Not till earth and not till heaven
> Pass away!"

Such unqualified assertions need proof. I am tempted to come up, but not till I know for a certainty that this life of self-denial will yield all you say:

> "Finding, following, keeping, struggling,
> Is he sure to bless?"

Yes, the proof is at hand that ever since holy Sabas founded this monastery three hundred years ago, men have reached this haven, followed the Rule, kept the faith, and fought the evil in their own hearts. Come up and I will show you the blue-domed tomb of the founder saint, the service books in the sacristy written by holy men of old, the hymns they composed in their tiny cells where every day was answered the prayer they had painted on the blue doors, "Christ, stay with us!" And even in the cave behind the saint's tomb I will show you the skulls of the martyrs slain here by the Persians: they sealed their devotion with their lives—

> "Saints, apostles, prophets, martyrs,
> Answer 'Yes.' "

## ANDREW OF CRETE (660–732)

ANDREW was a native of Damascus. He was mute from his birth up to seven years of age, and then after partaking of Holy Communion he began to speak. At fifteen he was brought to the Church of the Resurrection at Jerusalem, joined the clergy of the Patriarch's circle and thereafter lived for several years at Mar Saba. In spite of his youth he went as a delegate to the sixth Ecumenical Council at Constantinople (680–681) and presented to it a complete exposition of the questions that were to be decided at that Council. These were theological questions about the dual nature of Christ. It was decided that as Incarnate Word he had two complete natures: two wills and two energies. This was to silence the Monophysite heresy which held that Christ had only one nature (divine), one will and one energy.

After the Council Andrew stayed for a time in Constantinople. The Emperor was attracted to him, had him ordained a deacon of the grand church of St. Sophia, made him administrator of certain charitable foundations and finally promoted him to be Archbishop of Crete (hence the name by which he is known). Here he had to organize the island's defence against invasions of the Arabs. Since he attributed the invasions to the fact that the Church was falling away from its original orthodoxy, his best defence lay

Mar Saba Service Book, now in the library of the Greek Patriarch, Jerusalem. This is part of a hymn to the Saviour praying for the purification of the body from its desires and of the soul from its sinful thoughts. (Vol. 162, p. 41)

in resurrecting and preserving inviolate the orthodox faith, the tenets of which he had formulated for the Council. This militant note dominates the hymn which is found in our hymnals (see below).

Like the earlier propagandists he used hymns as a chief weapon. He is credited with writing a good many, using as his themes the saints, martyrs and even the Seven Jewish Maccabees (c. 165 B.C. See Books of I and II Maccabees in the Apocrypha). Incidents from the life of Christ were also drawn upon. One fragment that has survived may have furnished the imagery for the opening lines of Bernard of Cluny's *Hora novissima* (The world is very evil). Andrew's lines run thus:

> The end cometh, O Soul; it draws nigh,
>     And thou carest not, thou preparest not.
> The time is brief. Arise!

Close by, at the gate, is the Judge.
Like a dream, like a flower, the allotted span of life runs on.
Why do we vex ourselves vainly?
Awake, O Soul of mine;
Consider the acts thou hast done,
And bring them to the light.

To Andrew is attributed the invention of the Canon. This is a long liturgical poem divided into nine odes and these in turn into strophes or stanzas. It was based for the most part on Biblical songs and was sung at the Office of Lauds. Andrew's most celebrated "Great Canon" in four parts is sung in Lent just before Holy Week, "with much labor and weariness of the lungs"—for there are 250 stanzas in it and takes three hours to perform! It scans both the Old and New Testaments, gives examples of virtue rewarded and vice punished by the Lord, and offers the advice that Christians should shun evil and do good. John of Damascus perfected the Canon form. It still occupies an important place in the Greek liturgy.

Andrew died in Mytelene, ancient Lesbos, appropriately enough in the town where once lived the most famous lyric poetess of the ancient world—Sappho.

## Οὐ γὰρ βλέπεις τοὺς ταράττοντας

*Christian! dost thou see them*      Tr Dr. Neale, 1862

Wherever Andrew wrote this hymn it bears the stamp and imagery of the monastic life at Mar Saba. It pictures an existence utterly alien to this twentieth century, but in spirit it is as eternally ours as the art of sinning and the gift of Grace. To enter sympathetically into the poem you must feel the desolate loneliness of the Kidron canyon, you must realize the savage harshness of the times, you must feed upon the monk's fare and drink the stagnant water of his cistern. You must even undergo the penance and self-mortification of Lent—for this cry was wrung from Andrew by the second week of the Great Fast when the body was well-nigh fainting and the devils that assail the soul take visible shape before your eyes. You must picture your cell in the rock, the couch of stone, the rude crucifix on the wall, and repeat the piteous prayer painted on the door, "Christ! Stay with us!"

*Stanza 1.* Andrew has become aware of the onslaught of foes from over Jordan. Time and time again as he well knows they have raided the monastery and wiped out its defenceless inmates. In a cave behind the chapel are still the bones of the martyrs of the Persian invasion. The foes without were a fearful reality in those days. Andrew sees them in his imagination skulking around the monastery wall. He feels that his hour has come. The hymnal editors have erased this picture by changing the last two lines: "How the troops of Midian prowl and prowl around."

Now can you translate the picture into modern terms? Let it stand in your mind for the power of an evil environment; for the greed and the hatred, the vice and crime that stalk in city streets; that fasten themselves upon our young men and maidens and like vampires suck the blood of virtue from their souls. This is a picture of the man-destroying slum: of the tenement, the saloon, and the brothel; it is a picture of the gilded vice of the night-club where unearned wealth sports itself, a symbol of the race for position and power and the pride of life—of unredeemed society.

Andrew dispelled the horrid vision by a look at the Crucifix. And he doubtless thought also of Constantine, the first royal champion of the faith, who at the battle of Milvian Bridge saw a cross in the sky with the flaming legend, "By this sign conquer." What was fact to him is still truth to us: the cross is the only weapon with which the individual can conquer himself, or the Church the world. *Stanza 2.* The vision has now become inner. The lusts of the flesh have each assumed a separate demon personality and are warring with the soul for mastery. It is a picture of that conflict which man can no more escape by fleeing than he can outrun his shadow. It is the cry of the flesh, the lust for carnal delights such as beset St. Anthony and have crazed many a saint ere this; the hunger even for pleasures that God never meant man should deny himself but that the medieval soul resisted unceasingly with self-mortification and prayer.

For us it means the struggle against the beast within us, against the corrupting power of an undisciplined imagination, against the love of ease that kills our performance of duty, against selfishness that shuts the door in the face of need. The only hope in a never-ending struggle is a never-failing courage born of action. Again the un-monastic editors have taken liberties with the last couplet which should read

> Smite them by the virtue
> Of the Lenten Fast!

*Stanza 3.* The third episode in this battle of the soul is the fight against the Lesser Good. Stilled for the moment is the clamor of the flesh, and the voice of Reason is heard. There is plausibility in the plea, and the words are reminiscent of Ecclesiastes: " 'Be not righteous overmuch.' Prayers are all right occasionally, but vigils from midnight till sunrise are a little too strenuous. Give yourself a vacation now and then. The practical life demands something of a compromise with the frailties of the common man. Don't try to put on a halo till you get to heaven."

We do not need to translate this language. The good has always been the foe of the best—never more so than today when culture and polite society seem to make spirituality superfluous. But the Christian will not stop to argue this point.

*Stanza 4.* The monk is rewarded at last with the Supreme Vision:

This was the goal of every monk's desire—to have his Lord enter his cell in person and flood its bare walls with glory. To this end were the strivings and the agonies and the penances. Christ here speaks to Andrew the word of courage out of his own victorious peace (Rev 3:21).

This is also the true climax of our own spiritual struggles—to see Him. It is our crown and exceeding great reward. For us, that face is the symbol of all we have willed or hoped or dreamed of good, and whatever specific form of good we may have struggled for, a nearer glimpse of it will always reveal the Face of the centuries shining through.

## *JOHN OF DAMASCUS (EIGHTH CENTURY)*

UNDOUBTEDLY the greatest son of Mar Saba was John of Damascus. He was born c. 676 and died c. 780. This would make him one hundred and four years old. His period of productivity was in the eighth century.

Those were stirring times. Damascus, where John was born, was the seat of the Caliphate—the Caliph being the "Pope" and the leading civil ruler of the Mohammedan faith. John's father Mansur, a Christian of Damascus, was chief financial adviser to the Caliph Abd-el-Melik. When for political reasons the Sherif of Mecca refused access to the holy places to pilgrims who acknowledged the authority of the Damascan Omaiyads, Abd-el-Melik built at Jersualem that magnificent mosque called "Dome of the Rock" which still stands on the site of Solomon's Temple, and so created holy places of his own as a substitute for Mecca.

John grew up in wealth and luxury. When he reached the age of 23 his father tried to find a Christian tutor for him and his foster-brother Cosmas. Standing in the marketplace one day, Mansur saw for sale a slave recently captured by pirates in a raid on Italy—one Cosmas, a Sicilian monk. Investigation showed him to be a man of great learning. Through his influence with the Caliph, Mansur secured the slave's release, adopted him as a son and put him in charge of his other two sons. Under him John made rapid and extraordinary progress.

On the death of his father, John was made chief councillor to the Caliph. At this time the Byzantine Emperor Leo the Isaurian determined to suppress Christian art on the ground that it promoted idolatry; he issued decrees (726 and 730) that forbade all use of "images" in churches. John wrote three powerful protests and sent them direct to the Emperor. In anger, the Emperor is said to have forged a letter in John's handwriting, offering to betray the city of Damascus to the imperial forces, and sent it to the Caliph. The Caliph ordered John's hand to be cut off and displayed in the marketplace. However, the hand was miraculously restored through the intervention of the Blessed Virgin! Thus the legend.

The Caliph tried to keep John in his employ but John had had enough of the world. He sold all his property and gave it to the poor; he freed his slaves, went to Jerusalem, thence to Mar Saba (c. 740) accompanied by his tutor Cosmas the Elder and his foster-brother Cosmas (afterwards called "The Melodist"). Here John continued his polemic writing both in the realm of theology and of the arts. In fact, recent discoveries in the monastery of Mt. Athos in Greece have shown that John not only codified Byzantine music but propagated Byzantine painting in the face of the Iconoclasts, the "image-breakers." He preserved many ancient pictures that otherwise would be unknown (*New York Times*, May 1, 1945). By his huge compilations in the realms of science, philosophy and theology he may be said to have laid the foundation of Scholasticism, which became the dominant matter and method of instruction in the Latin West in the twelfth-thirteenth centuries (see above: Abelard). Because of these powerful and eloquent writings John became known as "Chrysorrhoas" (Golden Stream) and "Doctor of Christian Art."

John's chief accomplishment, however, was the impetus he gave to Greek hymnody and music. The Greeks have preserved a story of John's first experience with song. It seems that he composed a funeral hymn for an old fellow-monk who was reported near death. While he was rehearsing it lustily to see how it would sound, the monk for whom it was written came in, disgusted with the noise, and told John to get out. The abbot, brother of the would-be-deceased, then got angry and put John out, and John remembered how Adam had lost the Garden of Eden! But the Holy Spirit rebuked the abbot, revealed to him what John was destined to accomplish in the field of music, and induced him to make peace with John and encourage his further writing and singing.*

The subject that called forth John's hymns was the Incarnation, expanded to include the whole earthly life of the Saviour, and so he furnished the Greek liturgy with those hymns of the Christian Year which lend themselves so admirably to English liturgical needs. In this process he perfected the "Canon," an artistic liturgical chant and adapted choral music to church use. Quite possibly he did for the East what Gregory the Great did for the West (see above under Latin Hymns)—substituted notes and

---

* This story and other bits about the Mar Saba writers are obtained from a book written in modern Greek, called *The Sacred Laura of Mar Saba* by John Phokylides, Alexandria, 1927.

other musical characters for the letters of the alphabet in music notation. In this work he was seconded by his young foster-brother Cosmas, whose independent accomplishments in this line gave him the title of "Melodist," and in other lines made him bishop of Maiuma (the port of ancient Gaza in Palestine). One feature of these canons does not appear in our English translations: the final strophe of every ode is usually devoted to the Blessed Virgin whom the East adores equally with the West. The West is apt to devote it to the Blessed Trinity.

The most famous of John's canons is that for Easter—a song of triumph and thanksgiving. It is known as the "Golden Canon" or the "Queen of Canons"—said to be the grandest example of Greek sacred poetry. From it the following hymn is taken; the translation, however, is very free:

## 'Αναστάσεως ἡμέρα

### *The day of resurrection!*     Tr Neale, 1853

Easter has always been the Church's supreme festival. It surpasses Christmas because while Christmas is the beginning, Easter marks the culmination of the life on which our faith is founded. As Paul puts it, "If Christ be not risen, then is your preaching vain." Life after death, which is man's greatest hope, was for the disciples assured when they realized that Christ still lived, and that assurance has been the Church's most powerful lever in raising man out of his hopelessness and sin.

No wonder then that the Easter ceremonial has gathered to itself all the pomp of ritual, all the dramatic symbolism, the poetry, music and art the Church could produce. This is particularly true in the Greek Church. Even today, as a vital part of the ceremonial, they bury a cross under the high altar on Good Friday and dramatically resurrect it with paeans of rejoicing on Easter morning. And on Easter day the usual salutation of men on the street is, "He is risen!"

This Easter joy invaded the monastery. Many a monk tried his hand at Easter songs. Among all these attempts those of John of Damascus seemed to Dr. Neale most worth preserving.

*Stanza 1.* The word Passover shows that two ideas were in John's mind: first, that the Christian Easter coincides in date with the Jewish Passover which was celebrated at the first full moon after the vernal equinox. Second, that the proper method of interpreting the Old Testament was the allegorical, whereby incidents were all veiled prophetic accounts of incidents in the life of Christ, or typical of Christian ideas. Since in the old Passover the Israelites were saved from the stroke of the death angel by the blood of the Pascal lamb, so we are saved from condemnation by the blood of the Lamb of God who was slain on Good Friday and brought gloriously to life on Easter Sunday.

*Stanza 2.* Here John asks us to forget the Old Testament imagery and recreate imaginatively the resurrection scene—the garden, the tomb, the risen Christ at the door, surrounded by the dazzling whiteness of heavenly light; then the gathered disciples in the upper room on whom Christ's "All hail!" fell like heavenly music. How can we see these pictures? John says, by cleansing our hearts from evil: "Blessed are the pure in heart, for they shall see God." *Stanza 3.* The last stanza is a joyous exhortation to praise, embodying snatches of Biblical phraseology and filled with the spirit of victory. No better climax for an Easter hymn was ever written.

'Άσωμεν πάντες λαοῖ

*Come ye faithful, raise the strain*     Tr Neale, 1853

This ode was written for St. Thomas' Sunday, the first after Easter. As usual, John takes his inspiration from a canticle in the Old Testament, in this case the Song of Moses, Ex 15.

*Stanza 1.* The picture here presents Israel crossing the Red Sea. Israel stands for the Church or the individual believer, otherwise called "Jacob's sons and daughters." By "Pharaoh's bitter yoke" he means the hardships, failures, discouragements, persecutions of this world. By "Red Sea waters" he means Death. The whole incident means that just as God led Israel out of bondage, across the uncrossable sea to the Promised Land, so in the resurrection God has brought His Son out of this cruel world through the crucifixion to the glory of eternal life. And the Church now finds in Christ's triumph the promise of its own deliverance.
*Stanza 2.* This is a beautiful nature allegory. Every year the sun is forced to retreat farther and farther south until at the winter solstice, for northern lands at least, he is dead. Now he comes triumphantly back: the light grows brighter, the days grow longer, ice and snow melt, birds again sing and flowers bloom. Christ is like that sun: he went down into the darkness of death, but now he returns to give light and life to all who believe in Him.

How fortunate that Easter comes in the spring! In the fall or winter it would have no such meaning.
*Stanza 3.* This stanza tries to convey a sense of joy in the brightness of spring, the pageantry of the Easter ceremonial and the rejoicing throngs of Jerusalem, which city stands for the Church Universal.
*Stanza 4.* Here are added the realistic touches of the tomb, the watchers and the seal; then it closes with the episode of Christ's appearance to the disciples in the upper room (Lk 24:36).
*Stanza 5.* This is a later addition made for an early edition of the Anglican *Hymns Ancient and Modern,* 1861. It brings all worshippers into the picture with a burst of praise to the Triune God.

### THE MONASTERY OF THE STUDIUM

With the ninth century the center of gravity of Greek hymns shifted westward. It was a welcome change. From the weird desolation of a chasm in a Judean wilderness, the lyric spirit of the Church fled to the sparkling beauty of the Bosporus and the Golden Horn: to the crossroads of the world, to the New York and Washington of that still mighty Eastern Roman Empire, to the center of the world's commerce, learning, art and political power—in short, to the focal point of civilization, Constantinople (Istanbul).

As you sail northward today across the sea of Marmora the golden city climbs above the horizon, a long ridge thrusting eastward between the sea and the Golden Horn. Its seven hills are enclosed in a triangle, its four-mile westward base crowned by the marble walls and one hundred and fifty towers of the Emperor Theodosius II. The minarets of its countless mosques pierce the sky like needles, and its domes culminate near the triangle's point in the grand masses of Sultan Ahmed's mosque and St. Sophia. Approaching closer to the city you can make out at its southwestern corner where the western wall runs into the sea, the Fortress of the Seven Towers, and a little to the right among the spires of cypress trees what looks like an old factory chimney. This is the ruined minaret of the mosque into which the Turks turned the church of the monastery we are seeking, St. John of the Studium.

When your ship anchors in the Golden Horn, go ashore and hire a cab. You will first climb to the open square which once was part of the hippodrome built by Constantine in 330 A.D. and seating 100,000 spectators, then you turn right and enter the famous old road called the *Via Egnatia* which connected the golden milestone in the heart of Constantinople with the one by the Coliseum in Rome. Your car whirls along this highway until, as you near the Seven Towers, a lane leads toward the sea. Down it you see the low-lying wall surrounding the court of the mosque of Emir Akor, and above it a higher building and the old minaret you saw from the steamer. This is the place you have sought.

As you walk toward it the peace of the dead past descends. The centuries telescope together. The lintel of the gateway before you is upheld by pillars of red granite brought from Egypt by unknown hands twenty centuries ago to adorn some Greek shrine. They are among the oldest things in the city. Beyond the open door of the mosque cool shadows of vines and figtrees welcome you to a fore-court; in the center, the fountain of ablutions protected by a summer-house with seats around the inside. Near the outer walls, the tottering tombstones of Turkish saints and near-saints, some wearing stone turbans, while among them and hastening their downfall with their desecrating roots, grow figtrees and pomegranates, grapevines and towering cypresses. All these represent the centuries of Turkish rule, misrule and decay from 1453 to the present.

In imagination we must wipe all this away and in its place rebuild a paved atrium in the Roman style, surrounded with cloisters on lovely marble

*Top, left,* Entrance to the Studium, Istanbul. Ruins of the church are beyond the trees. *Top, right,* White marble narthex (foyer) to the church. The man against the tree is the present author telling the story of the hymns of the Studium. *Bottom,* View of the ruined church taken from adjacent minaret. Note the mosaic floor. Grave of Abbot Theodore was found at farther end of right aisle.

pillars. Silent monks pace the shadowy porticoes, reading their breviaries and telling their beads. Instead of the call of the muezzin from his minaret, we hear the solemn chant of the brothers in the church before us. This is one of the oldest churches in Constantinople, built by the Roman Senator Studius in 463 A.D., a wealthy patrician who probably had been consul in 454. He moved from Rome to this new capital of Constantine's and here dedicated his wealth to the service of God by building this parish church of St. John the Baptist—at that time in the country far beyond the city walls. This is his only title to immortality. After the Theodosian walls had included the church within the city, it was rebuilt on a larger scale and a monastic building was added capable of holding 1000 monks.

Before us now rises a lofty portal of white marble. Four columns bear a beautifully sculptured entablature in the late classic style. We pass through to the narthex, the long foyer that always precedes the church proper, and then the caretaker, unlocking a rickety wooden door which takes the place of the original bronze one, reveals the church itself. Alas! St. John has fallen upon evil days. The roof is gone, the top of the eastern wall has tumbled down, the side galleries have disappeared; the lovely veined marble which once sheathed the interior has either perished in flames or has been stolen to adorn some Turkish harem; the mosaics that once shed their golden radiance on altar and worshippers have long since been ground to dust beneath the heel of time. Only two things are left that give us a hint of past magnificence: on the north side a colonnade of six shafts of that precious mottled-green marble known as "verde antique," carrying the white entablature of a gallery; and a pavement of rare geometric patterns,—the deep red and sprinkled white of porphyry, the deep green and sprinkled light-green of serpentine, the rosy blush of "rosso antico," alternating with verde antique, veined Thessalian and Numidian marbles in white, black and alabaster. What must the glory of the house have been in the days of its prime!

More remarkable than the building was the record of the monks who lived in it. These monks were a variety of "sleepless": a group of them always were kneeling before the altar engaged in prayer or song. When the hour of their vigils was accomplished, another group came silently, picked up the service and allowed the first group to retire. Thus the service continued without a break. One is thrilled to think as one stands before the vacant chancel and the broken wall that here praise and prayer ascended 24 hours every day, 365 days every year, for no one knows how many years, probably a thousand.

For nearly 300 years the brothers, flitting between their cells and the chancel praying-circle, left hardly a ripple on the world's history. Then came to the Byzantine throne Leo the Isaurian, who by edict fanned to flame the hidden spark of heroism in the breasts of these peaceful ones. Leo forbade the use of images in worship. Images! they were the very life-blood of worship. Icons! they were focal points on which the scattering thoughts of worshippers might concentrate. Pictures! they helped make real the abstractions of theology, the personalities of the saints, the life of the Saviour and the Blessed Virgin in the adoration of whom stood man's eternal life.

But the Emperor was more powerful than the Abbot. During the persecution that followed under Leo's successor, Constantine Copronymus, (740–775) the monks were either killed or scattered. After 61 years of persecution peace was restored in 787 by the regent-empress Irene who once more allowed the icon-worship. An abbot named Theodore and twelve monks were brought from another monastery to take charge of the Studium.

Then began the period of the monastery's greatness. In the war against the icons which persisted intermittently for 116 years till 842 and shook the whole Christian world, the Studium at the center of it furnished the most martyrs. Abbot Theodore who was the spearhead of the opposition was banished and restored three times. He was a grand organizer and purifier of monastic life. He did for the East what Peter the Venerable did for Cluny and its subsidiary houses in the West in the twelfth century. In addition, he was himself an hymnist and an inspirer of hymns. He wrote the triumphal Canon for the great festival which commemorated the victory of the icons: "A song, a song of gladness," sung on "Orthodox Sunday," first Sunday in our Lent, and his Canon on the Judgment is called by Dr. Neale the grandest judgement hymn of the Church previous to the *"Dies Irae."*

The lyric spirit descended upon the monks also. Theodore's brother Joseph (called "Of the Studium") began to write hymns, but they cannot be distinguished from those of another Joseph (below). Still another monk of his named Anatolius added noble and passionate poems c. 810 A.D. Thirty years later came Joseph the Hymnographer, and finally Theoctistus who died about 890.

Theodore died in 826 and was buried in the island of Prinkipo in the Sea of Marmora. But eighteen years afterward in the final peace he was re-interred in his beloved Studium where his body was discovered during Russian excavations at the east end of the south aisle.

## ANATOLIUS c. 810

ALMOST nothing is known of this writer. A letter is said to be extant showing him to have been a pupil of Theodore. Over 100 hymns are ascribed to him, some of them celebrating martyrs of the sixth and seventh centuries, but only two have survived in English:

Τὴν ἡμέραν διελθῶν

*The day is past and over*      Tr Neale, 1853

This is a prayer still found in the Greek Orthodox Prayer Book, to be repeated upon retiring.

Neale makes a good deal out of little Greek. Here is a literal translation:

Having come through the day, I thank Thee, Lord.
I ask for the evening with the night (to be) sinless;
Grant (it) to me, Saviour, and save me.
     Glory to Father and Son
     And Holy Spirit.

Having come past the day, I glorify Thee, Lord.
I ask for the evening with the night (to be) temptationless;
Grant (it) to me, Saviour and save me.
     Both now and ever
     And into the age of ages, Amen.

Having crossed (the span of) the day, I hymn Thee, Holy (One);
I ask for the evening with the night (to be) free of any plot
          (against me);
Grant it to me, Saviour, and save me.
                    —Translated by Rev. Theodore Theodorides
                       Church of St. Constantine, Cambridge, Mass.

The original is repetitious, as if a formula or charm were being said over and over, sometimes with only a single word changed as in some of Poe's poems. This also helps produce a sense of the inexorable passing of time, the resistless coming of night in which, with the will relaxed in sleep, evil spirits ("the wakeful tempter") may enter, take possession and cause the soul to sin. That is why Anatolius prays that night may be "without guilt," "without falling or stumbling," "without treachery." After each stanza the same cry is repeated without change, "Grant me this, Saviour, and save me!" Neale preserves something of this repetition.

The hymn is based upon the elemental fear of darkness. Sidney Lanier has expressed something like this in his "Marshes of Glynn":

     And now from the Vast of the Lord will the waters of sleep
          Roll in on the souls of men,
          But who will reveal to our waking ken
     The forms that swim and the shapes that creep
          Under the waters of sleep? *

With us, night has lost most of its terrors, except to childish minds. This may be partly because we live in a stable society and have electric lights! and partly because the idea of demoniacal influences has happily been largely abandoned. The language of this hymn might perhaps be used to better advantage at the end of night and the beginning of day when most of our temptations begin.

Also by Anatolius we have

* *Poems,* Scribner's, New York, 1897.

Ζοφερᾶς τρικυμίας

*Fierce was the wild billow*      Tr Neale, 1862

OTHER POETS OF THE STUDIUM

*Joseph the Hymnographer*      fl. 840–883

Joseph left his native Sicily for the monastic life, first in Thessalonica then in Constantinople. During the resumption of the war against the icons he fled to Rome, was captured by pirates and held a slave many years in Crete. After gaining his liberty he returned to the Studium (after 842) and became the most voluminous of Greek hymn writers. More than 200 Canons of his exist out of the 1000 he is reputed to have written. Since most of them celebrate saints and martyrs, the result is prolix and repetitious prose. Dr. Neale has given us several paraphrases in which there is more of Neale than of Joseph.

*Stars of the morning so gloriously bright*
*O happy band of pilgrims*

*Theoctistus*      fl. A.D. 890

Nothing of him is known, but his monkish devotion to the crucifix is signalized by his *Suppliant Canon to Jesus,* out of which Dr. Neale has made one of the sweetest hymns of adoration in existence. Just as a work of hymnic art it should appear in more hymnals, especially if set to the music of J. B. Calkin. Its first line is

Ἰησοῦ γλυκύτατε

*Jesus, name all names above*

SUMMARY

To get a full perspective on the influence of the Oxford Movement on Hymnody we should make a comparative study of the number of Latin and Greek hymns found in our ten hymnals. The numbers vary greatly, depending upon the distance the different denominations have moved away from the Roman and the Anglican communions.

The Anglican Church had remained Catholic to the extent of preserving a liturgy, the Christian Year and the chief doctrines and sacraments of early Christianity, each of which is celebrated at its appointed time. In the first onrush of Protestant renunciation, all of the Church's ancient hymns were sacrificed. But after three hundred years of trying to satisfy their liturgical souls with the Psalms of David and the temporary expedients of private collections, the dam broke and the old hymns in translation came flooding back in an overwhelming tide. This amounted to a counter-revolution in which the splendid English hymns that had arisen as individual expressions of the soul of religion were combined with the resuscitated hymns of the past. This movement found expression in 1861 in the epoch-making *Hymns Ancient and Modern,* revised and enlarged in 1868, 1875, 1889 and 1916. While this hymnal was never officially adopted by the Church of England, it met so fully the subconscious demand for a well-rounded book of worship that it supplanted most other Anglican hymnals the world around. Dr. Benson * states that by 1905, out of 13,639 churches [in England?] no less than 10,340 used *Hymns Ancient and Modern;* it was also used in 28 cathedrals, universally in the Army and Navy, and almost universally in the Scottish Episcopal churches. Out of it also grew the Canadian *Book of Common Praise* (1908, revised 1938) which in this study, under the symbol A, takes the place of its parent English collection.

There is no denying that *Hymns Ancient and Modern* has been the most influential hymnal ever published. Not only had 60,000,000 copies been sold by 1912, but its spirit spread to all denominations. It increased the liturgical trend in all and opened for their use the rich storehouse of the hymns of the Church Universal. The extent of this influence is indicated in the following table:

SUMMARY OF LATIN AND GREEK HYMNS

|  | A | B | C | E | L | M | N | P | S | U |
|---|---|---|---|---|---|---|---|---|---|---|
| Latin Hymns Interpreted | 24 | 13 | 15 | 25 | 20 | 16 | 18 | 20 | 22 | 23 |
| Greek Hymns Interpreted | 9 | 4 | 5 | 9 | 7 | 8 | 8 | 7 | 5 | 5 |
| Total | 33 | 17 | 20 | 34 | 27 | 24 | 26 | 27 | 27 | 28 |
| Latin Hymns, other | 80 | 0 | 2 | 53 | 23 | 7 | 0 | 5 | 24 | 9 |
| Greek Hymns, other | 4 | 0 | 0 | 14 | 5 | 0 | 0 | 0 | 8 | 2 |
| Total | 84 | 0 | 2 | 67 | 28 | 7 | 0 | 5 | 32 | 11 |
| Grand Total | 117 | 17 | 22 | 101 | 55 | 31 | 26 | 32 | 59 | 39 |
| Ranking Order | I | X | IX | II | IV | VII | VIII | VI | III | V |

As might be expected, the Church of England in Canada (A) leads the way with a total of 117 ancient hymns. The official *Hymnal* (1940) of the Episcopal Church in America, full-blooded daughter of the Anglican Church, runs a close second with 101. Third in order, though with a little over half the number of ancient hymns (59), comes *Songs of Praise,* a modern Anglican hymnal that has met with wide approval in England. It draws heavily from *Hymns Ancient and Modern.* The last of the distinctively liturgical churches in our study is the Lutheran Church in America. In its hymnal, *Common Service Book,* the number of Latin and Greek hymns drops to 55.

Though composed exclusively of dissenting Churches, the United Church of Canada inherits very strongly the liturgical feeling of the mother

* *The English Hymn,* pp. 510–11, Doran, New York, 1915.

country. Its *Hymnary* includes 39 ancient hymns. But as we proceed farther away from the Anglican influence and reach those denominations which not only withdrew from Rome but rebelled against the Anglican Church, interest in ancient hymns drops. Had it not been for a few scholars among their clergy, educated in the Classical tradition and moved by an historical interest, the American dissenting Churches might have longer withstood the appeal of the past. But even before the Oxford Movement had attained its full momentum, these men independently began to translate, so that when their denominations were ready to subordinate Watts and Wesley, they found these translations ready to hand, though of course the success of the *Hymns Ancient and Modern* accelerated the tendency toward liturgical enrichment.

Last of all on the list are the Congregationalists and Baptists. These American denominations represent what Edmund Burke describes as "the dissidence of dissent." They had been persecuted and martyred by the Anglican Church. Their ministers had languished in prison, been whipped through towns at the cart's tail, had been sent as slaves to the Barbadoes to be worked to death. Why should their descendants embrace the literary labors of an Oxford Movement that continued to exclude them ideologically from the great Apostolic Church? So their hymnody sinks to an all-time low of 22 and 17 translations respectively. No doubt it was the musical setting of these hymns more than the words that won for them even that modicum of recognition.*

All in all, we must recognize the tremendous enrichment that came to English hymnody through the Oxford Movement. Probably more than any other factor it contributed to the broadened liturgical practices of all American Churches—the re-establishment of the chancel, the altar, the two pulpits, the processionals, the recognition of the Christian year, and one might add, the sense of dignity in worship, a realization that even a "meeting house" was also a "house of God." And the Oxford Movement became articulate beyond its own borders very largely through its rediscovery and translation of Greek and Latin hymns.

---

* In my boyhood, as late as 1880, our Baptist church in North Scituate, Massachusetts was using *The Psalmist*, published in 1843, which contained among its 1180 hymns not a single translation from any language.

# HISTORICAL SUMMARY

*German*
*Hymnists*

| | | |
|---|---|---|
| 1415 | John Hus burned at the stake beginning of Protestant Reformation. | |
| 1440–50 | Invention of printing, making possible wider education and Bible study. | |
| 1440–93 | Wars between German princes; hostility of free cities to both princes and the Church. | |
| 1453 | Church of Bohemian Brethren organized, parent of the Moravian Brethren; influenced Lutheranism. | |
| 1476–1513 | Four peasant insurrections in Germany; national life strongly disrupted. | |
| 1500 | Humanism (Classical learning) becomes influential in Germany; provides fertile soil for the Reformation. | |
| 1501–41 | Bohemian hymns; all suppressed. | |
| 1516 | Erasmus (Dutch) published Greek text of New Test.; leads to study of early Christian sources. | |
| 1517 | Luther posts theses, thus challenging Catholic Church; protected by Elector Frederick. | |
| 1518 | Melancthon, scholar and theologian, joins reform movement. | |
| 1520 | Papal bull excommunicates Luther. | |
| 1521 | Diet at Worms condemns Luther's teachings. Luther begins translation of Bible—to be basis of his teaching. | |
| 1527 | Lutheran Church organized; uniform belief and ritual demanded. | Luther, 1529 |
| 1535 | Peace of Augsburg gave equal rights to Lutherans and Catholics. | |
| 1548 | Theological division in Lutheranism; penetration by Calvinism. | |
| 1556 | Peak of Protestantism in Germany. Counter-Reformation by Catholics, led by Jesuits. | Herbert, 1566 |
| 1577 | Calvinistic Lutherans form Reformed Lutheran Church. | Nicolai, 1597 |
| 1618–48 | Thirty Years' War between Catholics and Protestants involving most of Europe. | Weissel, c. 1630 Rinkart, c. 1630 |
| 1635–1705 | Spener founds Pietism—a second Reformation, like Methodism in England. | Heermann, 1630 Löwenstern, 1644 Gerhardt, 1648–53 |
| 1691 | Pietist University of Halle founded; Francke inspirer. | Neander, 1680 Canitz, 1700 |
| 1722 | Zinzendorf refounds Moravian Brethren at Herrnhut; broad missionary enterprises started. | Schmolk, 1709 Zinzendorf, 1721 Tersteegen, 1729 |
| 1732 | Moravian missions to W. Indies; Georgia (1735); Pennsylvania (1741). | |
| 1757–1817 | Rationalistic period (contemporary with Goethe, Lessing, Herder). | Claudius, 1782 Mahlmann, 1815 Mohr, 1818 |

## CHAPTER ELEVEN

# GERMAN HYMNS

WHEN LUTHER NAILED HIS NINETY-FIVE THESES to the door of the Wittenberg castle church in 1517 he started something besides a Reformation: it was a beginning of a new Hymnody in the vernacular to be sung freely by all the people.

When Henry VIII of England used his divorce from Catherine of Aragon as a lever to pry the English Church loose from the grip of Rome, he too threw away Latin hymns but unlike Luther he put nothing in their place. Under the influence of John Calvin, the theologian, (as we have seen above) the newly-founded Anglican and Scottish Churches rejected all hymns of "human composure" but allowed the people to sing Biblical Psalms made metrical. This set back for nearly two hundred years the creation of genuine hymns in the vernacular.

The Protestant Church in Germany thus had the start on the rest of the world. German hymns at once became popular in their home land. As time went on, all phases of the religious life found expression: the fighting spirit of the Reformation, the misery and penitence of the Thirty Years' War, the inward-looking mysticism of the eighteenth-century pietists, the outward-looking missionary enthusiasm of the Moravians. German hymnody became the most prolific in the world. Its complete output must be near 100,000!

This vast popular expression of lyric religion did not begin to cross the national border to England until the eighteenth century. Then John Wesley discovered the treasure and was the first translator. How this happened has been told above in Chap. V. His translations have survived to the present day; five of them are interpreted in this chapter.

For a century no more translators gave us German hymns. The first to rediscover and translate was Miss Frances Elizabeth Cox, an Anglican and a native of Oxford. It is hard to imagine that she was uninfluenced by the Oxford Movement which was placing renewed emphasis on the ecumenical character of Christianity, not only on its Apostolic origin but its international ramifications. Her translations were published in 1841. Six of them appear in our list of hymnals, and one is analysed below.

Two Presbyterian sisters made the next contribution. They were Jane Borthwick and her sister Sarah (Mrs. Eric Findlater). Together they published in 1854, *Hymns From the Land of Luther.* Of these, Jane wrote sixty-one and Sarah fifty-three. The translations attained instant popularity and wide use both in England and America. They rank in quality second only to those of Miss Winkworth. Our hymnals contain nine, of which three are noted below.

The translator whose work has proved most popular and of the finest quality is Miss Catherine Winkworth, an Anglican. In 1855 appeared her *Lyra Germanica,* followed by other translations in 1858–69. Owing to her piety, which was not sentimental but deeply rooted, her interest was largely in devotional hymns. It was her work more than any other that acclimated German hymns in England. Twenty-four of her translations appear in our hymnals; eight are analysed below.

Of the other eight translators in our hymnals, one is anonymous, one is an American Unitarian, one Anglican-Roman Catholic, and five are Anglicans. Most of these translations were made when the Oxford Movement was in full swing. Altogether therefore we must conclude that the happy opening of this treasure of German song is attributable to the enlarged vision of the Church and the desire to enrich the liturgy that sprang from John Keble, John Henry Newman and their followers.

### THE REFORMATION

The German revolt against Rome was inspired by the same general conditions and the same specific abuses that obtained in England in the sixteenth century (Chap. I). Papal taxation was oppressive and unequally levied: the vast lands and treasure of the clergy and the monastic houses which brought no wealth to the people were exempted while the hard-working peasants and enterprising business men paid heavily. Many of the clergy were unworthy examples of Christian morality; the monks were lazy and corrupt. The Church's sale of Indulgences by which sins were forgiven in return for cash, without repentance or penance, shocked the moral sense. The Inquisition's stern repression of new ideas that now were coming into northern Europe like a tide—the Humanism resulting from the re-discovery of classical literature—angered the intellectuals; low standards of living and the hopelessness of any relief angered the peasants. These conditions combined with the stirrings of a popular religious awakening called for a leader with the courage of his convictions, one who would bring the smouldering unrest to a focus of action. This leader arose in 1517; people of all ranks flocked to his standard and in an incredibly short time the most gigantic revolution in the history of the Church was under way.

Luther posting his theses. From a painting by Vogel.

## Rev. *MARTIN LUTHER* (1483–1546)

MARTIN LUTHER was that leader. His parents were peasants of simple but genuine piety, ambitious that their son should be educated. By hard work they had him prepared for the University of Erfurt with a career in the law in view. But the sudden death of a friend and his own narrow escape from lightning coupled with a deep underlying consciousness of sin caused Luther to abandon law and become an Augustinian monk. Discovering his unusual ability, his superiors sent him to Wittenberg that he might prepare to become a professor in Theology. After securing his doctorate and making a trip to Rome he began lecturing on the Bible. At once his powers of intellectual penetration and of persuasive preaching became evident. He was made district vicar in charge of eleven monasteries of his Order.

But he was not at ease in his inner life. Gradually he discovered that salvation did not consist of holding an approved theology or of depending upon sacraments and penances, but upon a right personal relationship with God. For him the sum and substance of the gospel became the fact of God's forgiveness through the sacrificial death of Christ. One had only to trust the promises of God as given in His inspired word, the Scriptures, and to make Faith the foundation-stone of the religious life. It is easy to see what this conviction did to his relation to the Church: it swept away his loyalties to all that the contemporary Church stood for—absolute domination over men's thinking, absolute surrender to an institution which was largely political, selfish and corrupt.

The explosion came when Pope Leo X authorized the sale of Indulgences to help build the huge Church of St. Peter's in Rome. Luther preached against this abuse in general and against the monk Tetzel who was chief collector for his district. It was then, October 31, 1517, that Luther nailed up on the door of the Wittenberg castle church, which was the university bulletin-board, his ninety-five Theses that he would defend in argument against all comers. Excitement ran high. The Theses were copied and sent all over Germany and most of Europe. A leader had arisen to champion a people's cause against a tyrannical Church. The fight was on.

Luther was cited to appear in Rome and answer to the charges of heresy and insubordination. But a powerful political leader, the Elector Frederick of Saxony, sprang to his defence and secured a change of the trial from Rome, where Luther would certainly have been condemned, to Augsburg in Germany, where Luther had a fighting chance. The court ordered Luther to retract, but Luther refused and managed to escape to Wittenberg. In the controversies that now raged on all sides Luther declared that the Pope and Church councils were not infallible and that the Scriptures were supreme over both. This theoretically cut the ground from beneath the entire structure of Catholicism; Luther was excommunicated in 1520, but he publicly burned the "Bull."

At this juncture the Holy Roman Emperor died and a new one, Charles V of Spain, was appointed. He was soundly Catholic and hated Luther, but on the insistence of some of the leading princes of Germany that Luther had not had a fair trial, he summoned a court at Worms (1521) and promised Luther safe conduct thither. Here before the Emperor and the Reichstag Luther refused to retract, uttering, it is said, the famous words, "I cannot do otherwise. Here I stand. God help me, Amen." He was condemned to punishment and his books were burned. But his friend Elector Frederick took a bold hand in the game; he had him arrested (what we now call "protective custody") and secretly taken to the Wartburg castle near Eisenach. During this enforced residence Luther carried on his warfare with his pen, and in addition performed the notable service of translating the New Testament not from the Latin Vulgate but from the original Greek into German. This has remained the standard version of the German people.

Within a year the elector winked at Luther's escape from the Wartburg and his resumption of preaching. Luther's freedom from radicalism led many of the German rulers to favor his cause. The movement spread throughout Germany and into neighboring states. As new congregations formed, Luther helped them organize after a common pattern, and established an order of worship in which the singing of hymns in German instead of Latin held an important place. Instead of the Mass the central feature became preaching.

But hopeless divisions in the New Church, continual theological disputes, political jockeying and an endless series of wars between Emperor Charles V and the various components of his empire gradually sapped the vitality of the bold reformer and he died suddenly in 1546. However, the Lutheran Church he established had so far succeeded that by the peace of Augsburg (1535) it was granted by the Emperor equal political and civic rights with the Catholic Church.

The great accomplishments of Luther may be thus summarized: He established the Protestant Church in Germany known as Lutheran; he "gave the people in their own language the Bible, the Catechism and the Hymnbook so that God might speak *directly* to them in His Word, and that they might *directly* answer Him in their songs."

All these were important, but it was the Hymnbook that generated the power. Luther took the hymn out of a foreign tongue, away from the choir, away from an inelastic niche in a standardized liturgy; he gave it spontaneity, and, while requiring that the hymn be evangelical, he did not otherwise restrict the free imagination of any poet who was inspired to write. The result was a copious stream of hymnody that preached a gospel of joy; spiritual folk-songs which flooded the home and the school as well as the church and became a never-failing spring of spirituality in people's hearts and lives.

Luther no doubt knew that he was not the inventor of congregational singing. Though in the Roman Church the clergy as choristers had monopolized since before 1200 A.D. the singing function, and since 574 A.D. women had been forbidden to sing in church, wherever reform movements sprang up the tendency was for the people to sing. This spontaneous song had already reached full development among the followers of John Hus who

Martin Luther
from a portrait by
Lucas Cranach.

died singing as he was burned at the stake in 1415. These Hussites or Bohemian Brethren sang in their native Bohemian tongue; and when at last the survivors were driven into exile in Moravia and Saxony their songs were translated into German (1561, 1566, 1725–35) and were merged into the general stream of German hymnody. (See Moravian Hymns, below.)

While Luther himself composed 37 hymns only 10 have survived fitfully in our English hymnals, and only one has become a universal treasure.

*Ein' feste Burg ist unser Gott*    [1529]
*A safe stronghold our God is still*    Tr Thomas Carlyle, 1831
*A mighty fortress is our God*
Tr Frederick H. Hedge (Boston Unitarian) 1852
*A mighty fortress is our God*    (Composite) 1866

This hymn was written during a climax in Luther's struggle against the Roman Church. A couple of years previous, the Emperor Charles V had been at war with Pope Clement VII, had invaded Italy with an army which contained many German Lutheran soldiers, had shut up the Pope in the Castle St. Angelo and had barbarously looted the Holy City. The Pope was compelled to make peace. Then the Emperor turned his attention to suppressing the Lutherans. Accordingly the Reichstag assembled at Speier in February 1529, in which a Catholic majority resolved to put the revolting Lutherans in their proper place. It ordered that Catholic worship should be permitted in all the German principalities from which they had been excluded by the Lutheran-sympathizing princes, and that the prelates and the monkish orders should be allowed full enjoyment of their former properties and revenues. The Lutheran princes entered a formal protest, because of which action the Lutheran movement came to be called "Protest-ant." The hour was the darkest in the history of this fateful movement. This hymn, written at Coburg, was Luther's call to battle in that crisis. It takes its title and its spirit from Psalm 46: "God is our refuge and strength"; and then proceeds in Luther's striking imagery to summon all spiritual powers to the aid of the threatened cause. The world-famous chorale tune to which the words are universally sung may have been developed by Luther from an old Gregorian melody.

*Stanza 1.* In resisting the 1500-year-old Roman hierarchy with all its intrenched spiritual privileges and its political and financial power, Luther felt that he had only one helper—God. The "mortal ills" were not only those induced by the combat: they were social as well— the hopeless poverty of the peasants, the ignorance of the masses, the oppressions of barbarous laws. These Luther attributed to "our ancient foe," who was of course primarily the devil, as ancient as the Garden of Eden; but he was now incarnate in the worldly Pope Clement VII and in the ambitious, intriguing "Holy" Roman Emperor, Charles V. All these constituted a triangle of hate and power such as the world had seldom seen.

*Stanza 2.* Such odds might daunt the boldest. But Luther puts all his trust in a spiritual leader—Jesus Christ. On Him he confers the title which the ancient Israelites delighed to give to Jahweh, "Lord Sabaoth," commander of the hosts of heaven. This is a truly Protestant conception: we place our confidence of salvation not in an infallible Church with its sacraments, but in an unconquerable Man, clothed with the authority and might of God Himself.

*Stanza 3.* Luther of course believed in the existence of devils and their prince, Satan. In fact, the latter tried to get him while he was confined in Wartburg castle; but Luther threw his ink-bottle at him and the devil vanished. (The ink spot is still on the wall!)

The danger, as seen in the hosts of powerful enemies that encom-
passed Luther, was constant and dire. But, as men have always
believed, if you know the right formula you can exorcize the devil.
This "little word" of power is "the Name that is above every name"
—Phil 2:9–10.

*Stanza 4.* This is the quintessence of Luther's religion: personal contact with God, the source of spiritual power, through the divine
Saviour and the indwelling Spirit. And the gifts of the Spirit are
"love, joy, peace, long-suffering, kindness, goodness, faithfulness,
meekness, self-control" (Gal 5:22). Of what value are earthly things
compared with these priceless treasures?—which are the title-deeds
to a kingdom that shall never end.

So tremendous is the uplifting and sustaining power of this faith that
Luther's mighty hymn has been the battle-cry in many a national crisis.
Dr. Louis Benson writes of it:

It was, as Heine said, the Marseillaise of the Reformation. . . .
It was sung in the streets. . . . It was sung by poor Protestant
emigrees on their way into exile, and by martyrs at their death. . . .
Gustavus Adolphus ordered it sung by his army before the battle
of Leipzig in 1631. . . . Again it was the battle hymn of his army at
Lützen in 1632 in which the king was slain but his army won the
victory. It has had a part in countless celebrations commemorating
the men and events of the Reformation; and its first line is engraved
on the base of Luther's monument at Wittenberg. . . . An imperishable hymn! not polished and artistically wrought but rugged
and strong like Luther himself, whose very words seem like deeds.*

Following Luther's death the spate of German hymns continued. But
none from that century has survived in our English hymnals except two by

## PHILIPP NICOLAI (1556–1608)

HE WAS a Lutheran pastor, graduate of Erfurt and Wittenberg
Universities, a bold controversialist against both Catholics and Calvinist
Protestants. During his last pastorate at Hamburg he was universally es-
teemed as a popular and influential preacher, a pillar in the Lutheran
Church. While his prose writings were apt to be violent and bitter, his hymns
are concerned less with outer conflict and more with inner spiritual states.
Though he published four of these, only one finds a place in our study.

*Wie schön leuchtet der Morgenstern*    [1597]
Altered by J. A. Schlegel, 1768

* From *Studies in Familiar Hymns*, First Series, pp. 159–60, copyright, 1903. Used
by permission.

*O morning star, how fair and bright*     Tr Catherine Winkworth, 1863
*How brightly beams the morning star*     Tr William Mercer, 1859

The German of this hymn was altered seventy years after being written, and the two English translations of it have been altered almost beyond recognition. References below are to the latest version, found in the Episcopal *Hymnal*.

We have record of how the hymn came to be written. While Nicolai was pastor in the town of Unna, a terrible pestilence struck terror into all hearts and raged for seven months until more than 1300 had died. The parsonage overlooked the churchyard where the interments took place, sometimes thirty a day. It was inevitable that the poet's thoughts should dwell upon the hope of eternal life, on how that life is made sure through Christ, and how the assurance of it brings comfort in times of distress and tragedy. One morning as he thought of these things, "there welled forth from the inmost depths of his heart this precious hymn of the Saviour's love and of the joys of heaven. He was so entirely absorbed in this holy exaltation that he forgot all around him, even his midday meal, until the hymn was completed."

Behind the words and ideas of the hymn lie many scriptural reminiscences:

*Stanza 1.* Rev 22:16; 2 Peter 1:19; Jude 21; Job 38:7; Is 11:1; Lk 19:10; Jn 1:34; Is 40:9; Mt 11:29; Ps 69:18; James 4:8; Is 7:14. (Cf. "O come, O come, Emmanuel," Latin, 12th cent.)
*Stanza 2.* Heb 1:2; Col 1:15–16, 22.
*Stanza 3.* This conviction that Jesus the Saviour was high above all powers in heaven and on earth; that He would come to strengthen His loved ones in the hour of trial and redeem in the hour of death, had a comforting and uplifting influence in the presence of imminent dissolution (See Is 61:2–3).

No wonder the hymn became a favorite in the Germany of his day, "was reckoned indispensable at weddings [!] and was often sung around deathbeds." In our day we have to read new meanings into old words, but memories of the scriptural imagery give a halo to the truths that still endure.

### BOHEMIAN–GERMAN HYMNS

Meantime a small rill of foreign song had trickled into Germany, to be absorbed in the native stream. It came from Bohemia-Moravia, an extensive and fruitful area drained by the upper Elbe River and its tributaries.

Its center and capital was Prague, now the capital of Czechoslovakia. Around its circumference, clockwise from the north, lie Silesia (capital, Breslau), Hungary (capital, Budapest), Austria (capital, Vienna), Bavaria (present capital, Munich), and finally various small German states, chief

*Top,* Trial of John Hus of Bohemia at Constance, 1413, identical in spirit and method with that inflicted upon Luther. From a painting by Brozik. *Left,* John Hus preaching. From a painting by Liebscher.

among them Saxony, containing the important cities of Erfurt, Halle, Wittenberg, Leipzig and Dresden. Into this central region came the Slavic tribes of the Czechs in the late seventh to the late eighth centuries, superseding the Germanic peoples who had occupied it and would again filter in. The Czechs to the northwest grew into the strong medieval kingdom of Bohemia, the Czechs to the southeast grew into a semi-independent kingdom, the "Margravate" of Moravia. There was always a good deal of interpenetration between these. Both have been also the unfortunate football of politics and religion—a recent example, the partitioning and regrouping which followed World Wars I and II, and the contemporary seizure by communist Russia.

The Bohemians and Moravians were Christianized by missionaries from the Eastern Orthodox Church, but defeat in war brought them under the Church of Rome. Not taking kindly to the change they were quite ready to listen to leaders who scored the abuses of the Church. Such a leader arose in the person of John Hus (1369–1415). He had risen from the peasant class to become a professor and finally Rector of the University of Prague, and a strong preacher. Through Bohemian students returning from Oxford University he became acquainted with the writings of John Wyclif of England (1320–1384), which set his mind in the direction of reform in doctrine and morals. His archbishop began an investigation, found Hus guilty of heresy, burned two hundred volumes of Wyclif's books and excommunicated Hus. There was a long fight in which the peasants and many intellectuals lined up strongly behind their leader. Tricked at last into defending his beliefs at a Church Council in Constance, he was jailed, denied a fair trial, condemned, burned at the stake July 6, 1415, and his ashes thrown into the Rhine. So perished a great Bohemian who by courage and clear thinking handed the torch of reformation from the English Wyclif to the German Luther.

But Hus continued to live in his followers. They kept up their struggle not only against the rapacity and immorality of the clergy, but against their landlords and nobles who oppressed them economically and politically. Rebellion and war followed, the opposition drawn largely from neighboring countries egged on by the Church. The Hussites won and Rome was compelled to allow the moderate aristocratic wing to organize as the national Church of Bohemia (1433), which a century later was partly absorbed into the German Lutheran Church and partly slipped back into the Roman. But the more radical wing of the Hussites, still bent upon democratic reform, opposed the union of Church and State, demanded a complete break with Rome and a return to the simple teachings of Christ in the Sermon on the Mount. They founded a number of independent societies which shortly merged into a "Brotherhood" (c. 1453)—in Latin, *Unitas Fratrum,* the name by which they were oftenest called. We call them "Bohemian Brethren." They were a *singing* brotherhood. Hus himself was a singer. He had been a choirboy and as a man had not only translated Latin hymns into Bohemian but had written hymns of his own. It was natural, therefore, that contrary to the Roman Church's practice and law he should encourage congregational singing by his Brethren.

In 1501 they issued at Prague the first Protestant hymnbook in the world, its language Bohemian. When Luther arose in Germany (1517) the Brethren discovered a natural affinity with his teachings, and after the King of Bohemia began a bloody persecution, with confiscation of many estates on which the Brethren lived, a large block of them migrated *en masse* (1548) toward Germany, which they hoped would be a land of freedom. These fugitives took with them their precious hymnbook, either the Bohemian one or a German one compiled in 1531 by a certain Michael Weisse for the benefit of German-speaking families who had joined the Brethren. All the hymns were translated from the Bohemian and Latin by the editor, or composed by him.

A much more influential member of the Brotherhood and one who made a more lasting contribution to hymnody was

## PETER HERBERT (d. 1571)

HE WAS born in Moravia after the Brotherhood had fled thither from Bohemia. First a priest, then a member of the Select Council of the Brethren, he was sent on many important missions including one to John Calvin, the reform leader in Geneva. Herbert was one of the principal compilers of the Bohemian-German hymnal of 1566 which contained ninety of his own hymns, either originals or translations. One of the most beautiful of them has survived in our hymnals:

*Die Nacht ist kommen drin wir ruhen sollen*      [1556]
*Now God be with us, for the night is closing*
Tr Catherine Winkworth, 1863
*Now it is evening; time to rest from labor*
Tr Episcopal *Hymnal*, 1940

This hymn is so direct and simple, so free from theological dogmas and scriptural allusions, that it hardly needs interpreting. The chief thing to remember is that it was written under the shadow of oppression and persecution. To realize its full implications, imagine yourself to be the author, yourself a fugitive pursued by those who would not only imprison and kill your body but take away the faith which has been the mainstay of your life.

*Stanza 1.* The ancient fear of the night, which we saw emerging in Anatolius (Greek Hymns, above). But since God made the night as well as the day, it must be good. We will rest, trusting Him.
*Stanza 2.* Night is the time when our will is inoperative; evil spirits can enter our soul and work us harm. Send angels to ward them off and keep us sinless.
*Stanza 3.* As a further prophylactic, let our latest thoughts before sleeping and our earliest when awaking be of God and of our duty

to serve and praise Him. (Psychologically those two moments are most favorable for a "suggestion" to penetrate the subconscious and become operative.)

*Stanza 4.* The ravages of persecution are here suggested by such words as "sick and weeping," "prisoner," "griefs," "widows and orphans". The hunted need a friend.

*Stanza 5.* "Refuge" is a poignant word: the hunted have no place to go. Perhaps the poet recalls Psalm 46:1.

*Stanza 6.* The final petition is the immortal prayer of Jesus (Lk 11:2).

Not all the Bohemian Brethren migrated to Germany. Others stayed and grew steadily in number until within a hundred years this particular group formed half of the Protestants in Bohemia and more than half in Moravia. But alas! at the height of their success they were all but crushed out of existence by the Thirty Years' War. For the next hundred years a handful worshipped in secret in Moravia. Then in 1722 when a new persecution broke out, the German-speaking members fled in a body to Saxony and built a town called Herrnhut under the protection of Count Zinzendorf. Henceforth the group is known as Moravians, their spiritual ancestors having been Bohemian Brethren and, more remotely, Hussites. That portion of the story will be told later in this chapter.

## THE THIRTY YEARS' WAR (1618–1648)

Though this devastating war started as a quarrel over the throne of Bohemia it was primarily a religious war. The Protestant princes in Bohemia refused to elect Ferdinand of Austria to the throne and backed Frederick, Elector of the Palatinate; but Protestant princes in Germany refused to back Frederick, and so the latter found himself isolated between them and the Catholic Emperor who backed the Austrian. Soon the Emperor's forces began to invade and plunder—soldiers from Spain, from the Lowlands, Austria, Bavaria. In return the Protestant princes could not tolerate the tyranny of a Catholic Emperor, so they let loose their forces. Not being able to pay their troops, the latter lived by plunder; they literally ate up province after province—the Emperor's provinces if possible—even to Alsace and Lorraine in France, and Holland and Denmark in the north. The tide ebbed and flowed. Foreign interventions, Catholic and Protestant, prolonged the struggle and the suffering—England, Denmark, Sweden, Italy, France, were all dragged in. Under the iron heel of war, Germany, the chief battleground, was reduced to a state of misery that baffles description. Population dwindled from sixteen million to six, commerce and industry were destroyed, fields were wasted, all intellectual and moral life stagnated. The effects lasted for a century. When the struggle ended, Catholics and

Protestants found themselves relatively about where they stood at the beginning.

Out of this terrible epoch, however, were wrung some of the noblest hymns in the German language. Tragedy drove men to God. The first hymnist to survive from this period, however, shows only slight reaction to it.

## GEORG WEISSEL (1590–1635)

THIS Prussian scholar, school-teacher and pastor wrote about twenty hymns, most of which have to do with the festivals of the Christian year. Following is his hymn for Advent:

*Macht hoch die Thür, das Thor macht weit*     [Before 1635]
*Lift up your heads, ye mighty gates*     Tr Catherine Winkworth, 1855

> *Stanza 1.* The imagery is suggested by Ps 24 which supposedly celebrated the approach of the Ark of the Covenant to the gates of Jerusalem when David brought it from its twenty-year captivity.
> *Stanza 2.* The character of God described. A hint of the evil times is given in "distress," "woe."
> *Stanza 3.* The poet takes refuge from present misery in contemplating what his land would be if Christ were really ruler.
> *Stanza 4.* A prayer that this ideal condition may be realized, first in the poet's own heart, then in the larger realm of the Church and State, hinted in the words "our glorious goal."

## Rev. MARTIN RINKART (1586–1649)

AS A boy, Martin was chorister in the famous St. Thomas Church, Leipzig, where Bach was later musical director. A graduate of Leipzig University, he became a schoolmaster in the "gymnasium" (High School) of Eisleben and a "cantor" in the local church; then rose through Deacon and Pastor to Arch-deacon (bishop) in Eilenberg. His life in this last place was contemporaneous with the whole course of the Thirty Years' War. Since Eilenberg was a walled town it was a refuge for fugitives from far and near, became over-crowded and unsanitary, suffered from famine and disease. During the great pestilence of 1637, officials and clergy either died or ran away, leaving Rinkart alone to care for the dead. He read the burial service over 40 to 50 persons a day, in all about 4,480. At last the burials were in trenches, without service. The 8,000 persons who died included Rinkart's wife. Then came one sacking by the Austrians and two by the Swedes who levied 30,000 thalers on the town, finally reduced by Rinkart's prayers and labors to 2,000 thalers. His financial resources strained and his body worn out, he succumbed at the age of sixty-three.

With all this responsibility and tension, he was a musician and a prolific writer. Of his seven dramas of the Reformation period, two were acted. Of his sixty-six hymns, a few appeared in German hymnals, but one has found universal acceptance both in Germany and in English-speaking countries. It is

*Nun danket alle Gott*     [c. 1630]
*Now thank we all our God*     Tr Catherine Winkworth, 1858

Though frequently asserted, there is no evidence that this hymn was written to celebrate the Peace of Westphalia which ended the Thirty Years' War. The date forbids it. It was originally entitled, *"Tisch-Gebetlein,"* or a "short Grace before meals."

Rinkart received the inspiration for stanzas 1 and 2 from the Apocryphal Book of Ecclesiasticus (50:22–24) called also "The Wisdom of Jesus the son of Sirach." The last stanza is Rinkart's paraphrase of the *Gloria Patri*. This was originally composed in Greek, partly c. 95 A.D. and the rest before the fourth century, translated into Latin, then, following the Reformation, into the vernaculars of all Protestant sects, and today is used every Sunday in Anglican, Episcopal, Lutheran and whatever churches follow a liturgy.

These origins show that the impulse to thank and praise whatever gods there be, whether the one God of the Jews or the Triune God of the Apostolic Church tradition, is instinctive and universal. Rinkart merely gave voice to these ancient feelings in a form consonant with his time. And since meal-time seems to be most fitting for the remembrance of God's bounty and His love, he focussed them into this simple prayer which, with perhaps some mental reservations, may be said with sincerity by all religious people: God's greatness, His guidance, His bounty; the yearning for peace, for freedom from suffering, for assurance of salvation.

While the wretchedness of the Thirty Years' War is hinted in stanza 2, the whole tone is so triumphant that the hymn has become a second *Te Deum*. It is often sung on occasions of national rejoicing in Germany, England and America: as, for example, the completion of Cologne Cathedral (1880), the Diamond Jubilee of Queen Victoria (1897) and the ending of the Boer War (1902).

## *MATTHÄUS APELLES VON LÖWENSTERN (1594–1648)*

THOUGH of humble origin, Löwenstern became a notable musician, a high official in the State, and under Emperor Ferdinand III was made a member of the nobility. His thirty hymns, for which he composed melodies, are of uneven merit.

*Christe, du Beistand deiner Kreutzgemeine*     [1644]
*Lord of our life, and God of our salvation*     Tr Philip Pusey, 1834

If the general tone of Pusey's paraphrase at all represents the original German, we have here presented vividly and with strong feeling the tragedy of the Thirty Years' War. Even a nobleman like von Löwenstern could not escape the terror and the devastation, the fear that the Church he loved and served would be snuffed out of existence and the ancient tyrannies would return. This prayer is the groan of one in desperate straits.

No doubt that Philip Pusey, brother of the more famous Dr. Edward B. Pusey of Oxford Movement fame, sensed this desperation and saw the analogy to his own time, for the year 1834 was one to strike the hearts of Anglican churchmen with foreboding. (Re-read the first part of Chap. VIII—the Oxford Movement). Hence the appropriateness of the "Church's supplication" (st. 1). The "hungry billows," the "banners unfurling," the "darts envenomed" (st. 2) were the mobs of peasants wrecking the new farm-machinery, burning the palace of the Bishop of Bristol, insulting the Primate of All England on the streets of London; they were the Whig Party warning the bishops to "set their house in order," and cashiering half the bishops of the Established Church in Ireland; they were the Wesleyans and Congregationalists rapidly making converts in the industrial towns of Manchester and Leeds, and clamoring for an extension of the franchise. They were the "deadly sin" of stanza 3, the rejection by the unholy Whigs and Dissenters of the doctrine of Apostolic Succession, of the inviolability of the One and Only Church, and in these ways "being guilty of a direct disavowal of the sovereignty of God." * The "brothers engaging" in busy war (st. 4) was the strife between High and Low Churchmen, and between both and the Romanists. And to climax all, the smug prayer that "they may be forgiven" implies that though we may not forgive, God in His infinite mercy may be able to do so!

We, of course, more than a hundred years afterwards, would not realize the situation that lay behind these pious words. We therefore may interpret the hymn in purely spiritual terms and pray this prayer for the defeat of all foes of morality and religion, and the ultimate establishment of God's kingdom over all the earth.


### Rev. JOHANN HEERMANN (1585–1647)

HAVING lost four of her children, Johann's mother vowed that if God would spare the life of this her only surviving child she would educate him for the ministry even if she had to beg the money. Johann lived, the vow was fulfilled, and the boy became a scholar and a pastor. But trouble with both eyes and throat limited his usefulness and finally stopped his preaching. He too was a victim of the War. His village of Köben was plundered four times by Catholic hordes, was devastated by fire and ravaged by pestilence. Several times he lost all his moveable property, twice he was in imminent personal danger from sword and bullet. But his great consolation was poetry. In his younger days he wrote in Latin, then he

* See J. W. C. Wand: *A History of the Modern Church,* Chap. xvii (1938).

turned to German as the one effective means of expressing his spiritual states—his faith, his trust in God, and the emotions engendered by these qualities in conflict with the fearful tragedies of life. His poems met a general need and at once took a deserved place in the hymnody of his Church.

> *Herzliebster Jesu, was hast du verbrochen*     [1630]
> *Ah, holy Jesu, how hast thou offended*     Tr Robert Bridges, 1899

This translation by the former Poet Laureate of England compresses into five stanzas Heermann's original fifteen; Heermann got his inspiration from the so-called *Meditations of St. Augustine,* a medieval Latin work. In general, the ideas follow the traditional interpretation of the Crucifixion, namely, that by His sufferings and death Jesus took upon Himself the punishment due the sins of the world. More specifically, as we have seen in our study of Latin hymns (Chap. IX), the penitent sinner personalizes the general fact: it was for *my* sins He suffered:

> Jesus, clad in purple raiment,
> For my evil making payment.
> > —Theoctistus of the Studium, c. 890

> Faint and weary thou hast sought me,
> On the cross of suffering bought me.
> > —Thomas of Celano, c. 1250

> Mine, mine was the transgression,
> But thine the deadly pain.
> > Anon: *Salve, caput cruentatum,* 14th cent.

There are other interpretations of the Crucifixion and the Atonement, but this is the one promulgated by the Church:

> Hence the Priest, whenever he offers up the holy sacrifice [the Mass] recites this prayer: "Receive, O holy Father, . . . this immaculate victim which I, thy unworthy servant, offer to thee . . . for my innumerable sins, offences and negligencies, for all here present . . . that it may avail me and them to life everlasting."
> Whenever, therefore, we assist at Mass . . . let us acknowledge that our sins were the cause of that agony and of the shedding of that precious blood.*

Robert Bridges, following Heermann, presents this personalized point of view and gives what we must confess is one of the most affecting Passion hymns in our hymnals.

* Cardinal Gibbons: *The Faith of our Fathers,* p. 318, P. J. Kenedy & Sons, New York.

### Rev. PAUL GERHARDT (1607–1676)

GERHARDT is the most beloved of all German hymnists. In our list of hymnbooks he out-ranks Luther four to one, a ratio no doubt due to the less belligerent and more subjective tone that developed as the Thirty Years' War died down.

Student and tutor, with hope and opportunity deferred by war and poverty, Gerhardt had no settled position till he was forty-five years old. Then he was offered a living in a small village, was ordained to the ministry, married the woman he had long loved and began to publish the hymns he had for many years been writing. The hymns brought him fame and a larger opportunity. In 1657 he was called as "diaconus" (assistant pastor) to the great cathedral church in Berlin. There for a few years he enjoyed fame as a preacher and honor as a man of deep piety and good works. But in 1664 he refused to assent to an edict of Elector Frederick Wilhelm I which forbade free discussion of the differences between the Lutheran and the Reformed Churches, was deposed from his office and interdicted from performing any of his clerical functions.

But long before this happened he had undergone an inner transformation; he no longer thought of God as a fighter and a stickler for dogma—as Luther's God was—and took refuge in God as a loving person. Technically, of course, he held to the doctrines wrought out by Luther on the anvil of the Reformation, but he subordinated them to the more humanizing sentiments that common people who are not theologians can cultivate and utilize to transform human nature. His hymns are a reflection of this inner spiritual wealth, many of them written "under circumstances which would have made most men cry rather than sing."

*Fröhlich soll mein Herze springen*      [1653]
*All my heart this night rejoices*      Tr Catherine Winkworth, 1858

Gerhardt's original fifteen stanzas were reduced to ten by Miss Winkworth and have been reduced to four in most of our hymnals.

This is more a carol than a hymn. The meter is joyful, quite unlike the slow plodding rhythms of Dr. Watts' "common meter." Just to read the words apart from the music sets one's heart to dancing.

Christmas night in Bethlehem is pictured: the angel choir over the shepherd's field, an imagined invitation from the Babe in the manger, the response which dramatizes the journey to Bethlehem and the act of worship under the light of the Star, finally our personal promise to love and to serve through all eternity.

*O Jesu Christ, mein schönstes Licht*      [1653]
*Jesus, thy boundless love to me*      Tr John Wesley, 1736

John Wesley first heard this hymn sung by Moravians while on his voyage to America. When he compiled his first hymnbook for the use of the Georgia colonists he included it with three other Gerhardts and one of Tersteegen. Altogether John translated thirty-two German hymns. His *Journal* for May 7, 1737, reads: "Translated six hymns from the German while on a journey to another plantation" (probably walking!).

In his personal experience in Georgia John needed the support of this hymn. He was a misfit: his perfectionist doctrines did not suit the miscellaneous morals of the men and women of the colony; there were squabbles and lawsuits, sickness and death among them, and finally he made his secret flight to England while under indictment. This hymn suggested the only refuge open to him, a mystic union between Jesus and his own soul. In like manner Gerhardt needed that union. Such words as "fear," "care, anguish, sorrow," "suffering," "weakness," "storms of life," reveal to those who know the facts how desperately his soul demanded the mutual love-relationship here expressed between himself and Jesus.

We who for the most part live secure and prosperous can at least get an emotional glow from the hymn. But if and when the tragic trials of life come—as they did to thousands of our boys in the war—then the sentiment will deepen into something vital, and we will memorize and appreciate this hymn.

*Befiehl du deine Wege* [1656]
*Give to the winds thy fears*    Tr John Wesley, 1739
*Commit thou all thy griefs*    Tr John Wesley, 1739
*Commit thou all that grieves thee*
Tr Farlander and Douglas, 1939

The original was written in twelve stanzas of eight lines. Wesley cut them down to eight stanzas and printed them in his Georgia hymnbook. Our hymnals have divided these eight into two parts: I. "Commit thou all thy griefs"; II. "Give to the winds thy fears."

This hymn was published in 1656 during Gerhardt's first pastorate in the little village of Mittenwald, before he emerged from obscurity. It seems to be the expression of his own hopes long deferred, as well as of the hangover of misery from the War. No doubt he repeated these lines to himself many a time in after years when, one by one four of his five children died, his influential position in Berlin was taken away, and his wife succumbed after a long illness, leaving him with a single surviving son. Like the preceding hymn, this one is an expression of faith in the over-ruling God "who earth and heaven commands."

There are few today who hold the philosophy underlying this hymn: "Trust in God and everything will come out all right." Science indicates that "clouds, winds, seas" are subject to natural law which does not change its action to suit special human situations. Similarly, our conception of the freedom of man's will, even to do wrong, cannot be squared with, "Leave to his *sovereign sway* to choose and to command." How then can we be assured, "So safe shalt thou go on"?

In spite of our boasted science we are still very ignorant about both nature and human nature. There is ample evidence that the spiritual attitudes recommended in these two hymns have worked miracles—not in breaking nature's laws but in releasing unsuspected inner powers which have saved men when otherwise they surely would have perished. If this assertion needs documentation, read *The Great Answer* by Margaret Lee Runbeck (Houghton Mifflin, 1944), a compilation of stories out of the War illustrating the influence of prayer and faith on people and circumstances.

So let us read these two hymns again and enlarge our faith in God.

*Nun ruhen alle Wälder*     [1648]·
*The duteous day now closeth*     Tr Robert Bridges, 1899
*Now rest beneath night's shadow*
Tr Frances Cox, 1864 and Catherine Winkworth, 1855
*Now woods and fields are sleeping*     Tr Rev. George R. Woodward
*O'er field and forest stealing*     Tr Alfred H. Reynar (1840–1921)
*The day hath now an ending*     Tr Dean D. F. R. Wilson, 1935

The fact that six different translators have supplied versions for eight different hymnals shows what inspirational power Gerhardt had and still has. The original is probably the best-loved hymn in Germany: "Experienced and conceived in a truly childlike popular spirit, it unites with a rare simplicity of expression, a loftiness of thought, a depth of Christian experience, a grace of poetry, so that . . . it must rank as one enduring masterpiece among hymns."—So wrote Baron Bunsen in 1830.

But the inspired translators have felt free to reduce the nine stanzas to three or even two, and to eliminate ideas that are repugnant to twentieth-century thinking. In Bridges' translation, Satan is not allowed to devour us nor are angels allowed to defend us; prayer for our loved ones (Winkworth) is also omitted. By comparing Bridges with Cox and Winkworth, the differences between two different interpretations of prayer are evident: the seventeenth-century idea of prayer as a kind of charm which can ward off and protect, and the twentieth-century idea of prayer as a communion, as a merging, in which the mystic beauty of nature acts as a catalyst. Everyone will react to the poetry of Bridges' paraphrase. It might be well for parents to teach their maturing children this prayer instead of "Now I lay me."

We now enter a new period in German hymnody. The miseries of the Thirty Years' War are slowly being alleviated, the fighting of the theologians over dogmas and rituals is moderating, and hymnody responds with a more joyful note.

## FRIEDRICH RUDOLPH LUDWIG, FREIHERR VON CANITZ
### (1654-1699)

VON CANITZ was one of those fortunate persons to whom everything good came without spoiling him. Student at two universities, a traveller for further education, "gentleman of the bedchamber" to Elector Frederick William of Prussia, a chief magistrate, ambassador, privy counsellor, and finally made Baron by the Emperor—what more could a man desire! But withal he kept his life clean and his soul open to beauty and to spiritual communion with Christ. This deeply religious attitude found expression in twenty-four poems, of which only two have lived as hymns in the German Church and only one has been translated into English for our hymnals.

*Seele du musst munter werden*     Published 1700
*Come, my soul thou must be waking*     Tr Henry J. Buckoll, 1838

One is tempted to say that this is the finest rule of life ever put into a hymn: it is joyful, courageous, stimulating, challenging; a call to action, to self-control, to obedience. There is an absence of dogma; the presence of genuine piety as the inspiration to living.

> *Stanza 1.* The joy of waking to a new sunrise, which is a call to worship.
> *Stanza 2.* Offer "the incense of thy powers": that is, dedicate to the service of God your whole endowment of gifts. Let activity be your thank-offering for protection through the night.
> *Stanza 3.* A manly prayer for prosperity in right action, but for thwarting in wrong action. Who before ever prayed to be thwarted!
> *Stanza 4.* Prayer for a peaceful death and a joyous awakening.
> *Stanza 5.* A self-warning that he, who has received everything in life one could ask, must not misuse God's gifts but must be guided always by the inner Voice. Thus this morning's splendor will be extended into eternity.

### PIETISM

In the latter third of the seventeenth century there arose a movement within the Lutheran Church which was destined to have a great influence not only upon religion in general but upon hymnody in particular. Philip Spener (1635-1705) was its founder. It is called Pietism—originally a term of ridicule. The name came from the *collegia pietatis,* or cottage prayer-meetings which Spener began to hold in 1670 while he was pastor in Frankfurt-on-the-Main. Spener sensed the fact that Lutheranism as a spiritual force was slipping. With its establishment as a State Church in most of the northern Germanic principalities (there was as yet no "Germany"), the convictions that once had driven men to battle for their faith had hardened into a smug confidence that creeds and sacraments were all that was necessary for salvation, and that it was one of the State's functions to collect the taxes and pay for the unkeep of religious establishments and services. That waning enthusiasm was reflected in congregational singing. Whereas in Luther's day great congregations were inspired to sing with all their might the grand chorales in which their faith was expressed, in Spener's day formality and perfunctoriness had crept into the services, choirs began to take the place of popular singing, the organ expanded its function until it dominated the service, not only embroidering the chorales with jigsaw patterns of accompaniment and separating the stanzas with long-drawn-out frilly interludes, but literally covering up the rags of a poverty-stricken Christianity with a gorgeous cloak of thunder.* This down-curve had not yet reached its nadir, but it was under way. Spener recognized the danger and started a grass-roots reformation. He brought little groups of his people together in his home, or in other homes, talked with them about the inner personal nature of religion, encouraged them to talk and especially encouraged them to sing! There were hymns enough—from Luther to Gerhardt; they had a message for the soul: why not sing them!

Through his official position, his contacts in person and correspondence with men influential throughout Germany, by acting as father-confessor to hundreds of poor and middle-class men as well as those in high society, he stirred the whole Church to a sense of its spiritual poverty and to a resolve to deepen its spiritual life. Among its immediate fruits was the conversion of August Francke (1663–1727). He became the organizer and chief propagator of this movement. Among other things he began a charitable work among the orphans of the city of Halle, birthplace of the musician Handel. This enterprise grew into the great Francke Institution that has cared for and educated thousands of children. Its huge building still dominates the town. Francke and Spener then began to mold the University of Halle, just founded by Elector Frederick III (1694) and made it the leading center of Protestant theology and of Pietism, until, within Francke's own lifetime, it had graduated some 6000 preachers who spread religious fervor all over northern Germany.

Both Spener and Francke wrote hymns, but they were less poetry than metrical prose. Their movement, however, could not fail to produce real poets. The earliest was

### JOACHIM NEANDER (1650–1680)

NEANDER'S youth was spent as a student in Bremen. Student life in those days was riotous and immoral, and Neander participated in it with a

* See Rutland Boughton: *Bach, The Master,* 1930, Chap. III.

will. However, when a famous Pietist preacher named Under-Eyke came to
Bremen, Neander with a couple of friends went to hear him for the fun of it,
and the "fools who came to scoff remained to pray." Later, becoming tutor
to some sons of wealthy merchants, he went with them to the University of
Heidelberg, and in neighboring Frankfort became personally acquainted
with Spener, who confirmed him in the new spiritual emphasis. Then as
director of the Latin School at Düsseldorf, which was wholly controlled by
the "Reformed" or Calvinistic branch of Lutheranism, he ran into violent
opposition to his pietistic practices and was removed from his position. His
health gave way and death soon followed though he was only thirty.

Neander was one of the finest German hymnists and a genuine musician.
His hymns were published only after his death (1680), nineteen of them set
to his own chorale tunes. His love of nature was deep. No doubt his
familiarity with the lovely Heidelberg region, the Rhine, the hills and valleys
and streams of the Neanderthal region around Düsseldorf turned his
thoughts toward beauty as a revelation of God (See *"Himmel, Erde, Luft
und Meer"*—"Heaven and earth, and sea and air," L, N, P). The three other
hymns that are found in our hymnals dwell on the personal relationship of
the soul to God. Praise is the dominant note, as in

### *Lobe den Herren, den mächtigen König*     [Published 1680]
#### *Praise to the Lord, the Almighty, the King of Creation*
#### Tr Catherine Winkworth, 1863

The fact that all ten of our hymnals publish this hymn confirms the
judgement of the Julian *Dictionary:* "A magnificent hymn of praise to God,
perhaps the finest production of its author, and of the first rank in its class."
Praise is the opening word of each stanza.

The hymn is said to be based upon Pss 103 and 150, but the phraseology and imagery of many Psalms are here involved. The thought is simple
and straightforward:

*Stanza 1.* The Lord is here addressed as Creator, worthy of all
praise.
*Stanza 2.* The Lord as Sovereign, whose rule is founded on the
common good.
*Stanza 3.* The Lord as defender and befriender.
*Stanza 4.* The Lord as refuge in time of storm.
*Stanza 5.* The Lord as protector in time of persecution.
*Stanza 6.* A concluding summons to praise.

### ANONYMOUS     (seventeenth century)

#### *Schönster Herr Jesu*     [c. 1677]
#### *Fairest Lord Jesus*     Translator unknown, c. 1850

A good deal of mythology has grown up around this hymn. No one knows who translated it into English; one stanza did not appear in German until 1842, while other stanzas of that version differ markedly from the original text, which appeared first in print in 1677. So all the nonsense about its having been sung by boys and girls on the "Children's Crusade," or by any other Crusaders, or by German pilgrims on their way to the Holy City, is pure imagination. The most authentic note about it relates that it was "taken down from oral recitation in the district of Glaz" (Julian).

Now Glaz is a town in Silesia just over the border a hundred miles east by north from Prague, the home of John Hus. When the Hussites were driven out of Bohemia in the bloody anti-Reformation purge of 1620, one band went east into Silesia and there in country villages lived the life of obscure peasants—"weavers and cobblers," maintaining in secret their Protestant faith and holding to the tradition of hymn-singing. If we must have a "mythology," why not say that this lovely hymn which unites the fairest object in nature and the fairest Person in the history of religion is a true folk-song out of the soil of Silesia? It is a product of the peasant mind, fashioned for several generations in the mold of Hussite thought which had rejected the theology and ritual of the Holy Catholic Church, and was forced to live in obscurity next the soil. If any learned among them held views about the Incarnation, Eucharist, Atonement, these views did not percolate down to the peasants, except only that they saw in Jesus a son of both God and man (stanza 1) who, while ruling all nature, was fairer than all.

The hymn is a bouquet of lovely things taken from the Nature these people knew: meadows and woodlands in their lush spring green; sunshine, moonlight, the stars. And just as these objects steal into the heart, nestle there and keep us warm, so the Saviour, unadorned by the pontifical robes of the theologians, steals into our heart and makes His home there, Himself the crowning glory of life. This simplicity of thought about Jesus, like that of a little child, coupled with a child's unreasoning reaction to the beauty of the world, is what makes this hymn as dear to children as it does to grownups.

While the hymn has no apparent connection with Pietism, its date places it right next to Neander who held a similar point of view about nature and Jesus.

### Rev. BENJAMIN SCHMOLK (1672–1737)

ALTHOUGH Schmolk cannot be reckoned as a Pietist, he lived while Pietism was waxing and his attitudes were influenced by it. His Lutheranism was warmed by it. In his preaching he placed the emphasis not on doctrine but on living. It was fortunate this was so, for he held a difficult pastorate in Silesia for thirty-five years where he met constant opposition. Because of the Counter-Reformation effected within the Catholic Church to counteract the Protestant movement, Catholicism made some gains in Lutheran countries, noticeably in Silesia (the section between modern Czechoslovakia and Poland). In the principality where Schmolk was pastor, all the Lutheran Churches were suppressed but one. That one was tolerated outside the walls of the chief city, its place of worship a small timber and clay structure without tower or bells, where the population of thirty-six villages must worship if at all. Its three pastors of whom Schmolk was chief could not even serve Communion to a sick parishioner without permission of the Catholic priest. Many such restrictions so hampered them that the work became exhausting. As a consequence Schmolk suffered several paralytic strokes that laid him aside some years before he died, bedridden and blind.

This brief recital will help us understand the hymns of his that have survived in our books, only seven of the 900 he wrote, especially the one noted below.

> *Mein Jesu, wie du wilst*    [1709]
> *My Jesus, as thou wilt*    Tr Jane Borthwick, 1853

One of the hardest attitudes to maintain in time of adversity is submission to what seems to be God's will. This attitude of resignation is beautifully expressed in this hymn. We cannot suppose that the unsufferable conditions under which Schmolk lived and worked in Silesia were "God's will"; in fact, if God has as strong a sense of justice as most men have, He must have utterly condemned the treatment meted out by one branch of His Church to another branch. What under these circumstances should Schmolk, or any other man, do? Should he rail at his oppressor, try by every subterfuge to outwit and thwart him? That would have only brought down more active persecution, probably the complete extinction of the Protestant congregations in Silesia. Schmolk here says that it is better to submit and to accept as God's will the Law of Love—the Law of Christ, who Himself was a Man of Sorrows and who Himself prayed, "Thy will, not mine, be done." Only in that way will the "star of hope" not grow dim and disappear. So only can one entrust to God "each changing future scene" and "travel calmly, calmly on."

### PIETIST-MORAVIAN HYMNODY

In the year 1722 two important streams of hymnody met and coalesced. The first and younger stream was that of the Pietists who began their work of spiritualizing the Lutheran State Church about 1670 and who made notable contributions to the corpus of German hymns, as we have just seen. The other stream came from far-distant springs, both in time and place. It was the Hussite-Bohemian, dating from the martyrdom of Hus in 1415, called also that of the *Unitas Fratrum;* once strong and vocal but now through persecution almost dried up, it was in fact driven underground in Moravia but miraculously preserved in the hearts of a hunted few whom one of their bishops called "the hidden seed." Then in 1722 a new persecution made life so unendurable that this tiny underground brotherhood now calling themselves Moravian Brethren fled to Saxony and took refuge on the estate of a nobleman who had the reputation of being hospitable to oppressed peoples. They brought with them their ancient Bohemian-Moravian-German hymnbook, at which we have already taken a glance, and in their new home proceeded to use it with renewed fervor. This nobleman who henceforth became the protector, inspirer, organizer and poet of this group of Moravian Brethren was

## NICOLAUS LUDWIG, COUNT VON ZINZENDORF (1700–1760)

HIS father was a Saxon Minister of State, his god-father was Philipp Spener, founder of Pietism, his grandmother brought him up and saw that his education in school and university at Halle was exclusively Pietistic. Precociously religious and evangelistic, he set his heart on becoming a clergyman, but considering the station to which he was born, his family insisted on a public career. Accordingly he was bred to the law at the University of Wittenberg. After leaving the university at the age of nineteen he travelled extensively, his interest centering largely in observing all types of religion. He came to the conclusion that the one thing held in common by all sects regardless of differences in theology and government was personal religion, or, as he called it, "Christianity of the heart." Returning home at the youthful age of twenty-one he became Counsellor of State at the court of Saxony. Even in the midst of state affairs he managed to hold prayer-meetings at his house, as was the custom of Pietists, and to compose hymns for use on these occasions. Hymn-writing became with him almost a passion: before he died he had written some 2000. He had already published five volumes of them by 1735, all in the Pietist strain.

When he was twenty-two a new influence came into his life—the band of Moravian Brethren mentioned above. Zinzendorf, becoming interested in their plight, offered to let them remain on his large estate of Bertelsdorf and build a village on it which they named "Herrnhut"—the "Lord's shelter." Additional refugees came for ten years or more, so that by 1732 the Brethren at Herrnhut numbered 600.

This gave Zinzendorf the opportunity he had long sought to develop a "true Church," quite divorced from State Lutheranism, devoted to the cultivation of personal religion and to missionary activity. The first few years were spent in organizing, printing tracts, hymnbooks, catechisms and the like. Then in 1732, when considerable opposition to their Church was developing among Lutherans, the first missionaries started out—two men went to St. Thomas in the West Indies, with $6 in their pockets, determined if necessary to sell themselves as slaves. Another missionary colony arrived in Georgia in 1735, but shortly moved to Pennsylvania and joined another band from Herrnhut which had arrived on Christmas Day, 1741. The day accounts for the name of their settlement, Bethlehem. The aim was to do missionary work among the Indians and Negroes. Zinzendorf himself, exiled from Saxony for nine years because of his religious zeal, accompanied this group to Bethlehem and for a couple of years helped organize work in what we now call our Middle States. The Moravians were the first Protestant sect to maintain that the evangelization of the heathen was a duty of the Church —not an incident in the colonial policy of the State. The zeal and heroism of these missionaries was extraordinary. They selected the hardest fields possible and held themselves in readiness to go instantly to the ends of the earth. Men went to Labrador, Greenland, Alaska, Nicaragua, Cape Colony, Land of the Kaffirs, India—anywhere no one else dared to go. These missions still exist.

Zinzendorf was allowed to return to Saxony in 1747 and from his old home was able to direct the multifarious activities of his Moravians till his death.

Zinzendorf's influence on hymnody has been significant. Not only did he write hymns all his life—his first one when he was sixteen and the last at Herrnhut the year of his death—but he edited and published Moravian hymnbooks constantly. These hymnbooks were taken all over the world, were translated into such languages as Kaffre, Greenlander, North American Indian, Labrador Eskimo and West Indian Negro, and proved to be the most potent weapon in the arsenal of the missionary. But of equal importance was his Moravian hymnbook of the congregation at Herrnhut, 1735, which fell into the hands of John Wesley on his memorable voyage to Georgia, and inspired John to learn German in order that he might translate; it was the singing of the Moravians on that voyage through storm and calm which taught him the tremendous value of congregational singing both as teacher and inspirer, and so led him to compile his own first hymnbook in Georgia (See Chap. V, The Wesleys). It was a Moravian colony in London which brought about the conversion of the Wesley brothers, inspired Charles to write his first hymn and to begin that torrent of verse which swept Methodism along to victory. It was the Moravian habit of congregational singing that showed the great organizer John how essential was the collecting, editing, publishing and using of hymns as the means *par excellence* for creating and preserving the fervor which gave Methodism its revolutionary drive. And in turn, Methodist hymnody became a constant though long-resisted influence which finally helped change the Anglican Church from its devotion to the Psalter to its enthusiasm for the historic hymns and to new hymns as an inspiration to Christian living.

Two of Zinzendorf's hymns became the parent of two English translations which have proved to be very useful. The first is

*Seelenbraütigam, O du Gottes Lamm*    [1721]
*O thou to whose all-searching sight*    Tr John Wesley, 1738

*Top,* The Moravian Settlement at Herrnhut, Saxony. *Left,* Count von Zinzendorf aged 20 years.

Written before the Moravians had arrived at Herrnhut, this hymn was prophetic of things to come. At the time, Zinzendorf was only twenty-one and a Counsellor of State in the kingdom of Saxony. But his heart was not there. He had visions of something greater, something more in accord with his deeper yearnings to make religion a vital force in his native land and in the world. Out of these longings and unrealized resolves came this hymn of eleven stanzas. John Wesley found it in Zinzendorf's Moravian Hymnbook and included his six-stanza translation in his own little hymnbook in 1738.

Neither Wesley nor Zinzendorf had yet found his true vocation. What gave Zinzendorf courage, however, was the resolve (stanza 4) that he would walk in the footsteps of his Saviour, "dauntless, untired." This resolve Zinzendorf kept to the letter although his footsteps took him to far-distant lands and into the midst of great problems.

The strong appeal of this hymn and of the following one lies in the fact that the only attitude any Christian can take in this world of trials and tragedies is faith: "O let thy hand support me still."

It so happened that in 1778 a German hymnist saw in this hymn of Zinzendorf and in one other of his beginning "Glanz der Ewigkeit" the possibility of a more vigorous and challenging hymn. He, therefore, took stanzas from both and made a new German version beginning

### *Jesu, geh' voran*     [1721] (1778)

*Jesus, still lead on*     Tr Jane Borthwick, 1846, 1854
*Jesus, lead the way*     Tr Arthur W. Farlander, 1939

The prophetic nature of Zinzendorf's early hymn of 1721 is here most clearly seen, for by 1732 he had brought the education of his Moravians so far along the path that they were ready for their first missionary venture, that to the West Indies. Then in quick succession other campaigns were planned and executed along a far-flung battle line. This hymn in Miss Borthwick's vigorous English is a perfect campaign song. It is a challenge to the world to do its worst!

EIGHTEENTH AND NINETEENTH CENTURY HYMNS

### *GERHARD TERSTEEGEN* (1697–1769)

AN early checkered career in business, latterly the weaving of silk ribbons, finally brought young Tersteegen to a state of spiritual depression that lasted for five years. Finally, while on a trip to a nearby town, he had such an overwhelming "sense of the atoning mercy of Jesus that his heart was set entirely at rest." He thereupon wrote out a solemn covenant with God which he signed with his own blood, and withdrew from the Reformed Church. This branch of Lutheranism had seceded from the main stem (called henceforth "Evangelicals"), because they rejected some tenets of Luther's theology in favor of some of John Calvin's. Dominant in Calvinism was the doctrine of Predestination which holds that a person's salvation is not dependent upon his own will but on whether he had been "predestined" to salvation by Almighty God (Rom 8:29–30; Eph 1:11). The struggle undergone by conscientious souls who wanted to be saved, the agonies involved in trying to find out whether they were among the "elect," were crushing; they produced not only the melancholia such as young Tersteegen suffered, but sometimes lunacy and suicide.

After solving this problem in favor of his Election, Tersteegen became an independent religious teacher, supported by small contributions from friends and admirers. His main occupation was the translation of the works of medieval mystics, and the writings of books and hymns that would strengthen the faith of "awakened souls." He also did evangelistic work in the Ruhr region until a law against private religious gatherings was strictly enforced (1730–1750); then he devoted himself to helping the poor, until his death.

His collected hymns were published at various times between 1729 and 1768. They total 568. Only three of them have survived in our hymnals: one is generally accepted.

*Gott ist gegenwärtig! lasset uns anbeten*　　[1729]
*Lo, God is here; let us adore*
Tr John Wesley, 1798 (from Zinzendorf's hymnal)
*God himself is present: let us now adore him*
Tr F. W. Foster and J. Miller, 1789, Alt. W. Mercer, 1854
Tr Ditto, Alt. 1932
*God himself is with us: let us all adore him*
Hymnal Version; stanza 2 by Henry Sloane Coffin, 1940

This is the most widely used of all Tersteegen's hymns. It suggests a mystical approach to worship that appealed to a man like John Wesley. His translation and that of Miller and Foster show how similar temperaments can find widely different expression for the same original emotion.

*Stanza 1.* Entering the House of Prayer we remember the words of Jacob at Bethel (Gen 28:16–17); and the awe thus induced mingles with love, worship, and a prayer to serve (Wesley translation).

*Stanza 2.* When our poor hymns arise they seem indeed mean and halting compared with those perpetually chanted in heaven; but God will accept our imperfect praises.

*Stanza 3.* How our songs fill this earthly temple like the odors from the Tabernacle's altar of incense! Our prayers and resolves also ascend to the throne; when, lo, a translation takes place:

And he gathers the prayers as he stands,
And they change into flowers in his hands,
Into garlands of purple and red;
And beneath the great arch of the portal,
Through the streets of the City Immortal,
Is wafted the fragrance they shed.*

* H. W. Longfellow: *"Sandalphon"* in *Complete Poetical Works*, Houghton, Mifflin, Boston, 1893.

## MATTHIAS CLAUDIUS (1740–1815)

THOUGH son of a Lutheran pastor, Claudius was one of the few non-clerical writers of hymns. He was first a newspaper man and a literary editor at Hamburg; then in 1776 he was appointed a Commissioner of Agriculture and Manufactures in the Principality of Hesse-Darmstadt (north of Frankfort). There he became acquainted with Goethe and other free-thinking philosophers, and lost for a time the religious outlook of his youth. But after a severe illness he realized how empty of real values was the life he was living. He therefore resigned his lucrative position, went back to the little town near Hamburg where he had been literary editor, and resumed his old task with a new and actively religious spirit. After eleven years he was appointed auditor of a bank in the Danish city of Altona, now part of Hamburg. Twenty-five years later he was forced to leave home because of the Napoleonic wars and returned only in time to die.

This life is hardly a conventional background for hymn-writing; in fact Claudius wrote no hymns for Church use. But his poetry was filled with the spirit of religion to the extent that three of his poems have become hymns in Germany; only one in our American anthology:

*Wir pflügen und wir streuen*      [1782]
*We plough the fields and scatter*      Tr Jane Campbell, 1861

This universally favorite hymn was written as part of a descriptive poem called *Paul Eardmann's Festival.* In it he pictures a group of neighbors coming to a north German farmhouse for a get-together, in the course of which they sang this "Peasant's song," each of the seventeen stanzas a solo followed by a chorus. Some seventeen years after the sketch was published, a selection of stanzas roughly corresponding to our hymn appeared in a school song-book in Hanover; thence it sprang into fame through most of the school hymnbooks of Germany. It is found in all ten of our hymnals.

This is certainly an appropriate hymn for a Commissioner of Agriculture to write, for the land and its proper use have been his particular job. It did not occur to him to write about agriculture from a doctrinal or ecclesiastical viewpoint; only from the angle of a simple childish appreciation of the goodness of God. He may perhaps even have smiled to himself at the fancy that God too is a Commissioner of Agriculture on a grand scale; God provides not only the land but the other essentials—sunshine, air, rain and snow, which make the land fruitful. God goes even farther and throws in for good measure the wayside flowers and the birds, and even the stars to keep watch over the sleeping earth. All this to keep His children well-fed and happy. Surely thanks are a small gift to "render unto the Lord for all his benefits toward us." But the gifts and the thanks tie God and man together in one big happy project. Neither alone could attain to fullness of life and joy without the other.

## ANONYMOUS

*Beim frühen Morgenlicht*      [Between 1800 and 1828]
*When morning gilds the skies*      Tr Edward Caswall, 1853
Ditto Tr Robert Bridges, 1899

The writer of this fourteen-stanza hymn must have been a nature-lover. Well he might have been if the conjecture is true that he lived in Franconia. This part of Germany runs along the valleys and hills which follow the river Main and its tributaries flowing toward their junction with the Rhine at Mainz. It is a country of small mountain ranges and forests full of fairies (Jacob Grimm of the *Fairy Tales* was born here); full of little-to-medium towns with castles, ancient Romanesque churches and monasteries scattered around. Luther stayed once for three months at Coburg Castle, 500 feet above the town, and there translated the Prophets and the Psalms into German. Surely this is a region to arouse all the poetry in one's nature, and, if anyone is religiously inclined, to inspire hymns like this.

### *SIEGFRIED AUGUSTUS MAHLMANN (1771–1826)* German

*Gott segne Sachsenland!*      [1815]
*God bless our native land!*      Translators noted below

THIS hymn well illustrates the fact that wherever they live people normally love their country. The original German hymn begins, "God bless Saxony!" and in stanza 2 hails Friedrich Augustus, good King and father who raised his afflicted country "from Night to the Light." Today we may have our doubts about the patriotism of Friedrich, for he was off and on an ally of Napoleon, was made by Napoleon a Grand Duke of Warsaw, entertained Napoleon several times at his palace in Dresden, even on his disastrous retreat from Russia (1812), and Friedrich's army, fighting at Napoleon's side, was defeated at Leipzig by the Prussian and British allies. In 1814 he was allowed to resume his crown over a greatly diminished Saxony. The rest of his life was spent in repairing the damage caused by the wars and developing the resources and institutions of his little kingdom. His people stood by him through storm and calm, as this patriotic hymn testifies. This was first sung in the presence of the King, November 13, 1815.

Of course, all of the original hymn could not be translated into American—or any other national tongue. But the spirit of the original is certainly translatable into the language of any country where freedom, plenty, education and opportunity are the watchwords. Seeing this, several English-speaking writers have combined to give us the present version:

*Stanza 1.* Translated by Rev. Charles T. Brooks, 1813–83, native of Salem, Mass., student at Harvard College and Divinity School. Two stanzas were written while he was a student at the latter institution, 1832–35; but only the first five lines of stanza 1 have survived.

The last two lines were translated by Rev. John Sullivan Dwight, 1813–93, son of Pres. Timothy Dwight of Yale, native of Boston, graduate of Harvard College and Divinity School. His work comprises two lines of stanza 1 and all of stanza 2.

*Stanza 3.* Anonymous: first published in the Unitarian *Hymns of the Spirit*, Boston, 1864. Found in only two of our hymnals.

*Stanza 4.* Written by William E. Hickson (1803–70), an English boot manufacturer who in 1835 felt the need of a new national anthem to take the place of "God save our gracious King." England certainly had no reason to be proud of William IV; and the ferment over politics, the factory act, abolition of slavery, the poor laws, the revolutions in France and Belgium, wars of aggression by Austria and Russia, emphasized the need for a new inter-citizen and inter-national principle.

To these stanzas should be added a fifth, found only in *Pilgrim Hymnal*, No. 346. No indication of authorship is there given, though either Dwight or Brooks is implied.

As the poet surveys the shimmering landscape from the top of, say, 3100-foot Grosse Wasserkuppe, he lets his eyes and his emotions wander as they list: from the sunrise (stanza 1) to the bell pealing from a distant twelfth century church (stanza 2) which not only arouses a holy mirth (stanza 3) like that of St. Francis in his Canticle of the Universe, but stirs his recollection of antiphonal choirs chanting the Scriptures in the cathedral (stanza 4). Then in imagination sunset comes: night creeps through the forest and casts over his spirit the half-forgotten medieval fears of the dark (stanza 5), but the charmed words of his song exorcize the evil ones (stanza 6) and the sadness they have inspired (stanza 7). When these powers of darkness flee, earthly bliss will be like that of heaven (stanza 8), for both men and angels will join in the glad anthem (stanza 9).

Again, from his watch-tower he recalls the wars of old that have rolled like tides through the Franconian valleys—Frisian heathen hordes who murdered good St. Boniface now sleeping under near-by Fulda Cathedral; crusaders on their way from Mainz to Constantinople and the Holy City; the rabble routs of the Thirty Years' War;—Oh, if the nations of mankind would learn from Christ the secret of peace! (stanza 10). Then all the deeps of ocean and sky, even the distant stars, will echo the refrain (stanzas 11–12). Under the spell of the beauties without and the glories within, I too will sing through all eternity (stanza 13)!

The sentiments and prayers expressed in this hymn are well-nigh universal, but the world's attainment of the ideals expressed in stanza 3 is almost negligible. While we fervently pray for the brotherhood in stanza 4, its realization seems farther away than in 1835. We have not yet added works to our faith. God cannot make men brothers without the constructive cooperation of all nations. The impasses staged by Russia in the United Nations and Big Four conferences over the outlawing of the atomic bomb, represent the nadir of international relations. We need this hymn more than ever before in history.

### Rev. JOSEF MOHR (1792–1848) Austrian

MOHR was assistant pastor at the Roman Catholic Church of St. Nicholas in the tiny village of Oberndorf a little north of Salzburg. He has no title to fame except this hymn.

Oberndorf consists of a single winding street lined with ancient quaint houses, their outsides gay with window-boxes of flowers, frescoes of religious scenes and the owner's name in scrolls. In that village it was the yearly custom for a band of strolling players from a nearby village to put on a crude show illustrating the Christmas story. In the year 1818 a certain shipowner living in Oberndorf arranged to have the play given at his home, and as a compliment invited as a special guest young Mohr who had recently been appointed to his church. This unexpected hospitality and the touching simplicity of the performance so stirred the priest that instead of going home directly after, he climbed a small mountain overlooking the village and let the beauty of the night speak to him. Altogether it was such an inspiring experience that when Mohr returned to his house toward midnight he sat down and wrote what has proved to be one of the favorite Christmas hymns of the world:

### *Stille Nacht! Heilige Nacht!*     [1818]
*Silent night, holy night*     Tr Jane Campbell, 1863, and others

The relative simplicity of this Christmas hymn justifies its classification by the Lutherans as "For Children." It consists mostly of pictures from the Gospel, or rather, tiny suggestions out of which we who know the story can easily reconstruct the scene. Only in stanza 3 is there introduced an adult concept, its meaning obscured by poor translation and senseless punctuation. Literally rendered, lines 2–5 run

Son of God, O how love laughs out of thy charming mouth! There the hour of salvation strikes for us.

The mood of the whole is one of awed contemplation and silent joy, breaking at last into a chorus of praise.

Since the music we sing was immediately written for the hymn it will be interesting to hear that part of the story.

Next morning, December 24, Mohr took his carol to his friend Franz Gruber, school teacher and organist at the church, and asked him to set it to music. By nightfall the task was done—a melody arranged for two solo voices, chorus and guitar accompaniment. As a surprise to the people the composition was sung in the Oberndorf church at the Christmas Eve service. Since the organ was being repaired and could not be used, the guitar was the only instrument. Incidentally, the composer's grandson still has the original guitar with its long green ribbon shoulderstrap. The organ-builder from the nearby village of Zillerthal heard this première performance; carried the melody home in his head. From him the four Strasser sisters, famous for concert tours on which they sang native mountain songs, learned the music and soon spread it far and wide, starting it on its conquest of the world.

The little church in which "Stille Nacht" was first sung was washed away in a river flood in 1899. But a successor was soon built—a small six-sided chapel of stone and stucco. In the entry of the new building, on the right, a bronze bas-relief has been set in a frame of black marble. It represents Pastor Mohr looking out of a window of heaven, his face entranced as with hand to his ear he listens to children on earth singing his hymn. Standing behind him is Gruber playing his guitar and smiling in recognition of the grand welcome his music has been given the world over.*

### TABULAR SUMMARY OF GERMAN HYMNS

|                | A   | B   | C   | E   | L   | M    | N   | P   | S   | U   |
|----------------|-----|-----|-----|-----|-----|------|-----|-----|-----|-----|
| Hymns Analyzed | 15  | 17  | 18  | 19  | 22  | 17   | 21  | 18  | 12  | 17  |
| Other          | 9   | 2   | 0   | 13  | 40  | 3    | 6   | 3   | 13  | 8   |
| Totals         | 24  | 19  | 18  | 30  | 62  | 20   | 27  | 21  | 25  | 25  |
| Ranking Order  | VI  | IX  | X   | II  | I   | VIII | III | VII | IV  | V   |

As might be expected, L has the largest number; lowest in number is C. But confining the totals to analysed humns, S stands lowest (12); the highest is L (22) with N a close second. The choice seems to be based not on liturgical value but on broad general usefulness.

### A DANISH HYMN

The Danes are a branch of a prehistoric Scandinavian race that grew in the hardy Baltic and North Sea region. Archaeologists continue to dig up their stone implements, kitchen middens and inscriptions in Runic symbols scattered through five millenniums of pre-Christian time. The Danes come into history as Vikings or sea-warriors, who in the ninth–tenth centuries penetrated all the waterways of northern Europe, conquered England and reached as far west as New England. Christian monks converted some of them by the middle of the ninth century. Then in the tenth century Harold Bluetooth forced his warriors to settle down and become good Christians.

* Adapted from an article in the *New York Times Magazine* of Dec. 20, 1931, by Hazel G. Kinscella.

The Danes remained Catholic until the Reformation; then by a combination
of politics, economics and religion, Catholicism was abolished in favor of a
Lutheran State Church. Though at times merged politically with the kindred
kingdoms of Norway and Sweden, Denmark became independent in the
nineteenth century, democratic and progressive.

.      The Danes began congregational singing in Luther's time, their hymns
mostly translations from the Latin, German and Swedish. There was scarcely
any change for 150 years. Then the German and Danish hymns grew in
number, many of them in the Pietist vein. Not till the nineteenth century did
the hymnal become chiefly Danish. Perhaps the man who contributed most
to this modernization was

## BERNHARD SEVERIN INGEMANN (1789–1862)

HE was the youngest of five sons, his father a country pastor. He
managed to get a university education at Copenhagen, then became Professor
of the Danish Language and Literature and writer of both poetry and prose.
His historical romances, inspired by the novels of Walter Scott, are in great
vogue today. He was the editor and reviser of the old Danish hymnbook, to
which he contributed many hymns. "These are sung," as Dr. Percy Dearmer
says, "in every Danish home—which is perhaps why 90 per cent of the Danish
people are members of the National Church." One hymn by him is the only
Danish to survive in our English books:

*Igjennem Nat og Traengsel*      [1825]
*Through the night of doubt and sorrow*
Tr Sabine Baring-Gould, 1867

The imagery of this hymn is derived from the Israelite journey through
the Wilderness to the Promised Land, as described in various portions of
Exodus and Numbers. Thus we have to keep in mind a double picture—the
historic journey of old, and the ever-continuing march of the generations
from birth to death, or perhaps man's eternal progress from sin to redemption.

Of the "songs of expectation" sung of old, there are Miriam's Victory
Chant (Ex 15:1–18), the Song of the Well (Num 21:17–18), the paeans of
conquest over Moabites and Amorites (Num 21:27–30), and the Oracles of
Balaam (Num 23:7—24:24). These must be equated in our picture with
some of the Christian hymns we have been studying, the function of which
is to cheer us, comfort and inspire us on our Christian journey.

The "guiding Light" was originally the "Pillar of Cloud and Flame"
which the Israelites followed through the Wilderness (Ex 13:21–22). Our
correlative of that is Christ—as suggested by the capital letter L—and the
inspiration of human fellowship. This imagery is amplified into the two
halves of stanza 2. In stanza 3 we realize the oneness of our essential expe-

riences in spite of our many individual episodes: the song, the fight, the danger, the gladness of the final achievement of our goal. The fourth stanza is a call to press on, to endure what it takes, to rejoice in the hope of victory and the life everlasting.

There is a greater unity of structure, a finer feeling for form, and a sharper definition of imagery in this hymn than in most others.

### ANONYMOUS, 1625      Probably a Netherland Folk-song

## *We gather together to ask the Lord's blessing*
### Tr Theodore Baker (English) 1894

We cannot fully appreciate this hymn apart from its historical setting. Its birthplace was Holland. Its year was 1625. That year saw the accession of Frederick Henry, Prince of Orange, to the leadership of the Union of Dutch Provinces. He was the youngest son of William the Silent, the great leader in the revolt against Spain, who had been shot by a Catholic assassin. That great struggle for freedom, politically from Spain and religiously from the Catholic Church had come to a stalemate in 1609 and a twelve-year truce was established. This gave Protestant Holland a chance to breathe and to grow in stature. The prince now leading her destinies was a brilliant politician and an able soldier. During his stadtholdership of more than a quarter-century, a new golden age began. The Dutch East India Company developed a huge commerce which exceeded that of the English; Hals, Vermeer and Rembrandt raised Dutch art to its pinnacle; politics and religion became more harmonious, and finally the Spanish endeavor on land and sea to regain supremacy was smashed beyond recovery, 1648.

All this history was in the future, but the hope and promise of it were in the hearts of all Hollanders when Frederick Henry came to power in 1625, and this hymn was written. Echoes of the past, however, ring through this national anthem:

*Stanza 1.* "He chastens": There had been not only political but religious differences within the provinces of Holland. Calvinism, for example, had stubbonly fought the liberalizing tendencies of Arminius who taught that God did not doom the majority of mankind to an eternal hell. That inner conflict within Protantism might be termed God's chastening.

"The wicked oppressing now cease from distressing": This is an allusion to the frightful persecutions by the Catholic Church which directed the policies of the armies of Spain. For example: in 1576 Antwerp had been captured and plundered by the Spanish, six thousand had been massacred and eight hundred houses burned. In 1585 it was again captured by the Spanish after a long siege and all its Protestant citizens exiled. Many other cities suffered similarly.

But such catastrophes had not recurred in the fifteen years preceding the writing of this hymn.

*Stanza 2.* "So from the beginning the fight we were winning": It was the assured feeling of the Protestants that God had been backing their cause. The truce and cessation of hostilities in 1609 was proof of it.

*Stanza 3.* "And pray that thou still our defender will be": The fight has not yet been fully won, but with God's help we shall win.

There are times in the history of every nation when the use of this patriotic hymn becomes both appropriate and inspiring.

*High Church*
*Hymnists*

| | | |
|---|---|---|
| 1837–1901 | Queen VICTORIA | |
| 1838–48 | Chartist Movement for extension of franchise and social reforms. | |
| 1842 | Parliament Commission reports shocking working conditions in mines. | |
| 1843 | Free Church of Scotland formed. | |
| 1845 | Growth of Anti-Corn Law League. Three million die of famine in Ireland. Many Anglicans turn Catholic. | |
| 1846 | Repeal of Corn Laws—to the advantage of the poor. | |
| 1847 | Karl Marx: *Sketch of Communism.* Parliament prohibits women and children working more than 10 hours a day in factories. | |
| 1848 | Thackeray's *Vanity Fair* lambastes vice of great and wealthy. Christian Socialists found Queen's College for Women. | |
| 1851 | Earl of Shaftesbury presses for slum clearance and other reforms. | Alexander, 1848–52 |
| 1854 | Christian Socialists found Workingman's College. | |
| 1855 | Spencer: *Principles of Psychology* (materialistic). | |
| 1858 | East India Co. absorbed by British Government. | C. Wordsworth, 1858–63 |
| 1860 | Free Trade becomes England's policy. | Dix, 1858–67 |
| | | Whiting, 1860 |
| | | Pott, 1861 |
| | | Baker, 1861–8 |
| 1863–5 | Dean Stanley: *Hist. of Jewish Church*, applying development theory to Judaism and the Bible. | Monsell, 1862–3 |
| | | Pierpoint, 1864 |
| | | Plumptre, 1864–5 |
| | | Baring-Gould, 1865 |
| 1866 | Colenso Controversy over Higher Criticism. | Stone, 1866 |
| 1867 | Franchise extended to lower-income citizens. Karl Marx: *Capital*—textbook of social revolution. | |
| 1867–81 | Privy Council decisions adverse to High Church ritualists. | Pollock, 1871 |
| 1869 | Protestant Church in Ireland disestablished. | |
| 1871 | Religious tests for university degrees abolished. | Thring, 1873 |
| 1876 | Growth of Imperialism: Victoria proclaimed Empress of India. Compulsory education established in England. | Gurney, 1883 |
| 1886 | *Reform Act*; Universal manhood suffrage. | |
| 1897 | Queen Victoria's Jubilee celebration. | |
| 1898–1902 | Boer War. | |

## CHAPTER TWELVE

# THE VICTORIAN ERA:
# HIGH CHURCH HYMNS

VICTORIA CAME TO THE THRONE IN 1837 when the Oxford Movement was in full flood. Her reign was destined to see great changes in thought, secular and religious, and these changes affected all the various branches of the Church whether Anglican or Dissenting. Before we can appraise the hymnody of this period we must take a glance at these movements.

Some of the changes occurred in the political area. They were democratic in trend, aimed at the reduction of power in the hands of aristocracy, wealth and hereditary privilege. By successive hard-won victories of Whigs over Tories, liberals over conservatives, beginning before the Victorian Era, the franchise was extended to more and more people who owned less and less property. Non-conformist officeholders were released from the necessity of receiving Communion at least once a year at the hands of an Anglican priest (1828); the franchise was extended to Roman Catholics (1829), to Jews (1858). After 1871 one need not be an Anglican in order to get a university degree. Finally in 1884 full manhood suffrage was won and seats in Parliament were open to all without regard to wealth. As a whole the Anglican Church was hostile to this liberal movement, for its own preferred position in the state was thereby jeopardized.

Other changes were social and economic. The horrible conditions of the eighteenth century (Chap. V) had been gradually mitigated, largely through the efforts of Methodists, Evangelicals and other religious liberals, but the industrial and political revolutions spanning the change in the century brought new problems—unemployment, poverty, near-rebellion, repressions, the rise of Trade Unionism and Cooperatives. Most intense and long-sustained agitation of all of these mentioned was the Chartist Movement in the 1840's.

This movement came near precipitating another "French Revolution." It was an embryonic Socialism based on class struggle and hostile to the privileged classes. Chartists and their sympathizers held vast meetings in order to impress Parliament with the justice of their demands. They drew up petition after petition signed by millions of people urging upon the government new laws that would secure six specific benefits to the common man: manhood suffrage, voting by ballot, annual Parliaments, abolition of property qualifications for members of Parliament, payment to members, equal electoral districts on the basis of the census. During the decade of agitation a good deal of violence developed—burning of property, riots, smashing of machinery, and the like. The government became frightened and tried to suppress them, leading to the imprisonment, exile and death of nearly 500 Chartists. Organized religion was against these reforms. The Chartists responded with hatred: "More pigs and fewer parsons" was a famous Chartist slogan. While by 1850 the movement had spent itself, all of the political and most of the social changes demanded were ultimately won and became part of the British Constitution.

The social philosophers were meanwhile adding their ferment. The Frenchman Compte in his *Positivist Philosophy* (1830–42) bade goodbye to deism and all forms of supernaturalism and placed as the apex and crown of all the sciences the study of mankind. The word "sociology" was invented by him. But the real starting point for modern socialism and communism was Karl Marx who in his *Sketch of Communism* (1847) and *Capital* (1867) gave the working class its textbook of social revolution. Spencer aided with his huge *Sociology* which began to appear in 1876. You may be sure that the Church did not take kindly to these developments.

Perhaps the most critical changes of the Victorian Era occurred in the realm of science. They were revolutionary. They were based on the assumption that the universe was governed by law and not by the whims of a miracle-working deity. This concept led to an intensive preoccupation with the physical world as over against the religious or the theological. As James Harvey Robinson puts it: "When men of first rate ability turned from a consideration of the good, the true, and the beautiful, and of the precise relation of the three members of the Trinity to one another, and began to wonder what makes milk sour quicker in hot weather than in cool, . . . they had already made the transition from the old to the new attitude of mind." * Astronomy and geology led the way and opened up an infinite universe that was the product of changes covering millions of years. For those who gave heed to these teachings, the first chapter of Genesis had to be re-interpreted.

The universe of law thus opened up by science had a reflex influence upon philosophy. Matter and motion were raised to the rank of cosmic deities when Herbert Spencer tried to show in his *Principles of Psychology* (1855) that the human mind evolved in a wholly materialistic world where men's actions were the result of physical causes only. The biologist Darwin soon showed in his *Origin of Species* (1859) that all living forms are the product of a law of evolution working by the method of reaction to environment and the survival of the fittest. This book shook orthodoxy to its very

* *The Human Comedy*, p. 293, Harper's, 1937.

foundations: into the realm of myth went the second chapter of Genesis and with it Calvin's theology based upon it. Spencer buttressed Darwin in 1861 by his *First Principles,* which endeavored to state in a single formula and in terms of matter and motion the law of cosmic evolution. His doctrine of the "Unknowable," in the same book, was, to quote William James, "a polite attempt to bow religion out of the door." These books by Darwin and Spencer reshaped human thought in all realms and necessitated the rewriting of all books on science, history, philosophy and religion.

An even more devastating field for the religiously inclined lay in the new science of Biblical criticism. Once the whole Church taught—as some branches of it still teach—that the Bible is the revealed Word of God, inerrant in all its statements of fact and theology. The earliest intimation of a changing point of view and the first thorough-going attempt to establish the new science of Biblical Criticism arose in Germany. Inspired by this, Dean Stanley of the Anglican Church began to lecture at Oxford on the *History of the Jewish Church* (published 1863–5). Soon all the great English scholars were microscopically examining the Old Testament to discover its documentary sources and to arrive at their chronological order. The result was a conviction that, "like all living and life-giving systems of thought, belief and practice, the religion of Israel had been subject to development." When W. Robertson Smith in 1881 translated Wellhausen (*The Old Testament in the Jewish Church*), the Free Church of Scotland became so alarmed that Smith was tried for heresy. Though not convicted he was dropped from his teaching position. Nevertheless, at the end of his trial he was the most popular man in Scotland.

Even the common people caught a glimpse of this revolutionary science, argued *pro* and *con* on the subject of an inerrant Scripture. Henry Milman, the historian, walking through London early one morning, was held up by a group of porters and made to deliver his opinion: "Did God really command the Israelites to massacre the people of Canaan?"

If the man on the street was thus aroused, one can easily imagine what all this evolutionary science, philosophy and literary criticism did to the thinking people of the churches of England. Three-quarters of them became agnostics. Matthew Arnold has poignantly expressed the fact and his emotional reactions in his "Dover Beach":

> The Sea of Faith
> Was once, too, at the full, and round earth's shore
> Lay like the folds of a bright girdle furl'd.
> But now I only hear
> Its melancholy, long, withdrawing roar,
> Retreating, to the breath
> Of the night-wind, down the vast edges drear
> And naked shingles of the world.

Ah, love, let us be true
To one another! for the world, which seems
To lie before us like a land of dreams,
So various, so beautiful, so new,
Hath really neither joy, nor love, nor light,
Nor certitude, nor peace, nor help for pain;
And we are here as on a darkling plain
Swept with confused alarms of struggle and flight,
Where ignorant armies clash by night.*

We shall now consider the impact of these revolutionary movements upon the Churches of England and their Hymnody.

### THE HIGH CHURCH

Those Anglicans who resisted the drift both to Rome and toward agnosticism became more intensely High Church. They fought to retain Anglican supremacy over all other faiths and over the government. They fought social legislation and "shook off with well-bred impatience the humanitarian professions which had become associated with the Evangelical creed." On the other hand they intensified their devotion to the Church as a unique, divine institution, and, by ignoring the scientific trend of the times, were able to concentrate on their faith that the inerrant Bible, the Sacraments, the Liturgy and the faithful observance of the Christian Year would save England from atheism, democracy and degeneration. This uncompromising ecclesiasticism broke the unity of the Angelican Church: the clergy were more divided in opinions in 1870 than in 1815.**

Following the spate of translations in the early years of the Oxford Movement came a flood of original hymns beginning in the 1840's. As might be expected, almost all of these were written by clergymen. At the head of those whose verses still do service in many hymnals stands

## Mrs. CECIL FRANCES ALEXANDER (1818–95) Anglican, High

BORN in Dublin as Cecil Frances Humphreys she married the Anglican rector of a humble parish, the Rev. William Alexander, who, because of his preaching and executive ability, was made Bishop of Derry

---

* *Poetical Works of Matthew Arnold,* Macmillan, London, 1896.
** The division is still there. A New York paper dated Nov. 3, 1946, publishes this item, a United Press dispatch from London:

In London's St. Colombo's Church, Bishop John W. C. Wand was ascending the pulpit when a youthful member of the congregation sprang up shouting: "My Lord Bishop, I protest!"

Another worshiper punched the youthful member in the mouth. A moment later about 20 persons were embroiled, shouting, shoving and throwing hymnals. It lasted 10 minutes.

UP said it was Low-Church Episcopalian protest against "Romish" services.

and Raphoe in 1867, and after his wife's death was raised to Archbishop and Primate of all Ireland.

Before her marriage she had been a member of the Evangelical wing of the Anglican Church. That fact shows in her intense devotion to the religious education of children. Feeling that properly to teach children such abstractions as the Apostles' Creed and such Christian duties as are implicit in the Christian Year, one should put the substance of the Creed into verse, she wrote many hymns for her Sunday School class, read them at the sessions and finally published them in a book called *Verses For Holy Seasons* (1846). In a way this was reducing to the capacities of children the more mature concepts of Keble's *Christian Year* (1827) which she very much admired. Her book contained a hymn for every Sunday and for all the other days celebrated in the Prayer Book. Two years later (1848) appeared her more poetical volume, *Hymns For Little Children,* for which John Keble himself wrote a preface. From it three of the selections in our hymnals are taken.

Dr. Benson has described so appreciatively her later life as a pastor's wife that he should be quoted here:

> She was admirably fitted to be a pastor's wife. She was as far as possible from the dreamy ineffectual type of poet. She never posed, detested gush and sentimentality, had a direct tongue and incisive speech, and she turned a vigilant eye upon her husband's house, garden and farm. She kept her devotional life largely hidden in her heart, but was a strict "Prayer Book Christian," going to church every day and to communion every week. Beyond that her days were largely given over to errands of charity and helpfulness, from one poor Irish home to another, from one sick-bed to another, from one house of sorrow to another, no matter how remote. She knew all her neighbors and loved them.
>
> When her husband became Bishop in 1867 she was brought more into contact with society and large institutions. She became the hostess of many distinguished people and shared the publicity of a bishop's life. But she was as much at home in the back streets of Londonderry as in the Bishop's Palace. It was in the palace she died, and to her funeral a great throng gathered from England as well as from Ireland, thus paying a spontaneous tribute to a noble life.*

Of all Mrs. Alexander's hymns the best-beloved and most widely used is

### *There is a green hill far away*     [1848]

This is an attempt to make vivid and understandable to children a clause from the Apostles' Creed, "Suffered under Pontius Pilate." The only

* *Studies in Familiar Hymns*: Second Series, pp. 227–8, by Louis F. Benson, copyright, 1923. Used by permission of The Westminster Press.

descriptive feature is the "green hill . . . outside a city wall." Mrs. Alexander had never seen the rocky, barren hills of Judea, or heard of the impossibility of identifying the place of crucifixion or proving that it was on a hill, but according to Percy Dearmer, "When she went shopping in Derry she had to drive by a little grassy hill near the road, and she tells us that she used to fancy this was like Calvary." All the rest of the hymn is theological, the phrases not explained to children but merely asserted as true.

Her interpretation of the Crucifixion and the Atonement harks back to Anselm, Archbishop of Canterbury, 1093–1109. Dr. Williston Walker gives a brief explicit statement of Anselm's doctrine.* In quoting I have added in parentheses the stanza and lines of the hymn in which Mrs. Alexander has expressed his ideas:

> Man, by sin (3:1–2), has done dishonor to God; God's nature demands satisfaction (2). Man, who owes obedience at all times, has nothing wherewith to make good past disobedience (4:1–2). Yet, if satisfaction is to be made at all, it can be rendered only by one who shares human nature, who is Himself man, and yet as God has something infinite to offer (4:3–4). Such a being is the God-man (4:1–2). Not only is his sacrifice a satisfaction, it deserves a reward. That reward is the eternal blessedness of His brethren (1:4; 3:3).

The only detail that Mrs. Alexander has added to Anselm is the Blood (3:4; 5:3), doubtless because the New Testament writers, imbued with the ancient Jewish sacrificial system, insist that "without the shedding of blood there is no remission of sin" (Heb 9:22; 1 Jn 1:7; Rev 5:9).

More recent theories of the Atonement make all these ideas unacceptable to many: at any rate they are beyond the comprehension of children. While, therefore, its poetic fervor and the appealing tune (Green Hill), to which it is almost universally set, have made the hymn a great favorite with adults, one can only regret that it perpetuates an outworn theology.

## Once in Royal David's city    [1848]

In this hymn there is much less theology, more visualization and some preaching on a child's level. Its purpose is to present and interpret for children the clause in the Apostles' Creed, "(I believe) in Jesus Christ, our Lord, who was born of the Virgin Mary."

*Stanza 1* is a metrical version of the details given in Lk 2:4, 7.
*Stanza 2* begins with the theological concept of the pre-existence and deity of Jesus, then adds pictorial details of the Nativity. Luke, however, does not say that Jesus was born in a stable: every house-

---

* *History of the Christian Church,* pp. 263–4, Scribner's, New York, 1918.

hold had a manger for its donkey or goat. Some kind-hearted woman probably took Mary into her home.

*Stanza 3* paraphrases in lines 1–2 the statements of Luke 2:51–52. The deity of Jesus is suggested by the word "wondrous"; "lowly maiden" alludes to the creedal phrase "born of the Virgin Mary" and to the Catholic and High Church belief that Mary was "perpetual virgin"—the seven other children mentioned in Mt 13:55–56 being Joseph's by a former marriage.

*Stanza 4*, lines 1–4, enlarge the picture of a perfect child, Jesus the ideal. The suggestion for it comes from Lk 2:40. Lines 5–6 present two of the attributes of perfect character—sympathy, sharing.

*Stanza 5* expresses the hope of heaven which Jesus has promised to all those that love Him (1 Cor 2:9). The creedal statement reads, "(I believe in) the resurrection of the body and the life everlasting." Biblical parallels are Rev 1:7; Jn 14:2.

*Stanza 6* is a simplified glimpse of heaven as hinted in many New Testament passages and dramatized at full length in Revelation (Mk 16:19; Col 3:1; Rev 5:11–14). The "stars" in l. 5 come from Dan 12:3; the white garments from Rev 7:9–17.

The lovely poem is worth singing with our children for its poetical quality and its ethical suggestions. They will not discover the theology until they are old enough to question it.

### All things bright and beautiful    [1848]

The clause of the Apostles' Creed illustrated by this hymn is, "I believe in God, the Father Almighty, maker of heaven and earth."

For once Mrs. Alexander has forgotten her theology and lost herself in the beauty of nature. She has created a charming hymn for children: the aspects of nature she conjures up are all within the experience of the little people of the Emerald Isle—or anywhere. The only discordant note is stanza 3 (omitted in all hymnals but the Lutheran):

> The rich man in his castle,
> The poor man at his gate,
> God made them, high or lowly,
> And ordered their estate.

Here the Tory stratification of society is given the sanction of God Almighty. Belief in such a divine Order would make social and economic change impossible and would confine all philanthropic work to "medicating the symptoms," rather than eradicating the causes of poverty, crime and oppression. Fortunately there were in the Victorian era Evangelicals, Broad Churchmen and Dissenters who were bent on changing all this—as we shall see.

## *Jesus calls us o'er the tumult*    [1852]

Not written for children, this hymn appeared in a volume of *Hymns* issued by the Society for the Promotion of Christian Knowledge. In the liturgical hymnals it is placed under the caption *Special Days: St. Andrew*, and is indicated to be sung on November 30, which is St. Andrew's Day.

> *Stanza 1.* A beautiful picture in which the little lake of Galilee is expanded to a tumultuous ocean beating upon the shores of the world.
> *Stanza 2.* The scriptural foundation is Mt 4:18–20 which relates the calling of Andrew and Peter while they were fishing. Since Andrew is the patron saint of Scotland, and the oblique cross on which tradition has crucified him is part of the Union Jack of the British flag, it is appropriate that the hymn should be adopted by the Canadian Brotherhood of St. Andrew.
> *Stanza 3.* The call to us is particularized: following Jesus means giving up our worship of gold or any other object of desire.
> *Stanza 4.* Again the call comes to subordinate to the Christian way of life all merely worldly pursuits. They should be subsumed and transformed in our devotion to Jesus.
> *Stanza 5.* A prayer that we may hear the call and make it our heart's desire to be loyal to the Saviour.

One can have only praise for this exquisite lyric.

## *BISHOP CHRISTOPHER WORDSWORTH (1807–1885)* Anglican, High

CHRISTOPHER WORDSWORTH was well born and reared, son of a Master of Trinity College, Cambridge, and nephew of the poet William Wordsworth. Christopher often visited his uncle at Rydal Mount and kept up a constant correspondence with him, no doubt to the great enhancement of the young man's poetical insight.

Christopher prepared for the University at Bishop Ken's old school at Winchester (Chap. III), then went to his father's college at Cambridge. Here he won splendid honors, was elected a Fellow and finally when only twenty-nine years old was appointed Public Orator to the University. In this same year he became Headmaster of Harrow School, probably next to Eton in reputation. (Old boys: Lord Palmerston, Sir Robert Peel and two other Prime Ministers, Byron the poet, and in our day, Winston Churchill.) But Harrow boys in those days were young savages. Wordsworth tried to infuse into them a new spirit of law and order based on religion—

Pure religion, breathing household laws

as his uncle had once put it. "It will be my earnest endeavor," said the new Headmaster, "to make all of you, first, Christians, secondly, gentlemen, and

thirdly, scholars." But the village vicar who formerly had furnished religion
to the boys was much put out by Wordsworth's plan to build a chapel for
the school and to officiate himself, so he spread rumors that the Headmaster
was too High Church and was trying to introduce popery. Wordsworth
attempted to add singing to the chapel exercises, but there were no
hymnbooks and the attempt failed. His discipline finally became so strict
and untactful that the public got a wrong impression and withheld its
patronage: the numbers dropped from 190 to 69. Wordsworth was accordingly "kicked upstairs" into the Canonry of Westminster Abbey, and given
also the "living" of a minute village called Stanford-in-the-Vale cum Goosey.
After nineteen years of this humanizing he was elevated to the Bishopric of
Lincoln. Those of my readers who have seen the grand old cathedral of
Lincoln, its superb chapter house with its satirical sculpture, its famous
angel choir with its "Lincoln imp," and the grand bishop's palace, will
know what a joy it must have been to the bishop to pass the last fifteen
years of his life amid such intriguing medievalism.

It is inspiring to recall, however, that the hymns which perpetuate the
memory of this great and good man were all composed while he was vicar
of that humble parish of "cum Goosey." Having to deal with the joys and
sorrows and aspirations of simple if not unlettered people, the experience
brought to this scholar the gift of song. His hymns reflect his High Church
convictions because they center around the church year: they illuminate
every phase of that year and all the doctrines of the Prayer Book. He was
very conscientious in carrying out his point of view which was (to quote
J. H. Overton, his biographer) that

> materials for them should be sought (1) in the Holy Scriptures,
> (2) in the writings of Christian antiquity, and (3) in the poetry
> of the ancient Church. He held it to be the first duty of a hymn
> writer to teach sound doctrine and thus save souls.

As to his theory of the inspiration and interpretation of the Bible:

> We must lift up our eyes from earth to heaven and see the Bible
> in the hands of Christ: as subscribed by his Sign-manual, and sealed
> by his Seal, and delivered by his authority to the Apostolic Church
> Universal, the divinely-appointed Keeper and Interpreter of the
> Word of God.*

Therein speaks the pedagogue and the theologian, untouched by the modernism of the times.

These hymns, 127 in number, were published in a volume called *The
Holy Year* (1862–3). Many of them are prosaic, many are on themes which
do not interest modern Protestants, but some few have survived in almost
universal use. Chief among these are:

* Overton and Wordsworth: *Bishop Wordsworth*, Rivington's, London, 1888.

*Top,* Lincoln Cathedral, See of Bishop Wordsworth. *Right,* Christopher Wordsworth, Bishop of Lincoln.

## *O day of rest and gladness*     [1858]

This is a glorification of Sunday, appropriately placed first in *The Holy Year.* In the hymn are touches of genuine beauty, as in the opening apostrophe and all of stanza 3, where Sunday is extolled as having been through all the ages the satisfaction of a human need. But to give the day a greater

sacredness through its historical associations, the poet reminds us that Light
was first created on a Sunday (the first day of the week, Gen. 1:1, as over
against the Jewish Sabbath on which God rested, Gen 2:1–3); and that the
Resurrection and Pentecost both came on Sunday. He loves to find in these
facts, in the "triple light" and the three "Holys" of the Church's perpetual
praise a symbol of the "God triune." This theological doctrine he expands
to its full statement in the final quatrain. Thus the hymn combines the vital
and the dogmatic in a way very satisfying to a High Churchman.

### O Lord of heaven and earth and sea        [1863]

This hymn covers the Prayer Book prescription "Charitable Collections."
It is a reverent survey of the gifts of God in nature (stanza 2), in civilization (stanza 3), in Christ's redemption (stanza 4), in the Spirit's graces
(stanza 5), in the religious life as mediated by the Church, especially in
its sacraments which are the "means of grace" (stanza 6). Stanza 7 is
reminiscent of "he that hath pity upon the poor lendeth unto the Lord"
(Prov 19:17). This is Wordsworth's appeal for the "charitable collection"
of the day. Fortunately, the little community of "cum Goosey" was able to
act on the charitable suggestion of this hymn. In spite of a bad financial
crash in 1857, the farmers of England in 1863 were more prosperous than
ever before—no thanks to High Church legislation!—wages up 20% over
those in 1850 and food prices low.

Editors make different selections from the stanzas. The modern tendency
is to omit the theological ones.

### Alleluia! Alleluia! Hearts to heaven        [1872]

This resurrection hymn was of course written for the liturgy of Easter
Sunday. It is a series of Alleluias, exhortations to sing, shouts of victory, and
pictures taken or enlarged from Biblical metaphors.

Stanza 1. "He who on the Cross a victim" is suggested by Heb
9:13–14, 26; 10:12; 1 Cor 5:7.
Stanza 2. "Iron bars" is taken from Ps 107:16 or Is 45:2. Perhaps
the poet had in mind the pictures of "The Harrowing of Hell," in
which the medieval artists showed Christ breaking down the gates
and liberating the Old Testament worthies who had been imprisoned there.
Stanza 3. Based upon Paul's statement that Christ was the "first-
fruits," which in the Jewish ritual had to be offered to Jahweh
(1 Cor 15:20). This is enlarged by Paul's likening our resurrection
to the sprouting of wheat (1 Cor 15:35–38, 42–44).
Paul probably did not know that he was borrowing his figure

from the Egyptians. One may see in the Cairo museum what they call a "Vegetating Osiris." A couch was spread with a couple of inches of sand; wheat was then sown on it in the shape of a man; it was watered, placed in the sun, until the sprouting wheat was about six inches high; then the whole couch was placed in the tomb of the dead man as a perpetual reminder that "as in Adam all die, so in Osiris shall all be made alive."

*Stanza 4.* A rather unpleasant mixture of incongruous figures in which Christ has become the sun whose rays produce the harvest of saved souls. The "angel-hands" were suggested by Christ's explanation of the Parable of the Sower (Mt 13:36–43).

*Stanza 5.* The usual High Church Trinitarian formula in which the harvest and sun figures give place to a fountain.

Though this is one of the poorest Easter hymns, it is found in six of our hymnals. As far as I can recall I have never heard it sung in 60 years.

## WILLIAM CHATTERTON DIX (1837–98) Anglican, High

ONE of the few laymen who have written hymns. Dix was son of a surgeon of Bristol, England, became a business man and spent most of his life as manager of a Maritime Insurance Company in Glasgow. His church affiliations we know only through his hymns. Published as they were in *Altar Songs, Verses on the Holy Eucharist,* and *A Vision of All Saints,* we judge that he was High Church, yet their contents give partly, at least, an Evangelical emphasis. The last-named collection is horribly sentimental, High Church at its highest, as the titles show: "The Expectant Bride" (the Church), "Love and the Place of Rest Afar Off," "A Group of Virgin Martyrs," "The Embracing of the Body of Christ by His Virgin Mother," "On Seeing an Old Woman Telling Her Beads in Cheapside." However, his hymns are simple, reverent, sincere, imaginative, not above the average comprehension, and two of them at least have proved to be continuously serviceable.

## As with gladness men of old     [c. 1858]

A hymn for Epiphany celebrating the coming of the Wise Men (Mt 2:1–12), and since the fifth century interpreted by the Church as the first manifestation of Christ to the Gentiles. Dix himself has told us how, ill in bed, he began the hymn after reading the Gospel of the day, and before evening had finished it.

The arrangement is somewhat schematic: each stanza first draws a picture of some detail of the story, then makes the application to our own spiritual life.

*Stanza 1* pictures the joy of the Magi in seeing the star and in their feeling of being led; then our corresponding prayer for guidance.
*Stanza 2* pictures their joy as they worship before this representative of heaven and God; then our corresponding prayer for greater willingness to seek the throne of grace.
*Stanza 3* pictures the episode of giving—their costly gifts contrasting with the poverty of the Bethlehem shelter; then our prayer for willingness to offer to Christ sincerely our dearest possession—loyalty and love.
*Stanzas 4–5* abandon the story for a broader picture: the narrow way that leads to heaven, and heaven itself with its unspeakable glories; then the broader prayer that we may be kept, guided, and admitted to the heavenly country.

In our day a first-class hymn writer would be less likely to utilize two stanzas in describing a symbolic heaven, and more likely to bring the actual sinful world, wise men and all, to realize the necessity of laying its heart at the feet of Christ. But in Dix's time the social implications of the gospel had not yet assumed importance, except in a few minds.

## *WILLIAM WHITING* (*1825–78*) Anglican, High

A LONDON boy educated at Winchester, who through his musical ability rose to be Master of the Winchester College Choristers' School. Not another detail of his life has been recorded.

This school was the place where the "Quiristers" were trained for singing in the school chapel. Sixteen in number, they were an ancient institution created by William Wyckham, the founder of Winchester College (prep school), 1382. Besides singing, the boys had to wait on table in college hall; they also might study with the regular college boys. In their uniform of a hundred years ago—chocolate swallow-tail coats with brass buttons— they looked more like footmen than anything else. Now the waiting in hall and the uniform have been abolished. One who has seen the magnificent college chapel, fourteenth century, with its original wooden fan-tracery in the ceiling, will understand how important it was that Whiting and his Quiristers should prove not unworthy of their calling. (See also under Thomas Ken, Chap. III.)

### *Eternal Father, strong to save* [1860]

It is rather strange that this hymn of the sea should come out of an inland boys' school. We must remember, however, that, since Elizabeth's time at least, the English have been a seafaring people and that the whole channel coast is studded with harbors large and small from which fishing craft, cross-channel boats, merchantmen and great liners bound for New York, Cape

Town and Brisbane constantly sail. Southampton, next greatest of English ports to London, is only twelve miles from Winchester, and Portsmouth with its top naval base is only twenty. No Winchester boy would fail to respond to a hymn of the sea.

Only a few years after this hymn was written, one of the Winchester chaplains, Robert Dolling, established a mission in the slums of Portsmouth and two other towns, where the objects of its care were "thieves, felons, tramps, loafers," and, of course, sailors on shore leave. Senior boys from the school are still encouraged to visit these missions.

The hymn may have been inspired by that marvellous description of a sailor's dangers and deliverances given in Ps 107:23–32. It is constructed on the Trinitarian formula.

> *Stanza 1* is addressed to the Father who created the sea—"and marked out for it my bound, and set bars and doors, and said, Hitherto shalt thou come, but no further, and here shall thy proud waves be stayed" (Job 38:10–11).
>
> *Stanza 2* is addressed to the Saviour, second Person of the Trinity, whose power to quell the raging sea is told in Mt 8:23–27.
>
> *Stanza 3* appeals to the Spirit, the third Person, who at creation's dawn "brooded over the face of the waters" of chaos (Gen 1:1) as a prelude to the creation of light (1:3), life (1:20), and peace (2:2).
>
> *Stanza 4* unites the three separate agencies to receive the earnest prayer for protection against the dangers that beset sea-faring men, and closes with an echo of Ps 107:31, "O that men would praise the Lord for his loving-kindness, and for his wonderful works to the children of men."

This is the noblest and most widely-used hymn of the sea. It is used not only on English ships but at the U. S. Naval Academy at Annapolis, and a beautiful translation of it appears in the hymnbook of the French Navy. I have crossed the Atlantic forty-nine times, and to the best of my recollection this hymn was sung at Morning Prayer every Sunday we were at sea under the British flag.

### Rev. FRANCIS POTT (1832–1909) Anglican, High

BORN in Southwark across London Bridge from the City, the wretched suburb where lay Shakespeare's Globe Theater; educated at Brasenose College, Oxford, and from 1856 rector in a number of humble parishes until deafness caused him to retire. In his day he was best known as a translator of hymns from the Syriac and Latin. Universally used today is his translation, "The strife is o'er, the battle done," from the Latin of an anonymous writer of the seventeenth century. (See Chap. IX, *"Finita iam sunt proelia"*). He was also a member of the committee that compiled the famous *Hymns Ancient and Modern*. His one widely-used original hymn is

## *Angel voices ever singing*    [1861]

The original caption reads, "For the Dedication of an Organ, or for the Meeting of Choirs" (i.e., choir festivals so common in England). The hymn is reported as first sung in the Church of St. John the Evangelist at Wingate in Lancashire, but the rector of that church wrote me in 1938 that the history of the church revealed no such incident.

"Angel voices" (stanza 1) is a reminiscence of the pictures of the everlasting choirs of heaven given in Revelation: e.g., "And they rest not day and night, saying, Holy, holy, holy is the Lord God Almighty" (Rev 4:8). But the "thousands" who are now living rejoice that God will also listen to the songs of mortals (stanza 2). In stanza 3 the poet realizes that the present service of dedication is made possible only by God's provision for the coordinated powers of ears, hands, voices and the art of the craftsman who can make an organ. These gifts to us are now dedicated to Him in this musical service (stanza 4). The final stanza is the High Church formula in praise of the Blessed Trinity.

### Rev. SIR HENRY WILLIAMS BAKER (1821–77) Anglican, High

SON of a Vice-Admiral and Baronet, he was educated at Trinity College, Cambridge, ordained in 1844, became vicar of Monkland near Leominster in 1851, in 1859 inherited his father's baronetcy, and died at Monkland.

Monkland was so named because of a monastery once located there, owing allegiance to Normandy. The twelfth-century church was the old priory church, little changed except that Baker restored it in 1866—rebuilt the chancel and added a beautiful organ. The farmhouse just behind the church incorporates some of the monastery buildings. The day I visited it there were four calves in the yard beside the church, and evidences of cattle everywhere. It seemed as if the church itself were in a barnyard. The present vicarage, only thirty-odd years old, is not Baker's; his is about half a mile west of the church. It lies in well-wooded grounds, though now unoccupied and neglected. Baker, who was a bachelor, lived there with his sister for thirty years. The whole environs are lovely pastoral country, peaceful, with sweet-scented air in mid-July and distant views to the north and east.

Baker is another example of how a vicar with a good living and only nominal duties can devote himself to other congenial tasks. He became the prime mover in that epoch-making work, the compilation and publication

Henry W. Baker's parish, Monkland Priory Church, 12th century, restored by Baker.

Baker's abandoned vicarage at Monkland. Light duties in this parish enabled Baker to undertake editorship of Anglican *Hymns Ancient and Modern*, 1861, most widely-used hymnal ever published.

TYPICAL COUNTRY PARISHES, CHOICE SEATS FOR WELL-TO-DO "YOUNGER SONS" WITH SCHOLARLY TASTES.

of *Hymns Ancient and Modern* (1861), to which also he contributed translations from the Latin besides many hymns and tunes. Of these, fourteen
hymns are found in our ten hymnals; three of them are widely listed. He
continued as chairman of the Hymnal Committee for twenty years and,
therefore, is largely responsible for the *Appendix* of 1868 and the revised
edition of 1875 which remains the greatest English Hymnal produced.

### *The King of Love my Shepherd is*      [1868]

It is a far cry from the *Bay Psalm Book* to Baker. The former is bent
on giving the exact language of Scripture, modified only by the necessities
of meter; the Psalm remains Hebrew in all its connotations. Baker, on the
other hand, exhibits the grace of the Romantic poets of modern England,
and transforms a Hebrew Psalm into a Christian rhapsody.

The Christian transformation is effected by fusing into the Psalm
Christ's parable of the Good Shepherd (Jn 10:1–5, 11, 14–18) and John's
teaching that Christ is the incarnation of God's love (Jn 15:9–14; 1 Jn
4:8–11). The imagery is enriched also by remembered glimpses of the River
of the Water of Life and the Food Celestial (Rev 22:1–2); and the Parable
in which the lost sheep is brought home with rejoicing on the shepherd's
shoulder (Lk 15:3–7). The heavy "rod," which in darkness or mist the
shepherd clinks along the rocky path to comfort with its music the worried
sheep, is now transformed into a glowing cross that pierces the gloom.
"Unction" is a reminiscence of the Church's Sacrament of anointing by
which spiritual grace and salvation are ensured (James 5:14–15). The
"chalice" is the cup of the Holy Communion by which sin is expunged from
the souls of those who partake in faith. Such a fusion of the old and new,
metaphor with parable, the physical with the spiritual, the Judaic with the
Ecclesiastical, is well-nigh a work of genius.

This hymn of Baker's stood first in the 1868 *Appendix* to *Hymns Ancient
and Modern,* and thence it has spread to practically every hymnal in the
English language.

### *O God of Love, O King of peace*      [1861]

Written for *Hymns Ancient and Modern* under the caption "In Times of
Trouble." Its theme is congruous with such Prayer Book items as the prayer
to be offered "In Time of War and Tumults"; the Collect for the second
Sunday after Epiphany—"Mercifully hear the supplications of thy people,
and grant to us peace all the days of our life"; the beautiful Collect for
Peace beginning, "O God, who art the author of peace and lover of concord";
the prayer in the Litany, "That it may please thee to give to all nations
unity, peace and concord"; and the Versicle "Give peace in our time, O
Lord".

While Baker may have produced this hymn solely to fill a niche in the Hymnal, he had abundant reason to pray for peace. From 1859–61 the Italian War of Liberation was being fought, involving not only Italy but France, Austria, the Papal States, and of course producing tension and fear in Britain. By 1860 an imminent war between England and France caused corps of volunteer soldiers to be established in every county in England as permanent parts of the British Army. And in 1861 the American Civil War broke out, which vitally affected the economy of England. The unstable position of Great Britain as the leading imperial power of the world was a constant source of anxiety, as the numerous prayers for peace in the Prayer Book testify.

The hymn is doubtless needed in hymnals in case of emergency, but it lacks the necessary gripping quality to become a true prayer. Biblical phrases do not help much (Ps 46:9; Ps 76:10; Ps 78:3–4; Ps 34:22). And stanza 4, omitted by most editors, introduces saints and angels in heaven who do not help to solve the problem of peace on earth. On the whole, there are better prayers for peace in our hymnals, notably "God the Omnipotent! King who ordaineth."

### Lord, thy Word abideth    [1861]

This hymn is sometimes placed under the heading "Holy Scriptures," sometimes under "General," and is a chant of praise for the Bible as the inspired Word of God. However, it is not much more than a short list of the valuable qualities to be found there and the types of help one may derive therefrom. The most unusual feature is the rhyme-scheme—the rhyming syllable preceding an identical final syllable.

One has a feeling that the only Baker hymn destined to survive is "The King of Love."

### Rev. JOHN SAMUEL BEWLEY MONSELL (1811–75)

#### Irish Anglican, High

SON of an archdeacon of Londonderry, graduate of Trinity College, Dublin, he took holy orders in 1834 and became chaplain to Bishop Mant; then, after holding other preferments in Ireland, he was transferred to England as rector at Guilford. He died as the result of an accident while watching repairs on his church. Such is the brief and simple biography of one who was a true Christian; those who knew him pay tribute to his deep religiousness and the beauty of his family life in which sunshine and gaiety made his rectory a source of light and blessing.

Monsell was a prolific hymnist. He published eleven volumes of poems including nearly 300 hymns. The titles of the books indicate their slant toward High Church: *Spiritual Songs for the Sundays and Holy Days*

*Throughout the Year*, 1859; *Hymns of Love and Praise for the Christian Year*, 1863; *Litany Hymns*, 1870. In spite of the liturgical aims of his hymns, they follow in spirit the devotional character of the author. In this respect they contrast favorably with the theological hymns of Wordsworth.

## *Fight the good fight with all thy might*    [1863]

Monsell wrote this hymn for the nineteenth Sunday after Trinity, and named it "The Fight For Faith." On this day the Epistle to be read is Ephesians 4:17–32. There the apostle reminds his hearers that what Christ demands is a complete change of ideals and conduct, that they must "put off the old man and his deeds and put on the new man." He even particularizes the sins in a way that reminds one of the famous diatribe of Clement of Alexandria to which reference has been made above (Chap. XI: "Shepherd of tender youth"). It is this fight to accomplish a transformation of character that Monsell here describes in vigorous terms, some of which he borrows from the Epistles:

> *Stanza 1.* "Fight the good fight of faith; lay hold on eternal life" (1 Tim 6:12). "Wherefore . . . my joy and crown, stand fast in the Lord" (Phil 4:1).
> *Stanza 2.* "Wherefore . . . let us lay aside every weight, and the sin which doth so easily beset us, and let us run with patience the race that is set before us" (Heb 12:1). "I am the way, the truth and the life" (Jn 14:6). "I press on toward the goal unto the prize of the high calling in Christ Jesus" (Phil 3:14).
> *Stanza 3.* "Casting all your care upon him, for he careth for you" (1 Pet 5:7).
> *Stanza 4.* "In due season we shall reap if we faint not" (Gal 6:9). "He saith, be not afraid, only believe" (Mk 5:36). "This is the work of God, that ye believe on him whom he hath sent" (Jn 6:29). "Christ is all, and in all" (Col 3:11).

The fighting strength of the hymn lies in its imperatives—there are ten of them! Altogether the hymn shows much more of the Evangelical spirit than of High Church. It concerns not theology or the sacraments or the Church as a divine institution, but only the necessity for courage, endurance, faith. This is a hymn that will live.

## *(O) Worship the Lord in the beauty of holiness*    [1863]

This hymn was written for Epiphany beginning January 6, the season when the Church celebrates the Adoration of the Magi as the first manifestation of Christ to the Gentiles. In its unusual meter, richness of imagery and dominant purpose it reminds one of Heber's "Brightest and best of the sons of the morning" (*q.v.*). About them both there hovers an aura of opulence and beauty like that of Ormus and of Ind. To that extent, though we remember that we are watching the three Kings in their act of adoration, we are conscious of an unreality, and therefore a dissidence, which destroys the sincerity of our twentieth-century attempts to worship. Perhaps, however, it would be better for us if we could conjure up more of Monsell's romantic spirit.

> *Stanza 1.* "Gold of obedience"—a phrase that places obedience first in value over other acts; "incense of lowliness"—humility that gives an aroma to our act of worship.
> *Stanza 2.* "Carefulness"—not meticulousness, but carking care, overanxiety. "Casting all your care upon him, for he careth for you" (1 Pet 5:7).
> *Stanza 3.* "The slenderness of thy poor wealth"—a reminder of the widow's mite (Lk 21:1–3); more precious than gold are the attributes of truth and love.
> *Stanza 4.* "Mornings of joy . . . evenings of tearfulness"—a poet's paraphrase of Ps 30:5, "Weeping may endure for a night, but joy cometh in the morning."

## *On our way rejoicing*        [1862]

Appointed for the first Sunday after Trinity.

The first two stanzas fit the general theme of the Epistle for that Sunday (1 Jn 4:7–21), which is Love. In stanza 3 Christ becomes the supreme embodiment of God's love, while in stanza 4 is the Trinitarian doxology which typically closes High Church hymns.

## *FOLLIETT SANDFORD PIERPOINT* (1835–1917) Anglican, High

A GRADUATE of Queen's College, Cambridge. Became an occasional teacher of the Classics, and for the rest of his time enjoyed his patrimony and wrote as he felt like it. He contributed "Hymns for the Canonical Hours" to *Hymnal Notes*, edited by Neale, "a full realization of Tractarian dreams of a 'Catholic' hymnal." Others of his were published in *Lyra Eucharistica*, a High Church collection of hymns for the Communion. He is remembered only by the following hymn:

## *For the beauty of the earth*        [1864]

Written for the Communion Service. Its adequacy as a Communion hymn has been obscured by editors who have changed the refrain

Christ, our God, to thee we raise
This our sacrifice of praise

to

Lord of all, to thee we raise
This our hymn of grateful praise.

The original address was to Christ as God, and our offering was not mere praise but a sacrifice. Since Christ was sacrificed for us (Heb 9:26b) and that sacrifice is re-enacted in the Eucharist or Mass (Roman Catholic theory), this idea of offering a return sacrifice of praise is not far-fetched; in fact, it is suggested in Heb 13:15. A High Churchman would have no difficulty in accepting these interpretations.

Barring these theological details we have left such an acceptable lyric of joy in the beauties of eye and ear, heart and mind, that no hymnal can omit it.

The objects that arouse our gratitude are mentioned without much logical connection: the poet just thinks of as many sources of joy as possible and puts them down as they come to mind. They may be summarized as Nature with its magical sights and sounds—interpreted as signs of God's love (1:3): the power to understand the interrelations of mind and phenomena (stanza 3), the sacred bonds of human relationship and the emotions they engender (stanza 4), the lovable characteristics so generously bestowed upon men, that affect us like the beauty of flowers (stanza 5), the Church that, viewed the world around, is like the Sisters of the Perpetual Adoration kneeling in unbroken relays before the Blessed Sacrament (stanza 6); and finally (stanza 7) God Himself, who "so loved the world that he gave his only begotten Son" (Jn 3:16).

As we sing this hymn in shortened form we enjoy the memories and emotions aroused by the poet's pictures. Perhaps this is praise genuine enough to please God.

### DEAN EDWARD HAYES PLUMPTRE (1821-91) Anglican, High

EDUCATED at University College, Oxford, then Fellow at Brasenose College, Oxford. After ordination in 1846, because of his unusual intellectual and spiritual endowment he rose through successive positions as clergyman and scholar: Chaplain and later Professor of New Testament Exegesis at King's College, London; Dean of Queen's College, Oxford; Prebendary at St. Paul's Cathedral, London; rector of two parishes at different times; Dean of Wells Cathedral; select preacher often at Oxford; member of the committee for revising the Old Testament translation. His literary output includes the *Life of Bishop Ken, Biblical Studies*, translations of Aeschylus, Sophocles and Dante, besides several volumes of his own poetry. The wide range of his interests is hinted by the hymn collections or the occasions for which his hymns were written: the Evangelical *Church*

*Hymns,* the Jubilee of Queen Victoria, a Harvest Festival, processionals for Choral Festivals, processional for Thanksgiving, *Hymns for School and College,* for King's College Hospital, etc., etc. His hymns began their career of wide usefulness by being included in the ʾAppendix of 1868 to *Hymns Ancient and Modern.* Thence they spread into most of the hymnals of England and America. One is widely enough used at present to warrant its appearance here.

## *Rejoice, ye pure in heart*     [1865]

Written for a choir festival held at majestic Peterborough Cathedral. The untravelled American can hardly realize the emotional effect of a pro-

Peterborough Cathedral where Plumptre's "Rejoice, ye pure in heart" was first sung.

cessional made up of choirs from a dozen different communities, marching with full panoply of color through "long-drawn aisle" and under "fretted vault," while we hear

> The storm their high-built organs make,
> And thunder-music, rolling, shake
> The prophets blazoned on the panes.

The massiveness of the old Norman Peterborough makes a marvellous background and amplifier for such a processional.

The hymn is divided into two parts. Stanzas 1–5 are descriptive and suggestive. They enable us to see the long procession: first the processional cross and banner, always carried in front (stanza 1); then the mixed choirs of men and boys, girls and women (stanza 2); the music augmented in our imagination by angel choirs and in reality by the audience that participates (stanza 3), while ascending clouds of incense mingle with the echoes that fly from vault to vault, from pillar to pillar (stanza 4) until the vast volume of praise is like the Atlantic storm-waves beating on the shores of Tintagel (stanza 5).

Stanzas 6–8 transfigure the picture into symbol. Life is a processional path along which it is our privilege to sing from youth to age; it is an army's march, through toil and danger and sacrifice, from darkness into light, and like all marches it has a goal and an achievement to accomplish (stanzas 9–10). As we go, therefore, let us in imagination keep constantly before us the banner and the cross with which we started (stanza 1), and never fail to sing our praises to the Triune God whom we adore.

While ten verses are ordinarily too many for the needs of our small churches, we must remember that a choir festival processional in a great English cathedral takes from ten to thirty minutes! For such a feature this hymn is unsurpassed.

### Rev. SABINE BARING-GOULD (1834–1924) Anglican, High

BARING-GOULD was one of the most extraordinary men-of-letters of the Victorian Era. In the space of fifty-two years ending in 1906 he published eighty-five books on religion, travel, folk-lore, mythology, history, fiction, biography, sermons and popular theology. Perhaps his best-known work is his 15-volume *Lives of the Saints*. In addition he edited *The Sacristy*, a quarterly review of ecclesiastical art and literature. It is said that the literary catalogue of the British Museum shows more titles by him than by any other writer of his time. He never used a secretary: "The secret is simply that I stick to a task when I begin it."

Born in Exeter, educated first in Germany and France and then at Clare College, Cambridge, he took holy orders upon graduation in 1864 and served various parishes. The first was a curacy at Horbury, a smallish town three miles from Wakefield in Yorkshire. It occupies a high sandstone ridge above the Calder River, beneath which is a coal deposit; consequently a portion of the population are colliers. Below in the valley at Horbury Bridge are factories of yarn, cloth and shoddy, surrounded by cottages and hovels. These people were wholly neglected religiously, "even by the Dissenters"!

Baring-Gould was assigned to work among these people. He hired a small apartment in the present Post Office block consisting of a single room on the ground floor with a tiny back-kitchen. A stair led to a single bedroom above. The lower room he turned into a night-school, the upper into a chapel. Here he held sessions every evening in winter, service every Sunday in the chapel. "I had to stand on a stool before the chimney-piece, on which stood a cross and a pair of candlesticks. I wore no surplice, only a cassock. The congregation soon grew to fill the room and the stairs and the kitchen. Hymns were performed somewhat laggingly, as the singing had

*Top,* Horbury Bridge Post Office. The first cottage meetings were held by Baring-Gould in the apartment to the left of the letter-box. *Right,* Sabine Baring-Gould.

to bump down the stairs, fill the kitchen, and one strain of the tune after another came up irregularly through the chinks in the floor. . . . The notes from the stair also jostled." One old man used to pull out his pipe now and then for a few puffs. Some rowdies tried to disturb the school, but the master had a good helper, a bald-headed wool-comber: "If any roughs approached the door during school hours he would sally forth, crack a couple of walnuts in his fist and shout like the bellow of a bull: 'If you don't take care and be peaceable, I'll crack your heads as I do these here nuts.'" *

In 1867 he was transferred by Mr. Gladstone to another parish in Dalton. Not, however, until he had a romance. During one of the frequent floods of the Calder he saved a mill-girl named Grace Taylor from drowning, fell in love with her, sent her away to be educated, married her in 1868, spent the honeymoon in Interlaken, Switzerland, and lived with her happily many years till her death.

On his father's death in 1872 he inherited the estate of Lew Trenchard, north Devon, where his family had been settled for nearly three centuries. He therefore became squire, lord of the manor, justice of the peace, appointed himself rector of the parish, and there completed the ninety years of his life.

### Onward, Christian soldiers        [1865]

Baring-Gould himself has given us an account of how this amazingly-popular processional came to be written during the second year of his curacy at Horbury:

> It was written in a very simple fashion, without a thought of publication. Whitmonday is a great day for school festivals in Yorkshire, and one Whitmonday it was arranged that our school should join its forces with that of a neighboring village. I wanted the children to sing when marching from one village to the other, but couldn't think of anything quite suitable, so I sat up at night resolved to write something myself. 'Onward, Christian soldiers' was the result. It was written in great haste [less than fifteen minutes, it is said]. Certainly nothing has surprised me more than its popularity.

In trying to understand this hymn one must not be too critical. It was written for children who like to play soldier but have little notion of what soldiering involves or what war is about.

> Stanza 1. The war figure is found frequently in the Bible, especially in Paul who gave in detail the armor in which the Christian fights (Eph 6:13–17)—and that would look ridiculous even in 1865. Of course we have to interpret these figures in a spiritual sense, for "we wrestle not against flesh and blood" (Eph 6:12). The cross that goes on before is primarily the processional cross the children carried on the mile trek from Horbury Bridge to St. Peter's Church on the hill, and figuratively the symbol of the eternal crusade the Church must wage against the "armies of the aliens."
> Stanza 2. "The sign of triumph": Baring-Gould may possibly have told the children about the famous vision that Constantine saw blazoned in the sky on the night before his battle of Milvian Bridge that was to make or break him as the head of the Roman Empire

* From S. Baring-Gould: *Further Reminiscences,* Dutton, New York.

(312 A.D.)—the monogram of Christ and the words "In this sign thou shalt conquer." "Satan's host" would have to be explained to children. Possibly the author was thinking of Constantine's victory as a symbol of the rout of evil forces in the world, but that would be as meaningless to them as would "Hell's foundations quiver." In the latter phrase the poet may be recalling the clause in the Apostles' Creed, "He descended into Hell," and perhaps he coupled with it in his mind a picture by Fra Angelico showing Christ liberating the Old Testament worthies from a Limbo of Hell that had been wracked to destruction by the earthquake accompanying His crucifixion (Mt 27:51–53). At any rate, the children's "anthems" are supposed to do something of the kind to something or other.

*Stanza 3.* The army figure continues and recalls the phrase of the Creed, "I believe in the Communion of Saints." By this is signified the union between the faithful on earth and those in heaven: all are members of the same mystical body under Christ its head. That idea is continued in the remaining lines of the stanza. Of course, "we are not divided" is simply untrue, as Samuel Stone has stated in his famous hymn "The Church's one foundation" (see below). But perhaps the poet was referring to this group of children from two tiny villages who had been taught in common the Creed and Catechism and were now marching as one army to the mother-church on the hill.

*Stanza 4* expresses faith that the Church will never be extinguished. This has the warrant of certain Scripture texts: Dan 2:44; Mt 16:18; Mt 28:18–20.

*Stanza 5.* Omitted since 1868, it reads as follows:

> What the saints established
>   That I hold for true,
> What the saints believéd
>   That believe I too.
> Long as earth endureth
>   Men that faith will hold,—
> Kingdoms, nations, empires,
>   In destruction rolled.

This is Baring-Gould's confession of adherence to High Church principles which are said to be those of the Apostolic Church. In saying that this faith would never be changed he was shutting his eyes to the theological revolution then going on in England, destined to reinterpret or supplant many of the tenets in which he believed. (See under Broad Church, Chap. XIV.)

*Stanza 6* sums up the spirit of the previous verses in a fervent invitation to the onlookers to join in the children's profession of faith.

In this hymn written for children Baring-Gould has been less successful in getting down to the child's level than in the following hymn:

## Now the day is over          [1865]

This is one of the most exquisite and untouchable children's hymns in the English or any language. It is an evening prayer based upon Prov 3:24, "When thou liest down, thou shalt not be afraid: yea, thou shalt lie down, and thy sleep shall be sweet."

Stanzas 1 and 2 are an approach to God through nature. In these days of city life and sophistication many people have closed their minds and hearts to its appeal. But, in the childhood of the world, nature was man's environment, and there was a real emotion in Homer's oft-repeated line, "Then the sun sank and all the ways grew dark." A child still has that emotional contact: he wonders at a star, he cuddles when the dark descends; and if he is the product of a Christian home he welcomes the evening prayer. These two stanzas of nature-description give the environment and suggest the mood.

Stanza 3 is the invocation to Jesus: the contact with Him who is the only image of God the child can comprehend. It is the prayer of dominant desire for a tired child—placed first; it claims the promise, 'He giveth his beloved sleep" (Ps 127:2).

Stanza 4. Now follows the child's visualization of the Prayer Book petition, "We humbly beseech thee for all sorts and conditions of men" upon whom the stars look down. The first and most natural picture for a child would be that of other children kneeling by mother's side. For bed-time is the sweetest hour for children; then God is linked to home and loved ones. Then by contrast, those who are away from home and safety, on the ever-tossing sea, perhaps in the grip of a storm—"they that go down to the sea in ships, that do business in great waters" (Ps 107:23). Both halves of the stanza gain by this juxtaposition.

Stanza 5. The first half is a prayer for the sick, for whom night is the time of terror—the delirium, the long watching—"more than they that watch for the morning" (Ps 130:6). The second half is a prayer for the wicked: they who say, "Surely the darkness shall cover me" (Ps 139:11); they "who love darkness rather than light because their deeds are evil" (Jn 3:19).

Stanza 6 is a prayer for protection: from sudden alarms, from sickness or unforeseen violence. Angels are the most beautiful symbols of God's watchful care ever created. The Bible is full of these emblems: "He shall give his angels charge over thee to keep thee

in all thy ways" (Ps 91:11); "Thou shalt not be afraid of the
terror by night . . . He shall cover thee with his feathers, and
under his wings shalt thou trust" (Ps 91:5); "I will lay me down in
peace to sleep; for thou, Lord, only makest me to dwell in safety"
(Ps 4:8).

*Stanza 7.* A prayer for the new day. The truest thought about sleep
is that it prepares us for the fresh opportunities and service of
tomorrow, for night is only a prelude to morning. The Psalmist
appreciated that fact: "I laid me down and slept; I awaked, for
the Lord sustained me" (Ps 3:5). Dr. Watts' "If I should die before
I wake" is a wretched thought for a child's bed-time, compared
either with the Psalmist's or with this hymn's trustful and forward-
looking joy.

*Stanza 8.* A High Church poet must of course tag a perfect child's
prayer with a fourth-century Trinitarian formula, quite incomprehensible to a child. Fortunately, of the ten hymnals of our survey,
only A, L, S and U preserve it.

## *Through the night of doubt and sorrow*     [1865]

This is a translation from the Danish. See under Ingemann, Chapter
XI, p. 344.

### *Rev. SAMUEL JOHN STONE (1839–1900)* Anglican, High

STONE'S father was a learned and pious Evangelical. He sent his
boy to Charterhouse School in London (John Wesley's) and to Pembroke
College, Oxford, where Samuel became infected with High Church ideals.
Having "the muscles of a prize-fighter" he captained his college crew on
the Thames, and would have become a soldier but for an irresistible call to
the ministry. On graduating he became curate in Windsor and stayed eight
years (1862–70). His was a little mission church that had nothing to do
with the Royal Castle or with aristocratic Eton College across the river; it
was the chapel of a cemetery in the tough suburb of Spital. His athleticism,
if not his ethics, was equal to every occasion. Once he found a little girl
being maltreated by a bully. He beat the bully black and blue with his fists,
"like an avenging angel!" but some sober thought afterward showed him his
error.

Then followed thirty years in two parishes in the East End of London.
The first position was as curate to his Evangelical father (1870–90) at St.
Paul's, Haggeston, a very poor district with a population of 7000. After his
father's retirement he became vicar. Vigorous in mind and body, he used
to make his pastoral calls on a tricycle—before the days of bicycles. He was
devoted to his work with boys and girls, with women and their babies.
Benson says:

His combination of virility and sympathy gave him real power over the people. He was a churchman rather than a missionary, a shepherd rather than an evangelist.*

In his day the Established Church was practically the sole agent of education. Stone was bitterly opposed to the starting of Board (public) schools because they conflicted with his parochial schools. His fight was so strong that a supporter of the Board school system called him "the most tyrannical priest in East London."

Altogether his labors nearly wore him out. He was consequently changed to the rectory of All Hallows, London Wall (1890–1900). This was a small city church in an area that had a population of 10,000 by day and 150 at night!—consisting of the care-takers of the surrounding office buildings. Stone was equal to his opportunity: largely at his own expense he renovated the old church building and opened it at 6:30 in the morning as a place of rest and meditation for the crowds of office workers who had no place to go between the arrival of the commuters' trains at the nearby Broad Street station and the hour for opening the offices. This innovation was a huge success.

Though personally he was a man of spotless character and chivalrous toward the weak, he was a most pugnacious champion of the old order of thought that was so violently being shaken in his day. He refused to budge one iota before the Higher Criticism or Materialism or Evolution. Faith in the inspired Bible was enough for him. Here is a sample of his sarcastic reaction to the scientific and philosophic tendencies of his day:

### The Soliloquy of a Rationalistic Chicken

On the picture of a newly-hatched chicken contemplating the
fragments of its native shell.

(In the first two stanzas the chicken asked these questions: "How did I get in *there?*" Then, "Where was I of yore?" Besides, "Why didn't I get out before?") Follows stanza 3.

> I meet the notion with profound disdain;
> It's quite incredible; since I declare
> (And I'm a chicken that you can't deceive)
> What I can't understand I won't believe.
> Where *did* I come from, then? Ah! where indeed?
> That is a riddle monstrous hard to read.
>     I have it! Why, of course,
> All things are moulded by some plastic force
> Out of some atoms somewhere up in space,
> Fortuitously concurrent anyhow!—

---

* From *Studies of Familiar Hymns*, Second Series, p. 263, by Louis F. Benson, copyright, 1923. Used by permission of The Westminster Press.

There now!
*That's* plain as is the beak upon my face.*

A High Church chicken like Stone would say that God made him, 4004 B.C., on the sixth day after the vernal equinox, and that Adam named him "chicken." He would ask no further questions.

A Broad Church chicken (as we shall see) would say that God made him, but that it took several million years to do it, by processes the chicken hopes some day to find out.

Probably there is need for such divergencies of opinion in order that the intellectual discoveries of mankind may not destroy man's highest values but transform them. The fission of the atom must become a normal source of power by a slow chain-reaction if instead of annihilating mankind it is to serve its expanding needs.

Stone's hymns that have survived were all written while he was at Windsor, though his final volume of poetry containing fifty-five hymns was published in 1866 while he was in London. Julian in his *Hymnology* describes them as "strongly outspoken utterances of a manly faith, where dogma, prayer and praise are interwoven with much skill." The only hymn to be sung universally today is

### *The Church's one foundation*      [1866]

The hymn is a chain of Biblical phrases:
*Stanza 1. The Church's one foundation.* 1 Cor 3:11; Jn 3:5; Eph 5:26–27; Rev 21:2, 9; Acts 20:28; Phil 2:8.
*Stanza 2. Elect from every nation.* 1 Pet 1:1–2; Rev 5:9; Jn 11:52; Eph 4:5; Jn 3:3; Phil 2:10; Mt 26:26; Eph 4:4; 2 Cor 9:8.
*Stanza 3.* (Omitted from all hymnals):

> The Church shall never perish!
>> Her dear Lord to defend,
> To guide, sustain and cherish,
>> Is with her to the end;
> Though there be those that hate her,
>> And false sons in her pale,
> Against or foe or traitor
>> She ever shall prevail.

*Stanza 4. Though with a scornful wonder.* 2 Pet 2:1; Lk 12:37; Rev 6:10; Ps 30:5.
*Stanza 5. 'Mid toil and tribulation.* Rev 7:14.
*Stanza 6. Yet she on earth hath union.* See the Nicene Creed.

This hymn was written with a double purpose. First it was part of an attempt to interpret the Apostles' Creed for the benefit of certain cottagers in his Windsor suburb who were accustomed to repeat it as one of their private prayers, but with no clear idea of what it all meant. Stone accord-

* S. J. Stone, *Poems and Hymns*, London, 1903.

ingly wrote twelve hymns, one on each article of the Creed, and published them in a book, *Lyra Fidelium* (Lyre of the Faithful) that could be used at home or in the chapel. In that book the caption for this hymn reads

### Article IX

"The Holy Catholic Church; the Communion of Saints"
"He is the Head of the Body, the Church"

On the page opposite the hymn was his summary of the truths contained in Article IX, accompanied by proof-texts from the Bible.

The second and more fundamental purpose was to back up Bishop Gray in his controversy with Bishop John Colenso of Natal, South Africa, a struggle that was wracking the Anglican Church from one end to the other.

It seems that Colenso had espoused the cause of the "Higher Criticism," and was writing books on the subject: e.g., *The Pentateuch and the Book of Joshua Critically Examined* (1863), together with various defences of his position. His views were regarded as so dangerous that nearly every bishop of the Anglican Church called upon him to resign. On his refusal he was brought to trial for heresy in 1863 by his Metropolitan, Bishop Gray of Cape Town; he was condemned, deposed and prohibited from the exercise of any divine office. Colenso disregarded the sentence and was forthwith excommunicated. He appealed to the Crown, and the judicial committee of the Privy Council pronounced the decision null and void. Nevertheless the Church sought to undermine his work in every way, cut off his stipend— though that was made up by public subscription in England—and tampered with his converts, but he continued to preach to crowded houses and was greatly beloved. In all this he manifested "the deepest spiritual faith combined with the most advanced and searching historical criticism."

Stone's contribution to this controversy was this hymn. It consists of a strenuous assertion of High Church dogmas supplemented with mud-slinging against those who disagreed with him (see stanza 3, above), by which he means Colenso and all those who are accepting the Higher Criticism of the Old Testament. The "scornful wonder" of stanza 4 comes from the liberals in politics who resent the Church's opposition to political and social reform, the establishment of Board schools, the removal of disabilities from Catholics and Jews, and from the men of science and scholarship who believe the evidence of their reason over against the unproved assertions of the theologians. Thus was being re-enacted in England in the 1860's the tragedy that from the earliest Christian centuries has hindered the spread of the true gospel, and that still continues in the tensions between fundamentalists and liberals, Unitarians and Trinitarians, deists and humanists. This needless friction, waste and frustration could easily be eliminated if the Church would throw over its emphasis upon theology and accept as Christ's gospel his simple formula for the salvation of individuals and the world, "This is my commandment, that ye love one another." We then would see "the consummation of peace forevermore," and rejoice in the "vision glorious . . . of the great Church victorious"—which will never be the

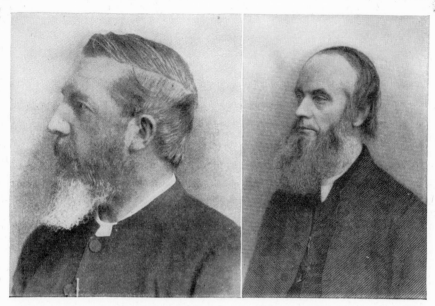

*Left,* Samuel J. Stone. *Right,* Henry Alford.

"Church at rest" but the Church devoted to the never-ending task of redeeming mankind.

### Rev. *THOMAS BENSON POLLOCK* (1836–96) Anglican, High

BORN on the Isle of Man, educated at Trinity College, Dublin, curate in three parishes including thirty years with his brother at St. Albans, Birmingham, until he succeeded him as vicar. Pollock was one of those saints who utterly sacrificed himself to his job. Though his "living" at Birmingham was worth only £150 a year, he refused offers of preferment in order to minister to the miserably poor people of his parish. He and his brother raised £100,000 to promote their work in church and school, and maintained a large staff to help them.

His special contribution to hymnody consisted of his *Metrical Litanies for Special Services and General Use* (1870). The Litany, originally a special form of processional prayer, has had a long history. In its earliest form it consisted of the repetition of the *Kyrie eleison* over and over hundreds of times: "Lord have mercy upon us! Christ have mercy upon us! Lord have mercy upon us!" St. Ambrose (fourth cent.) composed one of his own in which the whole community, fasting, clad in sackcloth, and walking barefoot, repeated the prayer incessantly. In 590 Gregory the Great, moved by a pestilence that had followed a flood, ordered a Litany to be sung by a seven-fold procession of clergy, laity, monks, virgins, matrons, widows, poor and children. This practice with variations was continued through the centuries, and in modified form was taken over by the Prayer Book of Edward VI, so that a Litany is found today in our Anglican and Episcopal Prayer Books. It consists of thirty short petitions chanted by the minister, with the repetition of the briefest of prayers by the people: "Good Lord, deliver us"; or "We beseech thee to hear us, Good Lord." To hear this Litany chanted by a great congregation, the alternate tenuous voice of the priest followed by the short tumultuous responses of choir and people, is like listening to the storm waves beating upon the shore. It is an insistent bombardment of heaven by those who refuse to take No for an answer. There is nothing quite so impressive in any Dissenting service.

Although thirteen hymns from Pollock's Litanies are found in our hymnals, only one qualifies for our special notice. Its petitions are different from any of those found in the Prayer Book:

### *Jesus, with thy Church abide*    [1871]

No one can dispute the rightness and urgency of most of these petitions in the original eighteen stanzas. We might even transfer the subject of them from the Church to the United Nations organization, without any omissions. It is only when we limit God to the Established Church, especially the High Church of Pollock's day, that we cannot see the absence of social vision which characterizes this litany.

### Rev. GODFREY THRING (1823–1903) Anglican, High

GODFREY THRING was a member of a distinguished family. His father was a rector, one brother was Lord Thring, another was Headmaster of Uppingham School for boys, which he brought up to effective rivalry with Harrow, Rugby and Eton.

Thring was a graduate of Balliol College, Oxford. Against his father's wishes but over-persuaded by his strong-willed mother, he became a clergyman and ultimately took over his father's "living" and rectory at Alford-with-Hornblotton. This place was an inconspicuous bit of country-side in south-central England not far from Glastonbury—King Arthur's ancient seat; and for ecclesiastical honors he was finally named in addition as Prebendary (honorary canon or member of the staff) of Wells Cathedral, associated with the names of hymnists Ken and Plumptre.

This community-with-the-double-name is typical of a good many English "livings." It is very old: the Alford parish preserves records back to about 1300 A.D. and its All Saints Church was built in the fourteenth century. The people were said to be "fighting farmers" and milk-men, rough and quarrelsome, though today they all seem peaceable enough. The second parish added to the first is Hornblotton. Its Church of St. Peter's stands in

One of Godfrey Thring's two churches, All Saints, Alford.

Prosperous farm at Hornblotton, Thring's other parish.

the midst of cow-pastures and hard by a huge manor-house belonging to the squire or the lord of the district. Whatever their former populations, Alford parishioners today number 50 people and Hornblotton 75. Yet the "living" is sufficient to keep a gentleman-rector in state and upkeep the fine old rectory surrounded by lawns and trees including an ancient Cedar of Lebanon. One can see that reading the service twice a day—attended by a handful or nobody—communions *ad lib.*, and a twenty-minute sermon once a week would leave plenty of time for hymn-writing and other scholarly tasks.

The famous Thring family are commemorated in Alford Church by beautifully-carved choir seats in the chancel, and two memorial windows.

While Godfrey Thring was rector here he wrote all his hymns and compiled at least four hymnals. The last of these (1882), which set a high literary standard, was intended to be an all-church book in protest against the sectarian and party hymnals that divided the Christian unity. Of it his schoolmaster brother wrote:

> Be sure that no painting, no art work you could have done, could have been so powerful for good. . . . As long as the English language lasts, sundry of your hymns will be read and sung . . . and many a soul of God's best creatures will thrill at your words. What more can a man want?

A little fulsome perhaps, but in a measure deserved.

Thring's High Church slant is shown in the title of his volume, *Hymns and Poems for the Holy Days and the Festivals of the Church.* Yet in general it must be said that his High Churchmanship is not obtrusive. Benson classifies him as representative of the Literary School, "as contrasted with the subjective and didactic method of the Evangelicals, the close adherence to scripture of Bishop Wordsworth and the tendency toward Liturgical verse in the Liturgical school." We can form a fair judgment of his contribution by considering the following hymns:

### *From the eastern mountains*     [1873]

Sometimes classified under "Epiphany" and, owing to the four-four tune to which it is set, sometimes used as a processional.

The first two stanzas visualize and emotionalize the story of the Magi given in Mt 2:1–2, 9–12; the remaining stanzas are a prayer to Jesus that He will accomplish certain things: viz.

*Stanza 3.* Bring the heathen into His kingdom.
*Stanza 4.* Reclaim the outcasts, the back-sliders and the unreached.
*Stanza 5.* Illumine Jew and Gentile alike (fulfilling the hopes of Paul: Gal. 3:14; 1 Cor 12:13; Rom 10:12).
*Stanza 6.* Redeem every nation, bond or free, and bring them all to heaven.

This makes therefore an excellent missionary hymn as well as a plea for the consecration of the individual life.

As a piece of literature it is a trifle ornate for modern taste, in the style of Heber and the Romantic School of fifty years earlier. In spite of its presence in eight of our hymnals, it is seldom or never sung today.

## Saviour, blessed Saviour    [1862]

Originally ten stanzas written under the title "The Goal," later changed to "Pressing Onwards." It is based upon Paul's words in Phil 3:14, "I press toward the goal unto the prize of the high calling of God in Christ Jesus."

The consciously artificial structure of the hymn is shown in the patterns of first lines: "Nearer, ever nearer" (2); "Great and ever greater" (3); etc. Throughout is also noticeable the tendency to stylize the pattern: "All, All, All" (stanzas 1:5, 6, 8); "Thou, Thou" (stanzas 2:5, 7); "Where, Where" (stanzas 3:5, 7); "Journeying, Journeying" (stanzas 5:2, 4). Though not obtrusively theological, Anselm and the Apostles' Creed peer at us through such items as "Cam'st on earth to die," "gone up on high"; the Communion of Saints is hinted in "worn by saints before us" (stanza 5) and "Saints with angels sing" (stanza 6); while the emphasis on personal salvation in heaven is always present. One would think that the political, economic and scientific revolutions that by 1862 had made great inroads on the old order would be hinted in at least some small detail in this glorification of the Christian ideal, but evidently these changes had not penetrated to the rectory of Alford-with-Hornblotton.

### ANONYMOUS

## Away in a manger, no crib for his bed

No trace of an author for this perfect child's hymn has been found nor has the date of its composition been established. It needs no interpretation, for both in thought and imagery it is on the child's level.

Somewhere between 1904–8 Methodist Bishop William Anderson asked his friend Dr. John T. McFarland, Secretary of the Methodist Board of Sunday Schools, New York, to write a third stanza. This is now printed in several of our hymnals. It breaks away from the descriptive-narrative point of view and simplicity of the original, and introduces ideas which are not yet part of a child's world.

## Mrs. DOROTHY FRANCES GURNEY (1858–1932) Anglican and Catholic

HER father and grandfather were both clergymen, the latter a bishop. In 1919 she and her husband Gerald Gurney were received into the Catholic Church at Farnborough Abbey.

### *O perfect love, all human thought transcending* [1883]

This, her one poem that has survived in popular use, was written for her sister's wedding while she was Miss Bloomfield. The writing took only fifteen minutes one Sunday evening while she was at Windermere in the English Lake region, haunt of Wordsworth and the other Lake Poets. In England it rapidly became the most popular wedding hymn.

Christ is here addressed under two titles that have special significance for marriage: perfect love and perfect life. These are the two great ideals—motive and performance—which when neglected in life's strenuous course will wreck any home. When measurably maintained they yield what stanza 3 calls joy instead of sorrow, peace instead of strife. This is another name for Heaven.

# HISTORICAL SUMMARY

*Low Church Hymnists*

| | | |
|---|---|---|
| 1837–1901 | Queen VICTORIA. | |
| 1838–48 | Chartist Movement for extension of franchise and social reforms. | Gurney, 1838 |
| 1843 | Free Church of Scotland founded. | |
| 1845 | Growth of Anti-Corn Law League. Three million die of famine in Ireland. Many Anglicans turn Catholic. | Alford, 1844–71 |
| 1846 | Repeal of Corn Laws, to the advantage of the poor. | |
| 1847 | Karl Marx: *Sketch of Communism.* | Maude, 1847 |
| | Parliament prohibits women and children working more than 10 hours a day in factories. | |
| 1848 | Thackeray's *Vanity Fair* lambastes vices of great and wealthy. | |
| | Christian Socialists found Queen's College for women. | Waring, 1850 |
| 1851 | Earl of Shaftesbury presses for slum clearance and other reforms. | |
| 1854 | Christian Socialists found Workingman's College. | Croly, 1854 |
| 1855 | Spencer: *Principles of Psychology* (materialistic). | |
| 1858 | East India Co. absorbed by British Government. | |
| 1860 | Free Trade becomes England's policy. | Bickersteth, 1860–75 |
| 1863–5 | Dean Stanley: *History of Jewish Church* applies development theory to Judaism and the Bible. | Em. Elliott, 1864 |
| 1866 | Colenso controversy over Higher Criticism. | Hankey, 1866 |
| 1867 | Franchise extended to lower-income citizens. | |
| | Karl Marx: *Capital,* textbook of social revolution. | |
| 1867–81 | Privy Council decisions adverse to High Church ritualists. | |
| 1869 | Protestant Church in Ireland disestablished. | |
| 1871 | Religious tests for university degrees abolished. | |
| 1876 | Growth of Imperialism: Victoria proclaimed Empress of India. Compulsory education established in England. | Havergal, 1872–7 |
| 1886 | *Reform Act*; universal manhood suffrage. | |
| 1897 | Queen Victoria's Jubilee Celebration. | |
| 1898–1902 | Boer War. | |

# THE VICTORIAN ERA:
# THE EVANGELICAL OR LOW CHURCH HYMNS

As OUTLINED IN CHAPTER VI, Evangelicalism began in the mid-eighteenth century. Connected with the founding are the names of Anglican George Whitefield, the Countess of Huntingdon and their group of helpers. Even more successful in reaching the unchurched and lower-middle classes were the Wesleys, who to the day of their death were Anglican clergymen. One of the purest leavening influences came from the humble John Newton and his friend William Cowper, who by example and through their Olney Hymns showed the average man how to be a Christian.

Throughout the later eighteenth and early nineteenth centuries the leaven was working strongly. It developed leaders among the upper classes. Most phenomenal was a congeries of extraordinary men whom Sydney Smith dubbed "The Clapham Sect" because their focal point was the aristocratic suburb of Clapham (now S.W. London). These men were rich Evangelical philanthropists. For example, there was banker Henry Thornton who between 1790 and 1793 gave to charity £20,400 while all his other disbursements were only £6,964. There was William Wilberforce who in 1801 gave away £3,000 more than his entire income. There was Zachary Macaulay, Governor of Sierra Leone in West Africa, a colony of emancipated Negroes whom the Clapham set wanted to raise to decency and citizenship. Among them also was a Governor-General of India, a Chairman of the East India Company, the Chief of the Colonial Office, several members of Parliament, and publicists, who together accomplished probably a greater amount of good to more millions of people than any other group England ever raised. While in that fellowship were Non-Conformists, Quakers and Independents, the members were predominantly Anglican, their common bond was Evangelical Christianity and their one aim was "to apply the ethic of Christ to personal, social, political, national and international affairs; . . . and especially to raise the level of underprivileged people who hitherto had been exploited and enslaved by vast mercenary interests for sordidly selfish ends." The historian Halévy says of them,

"Never in the history of Anglicanism had any party exercised so profound an influence."

These men were laymen, all students of the Bible, all men of prayer. They "gave freely of their time, talents and means that public life might be Christianized and that the very Empire might become an instrument of moral and social welfare to all peoples." Their effect upon Parliamentary legislation was out of all proportion to their numbers. Wilberforce, who had been converted from a life of respectable profligacy by reading a book by Doddridge, spearheaded the war against slavery which after more than thirty years was won throughout the Empire (1833). These men fought for the limitation of working hours, more humane factory conditions for pauper child labor, the humanizing of England's barbarous penal code, the launching and sustaining of the Trades Union movement. Nor did they neglect the reform of abuses within the Anglican Church, which the High Church group fought viciously to retain: "They sought to expel from the parsonages Parson Dolittle and Parson Merryman and to replace them by Parson Lovegood."

These men and those inspired by them founded the *Society for the Suppression of Vice* (1802); the *National Society for the Education of the Poor* (1811) which within twenty years was maintaining 13,000 schools. John Howard, the genius who reformed the prisons of England, though a Dissenter, was inspired by the Evangelical spirit. The 7th Earl of Shaftesbury, a self-styled Evangelical of the Evangelicals, was the chief power behind the factory reforms (1833–67), was president also of the *Ragged School Union* (1844) whose purpose was "to catch, befriend and educate human eels in the mud." Elizabeth Fry was a woman saint who created the *Association for the Improvement of Female Prisoners in Newgate,* and the *Ladies Association for Visiting Gaols* (c. 1813). Pressure on the East India Company to open India to missionaries, the formation of the great *Church Mission Society* and others (1795–1812), of the *Religious Tract Society,* the *British and Foreign Bible Society* (1804) and other similar enterprises, were also the work of Evangelicals.

But the essence of Evangelicalism is individual piety. It concerns the inner life, one's relationship not to a divine and historic institution but to God. The chief service the Low Church group rendered to its parent body was to infuse into it "a new fire and passion of devotion. . . . It raised the standard of clerical duty, completely altered the tone and tendency of its preaching . . . and became the undisputed center of religious activity in England." The emphasis was less on Sacraments, the Liturgy of the Church Year, and not at all on the esthetics of worship, but predominantly on the necessity of a New Birth and the guidance of the Holy Spirit in the individual life.

An example of the desperate need for an awakening was the condition of Cambridge University in the early 1800's:

THE ORIGIN OF SUNDAY SCHOOLS, HARE LANE, GLOUCESTER, 1780.

A typical picture of poverty and juvenile neglect such as the Evangelicals tried to remedy. Robert Raikes, founder of this school, stands in front of the court entrance.

> The discipline had sunk to the lowest point. The clerical society of many of the colleges was in not a few cases actually disreputable. A shameless intemperance was among the curses. . . . In the churches, even during the most solemn rites, confusion and disorder reigned. . . . Celebrations of the Holy Communion were miserably attended. Church life seemed dead.

It took the inspiring leadership of Charles Simeon to effect a revolution. He was the incumbent of Trinity Church in the center of Cambridge and a Fellow of King's College. For many years he was insulted and persecuted, but before his death in 1836 his church was packed to the doors and over-flowed into the street. His influence became measureless, for with Cambridge as a center it spread everywhere. It worked upward and downward through all ranks of society. Whereas when he began church attendance was spotty and irregular throughout England, within fifty years the majority of people in the average village or town were regular church-goers and their children were constant at Sunday School; Sunday games were forbidden, family prayers became common, the pervasive vices of gambling, drinking and prostitution were greatly reduced or driven under cover. It brought rectitude, unselfishness and humanity into high places, and at the top, the immoral court of William IV became in due time the righteous and almost prudish court of Victoria. When an African chief was once presented at court, he asked his queen to tell him the secret of England's greatness. Victoria gave him a Bible and said, "This is the secret."

Such in brief is the record of pre-Victorian Evangelicalism. But by the middle of the nineteenth century the fervor for reform that once characterized the Evangelicals had been taken over by different groups: by the Chartists, the second generation of Trade Unionists, by the Free Traders, the Christian Socialists, and the like. Then too, the "Golden Age" of British capitalism (1850–75) was easing life for all classes. But, though abandoning their reforming zeal, the Evangelicals retained their distinctive note of personal piety. It is that note alone that finds expression in their hymnody. In their hymns of this later period their Calvinism is disguised, is present by implication more than by assertion; the Bible is still the authoritative revelation of God and its reminiscent phrases crop out in most religious verse. But the inroads of science, of materialistic philosophy and Biblical Criticism are transferring intellectual leadership in Anglicanism from both High Church and Evangelical groups to Broad Church. The emergence of this third party we shall consider in the last section of this chapter.

### Canon *JOHN HAMPDEN GURNEY* (*1802–62*) Anglican, Low

SON of a baron, educated at Trinity College, Cambridge, curate at the old parish of Lutterworth made famous by the heroic ministrations, Bible translation and missionary work of John Wyclif (c. 1320–84). Though as a person of wealth and position he might have taken a number of superior posts elsewhere, the lovely country living at Lutterworth, with its inspiring memories, kept him seventeen years. In 1847 he became a London rector and in 1857 a prebend (honorary canon) of St. Paul's Cathedral. One of his main outside interests was the Society for the Promotion of Christian Knowledge; the other was hymnody. He compiled two collections, one for his Lutterworth and one for his London church. The following hymn is from his Lutterworth collection:

### *Lord, as to thy dear Cross we flee* [1838]

The hymn runs true to Low Church form. No ecclesiastical interest is in evidence; the one theological reference is, as usual, to the Cross as the means of salvation, and the last five stanzas are a description of the ideals of the transformed life.

*Stanza 1.* The beginning of the Christian life is forgiveness at the foot of the Cross. The rest of that life is imitation of Christ.
*Stanza 2.* The enumeration of particulars now begins: constancy in bearing our daily load; sympathy with others' afflictions;
*Stanza 3.* Altruism, spirituality, kindness;
*Stanza 4.* Acceptance of sorrow as God's will;

*Stanza* 5. Overcoming unjust accusations, slander and deceit, by love;

*Stanza* 6. Peace and tolerance; following in the footsteps of Christ.

Because these ideals of the Evangelicals were more and more embraced by the middle and upper classes of England, Victoria's reign saw an impressive advance in public and private morality.

## Dean HENRY ALFORD (1810–71) Anglican, Low

SON of a rector, educated at Trinity College, Cambridge; successively curate to his father, vicar, incumbent at Quebec Chapel, London, and finally (1857) Dean of Canterbury Cathedral. His instincts were literary. He started, and for some time edited, *The Contemporary Review,* published a volume called *English Descriptive Poetry,* another on *The Queen's English.* But he became preeminent for his Greek scholarship: he edited an edition of *Homer,* and his four-volume edition of the *Greek Testament* on which he labored for twenty years became the standard critical commentary. He was also a member of the committee which revised the New Testament, 1881. Greatly interested in hymnology, he translated hymns and himself composed, but his hymn-writing added little to his literary reputation.

His position in ecclesiastical matters is indicated by his book, *A Dissuasive Against Rome,* in which he rejected the High Church emphases that had led many like Newman and Faber into the Roman fold. He really occupied a middle position between High and Low, as is shown by his hymn, "In token that thou shalt not fear" (A, S). He entitled it, "Lines on the sign of the cross in Baptism":

> In token that thou shalt not fear
> Christ crucified to own,
> We print the cross upon thee here,
> And stamp thee his alone.

This is not the baptismal regeneration of the High Church but an act of dedication to Christ, as the concluding pious wish shows:

> And may the brow that wears his cross
> Hereafter share his crown.

As Benson puts it, "He was liturgical but not sacramentarian." Another writes, "A strenuous worker, never idle, at the end of a hard day's work he would stand up, as at the end of a meal, and thank God for what he had received. He was catholic-spirited, a supporter of the Evangelical Alliance, and throughout his life maintained cordial relations with Nonconformists. His unrealized longing to visit the Holy Land suggested the beautiful in-

Trinity College, Cambridge. While Cambridge produced fewer hymn writers than Oxford (16 in this book as against 37), some of them stand among the best.

Trinity College Bridge, Cambridge.

scription on his tombstone: 'The inn of a pilgrim travelling to Jerusalem.' " *
Of his surviving hymns the one universally used is

*Come, ye thankful people, come*    [1844]

In the liturgical books this hymn stands under "Harvest." Stanza 1 is
an invitation to thank God in His earthly temple for His bounty. The two

Canterbury Ca-
thedral: "Forward
be our watch-
word" was writ-
ten for a festival
here.

following stanzas are an elaboration of the Parable of the Tares and Christ's
explanation of it (Mt 13:24–30, 36–43). There good people are the wheat
which some day will go into the garner (heaven), while tares are bad people
who some day will be burned (in hell). The fourth stanza is a rather un-
welcome prayer that we may die soon and go to heaven. It is no wonder that
*Hymns Ancient and Modern* changed this stanza, but so unsuccessfully that
Dr. Alford would not accept it. There is no need of praying for angels to
help us sing a harvest hymn.

* Moffat and Patrick: *Handbook to the Revised Church Hymnary,* by permission of
The Oxford University Press.

## *Ten thousand times ten thousand*    [1867]

This is a processional for Saints' Days, but it is also classified under Life Everlasting, or even under General Hymns. It describes the pageantry of heaven on that great day after the Last Judgement when the gates of heaven are flung open and all the elect from every nation come thronging in for the endless eternity of bliss. Primarily it is based upon suggestions from the Book of Revelation, especially Chaps. 21–22.

The description stands as a late arrival in a long line. The earliest hymnic account is probably "Jerusalem, the blessed city," dating from the seventh century (See Chap. IX under Seventh Century, "Angularis fundamentum"). Then in the twelfth century arose the marvellous song of Bernard of Cluny, "*De contemptu mundi*" from which came "Brief life is here our portion" and "Jerusalem the golden" (Chap. IX, under Bernard of Cluny).

There is no denying that Dean Alford has painted a sumptuous picture filled with emotion—the numberless throng, the sparkling raiment, the mountain of light up which the elect float, the golden gates flung open to conquerors, the alleluias, the thousand harps, the raptured greetings, the union of those long separated, and finally the prayer that all this may soon come to pass. But while these visions of bliss may serve to soothe the suffering and dying they are a far cry from the true inspirations needed by men who are doing the world's work. They are all based upon Christian mythology, which in turn harks back to Jewish Apocalypse. The pictures are works of the imagination. Whether they correspond to fact we have no present means of finding out. Our concepts of God, of Jesus, of salvation, of the universe shot through with gamma rays, cosmic rays and radioactivity, have so changed within the last hundred years that modern man can find no place for such a heaven—except as a symbol of man's faith that

All we have willed or hoped or dreamed of good, shall exist;
     Not its semblance, but itself.

## *Forward be our watchword*    [1871]

The language and imagery of this hymn are largely scriptural. Here are the references and some comments:

*Stanza 1.* Phil 3:13–14
Ex 13:21–22. This description is based upon the march of Israel through the wilderness, led by Moses, guided by the fiery pillar, fighting the Amalekites and other tribes, at last crossing the Jordan to the Promised Land (the Christian symbols of death and heaven).
*Stanza 2.* Here is beautifully sketched the march from infancy to old age, inspired by the watchword "Forward!" Here is also a suggestion of modernism: nature interpreted by science is as much a part of education as is religion.
*Stanza 3.* Rev 21:1–3; 1 Cor 2:9; 2 Cor 3:14–16; 5:7.
*Stanza 4.* Rev 21:10, 14, 18–21; 22: 1–2; Heb 11:10, 13.

*Stanza 5.* A description of Canterbury Cathedral under the lofty vaults of which the processional was sung. Any other noble edifice can be substituted. Rev 7:4–12.

*Stanza 6.* Contrasting Canterbury with the city that needs no temple: Rev 21:22. "These courts" are Canterbury Cathedral. 1 Cor 3:1–2; 1 Pet 2:2.

*Stanza 7.* This Trinitarian formula is witness that Dean Alford is an orthodox churchman and that his Evangelicalism is only a difference in emphasis from that of his High Church brethren. Being Dean in the Archbishop's own cathedral, the mother-church of England, he would feel need of making his hymn acceptable to all.

Written for the tenth Festival of the Canterbury Diocesan Choral Union, June 6, 1871, and expanded from Ex 14:15, "Speak unto the children of Israel, that they go forward." In his exposition of the hymn in his *Songs of Praise Discussed,* Percy Dearmer gives an authentic account of its composition, which may be paraphrased as follows:

Mr. J. G. Wood, the "parson-naturalist" and the Precentor at the cathedral, insisted against the wishes of Dean Alford that they have a processional and suggested that the Dean write both words and music. The Dean graciously yielded and in due time sent in a hymn. Wood returned it with the comment that though excellent as poetry it was not adapted to marching: "Would he kindly go into his cathedral, walk slowly along the course which the procession would take, and compose another hymn as he did so?" The Dean was gracious enough to comply, and the result was the present hymn. In sending it the Dean wrote that he had put it into its hat and boots, and that Mr. Wood might add the coat and trousers for himself, which was his way of saying that he had supplied only treble and bass without the intermediate harmony. The hymn was accordingly sung by 900 choristers.

"The effect was almost overwhelming. It took a full half-hour for the entire procession to pass within the choir screen. Each pair of choristers started singing when they reached a specified spot, and ceased singing when they set foot on the last step of the ascent to the choir, so that there was a continuous and harmonious volume of praise." *

The Dean did not live to hear the hymn sung.

### Mrs. MARY FOWLER MAUDE (1819–1913) Anglican, Low

"WHILE yet in her teens she wrote three textbooks, based on the writings of Eastern travellers, on *Scripture Manners and Customs, Scripture Topography,* and *Scripture Natural History*—a rather ambitious program for

* H. Augustine Smith: *Lyric Religion.*

one so young. These, published by the (Evangelical) Society for the Promotion of Christian Knowledge were widely used for many years." At twenty-two she married a vicar assigned to a living in the Isle of Wight. When Mr. Maude was transferred to Chick in Wales she conducted crowded classes among the miners of the district, and after the death of her husband she taught in near-by Overton a Sunday class for young men. "When at ninety-three she lay dying, the young men begged leave to sing outside her door her own hymn, 'Thine forever' and another of hers, a favorite with them, 'Will your anchor hold?' Her message in farewell was, 'Tell them that it does not fail—it holds!' " *

### Thine forever, God of love    [1847]

The author writes: "Written for my class in the Girls' Sunday School [of her husband's church] and published in 1848 at the beginning of a little book called *Twelve Letters on Confirmation, by a Sunday School Teacher.*" The letters had been written week by week during Mrs. Maude's absence, and the original verses occurred almost impromptu at the end of one of them.

The confirmation ceremony (from the Latin, *confirmo*, to make firm) is that Sacrament by which after due instruction a young person ratifies the promise made for him at his infant baptism. A necessary preliminary is that he "can say the Creed, the Lord's Prayer, and the Ten Commandments; and can also answer to such other questions as in the short Catechism are contained." The purpose is given in the Prayer Book in these words: "To the end that children, being now come to the years of discretion, and having learned what their Godfathers and Godmothers promised for them in Baptism, may themselves with their own mouth and consent, openly before the Church, ratify and confirm the same; and also promise, that, by the grace of God, they will evermore endeavor themselves faithfully to observe such things, as they, by their own confession, have assented unto."

Then shall the Bishop say,
"Do ye here . . . renew the solemn promise . . . ratifying and confirming the same?"
And every one shall audibly answer,
"I do."

Perhaps the best commentary on the hymn, because it agrees with it in every petition, is the Bishop's prayer that follows:

Almighty and everliving God, who hast vouchsafed to regenerate these thy servants by Water and the Holy Ghost, and hast given unto them forgiveness of all their sins; Strengthen them, we beseech thee, O Lord, with the Holy Ghost, the Comforter, and daily increase in them thy manifold gifts of grace; the spirit of

* Moffat and Patrick: Handbook to the *Revised Church Hymnary*, by permission of The Oxford University Press.

wisdom and understanding, the spirit of counsel and ghostly
strength, the spirit of knowledge and true godliness; and fill them,
O Lord, with the spirit of thy holy fear, now and for ever. Amen.


### ANNA LAETITIA WARING (1820–1910) Anglican, Low

SHE was born in Wales and latterly lived in Bristol, England.
Though brought up in the Society of Friends, the impressive Sacraments
of the Anglican Church early drew her to unite with that body (1842). She
began to write hymns in her teens; completed thirty-nine of them by 1863.
In order to read Old Testament poetry in the original she learned Hebrew,
and, thereafter, daily read her Hebrew Psalter. She had a gentle but merry
spirit, was drawn into philanthropic work, and in the spirit of the Evangelicals used to visit in later years the prisons of Bristol. One of her special
interests was the "Discharged Prisoners' Aid Society." An outstanding trait
was a dislike for publicity; yet her long life of ninety years was a blessing
to all who knew her or read her poems.

### *In heavenly love abiding*     [1850]

In this hymn there are no Church, no Sacraments, no liturgy. The
author tells us that consciousness of God's love accomplishes various happy
results:

*Stanza 1.* The conquest of fear.
"Here" in line 4 does not mean the circumstances of life, but the
condition of abiding in God's love. Miss Waring was hunting for a
good rhyme-word!
*Stanza 2.* Consciousness of His guidance by means of His insight
and watchful care. A reminiscence of Ps 23.
*Stanza 3.* Confidence that the future has good in store.
"My treasure" is my heart, my supreme love.

Not only are these verses sung as a hymn, but more frequently than
many others they have been set to music as an anthem.


### Rev. GEORGE CROLY (1780–1860) Anglican, Low

SON of a Dublin physician, educated at Trinity College, Dublin,
curate in a small North-Ireland parish, he came to London about 1810 and
for twenty-five years engaged in literary work—biographical, historical,
scriptural, poetic, serious, humorous; he wrote tragedies, comedies, satires,
novels, songs. In 1835 Lord Brougham, a Whig patron and relative, gave him
a couple of "livings" in London, one of them St. Stephen's in the slum section
of the city. Here he reopened a pulpit that had been closed for a hundred
years, and proved to be a magnetic preacher.

He was a fundamentalist in theology, a fierce conservative in politics, opposed to all forms of liberalism. When his flock wanted a hymnbook he prepared one. It contained both Psalms and hymns, the majority of them from his own pen. His one surviving hymn would indicate that he was Evangelical rather than High Church.

## Spirit of God, descend upon my heart     [1854]

This is a passionate hymn, emotional and personal to the core. It is a prayer for the indwelling Spirit of God to take complete possession of body and soul. There is not a trace of Apostolic Church or Nicene Creed, and only a suggestion of theology in the brief reference to the Cross (stanza 2).

*Stanza 1.* The first effect of the Spirit's indwelling is to change the focus of life from things temporal (earth) to things spiritual—to love God.

*Stanza 2.* This love consists of the dedication of one's entire personality—soul, heart, strength, mind—to the King who rightfully claims loyalty, and to the Cross that saves. Notice the allusion to the lawyer's reference to the Great Commandment, Lk 10:27.

*Stanza 3.* The second effect of the divine presence is to quell the impatience of the soul when confronted by struggle, doubt, rebellion, delayed answer to prayer.

*Stanza 4.* The final petition is for an absolute and unqualified possession by love—the result of a baptism by the Spirit, of which the dove is symbol. The last line "My heart an altar, and thy love the flame," is one of the most beautiful metaphors found in any hymn.

The great world with its wickedness, its suffering, its struggles for a nobler civic and a juster economic life, is not present here. There is no science, no sociology, no Biblical Criticism. The poet has entered into his closet and shut the door.

## Bishop EDWARD HENRY BICKERSTETH (1825–1906) Anglican, Low

THE Bishop's father was a clergyman, at one time a missionary to West Africa and later the first secretary to the Church Missionary Society. He was also a poet and the editor of *Christian Psalmody,* the best Evangelical hymnal of its time.

Edward, his son, was a graduate of Trinity College, Cambridge, took holy orders in 1848 and rose by steady steps from curate to rector, vicar, Dean of Gloucester Cathedral and Bishop of Exeter (1885–1900). Following in his father's footsteps he became a poet (twelve volumes!) and editor of *The Hymnal Companion to the Book of Common Prayer* (1870). This book, in which the original text of hymns was tinkered with much less than usual, soon practically superseded all other Evangelical hymnbooks.

Bickersteth was a great lover of hymns. His son writes:

> It was his invariable custom to expect each one of us on Sundays at tea to repeat a hymn, and he did the same unless, as frequently happened, he wrote us a special hymn himself, in which way many of his hymns were first given to the Church.

Julian says of him:

> Joined with a strong grasp of his subject, true poetic feeling, a pure rhythm, there is a soothing plaintiveness and individuality in his hymns which give them a distinct character of their own. His thoughts are usually with the individual and not with the mass; with the single soul and his God, and not with a vast multitude bowed in adoration before the Almighty.

Theoretically this individual approach is not desirable in hymns, for the true hymn must be framed for the use of congregations. This may account for the gradual dropping of Bickersteth from our hymnals. Of all he wrote, A preserves the largest number, 14; U, 4; S none. Two are still widely used, as shown below.

### O God, the Rock of Ages    [1860]

*Stanza 1.* Ps 90:1-2.
The "Rock of Ages" as a figure for God is not scriptural and was probably borrowed by Bickersteth from Toplady's hymn. Nevertheless there are in scripture thirty-five allusions to God as Rock; e.g., 1 Sam 2:2; 2 Sam 22:2-3, 32; Ps 18:31.
*Stanza 2.* Contrasted with the immutability and eternity of God is the evanescence of human life. This is made vivid by figures from nature and our inner experiences. Scriptural allusions are Ps 90:4-6; 102:11.
*Stanza 3.* Practically a paraphrase of Ps 121:4; 90: 12, 14-17.
*Stanza 4.* The almost invariable ending for all pre-twentieth century hymns is a picture of heaven as compensation for all the deficiencies of temporal life. Most of the imagery is taken from Rev 21-22.

### Peace, perfect peace, in this dark world of sin?    [1875]

"Thou wilt keep him in perfect peace, whose mind is stayed on thee: because he trusteth in thee." Is 26:3.

The hymn was written under unusual circumstances. Bishop Bickersteth was visiting his aged relative, Archdeacon Hill of Liverpool, who was sick unto death and his mind greatly clouded. Eager to comfort him, the Bishop read to him the text from Isaiah quoted above, and then in a few minutes at the bedside composed this hymn and read it to the dying

Edward Henry Bickersteth, Bishop of Exeter.

man. Later the hymn was printed on cards and given by the hundred to young people at their Confirmation by the Bishop. His biographer says of it:

> Its popularity spread rapidly. It is loved and sung by persons of all ranks and conditions. It is said to have been a favorite of Queen Victoria. It has been translated into many languages; and the Bishop heard it sung in Japanese and Chinese on his tour in the East.*

The unusual form of question and answer given to each two-lined stanza adapts it to antiphonal singing.

The questions form a series of challenges to our faith: in each case Jesus is the key that resolves the dilemma. In plain prose these challenges and answers may be stated thus:

* F. K. Aglionby: *Life of E. H. Bickersteth,* Longmans, New York, 1907.

Is it sin that wrecks our peace? The answer is, Trust the Atonement.
Is it the pressure of work? Then let your acts conform to His will.
Is it sorrow? Take your sorrow to Him.
Is it separation? Trust Him to keep your loved ones.
Is it the unknown future? Trust the ruler of the universe, Jesus.
Is death staring you in the face? Remember Jesus' resurrection.
These specific answers are reassuring, for all will soon be over and
heaven is the final escape from all our problems.

These are the answers of a theologian and a mystic. The modern man
will question the Blood, our ability always to discover the will of Jesus, the
exact meaning of "On Jesus' bosom," the fallacy of thinking that accidents
will never happen to those we love, how Jesus' being on a throne is going
to tie in with the alleged freedom of the will, what "powers" were vanquished when Jesus survived death, and finally how all this, like the old
Chinese solution—saying, "This too will pass"—is anything more than
stoicism, and how the prospect of heaven can be a solution of present difficulties. The hymn sounds pious, but it offers only a Calvinist-Evangelical
traditional answer. Jewish Isaiah's statement (26:3) is more helpful because
it eliminates a doubtful theology and urges conformity to the laws of the
universe, physical and spiritual that constitute for him and us a personal
God. Perhaps that is what Bickersteth boils down to, but he clouds the issue.

## EMILY ELIZABETH STEELE ELLIOTT (1836–97) Anglican, Low

SHE was a clergyman's daughter and niece to Charlotte Elliott
(see above), like whom she was deeply interested in philanthropy and
Evangelical Sunday School work. For six years she edited a magazine called
*The Church Missionary Juvenile Instructor.* Forty-eight of her hymns were
printed in *Under the Pillow,* a book with tunes for the special use of people
in hospitals and infirmaries, or those sick at home.

### Thou didst leave thy throne and thy kingly crown      [1864]

The text for the hymn was Lk 2:7, "There was no room for them in the
inn."

The verses were privately printed for the choir and school children of
her father's church at Brighton. They are admirably suited to the level of
children, for they are descriptive and they use the imagery of the Bible.
Children would not discern behind the words such theological ideas as
Jesus' pre-existence in heaven, the doctrine of the Atonement, his restoration to heaven as God's supreme Vicegerent—all compressed by Paul into
Phil 2:5–11; also found in 1 Pet 3:22; Heb 1:2–8.

A contrast runs through four stanzas: Jesus, heaven's prince, became
a peasant for our sake.

*Stanza 1.* "Throne," "no room"; St. 2: "royal degree," "great humility";

*Stanza 3.* Creatures have homes, but for Him the desert (Mt 8:20);

*Stanza 4.* He came bringing redemption, but men gave Him Calvary.

*Stanza 5.* The contrast is reversed: death is changed into victory, and the ringing arches of stanza 2 here ring again. Finally—personalizing the story—if there was no room on earth for Him, yet there is room in heaven (for me).

The purpose of such a hymn is indicated by its classification in our hymnals: "Evangelistic Missions" (A); "Acceptance of Christ" (B); "For Children" (L); "Advent and Nativity" (M). Strangely, E classifies it as "General."

## ARABELLA KATHERINE HANKEY (1834–89) Anglican, Low

ARABELLA KATHERINE, familiarly known as Kate and now as Katherine, was daughter of a banker-member of the "Clapham Sect" (see above, Introduction to this chapter). While still in school she and her sister became enthusiastic Sunday School teachers in their home suburb. When she was eighteen she started a Bible class for shopgirls in London. It had an immense and lasting influence: some of the members became permanent religious workers. Later she started a class among her own social set, with similar lasting results. She became deeply interested also in Missions. This grew out of her trip to South Africa to look after and bring home an invalid brother, when that area was still primitive and transportation was by bullock-cart only. To the mission cause she contributed all the royalties from her various publications. These works included *Bible Class Teachings,* a booklet on *Confirmation,* and *The Old, Old Story and Other Verses.* Her ability and her consecration made her an outstanding member of the Evangelical group.

### *I love to tell the story* [1866]

The whole long poem entitled "The Old, Old Story," from which this hymn is excerpted, was written under three headings:

1. *The Story Wanted.* This part, from which the familiar hymn, "Tell me the old, old story" is taken, presents the sinner's desire to hear. The pictures drawn for the American Tract Society's edition, show children asking their mother for the story; a young man in trouble asking a clergyman in his study for the story; a man suffering from failure or disaster asking his wife for the comfort of the story; the family circle about the hearth listening intently to grandfather who reads the story from the Bible.

2. *The Story Told.* This is the section from which "I love to tell" came. Pictures show a gentleman-squire (member of the Clapham Sect?) reading at the bedside of a down-and-out man; Adam and Eve in the Garden, the cause of all our misery; the angels singing the good news of the Saviour to the shepherds; the shepherds adoring the Babe of Bethlehem; Christ blessing little children, preaching from a boat, talking with Nicodemus, healing the blind; the Crucifixion, the Resurrection. These of course illustrate the story that is being told in verse.

3. *The Story Welcomed.* The scholar in his study pressing a Bible to his heart; a girl reading from the book at an old man's bedside; and finally the hosts of heaven welcoming to glory a saved soul.

All this is a complete exposition, in language simple enough for a child to understand, of the religious beliefs of the Evangelicals—omitting the ecclesiastical non-essentials so dear to High Churchmen, and a picture as well of the religious activities of the Clapham Sect and Low Church in general. One must confess that to one brought up in a similar home and atmosphere, the hymn stirs profound memories.

### FRANCES RIDLEY HAVERGAL (1836–78) Anglican, Low

MISS HAVERGAL had an excellent heritage from her father. He was a humble clergyman who through a carriage accident was permanently injured and compelled to retire for a while. For nearly twenty years he devoted his talents to the improvement of church music in England, which in the 1840's was at a very low ebb. In his book, *Old Church Psalmody* (1844), he revived the use of the solid tunes of early English composers and so did much to improve the quality of singing. The American composer, Lowell Mason, who visited his church in 1852, reported that the music there was far in advance of anything he heard elsewhere in England.

All this was a great inspiration to his talented daughter who began to write verses at the age of seven and continued to write for thirty-five years. Owing to delicate health, Frances' education was sporadic, in England and then in Düsseldorf, Germany. Ultimately her devotion to self-improvement made her proficient in Hebrew, Greek, French, German and Italian. Her early life was overshadowed by the morbid fear of not being among the Elect—a common occurrence with children in Calvinistic households (*cf.* Isaac Watts' experience, Chap. IV). But as she entered adolescence the proper "conversion" took place and thereafter her religious life was secure, happy and fruitful.

She was a natural musician. Her voice was so pleasing and well-trained that she was sought after as concert soloist, and her piano playing was brilliant. Her personality too was charming, so that she might easily have been tempted into a gay social career. But the fundamentally religious set of her nature came to dominate her life and her ambitions: after 1873 she sang nothing but sacred music. "Singing for Jesus" was her mission. Added to her music was her gift of hymn-writing. She wrote incessantly and composed music also. Her themes were faith, consecration, service, and within those limits she produced hymns which the Church has cherished ever since. But

Frances Ridley Havergal.

she was never robust and her work told on her to the extent that she once said "she hoped the angels would have orders to let her alone a bit when she first got to heaven"!

Perhaps we should properly call her an evangelist, for the ultimate purpose to which she dedicated all her powers was to bring the unconverted to Christ. This is an Evangelical ideal. A devoted High Church worker would have depended upon Baptism, religious instruction in Creed and Catechism, Confirmation, regular church attendance, regular partaking of the Eucharist, and in general, faithfulness to all church duties as the proper means of grace. Evangelicals, on the other hand, demanded less emphasis upon these aspects of religion. They stressed surrender of the will to Christ, instantaneous "conversion," and a life of prayer and altruistic work. Miss Havergal devoted herself to the limit of her strength to the task of converting people, in which work her talents and great personal charm made her well-nigh irresistible.

Many of her hymns were originally printed on leaflets, which from time to time she transferred to volumes: *Ministry of Song* (1869), *Under the Surface* (1874), *Loyal Responses* (1878). After her death her sister gathered all her poetry into one huge volume. As the years pass it is becoming evident that the vibrant personality of the author rather than the intrinsic literary merit of her poetry is what gave her hymns their contemporary popularity. Their use is now on the wane. Our ten hymnals carry a total of nineteen hymns, only two hymns are in the six necessary for consideration here.

### *Lord, speak to me that I may speak*     [1872]

"For none of us liveth to himself, and no man dieth to himself"
—Rom 14:7.

Miss Havergal called this "a Worker's Prayer." While it surely is an ideal pattern for all who are interested in promoting the Kingdom of God, it is at the same time an intimate revelation of the author's inner life—so personal that one hesitates to sing it in public. It is a prayer for the wisdom and the will to hand on to another whatever blessing God gives to His worker. Did the Lord speak to me, then I will speak; did He seek me, then I will seek. This pattern underlies the whole hymn and organizes the emotions into constructive action: seeking the lost, leading back the wandering feet, feeding the hungry with celestial food; giving strength and stability to the storm-tossed; teaching and inspiring, soothing and kindling. The hymn ends with complete self-surrender, self-effacement, so that God may be all and in all. One might almost say that this is a kodachrome film of Miss Havergal's own life during the twenty years of her mature activity.

Incidentally, one should note the absence of certain elements: the Church is not mentioned, nor the Trinity, nor the Sacraments, nor the Christian Year, nor poverty and want, unemployment nor the slum. These were not Miss Havergal's concern—though some of them may have been the Lord's; she thought all that was necessary was to get people converted and keep them so. The lyric is not institutional nor social; it is personal, inner, Evangelical, evangelistic, saintly.

Because of its perfection of structure, idealism, devotion, it will undoubtedly live and be of use indefinitely.

### *Take my life and let it be*     [1874]

Miss Havergal has left an account of the circumstances of writing:

I went for a little visit of five days. There were ten persons in the house; some unconverted and long-prayed-for, some converted but not rejoicing Christians. He gave me the prayer, "Lord, give me all in this house!" And he just *did*. Before I left the house, everyone had got a blessing. The last night of my visit I was too happy to sleep, and passed most of the night in renewal of my consecration, and these little couplets formed themselves and chimed in my heart one after another till they finished with "*Ever*, only, ALL for thee."*

* Quoted in Percy Dearmer: *Songs of Praise Discussed.*

The hymn was originally arranged as a series of couplets, each one expressing one detail of the all-inclusive first-couplet word "life": these are time, hands, feet, voice, lips, wealth, mind, will, heart, love. It ends with a reintegration of these details: myself.

Again this hymn is autobiographical, another kodachrome film. We may see Miss Havergal continuously at work (couplet 2), writing poetry, traveling here and there in her evangelistic work (3–4), singing and speaking the gospel (5–6), giving away whatever she might earn, continuously thinking, solving her problems and those of others (7–8), having no personal ambition, placing Christ first in her affection (9–10), foregoing all earthly love (she never married—and that leaves an aching void in any woman's heart) (11)—"that Christ may be all and in all" (12).

In her letters Miss Havergal reveals the details of her life even more fully than in her hymns. As to her generosity (couplet 7 above), Miss Havergal writes:

> 'Take my silver and my gold' now means shipping off all my ornaments,—including a jewel cabinet which is really fit for a countess—to the Church Missionary Society where they will be accepted and disposed of for me. I retain only a brooch for daily wear, which is a memorial of my dear parents; also a locket with the only portrait I have of my niece in heaven, Evelyn. I had no idea I had such a jeweller's shop; nearly fifty articles are being packed off. I don't think I need tell you I never packed a box with such pleasure.*

This hymn has had a career of great usefulness. It has frequently objectified for even young children what practical ways of serving Christ may be theirs in their every-day lives. No doubt this is one reason why it has been translated into so many European languages, including Russian, and on the mission field into many African and Asiatic dialects.

* Quoted in Percy Dearmer: *Songs of Praise Discussed.*

# HISTORICAL SUMMARY

*Broad Church*
*Hymnists*

| | | |
|---|---|---|
| 1837–1901 | Queen VICTORIA. | |
| 1838–48 | Chartist Movement for extension of franchise and social reforms. | Tennyson, 1840–89 |
| 1843 | Free Church of Scotland founded. | |
| 1845 | Growth of Anti-Corn Law League. Three million die of famine in Ireland. Many Anglicans turn Catholic. | |
| 1846 | Repeal of Corn Laws, to the advantage of the poor. | |
| 1847 | Karl Marx: *Sketch of Communism.* Parliament prohibits women and children working more than 10 hours a day in factories. | |
| 1848 | Thackeray's *Vanity Fair* lambastes vices of great and wealthy. Christian Socialists found Queen's College for women. | |
| 1851 | Earl of Shaftesbury presses for slum clearance and other reforms. | |
| 1854 | Christian Socialists found Workingman's College. | |
| 1855 | Spencer: *Principles of Psychology* (materialistic). | |
| 1858 | East India Co. absorbed by British Government. | How, 1858–67 |
| 1860 | Free Trade becomes England's policy. | Hughes, 1859 |
| 1863–5 | Dean Stanley: *History of Jewish Church* applies development theory to Judaism and the Bible. | |
| 1866 | Colenso controversy over Higher Criticism. | Ellerton, 1866–71 |
| 1867 | Franchise extended to lower-income citizens. Karl Marx: *Capital,* textbook of social revolution. | Bode, 1868 Twells, 1868 |
| 1867–81 | Privy Council decisions adverse to High Church ritualists. | |
| 1869 | Protestant Church in Ireland disestablished. | |
| 1871 | Religious tests for university degrees abolished. | Kingsley, 1871 |
| 1876 | Growth of Imperialism: Victoria proclaimed Empress of India. Compulsory education established in England. | Hatch, 1878 Symonds, 1880 Butler, 1881 |
| 1886 | *Reform Act*; universal manhood suffrage. | |
| 1897 | Queen Victoria's Jubilee Celebration. | Kipling, |
| 1898–1902 | Boer War. | 1897, 1906 |

# THE VICTORIAN ERA:
# BROAD CHURCH HYMNS

The third variety of Anglican whose views have found expression in hymns is called Broad Church. As the term implies, this type partakes of the nature of both the others and then adds something. The Broad Churchman, like his brother High Churchman, loves his Church, its traditions, its Sacraments, its Litany and its mission of salvation. With the Low Churchman he believes in personal piety and the work that should accompany it, in devotion to Christ as the supreme expression of God in man and to His teaching that love is the foundation of all private and public virtue. But he takes account also of the changes that science, history and philosophy have wrought in man's point of view, changes so profound that so-called "Apostolic" statements of creed must be modified in the interest of intellectual integrity; that Calvinistic theories of salvation and Bible inspiration must be abandoned for truer ones; that Sacraments, liturgies, hierarchies are valuable only insofar as they truly minister to the spiritual life of a modern man in a contemporary world; and finally that the application of religion to the social problems which threaten our civilization with destruction is mandatory.

This concern for social progress was distinctively theirs. While High Church asked men to pray—with the Prayer Book—that they may be "content with that state in which it has pleased God to call them," and while Low Church recognized the stratification of society as a fact but sought to change the private lives of men so that God might reward them with heaven, Broad Church recognized that society was in a state of evolution, and so prayed and worked that through more humane laws, more liberal citizenship, wider participation in the profits of commerce and industry through co-operatives, trades unions and the like, God and man working together might direct their "divine discontent" toward fruition in a redeemed social order.

Broad Church is not a strictly defined group; rather it consists of all those, High or Low, who choose liberal churchmanship to agnosticism. If the choice lies between throwing away Adam or the science of evolution, they throw away Adam. If the choice is between the cosmology of Genesis

407

l and that of the astronomer Herschel, they keep Herschel. If these choices necessitate reconstructing their theories of Bible inspiration and inerrancy, they accept the Higher Criticism. If in church they are called upon to sing Heber's "Holy, holy, holy, . . . God in three Persons, blessed Trinity," they will sing it with a will, but they will think of the Council of Nicaea and its fighting bishops who formulated the doctrine of the Trinity, of the exiles, excommunications and exterminations administered through the ages by the "blessed Saints" to those who could not accept it, and they will then thank God that they are now privileged to interpret the old formula as a symbol of man's inadequacy as a thinker and of the living God as man's Creator, Saviour and Inspirer. One can see how such a position would tend to lessen the harshness of theological intolerance, broaden the mission of the Church to include the use of all knowledge as instruments in the transformation of character, and make the person and work of Christ shine forth as the supreme ideal of all the sons of God.

Naturally one finds within such a wide-ranging group a great variety of individual emphasis. It included such men as Thomas Arnold, Headmaster of Rugby, who wanted to include in the Established Church all Christian sects except Roman Catholics, Quakers and Unitarians, and who described the doctrine of Apostolic Succession, on which High Church depended for its legal and spiritual validity, as "a profane heraldic theory." On the other hand, Queen Victoria appointed as Archbishop of Canterbury, highest office in the Church, that liberal administrator, Archibald Tait, and took for her religious adviser Randall Davidson, "whose wisdom, courtesy and suavity appeased and reconciled the warring elements of his Church during troublesome years." These men endeavored to conserve everything vital to the Establishment.

This diversity of opinion has always been more productive of good results than compulsory uniformity of belief and government. That old ideal, worked out by lawyer Tertullian in the third century, did indeed help the Bishop of Rome climb to his ascendancy over his less favorably situated brethren; it gave Constantine a chance to salvage the whole Church as an instrument of imperial power; it was the formula that enabled the Pope in the Middle Ages to reach the heights of autocracy and eliminate the termites of Albigenses, Waldenses, Bohemian Brethren, who gnawed at his throne. But standardization never produced Democracy or Progress—unless by standardization we mean unflinching loyalty to truth as progressively we discover it. This last was the ideal of the Broad Churchman.

As we study the hymns of these people we shall discover through their piety a social concern which other hymns of the period do not contain. We shall recognize a change in fundamental theological concepts which dethroned a static and distant God in favor of an immanent and driving personal force, and a new emphasis upon a future state for men upon this earth that contrasts strangely with the mythical heaven of the Apocalypse. This is a brand new note in hymnody.

*ALFRED LORD TENNYSON* (*1809–92*) Anglican, Broad

THE life of Tennyson is easily summarized: son of a clergyman; a student at Trinity College, Cambridge, but not a graduate; a poet who grew from modest worth in his poems of 1830 to a place of eminence in 1842 and to a position of supremacy as the years went by; Poet Laureate, 1850; a peerage, 1884; buried in Westminster Abbey.

While in college Tennyson took a lively interest in politics, supported the anti-slavery movement, the abolition of Anglican restrictions on office-

*Left,* Alfred Tennyson, age 29. *Right,* Arthur Hallam, whose death is enshrined in *In Memoriam.*

holding; hated the narrow and ignorant toryism in the country districts which was largely responsible for the farmers' riots and rick-burnings; and, as representative of an informal discussion group called "Apostles," he and his friend Hallam went to the Spanish border with a contribution to aid an insurrection against government tyranny! But "the narrowness and dryness of college instruction, the absence of any teaching that grappled with the ideas of the age . . . or subjects of deepest human interest, stirred my father to wrath." * So he left Cambridge, 1831. While in later life Tennyson never became an active partisan, the spirit of inquiry into the deep things of life never left him. The man who most strongly influenced his early thinking was Frederick D. Maurice, the "Christian Socialist" (see below under Charles Kingsley), whose religious philosophy is summed up in his saying that God is moving in the present as fully as He has moved in the past. Tennyson shows his acceptance of that faith; as Stopford Brooke puts it:

* Hallam Tennyson: *Tennyson,* Macmillan, London, 1897.

"The necessary vitality of the present . . . man alive and nature alive, and alive with the life of God—these faiths lay at the root of the religion we find in the poetry of Tennyson." *

Strange as it may seem, Tennyson never wrote any hymns. He was frequently asked to write a hymn for some special occasion but he always declined. He felt that to write a good hymn was a very difficult task for which he was not fitted. Nevertheless, in most of our hymnbooks there are

Tennyson's home, "Freshwater," Isle of Wight.

three hymns by Tennyson. Two of these consist of selected stanzas from *In Memoriam,* and the third was written as a kind of confession of faith without any thought of its ever being sung in church. To understand the first two we must know something about *In Memoriam.*

This long poem embodies Tennyson's reflections on the early death of his college friend, Arthur Hallam, whom he regarded as the most perfect man he ever met—richly endowed, precocious, combining the sensitivity of a poet and the intellectual acumen of a philosopher. He left college without graduating, read a little law in London, became engaged to Tennyson's sister, and died suddenly in Vienna (1833) at the age of twenty-two. *In Memoriam* is a poem in which Tennyson enshrined his love, his sorrow and his struggle to resolve the meaning of death and life. Its composition was spread over sixteen years. The poem was written in various places in England as the thoughts within him ripened. All these unconnected sections were finally organized into a sequence that showed the poet's change from grief, to doubt, to reconciliation; then a Prologue was added and the whole published in 1850. It made a tremendous impression and has remained one

* *Tennyson,* Putnam's, New York, 1894.

of the great revelations of the poet's inner life, of the possibility of a helpful union of Reason and Faith. Out of this long poem of 700 stanzas the Church has selected for its hymnals parts of two sections. The first of these, original section cvi, is

### Ring out, wild bells, to the wild sky    [Early 1840's]
#### Ring out the old, ring in the new

*Stanza 1. Ring out, wild bells, to the wild sky*
This song of the bells marks the poet's transition from grief to hope. Tennyson has thought through his problem; the past is behind, the new year beckons with promise of new life.

*Stanza 2. Ring out the old, ring in the new*
The "old" of the first line is the "false" of the last; the "new" is the "true." The old grief and doubt, his struggle to accept death as part of a good universe, must be replaced with joy and faith—the belief that goodness is destined to conquer evil. The succeeding stanzas particularize these contrasting states.

*Stanza 3. Ring out the grief that saps the mind*
Personal grief is really too petty and too undermining to be harbored. The great social problems that are engaging the mind of philanthropists and statesmen are much more compelling. For example: all this uprising of farmers against their rich landlords which Tennyson saw while in Cambridge—engaged in with his friends as volunteer fire brigades to help save property. But this feud between the haves and the have-nots is more than a British affair; it is a world-wide problem.

*Stanza 4. Ring out the slowly dying cause*
The old wrong causes are dying slowly because so few men are helping to hasten the process. Political parties would rather fight each other for power than fight the wrongs under which men suffer. The Established Church is a sinner in this respect as much as Whigs and Tories. Men should raise their sights and aim at great social changes that will dignify and ennoble life for all classes.

*Stanza 5. Ring out the want, the care, the sin*
How can men be so cold and faithless when great abuses cry aloud for redress? In 1842–3 a report showed that the mines in Britain were worked with incredible disregard for humanity. Children began work in the mines at 5, 6, and 7 years of age. "Monotonous beyond measure was the labor of these mites who sat in the dark for a dozen hours a day to open and shut doors. A boy of 7 smoked his pipe to keep him awake. The children employed were of both sexes, and girls of tender age were compelled to labor like beasts of burden, harnessed to trucks of coal. Pauper apprentices were practically sold into slavery and treated occasionally with the

utmost ferocity . . . The consequences of this wholesale employment underground, considering the extreme ignorance and semi-
barbarism of the colliery population, is better imagined than
described . . . A state of filth, barbarism and demoralization which
both beggars description and defies belief." * These conditions
affected 750,000 people, the entire mining population. No wonder
the young and idealistic Tennyson wrung his heart over such bar-
barity. But the Established Church did nothing about it but oppose
humanitarian legislation!

*Stanza 6. Ring out false pride in place and blood*
The stratification of society is one of the evils which the bells should
ring out: the Norman blood that flows in the veins of kings and
dukes and earls; the grand thousand-acre estates—stolen long ago
by William the Conqueror or Henry VIII and made over to their
obsequious lords in return for their support—now withheld from
cultivation by the common people because the owner wants a deer-
park and a landscape; the *nouveaux riches*—the industrialists who
hold whole city populations in essential slavery while they wax fat
and arrogant; the bishops who have bought or intrigued their way
into lofty sees that yield them £ 100,000 a year and give them a seat
in the House of Lords; the hierarchy of deans, canons, prebends,
vicars, who pull wires for promotion and spend their time in indulg-
ing their literary tastes or wintering on the Riviera instead of feeding their flock.

Understand me: conditions in the Church have vastly improved in
the last hundred years; but in his day Tennyson had abundant
reason for thinking of the clergy when he wrote "pride in place and
blood."

"Civic slander and the spite" alludes to the lies that besmirch men
in public life, weapon of conscienceless politicians who value party
success more than the common good.

*Stanza 7. Ring out old shapes of foul disease*
Here are three of the major evils that beset mankind: disease,
greed, war. Think back a hundred years to Tennyson's time and
realize how relatively backward was the science of medicine; no
bacteria, no anesthesia, surgery in its infancy, no bio-chemistry, no
radiology, no penicillin; epidemics of smallpox and cholera frequent; infant mortality terrible; life expectancy about 40 instead of
the present 60–65. In the 1840's "no care was taken of the mass of
the population, not even of its children. 'In any large block of tenements,' stated the Glasgow superintendent of police, 'I should be
able to find a thousand children who have no name whatever, or
only nick-names, like dogs.' In Edinburgh the usual answer to 'When

* Mark Hovell: *The Chartist Movement*, p. 25, Longmans, New York, 1925.

The mob ransacking Mr. Robinson's house, London. Sketch by Cruikshank in a pamphlet about the Gordon Riots of 1778.

where you last washed?' was, 'When I was last in prison'; in Dumfries where one person out of every eleven died of cholera there were twelve bakers' shops and seventy-nine whiskey shops." *

Greed we still have with us, but in 1840 the discrepancy between rich and poor was much greater.

War still is the greatest devourer of wealth, lives and spiritual values. But England had not then wholly recovered from the misery caused by the Napoleonic Wars and was desperately afraid that the discontent of the lower classes, as evidenced by the Chartist Movement, would blaze out into an English French Revolution. Says Hallam Tennyson: "The Chartist and Socialist agitations were then alarming the country. My father thought that they should be met not by universal imprisonment and repression, but by a widespread national education [then a monopoly of the Established Church], by a more patriotic and less of a party spirit in the Press . . . and by an increased energy and sympathy among those who belonged to the different forms of Christianity." †

And the "thousand years of peace" have not yet begun to dawn in spite of the United Nations.

*Stanza 8. Ring in the valiant man and free*

* Cole and Postgate: *The Common People*, Methuen, London, 1938.
† See Hallam Tennyson, *op. cit.*

All these details are now summed up in the kindling phrases of the last stanza: the goal is the banishment of darkness, the creation of a nobler type of manhood. And the final phrase, "the Christ that is to be," gathers all these ideals, personal and social, into one glowing personality: not the Christ of the Creeds of long ago, not the Christ of the Liturgy, but Christ as a symbol of redeemed humanity—not redeemed in a future heaven of bliss, but living, working, suffering, conquering and advancing by the law of spiritual evolution in time and space.

This is a brand new note in Christian hymnody—so new and so beyond the vision of the Church that it was not recognized and admitted into our hymn books until the end of the nineteenth century when the Social Gospel became prominent. However, the High Church *English Hymnal* of 1906 did not contain it, nor does the latest revision of the great Anglican *Hymns Ancient and Modern* (1916), nor does the American Episcopal *Hymnal* of 1940.

We now turn from this passionate prayer for social change to a confession of faith so different from anything we have met hitherto that it is startling. It is the prologue which Tennyson prefixed to *In Memoriam* just before it was published:

### *Strong Son of God, immortal Love*     [1849]

From the eleven original stanzas the various hymnals select from four to seven. All omit the second. The last three are purely personal and therefore unsuited to congregational use.

As "Ring out, wild bells" was what might be called social idealism, so this later prologue is Tennyson's reaction to the science and philosophy that was fast making agnostics of professing Christians. It represents the mature judgment of a thinker—for Tennyson was now forty years old, and it summarizes the fruits of sixteen years of meditation.

*Stanza 1.* The hymn is a prayer to immortal Love, which is Tennyson's name for God (following 1 Jn 4:8). But because we cannot picture to ourselves either God or abstract Love, the poet thinks of Christ as the perfect expression of both, and in the first line calls Him Strong Son of God—strong because the greatest force that can move and inspire men is love.

The second couplet shows that Tennyson has reached an important conclusion, namely, that God's existence cannot be proved as one would prove a proposition in geometry, but that we can lay hold of Him by an act of faith: we believe where we cannot prove. He probably had in the back of his mind a word of Jesus found in Jn 20:29. In this statement he takes issue with all the materialistic atheists who rule out of existence every entity that cannot be appre-

*Top,* Shawell Rectory, near Rugby. Much of *In Memoriam* was written here during long visits. *Bottom,* Tennyson's "writing house," built by the Shawell rector in the garden to secure isolation. It is now used as a toolhouse.

hended by the senses or proved by mathematics or reason. This was a bold stand to take.

*Stanza 2.* In this quatrain Tennyson with equal boldness announces his faith in man's survival after death. Man cannot fathom God's reason for creating him, but he may rely upon instinct for survival, and upon God's justice in fulfilling man's instinctive desire placed in him by God Himself.

*Stanza 3.* In the first couplet Tennyson asserts that love is not merely a divine quality but is human also. It is the highest and holiest quality that persons possess, whether these persons are men or God. It is when we attain to perfect love that we become more than human, that we partake of the divine. Moreover, love is not merely a feminine quality; it has a strength we associate with manhood.

The second couplet, "Our wills are ours," etc., is a protest against the science of Tennyson's day which said that men are just mechanisms moved by external forces—like a football that goes where it is kicked. Men think they are making free decisions when really they are being pushed around. Tennyson does not believe this theory: he says that we are free personalities. How in a world governed by Law can we be free? Only by working within the limits set by law—the way Burbank made a new hybrid Loganberry or Vannevar Bush splits an atom. So in the spiritual world, if we want to get anywhere we have to operate within the limits of the moral law, laid down, like the physical, by God. "Our wills are ours, to make them thine."

Freedom of the will is so basic to the concept of morality that Tennyson goes to the trouble elsewhere of reiterating his belief: flings his defiance in the face of all the materialists. In that profound poem *De Profundis* written at the birth of his son, he writes (italics not his):

> [Thou a] shatter'd phantom of that infinite One,
> Who made thee unconceivably Thyself
> Out of His whole World-self and all in all—
> Live thou! and of the grain and husk, the grape
> And ivy-berry, *choose;* . . .
>> [i.e., choose between values—the good and the
>> worthless]
>>                    . . . and find
> Nearer and ever nearer Him, who wrought
> Not matter, nor the finite-infinite,
> But *this main-miracle,* that thou art *thou,*
> With *power on thine own act* and on the world.*

* *The Works of Alfred Lord Tennyson,* Macmillan, London, 1892.

*Stanza 4.* Here the poet hints that the pathway of science and philosophy through the centuries is strewn with broken theories and discarded systems of thought. From this fact we ought to infer that science today does not know everything and ought not to be so cocksure. At best, whatever science has found is only a part of the truth. This fragmentary knowledge is like the separate colors of the spectrum which are broken out of pure sunlight by a prism. Sunlight is more than red or green, so God is the whole truth and is greater than any single bit of it that man may have discovered.

If we wish proof that Tennyson was right, recall how much science has discovered in the hundred years since this was written: man's prehistory, non-Euclidian geometry, one short formula that governs every nebula and every atom (Einstein's "$E = mc^2$,") gamma rays, nuclear fission. The cock-sure scientists of the 1840's now look like babes in the woods!—and perhaps ours will a century hence.

*Stanza 5.* With the single faculty of our reason it is impossible to know everything. We can know facts, objects, things we can see and touch, but there is a whole class of realities which cannot be tested in a laboratory and known as we know the law of gravitation. Among these realities is love, human freedom in the sense of free will, immortality and God Himself. Such realities are recognized by intuition, by faith. And whatever we know by faith we believe comes from God: it is a real light in our darkness, though faint. We pray that this light will grow brighter.

*Stanza 6.* As our knowledge of the universe increases we should not be puffed up, for we know that there are greater mysteries which we have not fathomed. We should be reverent in the presence of these mysteries. *Mind*—that is, the power of reason and *Soul*—that is, the source of faith and intuition and feeling—should develop in perfect harmony, just as the parts of a song, though each different, make a single unified expression of beauty,—more vast and complex than any we have hitherto known.

*Stanza 7.*

> But vaster: we are fools and slight,
> > We mock thee when we do not fear:
> > But help thy foolish ones to bear;
> Help thy vain worlds to bear thy light.

A prayer for forgiveness for our cock-sureness and our vanity. Humility and a sense of dependence upon God are virtues to be cultivated.

If this hymn is Tennyson's philosophy and his religion, where is the Church with its Sacraments? Where is the Evangelical trust in the Blood of Christ and the eternal happiness in a heaven of gold?

When he repeated the Apostles' Creed with the great congregation he must have done it as a symbol of his allegiance to the cause which the Church was created to serve, but he must have made a mental translation of each doctrinal clause into terms he could honestly accept. If one seeks a name, one might call Tennyson's position mild Christian agnosticism. He remained a reverent Churchman till the day of his death.

The final selection made by our hymnal editors from Tennyson's poetry has to do with life after death. The poet considered this poem, "Crossing the Bar," the epitome of his life of faith, and requested that it stand at the end of all editions of his works:

### Sunset and evening star    [1889]

This poem is precious fruit from an old tree. The poet was eighty years old when he wrote it. On an October day his son Hallam was bringing him from his summer home at Aldworth in eastern England to his winter home at Farringford on the Isle of Wight. As they crossed the Solent—the narrow strait that separates the Isle from the mainland—the phrase "moaning at the bar" was apparently in his mind. Then after dinner the poet showed his son the poem completely written out in his shaky script. It "came in a moment," the poet said, by which he meant that the thoughts and emotions which had been in solution all day had suddenly crystalized into this gem.

The first step to understanding the poem is to visualize it, for a true poet always thinks in pictures. And the next step is to feel the emotions that always accompany the experience of seeing. The third step is to understand it.

Stanza 1. Sunset is one of the commonest and most beautiful of nature's panoramas. Among the emotions it stirs there is usually a tinge of sadness. By analogy we speak of the sunset of life. But in this picture there is also an evening star which not only adds to the beauty but changes the emotion. Through the ages, stars have been the symbol of hope. This applies especially to the evening star, because as day departs and darkness deepens the star shines brighter.

"Moaning" brings an auditory image. You who have lived somewhat inland from the ocean may have heard in the calm that precedes an easterly storm the dim roar of the sea. Tennyson's "moaning" is something like that, with the emotional charge of foreboding, anxiety, the portent of coming storm.

The next picture is a boat departing for a long voyage—always a solemn occasion. This sadness is doubtless an ancestral heritage from the days when going to sea was far more dangerous than now:

For men must work and women must weep

And the harbor bar be moaning.

*Stanza 2.* "But such a tide": An almost imperceptible silent motion by which all the streamers of seaweed that rise from the bottom of the harbor faintly stir, as in sleep, and point outward toward the great deep.

*Stanza 3.* "Twilight and evening bell": This is like the first picture but the pathos has deepened. Twilight comes later than sunset and is the vestibule to darkness. Curfew rings its solemn warning that it is time to cover the fire and say goodnight.

"The tide will bear me far": A picture of ships on distant seas. But as in the case of the migratory birds, "lone wandering but not lost"; there is a Pilot who knows the course and the haven.

*Stanza 4.* "I hope to see my Pilot": The last picture is the face-to-face meeting of the old poet and the strong Pilot who came aboard, to be sure, long long ago at the beginning of the poet's sea-faring, but who will not be seen until after they have left port for the final journey into unknown seas from which there will be no return. That meeting and recognition will be the ground of hope and courage for the uncharted voyage.

All these pictures come out of Tennyson's racial heritage, from the sea-farers who from time immemorial have voyaged and traded in the four corners of the world, and also from Tennyson's immediate environment. His home on the Isle of Wight lay in full view of the sea, which rolls in from the west and breaks on the shingle at the foot of his white cliffs. Every day he could see the ships passing up and down the channel, or through the Solent, taking and discharging pilots as they pass the sharp rocks of the Needles three miles away. And the sunset over the sea flooded his western windows, the evening star looked down, the sea moaned, the tide went out.

But in "Crossing the Bar" there is something deeper than mere nature-pictures: it is Tennyson's philosophy of life and death. For him the human soul was part of God. And just as the tide comes surging in from the great deep, crowding up into each river-mouth and creek until it is full to the banks, so God from the infinite deeps of His being comes flooding into the finite body of man, becomes the power behind his growth, his expanding personality, and then, when the life cycle is complete, the tide withdraws and with it takes the soul into the great deep again.

This figure runs through his *Idylls*—King Arthur, borne in on a mighty wave and laid at Merlin's feet; then at the end, from the western shore a huge dragon-ship guided by three Queens bore him away to the great deep. More specific yet is the statement in *De Profundis*:

> Out of the deep, my child, out of the deep,
> From that great deep, before our world begins,
> Whereon the Spirit of God moves as he will—
> Out of the deep . . . thou comest, darling boy!

And the sequel logically is a return of the soul to the deep from whence it came.

There is one further thought. Tennyson has himself explained the Pilot as the "Divine and Unseen who is always guiding us." He may have inferred that God was in the tide that bore him outward, or he may have felt Him, but he never *saw* Him direct as a person. Even so he believes that when he passes the boundary of "time and sense" he will see his Pilot face to face, that is, he will have the experience of God as a fully revealed personality. Inference, feeling, faith, will change the sight.

William Walsham How, Bishop of Wakefield.

This belief of Tennyson's was both a reasoned philosophy and an act of faith. It was his answer to a fighting materialism and a dawning evolution which were destined to destroy the faith of thousands. It was his answer to Compte who had pushed God out of his universe. Tennyson wrestled with these problems, "descended into Hell," and came up again; he emerged with the conviction that the universe was not a play of blind forces that "tumbled in a Godless deep" but the visible body of a Person whom he could know, trust and love.

### Bishop WILLIAM WALSHAM HOW (1823–97) Anglican, Broad

WHILE Tennyson was a layman and, therefore, had nothing to lose by embracing the doctrine of evolution and other findings of science, William How was a clergyman, whose career lay within the Church. It took courage for him to assert his modernism. Nevertheless, as he mounted the rungs of his clerical advancement his modernism grew, until he and John Ellerton became perhaps the most eminent Churchmen in the Broad fold and the most influential in keeping modernist laymen from throwing away their religion.

Born near Shrewsbury, Oxford educated, then successively curate, rector, dean, canon, Bishop Suffragan in London and Bishop of Wakefield. This is a thumbnail biography of a good man who had no purpose in life but to help his fellows. While his title of Suffragan Bishop of London seems high, we must remember that he was bishop of the slum section of East London, a position that carried a small salary and no social prestige. That did not worry How a bit: he declined the bishopric of the great city of Manchester without even mentioning the fact to his wife, and later, the bishopric of Durham with an enviable prestige and an income more than twice what he was getting. His only consideration was how much he could make his life count.

In London he was called "the poor man's bishop," though his influence was by no means confined to the poor. His large heart, untiring energy and genuine interest in the spiritual welfare of his flocks brought him the respect and love of all who knew him. Another nickname for him was "the omnibus bishop," because, unlike the typical bishop who lives in a palace and rides in a private coach, he rode the buses, lived and worked with his people.

All his hymns were written between 1858 and 1871 while he was rector at Whittington, a pleasant farming village on the Welsh border where the famous Dick Whittington, Lord Mayor of London, was probably born. Opposite the church is a castle built by the Normans to keep out Welsh raiders. Being a man of means, How rebuilt and enlarged the rectory to its present sumptuous dimensions, laid out extensive gardens and lawns including an archery range, planted trees (there is a thousand-year-old yew near the house), built barns and cultivated enough land to keep half a dozen men busy. In fact, the size of the estate has been quite an embarrassment to later incumbents. He also rebuilt the church which had moldered for a century and a half. He lies buried in the churchyard. The monument which once stood over the grave has been moved across the road and is known as How's Cross.

The hymns we shall now consider show How the Churchman rather than How the modernist. They were written for people who lacked education and, therefore, were not concerned with the reconciliation of science and religion. They fit the needs of the average church-goer who was using the Metrical Psalter or some inadequate compilation, before *Hymns Ancient and Modern* had arrived with its broader outlook. And they still fill a large place. How's hymns number about 60, of which 25 are found in our ten hymnals. Some of them are the best-loved in our hymnody. They embody his own ideal: "A good hymn should be like a good prayer—simple, real, earnest, and reverent."

## We give thee but thine own    [1858]

Written for the offertory. The hymn does not confine itself to our duty to give, but it opens up to our imagination the great needs of the world which our gifts are meant to fill—heartache, poverty, waywardness, woe, loneliness, captivity to sin; or more positively, the need of Christ's gospel. This vision changes a prosaic collection into an act of self-dedication.

This is a different approach from that of the usual offertory hymn in which giving is represented as a duty we owe to God or as an investment on which God will repay us a thousand-fold.

## For all the saints who from their labors rest    [1864]

Written for All Saints Day. It is a commentary on the clause of the Apostles' Creed, "I believe in the Communion of Saints"; *i.e.*, the solidarity of the faithful whether here—the Church Militant—or in heaven—the Church Triumphant. Its eleven stanzas have been edited down to six or fewer. It is the finest of all hymns written for this day, for it contains more of the purely spiritual element and less of pageantry and theology. The structure may be indicated in this prosaic way:

*Stanza 1.* Our thanks to Jesus for the saints.
*Stanza 2.* He was their inspiration and strength.
*Stanza 3.* May we prove worthy of them.
*Stanza 4.* Even now we have fellowship with them in spirit.
*Stanza 5.* Memories of their victories strengthen us.
*Stanza 6.* After the fight comes rest.
*Stanzas 7–8.* But our true reward will come in the grand review above, in which all earth's hosts will assemble to praise God.

While this logical progression of thought is commendable, the chief glory of the hymn is its exalted language, its sustained emotion and the feeling that we who are still fighting are carrying on a great crusade. For those of us who have lost sons in wars waged for righteous causes, memory adds its poignancy.

## O Word of God incarnate    [1866]

A hymn in praise of the Bible.

*Stanza 1.* The Bible is the "Word of God" in the Johannine sense of "Divine Intelligence" incarnated in the printed page (Jn 1:1). It is also divine Wisdom, which unlike scientific fact concerns itself primarily with conduct, human relationships and attitudes (Ps 119:9). It is Truth, which by nature is unchangeable—not so-called

*Left*, Whittington Castle, opposite How's church. Named for famous Dick Whittington, Mayor of London, born near here. The castle was a defense against Welsh raids (c. 1423). *Right*, How's church, Whittington. In the foreground, his tomb and memorial cross. All his hymns were written for use here.

scientific truth which is often theory that new investigations cause us to change. This truth has reference to spiritual values, not material (Jn 14:6; 17:17). It is Light, because by it we can walk without stumbling (Ps 119:105; Jn 1:4; 11:9–10).

*Stanza 2.* The Church is the institution by which the Bible has been transmitted to mankind. It took over intact from the Jews the Old Testament, and it selected and put its stamp of authenticity on the books of the New Testament. It is the agency behind the Bible Societies which have printed the Bible in all the principal languages of mankind, and behind the Missionary Societies which distribute the Bible to the dark places of the earth.

Wisdom is better than rubies (Prov 3:15).

In the Gospels alone is the portrait of Christ, who was the Wisdom of God (1 Cor 1:24).

*Stanza 3.* A series of metaphors that suggest the contributions the Bible makes to life. It is (a) a banner, symbol of the cause for which armies fight, unifying their purpose and giving courage; (b) a lighthouse that warns a ship off the sunken ledges or other dangers; (c) chart and compass: the one, to show the true destination of life and the course one must follow to reach it; the other, the instrument by which we are able to keep on the course.

*Stanza 4.* A prayer that the Church may be the faithful custodian and administrator of this treasure; its purpose, to guide men to God.

It may seem inconsistent that the person who wrote this hymn could at the same time believe in the "Higher Criticism" and the doctrine of evolution. But How reconciled the two positions. After he became Bishop he preached a sermon (1887) on "The Bible and Science." Gladstone, the statesman, and Huxley, the scientist, were both struck by it. In Huxley's book on *Science and the Christian Tradition* he mentions this sermon and says that the Bishop was one of the few people who so treated of religion and science that he felt he could go along with him.

About evolution How said that there were facts and arguments in its favor which it would be silly to dispute, and he warned people against saying, "All such-like speculations are straight against God's Word and therefore utterly untrue." God's Word, in abstaining from scientific revelations, is simply adapting itself to our understanding in the same way it does when it speaks of God Himself in anthropomorphic language. Religion and science revolve in different orbits, but these orbits cut one another at certain points. The origin of man is one of those matters on which God speaks to us both by His Word and His works. Evolution is the wonderful way in which "the Lord formed man out of the dust of the ground." (Condensed from How's biography by his son.)

### *O Jesus, thou art standing* [1867]

How has himself told us how he came to write this hymn. It was after reading a poem by Jean Ingelow called "Brothers, and a Sermon," in which she describes two brothers listening to an old parson preach to the people of a fisher village.

Quoting the text, "Behold, I stand at the door and knock" (Rev 3:20)—

> Then said the parson: "What! and shall he wait,
> And must he wait . . . ?
> Open the door with shame if ye have sinned . . .
> And take him in who comes to sup with thee."

How then goes on: "The pathos of the verses impressed me very forceably at the time. I read them over and over again, and finally . . . scribbled on an old scrap of paper my first idea of the verses beginning, 'O Jesus, thou art standing.' I altered them a good deal subsequently. . . . After the hymn left my hands it was never altered in any way."

It is probable also that How had seen Holman Hunt's famous painting "Light of the World," for the picture was painted in 1854 and within two years had all England talking. At any rate, the hymn is a close parallel to the imagery and the spirit of the picture.*

### Canon *JOHN ELLERTON* (1826–93) Anglican, Broad

THIS remarkable man came from an Evangelical family, but attending Trinity College, Cambridge, he came under the influence of Frederick D. Maurice, as did Tennyson and Charles Kingsley. As a result

* Both the picture and the hymn may be more fully understood if the reader will turn to A. E. Bailey: *Gospel in Art*, pp. 182–5.

he became better oriented toward the social problems of the times and so came to occupy an inclusive position in reference to the three Church parties: combining "the subjective piety of the Evangelical, the objective adoration of the High, the intellectual freedom of the Broad." At Cambridge, as ever afterward, he was "one of the best and noblest specimens of what a fine and

Ellerton's church at Crewe Green. Most of his hymns were written for use here.

pure Evangelical training can produce when it is widened out into the more excellent way of Maurician High Churchism."

Taking orders in 1850, he served in three curacies. From the first the condition of the poor and the education of the working people commanded his devoted service. In 1860 he became vicar of Crewe Green about thirty miles southeast of Liverpool. Here he found a population of about 500 mechanics employed in the steel works of the London and Northwestern Railway Company, supplemented by the farmers and laborers on the estate of Lord Crewe whose domestic chaplain he also was. The "living" was wretchedly poor. To obtain additional revenue, Ellerton used to conduct services in a hall in Crewe each Sunday, which gave him £1 more per week. His tiny brick church at Crewe Green still stands in a well-kept cemetery. Within is a neat auditorium seating perhaps 150 people, a fine stone chancel arch, timber roof and delicately-carved marble pulpit. A beautiful avenue of trees leads to the rectory, successor to the one where Ellerton wrote most of his hymns.

The Railway Company had a Mechanics Institute at Crewe. Ellerton became the chairman of its education committee, entirely reorganized the Institute and made it one of the most successful in England. He, himself, taught classes in English and in Bible History. He also organized one of the first Choral Associations of the Midlands. After a four-year service at another small country parish—"a kind of living grave," where he wrote his *Notes and Illustrations to Church Hymns* and helped W. W. How compile a hymnal for children, he was transferred to Barnes, a west suburb of London. The parish was large and populous; it broke him down and compelled him to go abroad for a year. On his return he took a smaller parish, his last. During his final sickness he was given the honorary title of Canon of St. Albans Cathedral—the only public recognition that ever came to him.

Ellerton's interest in hymns was a consuming passion. Not only did he write or translate eighty-six of his own, but "it is no exaggeration to say that his hand may be traced in every hymnbook of importance during the last thirty years before his death. . . . His mind was so steeped in hymns that on his death-bed, while he lay half conscious, they flowed almost unceasingly from his lips."

### *Saviour, again to thy dear name we raise*     [1866]

Written for the Choral Festival at Nantwich—the organization he, himself, had established. The original six stanzas are usually reduced to four, to its advantage. As it now stands it ranks among the greatest evening hymns of the Church. Benson says of it, "It seems the perfection of the blending of the corporate idea of worship with human individuality."

In stanza 1 we must picture the closing session of the Nantwich Festival; its dozen or so choirs robed in their variously-colored gowns and together singing their final prayer, then kneeling for benediction. In the remaining stanzas are three prayers for peace: peace of mind for the journeys to the several towns whence the singers have come, peace during the night, peace through the various vicissitudes of life until we attain the peace of eternity. Simple and heartfelt, universal in its application, it emphasizes that frame of mind which is essential for successful work—absence from worry. Because we all need this serenity, all hymnbooks contain this perfect expression of that need.

### *This is the day of light*     [1867]

This hymn for Sunday contrasts strangely with Christopher Words-worth's "O day of rest and gladness" (see above). The latter High Church hymn stresses the mystic symbolism of the first day of the week: it stands for Creation, the Resurrection, the Descent of the Spirit—a trinity of glories, and the hymn ends with the Trinitarian doxology. This hymn, on the contrary, ignores symbolism and theology, stresses what the day can do for our spirits as we gather in our places of worship. Thus Ellerton ministers to our spiritual needs, us common folk who need the sunshine of God's presence, release from toil, calmness of mind, contact with the Divine, and a quickening of our souls to greater love and more fervent praise. There are only two allusions: "Day-spring" (St. 1) which echoes Lk 1:78–79 and refers to Christ; and "Vanquisher of death," another allusion to Christ (1 Cor 15:56; 2 Tim 1:10).

### The day thou gavest, Lord, is ended    [1870]

An evening hymn, like "Saviour Again," but with a broader outlook. This world view arises from the fact that it was originally a missionary hymn, written for *A Liturgy for Missionary Meetings*.

This movement of the Church outward to the south and east was relatively something new for Protestants: William Carey, first missionary to India from England (1793) could not get the backing of the Established Church. The Anglican *Church Missionary Society* was not created until 1799. But now in the 1870's England was fully embarked upon her ideal of empire. She had outposts all over the world. The East India Company had gradually been taken over by the state until after the Indian Mutiny it had been wholly absorbed (1858). Only six years after this hymn was written, Victoria was to be proclaimed "Empress of India" (1876). It was fitting, therefore, and inevitable that the Church should cultivate a world-outlook and assume world-responsibility. This hymn is an expression of that concern and of the joy of hearing in imagination the ceaseless sound of prayer and praise breaking beneath the dawns and sunsets as they daily encircle the earth. The hymn is a series of pictures. The expanding British Empire thus becomes a symbol of the growing Kingdom of God that shall outlive all human institutions.

It is no wonder that Queen Victoria chose this hymn to be sung at the Diamond Jubilee Service in 1897, and sung it was on the same day by tens of thousands of churches throughout the world. Kipling wrote a hymn also, but it was not sung at the Jubilee. He foresaw that "earth's proud empires" would pass unless founded upon righteousness and humility. (See Kipling, below.)

### Behold us, Lord, a little space    [1870]

A hymn written for a mid-day service held in a London church—not on a Sunday but on a weekday. This was an innovation. The hymn too marks a new line, for instead of emphasizing Church, Sacraments, Theology, as a

High Churchman would have done, or the need for personal conversion
and mystic communion with Christ as the Evangelicals would have done, it
tells of the dedication to God of all our time and talents.

In stanza 1 we introduce ourselves to God—who was not expecting us!
In stanza 2 we hear "streaming London's central roar" and feel the pressure
of business. But (stanza 3) God's blessing is not won merely by going to a
church service: that blessing comes automatically to us, whatever our work,
if we work honestly and patiently. In stanza 4 we catch our first glimpse in
hymnody of our modern civilization: industry, business, production, commerce, science, art. This life is part of God's plan, and its successful prosecution is determined by God's own laws. Therefore (stanza 5), let us show
our Christianity by the way we tackle our job, and thus through the honesty
of our toil capture the world for God. To sum up (stanza 6): work and
prayer, if rightly understood, are one and the same thing. Carlyle had already
said this in his rugged prose; and if "Prayer is the soul's sincere desire," as
Montgomery wrote in his hymn (See above, Chap. VII) then we can see how
genuine devotion to the work in hand, if it be honest, is a religious act.

This is an extraordinary position for a Churchman to take. But it fits in
with Ellerton's personal life, with his devotion to the workers in his parishes,
with the scientific and philosophic trend of the times, and with the views
being stressed by the Broad section of Anglicanism. By way of contrast read
Stone's, "The Church's one foundation" (High Church), Charlotte Elliott's,
"Just as I am, without one plea," and Catherine Hankey's, "I love to tell the
story" (Evangelical).

## God the Almighty one! King who ordainest    [1870]

This hymn is a composite. Stanzas 1 and 2 were written in 1842 by
Henry F. Chorley (1808–1872), a musical critic and writer in London, under
circumstances undisclosed. Stanzas 3–5 are part of a hymn written by Ellerton on August 28, 1870, four days before the battle of Sedan in the Franco-
Prussian War. This combination seems to be preferred over the single work
of either. Hymnal editors, however, have done much tinkering. The unusual
meter is due to the fact that it was written for the tune, *Russian Hymn*, to
which it is always sung.

We cannot fail to be impressed with the majesty of the language and
with the nature-imagery derived presumably from the Bible. Read, for
example, the description of God in 2 Sam 22:7–18; or the words of Elihu in
Job 37:2–5. Memories of these passages may have shaped stanza 1 and its
opening characterization—"God the almighty one." In stanza 2, "God the
all-merciful," the other side of God's nature is stressed: we pray for that
mercy. Yet in stanza 3 we recall that God is "all-righteous," and that when
man defies Him, punishment cannot be arrested. God is also "all-wise"
(stanza 4): through His punishment for man's sins He is fulfilling in His

*own* time His purpose, and is building His kingdom. If, then, peace comes in *our* time (stanza 5) we can only praise Him for His power, His mercy, His justice and His wisdom. The refrain in stanzas 1–3 is taken from the Litany of the Prayer Book.

The Franco-Prussian War, in progress when Ellerton wrote his portion of the hymn, was not only a dire calamity for France but it threatened all Europe. It was a war of aggression fought by Prussia and her Germanic allies for the possession of Alsace and Lorraine, though the pretext was other. England had been euchered into a position of "benevolent neutrality," but with only the Channel between her and war, the people of England were on edge. All this is reflected in the hymn. "Man hath defied thee" (stanza 3) is Ellerton's judgment that there was no moral justification for Prussia's aggression. "Falsehood and wrong" could be laid at the feet of both parties; "the fire of thy chastening" is sign that God hates war and that the suffering caused by it is the inevitable result of someone's immoral decisions. The moral law lies behind most of the world's agony. As the present lines are written, following the greatest and most costly war in history, we are floundering in the morass of diplomatic insincerity, political chicanery, scheming for world power, impotent public opinion, while the atom bomb flings its lurid threat over the whole world. "Give peace in our time, O Lord" —based upon justice and the law of Love.

## *Now the laborer's task is o'er* [1871]

First sung at the funeral of the general manager of the Crewe Railway works, since then sung almost universally at funerals in England. It was first published in a hymnal by the Evangelical *Society for the Promotion of Christian Knowledge,* the church group that, longest of the three, held to the doctrines of Calvinism. However, by the time this hymn was written these doctrines had pretty well faded out of Anglican belief. While not offensively asserted we find here some of the old figures: the "farther shore" of Jordan (stanza 1. *Cf.* Watts' "There is a land of pure delight"), the Judgement Day (stanza 2), the eternity of bliss sitting at Christ's feet (stanza 3), the "powers of hell" that have been fighting for the possession of the soul but who have been foiled by Christ's death on the cross (stanza 4). In stanza 5 we who are still living will have to wait for our bliss till the "Resurrection Day." This confuses the picture, since that particular day is supposed to come at the end of the world, not when we individually die.

Behind the imagery of stanza 3 lies the incident of the Dying Thief (Lk 23:39–43). "Earth to earth . . . dust to dust" are words taken from the Prayer Book liturgy for the burial service. It is a pity that the Church does not revise its burial service to conform more nearly to modern ideas about matter and soul. Canon Ellerton's "New Theology" had not progressed far enough to substitute spiritual reality for the Apocalyptic imagery of the

Book of Revelation on which Evangelical beliefs were founded. His biographer says of the hymn: "It has been sung and will continue to be sung at the grave-side of princes, divines, statesmen, poets, artists, authors, as well as of many a Christian laborer in human life." * In America I doubt if it is ever sung—perhaps because congregational singing at funerals is not usual. Of the six hymns analysed above, this is poetically and theologically the poorest.

*Welcome, happy morning! age to age shall say*     [1868]

A translation from the Latin of Fortunatus. See above, Chap. IX.

### THE CHRISTIAN SOCIALIST MOVEMENT

The next two hymnwriters to be considered were organizing spirits in a piece of social propaganda known as Christian Socialism. This movement followed immediately upon the collapse of the Chartist Movement in 1848 (see above). The object was to enlist the Anglican Church in the work of social reform; "to bring the Church home to the people's hearts and to plead the people's cause before their masters, taking their stand on a return to the principles of Christianity freed from the later accretions of ossified officialdom and dogmatic harshness and the repellent self-assertion of class pride among the clergy and religious laity."

John Frederick Denison Maurice (1805–72) was the inspirer: son of a Unitarian minister, a student of Trinity College, Cambridge, though not being an Anglican he could not get a degree. Later, however, he became an Anglican (1834), was made chaplain of Guy's Hospital, London, and thenceforth became a most inspiring leader in improving the lot of workingmen. He helped found Queen's College for women, in London, and became its first Principal (1848); he also helped found Workingman's College (1854). Other leading spirits were Thomas Arnold of Rugby, Dean Henry Stanley, Charles Kingsley and Thomas Hughes. This group and their sympathizers promoted co-operatives and small self-governing workshops. But these attempts proved mostly abortive; the Anglican hierarchy was hostile, and though the movement paved the way for later similar enterprises, chiefly co-operatives, it never itself accomplished its ends. One of their early periodicals contained a phrase from Charles Kingsley, "Religion is an opium dose for the people"—which today is blazoned on the walls of the Kremlin in Moscow!

The first of these organizers to write a hymn was

### THOMAS HUGHES (1823–96) Anglican

EDUCATED under the famous Dr. Arnold of Rugby, and at Oriel College, Oxford, then becoming a lawyer, he rose to be a County Court Judge. While practicing law at Lincoln's Inn, London, he came under the

* H. Housman: *John Ellerton*, S. P. C. K., London, 1896.

*Top*, Rugby School, made famous by Headmaster Thomas Arnold and Hughes' *Tom Brown's School Days*. *Left*, Rugby School Chapel. *Right*, Thomas Hughes' statue in Rugby School Yard.

*Top*, Tomb of Charles Kingsley and his wife (left); his church at Eversley. *Below*, Charles Kingsley.

powerful influence of Frederick Maurice and in 1848 he joined the Christian Socialists. This movement led him to promote the founding of the Workingman's College in London, of which after Maurice's death he became Principal (1854). His great title to fame, however, is his *Tom Brown's School Days* (1857), the story of his life at Rugby under his ideal schoolmaster—probably the best picture of school life ever drawn. He also wrote other less famous books. He then sat in Parliament as a Liberal (1865–74) but did not succeed in securing any reform legislation.

Having made a lecture tour in the United States in 1870, he became so interested in the possibilities of finer social living in our country that in 1880 he became the moving spirit in founding an English co-operative settlement in "Rugby," Tennessee, named after his beloved "prep" school. This was not financially successful.

The only hymn Hughes ever wrote was the following, suggested, it is thought, by one of Maurice's sermons:

## O God of truth, whose living word    [1859]

The theme is the battle between truth and falsehood. Truth consists of ideas that correspond with reality; when expressed in conduct, it is called acting on principle. Falsehood is an ignorant or a willful shutting of our eyes to actuality, and so acting without principle.

*Stanza 1.* God is the living reality behind phenomena. Expressed in terms of action, He is natural and moral Law that never deviates from His will. That is why nature continues to exist. We who do not know Him and His truth are therefore, consciously or not, sinners and subject to death.
*Stanza 2.* Our duty is to enlist under God's banner of truth and with Him fight the lies that are now incarnate in society.
*Stanza 3.* A pious wish that we may join the army with our uniforms unstained; or, depending on the punctuation, this is a sarcastic question whether we would really join if we could!
*Stanza 4.* The sarcasm continues: we would make sorry fighters for truth, for in our nature we are untruthful, slaves to ignorance and willful rejection of truth, which is sin.
*Stanza 5.* God, get us out of this mess by slaying the falsehood in our hearts; then perhaps we would be fit to fight for truth.
*Stanza 6.* Smash and burn the falsehood entirely out of us; then heal our wounds with the dew of heaven (Hos 14:4–5).
*Stanza 7.* Burn out of us the dross of falsehood: then the residue will be pure gold—the truth of God dwelling in us.

This is a hymn of disgust at the shams of life. Pretending to be a Christian nation and to hold sacred the truth revealed in the Bible, we still are sunk in ignorance, sotted with drink, sodden in poverty, our leaders looking out for themselves—their pocketbooks and their social supremacy—rather than solving our national problems. This is the theme of the Christian Socialists of whom Hughes was one. It is a far cry from High Churchism or Evangelicalism.

The second Christian Socialist to write hymns was

### Canon CHARLES KINGSLEY (1819–1875) Anglican, Broad

THIS man exercised an extraordinary influence in his day along several lines: as poet, novelist, nature-lover, preacher, historian, humanitarian. When Charles was a boy his father was rector at Clovelly on the Cornish coast, so that, as a schoolboy in near-by Bristol, Charles saw the fearful riots that wrecked the town and burned the bishop's palace (1832). Soldiers shot down the rioters. "That sight made me a radical," he later said. When his father was transferred to Chelsea, a London suburb, Charles saw city life and became disgusted with the Church's attitude toward social inequalities and wrongs, and with the supercilious way in which "respectable" lady church-workers and dilettante curates went down to the slums to read the Bible to the wretches living there. By the Oxford Movement he was repelled rather than attracted, for it dissociated itself from the crying social needs of the times, "busy" as he said, "with their commenting and squabbling and doctrine-picking, while the world of labor turned away from the Church with disgust."

Kingsley entered Magdalen College, Cambridge, in 1838. Taking orders he began his work at Eversley on the edge of Windsor Forest, and remained thirty-three years. His parishioners were farmers and "poachers by instinct." Being an athlete and skilled at all country jobs, he often worked in the fields with his people. In epidemics of cholera and diphtheria he directed his sermons and his energies to draining swamps; he went from house to house with medicines and personal services. "What is the use of talking to hungry paupers about heaven? I assert that the business for which God sends a Christian priest in a Christian nation is to preach freedom, equality and brotherhood in the fullest, deepest, widest meaning of these three great words." As time went on he established all possible agencies for welfare and education among them.

The early morning hours of this versatile man were devoted to writing. From the first he used the themes dear to the heart of the newly instituted Christian Socialists: The *Saint's Tragedy* (1848), a dramatic poem about St. Elizabeth of Hungary, a Queen who devoted her life to the poor. This embodied his social gospel, following the great Chartist outbreak; *Yeast* (1849), his first novel, took up the problems of agrarian socialism. The hero of the book states the theme:

> The oppression, the want, that goes on all the year-round; the filth, the lying, the swearing, the profligacy, the sickening weight of debt, the grinding anxiety from rent-day to rent-day that crushes a man's soul down—"Oh, sir, the landlords never felt this!"

His second novel, *Alton Locke* (1849), presents the sweating system as found in the industrial cities. Again one of his characters presents the theme:

> And stopping suddenly before the entrance to a miserable alley— "Look!" says Sandy, "Look! there is not a soul down that yard but's either beggar, drunkard, thief or worse. Write about that! Say how

ye saw the mouth o' hell, and the twa pillars thereof at the entry—
the pawnshop-broker's shop o' one side and the gin-palace at the
other—twa monstrous devils, eating up men and women and bairns,
body and soul."

Kingsley's versatility is shown by his other titles: *Hypatia* (1853), a
novel of the conflict between heathenism and Christianity in Alexandria in
the fifth century; *Westward, Ho!* (1855), a rollicking tale of piracy on the
Spanish Main; *Water Babies* (1863), a charming series of nature-stories for
children; *Roman and Teuton* (1864), a historical study of the break-up of
the Roman Empire, embodying some of his work as Professor of History at
Cambridge University (1860–9), and a constant stream of essays and published sermons.

Fame and honors were now coming his way. Queen Victoria made him
her private chaplain (1859); he was appointed Canon of Westminster Abbey
(1873) and thereafter preached to great crowds in that venerable sanctuary.
He died while comparatively young (56) and was buried in his home
churchyard at Eversley. His wife lies beside him. The famous Latin inscription on the twin tomb, "We have loved, we love, we shall love," applies not
only to them but to the whole parish that had been so dear to his heart and
to the great world of toilers for whom he had toiled.

The one hymn by which he is remembered is

### *From thee all skill and science flow*      [1871]

Written for the laying of the corner-stone of the workingmen's block of
of the Queen's Hospital at Birmingham, and was sung by a choir of 1000
voices. It began,

### Accept this building, gracious Lord

The first two stanzas, which are of local interest, are omitted in all our
hymnals.

The hymn is a noble statement of the essence of Kingsley's philosophy
and religion: it was "to rehabilitate Christianity as the poor man's religion
and the workingman's friend."

*Stanza 1.* God is the source of all those human emotions and skills,
ideals and services, that unite to raise suffering man out of his
misery. God send us more of these precious gifts!
*Stanza 2.* And see that we all have a share in giving as well as
receiving—not the rich and talented alone, but the humblest of us.
Relief of suffering should be a universal enterprise.
*Stanza 3.* Hasten the day when men shall rule justly, for it is the
denial of justice on the part of the powerful that makes poverty,
sickness and most of the ills of mankind.

*Stanza 4.* It is not God who has spoiled the Paradise He had created for man, but man's own crude destructiveness. Restore the blueness of our smoke-blackened sky and the green of our trampled and factory-polluted sod.

We ought to have other hymns from Kingsley, but editors did not discover him until recently. If possible, read Kingsley's trumpet-call, "The day of the Lord is at hand, at hand!" (S), written in the throbbing days of the Chartist riots (1848–49).

Apart from the social and political movements in the midst of which the previous hymn-writers of this chapter lived, stand the more conventional religionists who have contributed something vital to our hymnody. In the later decades of the century, however, specific world situations will again became influential. (See Symonds, Kipling and Chesterton.)

### Rev. *JOHN ERNEST BODE* (1816–74) Anglican, Broad

EDUCATED at Eton, Charterhouse and Christ Church, Oxford. For six years after graduation he was tutor (Don) at Christ Church, then, entering the ministry in 1847, he served three parishes, of which the country peace of Castle Camps, not far from Cambridge, claimed fifteen years. He was honored in 1855 by being chosen Bampton Lecturer at Oxford. Though he published three volumes of verse, only one of his hymns has survived.

### *O Jesus, I have promised*     [1868]

Written for the confirmation of his daughter and two sons at his own Castle Camps Church, it originally read "we have promised."

It is a prayer for the constant presence of Christ throughout the vicissitudes of life:

*Stanza 1.* The hazards are battle—defending self and the right cause against assault from without; wandering from the straight and narrow way.

*Stanza 2.* A special danger is the alluring call to worldliness, supplied both by one's own instincts and by the provocation of environment.

*Stanza 3.* Safety lies in recalling the face of Jesus in two of its aspects: inspiration (Mk 1:16–20) and reproof (Lk 22:59–62).

*Stanza 4.* An allusion to the storm on lake Galilee (Mt 8:25–27).

*Stanza 5.* The candidate here claims heaven on the basis of mutual promises: Christ's to His disciples (Mt 24:12–13; Jn 12:26), and theirs now to Him.

*Stanza 6.* This is the final prayer for complete discipleship, strength, guidance.

In the hymn Jesus is addressed under the reassuring titles, Master, Friend, Guide, Guardian, Saviour.

Although Bode had the Anglican enthusiasm for the Christian Year, as is shown by his volume, *Hymns for the Gospel of the Day for Each Sunday and Festivals of Our Lord*, in this hymn he concentrates on personal consecration, without allusion to any theology or sacrament. A Quaker or a fundamentalist Baptist could subscribe to this hymn. It is almost universally used.

### Canon HENRY TWELLS (1823–1900) Anglican, Broad

A GRADUATE of Peterhouse (St. Peter's College), Cambridge, oldest of all the colleges (1281), and famous for training the poet Gray and Lord Kelvin the scientist. Twells divided his time between being schoolmaster and clergyman. One parish he served as sub-vicar was in Shakespeare's home-town of Stratford-on-Avon. After being Select Preacher at Cambridge, 1873–4, and Honorary Canon of Peterboro Cathedral, failing health sent him in 1890 to Bournemouth, the most-frequented resort for invalids on the Channel coast. In this town Mary Shelley was buried and there R. L. Stevenson wrote *Dr. Jekyll and Mr. Hyde*. Here Twells built and partly endowed the new Church of St. Augustine and served it as priest until his death. Like most Evangelicals this Broad Churchman was interested in missionary work among the poor and was a friend to all.

### At even e'er (when) the sun was set    [1868]

At the request of editor, Sir Henry W. Baker, Twells wrote this hymn for the Appendix to *Hymns Ancient and Modern*, the famous Anglican hymnal. The author has told the circumstances of writing:

> Being at that time headmaster of a large grammar school, I wrote it one afternoon while the boys were taking examinations, and I was supposed to be seeing "all fair." I am afraid I could not have been very energetic or lynx-eyed in my duties that day, but I little anticipated the popularity the hymn would attain. . . . Copies have been kindly sent to me in Greek, Latin, German, French, Welsh and Irish. I like to think that I have brought souls nearer Christ, and if so I heartily thank God for it.

Some discussion arose whether the Jewish law allowed cures to be made before rather than after sunset, but the author claimed that his word "e'er" was justified by Lk 4:40. At any rate, this evening hymn is based upon this text and expresses the value of our inner experiences with Christ, His power to meet the spiritual needs of all classes. The crowd of sick on Galilee's shore becomes ourselves, worshipping here at eventide in our church. See how many of our ills are listed (stanzas 3–5): we are sick, sad, have failed to love, or our love has gone out; we are worldly, slighted, restless, sinful, conscience-smitten. But Christ (stanza 6), "tempted in all points like as we, is able to succor them that are tempted" (Heb 2:18); and He has insight into even our hidden needs (Jn 2:25). So here we pray for Christ's healing touch, for though no longer on earth He still has this power (stanza 7).

All this is rhythmic prose; an expository sermon in rhyme. It lacks the emotion-conjuring imagery that is the vehicle of all true poetry. Perhaps the good schoolmaster should have chosen a more fitting place in which to woo the Muse.

### Canon EDWIN HATCH (1835–89) Anglican, Broad

EDUCATED at Pembroke College, Oxford, he came into close contact there with the artist, Burne-Jones, the arts-craftsman and socialist, William Morris, and the poet, Swinburne—surely a broadening experience. Before he left college he became a large contributor to magazines on a variety of topics. Though his parents were Dissenters he became an Anglican. For a time he took a parish in East London, the slum sector. For seven years he taught classics at Trinity College, Quebec, and was Rector of Quebec High School (1859–67); returning to Oxford he became Vice-Principal of St. Mary's Hall; then served the University successively as Bampton Lecturer, Reader in Ecclesiastical History, and Hibbert Lecturer. His great learning was acknowledged everywhere, especially as a result of the Bampton Lectures, "On the Organization of Early Christian Churches." These lectures were translated into German by Harnack, recognized as the world's authority on that subject at that time. In spite of this profound scholarship, his religion was "as simple and unaffected as a child's." His one surviving hymn shows this to be true.

### Breathe on me, Breath of God      [1878]

The hymn is based upon Jn 20:22 which gives John's description of the gift of the Holy Spirit—contrary to Luke's account in Acts 2:1–4. Whichever is historically correct, the important fact is that, according to the Bible, God's spirit came upon man as the differentiating mark of humanity over against lower forms of life (Gen 2:7; cf. also Michelangelo's "Creation of Adam" in which animal life is breathed into him by a nebulous face opposite his nostrils, while the spiritual quality is conveyed by an electric spark from God's finger to Adam's). All through Israelite history God's spirit is said to have descended upon man as inspiration to nobler living and heroic action (Num 27:18; Job 32:8; Ps 139:7; Is 48:16; Mk 1:10, etc.). We have ample warrant, therefore, for praying that God will extend this gift to us.

Stanza 1. What God's spirit accomplishes in us is to unify our desires and activities with His own.
Stanza 2. In particular it purifies our desires and gives our wills a divine direction and permanence.

*Stanza 3.* It sanctifies us: spiritualizes our animal nature and gives it a splendor which, though finite, is like God's.

*Stanza 4.* Only so can we share God's perfections and His eternity.

These achievements are all the supreme objects of prayer. How cheap beside them seem wealth, learning, beauty, power, fame! These lesser gifts may come as a result of the former, but if they are allowed to be primary objects of desire instead of secondary, they dwarf the soul.

The hymn gains in beauty and truth if contrasted with such others as "Ye watchers and ye holy ones," "The Church's one foundation," "Onward, Christian soldiers," "Alleluia! Hearts to heaven," or any of the theological High or Low Church hymns.

## *JOHN ADDINGTON SYMONDS* (1840–93) Anglican, Broad

EDUCATED at Harrow and Balliol College, Oxford, Fellow of Magdalen College, Oxford. A brilliant student, but over-work brought a breakdown in health which forced him to give up a professional career and to live in a more favorable climate. He spent much time in Italy and finally built a home at Davos Platz in the Swiss Highlands. He was one of the outstanding writers of the Victorian Era. Best-known of his works is a six-volume *History of the Italian Renaissance;* others are *Introduction to the Study of Dante, Studies of the Greek Poets,* besides translations of Michelangelo's *Sonnets* and other Italian works. Though his own poems filled two volumes, his surviving hymns are only two: a splendid bit of spiritual philosophy beginning "To God, the everlasting, who abides" (S) and

### *These things shall be! A loftier race*      [1880]

In Symonds' volume *Old and New* was a poem called "A Vista." No one recognized its hymnic value until twenty-four years later when the English Methodists published part of it in their Hymn Book. During World War I it came into extensive use in England as an expression of a nation's hopes, and now it is finding favor with American editors. It was the answer of Faith to the great problems posed by the changing social order and by a special crisis, and it still challenges the chaotic conditions of the world today. It can be better understood if the three opening stanzas are given:

> Sad heart, what will the future bring
>   To happier men when we are gone?
> What golden days shall dawn for them
>   Transcending all we gaze upon?
>
> Will our long strife be laid to rest?
>   The warfare of our blind desires
> Be merged in a perpetual peace,
>   And love illume but harmless fires?

Shall faith released from forms that chain
And freeze the spirit while we pray,
Expect with calm and ardent eyes
The morning of death's brighter day?

The poet knew that the realization of his hopes would long be deferred (stanza 1); that the delaying element would be the blindness of our desires —an ignorant and unseeing wish, and action untransformed by love (stanza 2); and that a religion of hard and fast forms and antiquated theology would chill the spiritual life.

The events of the time, which Symonds followed closely, must have suggested to him the need of better men and better nations. Russia and Turkey had gone to war in 1877. The situation was practically identical with that in 1946–48. Disraeli, British Premier, "was deeply convinced that only by maintaining the Turkish Empire . . . could Russia be prevented from obtaining a position in the Straits from whence ultimately she could threaten British dominion over India and elsewhere in the East." Russia had driven to the very outskirts of Constantinople and dictated peace on the battlefield, in which the fate of all the Balkan states was involved. Britain interfered, sent a fleet to Constantinople, seized Cyprus and Alexandretta and demanded that the victor submit the treaty to a congress of European powers. Disraeli manoeuvered Germany and Austria to his side and made Russia yield to British demands. So only narrowly was total war in Europe averted. The fear of that possible war cast a terrible gloom upon England, and lies at the bottom of this passionate cry of Symonds for a new principle of action for the individual and the nation, for a new and loftier race for whom war will be impossible.

*Stanza 1.* The two qualities that produce the new race are freedom, as opposed to enforced uniformity of belief or conduct; and knowledge, which alone can illuminate the path.

*Stanza 2.* The abolition of war coupled with the complete mastery of the powers of the universe. (Did he foresee nuclear fission and World Government by law?)

*Stanza 3.* The simple life for individuals, but the glorious life of public service, symbolized by music and hymns.

*Stanza 4.* Yes—World Government, the nations not only *un*-armed but *in*-armed, walking arm in arm in token of brotherhood.

*Stanza 5.* The bond of nations, as of individuals, is love—like that of angels in heaven, whose means of expression is chords of music without dissonance.

*Stanza 6.* Which suggests that the most complete expression of the ordered life is to be found in the Fine Arts. Back of his generalization lay the current teaching of John Ruskin, William Morris and Matthew Arnold.

*Stanza 7.* Suffering cannot be eradicated, nor the throes of passion, but sin and shame will be eliminated, for these arise only when God's law is broken.

*Stanza 8.* An affirmation of faith that these dreams will come true.

### Rev. *HENRY MONTAGU BUTLER* (*1833–1918*) Anglican, Broad

HERE is the almost ideal career of an English scholar: Son of a Headmaster of Harrow School; educated at Harrow and Trinity College, Cambridge; Fellow of Trinity; Headmaster of Harrow, 1859–85; Dean of Gloucester Cathedral, 1885; Master of Trinity College, Cambridge, 1886–1918; Vice Chancellor of the University, 1889–90.

Only twenty-five when he took charge of Harrow, he brought to his old school a vividness it had not known and a forward look that quite modernized the classic foundations on which Harrow, like all English schools, had been built. He introduced the study of science: "We want to get rid of the nonsense which regards Natural Science as naturally godless or at least uncanny." He was a great inspirer: he radiated a spiritual energy and high seriousness that boys felt and reacted to. Under his influence came, as boys, Prime Minister Stanley Baldwin, Lord Davidson (Archbishop of Canterbury), Galsworthy of the *Forsyte Saga,* 10 bishops including Bishop Gore, "the great thinker and theologian whose life and work was the reconciliation of faith and criticism in the Anglican Church," 17 judges, 4 viceroys, 12 governors, 12 ambassadors, 33 privy councillors, 64 generals. As successful builder and business manager he changed Harrow from a hide-bound and backward seventeenth century institution to a rebuilt and well-equipped contemporary school. Among the new buildings were a splendid library, gymnasium, science school, auditorium, a block of classrooms, besides football, cricket and tennis fields.

The hymn by which Dr. Butler is remembered was written for the *Harrow School Hymnbook,* one of the first of its kind. That book was the creation of a musical genius, John Farmer, school musical director; its use made inspiring by the unison singing he introduced into chapel.

### *Life up your hearts! We lift them, Lord, to thee*    [1881]

The theme is taken from the Prayer Book—part of the ritual for the Communion.

*The Priest:* Hear also what St. John saith, 'If any man sin, etc.' (1 Jn 2:1–2).
   *After which the Priest shall proceed, saying,*
   Lift up your hearts.
*The Answer:* We lift them up unto the Lord.

We must imagine ourselves in the splendid Harrow Chapel during a

Communion Service, the seats filled with the scions of the great families of England. The Headmaster as Priest stands at the altar, breaks the bread, lays his hand upon the cup and offers the invocation. Then when the rubric says, *Here may be sung a hymn,* before the elements are offered to the boys, the organ and the whole school raise this hymn of their Headmaster's. That indeed would be an inspiring moment.

*Stanza 1* is the invitation and the response.

*Stanza 2* prays that the dark levels of life may be lifted and illumined by the Lord of Light.

*Stanza 3* recalls the sins of cowardice and dishonor which need the lift that only the Lord of Truth can give.

*Stanza 4* prays that all the good gifts God has given us may be raised to an even higher level.

*Stanza 5* reminds the boys that some day as men they will still need this spiritual uplift to meet the challenges of life.

### RUDYARD KIPLING (1865–1936) Anglican, Broad

BORN in India, son of an artist and curator of the museum at Lahore which is described in the early chapters of *Kim;* educated in the United Services College at Westward Ho, England, Kipling then began his career in India, where from 1882–7 he was editor of two papers in English. For these he wrote his stories of Indian and Anglo-Indian life that later were gathered into the volumes, *Plain Tales from the Hills* (1887), and others. He showed himself from the first to be a masterful story-teller, and his light satirical verse caught on immediately. When this material was re-published in England the world became aware that another genius had arrived.

Travelling extensively (1887–9) he arrived in England, published his *Barrack Room Ballads* (1892) the racy slang of which added immensely to his popularity. Living some years in America, he married a Vermont lady in 1892 and published *Captains Courageous,* with other stories that reflect American backgrounds. In 1894–5 his genius showed another facet in his *Jungle Books* for children. Other poems and stories followed in a steady stream, the most popular being *The Day's Work* (short stories) and his fascinating novel of Indian life, *Kim.*

While visiting South Africa in 1898 during the Boer War he became an ardent imperialist, as his succeeding literary work showed. His last thirty years were spent in retirement, largely in England. During this time his genius was recognized by the award of the Nobel Prize for Literature (1907), numerous honorary degrees from universities all over the world, and the rectorship of St. Andrew's. He was regarded as the unofficial Poet Laureate of England—for it is alleged that he was kept from the official title because Queen Victoria took offense at his calling her "the Widow of

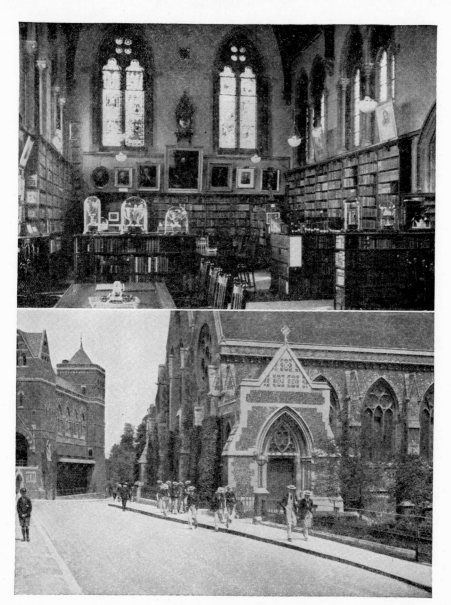

*Top,* The Vaughan Library, built 1863. "Lovers of books and lovers of chess are its patrons. All around are portraits and busts of famous Harrovians. Here one is in the heart of Harrow." *Bottom,* Harrow School Chapel. The first one was built in 1839 by Headmaster Christopher Wordsworth but the present one was built in 1857 around the old one. Here the greatest music-master of any school, Mr. Farmer, created unison singing which made the school services famous, and made the first school hymnbook. His successor, Mr. Faning, composed Harrow school songs that in later years became part of the most famous school song book in England.

*Top*, Kipling's house at Brattleboro, Vermont. *Left*, Rudyard Kipling. *From a photograph, copyright by Elliott and Fry, London.*

Windsor" in one of his poems. "He was a passionate patriot, an extoller of the virile virtues of clean living and manly duty and cheerfulness and stoic endurance."

While Kipling was descended from Methodist preachers—two grandfathers—and though he himself was a conventional Anglican, his literary work shows no particular interest in religion and he wrote practically no religious poetry. The two poems considered below were not intended for use as hymns but they were too valuable as pieces of work to be overlooked by editors.

THE RECESSIONAL

*God of our fathers, known of old*     [1897]

In 1897 the British Government held for Queen Victoria a "Diamond Jubilee" in recognition of her extraordinary reign of sixty years—longest in English history. In England a tremendous series of pageants of all kinds was arranged: her public servants came from their posts all over the world to do her homage; native princes from her imperial possessions, and kings, princes and representatives from all the nations of the world flocked to London. The culmination was the huge military and naval parade in which the might of England's vast empire was displayed in what was probably the greatest show in history.

Kipling had not been invited officially to write a poem, as would have been inevitable had he been Poet Laureate. Nevertheless the London *Times,* England's greatest newspaper, felt that Kipling should have the opportunity, and so asked him to write something. Kipling had considerable difficulty in doing it—more than with anything he ever wrote. The *Times* kept hounding him, but that didn't help. At last, spreading before him on the table his former scratchings, his eyes fell upon a single phrase that seemed pregnant with possibilities, "Lest we forget." That phrase finally evolved into the imperishable "Recessional."

It appeared on the front page of the *Times* after the celebration was over. It took the nation by storm and incidentally stirred up a hurricane of indignation. At the time when the glory of the British Empire had exhibited itself with all its pomp and power, how could a poet dare to suggest that the proper mood should have been a call for mercy to a just and righteous God! Kipling, the famed embodiment of imperialism, whose writings had nourished the pride of every Englishman, whose "white man's burden" had been a clarion call to the privileged race to serve the ignorant world through empire—that he should be recreant to his own ideals and pray for the forgiveness of heaven for their pride and boastfulness, that was not to be endured! Yet almost instantly the nation took the warning to heart. And while fifty years afterward Toryism and jingoism and power politics still exist, the logic of history is proving Kipling to be right and the Imperialists wrong. All their pomp of yesterday is following that of Nineveh and Tyre—and the ruin will be complete unless a deep spirit of religion can turn self-seeking into beneficence, and England raise the "lesser breeds" to the security and dignity that England has so long represented. Now someone should write a Recessional for Russia and the United States!

*Stanza 1.* God has been giving power to England for many generations—if the winning of many battles and peace congresses was God's gift. The result is an empire from the utmost northern and southern forests of Canada and Australia to the tropical forests that follow the equator around the world.

"Lest we forget" what? Forget the moral law that undergirds the universe: "What doth God require of thee, but to do justly and love mercy and walk humbly with thy God" (Micah 6:8).

*Stanza 2.* A masterful picture of the dissolving pageantry. That glory was fleeting, but the eternally enduring ideal is humility and repentance (Ps 51:16–17).

*Stanza 3.* The description of the dying glory continues: the fading of the 2500 beacon fires that flamed on the culminating night from Land's End to Ben Nevis, and their ashes are ghostly reminders of the buried cities of Nineveh and Tyre—centers of ancient empire over land and sea.

Nineveh is laid waste: who will bemoan her? . . . Thou hast multiplied thy merchants above the stars of heaven; thy princes are as the locusts and thy marshals as the swarms of grasshoppers [to devour] . . . There is no assuaging thy hurt. (See the entire Book of Nahum.)

Howl, ye ships of Tarshish! . . . Wail, ye inhabitants of the coast! . . . Who has purposed this against Tyre, the bestower of crowns, whose merchants are princes, whose taffickers are the honorable of the earth? Jehovah of hosts hath purposed it, to desecrate all the pride, to dishonor all the glory of the honored of the earth. . . . Howl, ye ships of Tarshish, for your stronghold is laid waste. (Is 23; Ezek 26:3–6.)

The refrain in this stanza changes to a frighted appeal for mercy.

*Stanza 4.* One recalls Lord Acton's words: "Power corrupts; absolute power corrupts absolutely." "Gentiles" reflects the emotional charge that the Old Testament Jew felt against those who knew not the Law of Jehovah which was Israel's distinctive glory. "Lesser breeds" are those who have never had the opportunity to rise to the dignity and power of England, which presumably has the "law" of God and uses it.

*Stanza 5.* The heart that puts its trust in guns ("reeking tube") and bombs ("iron shard") is heathen—has never caught sight of God's law! And the result, however valiant the fight, is "dust"— death and extinction instead of empire. (Ps 127:1; 69:5, 15.)

This hymn might have come out of the Old Testament prophets; compressed into it is the quintessence of the Book of Amos. In it there is no trace of ecclesiastical Christianity—only social morality founded upon religion.

### *Father in heaven, who lovest all*     [1906]

The original poem begins with this stanza, always omitted in our hymnals:

Queen Victoria stops at Temple Bar, entrance to medieval city of London, to receive from the Lord Mayor a pearl-studded sword. This was an episode in the Queen's Jubilee of 1897 which occasioned the writing of Kipling's hymn.

> Land of our birth, we pledge to thee
> Our love and toil in the years to be,
> When we are grown and take our place
> As men and women with our race.*

One of the poems in Kipling's *Puck of Pook's Hill* (1906). The book is a delightful combination of history and fairyland, written for children. Dan and Una playing at "Midsummer Night's Dream" on their country estate, somehow were surprised with periodical visits from a fairy named Puck. He told them snatches of ancient local history, from the visits of Phoenician and Greek traders, invasions by Romans, Saxons, Danes, Normans, down to Magna Charta (1215), with glimpses of the various weird religions that came and went. Between the stories are poems; last of all, this poem called "The Children's Song." It gathers up memories of the past and focusses all upon the lesson the children have presumably learned from the recitals, namely, religion and patriotism, the vital human achievements that they must accept and transmit. While not written as a hymn, its ideals are worth the Church's attention in the religious education of its children.

* From "The Children's Song" from *Puck of Pook's Hill* by Rudyard Kipling. Copyright 1905, 1906 by Rudyard Kipling. Reprinted by permission of Mrs. George Bambridge and Doubleday & Company, Inc.

In the preliminary stanza, bracketed in our hymnals or omitted altogether, the appeal is to patriotism: youth makes its pledge to the "Land of our birth," dedicates to it its love and toil. These energies are further particularized in the stanzas that follow. In the final stanza, bracketed or omitted, these various activities are summarized in a pledge to "Motherland." This appeal to the emotions under the figure of the family is appropriate to youth, which stands on the borderland between the sheltering home and the untried world.

In the central stanzas (2–7) the focal point is personal religion as the foundation and inspiration to patriotism. It is an appeal to God for His help in building character, as follows:

*Stanza 2.* A prayer that we may transmit undefiled the heritage of our fathers.

*Stanza 3.* That heritage demands taking responsibility now, while we are still in school; carrying on with it; searching for the truth which is the indispensable basis for national existence. "Grace" (the undeserved favor of God) is the source of that truth: patriotism is founded upon religion.

*Stanza 4.* That heritage demands self-control and purity of act and motive. Then when a crisis comes and our country calls on us for self-sacrifice, we may be a worthy sacrifice, one that really contributes something indispensable.

*Stanza 5.* That heritage demands a clear conscience in pursuing our ambitions. This enables us to stand alone, no matter what the world says: God alone is our judge.

*Stanza 6.* That heritage demands the exercise of mercy. Strength is granted us not for personal exploitation but to use for the social good, especially for the weak and suffering.

*Stanza 7.* That heritage is crowned by simplicity in our pleasures, fun that cheers but never hurts, a pure heart that can forgive wrongs done, an outgoing and unprejudiced love for all.

*Stanza 8.* The concluding stanza summarizes the ideal of patriotism as the dedication to our motherland of head—our intelligence, power of constructive thought; our heart—the emotions and the will motivated by them; and our hand—whatever skills we may have acquired. In fulfilling this pledge we become contributing members of our race and so carry on as our fathers did (stanza 1).

The unity of organization here exhibited is one of the necessary characteristics of a great hymn.

# HISTORICAL SUMMARY

|  |  | *Dissenting Hymnists* |
|---|---|---|
| 1837–1901 | Queen VICTORIA. | Bonar, 1836–55 |
| 1838–48 | Chartist Movement for extension of franchise and social reforms. | Wreford, 1837 |
|  |  | Duncan, 1839 |
|  |  | Adams, 1840 |
|  |  | Luke, 1841 |
| 1842 | Parliament Commission reports shocking working conditions in mines. |  |
| 1843 | Free Church of Scotland formed. |  |
| 1845 | Growth of Anti-Corn Law League. Three million die of famine in Ireland. Many Anglicans turn Catholic. |  |
| 1846 | Repeal of Corn Laws—to the advantage of the poor. |  |
| 1847 | Karl Marx: *Sketch of Communism.* Parliament prohibits women and children working more than 10 hours a day in factories. |  |
| 1848 | Thackeray's *Vanity Fair* lambastes vices of great and wealthy. Christian Socialists found Queen's College for women. |  |
| 1851 | Earl of Shaftesbury presses for slum clearance and other reforms. |  |
| 1854 | Christian Socialists found Workingman's College. |  |
| 1855 | Spencer: *Principles of Psychology* (materialistic). | Lynch, 1855 |
| 1858 | East India Company absorbed by British Government. |  |
| 1860 | Free Trade becomes England's policy. |  |
| 1863–5 | Dean Stanley: *History of Jewish Church*, applying development theory to Judaism and the Bible. |  |
| 1866 | Colenso Controversy over Higher Criticism. |  |
| 1867 | Franchise extended to lower-income citizens. | W. Smith, 1867 |
|  | Karl Marx: *Capital*—textbook of social revolution. | Clephane, 1868 |
| 1867–81 | Privy Council decisions adverse to High Church ritualists. |  |
| 1869 | Protestant Church in Ireland disestablished. |  |
| 1871 | Religious tests for university degrees abolished. |  |
| 1876 | Growth of Imperialism: Victoria proclaimed Empress of India. Compulsory education established in England. | Matheson, 1882 |
| 1886 | *Reform Act*; Universal manhood suffrage. |  |
| 1897 | Queen Victoria's Jubilee celebration. |  |
| 1898–1902 | Boer War. |  |

# THE VICTORIAN ERA:
# DISSENTING HYMNS

IN COMPARISON WITH THE VAST FLOOD of Anglican hymns in the Victorian Era, the contribution of the dissenting sects has been only a trickle. Of these, by far the largest number has come from the Presbyterians of Scotland.

### SCOTTISH HYMNISTS

In the Scottish Church the Muse awakened late. Our earliest Scottish hymn dates 1839, in spite of the fact that the Dissenting Church in Scotland was organized in 1560. This postponement was due to the Calvinistic dogma, accepted from the first by the Reformation Churches in Britain, that the only hymns acceptable to God were those found in Scripture, inspired by His own Holy Spirit (see Chap. II). The lyric spirit of Scotland, therefore, early produced a splendid metrical Psalmody which remained unchanged and in universal use until the nineteenth century. While here and there "hymns of human composure" were sung privately and as a supplement to the Psalter, the Church of Scotland did not even allow organs to be used in its kirks until 1874, and did not create a Hymnal until 1898!

This breaking of old bonds was the result of a gradual broadening of Church policy and a union of seceding groups.

At first the Presbyterian Church was "Established"—supported and controlled by the Government. The eighteenth century saw the beginning of a struggle for freedom; but not till an Evangelical revival began in the nineteenth century did a strengthening of the religious life and the establishment of independent Churches occur. Dr. Thomas Chalmers was the inspiring leader of a movement that by 1840 had built over 200 religious edifices. A renewed spirit of revolt against government control led in 1843 to the "Disruption": the Evangelicals pulled out of the national Church and established the Free Church of Scotland. It is this Church that produced all of the hymns listed below. Two other defections from the Established Church occurred, which by a merger formed the United Presbyterian Church. This in turn became united with the Free Church in 1900 under the name United Free Church of Scotland. By this time the Established Church was in the minority and, therefore, after long legal adjustments all the Churches of Scotland were given absolute self-government, free from State support and interference, and all became one under the title, "The Church of Scotland" (1929). It is democratically governed from the single kirk up to the highest representative body, the General Assembly.

This unified body now uses a common hymnal, *The Church Hymnary*, first compiled in 1898 and revised in 1928 and 1935. In it appear all the Scottish hymns of the nineteenth-twentieth century thought worthy of a place, and a generous selection of hymns from all other sources. Though not included in this study, the Hymnary contains a good many of our analysed hymns in its total of 727.

## Rev. HORATIUS BONAR (1808–89) Scottish Free Church (Presb.)

THIS greatest of Scottish hymn-writers was descended from a long line of ministers who aggregated 364 years in the Church of Scotland. He was trained in the University of Edinburgh and ordained in 1838 as pastor at Kelso near the English border. When the split came in the Established Church (1843) he entered the Free Church organization. His unusual powers won steady advancement in reputation. He edited the *Border Watch* that fostered the Free Church movement. Then after twenty-seven years at Kelso, which he had never intended to leave, he was persuaded to take over the large Chalmers Memorial Church in Edinburgh, erected in honor of Dr. Thomas Chalmers, his teacher at college and the leader in the Free Church Movement. Here he continued twenty-three years till his death. In 1883 he was honored with the Moderatorship of the Church's General Assembly.

Bonar was an enthusiastic Bible student, especially in the field of prophecy. For twenty-five years he edited the *Quarterly Journal of Prophecy*, in every issue of which he published one of his own hymns. To aid in this study he travelled in Egypt and Palestine (1855–6) and so obtained a factual background for his preaching and writing. His imaginative mind, however, led him into the vagaries of Pre-Millennialism: the imminence of the Lord's coming was the key-note of his preaching. His son writes:

> With the Saviour's return he associated the predicted restoration of Israel, destruction of Anti-Christ, the first resurrection, the translation of the Church, the marriage of the Lamb and the inauguration of the millennial kingdom. . . . He believed that evil men and seducers would wax worse and worse, that the poison of sin would become more and more deadly. . . . Immediately before the Return the dark energies of iniquity would recapitulate themselves in some person or institution or society which would be the

very Anti-Christ, and that the Lord would smite him by the breath of his mouth . . . and inaugurate the reign of grace.*

(If he had been living in the present age, what a fulfillment he would have seen in the rise of Hitler and Stalin!)

Bonar's fame and influence were solidified by his evangelistic tracts, devotional books and a prodigious correspondence with all sorts of people.

Horatius Bonar

He was unbelievably immersed in work. Though his Church inherited the Calvinism of the sixteenth century, his mind and heart were more generous than his theology; his love of mankind made his dominant interest the bringing of individuals to Christ without stopping to worry over their "predestination."

His imagination together with his flair for expression gave him his unusual power as a hymnist. No other Scot has approached him in the number and popularity of hymns. They were a spontaneous output. Though he kept a notebook in which jottings of ideas and of verse-fragments were written down as they occurred to him—chiefly on railway journeys—he could not tell the dates of many of his hymns. Some were composed on scraps of

* H. N. Bonar, Jr.: *Hymns by Horatius Bonar*, Oxford University Press, London, 1905.

paper accompanied by "doodles." Some of them were too spontaneous for literary perfection. That, however, is less important than the vital fact of their influence. They took the religious world of England and Scotland by storm, and thence covered the world. His total output was nearly 600. Over 100 are still in use in English-speaking countries; 41 are used in Roman Catholic churches; *The Hymnary* compiled to serve all the sectarian churches of Scotland still contains 15; the famous conservative Anglican hymnal, *Hymns Ancient and Modern,* latest edition, preserves 9. In the hymnals that comprise the present study there are 31, but contemporary general approval has dwindled them to only 3.

Of his hymns many beautiful things have been said:

His is always the accent of the singer who lives in his song.
Elevated and moving pathos.
The massive theology of the Reformation . . . breaks into deep and tender melody, a crystal river from the rock.

### Go, labor on: spend and be spent      [1836]

Written during his earliest period of service as student-assistant in a Leith mission church. Leith was a slum city where much social and religious work was needed. The object of the hymn was to encourage his faithful and hard-working helpers. It was his first hymn for adults, all the previous ones having been written for children in his Leith Sunday School.

As one might expect the hymn is full of scriptural allusions, and there are some hints of his preoccupation with the Second Coming. The incentives urged upon his workers run something as follows:

*Stanza 1.* Evangelism is the Father's will (2 Pet 3:9); the Master set the example (Lk 19:10).
*Stanza 2.* Though men may hate, the Master praises—a sure result (Mt 5:11–12).
*Stanza 3.* This approval of the Master is satisfaction enough (Lk 6:22–23).
*Stanza 4.* Though conscious of weakness and failure, the sure reward is heaven (Lk 13:29; Mt 10:22).
*Stanza 5.* There is need for haste, for the night cometh (Jn 9:4).
*Stanza 6.* Dying, hopeless men need you; take them the Light (Mt 8:12; 5:16; Eph 2:12).
*Stanza 7.* Toil, alertness, prayer, wisdom, are needed to save souls; go forth (Prov 11:30; Mt 26:41; Lk 14:23).
*Stanza 8.* Reward is sure (Mt 5:12; Rev 22:12); at Christ's coming, rest and heaven (Mt 25:6, 10; Jn 3:29).

### I heard the voice of Jesus say      [1846]

Of this hymn we fortunately have Dr. Bonar's original copy—a sheet of paper on which in pencil is the first rough draft—words abbreviated, changed, added to, and in the margins several "doodles," four faces partly sketched, and one expressive hat-to-shoulder drawing of a man.

This is undoubtedly Bonar's most popular hymn. Like "Go, labor on" above, it was written while he was student-assistant at Leith, but written for the children of his Sunday School. Those were the days when the churches of Scotland sang only metrical Psalms set to ponderous chorale tunes, neither the words nor the music of which aroused any interest in children. Bonar resolved to remedy this situation. He wrote simple words about Jesus and the Christian life, set them to popular airs and printed them on leaflets so that each child might have one. Grown-ups too were captivated, and as the stream of lyrics continued to flow from his pen their influence spread. In a way their appeal was similar to that of the *Gospel Hymns* so popular in America seventy-five years ago and still popular in the "Bible belt." In fact, Bonar actually wrote some hymns for Sankey when he and Moody were revivaling in Great Britain during the 1870's.

The present hymn presents three invitations followed by the human responses and the spiritual results:

*Stanza 1.* Come unto me (Mt 11:28): I came; found rest and gladness.

*Stanza 2.* Drink my living water (Jn 4:10, 13–14): I came, drank, and life revived.

*Stanza 3.* Look upon my light (Jn 8:12): I looked, and shall henceforth walk in that light.

It is all so direct and simple: no theology; a transcript of Christian experience which the wayfaring man, though a fool, can understand and appropriate.

### Here, O my Lord, I see thee face to face [1855]

Once a year Bonar visited his brother, Dr. J. J. Bonar, minister in Greenock, in order that they might together celebrate Communion. Dr. J. J. used to print a leaflet for each Communion Service and on that occasion, October 1855, Horatius supplied him with these verses. Of the eleven stanzas of the original only seven at most are found in our hymnals.

*Stanza 1.* The theology of the Sacrament is here not clearly expressed: it is neither the miracle of Transubstantiation, nor yet the Lutheran Consubstantiation, but more nearly like the Anglican "Real Presence." It is a mystic contact with "eternal grace," whether Christ Himself, or the gift of God which we call forgiveness, or salvation. The result of that contact is a burden rolled away.

*Stanza 2.* "Bread of God" and "wine of heaven" express the same truth in another way: the elements are something more than commonplace objects. The result of participation is, again, the burden of sin removed.

*Stanza 3.* "Banquet" suggests super-abundance; "song," the joy. The chief delight of all banquets is fellowship. In the Eucharist each one sits next to the "Master of Ceremonies"—the seat of honor.

*Stanza 4.* The essential spiritual blessing of the Table persists after the feast is done.

*Stanza 5.* That blessing is the continual presence and help of Christ.

*Stanza 6.* Here the Calvinistic interpretation is hinted: the blood of the Atonement shed once for all but memorialized in the cup is that which alone can cleanse from sin (1 Jn 1:7; Rev 7:14). Bonar probably knew John Wesley's translation of Zinzendorf:

> Jesus, thy Blood and Righteousness
> My beauty are, my glorious dress.
>
> .     .     .     .     .
>
> Fully through these absolved I am,
> From sin and fear, from guilt and shame.

*Stanza 7.* These recurring feasts hint at the eternal feast in heaven when the marriage of the Lamb and His bride the Church will be celebrated (Rev 21:1–5).

## Mrs. MARY DUNCAN (1814–40) Scottish Presbyterian

MARY LUNDIE was a beautiful girl, as fine in character and accomplishment as she was lovely. Her father was a parish minister at Kelso on the Tweed River not far from famous Melrose. Her younger sister married the famous Dr. Horatius Bonar (see above). She married Rev. William Wallace Duncan, Presbyterian minister at the obscure village of Cleish and died only three and a half years afterward, having in the meantime become the mother of two children. Her hymns, twenty-three in number, were written for her little children, too young then to understand them, and they were published after her death.

### Jesus, tender Shepherd, hear me     [1839]

The first hymn-prayer most children repeat is probably this one. It begins with Christ's own figure of the Good Shepherd who carries the lambs in His bosom—surely the most fitting that could be chosen, especially for Scottish bairns who saw shepherds and sheep every day of their lives. It continues with thanks for the Shepherd's guidance and provision; it ends with a prayer for forgiveness, for a blessing on loved ones, and for heaven when life is over. All these ideas except those of the last two lines are simple enough for a child to understand, appropriate and beautiful.

## Rev. WALTER CHALMERS SMITH (1824–1908)
### Scottish Free Church (Presb.)

EDUCATED at the Universities of Aberdeen and Edinburgh, ordained in 1850, he served churches in London, Glasgow and Edinburgh. He was honored in 1893 by being made Moderator of the General Assembly of the Free Church at its fiftieth Jubilee celebration. His poetry, which fills several volumes, was "the retreat of his nature from the burden of his labors."

### Immortal, Invisible, God only wise    [1867]

An apostrophe to God filled with phrases and ideas reminiscent of Scripture beginning with 1 Tim 1:17 and Ps 104:2. The basic metaphor is Light that reveals objects while it obscures its source. Coupled with that are other figures—mountains, suggesting the solidity and height of God's justice; clouds, symbolic of the constantly replenished source of goodness and love; vegetation, reminder of the tides of life that ebb and flow but that are ever renewed by the seasons.

One might say that the hymn is a rather florid attempt to express the inexpressible, and so rather a stimulus to the imagination than a clarifier of thought or an incentive to action. But no doubt our programs of public worship occasionally need hymns of this kind.

### ELIZABETH CECILIA DOUGLAS CLEPHANE (1830–69)
#### Scottish Free Church (Presb.)

HER father was a county sheriff, her mother a descendant of the famous Douglas family—

> My castles are my King's alone,
> From turret to foundation stone—
> The hand of Douglas is his own;
> And never shall in friendly grasp
> The hand of such as Marmion clasp!

She and her sister finally settled at Melrose near the old bridge which Scott mentions in *The Abbot* and *The Monastery*, and near Scott's home at Abbotsford. From her youth Elizabeth was in delicate health. Still to the limit of her strength she served the poor and the sick in Melrose, and together with her sister gave to charity all they did not need for family maintenance, even to selling their horse and carriage. She was known to the townspeople as "the Sunbeam." When her hymns were first published they were titled "Breathings on the Border" (of Scotland, or of life?). They contained the once popular "There Were Ninety and Nine," made famous by Sankey during his and Moody's revivals in Great Britain, 1873–4, and the following written shortly before her death.

### Beneath the cross of Jesus    [1868]

This hymn is appropriate for Good Friday or for any other day when evangelistic services are held. It centers attention upon the culminating fact in the life of Christ—His willingness to carry on His mission to men even to the death. Ever since that event in A.D. 30, the cross has been the constant symbol of the sacrificial life, commemorating, of course, the historic event but also challenging all men to match Jesus' heroism with a like heroism in His cause. Through the centuries thousands have risen to that challenge.

In most hymnals the hymn has been cut from its original five to three stanzas, largely because the Calvinistic theology they embody is now soft-pedalled. This viewpoint will be noted below. Other stanzas have been freely altered.

> *Stanza 1.* The cross becomes for this Scottish saint the symbol of rest for her soul on its last journey. For her now the world is a wilderness, a scorching desert; the cross is a place of rest for the weary and the heavy-laden. The imagery comes from the Bible: "the mighty rock," Is 32:2; "weary land," Ps 63:1; "home within the wilderness," Jer 9:2; "rest upon the way," Is 28:12; "noontide heat," Is 4:6; "burden of the day," Mt 11:30. The Scots knew their Bible!
> *Stanza 2* (usually omitted). The underlying figure is that of a storm threatening to overwhelm. It is the punishment due to sin, from which there is no shelter but the cross. *Cf.*

Rock of Ages, cleft for me, Let me hide myself in thee.

The cross is God's solution of an insoluble problem: how can justice that demands punishment be reconciled with love that demands forgiveness? That reconciliation makes possible a pathway to heaven—as in Jacob's dream (Gen 28:11–17).

> *Stanza 3* (always omitted). There are two shadows: one cast by the cross to protect the pilgrim from the heat (st. 1), the other lying beyond the cross, the shadow of death—not alone the death of the body but the "awful" death of the soul. The cross is both warning and rescue.
> *Stanza 4.* The cross now becomes more than a symbol. The saint actually sees the figure of Christ nailed to it, and realizes that His sacrifice is for her. Then the contrast comes driving home: His love, my worthlessness. (Editors have softened this last word to "unworthiness.")
> *Stanza 5.* The result of this vision and this realization is an acceptance of their meaning: I will stay within the shadow to mitigate the fever of life (stanza 1), but at the same time bask in the light of the Saviour's face, which is the symbol of His redeeming love (stanza 3). In the last analysis, all that counts is a recognition of my utter need and Christ's complete salvation.

## Rev. GEORGE MATHESON (1842–1906) Scottish Free Church

THE distinctive fact about this unusual man is that he was blind. From early childhood he was troubled with failing sight, but though physicians pronounced his eyes perfect in vision, he was wholly blind by his eighteenth year. Such an affliction must have come from psychological rather than physical causes—a form of hysteria. In spite of this handicap, however, he became a brilliant student at the University of Glasgow, head and shoulders above his fellows especially in philosophy, and he graduated at nineteen.

Beginning as an assistant pastor in 1866, he was called in 1868 to the pastorate of a small parish at Inellan, Argyleshire, on the Firth of Clyde. Here he stayed eighteen years, established a reputation as a preacher of the first rank, began his literary and theological writing, and won the absolute devotion of his people. While here he was honored by Queen Victoria with a summons to preach at Balmoral Castle. The Queen was immensely inspired and very grateful.

In 1886 Matheson was transferred to St. Bernard's Church in Edinburgh, where for thirteen years more he maintained his supreme place as pastor for its 2000 members. "The blending of imagination and reason in his preaching, and the breadth of his theology, made his ministry one of great and quickening influence, especially among young men." [*] Dr. Parkhurst, himself a famous preacher in New York, gives us a description of how this blind man conducted his services:

> He enters the pulpit not larger than a flour barrel. He has the face and form of Gen. Grant, but is taller. With natural open eye, you would not have thought he was blind. Now he rises, swaying a little until he gets his equilibrium. Announcing a psalm, he takes his verses without the mistake of a word, and throughout the service, calling for several hymns and Scripture references with chapter and verse, he never made an error. Then he prays, and such a prayer! It seems profane to write about it. Though his sight is eclipsed, he does see God, he does see into the hearts of his people. For forty minutes he preached. We were instructed, refreshed, inspired. [**]

Most of Matheson's work as scholar and theologian was published during this period beginning in 1874. But his blindness made painstaking research an impossibility and reluctantly he gave up the thorny path of scholarship. For a time he tried to find his way through the intricate paths of Biblical criticism, but this too was beyond him because of his eyes. Finally his writing changed to an area in which he was quite at home—the inner life, the mystical and devotional. Here he gave his spirit free rein and greatly enriched the life of his day. His writing continued into the period of his retirement which began in 1899. He published only one volume of verse, *Sacred Songs*.

[*] Moffat and Patrick: *Handbook to the Revised Church Hymnary*, by permission of The Oxford University Press.
[**] H. A. Smith: *Lyric Religion*, p. 301, Appleton-Century-Crofts, New York, 1931.

His own judgement on the quality of his verse is correct: the hymn below is the only one that is still remembered.

## O Love that wilt not let me go    [1882]

The occasion for the writing of this hymn has been the subject of much speculation. Perhaps to refute some mythical interpretations, Dr. Matheson finally gave all the information he felt the public should have:

> My hymn was composed in the manse of Inellan on the evening of June 6, 1882. I was at that time alone. It was the day of my sister's marriage, and the rest of my family were staying overnight in Glasgow. Something had happened to me which was known only to myself, and which caused me the most severe mental suffering. The hymn was the fruit of that suffering. It was the quickest bit of work I ever did in my life. I had the impression rather of having it dictated to me by some inward voice than of working it out myself. I am quite sure that the whole work was completed in five minutes, and equally sure that it never received at my hands any retouching or correction. I have no natural gift of rhythm. All the other verses I have written are manufactured articles; this came like a dayspring from on high. I have never been able to gain once more the same fervor in verse.*

This is an explanation that does not explain: the poet did not want us to know the details of inner suffering out of which the poem grew.

Perhaps we can gain some bit of insight if we approach the poem from the psycho-analytical angle. Modern psychology tells of the existence of a subconscious or unconscious mind that has a dynamic influence upon consciousness, of the fact of repressions resulting from "intra-psychical conflict," of "catharsis"—a cleansing, a clearing out of the emotional obstructions that cause mental suffering and even nervous and physical disorders. This cleansing occurs when the repression finds a definite and helpful channel of expression, sometimes through a new interest, sometimes in dreams, and usually in symbolism of some kind.

Apply this to Dr. Matheson and this hymn. In childhood—to which period Freud traces the origin of many later psychological disturbances—must have arisen the tensions and repressions that caused his hysteria of blindness. In adolescence came, it is reported, his consuming love for a girl, who jilted him when she realized he was going blind. This rejection sank into his subconscious and became a powerful repression, so much so that he never married. Now, more than twenty years after that experience, on the day *when his sister was being married,* and he was alone at home, something happened within him—a suffering so great that it broke the repressive bonds and issued, as one would expect, in a spiritual experience that could

* From H. A. Smith: *Lyric Religion*, p. 300 (no original source given).

be expressed only in symbolic form. What caused the release was probably an exceptionally poignant contact with God which brought the conviction that his personal frustrations and desires should be sublimated into God's will, that sacrifice was for him the only road to life. That is why the hymn seemed to be dictated: it welled up unbidden from the hidden reservoir of the subconscious as a catharsis and a release.

*Stanza 1.* Now what is the first symbol that expressed this new understanding?—Love. It is not the human love he has had and lost, but God Himself, the complete reality behind that word. It is God who has been pursuing him while he was trying to escape. But the fugitive now realizes the futility of the attempt, and, exhausted, surrenders. Then the flight-and-pursuit symbol is metamorphosed as in a dream into a different one that expresses the new love-union: the ocean receiving a river. What once was a turbulent and useless stream chafing within narrow banks has now become part of the ocean's infinite tide with limitless possibilities for power.

*Stanza 2.* The second symbol is light. It is the light that still pursues while his blind eyes are seeking it in the wrong direction. He has been wandering in a forest at night, trying to find the path but never striking it. Now the dawn has come, the sun rises. The flickering torch that originally had been lighted by the sun through a burning-glass ("borrowed ray") now merges into the infinite brightness that makes all things clear and beautiful.

*Stanza 3.* The third symbol is Joy. The pursuit now assumes in retrospect four different but related guises: it is joy overtaking pain, it is the rainbow painted against a cloud, it is tearlessness succeeding tears that endure but for a night, it is a closed heart opening.

*Stanza 4.* The next series of symbols begins with a cross. This is a glimpse of the reality from which the poet has been fleeing—the crucifixion of all that his soul longed for in its pursuit of Love, Light, Joy. Confronted now with this reality—that the historic Christ lost His individual life to save humanity—he raises his face to contemplate that suffering figure, and a revelation of how life can realize its highest hopes comes flooding down upon him. The flight from what is now recognized as his highest good ceases, the old ambitions die and are at once buried at the foot of the cross. Then, behold! a miracle: out of the dead earth springs a red flower! It is the symbol of passionate love and of self-sacrifice, endowed with the fadeless splendor of immortality.

It is a marvel that anything so unlovely as suffering can be transformed into a work of art so beautiful as this poem. This is poetry of the highest order; this is religion at its deepest and truest.

The value of poetic symbolism lies in the fact that it conceals what is intimate and personal. We do not know what caused Matheson's intense suffering: what has been written above is only conjecture about a process. But best of all, when we realize what areas of experience the symbols suggest, each of us can fill their general pattern with the intimate details of our own life though they may be entirely different from Matheson's, can sing this hymn feelingly and sincerely, and never reveal to another what is in the secret chamber of our heart. Tested by this touchstone, how few hymns of genuine poetic and religious quality are found in our hymnals.

### ENGLISH HYMNISTS

*Rev. JOHN REYNELL WREFORD* (1800–81) English Unitarian

EDUCATED at the Unitarian Manchester College in York, he became co-pastor of the Unitarian "New Meeting" in Birmingham (1826); then because his voice gave out he relinquished the ministry in favor of school-teaching. He opened a school in Egbaston, suburb of Birmingham (1831). His literary work consisted mostly of religious poetry. His zeal for the Unitarian form of Christianity led him to reject in his hymns—and in a hymnal he helped compile—all Trinitarian formulas and the sentiments in Evangelical hymns that savored of Calvinism, and "to reconstruct Unitarian hymnody out of materials exclusively Unitarian." Two of his hymns have survived but only one wins comment here:

## Lord, while for all mankind we pray     [1837]

Though Wreford here prays for his homeland of England, the absence of specific British references enables all peoples to use it without change.

*Stanzas 1–2.* While all men are brothers, we cannot help showing a special love for the land of our birth. The specific requests are listed in the succeeding stanzas.
*Stanza 3.* For security against invasion; for peace and prosperity at home.
*Stanza 4.* For devotion to education and religion; the realization of liberty—whatever that meant to an early Victorian.
*Stanza 5.* For the attainment of what religion promises: not the harsh gospel of Calvinism or the exclusive gospel of High Church Anglicanism, but the "pure and mild" gospel of Unitarianism that stresses only "piety and virtue."
*Stanza 6.* The prayer of stanza 1 in different words.

The hymn has no strong social message, as one might have expected from a Unitarian living in those revolutionary times (see under Ebenezer Elliott). Written in the year of Victoria's accession to the throne, it may well be that the author had in mind an ideal Coronation hymn, one in which all classes of loyal Britishers might join with genuine enthusiasm. Knowing as we now do the perils that were to beset the English modes of life and thought during Victoria's long reign, there was need for such a hymn with its prayer for the realization of the ideals of democracy. Compare with it, however, Kipling's "Recessional" written near the end of her reign, and observe the totally different emphasis and point of view.

### Mrs. SARAH FLOWER ADAMS (1805–48) English Unitarian

HER father, Benjamin Flower, who was editor of a radical weekly paper, *The Cambridge Intelligencer,* had the honor of being imprisoned in Newgate for six months by the House of Lords for criticizing the political conduct of the Bishop of Llandaff. While in jail he was visited by one of his admiring readers, Eliza Gould, a schoolteacher from Devonshire. Their political and personal outlooks so coincided that on Flower's release he married her. She thus became step-mother to his two young daughters, Elizabeth and Sarah, both talented girls.*

Sarah early showed a talent for writing. Her London pastor, Rev. William J. Fox, was one of the vigorous Unitarian reformers who fought for larger rights for women, freedom of the press, abolition of the Corn Laws, and who finally gave up the ministry to become a member of Parliament. To *The Repository* which he edited for his church people, Sarah Flower contributed many articles in prose and verse. Contributing also was an inventor and engineer, William B. Adams, who had a flair for political writing of the liberal type. In 1834 Sarah married him. Knowing her early ambition to be an actress and recognizing her dramatic ability, her husband encouraged her to make a try. Accordingly in 1837 she appeared as Lady Macbeth at the Richmond Theater, London. Her performance was so successful that she was sought by the Bath Theater, but finding her strength not equal to the profession she definitely gave up the stage for writing.

When in 1840–41 her pastor published for use in his South Place Chapel a collection called *Hymns and Anthems,* Sarah contributed 13 hymns and her sister Elizabeth wrote 63 out of 150 tunes, besides revising others. One of the hymns was "Nearer, my God, to thee." Besides a dramatic poem that dealt with the martyrdom in Carthage of a third-century female saint, she published *The Flock at the Fountain,* a catechism and song-book for children. She had numerous literary friends who often came to discuss religious matters with her, among them Leigh Hunt and young Robert Browning who was strongly attracted to both her and her sister. Elizabeth died of tuberculosis in 1846, and Sarah, who caught the disease while nursing her, died less than two years after. All who knew her acknowledged that she was a very lovely and highly talented person.

The only hymn that has survived in common use is

* There is conflicting opinion about this relationship. Benson says that Eliza Gould was the mother of these girls. Sarah was born in 1805 and Eliza Gould Flower died in 1810; no mention of Flower's previous marriage.

## *Nearer, my God, to thee*  [1840]

Mrs. Adams wrote spontaneously, on the impulse of some strong emotion.

*Stanza 1.* This hymn begins with an impulsive cry for fellowship with God, arising from some experience unknown to us. It was probably a sorrow, for the "cross" that raises her to the altitude of prayer is certainly not the Calvinistic "cross" by which sinners are saved from hell. Her salvation and her joy arise from drawing nearer to God.

*Stanza 2.* The shadow is still present. But now it takes on the figurative form of Jacob's experience at Bethel (Gen 28:10–22): Jacob is a "wanderer" seeking refuge from a revengeful brother; he has been overtaken by "darkness," his pillow is a "stone"; but his wretched plight is lightened by a "dream" released by the subconscious mind to relieve his defeats and repressions, in which impending catastrophe is illumined by the light of a God-directed future success.

*Stanza 3.* The figure continues, but is now personalized more vividly. The poet prays that her future path may become a "Jacob's ladder" that reaches heaven and reveals even her "crosses" to be God's promise of mercy.

*Stanza 4.* Jacob wakens and builds his altar out of the very rough stones ("stony griefs") on which he has slept. In this way the evanescent dream has become an enduring reminder of God's mercy: it is, hereafter, God's house (Beth-El) where at will he can renew contact with the divinity who pursued him without his knowledge and who has a glorious destiny in store for him.

*Stanza 5* grows out of the suggestion of flight implicit in "angels." As in the dream they "ascended," so some day shall she ascend to the immortality that the love of God confers. That heaven, in which life shall be consummated by eternal companionship with the object of her prayer, lies far beyond "sun, moon and stars" in the empyreum where dwells God, "in whose will is our peace."

Many editors and hymn-writers, including Bishops Bickersteth and How, have tried their hands at improving this hymn in the direction of Evangelical doctrine or emphasis, but all have failed. Mrs. Adams' original still stands.

### Mrs. *JEMIMA LUKE* (1813–1906) English Congregationalist

MISS JEMIMA THOMPSON inherited from her London father an interest in every good word and work. He was one of the founders of the

British and Foreign Sailors' Society, had given prizes for the writing of simple prayer-meeting hymns, and was noted for his broad Evangelical and philanthropic activities. At the age of thirteen Jemima used to write anonymously for *The Juvenile Magazine*. Once she surprised her father when he called for the singing of a certain hymn in his Sunday School: she was its author!

Though she had purposed to become a missionary in India, her health forced her to change her plans. However, her interest in missions continued. For a number of years she edited a missionary magazine for children. When she was thirty years old she married Rev. Samuel Luke, pastor of a Congregational Church in Bristol. The hymn here given is her monument.

### *I think, when I read that sweet story of old*    [1841]

The particular rhythm of this hymn was set by a Greek tune called "Salamis" which Miss Jemima chanced to hear at the Normal Infant School, London, whither she had gone to study teaching methods. She could not get the melody out of her mind, nor could she find religious words to fit it. She tells how at last the words came:

> I had to go one day on some missionary business to the little town of Wellington, in a stage coach. It was a beautiful spring morning, it was an hour's ride, and there was no other inside passenger. On the back of an old envelope I wrote in pencil the first two of the verses now so well known, in order to teach the tune to the village school supported by my step-mother, and which it was my privilege to visit. The third verse was added afterwards to make it a missionary hymn.

> *Stanza 1.* The first two stanzas are a unit: they take us in imagination to old Perea (Transjordan) and to the year 30 A.D. when mothers, hearing of the presence in their village of the great Prophet of Galilee, brought their children that He might bless them (Mt 19:13–15). As we realize the implications of the scene, we can only wish that our imagination were fact and that we were one of the children in His arms.
> *Stanza 2.* However, time and space do not sunder us from Jesus: by prayer we can still make contact with Him and be assured of eternal companionship with Him in heaven.
> *Stanza 3.* The outlook is broadened by the missionary interest: the children of all lands are equally welcomed by His arms. May the day come when the missionary's invitation shall be heeded and the Church shall be filled with His youthful followers.
> The last four lines do not necessarily refer to heaven, as most commentators suppose.

*Rev. THOMAS TOKE LYNCH* (*1818–71*) English Congregationalist

LYNCH began his career as usher (under-teacher) in school but later became a pastor in several small Congregational Churches in London, one of which, the Mornington Church, was built for him. His personal appearance was peculiar, his preaching was not of the popular variety, yet he had a gift of making people think in a new and intimate way about the deep things of the spirit. He was a great nature-lover, finding in the beauty of God's world an inspiration to holiness that ranked with other traditional sources. He tried to get this attitude across to his people and thereby provoked a quarrel beyond his parish, called from his published volume of poetry the "Rivulet Controversy." He named his book *The Rivulet* because "Christian poetry is indeed a river of the water of life, and to this river my rivulet brings its contribution."

Canon Percy Dearmer gives an account of the controversy in his *Songs of Praise Discussed:*

> He had poems sung from his book of poems which contained many references to nature: this was felt to be profane; and the scandal reached a climax when Lynch, being presented with a bunch of flowers one Sunday morning, took them into the pulpit and made them the theme of his sermon. Newman Hall, Binney, and Baldwin Brown stoutly defended Lynch, but Spurgeon condemned him for 'negative theology' and a 'non-doctrine scheme.' Lynch met the attack with admirable temper: 'The air will be all the clearer for this storm. We must conquer our foes by suffering them to crucify us rather than by threatening them with crucifixion.' But the controversy undermined his already feeble constitution and hastened his death.
>
> The fact that a large number of non-conformists could have violently objected to thus considering the lilies throws a flood of light upon the religious ideas of eighty years ago.*

The hymn of his that has survived is taken from *The Rivulet:*

### *Gracious Spirit, dwell with me*     [1855]

How differently would Christopher Wordsworth or any of the High Church writers have treated this theme! The subject is not the Holy Spirit as the third Person of the Trinity, but the non-theological spirit of God that pervades the universe and inspires the human spirit. Lynch characterizes it in four ways and devotes a stanza to each:

1. It is gracious: that is, outgoing in love and helpfulness. The prayer is that I may reproduce that quality in my life and so preach the gospel by act as well as word.

* Page 2. Used by permission of The Oxford University Press.

2. It is truthful: truth leads to wisdom, kindliness, sincerity—all echoes of Christ's character.

3. It is mighty: it reinforces my feeble strength and enlarges hope and courage.

4. It is holy: its presence will cleanse my heart and life, encourage the best and make my life sacrificial.

Lynch also wrote musical settings for twenty-five of his hymns, one of which he was heard softly singing as he lay dying. His last words were, "Now I am going to begin to live."

# HISTORICAL SUMMARY
## CHAPTER SIXTEEN: POST-VICTORIAN HYMNS

| | | |
|---|---|---|
| 1901–1910 | EDWARD VII, "by the grace of God, of the United Kingdom and Ireland, and of all the British Dominions beyond the seas, King, Defender of the Faith, Emperor of India." | Holland, 1902 |
| 1904 | Anglo-French Entente against possible German aggression. | |
| 1906 | Growing dissatisfaction with capitalism; socialism gaining. Forty-three Labor members elected to Parliament. | Chesterton, 1906 |
| 1907–9 | Important legislation to aid workers, increase education, health and unemployment insurance. | Oxenham, 1908 |
| 1910 | Union of South Africa formed. | |
| 1910–36 | GEORGE V. | |
| 1914–18 | World War I: a struggle between England and Germany for economic supremacy and colonial empire. | Bax, 1919 Fletcher, 1924 |
| 1936 | EDWARD VIII (Jan.-Dec.). | |
| 1936– | GEORGE VI. | |

## CHAPTER SIXTEEN

# POST-VICTORIAN HYMNS

QUEEN VICTORIA DIED IN 1901 but the social and religious movements that began in her reign have continued into the new century. To date there have been five twentieth-century British hymn-writers who have given expression to social ideals. Taken chronologically the first is

### Canon HENRY SCOTT HOLLAND (1847–1918) Anglican, Broad

THE product of Eton and Balliol College, Oxford, most of his life was given to serving his University. He was made tutor of Christ Church, a preacher during two different years, the Romanes Lecturer, and Regius Professor of Divinity (1910–18). From 1884 to 1910 he was Canon of St. Paul's, London. One of his valuable contributions was the founding, with others, of the Christian Social Union (1896), which he supported for twenty-two years till his death, and edited its magazine, *The Commonwealth*. As Canon of St. Paul's he was instrumental in raising the quality of its music. A writer of many valuable editorials, articles and books, he wrote only one hymn, which is

### *Judge eternal, throned in splendor*     [1902]

Suggestive of Kipling's "Recessional" (*q.v.*) in its reminder of imperial responsibility, it adds the note of social evils at home that demand attention. It is a powerful plea for reform, but its greatest limitation lies in placing the responsibility for betterment straight upon God.

*Stanza 1.* A majestic characterization of God as judge and ruler; a plea that He will descend as fire to destroy evil and then ease the pain of punishment with His own balm. The "wings" figure is from Mal 4:2.

*Stanza 2.* A vivid suggestion of social evils: overwork, the congestion, confusion and crime of cities, for the reformation of which the peace and quietness of the countryside mutely plead.

*Stanza 3.* A prayer for the spectacular intervention of God: let His "sword" be like a stroke of lightning at night; let the hungry heathen of the wide British Empire be fed by the word of God. [Does he mean to suggest more effective missionary effort in the spread of the gospel or the improvement of physical and social conditions by the application of gospel principles?]

How the Lord's "glory" can cleanse an empire is left to our imagination. That cleansing is a work for Christian statesmen.

Possibly the poet all along really meant that men have got to do the work, but he doesn't say so.

American hymnals of course change "empire" to "nation."

*GILBERT KEITH CHESTERTON* (1874–1936) Anglican, Roman Catholic

EDUCATED at St. Paul's School, London—the one John Milton attended—where he won the "Milton Prize" for English verse. After studying at the Slade School of Art he began his career as a writer of art criticisms for two magazines. From this field he branched out to miscellaneous journalism in which he became "one of the most vivacious, versatile and provocative figures in that field." His range of topics was broad, including some of the most penetrating literary appraisals of modern times (e.g., of Browning, Dickens, Swinburne), and a condemnation of the whole economic system of industrial capitalism, and equally strongly, of Socialism. Contemporary religious thought was attacked also in *Heretic* (1905), *Orthodoxy* (1908), and everything else in *What's Wrong with the World* (1910). To these were added detective stories, poetry, and a fanciful three-act play that was a success when presented.

Fairly early Chesterton came under the influence of Hilaire Belloc, a Frenchman, English educated, naturalized citizen and one-time member of Parliament. Belloc's enthusiasm for Roman Catholicism and for the civilization of the Middle Ages convinced Chesterton that Romanism was the true religion. When he was forty-eight years old (1922) he surprised everybody by changing to the Roman communion. The change made little if any difference in his views on most subjects. His *St. Francis of Assisi* was published after the change, but he would have said the same things had he been an Anglican.

## O God of earth and altar    [1906]

This was contributed to the High Church *English Hymnal*, though written earlier for a magazine. It represents Chesterton's scorn for the nineteenth century civilization which he regarded as degenerate, selfish and even cruel. The immediate cause for writing seems to have been the South African war (1899–1902) to which his friend Belloc, like many others, was bitterly opposed. In a way the hymn may be said to voice the aroused conscience of England against an unjust aggression. Though the Boers had begun hostilities, the deep-seated cause was the encroachment of English power upon the earlier Dutch settlers and the native African tribes. The discovery of diamonds and of vast gold fields to the north increased the struggle for control, encouraged and directed by Cecil Rhodes. It was he who financed

Gilbert Keith Chesterton

an unsuccessful raid into the Transvaal, which was the last straw. The Boers struck back.

After the victory it took a long time to reconstruct the shattered South African economy. England herself was divided on policy and it was not till 1910 that political and economic peace for these colonies was achieved under the new government, "Union of South Africa." During the long negotiations the subject was very much upon the English conscience. This hymn seems to be a product of that moral tension.

It may be added that the treatment of African natives and imported Indian labor in United South Africa is still a disgrace (1950) and a potential cause of war.

Stanza 1. "Earth and altar" (1) may stand for the two realms over which God is supreme: the physical and the spiritual. The hymn is a prayer for the supremacy of the latter. Our trouble is caused by the spiritual poverty of our rulers and the lack of idealism among commoners (3–4), by our lust for gold that makes our souls die (5), and by our haughtiness that severs friendship (6). "Thy thunder" is hint of coming storm—God's warning (7); "pride" is the summation of all our faults (8).

*Stanza 2.* A prayer for deliverence (8) from various spiritual evils: cowardice (1), duplicity (2), flattery of the powerful (3–4), veniality (5–6) desire for ease, which leads one on to destruction (7).

*Stanza 3.* We cannot be saved piecemeal: it must be all or none— the aristocracy, the Church, the commoners; salvation must come by divine chastisement (1–4). The nation is "living" when it can get angry with itself ("ire"), aflame with an exultant faith, and free 5–7); then it becomes a sword in God's hands to smite the evils of the world (8).

This is Chesterton's criticism of England, politically, economically, spiritually. History records that it has taken two world wars to force her to remake her ideals: she must now lose her imperialism by raising inferior races to her own level, and by socialism she is redistributing the wealth and economic power of her tycoons for the benefit of all. This would seem to be a tentative answer to Chesterton's prayer.

## *JOHN OXENHAM* (185?–1941) English, Congregational

MR. OXENHAM was very reticent about the date of his birth, but it was probably in the lower 1850's. He also changed his name from William A. Dunkerley. His career was amazing. Educated at Victoria University, Manchester—a late comer in the educational field (1880) compared with hoary Oxford and Cambridge—he was trained for a business career, travelled extensively as a business man in Europe, America, South Africa, lived several years in France, nearly decided to make his home in the United States and enter the cotton or the orange growing business. To relieve the tedium of his long journeys he began to write and soon discovered that he liked writing better than business. Soon writing became a passion and he gave up business.

His first book, *God's Prisoner*, was published in 1898. Following this came a list of forty-two novels besides twenty-five volumes of poetry and miscellaneous prose. When his first poem, *Bees in Amber*, was looked at askance by publishers he printed it himself and sold 285,000 copies! During World War I, becoming vitally interested in the religious life of the soldiers, he wrote for them several small volumes of verse which by 1919 reached an output of over a million copies. His *Hymns for Men at the Front* were sung all around the world: total circulation, 8,000,000 copies. After the war he wrote several interpretations of the life of Christ—all successful. His poem, *Chaos and the Way Out*, was adopted by the Methodist Church of the United States as a special service for its 20,000 churches.

Oxenham married a Scot, had two sons and four daughters, and died at his home in England during World War II, presumably of old age—for he was nearly ninety years old.

### In Christ there is no East or West    [1908]

Taken from *Bees in Amber* and used in the *Pageant of Darkness and Light* which was presented for a series of years in both England and America (1908–14). Oxenham wrote the entire text.

This hymn is the antithesis of Kipling's

> O East is East and West is West,
> And never the twain shall meet.*

It is the voice of a universal faith, a glowing ideal held up for the world to see and pursue. To have been more specific would have ruined the idealism and the poetry, but if Oxenham had been that reckless he might have written: "In Christ there is no Nicene or Arian creed, no Catholic or Protestant faith, no High or Low Anglican, no Methodist, Quaker, Nazarene or Pre-Millennarian sects." If these divisions represented organizations for efficiency in propagating the true gospel of Christ their existence would be pardonable and necessary, but in fact they represent internecine war that all too slowly and too late is being arbitrated. Oxenham's declaration is, therefore, an ideal not yet attained: there is no "one great fellowship of love throughout the whole wide earth." We have a Baptist Northern Convention and a Baptist Southern Convention, an Eastern Orthodox Greek Church and a Western Roman Catholic Church—stanza 1 notwithstanding. We have an obligatory Sacrament of the Mass and a recommended Sacrament of the Eucharist, salvation by Baptism and not by love and service—stanza 2 notwithstanding. We have an African Methodist Church that is not part of the white Methodist organization—stanza 3 notwithstanding, and in stanza 4 we must add parenthetically after "In Christ now meet," the words "in imagination only."

This situation is a Christian scandal. It is a contradiction of Christ's ideal and command, has been through the centuries the cause of martyrdoms and wars, and today renders the Church impotent to shape legislation toward a more righteous social order.

Let us continue to sing this hymn: it may sting us into repentance and action.

---

* From "The Ballad of East and West" from *Departmental Ditties and Ballads and Barrack Room Ballads* by Rudyard Kipling. Copyright 1892, 1893, 1899, 1927 by Rudyard Kipling. Reprinted by permission of Mrs. George Bambridge and Doubleday & Company, Inc.

## CLIFFORD BAX (1886–   ) Anglican ?

BAX was educated privately, studied art, lived much in Germany, Belgium and Italy, finally gave up painting for literature—poems, essays, a volume of memoirs, but especially plays in which music had a large part and which were successfully produced. In this realm he won distinction.

Eton College: Between Chapel and School: "You might spout me the construe!"

*Turn back, O man, forswear thy foolish ways*     [1919]

This poem is an aftermath of World War I. It is a magnificent call to men to make a right-about-face in their interpretation of religion and their ideals of life and stop crowning their heads with the flame of war. The nineteen Christian centuries have been devoted to propagating dogmas, persecuting dissenters, struggles for power in Church and State, wars for political and economic dominance and imperialistic control, scrabbles for personal wealth regardless of consequences to others (e.g., the 1947–8 gambling in foodstuffs when prices are putting the poor into bread lines, and Europe is starving). This is not religion. Man must totally change his emphases in religion; take oath that he will stop this betrayal of Christ.

More true than when this hymn was written is the line, "none may count her (earth's) days": for the atomic bomb, today a hundred times more powerful than when it turned Hiroshima into a dust wreath, will in the next war blot out New York and eight millions of people in a hundredth of a second.

> Earth *might* be fair (stanza 2): earth *shall* be fair under a World Federation ("all her people one," stanza 3) if we will implement God's will by our works! This is a clarion call to the twentieth century. It puts to shame the impotent demand of our previous centuries to accept a Church's theology and go to heaven when one dies.

### Sir *FRANK FLETCHER* (1870–1936) Anglican, Broad

AT Balliol College, Oxford, Fletcher had a brilliant career, winning three different scholarships. On graduation he devoted himself to the cause of secondary education: Assistant Master at Rugby (1894–1903), Master of Marlborough College, a fine boys' school founded in 1843 (1903–11), and Headmaster of Charterhouse School (1911–35). The Marlborough College appointment broke all precedent, for hitherto no layman had ever headed any of the great English preparatory schools. "He attained extraordinary success in the moulding of youth and in the management of schools for boys." The conferring of Knighthood was public recognition of this accomplishment.

### *O Son of man, our hero strong and tender*        [c. 1924]

Written for the boys of Charterhouse School. This famous institution began in London as a Carthusian monastery, founded near the east city wall in 1371. After the property had been seized by Henry VIII it was occasionally used as a royal residence, but in 1611 it was bought by a rich coal-merchant, who there established a hospital, chapel and school. The school, originally intended for forty boys, far outgrew these limits and became one of the great "public" schools of England. A few of its many famous graduates are Roger Williams, Richard Steele, Joseph Addison, John Wesley and William Thackeray. In 1872 it was removed to splendid new buildings near Godalming, thirty-five miles south-west of London. It was here that Fletcher served as Headmaster.

This is as fine a hymn for boys as was ever written. It is a paean of praise to Jesus, not as Son of God, or as Founder of the Apostolic Church, or as the creature of Nicene thinking, but as Son of Man—one who embodies all the ideals that make a boy's hero. These qualities are:

> *Stanza 1.* Strength, tenderness, sympathy, fun. "Our living sacrifice" means the sacrificial offering of our life's service.
> *Stanza 2.* The consecration of feet, for rugged ascents; of lips, for

*Top,* Charterhouse School at Godalming. *Bottom,* Headmaster Sir Frank Fletcher and his Sixth Form (seniors). "He was a magnificent teacher. The hours spent under him in the Sixth Form classroom will long be remembered by many generations of Carthusians."

inspired teaching; of eyes, conscious of beauty; heart, that loved a youth's enthusiasms (Lk 9:51–54; Mk 3:17).

*Stanza 3.* Lover of children (Lk 18:15–17), youth (Mk 1:16–20; 10:17–21; Jn 1:43–48), maturity (Jn 11:5, 36), and so one who welcomes whatever calls we make upon his sympathy and wisdom.

*Stanza 4.* Comforter and friend, whatever our state or need: one who welcomes the amenities of life (Lk 5:29; 7:36; Jn 2:1–2; 12:1–2) or the chance to share with the lowliest (Mt 8:20; 9:10–12).

There is nothing in this hymn that an adolescent cannot understand, and no ideal to which he cannot aspire.

# HISTORICAL SUMMARY

| | | *Evangelical and* |
|---|---|---|
| 1620–1789 | Colonial Period. | *Evangelistic* |
| 1740 | Whitefield begins the "Great Awakening." | *American* |
| 1782 | First Unitarian Church in America (Boston). | *Hymnists* |
| 1792–1817 | Jefferson and Madison fight for Democracy. | Dwight, 1800 |
| 1806–37 | American Missionary Societies founded. | |
| 1820 | Missouri Compromise on Slavery. | G. Doane, 1824–48 |
| | | Palmer, 1830–58 |
| 1831 | Garrison begins *The Liberator.* | S. F. Smith, 1832 |
| | | Bacon, 1833 |
| 1837–8 | Financial panic; growing misery in American cities. | |
| 1841–7 | Transcendental Movement: Brook Farm experiment. | Coxe, 1839 |
| 1841– | W. E. Channing (Unitarian) preaches social righteousness. | |
| | Bancroft, the historian, supports common people against privileged classes. | |
| 1846–8 | Mexican War. | |
| | Greeley and Charles Dana demand renovation of American society. | |
| | Lyceum Lectures popular (Emerson). | |
| 1847 | Horace Bushnell: *Christian Nurture* (against Calvinism). | |
| 1854 | Repeal of Missouri Compromise: All territories open to slavery. | Scriven, 1855 |
| | | Stowe, 1855 |
| 1857–8 | Widespread religious revivals. | Prentiss, 1856 |
| 1861–5 | Civil War. | Duffield, 1858 |
| 1868–82 | Many inventions; industrialization of the North. | Phelps, 1862 |
| 1868–80 | Four transcontinental railroads built; land frauds, bribery; great fortunes made. | Thomson, 1868–70 |
| 1870–1910 | Era of huge trusts, threat to free enterprise. | Wolcott, 1869 |
| | Foreign immigration increasing; slums, poverty. | |
| 1871 | Boss Tweed and his Tammany ring ousted. | |
| 1872 | Crédit Mobilier scandal. | Hawks, 1872 |
| | | Roberts, 1876 |
| | | Lathbury, 1877 |
| 1880–92 | Heresy trials (Presbyterian and Congregational). | Murray, 1880 |
| | | Rankin, 1880 |
| 1886 | American Federation of Labor organized. | W. Doane, 1886 |
| 1898–9 | Spanish-American War. | |

# AMERICAN HYMNS:
# EVANGELICAL AND EVANGELISTIC

## I. 1620–1823, THE ERA OF WATTS

AS IN COMMERCIAL AND POLITICAL MATTERS, so in religion, America began as a colonial dependency: she was largely a collection of English communities which were taking root in the New World. In their forms of local self-government, their social stratification, their education and lack of education, their dissenting and divided sects, they were quite English. Though they had rebelled at domination by the Established Church, Plymouth and Salem and New Haven brought with them the ideal of Establishment, and as for their Hymnody, they clung to the English-Calvinistic principle that God would be insulted if men offered to Him any hymns but those He had Himself dictated in Scripture. The Puritans of Salem, therefore, used Sternhold and Hopkins. The Pilgrims of Plymouth brought Ainsworth, and then, dissatisfied with the many unwarranted departures from the original Hebrew found in these Psalters, proceeded to make their own metrical version, the *Bay Psalm Book*. Some of this has been given more in detail in Chap. II.

While changes developed in the eighteenth century, they merely echoed the English evolution. Methodism brought the Wesley hymns to New Jersey, but the later comers to New England brought Isaac Watts. To be sure, Watts had to wage in America the same fight for acceptance that had raged in the mother country. It was a fight for "hymns of human composure" as well as for a less literal rendering of the Psalms, and that fight lasted into the second half of the nineteenth century.* For that reason our ten standard hymnals contain no American hymns written during the whole two hundred years of our early history from 1620 to 1820—with a single exception:

*Rev. TIMOTHY DWIGHT (1752–1817)* American Congregationalist

DR. DWIGHT was one of the outstanding men of colonial America, who, in spite of physical handicaps, became without question the New Eng-

* See H. W. Foote:*Three Centuries of American Hymnody,* chap. V.

lander best known and most influential in his day in education, theology and literature.

Born in Northampton, Massachusetts, his mother was daughter of Rev. Jonathan Edwards, famous preacher of Calvinistic hell-fire for unbaptized infants and those not predestined for salvation. Timothy was a most precocious youngster: at four he could read the Bible, at six he entered the grammar school, and, though supposedly too young to begin Latin, he borrowed *Lily's Grammar* from his mates and learned it by heart. When he was thirteen he entered Yale College.

After graduating he taught in a grammar school in New Haven, then became a tutor at Yale. When the American Revolution was on, he got a preacher's license, became chaplain of a regiment for a year and proved to be an inspiration to his men through his sermons and the songs he composed for them. From 1778 to 1783 he lived in Northampton, a farmer, preacher, student, and representative in the state legislature. Then he took a pastorate in Greenfield, Connecticut, augmented his meager salary by opening a private academy, which became so successful that in 1795 he was made President of Yale College.

His work at Yale was outstanding. He brought scholastic standards to a high level, inspired both students and professors by his learning, piety and genuine human interest. Not only was he President: he was Professor of Literature and Oratory, Professor of Theology, and College Chaplain. In the latter capacity he wrought a revolution. Most of the students had been infected with the "free thought" of Tom Paine, Rousseau and the French Revolutionists; professing Christians among them numbered not over five. But Dwight's frank discussions in chapel changed the whole complexion of the college: a revival ensued, the influence of which spread to other New England colleges as well.

In spite of imperfect eyesight due to the overstrain of study by candlelight in early morning hours and to the effects of smallpox, which made it impossible to read consecutively for more than fifteen minutes at a time, the amount of literary work he accomplished in forty years was amazing. Among his works are four volumes of travels in New England and New York, in which he gives details of local governments, popular customs, religious, social and economic conditions.

One solid piece of his literary work has to do with hymnody. In his day the churches of America were still wedded pretty strongly to Psalmody— either the "Old Version" or "Tate and Brady." But Watts was fast making inroads (Chap. V). A Connecticut enthusiast named Joel Barlow had revised Dr. Watts' *Psalms and Hymns* in a widely-used edition, but Barlow had gone to France, had dabbled with the French Revolution and had fallen, it was reported, into immorality. This spoiled his *Watts.* Accordingly in 1797 the Congregational and Presbyterian Churches of Connecticut requested Dr. Dwight to "demephitize and disinfect Barlow"! The result was so suc-

*Top,* Yale College in the days of President Timothy Dwight, engraved 1807. Notice the vanes designed as crosses. Compare the students' "football togs" with today's. Possibly the spectator (extreme right) may be the President. *Left,* Timothy Dwight, President of Yale 1795–1817.

cessful that *Dwight's Watts* was used in Connecticut almost exclusively for over thirty years. Of the thirty-three original hymns Dwight wrote for it, only one has survived.

### I love thy Kingdom, Lord     [1800]

A poem of eight stanzas suggested by Ps 137:5–6.

Since this is the only American hymn to survive of all those written between 1620 and 1824, it should be examined in the light of colonial religious and political history. So examined, "Thy Kingdom" proves to be a tight little closed-corporation of the Calvinistic saints-elect.

In the original Connecticut Constitution of 1639 the union of Church and State was presumed. The document clearly stated that the rules of Scripture should determine not only the ordering of the Church but the choice of magistrates, the making and repeal of laws, dividing of inheritances and all other matters of public import; that only Church members could become free burgesses and officials of the colony. This constitution was revised several times, and in the New Haven settlement "blue laws" were added that prohibited trial by jury, named the death penalty for adultery, commanded strict observance of the Sabbath, and imposed heavy fines for "concealing or entertaining Quakers or other blasphemous heretics." The Royal Charter of 1662 which united the Hartford and the New Haven colonies did not alter the theocratic law. This charter was confirmed in 1776 as the civil constitution of Connecticut. From 1789 to 1801 when the new United States Constitution was in operation, the Federalists were in control. Dwight was a Federalist. He was bitterly opposed to the democratic theories of Jefferson which would give equal rights to saints and sinners, college presidents and longshoremen. In a Fourth of July oration given about the time this hymn was written (1800) and aimed at the newly-elected President Jefferson, the Yale President said:

> The great object of democracy is to destroy every trace of civilization in the world and force mankind back into a savage state. . . .
> We have a country governed by blockheads and knaves. (And after giving some horrible particulars he adds) Can the imagination paint anything more dreadful this side of Hell?

But in 1817 the democratic sinners defeated the Federalist saints in the state election and established the present constitution of Connecticut.

This passionate belief in the supremacy of the Church over the State lies back of this hymn and must be read into it.

> *Stanza 1.* Kingdom, house and Church are apparently synonymous. It consists of all the people who have been predestined for salvation and have been saved by the Blood—according to the Calvinistic theory of the Atonement.
> *Stanza 2.* Dwight has substituted the Church for the Chosen People of the Old Testament as the special object of God's care. The language is borrowed from Ps 17:8, "Keep me (Israel) as the apple of the eye"; Is 49:16, "I have graven thee (Zion) upon the palms of my hands; thy walls are continually before me."
> *Stanza 3.* Complete dedication of all life's powers to the service of the Church. The social implication of these lines is elaborated in Dwight's Fourth of July Sermon, 1798: "The house of God is also the house of social prayer. Here nations meet with God to ask and to receive national blessings. On the Sabbath and in the sanctuary

the children of the Redeemer will, to the end of the world, assemble
to this glorious end. Here he is ever present to give more than they
can ask. If we faithfully unite here in seeking his protection, no
weapon formed against us will prosper."

*Stanza 4.* Three Church rites ("heavenly ways") are here suggested
as foci for emotions: the Communion Service, the "Right Hand of
Fellowship" (Confirmation, or the vows taken by adults before
baptism), and Hymns—a meager list when compared with the many
different celebrations in liturgical services. But that was Congrega-
tionalism.

*Stanzas 5–6* (Omitted in all hymnals.)

*Stanza 7.* The three titles given to Jesus suggest His love for
humanity, His sacrifice for man's sake, His claim to our allegiance
and obedience.

*Stanza 8.* The supreme place occupied by the Church in time and
through eternity. No doubt Dwight had in mind, for the last line,
the glorious spectacle of the City of God in Rev 21:1–22:5.

## II. 1824–1899, EVANGELICAL AND GOSPEL HYMNS

The Evangelical Movement in England represented a new emphasis in
religion—new and yet old as Christianity itself. The essence of it consisted
in cultivating the mystic, personal side: communion with God, fervent love
of Christ as God, prayer, contemplation of heaven as the reward for the
faithful endurance of the ills of life, nature as an approach to God, the winning of souls through conversion rather than through baptism, the spread
of the gospel to all lands.

The "Great Revival" that initiated it began in Wales under Howell
Harris (c. 1730) and swelled to epic proportions under Whitefield (1736–70)
and the Wesleys (1739–91). The Anglicans became infected and soon
found a humble leader in John Newton, the converted slave-ship captain,
who began his work at Olney in 1764 and with the cooperation of William
Cowper published the *Olney Hymns* (1779) which gave powerful lyric
expression to the movement. All this is given in greater detail in Chapter VI.

Whitefield brought revivalism to America in 1740 and America felt its
effects for more than a hundred years, though the domination of Watts
prevented lyrical expression until well into the nineteenth century. When
Evangelical hymns began, however, they increased to a fabulous number,
culminating in the so-called *Gospel Hymns* of the 1870's.

The Gospel hymn is a distinctively American phenomenon. It developed out of the camp meeting songs of the early decades of the nineteenth
century. It is, of course, Evangelical in spirit but focussed especially upon
the winning of souls through conversion, and while its primary use was in
revivals, it was taken over by Sunday schools, Christian Associations and
churches that in general were made up of less educated members to whom
literary form and quality had little appeal compared with emotion.

The modern Evangelistic as distinct from the Evangelical movement should be credited to the Young Men's Christian Association founded in London in 1844 and projected to Montreal and Boston in 1851. This organization took the leadership in a revival of some magnitude in 1858 that swept through the larger cities of America and helped popularize the Gospel hymn. During the Civil War the "Y" carried these hymns into the army and the *Soldiers' Hymn Book* became a leading instrument of army work. At least three great collections were used, containing, beside the newer type, the hymns found in the Church and Sunday school books at home. After the war the "Y" began a large revival work in the cities of the north and soon adopted the Gospel hymn as its distinctive type. These hymns gave to the evangelists of the postwar revival exactly the aid needed for their campaigns.

This revival movement culminated in the work of Dwight L. Moody (1837–99) who had worked among the soldiers during the war and in 1865 became President of the Chicago "Y." In 1870 a "Y" secretary, Ira D. Sankey, joined him. Together they undertook revival tours in America and England that "reduced the population of hell by a million souls." Moody never composed a hymn, Sankey hardly one, but Sankey was a composer and singer of extraordinary power. Sitting at his little reed organ on the platform he would lead vast audiences with his resplendent voice or sing solos with such pathos that sinners would be subdued and brought down the sawdust trail. Once in Edinburgh, called upon suddenly by Moody to cap a sermon on the subject of the Good Shepherd, he took from his pocket some verses clipped from a newspaper a few days before, placed them on the rack in front of him and improvised and sang the tune for

> There were ninety and nine that safely lay
> In the shelter of the fold;
> But one was out on the hills away,
> Far off from the gates of gold.

Any one who has heard Sankey sing that hymn will never forget it. His voice rose from a pianissimo recitative in spots to an Alpine horn crescendo that could be heard—actually once was heard—a mile way!

The songs these evangelists found effective were collected in a series of books. Sankey published one called *Sacred Songs and Solos,* of which it is said fifty million copies were sold. Then in 1875 came *Gospel Hymns and Sacred Songs.* Later collections by the same editors were numbered "Two" (1876), "Three" (1878) and so up to "Six" (1891). These hymns and songs are still extant in one volume containing 739 numbers. In this collection are found scores of the fine Evangelical hymns including twelve American given in this chapter, and many English hymns that go back even to Watts. Especially recognized are such English writers as Horatius Bonar, Emily Elliott, Charlotte Elliott, Miss Clephane, Kate Hankey, Frances Havergal, Charles Wesley and F. W. Faber. But American hymns make up the bulk of the collection—like those by blind Fanny Crosby (who wrote 8000! many of them for the *Gospel Hymns*), P. P. Bliss, A. T. Pierson, El Nathan, *et al.*, all of whom have practically disappeared from our standard hymnals.

Benson says of these:

> They carried the more emotional and less cultivated element of religious people off its feet, and furnished for a time the familiar songs of vast numbers hitherto unacquainted with hymns and unused to public worship. The new melodies penetrated even the music halls and were whistled by the man on the street. . . . Easy, catchy, sentimental, swaying with a soft or a martial rhythm and culminating in a taking refrain; calling for no musical knowledge to understand and no skill to render them; inevitably popular, with the unfailing appeal of clear melody.*

In a generation or two both hymns and tunes degenerated. The hymns became a repetition of old phrases, the tunes raggy and jazzy—the "oom-pa-pa" of a street band. A reaction finally set in and a return to the standard hymns of the Church. In some parts of America they still persist as the dominant lyric expression of religion.

In the pages that follow, the authors are given in chronological order, without regard to their classification as Evangelical or Evangelistic.

### Bishop GEORGE WASHINGTON DOANE (1799–1859)
### American Episcopal

THIS scholarly Christian gentleman was one of the great American prelates of his time. Educated at Union College, Schenectady, New York, and the General Theological Seminary of New York City; ordained in 1821, Assistant Minister at Trinity Church in down-town New York, at the age of twenty-five he was appointed Professor of Belles Lettres at Trinity College, Hartford, Connecticut. In 1830 he became Rector of Trinity Church, Boston —the church later to be served by Phillips Brooks. When only thirty-three he was made Bishop of New Jersey and remained there till his death.

As Bishop he was notably successful. The Oxford Movement in England was then in full swing. His sympathies were strongly with that renaissance of churchliness, as shown by his editing, in 1834, the first American edition of Keble's *Christian Year* (see Chap. VII, end; VIII, beginning), the contents of which fitted into his deepest life both as nature-lover and as churchman. His son, also later a bishop, writes thus of his father's impressionability:

> My father's poetical writings were simple necessities. He could not help them. His heart was so full of song. It oozed out in his conversation, in his sermons, in everything that he did. Sometimes in a

---

* L. F. Benson, *The English Hymn*, pp. 487–88, Doran, New York.

steamboat, often when the back of a letter was his only paper, the sweetest things came. And with his heart so full of it, nothing ever touched it but it pressed some out.

After his death his own works were published in four volumes. Three hymns therein preserved have perpetuated his influence to the present day.

### Softly now the light of day    [1824]

"Let my prayer be set forth before thee as incense; and the lifting up of my hands as the evening sacrifice."—Ps 141:2.

There is something about the fading beauty of sunset that deeply stirs the human spirit. It somehow gives pause to our feverish activity and turns our thoughts both inward to our deepest nature and outward till our spirit merges with the heart of the universe (*cf.* Tennyson's "Sunset and Evening Star"). This seems to be the experience recorded in this hymn.

*Stanza 1.* The dying day, the pause in our activity, make inevitable for the religious soul a period of communion with God.
*Stanza 2.* The introspective element is here uppermost: seeing one's life "under the aspect of eternity," from the impersonal viewpoint of eternity, leads to a prayer for forgiveness.
*Stanza 3.* The solemnity of the day's ending inevitably suggests the end of life. But that end, viewed also "under the aspect of eternity," can be glorious.
*Stanza 4.* This intimate intermingling of man and God brings to mind Jesus the God-man, who, looking at us "under the aspect of eternity," knows that we need pity and renewed strength more than condemnation.

The hymn was written for St. Mary's Hall, a girls' seminary founded by Bishop Doane. Traditionally this hymn is sung at the weekly chapel service throughout the year.

### Thou art the way; to thee alone    [1824]

The Fourth Gospel furnishes the inspiration for this hymn. In it Jesus is presented not so much biographically as philosophically. The author, John the Elder of Ephesus (c. 110 A.D.), was writing not to impress the superstitious commoners with whom Paul had such success (Acts 19:11–20), but the intellectuals who knew their Plato, and who believed in a Logos—the intelligent principle of the universe which also could descend into men as the Revealer of truth. In his gospel, therefore, we find clearly stated the functions of the Logos—identified in all its fulness with Jesus. Three of those functions are made the subject of this hymn: "I am the Way, the Truth, and the Life" (Jn 14:6).

*Stanza 1.* Thou art the Way:

Line 3: "He that heareth my word . . . hath passed from death into life" (Jn 5:24).

Line 4: "No man cometh unto the Father but by me" (Jn 14:6c).

*Stanza 2.* Thou art the Truth:

Lines 1–2: "Grace and truth came by Jesus Christ" (Jn 1:17). "Ye shall know the truth and the truth shall make you free" (Jn 8:32).

Lines 3–4: "That they might be sanctified through the truth" (Jn 17:19).

"The Spirit of truth shall guide you into all truth" (Jn 16:13).

*Stanza 3.* Thou art the Life.

Lines 1–2: "In him was life, and the life was the light of men" (Jn 1:4).

"And shall come forth; they that have done good, unto the resurrection of life" (Jn 11:25).

Lines 3–4: "I am the resurrection and the life" (Jn 11:25).

"That believing ye might have life through his name" (Jn 20:31).

*Stanza 4.* A summary of the teaching and a prayer that it may become part of us.

### *Fling out the banner! let it float*    [1848]

"Thou hast given a banner to them that fear thee, that it may be displayed because of the truth" (Ps 60:4).

A missionary hymn written at Riverside, Massachusetts, by request of the girls of St. Mary's Hall, Burlington, New Jersey, mentioned above. The school first used it at a flag-raising ceremony. Since then it has been sung at thousands of missionary meetings over the English-speaking world.

The hymn gains power by its repetitions: "Fling out the banner" is the bugle-call of each stanza; "skyward and seaward" (1, 5, 6) suggests the uplift and the wide outreach to all the world; "high and wide" (1, 5, 6) is a variant of the previous phrase.

*Stanza 1.* The cross is not a symbol of the sun in heaven that shines down on the banner, but the crimson emblem blazoned on the banner itself, which suffuses the whole with light.

*Stanza 2* suggests the mystery of salvation through the cross, which angels do not comprehend (though Augustine, Anselm and Calvin thought *they* did!)

*Stanza 3.* A vivid picture of the enthusiasm aroused by the Christian banner in heathen lands. After 150 years how many Christians are there in China, Japan, India? On the other hand, some islands in the Pacific have been almost entirely christianized, and their Christianity was a godsend to our GI's.

*Stanza 4.* A true insight into the therapeutic and inspirational value of the gospel. Line 3 was inspired by Mt 9:20, where a woman was healed by touching the hem of Christ's garment.

*Stanza 5.* Our emotion is intensified by the repeated view of the towering banner.

Line 3: "Far be it from me to glory save in the Cross of our Lord Jesus Christ." (Gal 6:14).

Line 4: "Christ in you, the hope of glory" (Col 1:27).

*Stanza 6.* Line 3 particularizes the "glorying" that is rejected in Gal 6:14 above.

Line 4 is an allusion to the legend about Constantine. Before the battle of Milvian Bridge, near Rome (312 A.D.) which was to decide for him the fate of the Empire, Constantine saw blazoned on the sky a cross and the words, *"In hoc signo vinces"*—"By this sign thou shalt conquer." He therefore vowed that if he won the next day he would become a Christian. Victory came, and after eleven more years of fighting, for better or worse, he became the first Christian Emperor, who founded Constantinople and pushed to acceptance the Nicene Creed, foundation of Catholic theology (325 A. D.).

These three hymns represent virtually the beginning of sacred song in America and stand in the best tradition of English hymnody.

## Rev. RAY PALMER (1808–87) American Congregationalist

BORN in Rhode Island, son of a judge who gave him his elementary education at home, young Ray first served as a clerk in a Boston dry-goods store, and, while attending the Park Street Church on "Brimstone Corner," he caught its evangelizing fervor and decided to become a minister. He prepared at Andover Academy, took his degree from Yale in 1830, and, to support himself while studying theology, he took a part-time job teaching in a girls' school in New York City and then in another at New Haven. Ordained in 1835, his first pastorate of fifteen years was at Bath, Maine, his second of fifteen years at Albany, New York; then he became Secretary of the Congregational Union of New York (1865–78) and on account of failing health retired to Newark, New Jersey, where he died.

The best of his thirty-eight hymns were written while he was still in the enthusiasm of youth, his most famous one (below) when he was only twenty-one, a few months after his graduation from Yale. In his more mature years, inspired no doubt by the example of the English scholars of the Oxford Movement, he used the leisure moments of a busy life in translating Latin hymns. He was thus the first to introduce this type to Americans. We have reason to be proud of him, for he matched the best of the High Churchmen in the beauty and inspirational power of his translations.

Dr. Palmer has been described as "a wise teacher, a simple-minded and devout Christian. He was a healthy, cheerful and buoyant man, loved by everybody who knew him."

### My faith looks up to thee　　[1830]

This hymn was written while Palmer was teaching at the girls' school in New York City. So many people later inquired how he came to write it that he felt it wise to publish a full account. Most of the minutiae are not pertinent to this study. The main point is that "it had no external occasion whatever." The poem was a spontaneous expression of a deep inner experience of the presence of Christ and a realization of what Christ meant to him and to the world. In writing he had no thought of ever showing it or of its eventually becoming a hymn. Jotted down on a loose sheet, it was afterwards transferred to a small morocco-covered book which he carried in his pocket for such purposes. No one ever saw it until a year or two later Lowell Mason, the musician, happened to meet him on the street in Boston and asked him to contribute some hymns for a book he was about to publish. Palmer showed him this hymn out of his little book. They stepped into a store and Mason made a copy. Then at home Mason wrote for it the tune "Olivet" to which it has been sung ever since. Meeting Palmer a few days later, Mason said to him, "Mr. Palmer, you may live many years and do a good many things, but I think you will be best known to posterity as the author of 'My faith looks up to thee.'" Mason was right.

The Congregationalists of America in Palmer's day were the inheritors of the English Evangelical tradition. Its theology shows a deep undercurrent of Calvinism which emphasizes the inevitability of human guilt, the sacrificial role of Jesus in salvation, and represents God as a hostile power that had to be appeased. These elements are here hinted in "Lamb of Calvary," "guilt" (stanza 1), "died for me" (stanza 2), "fear and distrust," "ransomed soul" (stanza 4). There is scriptural warrant for this view in Paul's allegorical interpretation of the Old Testament, in which Jesus is the sacrificial victim of the Hebrew Passover (1 Cor 5:7; 1 Pet 1:19). But countering the sense of guilt is the consciousness of Christ's redeeming and transforming power: "rich grace," "strength," "zeal," "living fire" (stanza 2); guide, bringer of light and joy, companionship (stanza 3). The final revelation of the Calvinistic undercurrent is the consciousness of death—the "cold, sullen stream" of Jordan that must inevitably roll: an ever-present fear, but relieved by the hope of being ransomed by the sacrifice of the Lamb (stanza 4).

Palmer's hymn is a perfect expression of nineteenth-century American religion; as yet untouched by Broad Church modernized insights as revealed, for example, in Canon Hatch's, "Breathe on me, breath of God"

(1878) or the Social Gospel emphasis that will soon emerge in England in Ebenezer Elliott's "When wilt thou save the people" (1832) and Tennyson's "Ring out, wild bells" (1842). In America the social note will not be struck with power until after the War between the States.

While still found in all our hymnals, this hymn is less and less frequently sung.

### Jesus, these eyes have never seen    [1858]

The hymn is based upon 1 Pet 1:8, "Whom not having seen ye love." Dr. Palmer has given us the incident that caused him to write the lines: He was

> preparing a sermon which had Christ for its special theme. Needing a volume from his closed book-case, he rose and opened the door, when the book appeared first in his hand. At once it occurred to him that in some such way the face of Christ would be unveiled to us; and the thought so filled his heart that he turned to his desk and composed the hymn.

Visualization is necessary to thought and an aid to emotion. This is why artists through the centuries have tried to picture Christ. Some have given us a simple portrait, some like the Byzantines have presented Him as a scowling dogma, a kind of focus for thought, some have put Him into a human situation so that we may see Him in action and realize His personality. But all these thousands of portraits are works of the imagination: they put into "a form not obliterated by the passing of time" the visualizations and the insights of the artist, and in turn they become focal points for the appreciation and emotion of others. This is one reason why Art has been called the handmaid of religion.

In Palmer's day in America there were few, if any, galleries containing old masters, nor had the printing arts arrived at anything like their present excellence. When, therefore, in the secret of his study Palmer undertook to visualize, he had no help from outside; he was thrown back upon pure emotion and found in the contact of soul with Soul the joy and the inspiration he sought. No doubt his heart was comforted with the latter part of the verse quoted above: "in whom, though now ye see him not, yet believing ye rejoice with joy unspeakable and full of glory"; or with that other in 1 Jn 3:2, "But we know that when he shall appear . . . we shall see him as he is." A few years later, Tennyson will restate stanza 3 thus:

> Whom we that have not seen thy face
> By faith and faith alone embrace,
>   Believing where we cannot prove.

And for stanza 4,

I hope to see my Pilot, face to face,
When I have crossed the bar.

Both Tennyson and Palmer are revealing the mystic side of religion in which the Nicene and Calvinistic creeds are both cancelled out by direct contact with reality.

Palmer's translations from the Latin have been touched upon in Chapter IX:

*Jesus dulcedo cordium, Jesus, thou joy of loving hearts*
*Rex Christe, factor omnium, O Christ, our King, creation's Lord*
*Veni Sancte Spiritus, Come, Holy Ghost, in love*

### Rev. SAMUEL FRANCIS SMITH (1808–95) American Baptist

SMITH was born in the "north end" of Boston under the shadow of the spire where hung Paul Revere's lanterns, and he graduated from Harvard in 1829. A classmate of his was Oliver Wendell Holmes, the "Autocrat of the Breakfast Table." This famous wit wrote in his Class Reunion poem of 1859:

> And there's a nice youngster of excellent pith,—
> Fate tried to conceal him by naming him Smith.
> But he shouted a song for the brave and the free,—
> Just read on his medal, "My country," "of thee!" *

After preparing for the ministry at Andover Theological Seminary he edited the *Baptist Missionary Magazine*, the function of which was chiefly to support the work of Adoniram Judson in Burma, the first Baptist missionary from America. In 1834 Smith became a Baptist pastor, first in Waterville, Maine, where at the same time he served as Professor of Modern Languages in Colby College of that town; then in Newton Center, Massachusetts, where he lived for fifty years in a frame house that is still standing. His missionary interest was so impressive that in 1860 he left the pastorate, was appointed Secretary of the Baptist Missionary Union, and in that capacity spent two years in visiting mission stations. Another great service to his denomination was the editing of their most popular hymnal, *The Psalmist* (1843), in use for more than thirty years.

His life was full of work—editing, preaching, managing, writing, and this continued till the very end. He died instantaneously as he was entering a train to keep a preaching engagement, aged eighty-seven years. One of his last poems (1891) was a school song for Worcester Academy, founded by Baptists to prepare boys for college and presumably for the ministry:

* The Poetical Works of Oliver Wendell Holmes, Houghton, Mifflin, Boston, 1891.

> Fair Worcester! enthroned on the hills in thy pride,
>   With the city domes gleaming below.

—in some respects a better poem than his famous national hymn.

## My Country, 'tis of thee      [1832]

This national hymn grew out of the fact that Smith was a linguist: by the time of his death he knew fifteen languages, and in his eighty-sixth year he was looking for a textbook to begin Russian! Dr. Benson tells the story of its composition: *

It seems that a certain Mr. Woodbridge had gone to Germany to study the school system and had brought back, among other things, some school song books. These he gave to Lowell Mason, then at the height of his revolutionary work of stimulating the love of music by founding singing-schools and training children to read a tune. Mason, not understanding German, asked young Smith to see what songs or hymns and what music would be suitable for translation, and he invited Smith to write some hymns of his own. As a result, Mason published two volumes, one of them, *Juvenile Lyre*, was the first song collection for children printed in America—most of the lyrics translated by Smith from the German.

While working at this, Smith's eye fell upon a tune he had never heard, and so did not know that the British had already pre-empted it for "God Save the King." The words of the German were patriotic. Then Smith says:

> I instantly felt the impulse to write a patriotic hymn of my own, adapted to the tune. Picking up a scrap of waste paper which lay near me, I wrote at once, probably within half an hour, the hymn "America" as it is now known everywhere.

The hymn was first sung at the Park Street Church, Boston, July 4, 1832, by a children's choir trained by Lowell Mason. From that beginning its use spread to the public schools and to patriotic celebrations everywhere. Thus was the wreath of immortality placed on Samuel F. Smith.

The hymn is no longer suitable for a national anthem. It is a New England product and its descriptions apply primarily to that corner of our vast domain. "Woods and templed hills" may be the characteristic charm of Connecticut, Vermont, and anywhere east of the Alleghanies, but they do not exist in Kansas or Louisiana. One has to hunt for "rocks and rills" in the prairie states. When Smith was composing his rhapsody the migrant settlers of Ohio and Indiana were forsaking for virgin soils the land where their fathers died; the English and German pilgrims had indeed been proud of Massachusetts and Pennsylvania, but their descendants now flocking to Los Angeles do not share their ancestors' search for freedom. We must confess, therefore, that what makes the hymn live is not its imagery of America but its passion, its ideals of "freedom," "liberty," "noble freedom,"

* L. F. Benson: *Studies of Familiar Hymns*, First Series, p. 98.

"sweet liberty," that spring from the heart of God. Our sentiment has so long entwined itself about these lines that to criticize them seems almost a sacrilege. We need not go as far as President Charles W. Eliot of Harvard who ejaculated, "Did ever a piece of doggerel win a man such fame!" There are far worse hymns in our hymnal. In spite of the adverse judgment of our head, our heart will still continue to throb under the wizardry of its emotion—it patriotism and religion indistinguishably blended.

## The morning light is breaking     [1832]

This hymn also was written while Smith was a student at Andover Seminary. It reflects his strong interest which later was to eventuate in directing the work of the Baptist Missionary Union and his two-year trip of inspection of mission stations.

We must remember that at this date Protestant missions were in their infancy. British William Carey had been the first to go (1793), Adoniram Judson had been the first American—a Congregationalist, but converted to Baptist views and immersed in Bow Bazar Church, Calcutta, by Carey. He began his work under the Baptist Union in 1814. When this hymn was being written Judson was erecting his church and school buildings at Moulmein, Burma ("By the old Moulmein Pagoda, lookin' eastward to the sea"), translating the Bible into Burman and laying the foundations for that grand evangelistic, educational and medical work so nobly represented in our day by Dr. Gordon Seagrave, the "Burma Surgeon," and his heroic band of native nurses. An inspiring report of Judson's work in Burma, which Smith had just read, was the immediate cause for writing this hymn. Smith's own son was destined to carry on the work begun by Judson.

The hymn is in some respects better poetry than "America." Its stirring imagery unveils the sunrise, the trade winds and the tropic seas; the jungle yields its denizens black and brown, who come crowding to where the gospel songs rise to heaven, and peace descends in showers of blessing. The final stanza is a fervent prayer that the gospel stream will swell to a mighty torrent that shall bestow its blessings upon all nations.

These verses have been sung over and over around the world. Dr. Smith wrote in 1883: "I have heard versions of it sung in Karen, Burman, Italian, Spanish, Portuguese, Swedish, German and Telegu."

## Rev. LEONARD BACON (1802–81) American Congregationalist

THIS man was the very incarnation of the evangelistic and missionary spirit. Well he might be, for his father had walked from Connecticut to Detroit—a three months' trek—leading a seventeen-year-old wife on horseback, sent by the Congregational Missionary Society of Connecticut to evangelize the Indians of Michigan. Leonard was born a few months afterward in the wretched frontier village of less than 2000 inhabitants. His father died not many years after, leaving Leonard to care for his mother and six brothers and sisters. But Leonard had the grit of a backwoodsman and the instincts of a scholar. He returned to Connecticut, put himself through Yale and Andover Seminary; then at twenty-three became pastor of the Center Congregational Church of New Haven.

His evangelistic spirit persisted through the forty-one years of his ministry there. Following the example of the late President Dwight, he sought to convert and inspire especially the students of Yale. With this aim he coupled a missionary zeal that led to his founding a monthly "Missionary Concert" in which other churches of the town joined, and in which he used the first collection of missionary hymns to be printed in America. He himself had compiled it while a student at Andover. Because of this sustained interest the Yale tradition of missionary service was established, which has in a century sent hundreds of graduates into the foreign field, led to the creation in 1886 of the Student Volunteer Movement, and in 1906 to the establishment of "Yale in China," a famous missionary college in Chang-sha that has survived the Japanese invasion.

After his retirement as pastor in 1866, Bacon served as Professor of Theology in the Yale Divinity School till 1871, and till 1881 he lectured there on Church polity.

## O God, beneath thy guiding hand    [1833]

Written for a celebration of the 200th anniversary of the founding of New Haven. As is natural, only the United States hymnals contain this best of Bacon's hymns.

It is fervently patriotic, conscious of the religious inspiration that drove our New England ancestors to these shores, and of the religious foundation beneath freedom, truth, law. In addition we have to notice the unusual absence of churchliness and of the Calvinistic theology still rife in Bacon's day. It deals only with the fundamentals to which no denomination or religion can take exception. For that reason, this hymn will never go out of fashion in America.

Probably the author had in mind the English people who settled in New Haven in 1638 and organized their government as a theocracy—God its ruler, its laws of the strict or "blue" type based on the Old Testament. But no doubt he also visualized the Puritans of Massachusetts Bay and the Pilgrims who landed on Plymouth Rock. He must have thought of the "Mayflower Compact." In that document, free men drew up a government in which authority was not a royal grant but was God Himself expressing through the instincts and ideals of His servants that respect for law and human rights which is the foundation of a free society.

"Thus," says E. S. Bates, "was set up a government by consent with the sovereignty residing in the whole male community, subject only to the ultimate authority of God and the King. . . . The sentiment of religious equality was carried over into political equality, and the government that was set up was made morally responsible for promoting 'ye generall good of ye Colonie.' " *

In stanza 4 of this hymn the love of God is the one enduring foundation of society. This is essentially the truth we are being taught by the aftermath of World War II and the revolutionary invention of the atomic bomb. The moral bases of civilization have been revealed as never before, and the challenge comes to us that we reconstruct our personal, social and political lives in accordance with these revelations. Failure to do so is destruction. So this hundred-year-old hymn has a message for all time.

## Bishop ARTHUR CLEVELAND COXE (1818–96) American Episcopal

HIS father was a Presbyterian clergyman, but the son seemed to have an inborn leaning toward liturgical religion. On graduating from New York University he added a final e to his name to distinguish him from his father, studied for the ministry at the General Theological Seminary (Episcopal) and after pastorates at Hartford, Baltimore and New York City was made Bishop of Western New York in 1865 with residence at Buffalo. He was an outstanding person, a militant Churchman, a passionate preacher and a modest poet, who as member of the Hymnal Commission of his Church insisted that any hymn of his own be not included in the Episcopal collection.

A generation ago the hymnals of many denominations included

> We are living—we are dwelling—
> In a grand and awful time

written in 1842 when the slavery question, intensified by the impending war with Mexico, was filling the nation with dread, and, the same year,

> In the silent midnight watches,
> List!—thy bosom door!

which was sung at every revival meeting and included in Moody and Sankey's *Gospel Hymns No. One*. The only hymn to meet the requirements of this study is

### O where are kings and empires now      [1839]

This hymn is excerpted from Coxe's earliest bit of poetry written when he was hardly twenty-one years old, a ballad called "Chelsea." It consists of four half-stanzas taken here and there to make up a unity of thought suitable for a hymn, and a splendid hymn it is. A superficial glance at history shows the wrecks of empires all along the shores of time, and a living, praying Church that has endured well-nigh irresistible forces of destruction and is

* *American Faith*, p. 110, Norton, New York. Copyright, 1940, by the publishers.

still militant. Stanza 2 likens her to a fortress—walls of granite laid upon immovable foundations (Ps 46; 1 Cor 3:11), her soldiers chanting their manly battle-hymns within their safe sanctuary. And though all the elements conspire to destroy her, she stands unshaken and unshakable (Ps 95:4; 46:5; Dan 2:35; 2 Cor 5:2).

This is an inspiring vision, but it is not true. The history of the Christian Church is a continuous battle and a continuous change: a civil war against heretics, protesters, non-conformists, puritans, theologians; an evolutionary change in which a Jewish concept of God as national Father becomes a Christian concept of Him as personal Father; in which Greek philosophy and Roman authority, asceticism, monasticism, ecclesiasticism, ritualism, sacramentarianism, deism, humanism, have produced a kaleidoscopic phantasmagoria of crashing patterns on the page of history. High Church brother Stone has given us a more accurate picture in stanzas 3–4 of his "The Church's One Foundation."

But, after all, Bishop Coxe has given us essentially the true picture. The marvel of the ages is that the Church still exists—and *is praying yet!* Through these prayers the true meaning of Christianity may yet be revealed, and the inner peace and outer transformation of persons and of society will some day justify the blood, sweat and tears that have been expended through the centuries by Christ and His followers.

## JOSEPH SCRIVEN (1820–86) Irish-Canadian, Independent

A GRADUATE of Trinity College, Dublin. He was engaged to be married, but his fiancée was drowned a day or two before the wedding. This tragedy induced a melancholia that afflicted him ever after. At the age of twenty-five he migrated to Canada and settled finally at Port Hope, Ontario. Though he was eccentric he was a born philanthropist and devoutly religious; he gave freely of what money he had, even his own clothing and his services to all poorer than himself who needed them. He was known as "the man who saws wood for poor widows and sick people who are unable to pay." At length he was found dead in a brook near Rice Lake where he had once lived. Whether it was an accident or suicide has never been determined. His neighbors thought enough of him to erect a monument to his memory.

### What a Friend we have in Jesus    [c. 1855]

Ira D. Sankey, the famous gospel singer who accompanied Dwight L. Moody on his revival tours, has given an account of how this hymn was written:

A neighbor sitting up with him (Mr. Scriven) during an illness happened upon a manuscript copy of "What a Friend we have in

Jesus." Reading it with great delight and questioning Mr. Scriven about it, Mr. Scriven said that he had composed it for his mother, to comfort her in a time of special sorrow, not intending that anyone else should see it. Some time later, when another neighbor asked him if it was true that he had composed the hymn, his reply was, "The Lord and I did it between us." *

The hymn was included in Sankey's *Gospel Hymns No. One* and was sung by revivalists and in prayer-meetings all over the English-speaking world. It is not good poetry. The rhymes are monotonous: "bear, prayer, bear, prayer; anywhere, prayer, share, prayer; care, prayer, prayer, there." It is what might be called doggerel. But if repetition is not a virtue, it is good teaching. Our criticism is made harmless by the tremendous service the hymn has rendered. Any unlettered person can understand it; the humblest saint can take its admonitions to heart, practice prayer, find his load more bearable and his spiritual life deepened.

### HARRIET BEECHER STOWE (1811–96) American Congregationalist

THIS person is known to fame for two reasons: she wrote *Uncle Tom's Cabin* which had a profound influence on the development of anti-slavery conviction, and she was a sister of Henry Ward Beecher, whose preaching was the inspiration of thousands, including Abraham Lincoln, and whose mission to England during our Civil War is said to have turned that country against recognizing the Confederacy.

Born at Litchfield, Connecticut, educated in her sister's school at Hartford, then moving with her sister to Cincinnati, Ohio, when their father, Lyman Beecher, was made president of Lane Theological Seminary, she helped the newly-established school and began writing stories and articles for the local papers, even compiling a school geography. In 1836 she married Prof. Calvin E. Stowe, a member of the faculty at the Seminary. To help with the family budget she multiplied her writings. Her sympathies with slaves multiplied also, for just across the river lay slave-holding Kentucky and she began to know first-hand what slavery meant, and to learn the schedule for the underground railroad. So when her husband was made professor at Bowdoin College, Maine, she knew her time had come to help the abolitionist cause. The result was *Uncle Tom's Cabin,* written serially for the Washington *National Era* (Whittier's paper) and published in book form in 1852. Not only did the book have a profound influence in America but it was translated into twenty-three foreign languages. In 1853 she went to Europe with the purpose of arousing the women of England to greater sympathy with the abolitionist cause.

From now on she was a literary woman. Her total output rose to forty

* *My Life and Sacred Songs,* p. 279.

*Top, left,* Ray Palmer. *Top, right,* Samuel F. Smith. *Right,* Harriet Beecher Stowe, portrait made in England, 1853.

volumes, concerned chiefly with social problems. Her religious poems also filled a volume. Her later homes were at Andover, Massachusetts, where her husband taught in the Theological Seminary, in Florida, and finally in Hartford.

Of her religious verse only one hymn has survived.

*Still, still with thee, when purple morning breaketh*    [1855]

Written at the request of her brother, Henry Ward Beecher, for his forthcoming *Plymouth Collection* of hymns. The hymn is a development of Ps 139:17–18, "How precious are thy thoughts to me, O God!"

On the whole, Mrs. Stowe is better than the Psalmist, for though the latter pays a wonderful tribute to the omniscience of God and His intimate penetration into the mind and heart of man, the effect is spoiled by an outburst of hatred against his enemies in *vv* 19–22. Mrs. Stowe keeps the wicked world out of her picture. She takes us into the silence of the dawn, and, like a nun kneeling in adoration before the crucifix, experiences with us that spiritual osmosis in which the soul and the Infinite intermingle. And that experience can be perpetually renewed "with each new-born morning"— Nature the ever-present priestess who administers the sacrament of communion to all who seek her reverently.

*ELIZABETH PAYSON PRENTISS* (*1818–78*) American Presbyterian

A NATIVE of Portland, Maine, and daughter of a saintly clergyman, Elizabeth Payson began writing both prose and poetry at sixteen and found an outlet in *The Youths' Companion* published in Boston, at that time the most widely-read publication for youth. After a period of school-teaching she married Dr. George L. Prentiss, a Presbyterian minister and afterward a professor at Union Theological Seminary in New York City. Though a life-long invalid she continued to publish at intervals; her best-known book is *Stepping Heavenward,* which outlines for young people what may be called the technique of the religious life and pictures the life hereafter. It reached a sale of over 200,000 copies—certainly a best seller for that day.

All her prose and poetry was religious. She was a mystic saint who lived constantly in and practiced the presence of Christ. Most of her 123 poems are addressed to Him. Of these, only one has survived in common use.

## More love to thee, O Christ     [c. 1856]

Written during a time of great personal sorrow, it was not shown to anyone, not even to her husband, for many years. But having been made public on a printed slip in 1869, it at once became popular. It was especially serviceable during the great revival of 1870. It has since gone all over the world and been translated into many languages including Arabic and Chinese.

The hymn does not require interpretation. The theme is expressed in the first line and is repeated over and over. The result is not ideas but emotion. In it the author renounces "earthly joy," rises superior to "sorrow, grief and pain," and has faith that her dying prayer will be unchanged from this.

*Rev. GEORGE DUFFIELD, JR.* (*1818–88*) American Presbyterian

HE was born at Carlisle, Pennsylvania, of a family distinguished in Presbyterian history: George I (d. 1790) was a chaplain in the Revolutionary army; his grandson, George II (d. 1868), was a pastor and theologian; the latter's son, George III, was the present author; Samuel, son of George III (d. 1887), was a noted hymnologist, author of *English Hymns* and *Latin Hymns*.

The present George graduated from Yale and Union Theological Seminary. Thereafter he held six pastorates in the East and Mid-West. His forte was preaching and pastoral work. In Philadelphia, during his third pastorate, his church was situated in a fast degenerating area and gradually grew impossible. It was while there he wrote his famous hymn, "Stand up for Jesus."

The tragic origin of this hymn has often been told. In 1857–8, Philadelphia, in common with many areas of the country, was experiencing a great revival. There the noonday meetings were held under the direction of the Y.M.C.A. in Jayne's Hall which seated 5000 people. The leading spirit in the revival was Rev. Dudley Tyng, a young Episcopal rector of unusual evangelistic power and nobility of life, a Low Churchman who believed in Church unity. Public sympathy was very much with Mr. Tyng, for he had recently been ousted from his parish for preaching a strongly anti-slavery sermon. When he was ejected many of his parishioners went with him and established a "Church of the Covenant" in a hall. Other clergymen had joined in the revival then under way, especially inspired by their admiration for Tyng. Mr. Duffield was among them.

Then came Tyng's sudden death. The previous Sunday he had preached a masterly sermon before the packed audience, and had converted a thousand of them. "The following Wednesday," wrote Mr. Duffield, "he left his study for a moment, went to the barn where a mule was at work on a horse-power machine, shelling corn. Patting him on the neck, the sleeve of his silk study gown caught in the cogs of the wheel and his arm was torn out by the roots." He died five days later. Several clergymen were present at his bedside. One of them asked the dying man if he had any message to send to his people. Tyng replied, "Tell them, 'Let us all stand up for Jesus.'" On the following Sunday Mr. Duffield preached to his own people from the text, "Stand therefore, having girded your loins with truth and having put on the breastplate of righteousness" (Eph 6:14), ending with the hymn that embodied the dying message of his friend. When published, the hymn became instantly popular especially among the soldiers of the Civil War. It has since gone all over the world in many languages.

## *Stand up, stand up for Jesus*   [1858]

The hymn is militant in spirit, based upon Paul's imagery of a Roman soldier's equipment. In a way this hampers its usefulness with the present generation, because modern warfare knows no "banners," trumpets have been superseded by "handie-talkies," and the gospel armor has been reduced to a mere helmet, while the "noise of battle" is now made by bazookas, bombs, tanks and machine guns. But our children will understand in spite of these anachronisms that the Christian life is a fight with evil within and without, that there is a Leader, that obedience and sacrifice are the order of the day, that courage and strength are still indispensable, that prayer helps and that victory is possible. This victory is won within us by letting the ideals of Christ dominate every thought and act; externally, by transforming the social life, now dominated by lust, greed and the will to power, into a brotherhood whose principle of living is the Golden Rule. Is there any other gospel but this or any greater challenge?

### Rev. SYLVANUS DRYDEN PHELPS (1816–95) American Baptist

BORN at Suffield, Connecticut, educated at Brown University and Yale Divinity School; then for twenty-eight years the pastor of the First Baptist Church in New Haven. While still in college he began writing hymns, among the first, temperance hymns for children. During his later life he published several books of poetry. As a result of extensive travels he wrote a volume on the *Holy Land* which ran through nine printings. Only one hymn has survived. His son, William Lyon Phelps, for many years the beloved Professor of English Literature at Yale, has this to say:
He was always deeply gratified by the success of one of his hymns, "Saviour, thy dying love," and he wished that "Author of the hymn" be put on his gravestone in the New Haven cemetery. It was.

### Saviour, thy dying love      [1862]

This hymn is a meditation in the form of a prayer.

*Stanza 1.* The supreme sacrifice made by Christ for me (the Calvinistic theory of the Atonement) suggests a counter-gift on my part: love and fidelity.
*Stanza 2.* My faith is fixed on Jesus, who (following Paul's imagery, Rom 8:34b) stands pleading with God to be merciful: to give me strength to endure whatever comes, and to make my contribution of love and testimony.
*Stanza 3.* A variant on stanza 2.
*Stanza 4.* A pledge of complete devotion and self-abnegation, ending with the usual expectation of an eternity in heaven.

Barring the outmoded Jewish concepts of God and sacrifice, the spiritual longings here expressed are valid for all earnest souls. When the hymn was written the wider function of religion in transforming the social and economic order had not yet risen above the horizon.

*Rev. JOHN HENRY GILMORE* (*1834–1918*) American Baptist

A VERSATILE and scholarly man who divided his time among preaching, teaching and writing—mostly editorial.

Born in Boston, educated at Andover Academy, Brown University and Newton Theological Institution, his teaching-subjects at various times were Hebrew (Newton and Rochester seminaries), logic, rhetoric and English literature (University of Rochester); his preaching was at Fisherville, New Hampshire, and Rochester, New York; his writings consisted of editorials for the Concord *Daily Monitor* and other papers, book reviews, hymns and a school textbook. For a time he was private secretary for his father, the Governor of New Hampshire. He is remembered today by one hymn.

## *He leadeth me! O blessed thought*    [1862]

Dr. Gilmore has left a record of the writing:

On a Wednesday evening he had been conducting a prayer-meeting at the First Baptist Church in Philadelphia; his topic, Ps 23. On returning to the house of friends who were entertaining him, he and they continued the discussion of the theme. "During the conversation," he says, "the blessedness of God's leadership so grew upon me that I took out my pencil, wrote the hymn just as it stands today, handed it to my wife and thought no more about it. She sent it without my knowledge to the *Watchman and Reflector*." The hymn has had continuous service ever since.

The house in Philadelphia where the hymn was written is now marked by a tablet commemorating the event.

Though the hymn was written in the midst of our Civil War it contains no hint of that fact.

The words are inspiring to those who believe them to be true. They are in a real sense true for those who are earnestly seeking to do God's will and who willingly follow the leadings of the Spirit. They are not true in the great external tragedies of life. When a boy is caught in the draft, sent overseas, gets smashed up in an airplane accident because of a pilot's mistake in judgement, his death in no way forwarding but rather retarding the great cause for which he is fighting, was he being led "by God's hand"? Were the twenty million Russians who were killed in the German invasion of their country being led "by God's hand"? Is the tragedy of the undeserved poverty and sickness of thousands of Christians in China and Japan the result of being led "by God's hand" and can these persons sing "Content whatever lot I see"? One has to eliminate most of the tragic events of life in order to believe this hymn to be true. It is hard to look at history "under the aspect of eternity," regard ourselves as expendable cells whose sacrifice is somehow necessary to a great evolutionary development, and still see God's hand in our obliteration.

Yet internally, in the development of one's personality, the earnest seeker after God's guidance can believe in it and find it, and the result is a Godlike person—even when that guidance leads to Gethsemane and Calvary. How many millions have found courage and joy in that fact! So we continue to sing this hymn.

### Mrs. MARY ANN (FAULKNER) THOMSON (1834–1923)
### American Episcopal

BORN in London. Since her father was an Anglican priest and her home a rectory, Mary Ann was from childhood deeply attached to the Church. When she came to America as the wife of Mr. John Thomson, librarian of the Philadelphia Free Library, she joined the Episcopal Church of the Annunciation of which he was a warden. She was the author of more than forty hymns, of which only one has survived.

### *O Zion, haste, thy mission high fulfilling*      [1868 and 1870]

This hymn is addressed to the Church under the fanciful name of Zion—originally applied to Jerusalem (2 Sam 5:7) and then by Christian metaphor transferred to the Church on earth (Heb 12:22) which eventuates in the New Jerusalem in heaven (Rev 21:2). The Church's mission is to reveal God as Light and Love—light to show the way of life, love to motivate the individual and to carry the message of the cross to the multitudes who need salvation. The last stanza proclaims the Second Coming of Christ, by which time the Church should have evangelized the whole world. The refrain expresses the fruits of the missionary endeavor: peace because of sin forgiven, knowledge of Jesus imparted to all, redemption from sin through the sacrificial death of Jesus, release from the consequences of sin (hell). This is thinly disguised Calvinism, which in a good deal of missionary work is still the dominant theology. It is time that a missionary hymn were written with a more modern approach to religion.

### Rev. SAMUEL WOLCOTT (1813–86) American Congregationalist

BORN at South Windsor, Connecticut, graduated at Yale College and Andover Theological Seminary, a missionary in Syria for two years but obliged to come home on account of ill-health; in America, pastor at Providence, Chicago and Cleveland. Strangely enough he never tried writing poetry until he was fifty-five years old; after that he wrote two hundred hymns, of which only one has survived. Of that one, the sentiment is praiseworthy but the poetry is inferior.

### *Christ for the world we sing*      [1869]

The hymn had an interesting origin. While Dr. Wolcott was pastor of the Plymouth Church in Cleveland, the Young Men's Christian Association of Ohio held a convention in the city. Directly over the platform was a large placard that blazoned the convention theme, "Christ for the World and the World for Christ." Having himself been a missionary and seen the need, he responded emotionally to the appeal and wrote this lyric that at once took its place among the standard missionary hymns of the Church.

Stanzas 1 and 2 picture the world's need; stanza 3, the ideal that new converts will share in still larger missionary enterprises; stanza 4 is filled with rejoicing at the prospective consummation of the Church's ideal of universal conquest.

### Rev. EDWARD HOPPER (1816–88) American Presbyterian

A NATIVE of New York City, a graduate of New York University and Union Theological Seminary, all of his active life with the exception of eleven years in Greenville, New York, and Sag Harbor, Long Island, was devoted to pastoral work in his home town. From 1870 till his death he was pastor of the Church of the Sea and Land, established as a mission for seamen, in whom Dr. Hopper was always deeply interested. He died of a heart attack while writing a poem on heaven. His various poems and hymns were usually written under assumed names or anonymously.

### Jesus, Saviour, pilot me      [1871]

Only three stanzas· have survived from a six-stanza hymn, published anonymously in *The Sailors' Magazine*. The hymn was first acknowledged to be his when he read it in 1880 at an anniversary service of the Seaman's Friend Society held in Broadway Tabernacle, New York. It is a fine expression of religion under the figure of seafaring, and because of its objectivity is especially dear to young people. The theme was of course suggested by the Gospel story of Jesus calming the storm on the sea of Galilee and quieting the fears of the disciples (Mt 8:23–27).

The hymn is beautiful in its simplicity and directness. Jesus is needed as a pilot over life's tempestuous sea. Only one who has a "chart and compass" can do this piloting, for he knows by his human experience where all the shoals and ledges lie that would wreck our lives, and where lies the harbor which all voyagers desire. The compass is that faith which points without variation to the true pole—the principle of life to which all must adhere who would survive the voyage: the Law of Love by which all actions must be judged. Such a statement of the essentials of Christianity is within the comprehension of even unlettered seamen, and is far more true and inspiring than any theological formula can ever be.

### Mrs. ANNIE SHERWOOD HAWKS (1835–1918) American Baptist

BORN at Hoosick, New York, a tiny up-state village, she began writing poems for newspapers when she was only fourteen. When she married and moved to Brooklyn in 1859 she united with the Hanson Place

Baptist Church over which, soon after, Dr. Robert Lowry became pastor. It was Dr. Lowry who started her on her career of hymn-writing and who wrote the music for several of her hymns, including the one given below. Her hymns were published in various popular hymnbooks of the Moody and Sankey type. After the death of her husband in 1888, Mrs. Hawks went to live with her daughter in Bennington, Vermont, until her death at eighty-three.

### I need thee every hour    [1872]

Mrs. Hawks tells us that the hymn welled out of her heart while she was doing her ordinary housework; it expressed her joy in the conscious companionship of her Master. She was not at all prepared for the almost universal use it won in Evangelical Churches and evangelistic services, and not until she experienced the loss of her husband did she realize how comforting the hymn could be in time of sorrow.

The thought of the hymn requires no exposition. It is an expression of the joy of divine companionship and can be used by any saint of the mystic type.

The refrain was added by Dr. Lowry, the composer of the music, to make it conform to the accepted type of gospel hymn.

The original final stanza has been omitted in all hymnals but the Presbyterian *Hymnal.*

### Rev. DANIEL CRANE ROBERTS (1841–1907) American Episcopal

BORN on Long Island, New York, educated at Kenyon College, Ohio, a soldier in the Union Army in the Civil War, beginning in 1866, rector of Episcopal Churches in Montpelier, Vermont, Lowell, Massachusetts, Brandon, Vermont, and for the final years, vicar of St. Paul's, Concord, New Hampshire. Besides being a faithful and well-loved pastor he carried outside interests: as President of the New Hampshire Historical Society, President of the State Normal School in Vermont, and Chaplain of the National Guard of New Hampshire. His one title to fame is his hymn, which slowly forged its way into popular acceptance. It is now found in all of our chosen hymnals that are published in the United States.

### God of our fathers, whose almighty hand    [1876]

The year 1876 was the hundredth anniversary of our Declaration of Independence. The event was celebrated all over the country, and in Philadelphia where the Declaration was signed it was made memorable by a Centennial Exposition, largest fair held in America up to that time. Though Brandon, Vermont, was a tiny village (only 1400 today), its people celebrated, and for that occasion Mr. Roberts wrote this poem to the tune "Russian Hymn." Not till 1894 was it published in a hymnal, and for it in the

Episcopal Hymnal the present music was written by Mr. Warren, a New York City organist. It is this music with its melodramatic trumpet calls that helped bring the hymn to public attention. The hymn is very serviceable for patriotic occasions, but offers nothing distinctive in the way of message or poetry. Stanza 1 emphasizes the majesty of God, stanza 2 is a prayer for national guidance in the future, as in the past, stanzas 3 and 4 enumerate the specific blessings desired. All this is general enough to fit into any kind of national celebration.

## MARY ARTEMESIA LATHBURY (1841–1918) American Methodist

SHE was born in Manchester, New York, daughter of a Methodist preacher and sister of two other Methodist preachers. She had many strings to her bow: She was a professional artist, having taught drawing and painting at Newbury Academy, Vermont, and in New York City; she was a writer of excellent verse and prose for children and young people, published in such periodicals as St. Nicholas and Harper's Young People. She was an editor for the Methodist Sunday School Union and a founder of the "Look Up Legion," based upon Unitarian Edward Everett Hale's famous Four Rules of Conduct:

> Look up, not down;
> Look forward, not back;
> Look out, and not in,
> And lend a hand,
> In his name.

But by far her most important contribution was made in connection with the Chautauqua Assembly in New York State.

Chautauqua is a tiny village of 300 people, quite swamped by the equipment and the summer patrons of the Assembly that for more than seventy years has been an outstanding American institution. The assembly grounds are situated among rolling hills on the shore of Chautauqua Lake, a beautiful expanse (seventeen miles by three) 1300 feet above sea-level. No more charming setting could be found for the work begun there by Rev. John H. Vincent (afterwards bishop). Originally a Methodist camp meeting, it was changed by Vincent into an annual ten-week assembly for the study of the Bible and Sunday School methods (1874). Its work grew rapidly, finally absorbing all the features that originally had been developed by the nation-wide Lyceums (1821–61); embraced the whole field of popular education, including music and drama. Some of the finest teachers, lecturers, artists, musicians and dramatists have served there.

Among the humbler members from the beginning was Vincent's assistant in the Sunday School Union, Miss Lathbury. Her lasting contribution proved to be the two hymns, both written for Chautauqua at Dr. Vincent's request. They are both used especially by young people in their evening services and summer conferences.

## Day is dying in the west    [1877]

The hymn is close to the heart of nature and expresses the feelings engendered by the sunset and twilight hours. It has been used as the opening hymn of the Sunday evening service at Chautauqua for over sixty years. The only part of the hymn that could be omitted or changed without loss is the final stanza where the thought of death intrudes. That is a hang-over from earlier evangelical writers who felt that no hymn could be complete without landing us in heaven.

The music has had a great deal to do with the popularity of the hymn. It is particularly appropriate to the mood of nature-inspired worship. The 6–4 time is not a dance rhythm, as one critic has asserted, but a lullaby rhythm. It rocks the soul into a mystic state where man, nature and God blend in quiet communion.

## Break thou the bread of life    [1877]

This so-called "Study Hymn" was written at Dr. Vincent's request for the Chautauqua Literary and Scientific Circle. This was a correspondence institute devised to supplement and extend to a wider circle the work of the summer conference. It offered courses not only in religion and the Bible but in any branch of learning a student might desire. As a home study course it could be taken by shut-ins, the crippled, the deaf, the aged. One New Jersey lady-student began French at seventy; Mr. and Mrs. Thomas A. Edison won their diplomas in 1930.

The hymn is based upon the incident of the feeding of the multitude by Jesus (Mt 14:13–21)—singularly appropriate to this Chautauqua Bible institute beside its own lake. It is frequently and quite appropriately sung also during a Communion Service. Used in this way it presents a theology contrasting with the traditional Catholic doctrine of Transubstantiation and the High Church Anglican theory of the "Real Presence." In fact, one can hardly classify the hymn as theological: it merely suggests that Jesus has something to offer us for the nourishing of our spiritual lives. That something comes to us first as words from the sacred page, but the true "Word" that really does the nourishing is the ever-living Christ Himself whom we contact by the outreach of our soul toward Him (stanza 1). The truth we find in this way needs consecration: that is, dedication through use in concrete situations. When so blessed it becomes fruitful in our lives, breaking fetters, opening the door to larger freedom, and yielding to the soul that peace which all men need. Such complete emancipation and inspiration with their resulting peace constitute the *summum bonum* of life, the "All-in-All" (stanza 2).

## Rev. ROBERT MURRAY (1832–1910) Presbyterian

DR. MURRAY was a Canadian. At ten he began writing poetry, and though ordained a clergyman his talent for writing led to fifty years of editorship with *The Presbyterian Witness*. His poetry usually took the form of hymns. The *Hymnary*, used by the United Church of Canada—Presbyterian, Congregationalist, Methodist and a few unclassified groups—contains besides the present hymn a "National Anthem" beginning, "Our loved Dominion bless." Dr. Murray was one of the leaders in trying to unite the various Presbyterian bodies of Canada, though he did not live to see the union.

### From ocean unto ocean    [1880]

The hymn is a fruitful blending of patriotism and religion, a contribution to the cause of Home Missions:

*Stanza 1*. Canada must be a Christian land that dedicates to Christ its God-given wealth.
*Stanza 2*. We pray for a more profound revelation of Christ, for that is the foundation of our temporal and spiritual welfare.
*Stanza 3*. It is Christ's gospel alone that can correct error with all it entails, and redeem all our diverse peoples.
*Stanza 4*. He must be our protector, inspirer and guide in the great Home Missionary task to which He calls us.

## Rev. JEREMIAH EAMES RANKIN (1828–1904)
### American Congregationalist

BORN in Thornton, New Hampshire, of Scottish pedigree, graduated from Middlebury College, Vermont, took his theological course at Andover, Massachusetts, held various Congregational pastorates and in 1889 became President of Howard University, Washington, D. C., an institution for Negro education, today a notable one. He wrote a good deal of verse and edited a number of song books of the Gospel Hymns type. He was a vivid preacher, "the deep voice speaking rapidly his characteristic short, sharp sentences with all his Scottish fervor and conviction." His congregations grew large; in the evening he conducted evangelistic services for which his one surviving hymn was written.

### God be with you till we meet again    [1880]

The hymn grew out of Dr. Rankin's interest in the derivation of the word "goodbye." The dictionary told him that it was a contraction of "God be with ye" and that was enough for the first stanza. After three musicians had cooperated in producing a singable tune for this stanza, Dr. Rankin composed the remaining stanzas, and a useful farewell hymn was on its way. It was popularized by a "Moody and Sankey" collection, adopted by the Christian Endeavor Society, then broke into three of the more conventional English hymnals, and now, with or without the refrain, is sung all around the world.

One realizes that this is not a literary hymn; it is a collection of phrases, almost ejaculations, embodying some of the homely pictures of the religious life drawn from contemporary evangelistic exhortations. The repetitions become wearisome. Dr. Benson has figured them up: "As sung there are thirty-three lines in all. Of these, just twelve are the first line over and over again, and in twelve other lines "till we meet" is read twenty times and sung forty times. Only eight lines are left which add any thoughts to the original theme, and most of these are turned from very familiar Scripture phrases." * The refrain is frequently and advisedly omitted.

Still, the hymn must have a strong emotional appeal or it would not have won such universal use.

### ANONYMOUS     [1881]     American?

#### *The wise may bring their learning*

*Stanza 1.* The imagery embodied in this stanza is evidently that of the three kings who brought gold, frankincense and myrrh. These gifts must be translated for children into terms they can understand and use.

*Stanza 2.* The "gold" turns into "love," the "frankincense" into songs of praise, the "myrrh" becomes a child's endeavor to live like Christ his King.

*Stanza 3.* The third gift is here enlarged and made definite: daily duties well done. Christian attitudes towards one's mates. The gifts of the kings were no better!

Contrast this simple statement of a child's religion with the High Church hymn of Baring-Gould—written also for children, page 372, in which boys and girls must become fighters, make "hell's foundations quiver," and subscribe to a belief in "Father, Son, and Holy Ghost."

### Bishop *WILLIAM CROSWELL DOANE* (*1832–1913*) American Episcopal

THIS son of Bishop George Washington Doane (see above) was born in Boston, Massachusetts, educated at Burlington College, New Jersey, founded by his father, ordained as assistant to his father in Burlington, then

---

* *Studies of Familiar Hymns,* Second Series, p. 287, by Louis F. Benson, copyright, 1923. Used by permission of The Westminster Press.

rector in Hartford and Albany, and finally elected Bishop of the diocese of Albany, 1869–1913. He wrote various works including a biography of his father and some poems of which only one hymn has survived. In his day he was so widely esteemed that honorary degrees were given him by Trinity, Columbia, Hobart and Union Colleges in the United States, and abroad by

A dramatic photo of Dr. Jeremiah E. Rankin, President of Howard University, Washington, D. C., and author of "God be with you till we meet again."

Oxford, Cambridge and Dublin Universities. From 1902 he was Chancellor of the Regents of the University of the State of New York.

### Ancient of Days, who sittest throned in glory     [1886]

When, in 1886, the city of Albany, New York, celebrated the 200th anniversary of its founding as the first American city, Bishop Doane was asked to write an appropriate hymn. The original version of this hymn was sung on that occasion, and when the Episcopal Church wished to include it in its new hymnal it was revised for that wider use. It is a stately prayer, written in the long slow rhythm that befits its dignity, and redolent of the churchly tradition that has come down from ancient times by way of the Anglican Oxford Movement of 1833 to the American daughter named Episcopal.

The hymn is full of Biblical reminiscences: "Ancient of Days" (Dan 7:9); "Eden," man's first home (Gen 2:8); "fire and cloud," the guiding manifestation of Jehovah as He led the Israelites through the Wilderness (Ex 13:21–22); "seas dry-shod" (Ex 14:22); "Prince of Peace" (Is 9:6); "Life-giver" (Jn 14:6). The hymn is also full of Nicene theology, revived and made standard in England by High Church Anglicans (see Chap. XII). Successive stanzas (2–4) are addressed to each of the three Persons of the Trinity and contain a prayer appropriate to each: the Father, who alone operated in Old Testament times and presides over the world's destiny, the Son, whose function is to save men from their own folly and passion as He once calmed the tempest on the lake, the Holy Ghost, inspirer and sustainer of our spiritual life, bringer of fellowship and peace. The final stanza unites the Three in One, the Triune God, who is the undivided Ancient of Days of stanza 1, refracted by the Nicene prism into his three functions, yet still One.

Our hymn cannot of course include everything. But it is singular that this one contains no hint of the social problems that in the United States in 1886 were pressing for solution, or of the growing conviction that the Church was obligated to do something about them. This is a backward-looking hymn: dignified, beautiful, but not prophetic or militant. The latest Episcopal hymnal (1940) shows some qualms about advertising our "plenty, wealth, prosperity and peace" (stanza 4:4), for it changes the line to "Our faith and hope, our fellowship and peace," and World War II compelled dropping "the peace that still prevails" in favor of the hopeful "shall prevail." A travesty of history is also written in stanza 1, every item is untrue— as are most of the assertions of the hymn. If we can manage to shut our eyes and ears to the past and present, perhaps we still can sing it with fervor.

# HISTORICAL SUMMARY

| | | |
|---|---|---|
| 1831 | Garrison begins *The Liberator*. | *Unitarian and* |
| 1841–7 | Transcendental Movement: Brook Farm experiment. | *Friend* |
| 1841– | W. E. Channing (Unitarian) preaches social righteousness. | *Hymnists* |
| | Bancroft, the historian, supports common people against privileged classes. | Lowell, 1844 |
| 1846–8 | Mexican War. | Sears, 1846 |
| | Greeley and Charles Dana demand renovation of American society. | |
| | Lyceum Lectures popular (Emerson). | |
| 1847 | Horace Bushnell: *Christian Nurture* (against Calvinism). | |
| | | Burleigh, 1848 |
| | | Whittier, 1848–72 |
| 1854 | Repeal of Missouri Compromise: all territories open to slavery. | |
| 1857–8 | Widespread religious revivals. | S. Longfellow, 1859–64 |
| | | Holmes, 1859 |
| 1861–5 | Civil War. | Chadwick, 1864 |
| | | Johnson, 1864 |
| 1868–82 | Many inventions; industrialization of the North. | |
| 1869–80 | Four transcontinental railroads built; land frauds; bribery; great fortunes made. | |
| 1870–1910 | Era of huge trusts, threat to free enterprise. | |
| | Foreign immigration increasing; slums, poverty. | |
| 1871 | Boss Tweed and his Tammany ring ousted. | |
| 1872 | Crédit Mobilier scandal. | |
| 1880–92 | Heresy trials (Presbyterian and Congregational). | Hosmer, 1876–1905 |
| 1886 | American Federation of Labor organized. | |
| 1898–9 | Spanish-American War. | |
| 1901–9 | Theodore Roosevelt President: Trust-busting and imperialism. | |
| | Rise of social philosophers: L. Ward, R. Ely, Veblen, B. Adams. | |
| 1902 | Ida Tarbell: *History of the Standard Oil Co.* | |
| | Frank Norris: *The Pit.* | |
| 1904 | Upton Sinclair: *The Jungle.* | |
| | Robert Hunter: *Poverty* (demanded more social legislation). | |
| 1907 | Rauschenbusch: *Christianity and the Social Crisis* | |
| 1909 | Hyde: *Outlines of Social Theology.* | Wile, 1911 |
| 1914–18 | World War I. | |
| 1923–33 | "Boom and Bust" period. | |

## CHAPTER EIGHTEEN

# AMERICAN HYMNS:
# THE REVOLT AGAINST CALVINISM

## I. UNITARIAN HYMNS

IN EARLIER CHAPTERS we have considered certain English Unitarian hymn-writers: Bowring (1825), Ebenezer Elliott (1832), Wreford (1837) and Adams (1840). The outburst of American Unitarian hymns occurred in the 1840's through the 1860's, though Hosmer, one of their best singers, came at the end of the nineteenth century. These American hymns are different from the English for they represent a new kind of Unitariansm which, while having some English inspirations, was in essence an American development.

American Unitarianism shows three phases of growth. The first, which ended about 1835, was based upon a rejection of Calvinism and all its works, in fact a rejection of all creeds on the ground that they were non-Biblical. The first church in America to accept Unitarianism as its principle was King's Chapel, Boston, 1782, James Freeman pastor. Harvard College was captured by the Unitarians in 1805, though its Divinity School was not founded until 1816. In this first phase, as in the later ones, America was following England in its ideal of religious liberty. The English Unitarians in 1792 had presented a petition to Parliament in which they declared that "they conceived it their duty to examine into and interpret the Holy Scriptures for themselves and their right publicly to declare the results of their enquiries." But they had to fight for their rights: penal laws against those who denied the Trinity were not repealed until 1813, and the Test and Corporation Acts which limited the political rights of all who dissented from the Established Church were not repealed until 1828.

In America under the newly created Constitution religion was politically free, but the Trinitarian Churches fought hard to keep their members from getting the liberal taint. The Calvinists founded Andover Theological Seminary in 1808 as an answer to Unitarian Harvard. William Ellery Channing was their *bête noir*—a Congregationalist who by 1819 had become a Unitarian, though he objected to the term as not expressing "the close fatherly relation of God to man." His article on "The Moral Argument Against Calvinism" was devastating: his conclusion was "Existence is a curse if Calvinism is true." On the positive side he put the liberal philosophy trenchantly: "The only God whom our thoughts can rest on and our hearts can cling to, is the God whose image dwells in our own souls."

As will be seen below, there are no hymns from this period. Something more positive than a rejection of outworn creeds was needed to make a Unitarian sing. That something, which produced the second phase, was the infiltration of French liberalism, which taught the excellence of human nature rather than its incurable sinfulness, and the more dynamic German Romanticism of Goethe and Schiller, which was given the name Transcendentalism. The latter was a philosophy of intuition based on the assumption that there is a world of reality beyond the world of experience which alone gives significance and value to the world we see. These ideas were not exactly new: they can be traced back through Kant (d. 1804) and the medieval Schoolmen to Plato, but as expounded by the contemporary Germans they brought an increase of mysticism that made the universal Soul an indwelling experience. In concrete terms this means "the inalienable worth of man."

One of the first to catch the import of this philosophy was Ralph Waldo Emerson. As early as 1832 he had gone to England to talk with Coleridge, Wordsworth, and especially Carlyle, who had already been set on fire by the German Kant. The visit wonderfully stimulated Emerson, only recently eased out of his Boston Unitarian pulpit because of his liberalism. Within a few years after reaching home he published his first series of Essays (1841), in which "The Over-Soul" contains his religious philosophy. A few excerpts will show his slant:

> Ineffable is the union of man and God in every act of the soul. . . . Yet forever and ever the influx of this better and universal self is new and unsearchable. . . . When we have broken our god of tradition, and ceased from our god of rhetoric, then may God fire the heart with his presence. . . . It is the infinite enlargement of the heart with a power of growth to a new infinity on every side. . . . He is sure that his welfare is dear to the heart of being. Let man, then, learn the revelation of all nature and all thought to his heart, this, namely, that the Highest dwells in him.

It was insight like this that led to the formation of the Boston Transcendental Club and this in turn to the Brook Farm experiment in West Roxbury, Massachusetts, that lasted from 1841 to 1847. Emerson did not join either one. Nevertheless he stood as the personification of one aspect of the philosophy they represented: a belief in freedom of thought, a mystic sense of God as the guiding idea and power behind human life and human history. Conversely, this liberated man refused to be bound intellectually and spiritually by any creed—even the Unitarian. Out of this new ferment was to come the intellectual renaissance which made Boston the "hub" of the American universe.

The hymnists noted below have been affected more or less deeply by this philosophy. Through it Lowell found his burning zeal for the anti-slavery cause, Sears his faith in the ultimate realization of the angels' song of peace and good will. Holmes is more deeply touched than these two by the metaphysics of transcendentalism; he puts Emerson's Over-soul into his appealing hymn, "Lord of all being," and in "O Love Divine, that stooped to share" he retains his reverence for the God-possessed Christ his Calvinistic father had taught him to love. Chadwick joins Lowell in finding inspiration in his liberal religion for the righting of social wrongs, and so do Burleigh and Hosmer, as the social problems that follow the Reconstruction period grow more and more insistent. But the young men, Samuel Johnson and Samuel Longfellow, were most fully possessed by the Transcendental spirit, and their hymns embody better than others of this Unitarian renaissance the full consciousness of the indwelling Spirit as the source of all that is noblest in life. More details of these men will be sketched in as we come to them in our study.

The third aspect of Unitarianism began about 1885. It is characterized by a full acceptance of the scientific method in ethics and religion, and an attempt to incarnate religion into the social order. These two tendencies finally issued, the one in humanism, which eliminates God entirely, the other in a strong interest in economic reform and in humanitarian enterprises like the Unitarian Service Committee that rendered essential help in Europe during the late war both in relief of the destitute and assistance to the underground forces in the invaded countries. It is this branch of the Unitarian Church that has written its later hymns and that also seems now to be returning to Jesus as the embodiment of man's higher ideals—an emphasis the absence of which in the past pretty nearly eliminated Jesus from its hymnbooks.

### JAMES RUSSELL LOWELL (1819–91) American, Unaffiliated *

THIS brilliant man-of-letters can hardly be called a hymnist: he was primarily a poet, next a literary essayist, in his early days an anti-slavery agitator, and always a cultured gentleman.

Born in Cambridge of the notable Massachusetts family, a graduate of Harvard, he made an unsuccessful try at the law and then turned to literature. His genius and especially his anti-slavery passion were stimulated by

---

* [Lowell] was unable to accept the dogmas of any Church, even the liberal and humane one of Channing, his uncle John and his father. F. Greenslet: *The Lowells and Their Seven Worlds*, 1946, p. 245.

his first wife, Maria White (m. 1845, d. 1853). His first editorial work was done on the *Pennsylvania Freeman,* which Whittier also served, then he contributed a weekly poem or prose piece to the *National Anti-Slavery Standard* of New York. His national reputation, however, was made by the first series of *Biglow Papers* (1846–8) called forth by the government's

James Russell Lowell

recruiting for the abhorred Mexican War. These papers in the New England dialect were both witty and stingingly satirical. They were first published in the *Boston Courier.*

Lowell's reputation as a literary critic was made by his Lowell Institute Lectures in Boston (1855), a series that won his appointment to the chair of Modern Languages at Harvard, just vacated by Longfellow. After a year of study abroad he began a teaching career that lasted twenty years. Contemporaneously he founded and edited the *Atlantic Monthly* (1857) as a mouthpiece for anti-slavery propaganda. Twice he was honored by his country with an ambassadorship: to Spain (1877) and to Great Britain (1880). Honorary degrees were conferred upon him by Harvard, Oxford, Cambridge, St. Andrew's, Edinburgh, and Bologna (Italy). Whittier wrote of him:

From purest wells of English undefiled
None deeper drank than he, the New World's child,
Who in the language of their farm-fields spoke
The wit and wisdom of New England folk,
Shaming a monstrous wrong. The world-wide laugh
Provoked thereby might well have shaken half
The walls of Slavery down, ere yet the ball
And mine of battle overthrew them all.*

### *Once to every man and nation*     [Dec. 1844]

An English hymnologist, Garret Horder, has the honor of discovering
a hymn in Lowell's long-lined poem, *The Present Crisis,* which begins

When a deed is done for Freedom, through the broad earth's
    aching breast
Runs a thrill of joy prophetic, trembling on from east to west,
And the slave, where're he cowers, feels the soul within him climb
To the awful verge of manhood, as the energy sublime
Of a century bursts full-blossomed on the thorny stem of Time.†

Out of the ninety lines of the original Mr. Horder in 1896 picked here and
there sixteen lines and arranged them into the hymn we are studying.

This poetry is a far cry from Watts, Newton and even Wesley. It is
imaginative, metaphorical, and passionate with something more than Evangelism or Evangelicalism; it is a clarion call to stop an international crime,
to repudiate a great social wrong. It is the earliest example in America of
the Social Gospel in a hymn.

*The Present Crisis* was written as a protest against the war with
Mexico, precipitated in 1846 by our annexation of the independent but
formerly Mexican territory of Texas. The admission was violently opposed
by the North because it greatly contributed to the extension of slavery. The
point of the poem is that the present hour is fateful: how we decide and
what we do about the territories now known as Texas, New Mexico, Arizona
and California will shape our country's future course for all time:

They enslave their children's children who make compromise
with sin.

Slavery, like a great Cyclops, is groping in new regions for its miserable
prey:
 Shall we guide his gory fingers where our helpless children play?

Did Lowell see the Civil War lurking behind the Mexican? the long iniquities of Reconstruction days, the present eruption of Huey Longs, Bilbos,
Ku Kluxers and Columbians? He remembered at any rate the stern courage

* *Complete Poetical Works,* J. G. Whittier, Houghton, Mifflin, Boston.
 † J. R. Lowell: *Poetical Works,* Houghton, Mifflin, Boston.

of his ancestors who sought in the New World a land of freedom and opportunity for all men:

> Lo, before us gleam Truth's campfires! We ourselves must Pilgrims be,
> Launch our Mayflowers, and steer boldly through the desperate winter sea,
> Nor attempt the Future's portal with the Past's blood-rusted key.

One word in the lines selected for the hymn our editors have not dared to retain. The first line of stanza 3 reads in the original,

> By the light of burning *heretics* Christ's bleeding feet I track.

The victims were of course martyrs because they died for what they regarded as truth. But they were really heretics because martyred by the Church, the result of internal, fratricidal war—a "death-grapple twixt old systems and the Word." Our beloved country, says the poet, should take warning and not kill off its bravest protesters who are willing to accept death rather than falsehood.

In stanza 4, lines 3–4, the original reads, more vividly:

> Truth forever on the scaffold, Wrong forever on the throne.

The poem is a clarion call for courageous fidelity to principle; it can be blown to the men of any era, especially our own.

### Rev. *EDMUND HAMILTON SEARS* (1810–76) American Unitarian

SEARS was a humble clergyman who lives only in two Christmas hymns. Born in the Massachusetts Berkshires, educated at Union College and the Harvard Divinity School (1837), he spent most of his life as pastor at Wayland, Massachusetts. In addition to his preaching he did editorial work for twelve years on the *Monthly Religious Magazine* and wrote several volumes on religious subjects. His first hymn, written while a divinity student, was "Calm on the listening ear of night"—still frequently used. His second is found in all our hymnals.

### *It came upon the midnight clear* [1846]

No Christmas is perfect without the singing of this hymn. It is one of the finest ever written, not only because of its melodious rendering of the Biblical story of angels and shepherds (stanza 1) but because it is one of the first to emphasize the social significance of the angels' message (st. 2–5).

In stanza 2 unrolls the never-ending procession of Christmas days. The remembered angels and their song are reminders that the world was not intended to be weary, its plains need not be sad and lonely, nor its sounds a Babel instead of a symphony. These angels are the very hope of man springing eternally in the human breast.

*Stanza 3* hints at the actuality rather than the ideal: the devastations, the slaughter, the hatreds, the vengeance, the struggle for power, the savage greed of men have drowned out the celestial music for two millenniums. As the poet was writing these lines his fellow-citizens were killing Mexicans in order that they might enslave more Negroes, and the Civil War was looming over the horizon.

*Stanza 4* becomes more personal. It urges all who find the burden of life too heavy—victims of poverty, disease, social injustice—to listen awhile to the angelic reminder that Good Will is heaven's law of life and can yet heal all their wounds.

*Stanza 5* relieves the picture of human wrongs by reminding us that the song is still valid. Eternal in the human heart springs the hope, the passionate faith, that what men so desperately have longed for —that "Age of Gold"—will surely come to pass. "Saints, apostles, prophets, martyrs" are all answering, "Yes!"

### *WILLIAM HENRY BURLEIGH* (*1812–71*) American Unitarian

A LINEAL descendant on his mother's side from William Bradford of the *Mayflower,* he was born on a farm in Woodstock, Connecticut. His boyhood was filled with long hours of manual labor, and with little schooling. As a young man he went to Pittsburgh (1837) where he was apprenticed to a printer, and that opened for him an outlet for the two passions that had seethed within him since his early days: the temperance cause and the abolition of slavery. He began his temperance campaign by publishing *The Christian Witness,* and later *The Temperance Banner.* His first anti-slavery paper, *The Christian Freeman,* was published in Hartford, Connecticut (1843), a little later he kept up his agitation against liquor by representing as Secretary the New York State Temperance Society at Syracuse (1849–55) and publishing *The Prohibitionist.* He supplemented the printed word by continued platform work, for he was an eloquent orator and a man of striking appearance. In fact, he was what people called a fanatic, preaching his gospels in season and out. "Mobs sought to intimidate him; society turned him out. For himself he cared nothing, but that his family should suffer cut him to the quick." * Personal bereavements including the death of his wife and two children added to his sorrow and gave a touch of poignancy to the hymns he wrote. His final occupation was as Harbor Master of New York City (1855–71) and he died in Brooklyn, New York. His wife was for some years a Unitarian minister in the little town of Brooklyn in the state of Connecticut.

*E. S. Ninde: *Nineteen Centuries of Christian Song,* Revell, New York, 1938.

His poems were published in various periodicals and gathered into a volume the year of his death. Some of them were used as hymns, especially by the Congregational, Baptist and the more liberal Anglican congregations in England where their merit was first recognized. Only one has survived in general use, and that one reflects only faintly his passion for social reform:

### Lead us, O Father, in the paths of peace      [Before 1859]

Written during the aftermath of the Mexican War and only a few years before the Civil War, this hymn betrays the anxieties of the anti-slavery agitator. The author's foreboding is expressed in a prayer for peace (stanza 1). The conviction that slavery is a moral and religious problem finds voice in lines 1 and 4: God must lead us, and Christ was the perfect embodiment of his perfect way.

At this early date in the development of Unitarianism, the author was not afraid to express his belief in Christ—not as a theological dogma but as a moral example and living force. The Transcendentalists (see below) and the humanists will later expunge His personal name and titles almost entirely from their hymnals.

In stanza 2 is expressed the need for right thinking on moral problems. Wrong thinking leads youth into sin (line 3): no doubt the author had particularly in mind the sin of drinking against which he preached so vehemently.

Stanza 3 emphasizes the need for righteousness in conduct as well as in thought. Here, without doubt, are hinted the legal injustices and personal cruelties involved in slavery—the second cause Burleigh fought.

Stanza 4 reflects the harshnesses of his public career and the personal bereavements he had suffered, but he relies on God for the ultimate peace—not rest in heaven, but a heavenly rest—that calmness of temper which comes only when our lives have consciously conformed to the Divine Will.


### OLIVER WENDELL HOLMES (1809–94) American Unitarian

THE most fascinating picture of this incarnation of nineteenth century blue-blood Boston is to be found in the early chapters of Catherine Bowen's *Yankee from Olympus*, written primarily about his son Justice Holmes. It tells of the father's boyhood in the strict home of his Calvinistic clergyman father, Abiel Holmes, in Cambridge, then a mere country village. When Oliver was eight his father used to take him as companion in the two-wheeled chaise when called to preach in Dorchester or Lexington—a Saturday-night to Monday-morning trip. On the rides the father taught his son all he ought to know about religion. By the time Oliver was ten he was "still afraid of the Devil, but the doctrine of transmitted sinfulness, justification, sanctification, meant no more to him than the mystic syllables by which his friends counted each other out in their games."

The virus of Unitarianism was in the air. It was creeping into Harvard College where Oliver went after finishing at the "dame-school" and Phillips Andover. When Oliver was a senior, father Abiel was deposed from his pastorate at the First Church, and the Unitarians took over. Oliver was sorry, but by now he had become a Unitarian.

Oliver made a beginning at law, but hated it. Suddenly he sprang to fame as a poet by writing *Old Ironsides*, and so saved the frigate *Constitution* from being scrapped. It is still at the Charlestown Navy Yard! But, not trusting poetry as a means of livelihood, he decided on medicine, took a room in Boston and began his studies at the Harvard Medical School, chiefly under his prospective father-in-law, Dr. Jackson. Then he went to Paris for further study and on his return began his career as a Boston physician. In 1847 he was appointed Professor of Anatomy at the Medical School and won fame not only as a pioneer researcher but as a teacher so fascinating that students were sent to him at the end of the day when they were fagged, because he alone could keep them awake!

"These, gentlemen," he is reputed to have said in one of his lectures, holding up a portion of a skeleton, "these are the bones on which Providence destined man to sit and survey the works of creation."

Holmes's fame rests not on his science but on his creative literature. *The Autocrat of the Breakfast Table* was something quite new—tangy, witty, New England through and through. The chapters came out serially in the *Atlantic Monthly* (1857) which Lowell had just founded; Holmes had named the magazine, and the Autocrat papers saved it to posterity through the days of the great financial panic. Holmes was now a member of the "Saturday Club," at the dinners of which he met intimately Emerson, Longfellow, Whittier, Lowell, Sumner, Agassiz and many other charming talkers. Henceforth he was less and less physician and more a charming man of letters. In 1886, when he visited Europe, he was showered with degrees; Litt.D. from Cambridge, LL.D. from Edinburgh, D.C.L. from Oxford. Harvard had already made him an LL.D.

In his day Holmes was often called a "free-thinker." He was far from that, for he was profoundly religious. "No irreverent word ever escaped his tongue or pen." His creed was very short—as he once put it in a letter to Harriet Beecher Stowe, "It is found in the first two words of the *Pater Noster*." That creed was profoundly held and emotionally cherished. Out of the character thus nurtured came two hymns, one of which few hymnals on either side of the Atlantic would care to omit.

### *Lord of all being, throned afar*      [1859]

Following the success of the *Autocrat,* Holmes wrote a second series for the *Atlantic* called *The Professor at the Breakfast Table.* It was like the

*Autocrat* but somewhat more restrained, or shall we say mature. The series closed with these verses entitled "A Sun-Day Hymn," introduced by a sentence that gives the author's point of view:

> Forget for the moment the differences in the hues of truth we look at through our human prisms, and join in singing (inwardly) this hymn to the Source of the light we all need to lead us, and the warmth which alone can make us all brothers.

Oliver Wendell Holmes,
c. 1859

The hymn is a cluster of metaphors each suggesting an aspect of religion—separate functions of God and their correlatives in human experience. All are drawn from the sun and stars.

*Stanza 1.* The sun is the source of life. In our day more than in Holmes's we realize how radiation from the sun has been imprisoned in atoms, grouped in molecules, organized into cells, structurally combined into grass and insect, bird and mammal, the life in which is constantly maintained by that same radiation. The sun is in truth "center and soul" of every planet and all that it holds.

That, says the poet, is exactly the relation of God to the spirit of man—infinitely removed yet inseparably near.

*Stanza 2.* God is light that illumines and quickens to action; God is also hope that like a star gives courage and direction in darkness.

*Stanza 3.* All human life can be described in terms of relationship to God: darkness comes to our spirit when sin blots out His shining; full illumination returns when again He dawns upon us; hope and the joy of His forgiveness are like the rainbow against the storm-cloud.

*Stanza 4.* What is our feeble light compared with His sun-burst? But we feel a kinship to it in two ways: His light becomes in us Truth, something intellectual, by which, in the language of Newton, "we think God's thoughts after Him," and when it strikes into us it becomes also something emotional, by which we learn that God is Love.

*Stanza 5.* A prayer that this alchemy of light may transform us: intellectually, to make us free from error and so open the doors to more abundant life; emotionally, to bind us in love to the infinite Sun of Righteousness. If that takes place there will be no divisions in our worship—no Protestant or Catholic, Buddhist or Hindu; there will be only one altar on which to lay our offerings, only one flame to consume the sacrifice.

This the poetic rendering of Holmes's creed—Our Father. Its basic truth is the only therapy for our ailing religiosity.

### Rev. *JOHN WHITE CHADWICK* (*1840–1904*) American Unitarian

BORN at Marblehead, Massachusetts, graduated at the Harvard Divinity School, 1864, minister of the Second Unitarian Church, Brooklyn, New York, for forty years, 1864–1904. During this pastorate he preached sermons that form a noble body of ethical teaching, later issued in printed form. He also found time to write considerable poetry and biographies of the two great Unitarian preachers, William Ellery Channing and Theodore Parker. Ten of his hymns are still to be found in the Unitarian-Universalist *Hymns of the Spirit* (1943), but only one wins consideration here.

### *Eternal Ruler of the ceaseless round*     [1864]

Chadwick wrote this hymn for his graduation day exercises at the Harvard Divinity School. It is one of the few hymns written during the Civil War, and almost the only one that shows traces of that conflict. Well it might, for only a few weeks previous Grant, hewing his way to Richmond, had fought the bloody battle of the Wilderness—a heart-breaking suspense of six days during which Grant wrote to the President, "I propose to fight it out on this line if it takes all summer." Against those backgrounds of fear and slaughter the lines of this hymn stand out like stars of hope.

*Stanza 1.* Those backgrounds are the "night profound," and faith in a God who rules the "circling planets singing on their way." Our feeble lives should be regulated by the cosmic laws that "preserve the stars from wrong."

*Stanza 2.* This prayer also reflects the fratricidal war. Men on both sides are children of God who need the constant presence and guidance of the Holy Spirit; they are brothers one of another and of Christ; all should be united in love. It is an echo of Christ's own petition on His last night with His disciples: "Holy Father, keep them in thy name which thou hast given me, that they may be one even as we are" (Jn 17:11). The allusion here to the three aspects of God as Ruler, Holy Spirit, Brother-Friend, is unusual in a Unitarian. In these present days of humanistic Unitarianism, Christ is practically never mentioned in hymns, even in those assigned to Advent, Christmas, Palm Sunday, Good Friday and Easter! The Holy Spirit, however, is more easily used as a synonym for God.

*Stanza 3.* "All wrong" includes slavery and war. The repetition of the word "one" gives the lines a driving force and emphasizes the supreme ideal on which our nation was founded and for which the war was being fought.

*Stanza 4* flames with the imagery of battle, yet asks for no victory but that which fulfils God's own purpose and proves our loyalty to Him.

## Rev. SAMUEL JOHNSON (1822–82) American Unitarian

JOHNSON and Samuel Longfellow stand at the fore-front of the Unitarian Movement for more and better hymns of a liberal faith. In their youth, Watts and his various revisers had held imperial sway over Church hymnody in America. But his hymns were strongly Calvinistic, a point of view that liberals in America were rejecting with increasing vigor during the middle decades of the nineteenth century. Nor could they follow the high-churchliness of contemporary Anglicans, at that time revelling in the new-found treasure of the Latin and Greek service books and composing hymns of their own after the Nicene pattern. This left the Liberals without any hymns.

These two friends, fellow-students at the Harvard Divinity School, brought out their first *Book of Hymns* the year of their graduation (1846), and another, *Hymns of the Spirit* in 1864. In these books they eliminated all hymns that would offend the intellect of liberals, and at the same time tried to meet their spiritual needs with new ones. Dr. H. W. Foote gives a fine appreciation of their work:

> A *Book of Hymns* was first used by the Church of the Unity in Worcester of which Edward Everett Hale was minister, and by Theodore Parker's congregation in the Music Hall in Boston. Parker, on receiving a copy, is said to have remarked, "I see we have a new books of Sams!" It ran to twelve editions and marked a new epoch in American hymnody because of the freshness and originality of its viewpoint, and even more because of the new materials which it introduced and upon which later editors drew heavily. The young editors were the first to see and make use of the hymnic possibilities of Whittier's poems. And they were the first to introduce into an American hymnbook Newman's "*Lead, kindly Light,*" which they found printed anonymously in a newspaper.*

Johnson was born in Salem, Massachusetts, graduated from Harvard College and Divinity School, was minister for seventeen years of an independent congregation in Lynn which he had formed and which ceased to exist when he left. While he never acknowledged connection with any denomination, the Unitarians naturally claim him. The work of scholarship which brought him fame was *Oriental Religions;* he published another work on *The Worship of Jesus, in its Past and Present Aspects* (1868). Though he wrote fewer hymns than his partner, Longfellow, the current Unitarian-Universalist hymnal contains five, two of which are included in this study.

### City of God, how broad and far      [1864]

Underlying the imagery of this hymn is John's vision of the New Jerusalem (Rev 21:2; 27). A comparison of the two poems will accentuate the differences—one a miraculous city coming down out of heaven, walls of jasper, foundations of precious stones, gates of pearl, streets of gold, its people saints who had died; the other an earthly city embracing all living men whose character qualifies them for citizenship. Earthly is not quite the word; let us rather say spiritual: a fellowship that embraces throughout the world all who give obedience to the one King, and therefore by right of charter are free men (stanza 1).

> *Stanza 2.* The solidarity of this band is emphasized by "one" four times repeated. The Church, from the author's point of view, is a group that has rejected all divisive creeds, and under God relies for its strength on a united purpose to attain a common noble end. *Stanza 3.* The speech of its citizens is "pure" because it is untheological, the direct and disingenuous speech heard in the childhood

* *Three Centuries of American Hymnody*, p. 237, Harvard University Press, Cambridge, 1940.

Samuel Johnson

of the world (?—the figure is not clear). The empire of which the
city of God is the capital consists of all whose lives are governed
by "freedom, love, and truth."

*Stanza 4.* No night can quench its outlines; each dawn reveals its
battlements unscathed.

*Stanza 5.* Finally the city is impregnable to time or change, force
or oblivion. Reverting to Christ's own figure: "the rains descended,
and the floods came, and the winds blew, and beat upon that house,
and it fell not: for it was founded upon the rock" (Mt 7:25). Since
those that thus endure the shocks of life are those "that heareth
these words of mine," the writer of this hymn was a Christian—one
who takes the gospel preached by the lips and the life of Jesus as
his law of life. But this total rejection of the theologies which the
Church of his day insisted upon as the irreducible minimum for
membership threw the author out of even the Unitarian fold. The
Church of his hymn was thus not a reality but an ideal. It is still
an ideal—though more and more clearly seen or adumbrated on the
horizon.

Though written during or immediately before the Civil War there is
strangely no allusion in this hymn to that national catastrophe or the great
moral problem underlying it, and no suggestion of any interest in the social

movements that contemporaneously were energizing the Unitarians of England. Felix Adler of Jewish extraction will soon (1878) take up this theme from the social angle in his, "Hail the glorious golden city," and so will Frederick Hosmer the Unitarian (1876–1905). See below under *Social Gospel*.

### Life of ages, richly poured     [1864]

There is here just a hint of the great national struggle of the Civil War, but the same words could be used in any age. The writer is expressing fervently his faith in Transcendentalism and is coupling with it his belief

*Left*, Samuel Longfellow. *Right*, Frederick Lucian Hosmer.

in the evolutionary theory recently formulated by Charles Darwin (*Origin of Species*, 1859) and Herbert Spencer (*First Principles*, 1861). But he extends the scope of evolution into the spiritual realm and utterly rejects the thesis of Spencer's *Principles of Psychology* (1855) which tries to show that the human mind evolved in a wholly materialistic world where men's actions are the result of physical causes only. The poet holds that without God was "not anything made that hath been made," and God is Love.

The hymn is an elaboration of that truth. God is the urge behind the prophet's word (as the Orthodox confess, if the prophet is Biblical), and in the people's liberty—as Hamilton and Timothy Dwight would not confess. The "Chosen Race" was not his sole concern—as Israel sometimes has asserted; he has been a fountain of living waters in all races. He breathes in the "thinker's creed"—not that the thinker is always right, but feels the urge to find truth and to state his findings adequately. He is the basis of heroism when right is on the scaffold and wrong on the throne. He is the urge behind the soaring cathedral and its glowing windows, behind Apollo's lyre and Handel's Halleluia, behind all the Holy Books ever written and all pilgrimages to the shrines of all saints, Christian or otherwise. He is the courage and the wisdom that arbitrates differences and avenges wrongs, that writes the constitutions of democracies and United Nations. He is the life of all ages, richly poured.

All this is a far cry from "the faith once delivered unto the saints." Religion, like all the rest of life, is not cut and dried, pre-determined, departmentalized into heathen and Christian, unsaved and saved. Life is a flux, a tide in which, to be sure, large areas are bound fast by physical and mental laws, but nevertheless permeable by the infinite, creative, evolutionary spirit that will not leave us in the dust, but that pushes and pushes with the insistence of a sprouting seed until our clod feels a stir of might and climbs to a soul.

This hymn is a true insight into religion. It deserves wider use.

## Rev. SAMUEL LONGFELLOW (1819–1892) American Unitarian

SAMUEL, youngest brother of the more famous poet Henry Wadsworth Longfellow, was the partner of Samuel Johnson in establishing a Unitarian hymnody in America. He was a more prolific writer than Johnson, and in his editing he did a good deal of tinkering to fit Calvinistic and Trinitarian hymns into Unitarian modes of thought.

Born like his brother in Portland, Maine, educated, unlike his brother, at Harvard College (1839) and Divinity School (1846), he became minister of the Unitarian Church at Fall River, Massachusetts, and in 1853 of the Second Unitarian Church of Brooklyn, New York. After seven years of service and a gap of eighteen years, he became pastor of the Unitarian Church of Germantown, Pennsylvania, 1878–83. The rest of the time he was a free lance—preaching, writing and editing. Poor health was largely the cause of his intermittent pastorates. As he grew older he became less and less sectarian, refused to be called a Unitarian, and finally adopted a position that he called theistic but which we should call more exactly Transcendental—that is, eliminating from his teaching all strictly Christian concepts.

Of the twenty-seven hymns to the current Unitarian-Universalist *Hymns of the Spirit* written or adapted by Longfellow, only one has survived in enough selected hymnals to be considered here:

### Holy Spirit, Truth divine [1864]

A good Trinitarian would not discover anything wrong with this Unitarian hymn. Ostensibly it is addressed to the third Person of the Trinity. But in Longfellow's philosophy the Spirit is the only Person there is in the God-head. To be sure, this Spirit has fatherly traits, as we know from some

Summer Costume of the Cambridge Students

*Top*, Harvard Divinity School. *Left*, Sketch by Samuel Longfellow, 1838, showing Harvard boys' summer clothes.

of his other hymns, and he appeared historically in Jesus—as he did and does appear in every prophet and saint. But these are only temporal manifestations of the one and indivisible Eternal Spirit in whom all things consist. This is not the Nicene conception; rather it is Transcendentalism.

The hymn is an enumeration of the aspects under which the one God can be discerned, and a prayer that we may discover and appropriate them:

> *Stanza 1,* as Truth. It is a common figure to say that truth makes things clear, sheds light. John the Evangelist used it almost in the Transcendental (Platonic) sense when in his Gospel (1:1) he refers to Christ as the Word—the divine Intelligence or Truth of God made manifest in the flesh (1:14). He also refers to Him as Light (1:4–5; 8:12; 12:46).
>
> It is well to remember that the Gospel of John, written c. 110 A.D., is based on the Platonic concept of God as the *Logos* who pervades the universe and can make Himself known to men by the process of incarnation. It was John's method of making a peasant-teacher of Galilee acceptable to the Greek intelligentsia of Ephesus. Longfellow is doing the same for Boston tories.
>
> *Stanza 2,* as Love, which warms and enkindles (Jn 13:35; 17:26; 1 Jn 4:7).
>
> *Stanza 3,* as Power (Acts 1:8; 10:38; Eph 3:20; 2 Tim 1:7).
>
> *Stanza 4,* as Right: that is, a knowledge of what the right is, the law we must obey. It is revealed to us by conscience. Obedience to this law is the only way to be free—just as an inventor can get nowhere if he goes against natural law, but can accomplish new wonders in a thousand ways if he works within the law. (Rom 8:1–4; Jas 1:25).
>
> *Stanza 5,* as Peace—the result of working within the law, not against it (Jn 14:27; 16:33; Rom 8:6; Phil 4:7).
>
> *Stanza 6,* as Joy—the result of peace in the heart and of possessing the other qualities previously mentioned (Rom 14:17; Gal 5:22; Jn 15:11). The figure of the well is taken from an incident in the desert journey of the Israelites to Canaan (Num 21:16–17).

*Rev. FREDERICK LUCIAN HOSMER (1840–1929)* American Unitarian

BORN in Framingham, Massachusetts, of early colonial stock (1635), a graduate of Harvard College in 1862 and Harvard Divinity School in 1869, and a Unitarian minister with pastorates in Massachusetts, Ohio, Illinois, Missouri and California. Himself one of the finest of the Unitarian hymn writers, he was also a student of hymnody so scholarly that in 1908 he was invited to give a series of lectures on the subject at Harvard University. In conjunction with W. C. Gannett he wrote two books on *The Thought of God in Hymns and Poems* (1885, 1894). In fact, this pair of friends, fellow students at the Divinity School, did the same type of work which an earlier pair accomplished (Johnson and Longfellow, above) in adapting the old type of hymn to the growing liberal spirit of the times and of writing new hymns out of their personal experience and convictions. The Unitarian-Universalist *Hymns of the Spirit* (1943) contains eight of Gannett's and thirty-five of Hosmer's, though our list of hymnals presents none of Gannett and only three of Hosmer.

Dr. Foote has a fine appraisal of Hosmer's workmanship:

> He studied carefully the technique of his art, each hymn expresses a definite mood or thought, wrought out with care, and finished with the artist's love of perfection. Each one is a lyrical phrasing of some religious emotion, of some universal and eternal theme, but the speech is vernacular, not anachronistic; simple and not theological; natural and not pietistic.*

### *O Thou, in all thy might so far*     [1876]

First published in the New York *Inquirer* and later in his book, *Thoughts of God* (second series), this hymn is one of the simplest and clearest expositions of religious faith to be found in our hymnals. It was written in the full light of nineteenth-century science, with knowledge of the agnostic philosophies that were in flood in his day, yet it preserves in unabashed strength the religious consciousness of God as a force both without and within human personality.

> *Stanza 1.* The transcendence of God is here asserted: His existence and power attested by the universe of stars that with every increase of telescopic range grows bigger until it passes man's mental grasp. But also the immanence of God is asserted: His residence in the world He has made, and in man—in me!
>
> *Stanza 2.* The unsearchableness of God is here asserted (Job 9:10; Rom 11:33), whether sought emotionally ("heart") or intellectually ("searching"); yet the experience of a religious soul makes certain two things: that He somehow works within us as an illuminating and quickening spirit, and works in the world around us (as the guiding force in social evolution?).
>
> *Stanza 3.* Here expressed is the assurance that comes to the soul in consequence of this recognition of God: one does not have to know all—that would be impossible, but one is privileged to love the Person so experienced, and to worship Him for His goodness.
>
> *Stanza 4.* This faith that is not dependent upon intellectual processes but supplements them with something intuitive ("childlike") is the *summum bonum* of life—the greatest good; it leads one direct to God, no matter how dark may be the guidance of reason.

* *Op. cit.*, p. 296.

Contrast this with the average theological or evangelical hymn and it reveals two excellencies: it does not hit you with an interpretation of God you cannot accept, for it presents no dogmas, nor does it stress an invitation to you as a sinner to change your ways. Its intellectual modesty and its emotional assurance give you an illustration of what religion can mean to a modern cultured man. Perhaps it makes you wish you had the author's faith.

### Thy Kingdom come! on bended knee    [1891]

Written for the Commencement of the Meadville Theological School, Pennsylvania (Unitarian)—now removed to Chicago and affiliated with the University of Chicago.

In this hymn we get one of our earliest glimpses of the Social Gospel, soon to become a dominant note in American preaching and hymnody. This social note is expressed in generalities; in later hymns we shall find mentioned the specific abuses that the gospel should remedy. Hosmer's general approach might be called the cosmic: there has been through the ages a trend, postulated by man's yearning and prayers; it is a slow progress from darkness through dawn to day.

> *Stanza 1.* The opening phrase sets the theme of the hymn: it is the first clause of the Lord's Prayer. In swift suggestion the whole history of man passes in review—humanity praying that the night of ignorance, fear and suffering may become the full day when God shall be King.
>
> *Stanza 2.* But night has its promise: there are the stars! They are the symbols of God's unchanging purpose and His sustaining might.
>
> *Stanza 3.* But night is passing! the dawn is flaming, and those gifted with insight know what it means for man:
>
>> "Watchman, what of the night?"
>> The watchman said, "The morning cometh.
>> Enquire ye; turn ye, come!" (Is 21:11)
>
> *Stanza 4.* What happens when the day comes? We shall be able to see what is wrong. Only so can justice have the power to correct evil and heal man's sicknesses.
>
> *Stanza 5.* In that broad daylight knowledge will bring peace instead of war, righteousness instead of evil.
>
> These conditions constitute the promised Kingdom.

### Thy Kingdom come, O Lord    [1905]

Again a hymn that ignores except by implication the specific evils that need eradication, and centers upon the glories of the kingdom of righteousness for which men pray. It is a kind of glorified wishful thinking.

*Stanza 1.* The first prayer is for international unity, made possible by all nations subjecting themselves to the law of righteousness, as the Scripture has foretold in many places (Ps 72:7–17; 82:8; 22:27–28; Jer 4:1–2; Gal 3:8).

*Stanza 2.* A list of the particular activities and attitudes that yield international unity. The United Nations please take notice!

*Stanza 3.* In addition to the Bible prophecies cited above, many non-Biblical seers have painted the millennium of the nations. Tennyson proclaimed it in "Locksley Hall":

> For I dipped into the future far as human eye could see,
> Saw the vision of the world, and all the wonder that would be.
>
> .     .     .     .     .     .     .
>
> Till the war-drums throbbed no longer, and the battle-flags
>         were furled,
> In the Parliament of man, the Federation of the world! *

*Stanza 4.* An echo of the vision of the New Jerusalem coming down out of heaven (Rev 21:1–5a, 10–22:50), but in the hymn the new city will be built by men, on earth, with God's help—that "alabaster city, undimmed by human tears."

It seems ungenerous to criticize so fine a hymnist as Hosmer, but a serious limitation which has ruled out his hymns from most hymnals is the absence of a distinctively Christian note. In his thirty-five hymns in the current Unitarian-Universalist *Hymns of the Spirit* there are only four vague references to Jesus: "Spirit of Jesus," "one the Shepherd that doth lead" [which may be God], "Now [today] the Christ of larger faith is born" [not Jesus], "Jesus's motto" [probably the Golden Rule]. There are plenty of allusions to prophets, seers, martyrs, poets, but no appreciation of the supreme Prophet of all time who was the founder of the Christianity that Hosmer professes to follow. His hymns might as well have been written by the Stoic Greek poet, Cleanthes, third century B.C. It will be enlightening to compare these two.†

## Cleanthes: *Hymn to Zeus*

Thou, O Zeus, art praised above all gods: many are thy names and
        thine is all power for ever.
The beginning of the world was from thee: and with law thou
        rulest over all things.
Unto thee may all flesh speak: for we are thy offspring.**

---

* *The Works of Alfred Lord Tennyson,* Macmillan, 1892.

† For a passable exposition of Unitarian faith, with of course some exceptions, read Will Durant's account of Stoicism in *The Life of Greece,* pp. 652–6.

** St. Paul quoted this line at Athens, Acts 17:28.

Therefore will I raise a hymn to thee: and will ever sing of thy
power.

The whole order of the heavens obeyeth thy word: as it moveth
around the earth:

With little and great lights mixed together: how great art thou,
King above all for ever!

Nor is anything done upon the earth apart from thee: nor in the
firmament, nor in the seas:

Save that which the wicked do: by their own folly.

But thine is the skill to set even the crooked straight: what is
without fashion is fashioned and the alien akin before thee.

Thus hast thou fitted together all things in one: the good with the
evil:

That thy word should be one in all things: abiding forever.

Let folly be dispersed from our souls: that we may repay thee the
honor wherewith thou hast honored us:

Singing praise of thy works for ever: as becometh the sons of men.†

We realize, of course, that Unitarian hymns represent a reaction against
the fine-spun intellectual impossibilities of Athanasius and against the rigors
and unethical distortions of Calvin, but their rejection of the Hero of Christianity need not have been so absolute. English Unitarian John Bowring
could write in 1825:

> In the Cross of Christ I glory,
> Towering o'er the wrecks of time.

But the American Transcendentalists have reduced the cross to a metaphor
for the hardships of life, and Jesus himself to a non-entity not worth mentioning—except that he once had a "motto." One wishes that the Unitarians
could have preserved something of the passionate devotion of Whittier,
whose intellectual position was like theirs.

This coldness toward the founder of their faith, whose ethics and hopes
the Unitarians accept, may account for the fact that in my seventy years
of church attendance (mostly in Congregational and Baptist Churches) I do
not recall ever having heard a Hosmer hymn sung until February 9, 1948!

*Mrs. FRANCES WHITMARSH WILE* (*1878–1939*) American Unitarian

MRS. WILE was born in Bristol Valley, New York. She was a
parishioner of Dr. William C. Gannett in Rochester, New York, at the time
when he and Dr. Hosmer (q.v.) were compiling their hymnal. Knowing
Mrs. Wile's poetic talent they asked her to write a hymn that reflected the
spiritual values of the winter season. The following was the result:

† Quoted in Walter Pater: *Plato and Platonism*, p. 50, Macmillan, London, 1910.

## *All beautiful the march of days*      [1911]

This is lovely poetry: clear-cut in its imagery, unified in organization, and religious without being either theological or sentimental.

*Stanza 1* suggests that winter has its beauty quite as much as June: both seasons came from the same Hand.

*Stanza 2* continues the picture-panorama of the cold, and our heightened response: invigoration, intensified home life—and Christmas!

*Stanza 3* recalls the inevitable stirring of mother earth with the promise of spring until at Easter the miracle of new life is re-enacted for the millionth time and the cycle is complete.

*Stanza 4* is an apostrophe to God as the reality incarnate in crystal and rose, in the rhythmic law of the seasons. It ends quiet inevitably in the words of the Psalmist (Ps 19:1–2).

Only northerners can appreciate winter, which is the main theme of this hymn. Those who with Whittier have lived through fifty years of "Snow Bound" can forget the discomforts and remember only the delights of form and color, the purity, the silences—even "the tumultuous privacy of storm." That is why our poets of winter are all northerners.

II.  POET LAUREATE OF AMERICAN HYMNISTS

## *JOHN GREENLEAF WHITTIER* (1807–92) American Friend

WE shall now consider the hymns of the greatest American hymn writer—great not because he wrote many, for he did not, and what he wrote as hymns were not great. He is greatest because of the depth of his religious insights, the transparent sincerity of their expression and the absence of those divisive views that have in others obscured the underlying unity of our historic faith. All hymnals could contain Whittier—Unitarian to High Church.

Like Holmes and Lowell, Whittier was pure New England. The two former were city-bred, cultured men of the world. Whittier was country born and reared, without a schooling beyond the middle grades. Yet he left upon our literature the stamp of genius and upon our religion the touch of sanctity.

Whittier was born in the Merrimac Valley at East Haverhill, Massachusetts, in a big farm house that today is a pilgrim shrine. The savor of those pioneer acres pervades his "Snow Bound," they and it give a graphic picture of the environmental influences that shaped this rare spirit. His immigrant ancestor who built the house in 1688 was a Quaker and in that faith this boy was reared. The plain meeting-house still stands in which his neighbors waited in silence for the Spirit to move; they never sang hymns. There has

*Top,* Winter at Whittier's birthplace, Haverhill, Massachusetts. *Left,* Whittier's Quaker meeting-house in Amesbury, Massachusetts. *Right,* Whittier in his fighting years.

survived also one wooden desk from the schoolhouse in which he learned to read and write. It was the schoolmaster there who first fired his poetic muse by lending him a copy of Burns's poems, and though John began at once to write verse, no notice of him was taken until his sister sent one of his poems to William Lloyd Garrison of Newburyport who published it in his weekly *Free Press* and then rode over to Haverhill to see the budding poet. He urged John's father to give him an education so that he might become a writer. "Sir," the father answered, "poetry will not give him bread." The friendship and cooperation with Garrison thus started continued unbroken through the thirty-seven years of anti-slavery agitation.

Two years of schooling at Haverhill Academy, through which he worked his way, enabled Whittier to take up journalism. He contributed to many papers, became editor of some, but his father's death recalled him to the farm, where through over-work and exposure his health broke, and until he sold the property and moved to Amesbury in 1836 he was desperately unhappy. He served a term in the Massachusetts Legislature. His shrewd mind would have carried him far in politics, but he gave up probable election to Congress (1833) in order to join the anti-slavery cause.

Now began his career as agitator. Says the *Britannica:* "Although a Quaker he had a polemical spirit. Men seeing Whittier only in his saintly age knew little of the fire wherewith, setting aside ambition and even love, he maintained his warfare against the 'national crime,' employing action, argument, and lyric scorn." He wrote articles continuously during the 1830's, at home, in Harrisburg (Pa.), New York, Boston and Philadelphia. At one time he was hunted by a Philadelphia mob and stoned. When heart trouble confined him to Amesbury he still served as corresponding editor of the Washington *National Era,* in which he rose to his highest pitch of power. Periodically his lyrics were published in small volumes from 1831 to 1865, and other works in the *Atlantic Monthly* with which he was closely associated. The publication of "Snow Bound" in 1866 put him beyond anxiety in financial matters; other volumes followed until the final collection, *At Sundown,* in 1890. Thus his period of literary activity covered sixty years.

Whittier has himself given the best appraisal of his "ballad" poems: "They were written with no expectation that they would survive the occasions which called them forth; they were protests, alarm signals, trumpet-calls to action, words wrung from the writer's heart, forged at white heat, and of course lacking the finish which reflection and patient brooding over them might have given." His true genius reaches perfection of expression in his religious poetry, some selections from which writings we shall now consider.

We get our best view of Whittier's type of religion in his poem "The Meeting"—meaning a Quaker religious service. In the poem he pretends that a friend is objecting to such an uninspiring custom and recommends the great out-of-doors as the best place to worship. Then the poet justifies his Quaker-meeting in remarkable lines, selections from which are here given as a preparation for the study of his hymns.

I ask no organ's soulless breath
To drone the themes of life and
   death,

No altar candle-lit by day,
No ornate wordsman's rhetoric-play,
No cool philosophy to teach

Its bland audacities of speech
To double-tasked idolaters
Themselves their gods and worship-
    pers,
No pulpit hammered by the fist
Of loud-asserting dogmatist,
Who borrows for the hand of love
The smoking thunderbolts of Jove.
I know how well the fathers taught,
What work the later schoolmen
    wrought;
I reverence old-time faith and men,
But God is near us now as then;
His force of love is still unspent,
His hate of sin is imminent;
And still the measure of our needs
Outgrows the cramping bounds of
    creeds;
The manna gathered yesterday
Already savors of decay;
Doubts to the world's child-heart
    unknown
Question us now from star and stone;
Too little or too much we know,
And sight is swift and faith is slow;
The power is lost to self-deceive
With shallow forms of make-believe.

.    .    .    .    .

God should be most where man is
    least:
So, where is neither church nor priest,
And never rag of form or creed
To clothe the nakedness of need,—
Where farmer-folk in silence meet,—
I turn my bell-unsummoned feet;
I lay the critic's glass aside,
I tread upon my lettered pride,
And, lowest-seated, testify
To the oneness of humanity;
Confess the universal want,

And share whatever Heaven may
    grant.

.    .    .    .    .

So sometimes comes to soul and
    sense
The feeling which is evidence
That very near about us lies
The realm of spiritual mysteries.
The sphere of the supernal powers
Impinges on this world of ours.

.    .    .    .    .

The breath of a diviner air
Blows down the answer of a prayer.

.    .    .    .    .

Then duty leaves to love its task,
The beggar Self forgets to ask.

.    .    .    .    .

So to the calmly gathered thought
The innermost of truth is taught,
The mystery dimly understood,
That love of God is love of good,
And, chiefly, its divinest trace
In Him of Nazareth's holy face;
That to be saved is only this,—
Salvation from our selfishness;

.    .    .    .    .

That worship's deeper meaning lies
In mercy, and not sacrifice,
Not proud humilities of sense
And posturing of penitence,
But love's unforced obedience;

.    .    .    .    .

That the dear Christ dwells not afar,
The king of some remoter star,

.    .    .    .    .

But here, amidst the poor and blind,
The bound and suffering of our kind,
In works we do, in prayers we pray,
Life of our life, He lives today.*

## Whittier's Hymn-Poems

I. From "Worship," 1848: a poem of fifteen stanzas. The numbers
below indicate the original stanzas used.

* *Complete Poetical Works of J. G. Whittier,* Houghton, Mifflin, Boston.

Under the title Whittier made this comment and quoted the New Testament.

> Pure religion and undefiled before God and the Father is this,
> To visit the fatherless and widows in their affliction, and to
> keep himself unspotted from the world.—James 1:27.

He then reminds us of the pagan faiths, now enshrined in myths and in shattered statues and temples, in Druid woods where human sacrifices once smoked, fear the only urge to worship. Then the panorama of Christian temples passes in review: the music, "pale wizard priests, o'er occult symbols droning," the savor of incense, the roll of organ music, while some tyrant fresh from the field of carnage strides to the altar and kneels before the priest. Then Whittier's scorn breaks forth at such travesties of religion, and the stanzas follow from which our hymn is taken.

## O brother man! fold to thy heart thy brother

In this and the succeeding hymns the original stanzas selected are indicated by number and first lines; an asterisk indicates the first line of the hymn as found in the indicated hymnals.

8. Not empty worship the benignant Father   * C
11. For he whom Jesus loved   A B C M N P U
13. O brother man! fold   C * A B E M N P S U
14. Follow with reverent steps   A B C E M N P S U
15. Then shall all shackles fall   A E N P S U

Although this poem was written during the Mexican War and in the midst of the anti-slavery struggle, nothing of the militant Whittier appears in it; rather the deep-seated realization of the ends for which he was fighting—to make brothers of all men, black and white. This is perhaps the reason why all the hymnals but one begin with "O brother man."

II. From "Our Master," 1866, a poem of 38 stanzas beginning

## Immortal love, forever full

The poem is an interpretation and an exaltation of Jesus as the Incarnation of Immortal Love. Whittier here duplicates Tennyson's insight as given in "Strong Son of God, immortal Love." His purpose is to show how far Christianity has misinterpreted Jesus: the theologies, the learned tomes, the forensics, have quite missed the point. Christ is not found in heaven, nor in the Eucharist, nor as a King or a final Judge; not in systems or symbols, fable, myth or seer's dream, not in incense or cathedral piles of stone, only in the heart—in faith, hope, obedience.

1. Immortal Love, forever full   * A B C E N P S U
2. Our outward lips   C E S
3. Blow, winds of God   A C U

5. We may not climb   B C E N P S U * M
7. He cometh not a king to reign   C
9. The letter fails, the systems fall   C U
13. But warm, sweet, tender   B C E M N P S U
14. The healing of his seamless dress   A B C E M N P S U
15. Through him the first fond   C E M N S
16. Our Lord (O Lord) and Master   B E M N P * C E S U
17. Thou judgest us; thy purity   S
18. Our thoughts lie open   A E S U
20. Yet, weak and blinded   A E S U
21. To thee our full humanity   A E S
22. Who hates, hates thee   C E S
23. Deep strike thy roots   C
26. We faintly hear   C U
28. To do thy will is more   C
30. Apart from thee all gain   A E U
31. Alone, O Love ineffable   A S
34. Our Friend, our Brother   C U
36. Thy litanies, sweet offices   C

III. From "The Eternal Goodness," 1865, a poem of twenty-two stanzas beginning

> O friends! with whom my feet have trod
> The quiet aisles of prayer.

Whittier here acknowledges that people have different ways of looking at religion and of living it, but he cannot accept the creeds for which men argue—the "iron" creeds by which thought is irrevocably bound. His mind is unwilling to fix limits to either the power or the love of God: it cannot divorce justice from love, sovereignty from service; it rejects the "curse" and claims the Beatitudes and Christ's dying forgiveness; it rejects God's hatred and claims His goodness. Though utterly unworthy of His mercy, he trusts Him now and for the immortal life beyond.

> O brothers! if my faith is vain,
> If hopes like these betray,
> Pray for me that my feet may gain
> The sure and safer way.

Our hymns are made up of nine of Whittier's twenty-two stanzas, beginning for the most part with the line

*I know not what the future hath*

9. I bow my forehead in the dust   * P
10. I see the wrong that round me lies   A
11. Yet in the maddening maze of things   A * C

14. I dimly guess from blessings known   A
15. I long for household voices gone   C
16. I know not what the future hath   A C P * B E M N S U
17. And if my heart and flesh are weak   B E M N S U
18. No offering of my own I have   A E
19. And so beside the Silent Sea   A B C E M N S U
20. I know not where his islands lift   A B C E M N P S U
22. And thou, O Lord! by whom are seen   B M N

IV. From "The Brewing of Soma," 1872. A poem of seventeen stanzas beginning

The faggots blazed, the caldron's smoke

Beneath the title was this quotation from *Vashista*, translated by Max Müller:

These libations mixed with milk have been prepared for Indra:
offer Soma to the drinker of Soma.

The first eleven stanzas describe the various ways men have devised to get in touch with their god. The Hindus prepared a drink called "soma" made from honey and milk, brewed by their priests who, after consecrating it with their rods, declared it to be the "drink of the gods." This drink produced a frenzy, a storm of drunken joy that made the old forget their age, the sick and lame their pains.

Then knew each rapt inebriate          Soared upward, with strange joy elate,
    A winged and glorious birth,          Beat, with dazed head, Varuna's gate,
                    And sobered sank to earth.

This orgy of religion, originating in the childhood of the world, has been re-enacted in various ways down through the centuries: by the use of music, incense, vigils, trances, self-scourging like the Penitentes, the dance of the Dervishes, the mysteries of Orpheus, of Bacchus, the ascetic practices of Christian hermits and monks and pillar-saints, the hashish smoker, the fakir on his bed of spikes, and the transports of Christian sects in the camp-meetings and churches of Whittier's day. A particularly obnoxious revival service in his neighborhood is said to have moved Whittier to write the poem.

When this recital of man's insane religious vagaries is ended, the poet paints the finest picture of true worship we have in literature, in six stanzas beginning

*Dear Lord and Father of mankind*     [1872]

*Stanza 1.* Part of the beauty of this hymn lies in suggested pictures from the Bible. "Re-clothe us" is taken from the story of the naked

Gadarene demoniac out of whom Jesus had cast a "legion" of devils. "Then his fellow-villagers found him clothed and in his right mind" (Mk 5:15). We serve God when we live pure lives; we praise him not by orgies but by reverence.

*Stanza 2.* Here is recalled the Gospel story of the simple invitation and response of certain men on the shore of Lake Galilee (Mk 1:17).

*Stanza 3.* Jesus set the example of the quiet retreat for prayer and communion (Lk 6:12). The last two lines are a superlative expression of the essence of prayer: a "recovery of values" from the viewpoint of eternity.

*Stanza 4.* "With that deep hush subduing all" (U only) Manna: an allusion to the "bread from heaven" by which the Israelites were kept alive during their forty-year wandering (Ex 16:4–5, 14–18). This incident is transformed in the Fourth Gospel to mean that Jesus is the true manna (Jn 6:30–34).

*Stanza 5.* Dew falls only when the air is still: so only when we cease striving and straining can we realize the peace of soul which is so constructive and beautiful.

*Stanza 6.* As an ocean breeze in the swelter of summer so is the balm of the presence of God. Only when we retire from the world as Elijah did on Horeb, and listen to the "still, small voice" can we learn the inner meaning of the forces which wreck the world—and us (1 Kgs 19:9–13).

V. Hymn for the opening of Plymouth Church, Minneapolis, Minnesota.

### *All things are thine: no gift have we*      [1872]

A good many dedication hymns have been written, first and last, but few have survived the special occasion. The Episcopal *Hymnal* (E 228) has a beautiful translation from a ninth-century Latin hymn. Its limitation is that it is filled with medieval theological phrases that will not be acceptable to many. Bryant's "Thou whose unmeasured temple stands" is free from theology but dwells on what God may do for us who worship here. Whittier takes the point of view we have seen in Charles Kingsley's dedication hymn for a hospital beginning "From thee all skill and science flow" (see above), namely, what man offers to God is only what God has given to men in the way of endowment. Creativity of mind, artistic and mechanical skill, motives, are all expressions of God-implanted powers. God does not need this gift of our handiwork, but we need to give: it is our only possible expression of gratitude. The house will be also a perpetual gateway to God.

Such a hymn deserves wide use. It is found in seven out of our ten hymnals.

VI. From the poem "At Last."

*When on my day of life the night is falling*    [1882]

As Whittier grew old he seemed to grow more saintly. The flaming spirit that fought the mighty wrong of slavery died down with the years, but the coals glowed with an incandescence that seemed almost unearthly. Phoebe Cary wrote of him in one of her last poems:

> But not thy strains, with courage rife,
>   Nor holiest hymns, shall rank above
> The rhythmic beauty of thy life,
>   Itself a canticle of love.

When he reached his seventy-fifth birthday and the inward hints grew more insistent, he wrote this exquisite poem, "At Last." How its "heaven" contrasts with the countless pictures enshrined in the hymns of the centuries!—ecstatic visions of a city of gold filled with saints and angels whose only occupation is to sing Alleluias to God and Christ through all eternity. Quaker though he was, the science of the nineteenth century had made its impact upon his thought, as it had upon the Victorians of England:

> The manna gathered yesterday
> Already savors of decay;
> Doubts to the world's child-heart unknown
> Question us now from star and stone.

But agnosticism was not the result in his case, for he had not cherished those unchangeable clauses of the ancient creeds or that view of an inerrant Scripture which left to the average Churchman nothing but a desperate choice. As we read again his earlier poems we can easily discern that the basis of his faith had never been intellectual but instinctive.

So now as the end draws near we hear this inspired lyric of humility and hope in the presence of the unknown. The very last line is the essence of his faith—that, whatever the environment of the future may be, its function is to give "the life for which I long," the life so beautifully sketched in the last three stanzas of his hymn.

Whittier lived to be eighty-six and died peacefully while visiting friends at Hampton Falls, Massachusetts, near the sea he had loved. At his bedside when the last moments approached, a friend read this poem.

. . . .

# HISTORICAL SUMMARY

|  |  | *New Theology Social Gospel Hymnists* |
|---|---|---|
| 1861–5 | Civil War. | |
| 1868–82 | Many inventions: industrialization of the North. | Brooks, 1867 |
| 1869–80 | Four transcontinental railroads built; land frauds; bribery; great fortunes made. | |
| 1870–1910 | Era of huge trusts, threat to free enterprise. Foreign immigration increasing; slums, poverty. | |
| 1871 | Boss Tweed and his Tammany ring ousted. | |
| 1872 | Crédit Mobilier scandal. | |
| 1880–92 | Heresy trials (Presbyterian and Congregational). | Shurtleff, 1877 |
| 1886 | American Federation of Labor organized. | Gladden, 1879 |
|  |  | Lanier, 1880 |
|  |  | Bates, 1893 |
| 1898–9 | Spanish-American War. | Babcock, 1900 |
| 1901–9 | Theodore Roosevelt President: Trust-busting and imperialism. | |
|  | Rise of social philosophers: L. Ward, R. Ely, Veblen, B. Adams. | |
| 1902 | Ida Tarbell: *History of the Standard Oil Co.* | |
|  | Frank Norris: *The Pit.* | Hyde, 1903 |
|  |  | North, 1903 |
| 1904 | Upton Sinclair: *The Jungle.* | |
|  | Robert Hunter: *Poverty* (demanded more social legislation). | |
| 1907 | Rauschenbusch: *Christianity and the Social Crisis.* | van Dyke, 1907 |
| 1909 | Hyde: *Outlines of Social Theology.* | |
|  |  | Bowie, 1910 |
|  |  | Merrill, 1911 |
|  |  | Stocking, 1912 |
| 1914–18 | World War I. | |
| 1923–33 | "Boom and Bust" period. | Tweedy, 1925–9 |

## CHAPTER NINETEEN

# AMERICAN HYMNS:
# THE NEW THEOLOGY AND
# THE SOCIAL GOSPEL

## I. THE NEW THEOLOGY

THE CIVIL WAR WAS A NODE IN AMERICAN HISTORY. The emancipation of the slaves was of course an event of the first order, but the religious, social and economic changes that followed in the next fifty years were revolutionary—and the end is not yet.

The religious changes are attributable to the infiltration of ideas from England that have already been described in Chap. XII under the heading "Broad Church." The impact of the evolutionary sciences and philosophies, of the historical and literary criticism of the Bible, forced educated laymen to reformulate their religious principles, and Trinitarian theologians their theology. As early as 1847 Rev. Horace Bushnell, Congregational pastor in Hartford, Connecticut, began to attack Calvinism, especially the damnation of infants and the necessity of spectacular conversion. In his *Christian Nurture* (1847) he deplored the revivalism that had been almost the sole means of recruiting new members for the Church, and substituted for it the religious education of children. In *God in Christ* (1849) he modified the doctrine of the Trinity in the direction of separate functions rather than Persons; in *The Vicarious Sacrifice* (1886) he argued for a moral view of the Atonement as over against the "penal" or "satisfaction" theories of Calvin. Attempts were made to try him for heresy but his faithful congregation saved him by pulling their church out of the jurisdiction of the Congregational Association—though still remaining Congregational.

But reformers were few; non-conformity was dangerous especially for clergymen. Heresy trials began. Dr. Charles Briggs was ousted from his professorship at Union Theological Seminary after two trials (1892); five professors of Andover Theological Seminary (Congregational) were likewise cashiered. Popular indignation among pious people ran high against such preachers as Lyman Abbott, famed successor of Henry Ward Beecher at Plymouth Church, Brooklyn (Congregational, 1888–99), when he gave over his Sunday evening services to lectures on the Bible as literature, before crowded houses, and still more so when he published his Lowell Institute Lectures, *The Evolution of Christianity* (1896), *Theology of an Evolutionist* (1897), *Christianity and Social Problems* (1897), *Industrial Problems* (1905) —strange subjects for a Christian minister to handle! More and more Protestant thinkers turned from conventional religious concepts to reinterpret the old theology in terms of philosophy, psychology and sociology, and so attempted to translate metaphysics into vivid, concrete, human terms.

In the college field, perhaps one of the most stimulating leaders in the New Theology, as it was called, was President William DeWitt Hyde of Bowdoin College, Maine. In his Preface to his *Outlines of Social Theology* he thus reinterprets, for example, the ancient dogma of the Atonement:

> The cross of Christ is the symbol of the consequences of sin writ large. . . . Christ, in coming into the world full of hypocrisy and avarice and pride and malice, had his life embittered, and finally was brought to death, as the inevitable consequence of being a good man in an evil world. He loved the world, and in trying to do it good won its hate. In seeking to save it he laid down his life. Hence he stands as the great historic representative of suffering love seeking to save the world. . . . Christ stands therefore as the revealer and interpreter of God in terms of the highest and holiest human experience we know—that of suffering love bearing the consequences of sin, and appealing to the sinner, who has caused the sorrow, to be a better man.[*]

These changes in theological interpretation, as we shall see, will be reflected in a diminishing emphasis upon evangelical and evangelistic hymns, and the composition of a new type of untheological but deeply religious and thoroughly Christian hymns. These hymns we shall now consider.

### Bishop PHILLIPS BROOKS (1835–93) American Episcopal

BOSTON born, Harvard educated, then trained for the ministry at the Episcopal Theological Seminary at Alexandria, Va., pastorates in Philadelphia (1859–69) and finally in Trinity Church, Boston (1869–91). Here he truly found himself as a humanitarian and a preacher. He drew such large crowds that his parish had to build a new church to hold them— the stately brownstone structure in Copley Square, designed by Richardson, apostle of the American resurrection of Romanesque. Brooks was wonderfully successful as a pastor and won the devotion of his people as few clergymen have ever done. Perhaps his dominant personal characteristic was his love for children. Himself a bachelor, he took to his heart all the little ones of his parish, and they reciprocated. His last social engagement

[*] Copyright 1895. By permission The Macmillan Company, publishers.

was with the choir boys of the Episcopal Church in Newton, Massachusetts.

As a preacher Brooks was preeminent, rivalling in substance his philosophical neighbor across the square, Dr. George A. Gordon of the Congregational Old South Church, and surpassing him in the intensity of his de-
livery. His words poured from him with the impetuosity of a mountain
torrent—two hundred and fifty words a minute, too fast for any stenographer
to take down. And his message was not mere moralizing sentiment, such as
characterized so many Boston pulpits of his day; it was the evangelical
gospel of Jesus Christ. Augustus St. Gaudens caught this dominant trait in
his statue erected just outside the church after Brooks' death: the stalwart
form with one of his characteristic preaching gestures, Christ standing behind him with his hand on Brooks' shoulder. In 1891 Brooks was made
Bishop of Massachusetts, but died less than two years after.

Tradition has preserved several anecdotes that reveal his kindly and
humorous characteristics:

> One April Fool's Day, as he was walking along Boylston St., Bos-
> ton, he saw a little fellow trying in vain to reach a door bell.
> Brooks went up the steps, saying, 'Let me help you, my little man!'
> He pulled the knob; the boy scampered down the steps, saying,
> 'Now run like the devil!'
>
> His customary remark to a mother when he visited a home
> where a new baby had just arrived: "Well, well, this *is* a baby!"
>
> Busy with sermon-writing one Saturday, he told his maid not
> to admit any visitors, 'not even if it were St. Peter.' By chance
> Robert Ingersoll, the famous atheist lecturer, called. The maid re-
> peated Brooks' order, but Ingersoll said, "Oh, he will see me all
> right," and pushed into the study. Brooks greeted him warmly—
> "Glad to see you, Mr. Ingersoll!" "Come now," said Ingersoll, "I
> thought you said you would not see even St. Peter this morning."
> "Never mind," replied Brooks, "I'll have plenty of time to see him
> in the other world. Sit down."

Dr. R. G. McCutchan has recorded two bits that are worth repeating:

> When told of Bishop Brooks' death, a little girl of five exclaimed,
> "Oh, mama, how happy the angels will be!"
>
> Posterity will never see his princely form towering six feet and a
> half in height; and his majestic face, combining the thoughtfulness
> and fire of Webster with the sweetness of Fénelon or Fletcher; and
> his massive frame, impressing one at first as a giant, yet so filled
> with light and life that he seemed as radiant as an angel.\*

Bishop Brooks had a poet's instinct and wrote a number of carols for
Christmas and Easter. Only one has survived:

\* *Our Hymnody*, p. 135, Abingdon-Cokesbury Press.

## O little town of Bethlehem    [1867]

While a young rector in Philadelphia in 1865, Brooks went abroad for a year of travel and made a pilgrimage to Palestine. The day before Christmas he rode on horseback from Jerusalem to Bethlehem and visited not only

*Left*, Phillips Brooks at about the time he wrote "O little town of Bethlehem." *Right*, Statue of Phillips Brooks by St. Gaudens at Trinity Church, Boston. Christ, holding his cross, places his hand upon Brooks' shoulder. This is the source of the preacher's inspiration.

the usual sights in the village but went eastward down to the traditional Field of the Shepherds:

> Before dark we rode out of town to the field where they say the shepherds saw the star. It is a fenced piece of ground with a cave in it, in which, strangely enough, they put the shepherds. . . . Somewhere in those fields we rode through, the shepherds must have been. As we passed, the shepherds were still 'keeping watch over their flocks,' or leading them home to fold.

Finally he joined in the service conducted with such pomp in Constantine's ancient basilica (326 A.D.) built over the traditional site of the Nativity, a cave. The service lasted from 10 P.M to 3 A.M.! With these experiences in mind it is not strange that on his return to Philadelphia he wrote for a

Christmas celebration in his Sunday school the exquisite lyric now sung all over the world, the music composed by his organist who was also superintendent of the school. It is a perfect combination of the Bethlehem background, the gospel story, the spiritual message for children, and poetic beauty of expression.

*Stanza 1.* An apostrophe to the little town. Bethlehem is "still," "asleep," "dark," because in all Palestine villages in 1865—as largely today—there were no street lights, no night clubs, no students burning the midnight oil. People worked outdoors from sunrise to sunset, went to bed at dark and slept till dawn. The "everlasting Light" was not the star of the Magi but the "Light of the World" (Jn 1:9; 8:12). The "hopes of all the years" were the Jewish hopes of their Messiah and the world's hope for release from poverty, misery and war. The "fears" were based upon the experience that help never yet came to stay. Tonight both hopes and fears were answered (potentially) in the Nativity of the Light of the World.

*Stanza 2.* A narrative that puts the Scripture story into poetic form. The "wondering love" of the angels reflects their participation in God's outgoing beneficence (Jn 3:16), and at the same time the mystery of the Incarnation (1 Pet 1:12c). The "morning stars" are not the Star which later guided the Wise Men, but the angels themselves—a reminiscence of the morning stars that sang together at the creation (Job 38:7).

*Stanza 3.* A meditation: The silence that shrouds the night is symbolic of the noiseless coming of God's spirit into the human heart—of Christ's presence in the soul of all who desire Him.

*Stanza 4.* A prayer that children can understand, perhaps better than their elders. What a grown-up would call sin a child would call naughtiness. The metaphor being "born" means to a child a feeling of love suddenly filling the heart, which is all that is needed to cast out the naughtiness. But that love must stay if one is to be permanently good. The Bible has the right word for it—"Emmanuel," God with us.

Thank God, Christmas comes every year, for we need to be reminded.

### Rev. ERNEST WARBURTON SHURTLEFF (1862–1917)
### American Congregational

A BOSTON boy, a graduate of Harvard and of Andover Theological Seminary (1887), a pastor in California, Massachusetts and Minnesota. His most distinctive and productive work was done in Europe. In 1895 he organized the American Church in Frankfort-on-the-Main, Germany, and from 1906 to 1917 had charge of the American Students' Atelier Reunions in Paris. During World War I he and his wife were active in relief work.

Even before graduating from Andover he had written two volumes of poetry. He was also a good amateur musician. The hymn by which he lives was written at request of classmates at Andover for their Commencement.

## Lead on, O King eternal     [1877]

This is a superb hymn not only for the original occasion, but for all days. It is a young man's chivalric dedication to the great spiritual warfare to which God calls us. It is the eager cry of the knight who has been kneeling through the hours of darkness in vigil at the altar where his sword and armour are being impregnated with the power of heaven, and who now with the dawn rises to receive the accolade of his King and goes forth to combat. No wonder that young people love to sing these words to the martial music provided for them.

*Stanza 1.* One sees through the metaphors the appropriateness of the hymn to its original setting: The "days of preparation" are the years of training in college and divinity school, "the fields of conquest" are the pastorates to which the young men will be called; the "tents" are the parsonages and churches, dedicated to the work of God, in which they will live and work, the "battle-song" is this hymn. It is hard to imagine a finer transformation of prosaic fact into inspiring verse.

*Stanza 2.* Here the whole purpose of the ministry and of the Christian life in general is compressed into eight lines. It is the war against sin, carried on by deeds of love and mercy; peace comes only when holiness has been attained. The author's later life was an incarnation of this theory of religion, so different from the theological or evangelistic approaches that through the centuries have characterized the Church.

*Stanza 3* echoes the courage of the young crusader: the gladness of the dawn—the recognition that Christ is leading, the courage so inspired, the cross with Constantine's motto in the sky, "By this sign thou shalt conquer," and the waiting crown—sign and reward of victory. In the final line the previous "King eternal" has been changed to "God of might." It is the warrior's faith that the power of God is able to accomplish anything—with human cooperation.

All this imagery, purpose, fight and conquest need not be confined to the ministry. It is the battle-plan for humanity.


*SIDNEY LANIER* (*1842–81*) American (Presbyterian) Liberal

THE only Southern hymnist in all our hymnbooks was born in Macon, Georgia. His unusual qualities seem to derive from a mixed ancestry—Huguenot on his father's side and Scottish-American on his mother's. From early childhood he showed exceptional talent as a player of violin and flute. His poetic gifts became evident also in his eagerness to read imaginative literature. By himself he prepared for college, entered Oglethorpe at Milledgeville, Georgia, when only fourteen, was tutor there for a while after graduation and then volunteered in the Confederate Army. There he served as private, scout, signal officer and blockade runner, was captured and held in prison till 1865, and suffered a breakdown in health.

After the war his life was a hard and precarious struggle. Lanier once wrote to a friend: "Perhaps you know that with us of the younger generation in the South since the war, pretty much the whole of life has been merely not-dying." After trying several kinds of jobs, including the law, his health compelled him to live in Texas for a while. There he made many friends among musical people who urged him to devote himself to music and poetry. Accordingly he went north to Baltimore and joined the Peabody Orchestra as a flutist (1873). He became the leading flutist in America, in spite of the tuberculosis that made playing a dangerous activity. Of one concert he recalled: "When I allowed the last note to die, a simultaneous cry of pleasure broke forth from men and women that almost amounted to a shout."

On the side he wrote a guidebook to Florida, and tales for boys from such medieval works as Froissart, Malory, the Mabinogion Welsh tales and Percy's *Reliques of Ancient Poetry*, "expurgating them of all uncleanness." At last his creative output and his growing scholarship led to his appointment (1879) as Lecturer on English Literature at Johns Hopkins University, but again his health gave way; he was compelled to retreat to the North Carolina mountains and there died, aged only thirty-nine. It is inconceivable that in spite of all his handicaps he produced fourteen volumes of prose and ten of poetry.

The poet himself had some intimations of immortality: "Let my name perish," he once wrote his wife, "—the poetry is good poetry and the music is good music, and beauty dieth not, and the heart that needs it will find it." This prophetic conviction was realized when New York University placed his bust in its Hall of Fame with its other great Americans.

In spite of his early rigid Presbyterianism, Lanier's acquaintanceship with the development of science destroyed his Calvinism. He writes:

The Church is too hot, and Nothing is too cold. I find my proper temperature in Art. Art offers me a method of adoring the sweet master Jesus Christ, the beautiful-souled One, without the straitness of a Creed which confines my genuflections, a Church which confines my limbs, and without the vacuity of the doubt which numbs them. An unspeakable gain has come to me in simply turning a certain phrase the other way: the "beauty of holiness" becomes . . . in reverse the "holiness of beauty." This is like opening a window of dark stained glass and letting in a flood of white light. I thus keep upon the walls of my soul a church-wall rubric which has been somewhat clouded by the expiring breaths of creeds dying their natural death. For in Art there is no doubt.*

Lanier has been called "a tardy Transcendentalist." But he went beyond Transcendentalism in his exaltation of Jesus. He wrote:

Than Christ there has been no man more dear and friendly and helpful and strong and human and Christly. . . . For the scientist, He sets the goal for spiritual evolution; for the artist, He is the artist of conduct; for the democrat, He is the brave, democratic hero; for the poet, He is a symbol without which our poetry would be poorer.*

In his poem "The Crystal" he surveys briefly the qualities of the great leaders of mankind, always finding some flaw; then ends with this apostrophe:

> But Thee, but Thee, O sovereign Seer of time,
> But Thee, O poets' Poet, Wisdom's Tongue,
> But Thee, O man's best Man, O love's best Love,
> O perfect life in perfect labor writ,
> O all men's Comrade, Servant, King, or Priest,—
> What *if* or *yet*, what mole, what flaw, what lapse,
> What least defect or shadow of defect,
> What rumor, tattled by an enemy,
> Of inference loose, what lack of grace
> Even in torture's grasp, or sleep's, or death's,—
> Oh, what amiss may I forgive in Thee,
> Jesus, good Paragon, thou Crystal Christ? †

All this adoration of Jesus comes to a climax in what is now recognized as perhaps his most perfect gem, "The Ballad of the Trees and the Master." Though of course not written for a hymn, it is fast finding acceptance in our hymnals:

### *Into the woods my Master went*      [1880]

This was written during Lanier's last hand-to-hand battle for his life. It is an expression of the comfort and inspiration that trees bring, "the healing effect of nature on the human spirit":

It was into the woods that Lanier went continually to escape the desolating sense of defeat that contact with society brought; it was into the woods that he goes again as death approaches, into re-

---

* Reprinted from *Sidney Lanier*, pp. 399–403, by Aubrey Harrison Starke, by permission of The University of North Carolina Press. Copyright, 1933, by The University of North Carolina Press.

† From *The Poems of Sidney Lanier*, Scribner's, New York.

membered woods of the Georgia sea-coast where he receives, in ecstacy, the inspiration for the poem that is his supreme poetic vision.*

Now that his end was approaching he thought of the final hours of Jesus, also doomed to die before His time, and the Garden where He had attained the ultimate peace and fortitude that stayed by Him till the end.

Only one allusion may perhaps need clarifying: "The thorn-tree had a mind to him"—its sympathetic yearning for forgiveness, for it knew that on the morrow it would have to form his mocking crown.

The hymn is appropriately sung on Good Friday eve.

### Rev. MALTBIE DAVENPORT BABCOCK (1858–1901)
### American Presbyterian

ONE of the outstanding Presbyterian ministers of his generation He was born in Syracuse, New York, and graduated at Syracuse University. While there he was an athlete, a leader of the glee club and the orchestra, member of the dramatic club, and an earnest worker in all the religious activities of the college. E. S. Ninde gives an admiring sketch of him:

> He grew up tall, broad-shouldered, with muscles of iron, a superb specimen of physical manhood. He was champion base-ball pitcher and swimmer, and at the front in all athletic contests. The young men as well as the boys fairly idolized him, but they all knew where he stood. He was as full of fun and mischief as the next man, but some things he would not tolerate. One day when an older fellow was trying to bully one younger than himself, and was indulging in some unsavory language, Babcock quietly seized him by the nape of the neck and the seat of the trousers and with a word of forceful warning pitched him over the fence.**

After training at the Auburn Theological Seminary, New York, he served as pastor at Lockport near Lake Ontario, and was then called to the Brown Memorial Church at Baltimore. There he began a work among the students of Johns Hopkins University, so valuable that a room was especially set aside for his use in student conferences. He was also in great demand as a college preacher. Recognition of his power was given when he was elected to succeed Dr. Henry van Dyke at the Brick Church, New York City. Dr. Babcock died in a hospital at Naples, Italy, after a trip to the Holy Land.

### This is my Father's world      [1900?]

Though published in 1901, the year of Dr. Babcock's death, the hymn was probably written much earlier. The original from which the above verses

---

* Starke, *op. cit.*, pp. 402–403.
** *Story of the American Hymn*, p. 373, Revell, New York.

were selected for a hymn consisted of a sixteen-stanza poem called "Thoughts for Everyday Living." It reveals the author as a great lover of nature. The pictures in the first stanzas need no comment, except to note that the Creator is not a "First Cause" or a Transcendental "Over-Soul," but one best called, because of his personal interest in man, "Father."

In stanza 3 the author realizes that all's not right with the world, but has faith that God's moral law will be upheld, Jesus' sacrifice to be justified,

*Left,* Sidney Lanier, age 32. *Right,* Henry van Dyke.

and ultimately earth and heaven will be indistinguishable—a hope that it may take eternity to realize, but a grand and necessary one.

*Rev. HENRY VAN DYKE* (1852–1933) American Presbyterian

DR. VAN DYKE was one of our most versatile men of genius, eminent in many fields. Born in Germantown, Pennsylvania, he was trained at the Brooklyn Polytechnic Institute, Princeton University (A.B. 1873; M.A. 1876), Princeton Theological Seminary, and University of Berlin. He served as Presbyterian minister from 1879 to 1900, his most important charge being the Brick Church in New York City. Here he became famous as one of the great preachers of America. Like Washington Gladden, and at about the same time, he was a member of the Board of Preachers of Harvard University; he served other universities as well. A change came when in 1900 Princeton University called him to the professorship of English Literature, an interruption when in 1908–9 he was American lecturer at the Sorbonne, Paris, and still another when in 1913 President Wilson appointed him United States Minister to Holland and Luxembourg. In this capacity he served with distinction during World War I until 1917 when the United States entered the war. He was chaplain in the U. S. Navy during the hostilities.

Throughout his life he was a student in many departments, a lover of nature, a wide traveller, a writer of many books, and a poet of exceptional ability. His more popular nature studies are *Little Rivers* (1895), *Fisherman's Luck* (1899), the short story, *The Other Wise Man* (1896), *Out of Doors in the Holy Land* (1908), *Collected Poems* (1911). High honors in many lines came to him. From his resignation as Professor in 1923 he spent his remaining years in retirement at Princeton.

Dr. van Dyke's ideal of hymn-writing is thus stated by him:

> These verses are simple expressions of common Christian feelings and desires in this present time,—hymns of today that may be sung together by people who know the thought of the age, and are not afraid that any truth of science will destroy religion, or any revolution on earth overthrow the kingdom of heaven. Therefore these are hymns of trust and joy and hope.

## *Joyful, joyful, we adore thee* [1907]

While serving as preacher at Williams College among the Berkshires, Dr. van Dyke undertook to write suitable words for the "Hymn of Joy" in Beethoven's Ninth Symphony. The melody of that composition had already been used as a hymn-tune but lacked an adequate text. The Doctor seems to have provided one. The intricate interweaving of fact and metaphor may need a little interpretation for our younger readers.

*Stanza 1.* A joyful interplay between the outer world and the inner: God manifest in creation, the Lord manifest in human life, illustrated by the simile of flowers unfolding under the rays of the sun (lines 1–2). Line 3 shows the "expulsive power of a new affection"; line 4 the transforming radiance of the divine presence in the soul.

*Stanza 2.* Again two points of view: Creation itself cannot conceal its joy, and that joy is appreciated by God the center of it all (lines 1–4); likewise all nature fills us with joy, caused fundamentally by our recognition of God as the giver (lines 5–8).

*Stanza 3.* A series of contrasting doubles: the outgoing ("giving," "blessing") and the incoming ("forgiving"—God accepting our repentance; "blest"—God accepting our praise (lines 1–2). Action, as of a fountain; rest, as of the "sunless retreats of the ocean" (lines 3–4). God, our father on high; Christ, our brother on earth: relationships that are meaningful only if we love (lines 5–6). We pray therefore that this love with its accompanying joy may be ours (lines 7–8).

*Stanza 4.* An invitation to join the chorus of joy begun at creation's dawn (Job 38:7). Both the cause and the theme are love—Father-love from heaven, like the sun; Brother-love on earth uniting all in the same warmth (lines 1–4). And the total effect of this radar interpenetration and inter-reflection is conquest over life's ills and a triumphant upsurge of the soul towards God.

Such an attempted interpretation doubtless rubs the down off the butterfly's wing, but the poet must have meant something as well as felt something. Perhaps his thought was something like the above.

### *Jesus, thou divine companion*     [1909]

### *They who tread the path of labor*

This is Dr. van Dyke's reaction to the growing social and economic problems of our age. It is his endeavor to rescue Christianity from the sacerdotalism with which the centuries have encrusted it, and restore it to its original vitality. True Christianity, says the famous preacher and teacher, is following Jesus. Jesus had two sides to His nature, the physical and the spiritual. With the physical He had to work hard to support His widowed mother and at least five younger brothers and sisters; on the spiritual, He lived in constant companionship with His Father and on terms of self-forgetting service with His fellows. This sets the pattern for all who have to work: they must work, but also live in companionship with the Carpenter of Nazareth, absorb His sacrificial spirit and make life an offering of love to Him.

But Dr. van Dyke, the theologian, hints that Jesus was something more than a carpenter. He is a "divine" companion, who "hast come" (from heaven?); the "Bread of Heaven" broken for us in sacrifice and "with thee everywhere." Then to make His mysticism complete, in stanza 1 he quotes verbatim from a third century fragment of papyrus called "Logia" or "Sayings" found in Oxyrhynchus, Egypt, not long before this poem was written: "Jesus saith, 'Wherever there are two they are not without God, and if one is alone anywhere, I say I am with him. Raise the stone, there thou shalt find me; cleave the wood and there I am.'"

This interpretation of Jesus as an emanation from God is one of the earliest attempts of the Church to account for His extraordinary personality. It was known as Gnosticism, soon to be classed as a heresy. It is doubtful if the average stone mason or lumberman could get any comfort or help out of this subtlety.

There is another sentence in this poem which would tend to alienate workers from full acceptance of Dr. van Dyke's gospel:

> They who work without complaining
> Do the holy will of God.

This attitude if adopted would rule out complaints about unhealthy working conditions, poor pay, long hours, and whatever else leads to strikes, picketing and other attempts to force employers to share profits with those who create them.

On the whole, therefore, we must conclude that this brilliant Princeton professor has not too successfully brought the religion of Jesus within the sympathetic grasp of the American Federation of Labor and the Congress of Industrial Organizations. His friends William Merrill ("Rise up, O men of God"), Walter Russell Bowie ("O holy city, seen of John") and Frank North ("Where cross the crowded ways of life") have done a better job. It is probable that Dr. van Dyke realized this, for the poem from which this hymn is taken cannot be found in the two volumes of his collected poetry published by Scribners in 1922.

## II.  THE SOCIAL GOSPEL

The hymns we have just examined are a reflection of changed theology. But in the fifty years following the Civil War a social situation also demanded a new emphasis. We must now review briefly the men and events of this period to realize how desperately was needed an application of the gospel to our corporate life and a corresponding change in the viewpoint of our hymns.

This post-war period produced what has been called a "moral debacle that succeeded the idealism of the war years." The down-curve took its start in the disgraceful handling of war equipment in which men without conscience traded human life for gold. With the opening of the West, the construction of trans-continental railroads, the discovery of oil, the stealing from a Frenchman of the Bessemer process for making steel cheaply, began what James Truslow Adams calls "The Age of the Dinosaurs," and Matthew Josephson calls the epoch of the "Robber Barons." It is a sordid tale of greed and the will to power. When these men began operations, America was an agrarian-mercantile democracy; before they passed on, it was an industrial and financial fascism. The manipulators were mostly young men in their early twenties: Jay Gould, Jim Fiske, J. P. Morgan, Philip Armour, Andrew Carnegie, J. J. Hill, and John D. Rockefeller. All but Morgan were born poor; all but Fiske were Protestants from pious homes, some of them leaders of Sunday school classes, and church attendants all their lives.

These men and their immediate elders proceeded to get what they wanted despite morality. Old Cornelius Vanderbilt had a characteristic expression, "What do I care about the law? Haint I got the power?" His New York Central Railroad was so constructed that "each mile of track from New York to Buffalo represented $50,000 of pure water."

Daniel Drew wrecked the Erie Railroad and made a fortune by it. For a generation he dominated the stock-gambling world. But he spent an hour each day with his Bible and on his knees, and founded Drew Theological

POLITICAL REASONS FOR GLADDEN'S NEW DEAL RELIGION.

"Blindman's Buff: How long will the game last?"—Justice, blindfolded, is trying to locate Boss Tweed (squeezing against the wall). "Tricks of the Law" is trying to trip her. The man behind her has "Verdict of the Jury" in his pocket.

Seminary with a gift of $250,000. The gift was in the form of a note which, as his fortunes shifted, was never paid.

Land grabbing and land speculation after both the Mexican and the Civil Wars was a great game, practiced preeminently by the trans-continental railroads. The scandal reached a climax in the Crédit Mobilier—a construction company organized by the stockholders of the Union Pacific to build their railroad. As stockholders of the railroad they voted to themselves as stockholders of the construction company contracts at excessive figures so as to get immediate profit for themselves regardless of the railroad's future earning power. The railroad was subsidized by the federal government to the tune of $27,000,000, together with a gift of twelve million acres of land along the line, on which the road speculated outrageously. Then to keep from being investigated, Congressman Oakes Ames, a director, distributed 343 shares of Crédit Mobilier among influential congressmen and senators, in- cluding the Speaker of the House, a senator who soon became Vice Presi- dent, and a representative who later became President. Senator Hoar of Massachusetts said, "Every step of that mighty enterprise had been taken by fraud."

The elder Rockefeller crushed out his competitors in oil by a secret deal with the railroads whereby not only did he get a rebate on transporting his own oil but also a kick-back from the oil transported for his competitors! His company finally grew by absorbing his competitors. He took in only the big concerns: "As for the others, unfortunately, they will have to die." He kept the Sabbath, contributed to the churches and to missions. "God gave me the money," he said.*

Big business finally headed up in huge banking and insurance aggre- gates in which the deposits of millions of small fry could be used to buy stocks and bonds for themselves and to secure control of boards of directors, "transforming the pigmy property of the many into the titan property of the few." Members of the Morgan and Rockefeller groups together held, in 1911, 341 directorships in 112 corporations whose resources aggregated more than 22 billions of dollars.

In the 1870's also, politics became a scandal. The conspicuous example, of course, was Boss Tweed's Tammany ring in New York City. They doubled the city's debt every two years, and for every dollar they spent on the city kept ten for themselves! They were hooked up also with the Erie Railroad wrecking. But state and national governments did not escape pollution. Men were elected to office by the financial assistance of the Robber Barons, and in return they voted as directed. In 1871 Henry Ward Beecher declared:

> We are today in more danger from overgrown organized money than we ever were from slavery; the battle of the future is to be one of gold.

Industry created slums. The demand for cheap labor brought an influx of countrymen into the industrial cities, but more significant, it brought a horde of immigrants from abroad, the tide artificially stimulated by steam- ship agents and big corporations who wanted a cheap "labor pool." Between 1881–90 the influx from abroad was 4,700,000; between 1901–10 it reached

---

* Of Ida Tarbell's *History of the Standard Oil Co.* that came out serially in *Mc-Clure's Magazine* (1902–4) a reviewer wrote: " A fearless unmasking of moral crimin- ality masquerading under the robes of respectability and Christianity."

TWO CARTOONS BY THOMAS NAST LEVELLED AT POLITICAL CORRUPTION
OF THE TIMES.

*Top,* JUSTICE (to the Saints of the Press): "Let him that has not betrayed
the trust of the people, and is without stain, cast the first stone." (Inscription
over the door of the Capitol) DISGRACED in the EYES of the PUBLIC for
owning CREDIT MOBILIER STOCK, which was in fact and intent a FRAUD
UPON THE GOVERNMENT, Also for DECEIT AND EVASION—the high
trust of Legislators MISUSED—The people will not long respect the Laws if
they lose respect for the Law-makers. *Bottom,* Farmer "Granger": "I say, Mr.
Wildcat Speculator, what am I to do now?" Railroad "Monopolist": "Solve your
own problem, Mr. Farmer Despot."

8,130,000. Where could these people live? They swarmed into the industrial cities, driving well-to-do residents to seek homes in up-town or suburban areas, while the brownstone fronts of down-town were crowded with a family in every room. This was a gold mine for owners and real estate companies who were willing to let the property degenerate while quadrupling their income. One of the most aristocratic churches in New York City was among the largest owners of rotten tenements and fought hard to prevent remedial legislation. If the city government were properly manipulated, fire traps could still be maintained: there were in 1947 70,000 houses in New York City that had been condemned but continued to operate profitably.

What has all this to do with hymns?

These conditions became a challenge to the Christian religion. They were a denial of the basic aims of the gospel of Jesus and His Kingdom of God. The "New Theology" and the "Social Gospel" found themselves at one in their purpose to change society. As in the former days of the Reformation, the Methodist Revival, and the intolerable industrial situation that produced the Chartist riots in England and called forth Thomas Hood's "Song of the Shirt" (1843), so now again, hymns could become a potent weapon of propaganda.

As we study the hymns of the last seventy years we realize how completely they differ from the Evangelical hymns with their mystic approach, their zeal for individual conversion, their ideal of God's Kingdom as an Apocalypse or an eternal city in heaven; from the High Anglican hymns that looked back with nostalgia to the historic Church, its theology, its liturgy, and from the Unitarian Transcendental approach in which enthusiasm for the Kingdom took the form of vague wishful thinking. These modern hymn-writers have their eye on the object. They want the slums abolished, poverty and sickness banished, the will to grab transformed into the will to serve, and all our faith and energy devoted to bringing into being a brotherhood on earth. Taken together in their historic milieu they are a remarkable testimony to the distance we have travelled since the days of Watts and Dwight.

We are now ready to consider some of the more prominent hymnists of the Social Gospel.

### Rev. WASHINGTON GLADDEN (1838–1918) American Congregationalist

BORN on a farm in Potts Grove, Pennsylvania, a graduate of Williams College under President Mark Hopkins, Gladden was ordained in 1860 and took his first pastorate in Brooklyn, New York. Called to a North Adams, Massachusetts, church in 1866, he began to show the stuff in him by preaching the anti-Calvinist theology of Dr. Horace Bushnell, at that time anathema in the conservative Church. In 1871 he interrupted his pastoral work to serve as religious editor on the then influential New York

*Independent* and got his baptism in politics by fighting the notorious Tweed Ring. In fact, it was his insistent editorials that started the prosecution which sent Tweed to jail. Gladden finally resigned because of his disapproval of the chief editor's advertising ethics.

From 1874–1882 he was pastor of the Congregational Church in Springfield, Massachusetts. There he began to preach Sunday evenings on labor-management problems. This was one of the first intimations of the social

Washington Gladden

implications of the gospel to come from a pulpit. He aroused opposition: "The business of a minister is to save souls, not to regulate business." Gladden ignored the jibes and continued to preach cooperation between men and their employers. In this pastorate also he began to champion the heretical theory that the Bible was not inerrant science and history but a book of religion. He found his fellow-clergymen without courage to follow him, for heresy trials were beginning in the Congregational Church. His theory was that liberal men should stay in the Churches where they belong —not leave them.

In 1882 he was called to the First Congregational Church in Columbus, Ohio, where he remained thirty-two years. There he became not only one of the most powerful preachers in the country, but he must be reckoned a pioneer in insisting upon the application of the gospel to the social, political and economic life of America and the world. His Sunday evening sermons were aimed at bringing reason and conscience into labor disputes. He became involved in the telegraphers' strike of 1883 and in the Hocking Valley coal strike of 1884. The vice-president and general manager of that company was a member of Gladden's church board. Gladden was called to Cleveland and to Boston to address strikers and near-strikers. His sermons and addresses on these occasions were published by the *Century* magazine and later in *Working People and their Employers* (1885) and *Applied Christianity* (1886). "The one thing needful is a change in the direction of the ruling motive from self-aggrandizement to service."

Students from the State University at Columbus flocked to his evening services. Gladden was convinced that he ought to tell them the truth about the origin and nature of the Bible and so counteract the distortions of Robert Ingersoll who was confounding the religious world by his lecture on "The Mistakes of Moses." These sermons were published in *Who Wrote the Bible?* —which proved to be his best seller.

His services were continually sought by universities. At the Yale Divinity School he delivered lectures afterward published as *Tools and the Man* (1893), again delivered at Cornell, Mansfield College, Oxford, and Meadville Theological Seminary (Unitarian). Beginning in 1893, he was one of the Harvard University preachers for three years. As the depredations of intrenched capital increased and the elder Roosevelt began his attacks on "malefactors of great wealth" (1901–9). Gladden let his voice be heard in no uncertain tones: *Social Facts and Forces* (1897) and *Organized Labor and Capital* (1904).

Naturally he became the object of bitter criticism and misrepresentation. On account of his economic views he was twice blocked from becoming president of large universities. He was also nearly repudiated by his own denomination when in 1905 he condemned his American Board of Foreign Missions for soliciting and accepting a gift of $100,000 from the senior Rockefeller: "tainted money" he called it, because of the unfair and illegal monopolistic practices of the donor. His position was clearly stated in articles in *The Outlook*, later published in *The New Idolatry* (1905), two chapters of which are "Tainted Money" and "Standard Oil and Foreign Missions."

Nothing stayed his steady purpose. But as social reforms gained headway, popular reaction to Gladden by his fellow-preachers became more favorable. By the time he died most of the harsh judgments had been forgotten, and today he is honored, with Walter Rauschenbush, as the outstanding clergymen of their generation in the field of social philosophy.

His hard-hitting gospel is adequately summarized in this seemingly harmless quotation from his *Recollections* (p. 429):

The simple truth is that Religion is nothing but Friendship: friendship with God and with man. . . . Friendship first with the great Companion, of whom Jesus told us, who is always nearer to us than we are to ourselves and whose inspiration and help is the greatest fact of human experience. . . . This is religion on its Godward side. Then, turning manward, friendship sums it all up. To be friends with everybody; to fill every human relation with the spirit of friendship; is there anything more than this that the wisest and best of men can hope to do?

And by way of contrast to the vague doctrines of the Transcendentalists who tend to ignore Jesus, this further quotation will suffice:

Religion at the beginning was largely a matter of tradition; today I am resting on what I have verified. Of some things I am much less sure than I was once; but what Jesus has taught us about the Father in heaven and the Brother on the earth looms large. . . . The things that men have said about Him concern me less and less; the things that He Himself has said concern me more and more. A correct theory of His person is of much less consequence than obedience to His word. Has He not told us so? "Why call ye me Lord, Lord, and do not the things which I say?" . . . Yet there are millions who are deeply exercised over metaphysical theories of His nature, but who are utterly skeptical concerning His explicit counsels about living together.*

Gladden will live for future generations in his one immortal hymn:

### O Master, let me walk with thee      [1879]

This poem was written not as a hymn but as a meditation. It first appeared in a publication called *Sunday Afternoon* of which Dr. Gladden was editor, under the caption "Walking with God." When it came to be used as a hymn the second stanza was cut out (this would be stanzas 3 and 4 as the hymn is now printed) on the ground that it was not suitable for the worship services of a church:

> O Master let me walk with thee
> Before the taunting Pharisee;
> Help me to bear the sting of spite,
> The hate of men who hide thy light,
> The sore distrust of souls sincere
> Who cannot read thy judgments clear,
> The dullness of the multitude
> Who dimly guess that thou art good.

* W. Gladden: *Recollections*, p. 418, Houghton, Mifflin, Boston, 1909.

As it stands in the hymnals, this hymn represents the high-water mark of religious poetry. It contains no challenging theology out of the past, only a yearning for that constant companionship with the Master, that sharing of his spirit, which when accomplished assures the acme of Christian character.

*Stanza 1.* A prayer for greater efficiency in service; a prayer also that will enable a disciple to fight successfully the two major enemies of a happy life—the strain and the fret that seem inseparable from aggressive living.

*Stanza 2.* The prayer of a pastor for more intelligible, persuasive and sympathetic preaching, for more penetrating analysis of a friend's problems, and wisdom to map with him life's true course.

*Stanzas 3 and 4.* A personal revelation of what Dr. Gladden had lived through: scorn of religious high-brow for social reformer, of the citizen whose secret life is false but who keeps up appearances; the open hostility of those whose under-cover transactions he had helped bring to light—some of them members of his own church! the anxiety of his friends who could not see things as he saw them and so suffered vicariously for him; the inability of the crowd to understand at all, and so fall back on the hunch that things are probably all right anyway.

On reading this stanza we come to realize that sixty-five years after the hymn was written there still exists in our beloved land the same intolerance of the prophet-citizen, the same under-cover tactics of slander and innuendo, by greed and the will to power, that existed in the days of the "Robber Barons."

*Stanza 5.* A prayer for patience. We shall learn patience if we keep company with Christ who has already waited 2000 years for His gospel to be implemented in the social order. We shall learn it if we keep working, because "faith without works is dead," and with works faith will be kept healthy. We shall learn patience if we keep trusting, because otherwise we shall lose our bearings, and that means defeat.

*Stanza 6.* The same thought continues: We must keep company with Christ to strengthen our hope, which like a beacon lightens the expanding future; to strengthen our peace of mind, for as we view this warring world the only guarantee of serenity is companionship with Christ.

Most of us are not pastors as Dr. Gladden was. Most of us will not, like him, become consultants or arbitrators in labor disputes. Most of us will not be denied the presidency of great universities because of our passion for reform. But in our separate tiny spheres we need exactly the help here prayed for—the presence of Christ in all life's relationships and decisions.

### KATHARINE LEE BATES (1859–1929) American, Undenominational

HER biography is short out of all proportion to the life of the hymn that has immortalized her. She was born in Falmouth, Massachusetts—or as we Yankees say, "down on the Cape," was educated in Wellesley College, Massachusetts, and all her life taught English there. She wrote and edited many books in her field. Her heritage was thus like that of another New Englander who wrote the only other national anthem that has survived in hymnals—S. F. Smith. She appears not to have been connected with any church. Wellesley College itself was maintained, in accordance with the wish of its founder, as "undenominational, but distinctively Christian in its influence and instruction."

There is no doubt of Miss Bates' deeply religious nature, for she wrote not only a lovely Christmas carol beginning

> The Kings of the East are riding
> Tonight to Bethlehem

but a deeply spiritual hymn

> Dear God our Father, at thy knee confessing,

filled with a mystic rapture at the beauty of the world and an evangelist's passion for the redemption of humanity. Perhaps this hymn is too fragile for the rough demands of a hymnal, but it ought to be tried out more fully.

### O beautiful for spacious skies      [1893]

This hymn grew out of two exceptional experiences. In 1893 Miss Bates visited an "alabaster city" on a Chicago lagoon—the Columbian Exposition, the buildings of which were of Pentelic whiteness and as dignified as the Parthenon. As she herself has written,

> The White City made such strong appeal to patriotic feeling that it was in no small degree responsible for at least the last stanza of 'America the Beautiful.' It was with this quickened and deepened sense of America that we went on, my New England eyes delighting in the wind-waved gold of the vast wheat-fields.

The second experience was the ascent of Pike's Peak, Colorado. The view from this 15,000-foot summit is magnificent and a sunrise there is overwhelming—the whole panorama of which is compressed by the poet into the phrase "purple mountain majesties." Thus the combination of art and nature impressed upon the author the perfection of God's gifts to America, and suggested to her the providential guidance that had shaped its history. The hymn was written at once, in Colorado Springs.

The idea of guidance, with its emotions, finds expression in stanzas 2 and 3. The "pilgrim feet" are not only those that landed on Plymouth Rock, but the feet of thousands who had trekked across the Alleghanies, the great plains, the Rockies, to the Golden Gate. "Stern" these feet were to meet the hardships of an untamed land and hostile Indians; "impassioned" because the drive behind the trek was a search for greater freedom—from debt, from poverty, from denial of voting rights by the privileged property-men and men of education. Some who thought about political theory were Jeffersonians; some were Jackson men; others were just looking for opportunity, and in the end they won the freedom they sought. "Liberating strife" recalls Patrick Henry, Bunker Hill and Valley Forge. It hints the moral purpose behind the anti-slavery struggle culminating in the Emancipation Proclamation.

But these ideas are only backgrounds and inspirations for a deep-yearning prayer, parts of which are found in each stanza: May God supplement His gifts and man's accomplishment with something not yet attained—brotherhood, self-control, liberty within law, success that does not destroy character, and still greater patriot dreams of brotherhood.

As Miss Bates stood on the shores of that shining lagoon, surrounded by beauty created by men's hands, she must have known that Chicago was not all an "alabaster city." Four miles northwest of her lay the Stock Yards, in the stench and blood of which thousands of Negroes and immigrant workers toiled long hours for miserable pay and at night slept in a slum that was a disgrace to Christian America. Soon after (1904), Upton Sinclair will expose all that in *The Jungle,* and Jane Addams, in her recently-founded Hull House (1889) is already arousing the public conscience.

Six miles north of White City lay—and still lies—the Black Ghetto with its crowded squalor, some day to be held up in horror by Richard Wright's first novel, *Native Son* (1940).

Two miles further on, Miss Bates could have toured the blighted flophouse area where hoboes and dope-fiends, gangsters and prostitutes cluttered—and still clutter—the fair city with their moral refuse.

And in the Loop itself only half a mile from "hobohemia," amid the great buildings of the mid-west financial empire, rises the Grain and Produce Exchange. There in 1897 Joseph Leiter will corner the wheat market and send the price to astronomical heights. Plenty of tears will be shed from New York to Moscow and Shanghai when housewives scrape the bottom of their flour barrels—until with the outbreak of the Spanish-American War the market will break and 60,000,000 bushels of wheat will come tumbling down on Leiter's head! "Success" is never "nobleness" when it brings starvation.

Four miles south of White City Miss Bates could see the smoke of an infant steel industry, expanding with utter disregard of humane working

*Top,* "The Alabaster City," World's Columbian Exposition, Chicago, 1893. *Left,* Katharine Lee Bates. *Right,* William DeWitt Hyde.

conditions in plants full of hazards to life and limb, with a sacrosanct twelve-hour day, and forty years afterwards in the same area pickets on the public highway will be set upon by thugs, beaten up and some of them killed because management does not propose to have its autocratic power curbed by labor unions.

"God shed his grace on thee!" Our alabaster cities will continue to be dimmed by human tears until men realize that all are brothers in fact as well as in song.

### Rev. *WILLIAM DE WITT HYDE* (*1858–1917*) American Congregationalist

BORN in Winchendon, Massachusetts, graduated from Harvard (1879) and Andover Theological Seminary (1883), Hyde was pastor at Paterson, New Jersey (1883–5), then only three years after beginning his ministry he became President of Bowdoin College, Maine, and Professor of Philosophy (1885–1917). "The Boy President," he was nicknamed. In that position he stayed until his death—a fine administrator, a wise counsellor of his students, and a beloved and honored citizen. He was author of books on educational and religious subjects, a Fellow of the American Academy of Arts and Sciences, and University Preacher at Harvard (1897–9), Chicago, 1902, and Yale at various times.

### *Creation's Lord, we give thee thanks* [1903]

This hymn was written with his college students in mind. It is a call to battle, a challenge to the young men and women who came, almost all of them, from the humbler walks of life, for Maine is predominantly an agricultural, fishing and forest state. The challenge is for them to become part of the national life and to pledge their loyalty to the moral principles that alone can make a nation great.

*Stanza 1.* A prayer that thanks God for an incomplete world! But its incompleteness is a challenge to us to work for its advancement.
*Stanza 2.* Thanks continue that the individual is incomplete! These college girls and boys are only in the making, but with the training the Christian college can give we can grasp the Maker's idea and conform to His plan.
*Stanza 3.* (usually omitted)

> Beyond the present sin and shame,
> Wrong's bitter, cruel, scorching blight,
> We see the beckoning vision flame,
> The blessed kingdom of the right.

The prayer now changes to a meditation on present-day conditions—A.D. 1903. The college President has no rosy view of this year of grace. President McKinley had recently been assassinated (1901). Young Theodore Roosevelt had taken over, resolved to tackle the immense and growing problems. "Trust busting" was fast becoming his object—huge aggregations of capital that were controlling national resources and stifling competition: steel, Standard Oil, the railway empires, the huge insurance companies. The year this hymn was written, Roosevelt ordered the Attorney General to bring suit against the Northern Securities Company as a combination in restraint of trade. In 1902 a strike in the coal mines paralyzed the nation. Roosevelt made labor and the owners arbitrate, secured shorter hours and more pay. These are only samples of the advances the fighting President was securing. See how all these details are reflected in the phrases of this stanza.

*Stanza 4.* The challenge of this stanza is, Don't be discouraged! The foes may be haughty—like the $1,400,000,000 United States Steel Corporation just pulled together by Morgan; but that is a challenge, students of mine, to your ability, your faith in God and your optimism!

*Stanza 5.* That is what makes us men: our choices produce character, our affections transform us into the thing we love, our determination alone can win and keep our freedom.

To realize how far our leaders have travelled in a hundred years, one might contrast this hymn with Timothy Dwight's smug satisfaction in "I love thy kingdom, Lord"! (1800).

### Rev. FRANK MASON NORTH (1850–1935) American Methodist

BORN in New York City, educated at Wesleyan University, Connecticut, ordained in 1873. After serving a few small Methodist parishes, a chapel on the East Side, New York (1879–81), and the Calvary Methodist Church, New York (1882–4), he was called to his university city of Middletown, Connecticut, where he stayed five years (1887–92). Then he was made Corresponding Secretary of the New York City Mission and Church Extension Society, and served in that capacity for twenty years (1892–1912). He was then transferred to the Secretaryship of the Methodist Board of Foreign Missions (1912–24). He performed other functions as well: Corresponding Secretary of the National City Evangelical Mission, New York City (1896–1912); editor of *The Christian City,* New York (1892–1912); President of the Federal Council of Churches (1916–20); Chevalier of the Legion of Honor, 1919; Officier de l'Instruction Publique in France, 1920; Officer of the Royal Order of George I, Greece, 1920. His faithful and devoted service in whatever work he tackled made him one of the outstanding members of his denomination. His Alma Mater recognized his worth by electing him a Trustee.

## *Where cross the crowded ways of life*    [1905]

Back of this hymn are a few causative incidents and a deep concern for the people of the slums of New York City.

The Methodists were compiling a new hymnal. Prof. Caleb Winchester of North's Alma Mater was one of the editorial committee. By chance one day in New York he met Dr. North at the Methodist headquarters and asked him to write a hymn on some missionary theme. North protested that he was no hymn-writer, but promised to try.

Shortly before this meeting North had preached a sermon from Mt 22:9, using the more accurate translation, "Go ye therefore into the parting of the highways." Caught by the new phrase his imagination called up the great centers of traffic in our cities, foreign and American. These pictures with tides of life flowing through them are the inspiration of the first two lines of the hymn.

For years before the meeting with Prof. Winchester the crowded streets of New York had been perfectly familiar to Dr. North. They were the center of his interest, the field in which his Missionary Society was working. He knew all the needy areas, the people of all nationalities, the desperate problems that confronted them. To find his hymn he had merely to review his personal experiences and select the high spots that could be organized into liturgical form.

> *Stanza 1.* The essence of this stanza lies in the final line: We hear thy voice above the city's clamor and strife. And what does that voice say? We may well guess: "Come unto me, all ye who are weary and heavy laden, and I will give you rest."
>
> *Stanza 2.* Now comes the enumeration of details implicit in Stanza 1: the squalid tenements of the slums, the dumbell-shaped apartments where the only light and air for inner rooms is a narrow shaft into which tenants throw their rubbish, dark basement one-room apartments cluttered with all the family's gear, the one hall toilet serving half a dozen families (the old and the tiny ones, of various races, languages and characters), shared by degenerates, VD's and innocent children. We middle-class respectables *have no conception* of the way people in our great cities have to live. Even Christ weeps when He sees such misery.
>
> *Stanza 3.* Recalls the Gospel record of Christ's ministry to such people: a friend of publicans and sinners (Mt 11:19); one who ate with those who had unwashed hands (Mt 9:10–12); a lover of children (Mt 19:13–15); hope of the over-borne (Mt 11:28–30) and the sorrowing (Lk 7:12–15), the hungry (Mt 15:32), the sick (Mt 4:23–24). A "vision of thy tears" is given us in Jn 11:33–35.
>
> *Stanza 4.* If we give our cup of water, Jesus says we give it unto

Him (Mt 10:42; 25:40); "The sweet compassion" of His face (Jn 11:36).

*Stanza 5.* As the Master once came down from the Mount of Transfiguration to heal the epileptic (Mk 9:21–27) so may He come down again to heal man's wretchedness.

*Stanza 6.* The driving power behind sacrificial service is love, and love some day will build the city of God where now is our wretched city of slums.

*Rev. WALTER RUSSELL BOWIE* (1882–  ) American Episcopal

BORN in Richmond, Virginia, a graduate of Harvard and the Episcopal Theological Seminary at Alexandria, Virginia. His first two rectorships were in Virginia. From 1923–39 he was rector of Grace Episcopal Church in New York City. There he won the reputation of being a great preacher and a leader in the fight for social righteousness. He declined elevation to a bishopric on the ground that he still had work to do in New York. During World War I he was chaplain of Base Hospital 45. Since 1939 he has been a professor at Union Theological Seminary, New York. The Handbook to the Presbyterian Hymnal says of him: "His ministry is marked by the sympathy and breadth of his churchmanship and his courage in confronting social and industrial situations with the uncompromising standards of the Christian religion."

Dr. Bowie is a trustee of many religious and educational institutions, and the author of several widely-read books and a few poems. He is represented in our hymnals by one prophetic hymn:

## O Holy City, seen of John    [1910]

Written during his first rectorship at Greenwood, Virginia. The inspiration for the hymn and its underlying imagery came from John's vision on Patmos (Rev 21–22).

*Stanza 1.* "The Lamb doth reign": Rev 21:22; 22:9; 11:15.
"Four-square walls": Rev 21:12, 16
"No night, nor need, nor pain, nor tears": Rev 21:23, 25; 22:3; 21:4
*Stanza 2.* Against the idealism of Stanza 1 is pitted the realism of Stanza 2. While as yet the young rector in his tiny hamlet in the Shenandoah Valley had not experienced the woes of life in great cities, this picture is prophetic of the realities he will later be called to fight.
*Stanza 3.* A cry of protest against the shame of sweatshops, the slum tenement, the pauper wage in the South particularly. These conditions would seem to indicate that Christianity had been a failure.
*Stanza 4.* The unrealized vision of stanza 1 is now turned into a

prayer for strength. And the prayer puts the blame where it belongs —upon us who have not builded our cities on Christ's law of love, his principle of brotherhood. The sun of God's grace is useless unless it produces fruit in us.

*Stanza 5.* God is the architect of that future city, challenging in its splendor. It is our high obligation to turn the blueprints into a reality in time and space, to make human life one grand cathedral to His glory.

### Rev. WILLIAM PIERSON MERRILL (1867–  ) American Presbyterian

BORN in Orange, New Jersey, educated at Rutgers College and Union Theological Seminary, New York City, began his pastorate (1890) at Philadelphia (five years), then Chicago (sixteen years) and finally at the Brick Presbyterian Church, New York City (1911–38). His experience has been that of city pastor, and as such he has had to wrestle with the spiritual and economic problems that arise in present-day metropolitan areas. He has not only nobly filled this primary function but has become an author of repute on subjects pertaining to liberal religion, especially "world brotherhood through an internationalism transformed by the Christian spirit and ideals." He is also an outstanding authority in the field of hymnody and a composer of hymn tunes; an active leader in movements for civic betterment. Since 1915 he has been president of the Trustees of the Church Peace Union and author of many books of sermons and essays.

### Rise up, O men of God    [1911]

The rise of the Brotherhood movement in the Presbyterian Church in the early years of this century is the underlying cause of this hymn. A more immediate cause was a request for a hymn by the editor of *The Continent* and reading an article by Gerald Lee called "The Church of the Strong Men." With these ideas incubating in his mind, Dr. Merrill was returning to Chicago on a Lake Michigan steamer when this hymn suddenly welled up almost without conscious effort.

The words are a trumpet call to men. Appropriate, therefore, is the unadorned, hard-hitting style in which there are no poetical metaphors to intrigue the mind and diminish the voltage.

*Stanza 1.* "Lesser things" may refer to church suppers, entertainments, bowling teams or whatever activities only vaguely suggest the objects of Christian living. All the energies of the soul must be devoted to implementing the rule of God in human society.

*Stanza 2.* Two thousand years of theological wrangling and the drive for power have only postponed the kingdom of God; the rule of God is secured only by cultivating the attitude of brotherhood, for that alone will cure the ills of society.

*From Riesenberg and Alland: "Portrait of New York," copyright 1939 by The Macmillan Company and used with their permission.*

A "hotel" of the East Side, New York.

*Stanza 3.* The Church is impotent without the help of strong men of principle. This stanza has bothered some churchmen, particularly Anglicans. Dr. Merrill now insists that this stanza be included whenever the hymn is used.

*Stanza 4.* The standard around which we rally must be the cross of Christ, symbol of self-sacrifice. The line of march has been determined by Christ's own feet—the path of the common good. We conquer only by being brothers with Him who, as his title "Son of Man" shows, represents the possibility that the humblest of us may acquire something of the divine.

### *Not alone for mighty empire*  [1911]

Written like the former hymn while Dr. Merrill was pastor in Chicago, this hymn is a kind of mountain-top survey of history—of past empires and of America. It is also an appraisal of what really makes a nation great. The secret is not physical power or wealth; it lies in the realm of spirit (stanza 1). We may sometimes be tempted to glory in our military strength and in the victories we have always won in our wars, but what are they compared with our priceless heritage of freedom as expressed in our every-day institutions, in opportunity for all (stanza 2)? How thankful we ought to be for our heroes of the spirit—the nameless ones, the outstanding ones, the forward-looking prophetic souls and teachers of our nation, and those who have suffered for the truth (stanza 3). We are thankful for both the past and the present—but how about the future *which lies in our hands?* Pray God that we may see clearly the goal and be wise and brave enough to achieve it:—justice for all, for black or red, yellow or white; for Protestant, Catholic, Jew, Mohammedan, Hindu; for capitalist or worker, rich or poor, cultured or ignorant. Freedom for all, whether political, religious or eco-nomic. If we have faith enough in these fundamental human rights to work for them, then we shall achieve the ideal goal of humanity—brotherhood (stanza 4).

As a working formula for salvation, how superior this gospel is to the former preachments of theologians and evangelists! Something has happened to old-fashioned Calvinistic Presbyterianism.

*Rev JAY THOMAS STOCKING (1870–1936)* American Congregationalist

BORN at Lisbon, New York; trained at Amherst College, Yale Divinity School and the University of Berlin. His pastorates covered thirty-five years in New England, New Jersey, Missouri and Washington, D. C. In addition to his pastoral work he was active in wider Church affairs: trustee of Oberlin College, member of the executive committee of the Fed-eral Council of Churches in which he served on the Commission on Inter-national Justice and Good Will, member of the Congregational American Board of Foreign Missions, a director of the American Peace Society, and in 1934 he was elected Moderator of the Congregational National Council. He was also author of several volumes of sermons and studies. His final pastorate of a few months was at the First Church, Newton Center, Massa-chusetts. The hymn given below is the one contribution by which he will be gratefully remembered.

### O Master-workman of the race [1912]

The theme was suggested to Dr. Stocking by watching carpenters at work on his summer camp in the Adirondacks while he was there on a spring fishing trip. He wrote the hymn for a forthcoming *Pilgrim Hymnal* and gave it the title "The Carpenter of Nazareth." It was meant to appeal especially to young people.

The real theme is the lesson we may learn from the Carpenter of Nazareth—the necessity of finding and doing God's will.

*Stanza 1.* Jesus as a boy had the insight that just being a carpenter like His father was not enough: there is a spiritual task that is re-

Thomas Benton: The Age of Jazz, mural in the New School for Social Research, New York City. The only religion suggested here is in lower center.

quired of every person. We gather this from the Jerusalem incident when he was twelve, culminating in the words paraphrased in line 4 (Lk 2:41–49).

*Stanza 2.* As the boy grew He fulfilled this divine mission and builded Himself a character in accordance with the divine blueprint. We need His insight, His breadth of view as from a mighty tower, in order that we too may accomplish the "Father's business."

*Stanza 3.* May He, the source of our visions, our urges and our endurance, add also the guidance of conscience and the definiteness of specific tasks.

While the hymn does not qualify as high poetry, it has a picturesque appeal to the idealism of youth.

*Rev. HENRY HALLAM TWEEDY (1868–   )* American Congregationalist

BORN in Binghamton, New York; trained at Yale University, Union Theological Seminary and University of Berlin. Served churches in Utica, New York, and Bridgeport, Connecticut, and from 1903–37 was professor of Practical Theology at Yale Divinity School. His courses led him to study with his students the various hymnals in common use and to appraise hymns for their religion, their poetry, and their value in public services of worship. This led to his own writing of hymns, one of which is below.

*Eternal God, whose power upholds*     [1929]

In November, 1928, the Hymn Society of America announced a prize to be given for the best Missionary Hymn. Over a thousand manuscripts were submitted, from which this one of Dr. Tweedy's was selected as the winner. The thesis is that in the nature of God Himself we find the justification for missions. He is the reality behind all phenomena, physical or spiritual; He is love, truth, beauty, righteousness and benevolence.

> *Stanza 1.* The thought of the omnipresence and eternity of God eliminates all racial distinctions, all thoughts of deserving or undeserving, all boundaries. A missionary is God's ambassador of reconciliation to all the world.
> *Stanza 2.* The method of reconciliation is to develop love, which exists potentially in every heart. That is the only remedy for greed and hate, the two deadliest sins; the only assurance of kindness and peace.
> *Stanza 3.* Since the mind is given to man that he may find God, instruction and illumination are essential missionary methods; ignorance and fear are to be replaced by wisdom.
> *Stanza 4.* Man's distorted view of God issues in ugliness, whereas a right view of Him as the inspirer of art and music would make Beauty the characteristic of all our living.
> *Stanza 5.* The true missionary holds up Christ as the embodiment of God's ideal of human character. He should, therefore, himself live the Christ-life as an example, until all the races of earth have been transformed into His likeness.

---

We have now surveyed the currently-used hymns of the Church from their beginning c. 200 A.D. to 1929. Our thesis has been that hymns embody more than a personal expression of religion; they reflect also the religious and social beliefs and practices of the ages that produced them.

Fortunately time does not stop. Changes are still going on at a revolutionary pace, especially in the direction of implementing the Social Gospel among all races and conditions of men throughout the world. The tendency is toward unification. Small sects are merging, larger sects are negotiating, Lambeth and Amsterdam World Councils are being held, and rising above the horizon are fears of world destruction and visions of world unification—even of an over-all political and economic World Federation.

Hymns expressing these hopes have not been fully embodied in the ten collections we have studied; that will require another generation. Yet hymns extolling world fellowship and federation along democratic lines are being written. Here is one, first published in 1946, which more forcefully than others embraces this ideal of a Christian World Unity:

## World Hymn

God of all nations, Thy chastened children meet,
Drawn by a common anguish to Thy feet.
Curbed are the strident tongues, the myriad flags are furled.
Help us, O God, to save our stricken world!

Spirit of Brotherhood, our captive souls unbind;
Loosen the grasping hand, unwarp the mind;
Burst bars of race and creed, the patriot dream transcend.
Build us one world, one kinship to defend!

Spirit of Liberty, refine the laws that be;
Teach us the disciplines that make men free—
Fearless to speak and pray, and strong to work and plan.
Clear Thou the pathways of the common man!

God of all nations, forspent with thirst we meet,
Driven from waste and jungle to Thy feet.
Tuned are the divers tongues, the flags of hope unfurled.
Help us, O God, to save our waiting world! *

* By Lois B. Wills.

# SELECTED BIBLIOGRAPHY

## GENERAL

John Julian: *Dictionary of Hymnology.*
Louis F. Benson: *The English Hymn,* 1915
*Encyclopaedia Britannica.*
*Catholic Encyclopedia.*
*Dictionary of National Biography* (for all English hymnists).
F. J. Gillman: *The Evolution of the English Hymn,* 1927.
*Cambridge History of English Literature.*
S. R. Gardiner: *Students' History of England,* 1895.
J. C. Wand: *History of the Modern Church,* 1938.
Williston Walker: *History of the Christian Church,* 1918.
Elie Halévy: *History of the English People,* 1915, Vol. III, 1924.
Louis F. Benson: *Studies in Familiar Hymns,* 2 vols. 1903, 1923.
R. G. McCutchan: *Our Hymnody* (Methodist) 1937.
W. G. Polack: *Handbook to the Lutheran Hymnal,* 1942.
W. C. Covert: *Handbook to the Hymnal* (Presbyterian), 1935.
Percy Dearmer: *Songs of Praise Discussed* (Anglican), 1933.
H. A. Smith: *Lyric Religion,* 1931.

## CHAPTER I

Gustav Constant: *The Reformation in England,* 1934.
*Hymns Ancient and Modern,* Historical Edition: Introduction, 1909.
*The First Prayer Book of King Edward VI* (a reprint), 1903.
Percy Dearmer: *Everyman's History of the Prayer Book,* 1912.
*Sarum Primer:* reprinted in Maskell: *Monumenta ritualia Ecclesiae Anglicanae,* Vol. III.
*The Day Office of the Monastic Breviary,* Peekskill, N. Y., 1918.
H. H. Milman: *Annals of St. Paul's Cathedral,* 1869.

## CHAPTER II

Gustav Constant: *op. cit.*
Isaac D'Israeli: *Curiosities of Literature,* 1882 (Article on Psalm Singing).
John Strype: *Historical Memorials, Chiefly Ecclesiastical,* Vol. II, 1721.

579

## CHAPTER III

Isaac Walton: *Lives of Donne, Wotton, Hooker, Herbert*, 1670.
———— *Reliquiae Wottonianae*, 1651.
F. J. Gillman: *The Evolution of the English Hymn*, pp. 164–175.
E. H. Plumptre: *Life of Thomas Ken*, 1890.

Edward Calamy: *An Abridgement of Mr. Baxter's History of His Life and Times* (2nd ed., 1713).
A. H. Drysdale: *History of the Presbyterians in England*, 1889.
John Bunyan: *Grace Abounding to the Chief of Sinners* (Autobiographical).

## CHAPTER IV

Thomas Gibbons: *Life of Rev. Isaac Watts*, 1780.
Thomas Watts: *Memories of Dr. Isaac Watts*, 1780.
Frederic Palmer: Isaac Watts (*Harv. Theol. Rev.*, Vol. VII, 1919). Also chapter in his *Heretics, Saints and Martyrs*.
A. P. Davis: *Isaac Watts*, 1943.
William Romaine: *Essay on Psalmody*, 1775 (attacking Watts).

## CHAPTER V

G. D. H. Cole and R. Postgate: *The British People* (*1746–1946*), 1947.
John Wesley's *Journal*.
Charles Wesley's *Journal*.
C. T. Winchester: *Life of John Wesley*, 1906.
Arnold Lunn: *John Wesley*, 1929. Chap. xiv for organization of Methodist Classes, etc.; John Cennick's work, etc. Chap. xviii, The Day's Round.
Rattenbury: *Wesley's Legacy to the World* (Chapter on Hymns), 1928.
J. Wesley Bready: *England Before and After Wesley*, 1938.
Maldwyn Edwards: *John Wesley and the Eighteenth Century*, 1933 (a study in his social and political influence).
D. M. Jones: *Charles Wesley, a Study* (n.d.).
Thomas Jackson: *Life of Charles Wesley* (Cennick, vol. i, p. 248 ff.), 1841.
James Heath, R. A.: *The Works of William Hogarth, from the Original Plates*, 1822. Plates explained by J. Nichols.

## CHAPTER VI

G. D. H. Cole and R. Postgate: *op. cit.*
J. Wesley Bready: *op. cit.*
*Life and Times of Selina, Countess of Huntingdon*, by a member of the houses of Shirley and Hastings, 1844.
*A Brief Account of the Life of Howell Harris*, Trevecka, 1791 (interesting letters of his; also about Cennick).

Hay Aitken: *Introduction to Whitefield's Journal.*
Howell E. Lewis: *Howell Harris and the Welsh Revivalists,* 1912.
*Olney Hymns.* (See Benson: *English Hymn;* Julian: *Dictionary*).
T. Wright: *Life of Cowper,* 1892.
M. Haweis: *Authentic Narrative . . . of Life of John Newton,* 1765.
Sir James Stephen: *Essays on Ecclesiastical Biography.*

### CHAPTER VII

George Smith: *Bishop Heber,* 1895.
Geoffrey Faber: *Oxford Apostles,* 1934.
Verne Dyson: *A Hong Kong Governor and His Famous Hymns,* 1930.
E. C. Vaughan: *The Romantic Revolt,* 1907.
Arthur Symons: *The Romantic Movement in English Poetry,* 1909.

### CHAPTER VIII

J. H. Newman: *Apologia Pro Sua Vita,* 1864.
Richard H. Hutton: *Cardinal Newman,* 1891.
John Keble: Sermon on *National Apostacy,* 1833.
Frederick Oakeley: *Personal Reminiscences of the Oxford Movement,* 1855.
Walter Walsh: *History of the Romeward Movement,* 1900.
S. L. Ollard: *Short History of the Oxford Movement,* 1915.
Geoffrey Faber: *op. cit.*

### CHAPTER IX

*Cambridge Medieval History,* 1911–1936.
F. J. E. Raby: *A History of Christian Latin Poetry,* 1927.
Hartmann Grisar: *History of Rome and the Popes in the Middle Ages,* 1911.
*Catholic Encyclopedia, sub* various hymnists.
A. S. Walpole: *Early Latin Hymns,* 1922.
Thomas Wright: *Anglo-Latin Satirical Poets of XII Century,* Vol. ii (contains Latin text of *Hora Novissima*).
F. G. Holweck: *Biographical Dictionary of the Saints,* 1924.
Kenneth J. Conant: authority on the architecture of Cluny. See pictures and text in *Medieval Studies* in memory of Arthur Kingsley Porter, Vol. ii, pp. 339, 349; *Speculum* xvii, #4 (Oct. 1912).
Paul Sabatier: *Life of St. Francis of Assisi,* 1894.
Henry Adams: *Mont St. Michel and Chartres,* 1913. The Virgin, chaps. vi, viii–x; Abelard, xiv; the Mystics, xv.

### CHAPTER X

*Encyclopaedia Britannica, sub* "Orthodox Eastern Church."
John Julian: *Dictionary, sub* "Greek Hymnody."
J. M. Neale: *Intro. to History of the Holy Eastern Church,* 1863.

William Smith and Henry Waco: *Dictionary of Christian Biography*, 1911, for individual Hymnists.
John Phokulides: *The Holy Laura of Saba*, 1927 (in modern Greek).

## CHAPTER XI

John Julian: *Dictionary, sub* "Moravian Hymnody," "German Hymnody," and each hymn-writer.
*Hymns Ancient and Modern, Historical Edition*, 1909, Intro. sec. xiii.
Luther D. Reed: *Luther and Congregational Song*, 1947. (Am. Hymn Soc.).
James F. Lambert: *Luther's Hymns*, 1917.
T. B. Hewett: *Paul Gerhardt as a Hymn Writer*, 1918.
W. G. Polack: *Handbook to the Lutheran Hymnal*, 1942.

## CHAPTER XII

*Oxford History of England*, "The Age of Reform, 1815–1870."
G. H. D. Cole and R. Postgate: *The British People*, 1947, sections V–VII.
G. M. Young: *Victorian England*, 1937.
S. Baring-Gould: *Further Reminiscences*, 1925.
A. Clifton Kelway: *George Rundle Prynne*, 1905.
G. F. Ellerton: *Samuel John Stone*, 1903.

## CHAPTER XIII

(See Chap. XII.)
Mrs. Alvord: *Life, Journal and Letters of Henry Alvord*, 1873.
Francis K. Aglionby: *Life of Edward H. Bickersteth*, 1907.

## CHAPTER XIV

Wm. E. Smyser: *Modern Poets and Christian Thinking*, 1906.
Hallam Tennyson: *Alfred Lord Tennyson*, 1897.
Stopford Brooke: *Tennyson*, 1895.
A. C. Bradley: *A Commentary on Tennyson's "In Memoriam,"* 1929.
F. W. How: *Bishop Walsham How*, 1898.
W. C. Ingram: *Memoir of Henry Twells*, 1901.
Henry Housman: *John Ellerton*, 1896.
M. Kaufmann: *Charles Kingsley: Christian Socialist and Social Reformer*, 1892.

## CHAPTER XV

R. V. Holt: *The Unitarian Contribution to Social Progress in England*, 1938.
(See also under XII–XIV.)

## CHAPTER XVI

(See under XII–XV.)

## CHAPTERS XVII–XIX

Charles and Mary Beard: *Basic History of the United States,* 1944.

H. W. Faulkner: *American Political and Social History,* 1945.

James Truslow Adams: *Epic of America,* 1932.

V. L. Parrington: *Main Currents in American Thought,* 1927, 1930.

E. S. Bates: *American Faiths,* 1940. Chaps. 20, 26, 28.

*Cambridge History of American Literature,* 3 vols. 1917–43.

Henry W. Foote: *Three Centuries of American Hymnody,* 1940.

W. DeWitt Hyde: *Outlines of Social Theology,* 1895.

Washington Gladden: *Recollections,* 1909.

Matthew Josephson: *Robber Barons,* 1934.

C. H. Hopkins: *The Rise of the Social Gospel,* 1940.

Walter Rauschenbusch: *Christianity and the Social Crisis,* 1907.

———— *The Social Principles of Jesus,* 1916.

Charles Howard Hopkins: *The Rise of the Social Gospel in American Protestantism, 1865–1915.* 1940.

Ferris Greenslet: *The Lowells and their Seven Worlds,* 1946.

# INDEX OF FIRST LINES AND HYMNAL REFERENCES

## NOTE

The letters immediately following the first lines of the hymns in the index refer to the hymnal indicated in the following Key:

| Symbol | Denomination | Title and Date |
|---|---|---|
| A | Anglican (Canadian) | The Hymn Book, 1938 |
| B | Baptist-Disciples | Christian Worship, 1941 |
| C | Congregational Christian | Pilgrim Hymnal, 1935 |
| E | Episcopal (United States) | The Hymnal, 1940 |
| L | United Lutheran | Common Service Book, 1918 |
| M | Methodist | The Methodist Hymnal, 1939 |
| N | Undenominational | New Church Hymnal, 1937 |
| P | Presbyterian | The Hymnal, 1937 |
| S | Anglican (English) | Songs of Praise, 1931 |
| U | United Church of Canada | The Hymnary, 1930 |

The figures refer to the number of the hymn. (For basis of selection of hymns in this book see page vii.)

## INDEX OF FIRST LINES AND HYMNAL REFERENCES*

* The index to the original first lines of translated hymns appears on page 597.

585

PAGE

# INDEX OF ORIGINAL FIRST LINES OF
# TRANSLATED HYMNS

## GREEK

Ἄσωμεν πάντες λαοί, 299
Ἀναστάσεως ἡμέρα, 298
Ζοφερᾶς τρικυμίας, 305
Ἰησοῦ γλυκύτατε, 305
Κόπον τε καὶ κάματον, 290
Μνώεο Χριστέ, 286
Οὐ γὰρ βλέπεις τοὺς ταράττοντας, 294
Σιγησάτω πᾶσα σὰρξ βροτεία, 287
Στομίον πώλων ἀδαῶν, 283
Τὴν ἡμέραν διελθών, 303
Φῶς ἱλαρὸν ἁγίας δόξης, 285

## LATIN

Adeste fideles, 278
Altissimu, onnipotente, bon signore, 264
Angularis fundamentum, 234
Audi benigne conditor, 227
Corde natus ex parentis, 223
Ecce tempus idoneum, 227
Finita iam sunt proelia, 278
Gloria, laus et honor, 236
In dulce jubilo, 275
Jesu, dulcedo cordium, 255
Jesu, dulcis memoria, 252
Jesu, Rex admirabilis, 354
Mater Hierusalem, civitas, sancta Dei, 277
Nocte surgentes vigilemus omnes, 241
O Deus ego amo te, 277
O filii et filiae, 276
O Lux beata Trinitas, 221
O quanta qualia sunt illa Sabbata, 247
Rex Christi, factor omnium, 227
Salve, caput cruentatum, 274
Salve, festa dies, 233
Splendor paternae gloriae, 220
Stabat Mater gloriosa, 270
Surrexit Christus hodie, 271

Te Deum laudamus, 215
Urbs Syon aurea, 258
Veni, Creator Spiritus, 239
Veni, veni, Emmanuel, 272
Vexilla regis prodeunt, 230

## GERMAN

Befiehl du deine Wege, 327
Beim frühen Morgenlicht, 340
Christe, du Beistand deiner Kreutzgemeine, 323
Die Nacht kommen drin wir ruhen sollen, 320
Ein' feste Burg ist unser Gott, 314
Fröhlich soll mein Herze springen, 326
Gott ist gegenwärtig! lasset uns anbeten, 338
Gott segne Sachsenland!, 340
Herzliebster Jesu, was hast du verbrochen, 325
Jesu, geh' voran, 337
Lobe den Herren, den machtigen König, 331
Macht hoch die Thür, das Thor macht weit, 322
Mein Jesu, wie du wilst, 333
Nun danket alle Gott, 323
Nun ruhen alle Wälder, 328
O Jesu Christ, mein schönstes Licht, 326
Schönster Herr Jesu, 331
Seele du musst munter werden, 329
Seligbraütigam, O du Gottes Lamm, 336
Stille Nacht! Heilige Nacht!, 342
Wie schön leuchtet der Morgenstern, 316
Wir pflügen und wir streuen, 339

## DANISH

Igjennem Nat og Traengsel, 344

597

# INDEX OF AUTHORS AND TRANSLATORS